Southern Biography Series
BERTRAM WYATT-BROWN, EDITOR

Published with the assistance of the V. Ray Cardozier Fund,
an endowment created to support publication of scholarly books

EDITOR FOR JUSTICE

The Life of Louis I. Jaffé

ALEXANDER S. LEIDHOLDT

LOUISIANA STATE UNIVERSITY PRESS *Baton Rouge*

11   10   09   08   07   06   05   04   03   02
5   4   3   2   1

Designer: Amanda McDonald Scallan
Typeface: Sabon
Typesetter: Coghill Compostion
Printer and binder: Thomson-Shore, Inc.

Library of Congress Cataloging-in-Publication Data:
Leidholdt, Alexander.
  Editor for justice : the life of Louis I. Jaffé / Alexander S. Leidholdt.
      p. cm. — (Southern biography series)
Includes bibliographical references (p.) and index.
  ISBN 0-8071-2751-5 (cloth : alk. paper)
  1. Jaffé, Louis I. (Louis Isaac), 1888–1950. 2. Journalists — United States — Biography. 3. Norfolk
(Va.) — Race relations. I. Title. II. Series.
  PN4867 .J345 2002
  070.92—dc21

2002003273

To JoAnne: for her love
and
In memory of my friend and teacher Robert Mason (1912–2001)

CONTENTS

ILLUSTRATIONS

following page 234

All photographs courtesy Louis I. Jaffé Jr.

ACKNOWLEDGMENTS

Many former *Norfolk Virginian-Pilot* reporters and members of its editorial staff, including Staige Blackford, Luther Carter, Alonzo Dill, Robert Smith, Harold Sugg, and Widdy Tazewell, gave freely of their time and provided vital information that informed my research on this book. The numerous published works of veteran columnist Guy Fridell, an authority on Virginia journalism and history, contributed valuable background on my topic. Frank Batten Sr., founder of Landmark Communications, chairman of the board's executive committee, and former publisher of the *Virginian-Pilot,* took time out of his very busy schedule to share his memories of Louis Jaffé with me. The *Virginian-Pilot* and *Norfolk (Va.) Ledger-Dispatch* editorials in this book are reprinted with the permission of Landmark Communications.

Robert Mason, who knew and admired Louis Jaffé and kept the faith during his own seventeen-year stewardship as editor of the *Pilot,* deserves special mention. Mr. Mason, who began his impressive newspaper career at the *Sanford (N.C.) Herald* in 1933 and continued it through most of 2001 with regular contributions to the *Southern Pines (N.C.) Pilot,* was an authority on southern journalism, as well as southern and naval history. He was also a book author and a prolific contributor to journals. He suggested many scholarly sources, consented to numerous interviews, corresponded with me throughout my many years of research and writing, and reviewed each chapter. I could not have completed this project without the benefit of his wisdom and input.

I am deeply indebted to the many reference librarians and archivists who assisted me in my research. At the University of Virginia's Special Collections Department, Mike Plunkett, director, and Ervin Jordan, research archivist, provided invaluable assistance. At the University of North Carolina's Southern Historical Collection, Richard Schrader, reference archivist, and John White, assistant reference archivist, graciously guided me through their extensive holdings. Robert Anthony, curator of the University of North Carolina's North Carolina Collection; Conley Edwards, state archivist at the Library of Virginia; William E. King, university archivist at Duke University; and John Haskell, associate dean for administration and director of manuscripts and rare books in Special Collections at the College of William and Mary's Earl Gregg Swem Library, all made their resources available to me and guided me through my study.

Lawrence Mykytiuk, associate professor of library science and a reference librarian at Purdue University, and Frances Goins Wilhoit, librarian at the Journalism Library and assistant professor in the School of Journalism at Indiana University, consulted with me throughout my research. Tommy L. Bogger, archivist at the Harrison B. Wilson Library at Norfolk State University, and Janice Halecki, head of Special Collections at Old Dominion University's Perry Library, availed me of their expertise. Peggy Hale, city historian at Norfolk's Kirn Memorial Library, made available to me reference materials contained in the Sargeant Memorial Room. Vincent Fitzpatrick, curator of the H. L. Mencken Collection at the Enoch Pratt Free Library in Baltimore; Lucious Edwards, archivist at Virginia State University's Johnston Memorial Library; Ann Kinken Johnson, director of the *Virginian-Pilot* library; Julia Carrington, children's coordinator at the Halifax County (Va.) South Boston Regional Public Library; Julia Randle, archivist at the Virginia Theological Seminary's Bishop Payne Library; Marilyn Berry, librarian at the Bad Axe (Mich.) Public Library; Lina Tindal, director of the Harry M. Caudill Memorial Library in Whitesburg (Ky.); Janet Whitson, manager at Detroit Public Library's Burton Historical Collection; Daniel Bowell, director of King College Library; and the staff of the news library at the *Greensboro (N.C.) News and Record* all provided essential assistance.

At the American Jewish Historical Society, associate director for administration Stanley Remsberg and his research staff provided important help. Nancy Levin Arbeiter, who directs AJHS's Genealogical Research Service, worked tirelessly and heroically on this project for several years. Her diligence and expertise resulted in many contributions to this book and inspired me throughout my work. Robert A. Rockaway, senior lecturer in Tel Aviv University's Department of Jewish History and Diaspora Research

Institute and the author of *The Jews of Detroit,* read and commented on a crucial section of this manuscript. James D. Grey, president of the Jewish Historical Society of Michigan, reviewed an early chapter of this book and provided assistance, as did Leon Dworsky and several other senior citizens in Durham's Jewish community. I would also like to acknowledge the significant contributions made by the archivists and congregants at Detroit's Congregation Shaarey Zedek and Temple Beth El, Richmond's Congregation Beth Ahabah, and Danville's Temple Beth Sholom.

Local historians Celestyne D. Porter of Norfolk, John M. Johnson of Wytheville, Virginia, and Bud Phillips of Bristol, Virginia, shared their extensive knowledge of their communities with me, as did confidential sources in these localities.

John Egerton's monumental *Speak Now Against the Day* and John Kneebone's extensively researched *Southern Liberal Journalists and the Issue of Race* greatly influenced my approach to this topic. Media historian James Startt, senior research professor in Valparaiso University's history department and co-author of *Historical Methods in Mass Communication,* who patiently oversaw my education in the craft of historical research, corresponded with me and helped me address methodological concerns.

Many colleagues in the American Journalism Historians Association, including David Davies, chairman of the Department of Journalism at the University of Southern Mississippi, and Louise Benjamin and Wallace Eberhard, in the University of Georgia's Grady College of Journalism and Mass Communication, shared their expertise in media history with me.

I received support for this project from the Virginia Foundation for the Humanities in Charlottesville, where I spent a thoroughly enjoyable and undistracted semester as a resident fellow while writing the first chapters of this book. I was befriended by staff members Robert Vaughan, Roberta Culbertson, and Carol Hendrix, who continue to play a vital role in nurturing scholarship in Virginia and throughout the South. Linda Hyatt, executive director of the Landmark Communications Foundation, awarded me a very generous grant that allowed me to travel to research collections and lent enthusiastic support throughout my work on this project. Purdue University's Research Foundation, School of Liberal Arts, and library awarded me many grants that funded my travel to manuscript collections.

Charles Stewart and Cynthia Stohl, who served as my department heads in Purdue University's Department of Communication, took an early interest in my work and never wavered in their support. Margaret Rowe, dean of the School of Liberal Arts, and associate deans William Schaeffer and Howard Zelaznik worked hard to provide me with the resources I needed to conduct my research. The administration of James Madison University lent their full support to this project after I transferred there. Richard Whitman, dean of the College of Arts and Letters, and associate deans David Jeffrey, Marilou Johnson, and A. J. Morey strongly encouraged my efforts. George Johnson, director of the School of Media Arts and Design and a former journalist, expressed a strong interest in my work and facilitated my research and writing.

Departmental colleagues and native southerners Linda Perry and Robert Ogles shared their expertise with me, as did graduate student Changfu Chang, now a professor at Millersville University. Maurice Berube, Eminent Professor of Urban Services at Old Dominion University, who introduced me to scholarship, continues to serve as a valued mentor and close friend.

The Jaffé family played an indispensable role in the research and writing of this book. Louis Jaffé Jr. and Kitty Whitman encouraged me to undertake this project, provided me with access to personal papers that had not been examined by other scholars, shared their interpretations with me, reviewed the manuscript, and suggested important changes that vastly improved its quality. They also selected the photographs for this book and oversaw their reproduction. The photographs and the quotations from Louis Jaffé's personal papers and the Jaffé Papers at the University of Virginia's Special Collections Department appear here with their permission.

Louis Jaffé's wife, Alice, who died shortly before I began work on the book and who herself played a notable part in advancing civil rights in the Hampton Roads area, made the most important contribution to this book. She compiled and cataloged her husband's papers and researched his past. Her marginalia, notes, letters, and essays proved invaluable. I wish I could have known this remarkable woman.

I have long admired Louisiana State University Press, and I am gratified that its editorial staff elected to publish this book. Maureen G. Hewitt, associate director and editor-in-chief, supported my project early on and wisely guided it to completion. Bertram Wyatt-Brown, editor of the Southern Biography Series, made many useful suggestions and influenced my work through his important book, *Southern Honor: Ethics and Behavior in the Old South*. Sylvia Frank Rodrigue, acquisitions editor, played an important role in coordinating the book's production. Editor Gerry Anders oversaw the editing process with wisdom and good humor. Alisa Plant, with meticulous attention to detail, copyedited the manuscript and made many important changes. I would also like to acknowledge the crucial contribution made by the anonymous scholar who so thoroughly reviewed my manuscript for the press and encouraged me to make revisions that decidedly strengthened its quality.

My family sustained me throughout my work on this book. My sister, Dorchen, through her social activism, international human rights advocacy, and scholarship provided a source of inspiration. My mother, Louise Leidholdt, whose Virginia upbringing, deep understanding of the South, and personal experiences helped inform this project, meticulously reviewed each chapter and suggested important changes in terms of content and writing. I have immense respect for my mother and my father, Edwin, who has served as my lifelong role model. My wife, JoAnne, a colleague formerly in Purdue University's Department of Communication and now at James Madison University, traveled with me numerous times to research collections, discussed with me many issues of interpretation, and subjected my work to close inspection. Her own scholarship, which focuses on enhancing public participation in the formulation of media policy and advancing the public interest, significantly informed my approach to this book. I could not have completed this project without her love and support.

EDITOR FOR JUSTICE

INTRODUCTION

Black American soldiers returning to the South from service overseas in World War I found no improvement in conditions at home. After risking their lives to make the world safe for democracy, most returned to the same substandard housing and subservient status they had left. After mingling freely with whites in Europe, blacks now found the segregation of facilities and the restriction of movement as firmly entrenched as ever. The most sympathetic of whites, passing along their hand-me-downs, still only clucked over the economic plight of blacks. What a shame that they innately lacked the ability to better their circumstances—but how convenient that they remained available for menial service at affordable wages!

Southern Jews, too, walked a narrow line, sometimes reminded frighteningly of the precariousness of their societal acceptance and their actual safety. While managing not to look as deprived as blacks, first- and second-generation American Jews often lived in penury and operated their businesses on narrow profit margins. Boycott spelled disaster.

Most southern women still cooked and scrubbed their days away or supervised their underpaid domestic help from the politically voiceless and occupationally repressive pedestal assigned to their sex in purported veneration of womanhood.

Post–World War I Norfolk, Virginia, suffered all these ills and more. The city's business and port facilities, having lost much of their workforce to military service and straining to meet wartime demands, had recruited hordes of new workers, many of them from rural areas where racial animosity ran deep. And lured by the city's notorious nightlife, sailors from the world's largest naval base poured downtown in the evenings and on the weekends. Violence, often racially motivated, erupted with predictable regularity and frequent scapegoating of blacks.

To present their cases in these and other inequities, blacks in Norfolk had only the ministers of their segregated churches and a single small press with virtually nonexistent circulation outside the black community. No white spokesperson consistently or frequently served as a voice for blacks or other underdogs.

Enter young, unknown Louis Isaac Jaffé, fresh off the boat from war-torn Europe, to step behind the editorial desk of one of the state's leading newspapers.

But the Jaffé story begins a generation earlier in a distant land, where a beleaguered people envisioned a better life. This narrative identifies two people who acted on that dream, follows them to the New World, and tracks their journey there, with its formidable hardship, uncertainty, and repeated starting over. It investigates the forces that assisted and beset them and their children in their struggle for survival. It traces the progress of an upwardly mobile second-generation American Jew, looks inside a Jewish-Gentile marriage, and reveals the painful confliction that the departure of a family member from the traditional fold could generate.

The story of Louis Jaffé depicts life in three major southern cities at different stages of development and chronicles the amassing of the Duke fortune and the birth of a prestigious university. It spans two world wars, from ominous first rumblings to aftermath. It documents the genesis and proliferation of hate movements and persecution in the names of race, religion, and chivalry. It disinters some long-buried atrocities and dissects several particularly lurid lynchings of minorities. It personalizes the catastrophe of the Great Depression.

Louis Jaffé's decades-long battle for human rights did not confine itself to the city of Norfolk. His most illustrious victory, which helped put an end in Virginia to perhaps the cruelest discriminatory act practiced in the South, resounded throughout the southern states. Continuing his attack on other violations of human rights, he pointed out many injustices and dangers and fired at them without letup.

This account illuminates Jaffé's editorial campaigns in all their intensity and dips intimately into his personal life as well, exposing its joys and its agonies. His story encompasses a broad spectrum of life in the South in his time: the ethnic, religious, and gender divisions and the complexities of the interplay among them.

The story of Louis Jaffé is at once the odyssey of a courageous newspaperman, a chapter in the annals of human rights, an expansion of the history of liberal journalism, and a panoramic portrayal of the way it was in the American South in the first half of the twentieth century.

1   THE LAST STRAW

For Louis Jaffé, editor of the *Norfolk Virginian-Pilot,* the news from Wytheville on August 15, 1926, was profoundly troubling. The Bird lynching could easily have been prevented. Jaffé had warned, as had many other southern newspaper editors, of the need for local officials to exercise extreme caution in volatile cases such as this one. Raymond Bird should never have been locked up in the flimsy Wytheville jail; he should have been rushed to Bristol or Roanoke, each well under a hundred miles away. Now the town fathers would play out the charade, the chamber of commerce and the local press would halfheartedly condemn mob justice, and a pro forma investigation would produce nothing of substance.

Virginia's modern business-minded governor, young Harry F. Byrd Sr., despite his admirable energy and efficiency, would be hamstrung in his attempts to launch an investigation. The governor would fret about the negative publicity and its impact on his efforts to entice northern businesses to Virginia, but the law was the law. Unless local authorities requested its assistance in conducting the investigation, the state had to steer clear. And the last thing Wytheville's commonwealth's attorney, H. M. Heuser, wanted was the state's Department of Justice snooping around. God knew what it might find. Despite Harry Byrd's pressure and despite the barrage of editorials from Virginia newspapers, Heuser had no intention of letting the state get its foot in the door. He knew that with a little time the clamor would die down, and outside attention would turn elsewhere. If one discounted the blacks living in Wythe County's isolated black settlements, people would soon forget about the unpleasantness and go on with their lives.

Although Jaffé intended to keep the heat on Wytheville, he knew nothing would come of Heuser's inquiry. Throughout his career, Jaffé had observed the inefficiency of local law authorities in preventing and investigating lynchings. Ineptitude, fear, and at times actual complicity virtually guaranteed the bungling of such cases.

Bird's death distressed Jaffé intellectually and emotionally. The remedy for the problem seemed simple. If the state's General Assembly directed that suspects of offenses likely to provoke lynchings be rushed to city jails, mob justice could frequently be avoided. If the state would employ its powers to apprehend and punish lynchers, mobs would think long and hard before taking the law into their own hands.

Jaffé felt a visceral revulsion in cases like this. Social and racial wrongs—lynchings in particular—appalled him and affected him deeply. Most southern editors lashed out at lynch mobs, but Jaffé felt outrage on a personal level, far exceeding that of his peers in the white press. Jaffé was intensely private, and few knew of the experiences in his own life that drove him to battle such injustices.

Raymond Bird had lived with his wife and their three young children in an isolated pocket of about thirty black families in the western end of Wythe County, in an area known to some whites as Nigger Ridge. Bird, in the prime of life at thirty-one years of age, was so tall that his feet nearly touched the ground when he rode his horse and so strong that he could effortlessly lift a hundred-pound sack of sugar and hold it high above his head.[1]

For five years Bird had worked as a farmhand for Grover Grubb, who lived across the ridge. Grubb owned a small farm of about sixty acres and worked at a sawmill some distance away. During the workweek he would spend nights at the mill, returning home on the weekends. His wife, an invalid, was confined to the farmhouse. As a result of their father's absence and their mother's illness, the Grubbs' three daughters and son went largely unsupervised.[2]

On August 7, 1926, Bird was charged with raping the older two girls, Minnie and Essie May, ages nineteen and twenty-two, and with fondling their twelve-year-old sister. Grover Grubb had filed charges with

1. Confidential interview in possession of author, 4 December 1985; Paul G. Beers, *The Lynching of Raymond Bird* (n.p., n.d.), 3–4; Stuart Campbell to Harry Byrd, 20 August 1926, Byrd Executive Papers.

2. Campbell to Byrd, 20 August 1926; Beers, *Lynching of Raymond Bird,* 4.

Heuser and retained a prominent local lawyer, future state legislator Stuart Campbell, to press his claims. Yet, as is so often the case in the history of southern race relations, the story was not as simple as the charges against Bird might suggest. Bird's testimony and even a cursory cross-examination of Minnie and Essie May Grubb would have brought to light circumstances suggesting that the most fundamental notion of southern racial hierarchy might have been contravened. That Raymond Bird had violated the penultimate taboo of southern society by crossing the "color line" was certain, but the possibility that the Grubbs' older daughters had been willing participants in sexual liaisons with a black man transgressed the South's most powerful racial dictum and would have heaped dishonor on Grubb and his family.[3]

None of this background appeared in the white presses' newspaper reports; but in a lengthy confidential letter, Grubb's attorney told Governor Byrd many of the details that led up to Bird's arrest. The *Richmond Planet,* a black weekly newspaper that had acquired a reputation for bold journalism and concerned itself little with offending the sensibilities of white readers, printed another account.[4]

Minnie and Essie May admitted that they had begun to engage in sexual relations with Bird in the fall of 1925. Both daughters became pregnant, Minnie first. They managed to conceal their conditions from their parents and neighbors; even Minnie's physician, who was treating her for a chronic health condition, discovered her pregnancy only two weeks before she gave birth. The baby was born in a car as Minnie hurried to the hospital in nearby Abingdon, where nurses declared the baby to be black, despite Minnie's insistence otherwise. She tried without success to give the baby away in Roanoke; when she returned home, Bird took the baby and gave it to a black woman in Wytheville. "It is a pretty baby, being a brownie," an informant told the *Planet.*[5]

3. Campbell to Byrd, 20 August 1926; W. Fitzhugh Brundage, *Lynching in the New South: Georgia and Virginia, 1880–1930* (Urbana: University of Illinois Press, 1993), 61–2; Gunnar Myrdal, *An American Dilemma: The Negro Problem and Modern Democracy,* vol. 2 (New Brunswick, N.J.: Transaction, 1996), 586–7.

4. W. Fitzhugh Brundage, "'To Howl Loudly': John Mitchell, Jr. and his Campaign Against Lynching in Virginia," *Canadian Review of American Studies* 22, no. 3 (winter 1991): 325–41.

5. Campbell to Byrd, 20 August 1926; *Richmond Planet,* 4 September 1926.

It is unclear from Campbell's account of his interview with the Grubbs how the two women described the nature of their sexual relationship with Bird, but both maintained that he had threatened to kill them if they revealed that he had impregnated them. Heuser and Campbell concluded that Bird could not be charged with rape but that he could be prosecuted for allegedly attempting to molest the youngest of the three Grubb daughters.[6]

The *Planet*'s source asserted that no rape had occurred. The source reported a long history of interracial sex between Grover Grubb's relatives and blacks: "The girls love Raymond and [Minnie] told the officer that she would die and go to h . . . before she would go against Raymond. Those Grubbs have been mixing up with Negroes ever since before the War. They were good livers."[7]

Southerners had long winked at miscegenation between white men and black women, so long as it was kept discreet; but the purported raison d'être of Jim Crow was the protection of "southern womanhood," enforcing an inviolable proscription against sexual relations between black men and white women. The rest of segregation's taboos were predicated on this dictum.[8]

Bird's violation of Grover Grubb's honor set in motion the train of events that culminated in the lynching. A quarter century earlier an alleged rape of a white female by a black man had affronted the collective honor of Wythe County to such a degree that the larger community had openly participated in a mass mob lynching. Had the reputation of Grover Grubb's family been less dubious and Wytheville slightly less cosmopolitan, perhaps the passions of the citizenry could have been stoked to such an extent that that ritual could have been reenacted. But the slight to Grubb's honor, however much it may have enraged his friends in the west end of the county, was of minor concern to the townspeople. His lust for revenge would have to be satiated by a clandestine mob of his neighbors. Raymond Bird's killers may have believed that if they constituted themselves as a lynch mob, their

6. Campbell to Byrd, 20 August 1926.
7. *Richmond Planet*, 4 September 1926.
8. Betram Wyatt-Brown, *Honor and Violence in the Old South* (New York: Oxford University Press, 1986), 105; Myrdal, *An American Dilemma*, 586–7.

actions would be given legitimacy and the murder would be sanctioned as an expression of communal will. It was not.[9]

Before arresting Bird, Wythe County's sheriff, W. C. Kincer, and his deputies, along with law officials from nearby Rural Retreat, met at Grover Grubb's house. There they found a mob, armed with shotguns and pistols, who wanted to assist the officers in their duties. Fearing that the situation could easily deteriorate into a lynching, Sheriff Kincer concocted a ruse. He directed the mob to accompany a deputy to apprehend Bird at his home, while the sheriff and the remaining deputies traveled to a wake their suspect was attending and arrested him. Bird was escorted back to Grubb's house, but when Kincer learned that the mob had grown, he sped his prisoner to Wytheville's jail by way of a back road. One of the deputies stayed at the Grubb farm and attempted to calm the crowd. That night Kincer spoke with Heuser and apprised him of Bird's arrest and of the volatile atmosphere brewing in the western end of the county. Kincer and his deputies allegedly advised Heuser that their prisoner should be transferred to a more secure jail.[10]

The sheriff had good reason for concern. Grover Grubb and his friends were known for their violent tempers and their racism. Grubb had shot a neighbor in the wrist during an argument over horses; in another dispute, he and his son had waylaid and shot a relative. (One hates to think of the rebuke Grubb administered to his daughters upon learning of their sexual liaisons with Bird.) Members of Grubb's social group hated blacks and believed that they could be controlled only through violence. Grubb's circle also included some known Ku Klux Klan members. The Klan was particularly active in southwestern Virginia, where social and racial tensions were heightened by the development of modern transportation and rural industrialization, which in many localities had swollen the area's population through importation of black and foreign-born workers. Klansmen threatened to beat blacks and whites they suspected of transgressions by propping switches against their doors. Cross burnings were reserved for the most serious cases and warned of more severe punishment.[11]

9. Brundage, *Lynching in the New South*, 32–3, 282.

10. *Smyth County (Va.) News*, 26 August 1926.

11. Confidential interview, 4 December 1985; David M. Chalmers, *Hooded Ameri-*

Heuser refused to order Bird's transfer to another jail, urging Sheriff Kincer to rely on his own judgment as to whether the prisoner should be moved. Kincer and his deputies insisted that such a decision was beyond the scope of their duties and that Heuser should accept responsibility for the transfer. The stalemate resulted in Bird's remaining in the Wytheville jail.[12]

The prisoner—well aware of his dangerous predicament and of the precarious security Wytheville's jail afforded him—nervously awaited his preliminary hearing, which was set for August 18. He surely would not have been surprised early on the morning of August 15, if he was awake, when a mob silently descended on the jail, tricked the jailer into opening the wire-mesh door, and clipped the single telephone line.[13]

Once inside, members of the fifty-man mob, all of whom were masked and some of whom had dressed in women's clothes to disguise their identities further, quickly subdued the jailer and located the keys to Bird's cell. Holding the jailer at gunpoint, the men shot Bird, perhaps killing him. Then they entered his cell and beat his head to a pulp with rifle butts and clubs. After pulling his body outside to the street by a noose tied around his neck, they tied the rope to the rear axle of an automobile and dragged the body ten blocks to the outskirts of town. They then placed the bleeding corpse in the car, and the caravan proceeded nine miles to Grubb's farm. (Later that morning, the son of the driver would observe his father and a neighbor carefully washing the vehicle inside and out to remove all incriminating traces of Bird's blood.) About a quarter of a mile from the farm, the mob strung Bird up in an oak tree near the scene of his alleged crime and left him there to terrorize the black community. At dawn, a boy tending his father's cows received the scare of his life when he nearly walked into the body's dangling legs.[14]

---

canism: The First Century of the Ku Klux Klan, 1865–1965 (Garden City, N.Y.: Doubleday, 1965), 231; Brundage, Lynching in the New South, 149.

12. Smyth County News, 26 August 1926; Campbell to Byrd, 20 August 1926; Mary B. Kegley, Wythe County, Virginia: A Bicentennial History (Marceline, Mo.: Walsworth, 1989), 179–80.

13. Confidential interview, 4 December 1985; Campbell to Byrd, 20 August 1926; Norfolk Virginian-Pilot (hereafter cited as Pilot), 20 August 1926; Richmond Planet, 21 August 1926.

14. Confidential interview, 4 December 1985; Beers, Lynching of Raymond Bird, 6; Richmond Planet, 21 August 1926; Pilot, 18 August 1926.

Word of the lynching spread like wildfire among the churchgoers arriving at a nearby Lutheran church. After the services, the sheriff and members of the congregation cut Bird down, while some observers bickered over scraps of the rope and other souvenirs. Instead of transporting the body to a coroner for an autopsy, which would have proved useful in the ensuing investigation, the sheriff turned the body over to an undertaker for burial.[15]

Bird's lynching happened to coincide with the Virginia Press Association's summer meeting, which was taking place in nearby Pulaski. A number of reporters and editors had toured Wytheville, where the region's chamber of commerce maintained its headquarters, the day prior to the lynching. A spirit of boosterism had prevailed at the meeting. Attendees had been welcomed by a local official "reviewing the power which the press exercises and telling something of . . . Southwest Virginia." In response, the presiding officer of the association, Colonel Walter Copeland, editor of the *Newport News Times-Herald,* ironically had "emphasized the attitude of Virginia newspapers toward all things which are elevating."[16]

Jaffé likely learned of the lynching when he arrived for work at nine o'clock that Monday and read the Associated Press's story in the morning's *Virginian-Pilot.* He was doubtless dismayed by the lackadaisical attitude imputed to Wytheville's citizenry and by indications that the lynch mob would go unpunished. "Wytheville, according to advices here, seems undisturbed over the affair," the report read. "The identity of the mob is shrouded in mystery. . . . No arrests have been made although an investigation has been launched by Wytheville authorities." Jaffé promptly began work on his lead editorial that would run the following day.[17]

In "Another Virginia Lynching," Jaffé recounted Bird's murder in grisly detail, brushing aside the veneer of courtliness and gentility that many

15. Confidential interview, 4 December 1985; Beers, *Lynching of Raymond Bird,* 1; *Pilot,* 16 August 1926; *Southwest Virginia Enterprise,* 17 August 1926; Campbell to Byrd, 20 August 1926.

16. *Southwest Virginia Enterprise,* 17 August 1926; Lester J. Cappon, *Virginia Newspapers, 1821–1935: A Bibliography with Historical Introduction and Notes* (New York: D. Appleton-Century, 1936), 133; Leland B. Tate, comp., *The Virginia Guide: A Manual of Information About Virginia* (Lebanon, Va.: Leland B. Tate, 1929), 51.

17. *Pilot,* 16 August 1926.

Virginians believed distinguished them from their coarse brethren in the Deep South. "No more barbarous exhibition of the mob spirit has been reported from any State in many a month," he wrote, concluding his editorial with a call for action. "Failure to take measures against those responsible for this outrage will tend to encourage similar occurrences in the future. Prompt and vigorous efforts to identify those responsible for this offense would, on the contrary, put all lawless elements on notice that Virginia intends to ban private justice and make the laws of the Commonwealth supreme."[18]

In contrast, Wytheville's semiweekly *Southwest Virginia Enterprise* attached little news value to the lynching, allocating only three paragraphs to the report, which ran with the same size headline as an adjoining story, "How Tourists Benefit Our City." The *Enterprise* mildly condemned both Bird's alleged crime and mob justice. Influenced by town officials' concerns over negative publicity, the paper's editor had clearly decided to downplay the story. The unsavory prospect of encountering Grover Grubb and members of the mob likely contributed further to his reticence. Journalists working for small-town papers labored under these sorts of pressures on a daily basis and to a much greater extent than did their big-city counterparts.[19]

On August 18, Jaffé confronted what he perceived to be the indifference of Wytheville's townspeople. In "Wytheville Is Quiet!" he reprinted a segment of an Associated Press report concluding that the lynching had created no excitement. Adopting a sarcastic tone, Jaffé chided the town's residents. "If the cashier of the leading bank had absconded with the burghers' savings, if a leading citizen had been apprehended in flagrant dereliction with the town Jezebel, . . . if the Methodist pastor had boldly in his pulpit defended the teaching of organic evolution," he charged, residents would have been profoundly upset, and Sheriff Kincer and his deputies would have conducted an energetic investigation.[20]

Throughout the week nearly all of Virginia's principal dailies, as well as the state's two major black presses, the *Richmond Planet* and the

18. Ibid., 17 August 1926.

19. *Southwest Virginia Enterprise*, 17 August 1926; Robert Mason, *One of the Neighbors' Children* (Chapel Hill: Algonquin Books of Chapel Hill, 1987), 36–43; Brundage, *Lynching in the New South*, 32.

20. *Pilot*, 18 August 1926.

Norfolk Journal and Guide, denounced Bird's lynching. The event had tarnished the region's reputation, the *Newport News Daily-Press* declaimed, and "would be used against the county and State by enemies of Virginia in other sections of the country." (During recent congressional hearings on the need for federal antilynching laws, many witnesses and legislators had criticized the South's propensity for mob violence. A few years earlier, southern senators had been hard pressed to derail the Dyer federal antilynching bill with a filibuster.) The *Petersburg Progress-Index* implored Wytheville's residents to remove the stigma of Bird's lynching by pressuring Heuser and Kincer to investigate the incident thoroughly. The *Richmond Times-Dispatch* lampooned the slowness with which the Bird investigation was proceeding by picturing Lady Justice balancing her scales while seated astride a giant tortoise labeled "Wytheville Lynching Case."[21]

Despite the media outcry, Wytheville's authorities refused to press the investigation. They had displayed a seamless record of incompetence and lethargy from the moment of Raymond Bird's incarceration. The jailer, who may have been complicit in the attack, had taken an hour and a half to telephone Heuser, who then had ordered a single policeman to pursue the mob. Stuart Campbell, Grover Grubb's attorney, confided to Governor Byrd that Kincer and his deputies lacked initiative and could not be relied upon to apprehend suspects. "Nothing seems to have been done that night," he wrote, "or for that matter, at any other time by the Sheriff's Office to endeavor to ascertain any of the participants of the mob." Horace Sutherland, the local circuit court judge, cautioned the governor that Wytheville's law officials might actually be in league with the mob. Acting on this information and spurred to action by the press, Byrd offered Heuser the assistance of state detectives, but the commonwealth's attorney refused the offer of help, claiming that the "situation was quiet." Heuser, who resented the newspapers' criticism of his performance, dug in his heels and blamed the press for obstructing the investigation.[22]

21. George B. Tindall, *The Emergence of the New South, 1913–1945,* vol. 10, *A History of the South,* ed. Wendell Holmes Stephenson and E. Merton Coulter (Baton Rouge: Louisiana State University Press, 1967), 173–4; *Norfolk Journal and Guide* (hereafter cited as *Guide*), 28 August 1926; *Richmond Times-Dispatch,* 29 August 1926, 1 September 1926.

22. Campbell to Byrd, 20, 28 August 1926, Byrd Executive Papers; *Guide,* 21 August 1926; Confidential interview, 4 December 1985; Horace Sutherland to Harry Byrd,

All in all, Wytheville's residents seemed much more disturbed by the negative publicity they were receiving than by the lynching itself. The *Baltimore Evening Sun* reported that the "criticism which the affair has aroused and the editorial attacks on the county, which have appeared in virtually all newspapers of the state, appear to have aroused the residents of this section more than the actual lynching." Indeed, less than two days after the lynching, fifty townspeople held a meeting to complain about the economic consequences of the media's unflattering portrayal of Wytheville.[23]

As the week wore on, the *Pilot*'s fierce criticism of the investigation continued, and Jaffé's recommendations grew more explicit. From his editorial page he both flattered Byrd and warned him that his stature and reputation depended on bringing the members of the lynch mob to justice. Applauding the governor's offer of state assistance, Jaffé urged Byrd to overrule Heuser's objections and assign detectives to augment Wytheville's investigation. The editor argued that prisoners accused of offenses likely to inflame mob passions, such as Raymond Bird, should be rushed—by military force, if warranted—to the nearest city with a large professional police department and a sturdy jail able to withstand a mob siege. Modern transportation and paved roads allowed prisoners to be conveyed to county courthouses for trial during the daytime and returned to secure jails for lodging.[24]

Despite the fact that Jaffé had supported Byrd's opponent, G. Walter Mapp, in the 1925 Democratic primary, the governor read the *Pilot*'s editorials every day and sought Jaffé's advice on policy matters. "I have been impressed with your accurate knowledge and the study you have given State questions," Byrd wrote the editor. "You . . . wrote the most effective editorials against me in the last campaign, but at all times you were fair and courteous. . . . I want you to feel your suggestions will be received by me gladly and I will appreciate having them."[25]

As the nephew of a former long-term congressman from Virginia, Henry "Hal" D. Flood, and the son of Richard Evelyn Byrd, a former

Byrd Executive Papers, 24 August 1926; *Pilot*, 18 August 1926; H. M. Heuser to Harry Byrd, 23 August 1926, Byrd Executive Papers.

23. *Roanoke Times*, 3 September 1926; Beers, *Lynching of Raymond Bird*, 8.

24. *Pilot*, 19, 20 August 1926.

25. Harry Byrd to Louis Jaffé, 28 August 1925, 24 March 1926, Jaffé Papers.

speaker of Virginia's House of Delegates, Byrd claimed an impressive political lineage. But Jaffé had also known the governor as the editor and publisher of the *Winchester Evening Star*—a lesser paper than the *Virginian-Pilot*—prior to his political ascendancy. The *Pilot*'s editor therefore felt little compunction in advising the governor, but he had saved his direct input for an especially vital matter. The situation in Wytheville more than met that criterion. He ended his silence.[26]

"The crime of lynching," Jaffé wrote Byrd, "has always seemed to me to be particularly atrocious and degrading. The Wytheville performance added a touch of savagery that must add to every Virginian's humiliation." Reiterating the content of his editorials, Jaffé urged the governor to support legislation that would require local authorities to rush suspects of crimes likely to provoke lynchings to city jails, and would enable the state to "employ all the power and resources at its command to apprehend and punish lynchers" when local investigations appeared inadequate.[27]

Jaffé would have to bring Byrd along slowly; localism was revered in Virginia, and the state's electorate regarded heightened executive authority with suspicion. Byrd's gubernatorial tenure, characterized by a consolidation of state departments and by a shortened ballot that greatly increased his powers, flew in the face of this sentiment. Even though he continued to enjoy popular support, the governor was wary of overstepping his bounds. Nonetheless, responding to Judge Sutherland's concern that Heuser's investigation would lead nowhere, Byrd appointed Leon Bazille, an assistant attorney general, and Joseph Chitwood, a Roanoke attorney, to assist the commonwealth's attorney. Ultimately, Heuser had been forced to accept the state's offer of help.[28]

On September 1, Sutherland convened a special grand jury comprised entirely of white men. Kincer, his deputies, the jailer, and many other

26. Ronald L. Heinemann, *Harry Byrd of Virginia* (Charlottesville: University Press of Virginia, 1996), 13.

27. Louis Jaffé to Harry Byrd, 30 August 1926, Jaffé Papers.

28. Brundage, *Lynching in the New South,*161; J. Harvie Wilkinson III, *Harry Byrd and the Changing Face of Virginia Politics, 1945–1966* (Charlottesville: University Press of Virginia, 1968), 7; George C. Rable, "The South and the Politics of Antilynching Legislation, 1920–1940," *Journal of Southern History* 51, no. 2 (1985): 207; Brundage, "To Howl Loudly," 325–41.

witnesses were examined. Although an atmosphere of secrecy prevailed, the *Southwest Virginia Enterprise* reported, "It seems the consensus of opinion that the investigation may extend over some time."[29]

From the outset Sutherland's investigation was stymied. Throughout the inquiry Bazille and his colleagues issued pessimistic statements to the press. The judge, who had opened the trial by declaring that the lynchers had shamed the region and Virginia, was forced to suspend the proceedings after only four days because the prosecutors had run out of evidence. Byrd attempted to jump-start the investigation by offering a state reward of $1,000. Wythe County's board of supervisors—in an attempt to control the negative publicity Heuser's lethargic investigation had aroused—posted a reward of $100 (a sizable inducement, at a time when a postage stamp cost two cents) for information that led to the conviction of a member of the lynch mob. No one came forward.[30]

The sheriff and his deputies were summoned again on September 16, and the investigation reached a climax two days later when Grover and Minnie Grubb and many of their neighbors appeared before the grand jury. In all probability several members of the lynch mob were among the witnesses called that day. Sutherland and the jury members must have listened skeptically to much of the testimony, but Raymond Bird's murderers walked away from the courthouse free men. Many in Wytheville knew who was responsible for the lynching—the town's newspapers said as much when they identified the region of the county from which the mob came—but they chose to keep silent. In the end, just as the lynch mob intended, Wythe County's black citizens were terrorized. In an effort to protect its correspondent, the *Richmond Planet* withdrew him, writing: "There is a tense feeling, no colored person knowing just what will happen after the outside influences exerted by the Governor, the Attorney General's office and the state press have been withdrawn."[31]

29. Circuit Court of Wythe County summons, 31 August 1926; *Southwest Virginia Enterprise,* 3 September 1926.

30. Beers, *Lynching of Raymond Bird,* 9–10; *Southwest Virginia Enterprise,* 10 September 1926.

31. Circuit Court of Wythe County summons, 15 September 1926; Circuit Court of Wythe County summons, 17 September 1926; Confidential interview, 4 December 1985; *Southwest Virginia Enterprise,* 24 August 1926; *Richmond Planet,* 4 September 1926.

Mob violence occurred much more rarely in Virginia than in the Deep South, but a number of lynchings had been committed in the state since Jaffé had assumed the editorship of the *Virginian-Pilot* in 1919. The year before Raymond Bird's lynching, a particularly heinous lynching in the *Pilot*'s own backyard in little Waverly, just sixty miles from Norfolk, drew a much less spirited response from Jaffé. A mob—variously estimated at between five hundred and two thousand, and comprised of nearly every adult white male who lived in the county—held law authorities at gunpoint, battered its way into the jail with a water main, and lynched James Jordan, who was accused of raping a young white woman. A train from Norfolk pulled into Waverly's Norfolk and Western Railway depot, where the mob hanged Jordan, riddled his corpse with bullets, and burned his body. Horrified passengers received a clear view of the carnage.[32]

Responding to Jordan's brutal death, Jaffé had downplayed the idea that legal reforms could help end lynching. "Punitive measures against members of a lynching mob are notoriously ineffective," he wrote. "We shall have an attempt at it, no doubt, in Waverly. A solemn jury may return indictments or may return the usual finding: 'Shot to death by parties unknown.' It makes little difference either way. In forty years more than forty hundred persons have been lynched in the United States, and at least forty thousand persons were direct participants in the lynchings. Not forty of this number have been indicted for murder in the first degree." Jaffé called for a concerted education campaign to reshape the public's attitude toward mob violence: "Our schools, our churches, our publicists, our politicians and all who are concerned with the ennoblement of American civilization have a part to play in establishing this rule of order."[33]

During his Wytheville editorial campaign, Jaffé's advocacy grew much more dynamic, and his antilynching recommendations evolved considerably. Bird's lynching may have appeared more preventable to him than Jordan's had been. Waverly's commonwealth's attorney and sheriff had attempted to spirit the suspect out of the county to a more secure jail only

32. *Pilot*, 21 March 1925; *Richmond Planet*, 28 March 1925; *Richmond Times-Dispatch*, 21 March 1925.
33. *Pilot*, 22 March 1925.

to find the roads blocked by armed men, and when conditions degenerated in town, they had requested troops from then-governor Elbert Lee Trinkle. But Jaffé's heightened activism sprang from more than ire brought on by the ineptitude of Wytheville's authorities and the apparent indifference of its citizenry.[34]

The editor saw great potential in Trinkle's successor, Harry Byrd Sr. In the ambitious new governor's plans to increase the authority of Virginia's chief executives and in the strong mandate awarded him by the public in the recent election, Jaffé discerned a previously unavailable opportunity for the state to take steps to eradicate lynching. He knew that a committed governor could deter mob violence. Contemporaneously to Byrd's inauguration, Jaffé had lauded North Carolina governor Angus W. McLean for denying pardons to rioters who had attempted a lynching in Asheville; despite intense political pressure to grant clemency, McLean had stood his ground. Jaffé now quoted him in "War on Lynching to the End": "The only way to suppress lynching is to let those who engage in it understand that they will be punished and punished severely." Jaffé also praised North Carolina's willingness to call out the militia to protect black prisoners. "If every state would follow the example North Carolina has set during the past five years," he concluded, "the lynching practice would soon be extinct."[35]

Jaffé was ambitious, and in such a critical issue he may have seen an opportunity to showcase his talents and advance his professional career. He was aware of the growing reputations of other leading progressive southern journalists. Robert Lathan of the *Charleston News & Courier* had been awarded the Pulitzer Prize in 1925 for "The Plight of the South," an editorial decrying the region's lack of political leadership. Editors Grover C. Hall of the *Montgomery (Ala.) Advertiser* and Julian Harris of the *Columbus (Ga.) Enquirer-Sun* were—with the assistance of H. L. Mencken of the *Baltimore Sunpapers*—beginning to develop national reputations among their peers. Jaffé, who along with Hall and Harris had battled the Ku Klux Klan from the beginning of its spectacular ascendancy in the early 1920s, had been omitted from the leading book on southern liberalism, *The*

34. Ibid., 13 February 1926, 21 March 1925.
35. Ibid., 7, 13 February 1926.

Advancing South, written by one of his former professors. His bold and pioneering criticism of the Klan early in the decade had enhanced his reputation in Virginia but had not earned him national renown.[36]

But Jaffé's antilynching advocacy arose primarily from much more than professional ambition. His struggle against mob justice was entirely consistent with his life's work as a journalist. Much that had occurred in his own history had imbued him with acute sensitivity and aversion to social injustice. He had shared few of these details, even with intimates. In the words of a close friend, the *Pilot*'s editor placed "self revelation . . . on a par with nudism," an observation that Jaffé himself acknowledged was a "shockingly penetrating observation on the brittleness of the shell of reserve that shuts me in."[37]

However frustrating those who cared about him may have found Jaffé's reticence in personal matters, his reserve did not lack for motivation. Much about the man quite literally set him apart.

36. Wm. David Sloan and Laird B. Anderson, comps., *Pulitzer Prize Editorials: America's Best Editorial Writing, 1917–1933,* 2nd. ed. (Ames: Iowa State University Press, 1994), 29–30, 37–8; Virginius Dabney, *Liberalism in the South* (Chapel Hill: University of North Carolina Press, 1932), 400–2, 408; Edwin Mims, *The Advancing South: Stories of Progress and Reaction* (Garden City, N.Y.: Doubleday, Page, 1926); *Roanoke World-News,* 19 May 1926; *Pilot,* 8 August 1921; Ku Klux Klan to Louis Jaffé, 24 July 1922, Jaffé Papers; Edward Clarke to Louis Jaffé, 19 October 1920, Jaffé Papers; Grover Hall to Louis Jaffé, 25 April 1927, Jaffé Papers.

37. Eleanor King to Louis Jaffé, [October 1936], Louis Jaffé to Eleanor King, 15 October 1936, both in Jaffé Papers.

2 A POIGNANT JOURNEY

Louis Jaffé's roots lay not in America's Dixie or even in the western European countries to which nearly all of the South's white population could trace its ancestry, but in the remote and ancient Jewish *gubernia* (province) of Kovno, Lithuania. His ethnic heritage, which he neither volunteered nor attempted to conceal, set him apart from most southerners.

Jaffé's parents, Philip and Lotta (also called Lena, Lotte, and Lottie), appear to have been born in the early to mid 1860s in or near the city of Panevezys (also known as Ponevezh and Ponevetz) in central Lithuania. Panevezys served as a district center for the towns and villages in the surrounding area. The upper reaches of the Neviazha River divided the city, and the Jews settled in a quarter on the southern bank. In 1850 about fifteen hundred Jews lived there.[1]

The larger city of Kovno (also called Kovna, Kovne, and Kaunas), about sixty miles south of Panevezys, functioned as the provincial capital. In the second half of the nineteenth century, Kovno grew into a center for Jewish cultural and educational activity in Lithuania. Its Jewish community

1. 1900 census entry for Philip Jaffe's household, Durham Township, Durham County, N.C.; 1910 census entry for Philip Jaffe's household, South Boston, Halifax County, Va.; 1920 census entry for Phillip [sic] Jaffe's household, South Boston, Halifax Co., Va.; Philip Jaffe, petition for naturalization #101 (admitted 5 March 1928), U.S. District Court, Western District of Virginia; Lottie Jaffe, death certificate (9 October 1946), Baltimore City Health Department; Philip Jaffe, death certificate (19 March 1933), Commonwealth of Virginia; Alexander Beider, *A Dictionary of Jewish Surnames from the Russian Empire* (Teaneck, N.J.: Avotaynu, 1993), xxii; *Encyclopaedia Judaica*, s.v. "Panevezys"; Nancy Schoenburg and Stuart Schoenburg, *Lithuanian Jewish Communities* (New York: Garland, 1991), 224–30; Masha Greenbaum, *The Jews of Lithuania: A History of a Remarkable Community, 1316–1945* (Jerusalem: Gefen, 1995), 120–2.

contained numerous schools and libraries, a number of renowned yeshivot, and many celebrated Hebrew writers and literary critics.[2]

But despite the city's flowering culture, Jews living there and throughout the surrounding one million square kilometers along the western border of Russia known as the Pale of Jewish Settlement labored under dire economic conditions. Unemployment was endemic, and most Jews fortunate enough to find work received only subsistence wages. The average worker earned fifteen kopecks per day, a few pennies in today's terms. Many Jews in the Pale suffered from hunger, illness, overcrowding, and despair. Nearly 40 percent of Jewish families residing there received some sort of assistance, most of it from overseas Jewish communities.[3]

To a large extent, the Jews' marginal existence resulted from an official policy of discrimination. Perceiving them as a parasitic and foreign element that exploited farmers, Russian czars had confined Jews to the Pale. Under the reigns of Alexander I (1801–1825) and especially Nicholas I (1825–1855), anti-Semitism became institutionalized in Russia. Laws barred Jews from many occupations, restricted their right to own land, and forced them to pay special taxes. The hated Cantonist Act required Jewish communities to supply quotas of their male population aged twelve and over for military service. Christian foster families raised the boys in camps until their eighteenth birthdays, when they began to serve twenty-five-year periods of military service.[4]

Misunderstanding and suspicion often characterized the daily interactions between Christians and Jews. Many factors contributed to this tenuous relationship. Despite brutal attempts by the czars to assimilate Jews, they retained their traditional ways and stood out from their Gentile neighbors. They spoke Yiddish, learning just enough Lithuanian, Russian, or Ukrainian to conduct commerce. They observed a different day of rest and different holidays. They dressed in a distinctive style and conformed to spe-

2. "Kovno" [cited 1 February 1997]. Available from http://www.jewishgen.org/shetlinks.kovno.html; *Encyclopaedia Judaica,* s.v. "Kaunas."

3. Greenbaum, *Jews of Lithuania,* 185; *Encyclopedia of Jewish History,* s.v. "The Jewish Community in Russia: 1772–1881."

4. I. Michael Aronson, *Troubled Waters: The Origins of the 1881 Anti-Jewish Pogroms in Russia* (Pittsburgh: University of Pittsburgh Press, 1990), 29–43; *Encyclopedia of Jewish History,* s.v. "The Jewish Community in Russia: 1772–1881."

cial dietary laws. In the already overcrowded Pale, their swelling numbers aggravated tensions and made their community even more conspicuous. The powerful Russian Orthodox Church fueled these tensions by assigning all nonbelievers inferior status and sanctioning their persecution.[5]

The coronation of Czar Alexander II had filled Jews with optimism. Upon assuming power in 1855, Alexander immediately repealed the Cantonist Act and reduced the term of military service from twenty-five to sixteen years. He allowed Jews to move freely within the region and permitted educated and advantaged Jews to settle outside the Pale. For a brief period, Jews in Lithuania could purchase land. But badly frightened by a rebellion in Poland in 1863 and an attempt on his life in 1866, Alexander II drew inward and surrounded himself with reactionary advisors, who persuaded him to end his reforms. During the 1870s, the anti-Semitic Russian press, with tacit government approval, began to agitate against Jews, accusing them of exploiting the Christian working class and of fomenting revolution.[6]

The assassination of Alexander II in 1881 provided the spark needed to set off this tinderbox. When a group of radicals from the revolutionary organization Will of the People detonated the bomb that mortally wounded the czar, the inner circle of conspirators included Hessia Helfman, a Jew. Some of the Russian press seized on the issue of Jewish involvement in the plot. Although none of these reports called for attacks on Jews, they inflamed anti-Semitic passions. The press further incited lawlessness by printing rumors of impending riots against Hebrew communities. Government tolerance of Jew-baiting press tactics was commonly interpreted by readers as official endorsement of anti-Semitism. Jews shared a widespread conviction that irresponsible reporting contributed mightily to the outbreak of mob attacks in 1881.[7]

During the first wave of pogroms (1881–1884), devastating violence, concentrated primarily in the southern and southwestern regions, broke out in the Pale. Mobs comprised of peasants, industrial and railroad

5. Uri D. Herscher, *Jewish Agricultural Utopias in America, 1880–1910* (Detroit: Wayne State University Press, 1981), 16.

6. Greenbaum, *Jews of Lithuania*, 179–84; Aronson, *Troubled Waters*, 67–8.

7. Aronson, *Troubled Waters*, 68–70.

workers, and rabble from towns beat, raped, and murdered Jews and ransacked and burned their homes. Frequently, civil and military authorities stood by and did nothing to end the violence. Lithuania's governor general made clear that he would not condone rioting and thus protected that territory's Jews from life-threatening violence. Nevertheless, Gentile arsonists there terrorized Jews by burning down many of their homes and shops.[8]

Precisely how the deeply entrenched anti-Semitism of the Pale manifested itself in the daily lives of Philip and Lotta, etched itself into their personalities, and shaped their world views is not known. But in some ways, their lives resembled those of the blacks they would one day encounter in the American South. Louis Jaffé's parents experienced discrimination and deprivation firsthand, and they lived their lives in Lithuania uneasily, knowing that the dominant majority could target them for violence. As Alexander III ascended to the throne in 1881, frantic Jews began to flee the Pale. Many emigrated to the United States, while others fled to South Africa and western European nations.[9]

Few details survive about the Jaffes' lives in the Pale and their emigration to the United States. Many years later, in an incidental entry in his diary, Louis mentioned that his parents had crossed the ocean in "steerage in 1880." A petition for naturalization that Philip filed in 1917 provides an exact and probably more accurate emigration date. According to this document, he embarked from Hamburg, Germany, in September 1884 and arrived at the port of New York later that month. If he followed the traditional procedure for eastern European Jewish immigrants, he traveled alone and later sent for Lotta, who may have retraced his route.[10]

The Jaffes probably arrived in New York City with meager means and with appearance and mannerisms drastically different from German Jews, who by now had become nearly completely assimilated. Like most Russian Jews, the Jaffes retained their traditional Jewish beliefs and customs. They continued to speak Yiddish, although Philip probably could

    8. *Encyclopaedia Judaica*, s.v. "Pogroms"; Greenbaum, *Jews of Lithuania*, 187.
    9. Greenbaum, *Jews of Lithuania*, 189.
    10. Louis Jaffé war diary, 26 July 1918, Jaffé Papers; Philip Jaffe, declaration of intention #41 (filed 8 March 1917), U.S. District Court, Western District of Virginia.

read Hebrew. (They did not accent the second syllable of the family sur-name, as their son Louis would later choose to do.)[11]

The Jaffes may have remained in New York for a brief time, resid-ing in one of the crowded, dark, and unsanitary East Side tenements that housed the hordes of Jews pouring into the city. A large number of these refugees labored in factories and the needle trades, changing jobs frequently. German Jewish employers regularly exploited their coreligionist workers, who toiled in unsafe and terribly overcrowded conditions. Many Jews, par-ticularly the Jaffes' countrymen, became peddlers, spending their last ten dollars for a peddler's box, three or four dollars worth of cheap household and personal goods, and a basket for displaying wares. Encouraged by rags-to-riches stories of American capitalists, they shouldered their burdens with the cry, "Be on the march, you Lithuanian."[12]

In the mid- to late 1880s, the Jaffes moved to Detroit, Michigan, which was then transforming itself from a modest manufacturing center to a great industrial city. Its opportunities for employment would have attracted the Jaffes, and a desire to escape the tenements of New York may have provided additional impetus. "If one wants to work, there is no short-age of work," one Jewish immigrant later wrote. "The working class does not live in foul, airless rooms, as in New York, because the rent is cheaper here. Detroit is to be marveled at for her freedom and her clean air, which is like that found in a park full of beautiful trees."[13]

Indeed, the city had much to recommend it. Residents of "New Jerusalem," the Jewish quarter of Detroit's East Side where many Russian Jews had settled, lived in single-family dwellings, not in cramped tenements

11. 1900 federal population census for Philip Jaffe's household, Durham Township, Durham Co., N.C; *Halifax (Va.) Gazette,* 23 March 1933; Lee J. Levinger, *A History of the Jews in the United States* (Cincinnati: Department of Synagogue and School Extension of the Union of American Hebrew Congregations, 1930), 266–7; Robert Rockaway, letter to author, 8 April 1998; Charles S. Liebman, "Orthodoxy in American Jewish Life," *American Jewish Year Book* 66 (1965): 21–98.

12. Levinger, *History of the Jews,* 275–6; George M. Price, "The Russian Jews in America," *Publications of the American Jewish Historical Society* 48, no. 1 (1958): 46–52; Rockaway, letter to author, 8 April 1998.

13. *Halifax (Va.) Gazette,* 23 March 1933; G. Uhrman to A. Jaffé, n.d., in posses-sion of Louis Jaffé Jr.; Robert Rockaway, *The Jews of Detroit: From the Beginning, 1762–1914* (Detroit: Wayne State University Press, 1986), 53, 56.

owned by absentee landlords. And although Detroit's Jewish quarter suffered in comparison to other regions of the city, many Jews preferred it for the sense of community they found there. "A Hebrew might live his lifetime in the quarter and never leave its confines," one observer marveled. According to a local newspaper, one could find "Hebrew stores of every description: butchers, grocers, bakers, clothiers, shoemakers, printing shops, and restaurants."[14]

It is not known how the Jaffes earned a living in Detroit. They possibly worked as peddlers, as did many of the city's Jews, or they may have engaged in business or factory work. Detroit's Jews achieved particular success in the waste industry, dealing in junk, rags, scrap, and paper.[15]

The Jewish quarter's residents rarely stayed long at an address. They moved frequently, both within New Jerusalem and to other cities. Perhaps this accounts for the fact that the Jaffes left no mark of their residence in Detroit's municipal, commercial, and religious records. The Detroit City Directory and other standard reference sources of this period provide no listings for the family. Nor do documents surviving from Detroit's two great synagogues of this era, Congregation Shaarey Zedek (Conservative) and Temple Beth El (Reform)—both of which sponsored a wide range of activities involving the city's Jewish community—mention the Jaffes. They may have worshiped at one of the city's numerous Orthodox synagogues, whose records no longer exist.[16]

Throughout his life Louis Jaffé listed Detroit as his birthplace and February 22, 1888, as his date of birth. Many official documents, such as Philip's naturalization papers and Louis's World War I draft registration, support this information. The 1910 and 1920 censuses place and date his birth more generally—in Michigan, within a year or two of 1888. Intriguingly, however, the 1900 census entry for the Jaffe household—the earliest extant documentation regarding Louis's birth—states that he was born in Russia in December 1884. Similar materials (including the 1900 census) pertaining to Louis's younger brother Hyman, the only other Jaffe offspring

14. Rockaway, *Jews of Detroit,* 62–3.

15. Ibid., 65–7.

16. *Detroit City Directory* (Detroit: R. L. Polk, 1880–1895); Sharon Cohen, interview by author, 19 May 1997; Heidi Christein, letter to author, 14 April 1997; Rockaway, letter to author, 8 April 1998.

to survive childhood, uniformly substantiate his birth in Bay City, Michigan, in April 1889. The failure of multiple searches of Detroit records to unearth a certificate of Louis's birth means little; Michigan authorities did not enforce the registration of newborns at that time.[17]

A search of Hamburg embarkation records and passenger indexes for arrivals to New York (and also Baltimore, Philadelphia, and Boston), which could confirm the location of Louis's birth, has revealed no trace of the family. But it seems unlikely that Philip would have left his pregnant wife to bear their child in Russia if he emigrated in September 1884, or that a discrepancy of more than three years in Louis's age would have gone undetected and uncorrected during his childhood and puberty. The birthdate supplied in 1900, probably by Lotta, could represent a misunderstanding of the census taker's question and refer to a different event, possibly her marriage. Nevertheless, the circumstances of Louis Jaffé's birth retain an element of mystery.

As eastern European Jews continued to pour into America in the wake of the pogroms, relations between the established German Jewish community and the eastern European newcomers grew strained. Detroit's assimilated German Jews regarded the destitute refugees with mixed feelings. Although the city's Jewish elite were moved by the immigrants' plight and gave generously to a number of charities to aid their settlement, the newcomers with their Old World ways accentuated the differences between Jews and Gentiles and revealed to the German Jewish community the precarious nature of its own status. At first, Detroit's Gentiles sympathized with the refugees and denounced the governments responsible for their persecution. But as the Jewish population in the city grew and as the visibility of the unacculturated eastern European Jews increased, anti-Semitism rose here also.[18]

17. Louis I. Jaffé, World War I draft registration (filed 5 June 1917, First Lee Ward, Richmond, Va.); 1910 federal population census for Philip Jaffe's household, South Boston, Halifax Co., Va.; 1920 federal population census for Louis Jaffé, Norfolk, Norfolk Co., Va.; 1900 federal population census for Philip Jaffe's household, Durham Township, Durham Co., N.C; 1920 federal population census for Hyman Jaffe's household, South Boston, Halifax Co., Va.; Hyman Jaffe, World War I draft registration, 5 June 1917; Alice Eichholz, *Ancestry's Redbook: American State, County & Town Sources* (Salt Lake City: Ancestry, 1992), 370.

18. Rockaway, *Jews of Detroit*, 58.

By the time of Louis Jaffé's infancy, the city's press was helping fuel religious hostility by referring to the mass immigration of Jews as a "threatening tide." The *Detroit News* accused Jewish newcomers of posing a health risk to the city because "they came from cholera infested cities of Europe and carried the plague with them." While Detroit's "better classes of American citizens" would be spared infection, cholera would surely spread among the "foreigners whose houses and clothing are absolutely filthy, and who go down to garbage heaps and jerk out the choicest bits of old meat and decaying fruit for food." Perhaps inspired by such attacks, one minister labeled Jews a "pauper and lawless class" who would "combine with our own worst elements" to destroy Christian traditions. Another clergyman, visiting the city, charged that Russian Jewish immigration posed a greater threat to the country than the "yellow peril."[19]

This sort of rhetoric, coupled with tensions brought on by the economic panic of 1893, the depression that followed, and the popularization of European theories of racial development, created an environment in which anti-Semitic violence flourished. Polish and Irish hooligans, themselves recent immigrants who faced discrimination, regularly accosted Jewish peddlers within the city. The police took no concrete steps to end the attacks, which cost the lives of several victims and resulted in the formation of a Jewish self-defense organization, the Jewish Peddlers Protective Association.[20]

As the situation worsened, the *Detroit Evening News* provided a classic example of irresponsible journalism when it ran an editorial with the incendiary title "Why is the Jew Hated?" Although the paper claimed it wished to provoke a constructive discussion, the exchange of letters and subsequent editorials—in which one of the editors charged, "There is absolutely no prejudice against the Hebrew in this or any other country which they themselves have not invited but made mandatory by the rest of the world"—did much to exacerbate tensions between the city's Gentile and Jewish communities. Detroit's Jewish leaders closely monitored the *Evening News*'s editorials, and the press's role in fomenting anti-Semitism probably

19. Robert Rockaway, "Anti-Semitism in an American City: Detroit, 1850–1914," *American Jewish Historical Quarterly* 64, no.1 (1974): 46; Rockaway, *Jews of Detroit*, 58.
20. Rockaway, "Anti-Semitism in an American City," 47.

would have filtered down to many settlers like the Jaffes via synagogues and the grapevine.[21]

At some point during their years in Michigan, the Jaffes moved north to Bay City. A large Jewish community had begun to develop there, surpassed in size in the state only by Detroit's. Bay City served as a gateway to Michigan's northern and thumb areas, and a number of Jews worked there as peddlers, supplying household goods and notions in exchange for scrap, which they sold to the city's salvage yards. The Jaffes may for a time have engaged in this business. Peddlers at first traveled by foot with their packs. Those who encountered success acquired horses and wagons. Some of these Jews discovered that they could earn a living more comfortably by plying their trade within the growing city than by traveling to the lumbermen, farmers, and villagers living in the surrounding rural areas. Peddlers drove their wagons along scheduled routes, selling produce as "fruit peddlers" or collecting scrap as "junk peddlers." The depression that preceded the economic panic of 1893 had begun, and many Jews barely managed to eke out a livelihood.[22]

While living in the Bay City area, the Jaffes may have become involved with a Jewish agricultural colony that sprang up in the nearby village of Bad Axe. The support for this possibility comes from a notation made eighty-odd years later by Louis Jaffé's widow, Alice, in an attempt to reconstruct from a few cryptic clues the travels of her father-in-law, Philip. She wrote, "The idealistic farming venture which brought him, as a young man, newly married, to Michigan, outside of Detroit, was a failure (a sort of communal farm), and after [sic] they moved to Durham, N.C."[23]

Almost certainly this chronology and geography are incorrect. The Bad Axe settlement arose in 1891, well after the Jaffes' arrival in Michigan. Moreover, it was located over one hundred miles from Detroit. Although two other Jewish farming settlements had sprung up in the state (Mackinaw City and Benton Harbor, both quite distant from Detroit and Bay City), Bad

21. Ibid., 48–9.

22. Gladys Uhrman to Alice Jaffé, n.d., Louis Jaffé Jr.; Lillian R. Greenstein, "The Peddlers of Bay City," *Michigan Jewish History* 25, no. 1–2 (1985): 11–7.

23. *Catholic Weekly*, 9 July 1965; Gabriel Davidson, "The Palestine Colony in Michigan: An Adventure in Colonization," *Publications of the American Jewish Historical Society* 29 (1925): 61–2; Jaffé family tree, Louis Jaffé Jr.

Axe is the most probable candidate, because the colony with one exception consisted of peddlers drawn from Bay City's Jewish community during the time the Jaffes appear to have lived there. Although the Jaffes do not appear to have been principal members of Bad Axe, a number of settlers either joined briefly or flirted with affiliation but changed their minds when they observed the hardships of involvement in the experiment.[24]

For Russian Jewish immigrants, forbidden to own land within their former homeland's Pale, farming made an unqualified political statement. The occupation represented a radical break with the past and the czars' anti-Semitic policies. For Jewish resettlement and philanthropic agencies and for leaders in the Hebrew community, farming, which was generally perceived as the most important industry in the United States, also represented a means by which Jews might escape the unhealthy living conditions of crowded cities and learn a vocation that would accord them respect. A New York weekly, the *American Hebrew,* optimistically believed that the "healthy, invigorating and independence-fostering avocation of the farmer" would rescue the "thousands of poor Israelites who live and die as pedlers and small hucksters . . . from the slough of pinching privation and mind-debasing penury."[25]

The Jewish settlers in the Bad Axe community (known to its colonists as Palestine) arrived there in the summer of 1891, nearly penniless. Lacking the means to purchase the land, they borrowed money from the landowner, a wealthy banker, who retained the deed. They had received bad advice regarding the suitability of the land for agriculture; a forest covered it, and clearing the trees confronted the unskilled and poorly equipped colonists with a daunting task. At first the settlers slept on the ground and focused their energies on cultivating the land. After obtaining additional loans, they erected homes, barns, and granaries and purchased livestock.

---

24. Herbert Friedenwald, ed., "Agricultural Activities of Jews in America," *American Jewish Yearbook* 14 (1912): 92–3; Gabriel Davidson, *Our Jewish Farmers and The Story of the Jewish Agricultural Society* (New York: L. B. Fischer, 1943), 241–4; Herscher, *Jewish Agricultural Utopias,* 61; Bad Axe Colony Records, American Jewish Historical Society, Waltham, Mass.; Heidi S. Christein, letter to author, 14 April 1997; Sheri Stanton, letter to author, 23 October 1996; A. James Rudin, "Bad Axe, Michigan: An Experiment in Jewish Agricultural Settlement," *Michigan History* 56, no.2 (1972): 121.

25. Herscher, *Jewish Agricultural Utopias,* 22–6.

Although the colony consistently teetered on the brink of insolvency, by all accounts the settlers displayed industriousness and courage. According to a report on the colony for the Baron De Hirsch Fund, even "their Christian neighbors testify to their pluck, energy and determination." Residents of the village and the farms near Bad Axe knew of the tragic circumstances surrounding the colonists' arrival; the local paper repeatedly reported on the pogroms in Russia and the czars' unjust treatment of Jews.[26]

In the early days of Bad Axe, Martin Butzel, leader of Detroit's Temple Beth El Hebrew Relief Society, learned of the settlers' dire conditions and arranged for Emanuel Wodic, an experienced farmer in his congregation, to travel to Bad Axe to advise them. Beth El provided the colonists with an emergency supply of clothing, groceries, and matzoh and raised $1,200 for Wodic to purchase livestock, equipment, and supplies. While Wodic remained in Bad Axe throughout the spring and summer of 1892, acting as the community leader, Butzel successfully appealed to the Baron de Hirsch Fund for funding.[27]

With the generous assistance of Beth El and with additional loans from the Baron de Hirsch Fund, the colony weathered severe winters and crop failures. The most critical period occurred during the fall of 1895—the approximate time the Jaffes moved to North Carolina—when the settlers defaulted on their loans from the landowner. With Butzel's continued intervention, the settlement lingered on until 1900, when the last of the colonists abandoned their farms.[28]

Young Louis Jaffé had completed the first year of his education, which required lengthy walks to and from school in the frigid Michigan winter, when around 1895 the Jaffes moved south to Durham, North Carolina. Word of the town's phenomenal expansion, sizable Jewish community, and moderate climate must have reached Bay City. The Jaffes aspired to become prosperous members of the merchant class, and Durham was an ideal place to try to realize their dreams. Propitiously located in the center of the state's

26. E. Marx to A. Solomons, 7 October 1897, Bad Axe Colony Records, American Jewish Historical Society, Waltham, Mass.; *Bad Axe (Mich.) Democrat,* 7 August 1891, 30 October 1891.

27. Rudin, "Bad Axe, Michigan," 121–4.

28. Davidson, "Palestine Colony in Michigan," 70–3.

Bright Tobacco Belt and boasting a rapidly growing textile industry, Durham nonetheless presented a study in contradictions.[29]

Tobacco barons William Blackwell and Julian Carr (of Bull Durham fame) and Washington Duke and his three sons, Brodie, Benjamin, and James "Buck"—who pioneered the mass production, modern packaging, and international marketing of cigarettes and created the American Tobacco Company trust—had built the city. Now these founding fathers had begun to diversify their interests, branching out into banking and, most notably, textiles. Tobacco money had created the Durham Cotton Manufacturing Company, the Commonwealth Manufacturing Company, the Erwin Cotton Mills, two hosiery companies, and the surrounding mill villages for workers.[30]

Capitalists and "mill folks" alike frequented the shops and businesses that lined the merchant section of Main Street, which was bisected by tracks for the horse-drawn streetcars. Each fall the town's retailers eagerly awaited the arrival of tobacco farmers from the hinterlands for the auctions hosted by Durham's warehouses.[31]

Dressed in rough work clothes, the farmers streamed into town on a motley array of mule- and horse-drawn wagons piled high with their gingerly packed cargoes. Most had staked nearly everything on a harvest grown from a teaspoonful of tiny seeds. On freshly cleared and fertilized land, they had planted their fragile crop and prayed for enough rain and not too much sun. Hail, blue mold, or tobacco worms spelled catastrophe. The

29. Jaffé family tree, Louis Jaffé Jr.; *Hand-Book of Durham, North Carolina: A Brief and Accurate Description of a Prosperous and Growing Southern Manufacturing Town* (Durham: The Educator Company, 1895), 3; Jean Bradley Anderson, *Durham County: A History of Durham County, North Carolina* (Durham: Duke University Press, 1990); James L. Hunt, "Law and Society in a New South Community: Durham County, North Carolina, 1898–1899," *North Carolina Historical Review* 68, no. 4 (1991): 429.

30. William Kenneth Boyd, *The Story of Durham, City of the New South* (Durham: Duke University Press, 1927), 60–96; William S. Powell, *North Carolina Through Four Centuries* (Chapel Hill: University of North Carolina Press, 1989), 408–9; Anderson, *Durham County,* 211–3.

31. Anderson, *Durham County,* 187; Joel A. Kostyu and Frank A. Kostyu, *Durham, A Pictorial History* (Norfolk, Va.: The Donning Company, 1978), 36–44; Eli N. Evans, *The Provincials: A Personal History of Jews in the South* (New York: Atheneum, 1974), 23–4.

fields required constant hoeing and weeding and, in the frequently dry weather, hand watering.[32]

Farmers topped the stalks when they reached the right height, and pulled—"suckered"—the excess growth off by hand. When the leaves ripened, the plants were cut, hauled to small log barns, and hung for curing. For four days or so, assiduously tended wood or charcoal fires smoldered as the tobacco dried. When the leaves turned deep yellow, they were graded and stored. After a particularly good harvest, the rooms of the growers' shacks and little houses served as extra storage.[33]

Arriving in Durham, farmers went straight to the immense warehouses, where black workers unloaded the wagons at the driveways, placed the tobacco on carts, and wheeled it to the scales for weighing and then to the floor for display in long rows. Tags listed the weight of individual piles and the names of their owners. Farmers stayed close by their harvests, sometimes sleeping on them, to guard against "pinhookers"—speculators who stole "hands" of leaves to "feather" atop undergraded tobacco that they would later market at another warehouse.[34]

Perched on a small rolling platform, the auctioneer, with great volume, great dispatch, and—for the untrained ear—great inaudibility, "knocked out" the piles to the highest bidders. The excitement attracted spectators, perhaps including young Louis Jaffé. Clerks recorded the sales, and the farmers hurried to the sales office, where they received their money, less the auctioneer's fee and the warehouse commission. With wads of bills

32. Robert Stevens, interview by author, 10 July 1996; J. B. Killebrew and Herbert Myrick, *Tobacco Leaf, Its Culture and Cure, Marketing and Manufacture: A Practical Handbook on the Most Approved Methods in Growing, Harvesting, Curing, Packing and Selling Tobacco, Also of Tobacco Manufacture* (New York: Orange Judd, 1906), 105–50, 251–5; W. B. Barbour, *"Halifacts"* (Danville, Va.: J. T. Townes, 1941), 32–5.

33. Stevens, interview, 10 July 1996; Killebrew and Myrick, *Tobacco Leaf,* 209–19; Barbour, *"Halifacts"* 32–5; Powell, *North Carolina Through Four Centuries,* 310–1; John Shelton Reed and Dale Volberg Reed, *1001 Things Everyone Should Know About the South* (New York: Doubleday, 1996), 211–2.

34. Killebrew and Myrick, *Tobacco Leaf,* 263–9; A. B. Bradsher, "The Manufacture of Tobacco in North Carolina," *Trinity College Historical Papers* 6 (1906): 12–21; Robert Mason, letter to author, 15 January 1998; Joel A. Kostyu and Frank A. Kostyu, *Durham, A Pictorial History,* 51–3.

securely buttoned away in pockets or purses (sometimes concealed in a boot), farm families walked to Durham's stores and shops. After a good auction, they bought shoes, kitchenware, tools, and dresses. A poor harvest or falling prices boded ill for the town's commerce.[35]

Booster literature for the city of Durham made the sweeping and unsupported assertion that the town's "percentage of idleness . . . is as small as can be found anywhere." Promoters ascribed this to the "fact that both the rich and poor are constantly employed and find little time to brood and fret over their condition in life." Certainly, given the economic climate of the day, this claim held bright promise. Durham's promoters also lauded the town's healthful conditions, which they attributed directly to tobacco manufacturing. "It is a matter of record that an atmosphere permeated with the odor of tobacco will ward off contagious diseases," publicists declared, sounding just a trifle defensive in the wake of the increasing criticism that churches, women's groups, and physicians were leveling at tobacco. A local physician's recollection from this period that the town "smelled to high heaven" probably describes the situation more accurately.[36]

Many of the Jews who settled in Durham at this time—perhaps including the Jaffes—came at the urging of friends and family who had arrived earlier. A half-dozen German-Jewish and two Polish-Jewish families had moved to the town in the 1870s; by the 1880s they had established themselves as grocers and dry-goods merchants on Main Street. In the late 1880s and the 1890s, this small population was augmented by the arrival of a number of eastern European families like the Jaffes. These newcomers swelled the town's Jewish population to two hundred by the year 1900.[37]

This enclave of Jewish merchants constituted a petite bourgeoisie. Concurrently with the development of this cohort of socially conservative small businessmen, however, a sizable population of militant Jewish work-

35. Killebrew and Myrick, *Tobacco Leaf,* 277–81; Bradsher, "Manufacture of Tobacco in North Carolina," 12–21; Evans, *Provincials,* 23–6.

36. Ibid., 18; *Hand-Book of Durham, North Carolina,* 5–6; Anderson, *Durham County,* 190.

37. Robin Gruber, "From Pine Street to Watts Street: An Oral History of the Jews of Durham, North Carolina" (honors thesis, Duke University, 1986), 15; Leonard Rogoff, "Jewish Proletarians in the New South: The Durham Cigarette Rollers," *American Jewish History* 82, no. 1–4 (1994): 141–2.

ers, skilled in the art of cigarette rolling, had been transported en masse from New York to Durham by the Dukes, who had seen a niche for them in the tobacco industry. Frustrated with butting their heads against what Buck Duke termed the "stone wall" posed by Bull Durham's dominance of the market—then overwhelmingly consisting of pipe tobacco—the Dukes intended to capitalize on the European-born cigarette fad.[38]

To this end Buck Duke traveled in 1881 to New York, where on a lower Manhattan dock he met nineteen-year-old Moses Gladstein, a recent immigrant who had been fired for leading a strike at one of the city's cigarette factories. Gladstein—like many of his co-workers—had learned his craft in Russia, where he had rolled gold-tipped cigarettes for a count and countess. On Duke's behalf, he recruited many of the factory's striking workers right off the picket line. Accustomed to the compliancy that characterized southern labor, Buck Duke foresaw no difficulty in managing the newest additions to the Dukes' work force.[39]

The imported workers established a ghetto called Yiddisha Streetal on Durham's Pine Street, and an informal synagogue above a Main Street drugstore. The New Yorkers rolled premium-brand cigarettes at a rate of seventy cents per thousand, ten to fifteen cents more than the scale for the less dexterous indigenous employees. Working long hours, six days a week, the Jewish rollers earned between eight and ten dollars per week.[40]

For several years the arrangement between the New Yorkers and the Dukes proved mutually profitable. In 1883, however, Buck Duke traveled to Richmond to examine a cigarette-rolling machine developed by James Bonsack, a young Virginia inventor. Despite industry insiders' predictions that the temperamental contraption would never work properly, and regardless of a consumer prejudice against machine-rolled cigarettes, Duke arranged to lease one of the machines at a reduced rate. Bonsack and his workers installed the machine in 1884, and the Dukes hired away one of Bonsack's mechanics and assigned him the daunting task of perfecting the finicky and screeching piece of machinery.[41]

38. Rogoff, "Jewish Proletarians in the New South," 142–3.
39. Ibid., 143; Evans, *Provincials,* 15; Gruber, "From Pine Street to Watts Street," 7–8.
40. Rogoff, "Jewish Proletarians in the New South," 145.
41. Boyd, *Story of Durham,* 88–9.

Over a year later the machine began to run reliably, and the rollers saw the writing on the wall. They organized the state's first chapter of the Cigarmaker's Progressive Union (CMPU), harassed the Duke mechanics, and threatened to sabotage the machinery. Unintimidated, Buck Duke installed a second rolling machine and announced to the CMPU's board in New York his intention to limit severely the number of cigarettes the unionized rollers could produce, in effect reducing their wages by two-thirds. Non-unionized workers were given higher quotas. With an eye to the bottom line and the displacement of the now-troublesome Jews, the Dukes offered incentives for local boys and girls to learn the trade and roll the slack the machines could not process.[42]

The New Yorkers found themselves in an untenable position. When the local union chapter folded, some of its former members affiliated with the biracial Knights of Labor, scorned by white racists as a "nigger" organization. The Dukes' foremen vowed to fire any of their employees who joined the Knights. By 1886 nearly all of Durham's Jewish tobacco workers had melted away. With twenty-five dollars in severance pay, most had returned to New York. A few former rollers remained in town, and they quickly metamorphosed from labor militants to merchants. Moses Gladstein opened a clothing store that one day would compete for business with the Jaffes' dry-goods store, just a few doors away on the same block of Main Street.[43]

Durham's Jewish community developed a lasting fascination with the Dukes' rags-to-riches story. The family might have exploited their imported workers and coldly cast them aside, but the Dukes had started with as little as the Jewish peddlers who drifted throughout the South, and within a single generation had built an empire. Washington Duke, with his farm in ruins and fifty cents in his pocket after his release from a Union prison camp at the end of the Civil War, had pounded, sifted, and bagged tobacco in a log cabin. Twenty-five years later his son Buck headed the American Tobacco Company trust, which now controlled the majority of the product in the nation.[44]

42. Rogoff, "Jewish Proletarians in the New South," 146–7.
43. Ibid., 148–9, 151–2.
44. Evans, *Provincials*, 17; Boyd, *Story of Durham*, 80–96.

In time the animosity between the Dukes and the New Yorkers faded from the memories of Durham's remaining Jews, and the reputation of the town's first family would rest on its Horatio Alger success and its philanthropy. As Washington Duke aged and as American Tobacco came under increased scrutiny from "trust busters" and critics of tobacco, the Dukes grew concerned about their legacy. They began to give generously to Durham and on occasion to the Jewish community. Sharing ambition, a spirit of civic loyalty, and pride in their humble origins, the Dukes and the town's Jewry had much in common.[45]

When the Jaffes arrived in 1895, Durham was in the midst of a depression. The wealth of the Blackwells, Carrs, Dukes, and other capitalists contrasted shockingly with the poverty of the urban poor and the farmers in the surrounding region. As the town's population had shot up with the influx of mill workers, so had the prevalence of crime, hunger, disease, and other social problems. One contemporary chronicler of Durham's legal and judicial affairs wrote, "However much town boosters sought to promote the citizenry as a hardworking and sober folk, thrift and industry were frequently less on the public mind than violence, theft, hard drink, and lust." During 1898 and 1899, the town's courts heard over four hundred criminal cases. Despite the fact that blacks comprised only one third of the county's population, they were charged with two thirds of the offenses and sentenced much more severely than whites.[46]

A host of other problems plagued the town. Slum landlords exploited their tenants. No arrangements existed for garbage collection or clearing the streets of manure and mud. Soon after the Jaffes' arrival, pellagra—thought to be associated with filth rather than diet—would become the leading cause of death in Durham.[47]

The town's first families tried mightily to change its image. Attempting to entice a Baptist women's college to locate in Durham, city leaders put together an impressive offer of fifty thousand dollars and sixteen acres of land, a package far exceeding other suitors' bids. Nevertheless the Baptist State Convention, judging Durham an unsuitable environment for

45. Rogoff, "Jewish Proletarians in the New South," 157; Evans, *Provincials*, 18.
46. Hunt, "Law and Society in a New South Community," 446, 452.
47. Anderson, *Durham County*, 206–7, 251.

impressionable young ladies, chose Raleigh instead. Durham's civic leaders did, however, best Raleigh in their courtship of Trinity College, then located in rural Randolph County. With Carr providing the land and the Dukes the lion's share of the money, little Trinity—Louis Jaffé's alma mater-to-be—with its progressive Pennsylvania-born president, John Crowell, came to town in 1892.[48]

Displaying a growing spirit of public uplift, Durham built a public library, the first in the state, in 1898. In that same year, Benjamin Duke provided the funds to build the Southern Conservatory of Music, replete with a gallery, an auditorium, and living quarters for fifty young women. Touring theatrical companies performed there regularly. Durham was especially proud of the luxurious seventy-room Carrolina Hotel (named for Julian Carr, its owner), one of the South's finest.[49]

The town's leaders probably best expressed their civic-spiritedness through the creation of and commitment to the public school system. Durham's grade and high school for white students opened in 1882 in an old factory building, which quickly grew inadequate for the burgeoning school population. Ten years later a school bond issue funded the construction of Morehead School, where high school classes met on the second floor of the two-story building. In 1906, after another special election and bond issue, the town built its first real secondary school. Red-brick neoclassically designed Durham High School, by all accounts the best in the state, boasted a superb plant, state-of-the-art equipment, and the highest paid teachers in North Carolina. Young Louis and his brother attended the new school, where boys had to enter through doors on the left side of the building and girls on the right. Classrooms were segregated by sex, and if a boy at recess was caught peeking through the playground's high wooden fence that walled off the girls' portion of the exercise yard, he was punished with detention.[50]

48. Boyd, *Story of Durham*, 80–96, 167–71; Earl W. Porter, *Trinity and Duke, 1892–1924: Foundations of Duke University* (Durham: Duke University Press, 1964), 22.

49. Anderson, *Durham County*, 202–4; Joel A. Kostyu and Frank A. Kostyu, *Durham, A Pictorial History*, 39, 45; *Hand-Book of Durham, North Carolina*, 15; Betsy Holloway, *Unfinished Heaven, Durham, North Carolina: A Story of Two Schools* (Orlando: Persimmon Press, 1994), 8.

50. Holloway, *Unfinished Heaven*, 7–8, 15; Anderson, *Durham County*, 230–4, 282–4; Joel A. Kostyu and Frank A. Kostyu, *Durham, A Pictorial History*, 91.

This, then, was the town that provided the Jaffes with their introduction to the South, the town in which young Louis would spend his most formative years. Steeped in dichotomies—rich and poor, black and white, propriety and hedonism—Durham, a grand experiment, a prototypical New South city, depended in approximately equal measures on the noblesse oblige of a clique of moralistic millionaires (Blackwell, Carr, and Washington Duke all taught Sunday school), the submissiveness of the mill and plant workers who kept the machines humming, and an ambitious merchant class.

Protestantism and industriousness permeated the air every bit as much as the smell of tobacco. The tragedy of the Civil War, personified in the shuffling gaits and scarred faces of the town's wounded soldiers and in the eyes of its blind beggar veterans, receded into the past. Most blacks in the Bottoms and Hayti sections of town lived in hopeless poverty. At this time, the state's dominant Democratic Party, headed by a former Trinity student, Furnifold M. Simmons, waved the bloody shirt and launched a vicious campaign of racial hatred that would sweep aside the last vestiges of Reconstruction and culminate in the near-total disenfranchisement of blacks.[51]

When the Jaffes arrived in town, they probably owned few material resources. Philip and Lotta initially may have peddled and operated a small-goods stand; most of the town's Jewish storekeepers began their businesses that way. Jews during this period regarded Durham as a merchant's town brimming with opportunities for hard workers.[52]

Young Louis almost certainly spoke English better than his parents. (The 1900 census indicates that Philip could speak but not read or write English; a naturalization petition filed by him late in his life in 1928 specifies that he did not read English.) We have no record of Louis's first impressions of the South or of southerners, some of whom may have gawked at the young Jewish boy and his family. Relations between the two communities were complex and nuanced.[53]

51. Rogoff, "Jewish Proletarians in the New South," 150; Joel A. Kostyu and Frank A. Kostyu, *Durham, A Pictorial History*, 43; Powell, *North Carolina Through Four Centuries*, 433–9.

52. Gruber, "From Pine Street to Watts Street," 15.

53. 1900 federal population census for Philip Jaffe's household, Durham Township,

Harry Golden, editor of the *Carolina Israelite,* drawing on extensive personal experience, maintained that by and large Jews received better treatment in the South than in other regions of the country. He also noted that the experiences of southern Jews varied according to whether they lived in rural or urban areas. According to Golden—himself a Jewish immigrant from eastern Europe—Jews and Gentiles living in southern cities had little genuine social interaction. The consequent inability of metropolitan Jews to gauge accurately the extent to which anti-Semitism existed in their communities created gnawing insecurity. As they exchanged pleasantries and conducted commerce with their Gentile neighbors, Jewish merchants fretted over how they were perceived and the degree to which they were accepted by the dominant majority.[54]

Even if an urban Jew could be virtually certain of the disposition of a particular Christian, the Jew could never predict with confidence whether other members of that person's social circle harbored prejudice. Only when Jews interacted with the top strata of the Gentile social structure did they feel entirely safe from direct expressions of anti-Semitism. Day-to-day interchanges with lower- and middle-class whites exposed southern Jewry to countless opportunities for misunderstandings and clashes. As southern shoppers entered Jewish stores for the first time, frequently they would inquire, "Is this a Jew store?" The question was often the result of natural curiosity and stemmed from a widespread perception that Jewish merchants could be bargained down, particularly when it came to the first sale of the day. But exchanges such as this and the often asked "How is the Jew today?" set Jews on guard and underscored the profound differences that existed between them and members of the Christian community.[55]

Golden believed that there was little or no social segregation between Jews and Gentiles in the region's rural areas. Small-town life forced the two groups to live closely together and depend on each other. Jewish merchants regularly served as presidents of chambers of commerce and Rotary, Kiwanis, and Lions clubs. Often these Jews enjoyed personal influ-

---

Durham Co., N.C.; naturalization petitions recommended to be continued (28 February 1928), U.S. District Court, Western District of Virginia; Evans, *Provincials,* 16.

54. Harry Golden, *Jewish Roots in the Carolinas: A Pattern of American Philo-Semitism* (Greensboro, N.C.: Deal, 1955), 50.

55. Ibid., 38, 50.

ence with important politicians. Early in their careers—as they had mounted bids for sheriff, county attorney, and other minor offices—many political leaders had campaigned in Jewish stores and had gotten to know the owners. These ties grew stronger as they were renewed over time in subsequent elections. Friendships developed over years of repeated contacts, and Jewish storekeepers were often on a first-name basis with congressmen, senators, and governors. (Future Virginia governors and federal legislators Harry F. Byrd Sr. and William M. Tuck would visit with Philip, Lotta, and Hyman at a store they later operated in South Boston, Virginia. Although Tuck would refer to Hyman as "one of my best friends," the popular politician undoubtedly had a superabundance of such relationships.)[56]

Factors like these resulted in rural communities' forming strong—if often patronizing—attachments to their Jewish residents. As Golden wrote, "He is 'our' Jew to small-town Southerners, and they often take care of him with a zeal and devotion otherwise bestowed only on the Confederate monument in the square." Golden labeled the relationship between the two groups "philo-Semitism." Southern Protestant fundamentalists respected Jews' Old Testament traditions. For many people in the rural South, Jews represented a direct link to sacred history and to Biblical prophets. On occasion Christian religious leaders would call on Jews to clarify fine points of Biblical exegesis.[57]

Business competition between Jewish and Christian merchants rarely caused discord. When Jews started out in business, they almost always sold soft goods (ready-to-wear clothing and accessories) to blacks. They thus posed little economic threat to Gentile merchants, who catered primarily to whites. Jewish proprietors did not caution their black customers, "Don't touch it if you're not going to buy it," or insist that they cover their heads with tissue paper before trying on hats. By the time Jewish merchants attained success and began to cater to the white consumer, they had become so embedded in their communities by virtue of their charitable and civic activities that business competition rarely escalated to anti-Semitism.[58]

56. Ibid., 56; Lotta Jaffe to Louis Jaffé, 4 June 1929, Louis Jaffé Jr.; William M. Tuck to Louis I. Jaffé, 20 December 1940, Jaffé Papers.

57. Golden, *Jewish Roots in the Carolinas*, 55, 57.

58. Ibid., 47; John Dollard, *Caste and Class in a Southern Town* (Madison: University of Wisconsin Press, 1988), 128–30.

Golden's observations are generally confirmed by more recent scholarship that, while pointing to many examples of anti-Semitism, finds relations between Jews and Christians no worse in the South than in other regions of the country and considerably more advanced than in the Northeast and Midwest. Historian Howard Rabinowitz cited three reasons for this phenomenon. He contended that Jews, particularly the later wave of Russian emigrants, presented little threat to southerners because of their mercantile ambitions and their paltry numbers. Rabinowitz asserted that other ethnic and religious groups posed a greater threat to Gentile whites and thus served as better scapegoats. "It takes perseverance to hate Jews, Negroes and Catholics all at the same time," observed Hodding Carter, editor of the *Greenville (Miss.) Delta Democrat-Times*. Finally, Rabinowitz maintained that the South's Jews took care to conceal whatever private reservations they may have held about southern society, particularly in regard to white supremacy. Publicly they embraced the status quo.[59]

Like other scholars exploring anti-Semitism in the South, Leonard Dinnerstein believed that political and social crises exacerbated anti-Jewish feeling. He cited the case of Judah Benjamin, who as Confederate secretary of state during the Civil War served for many southerners as a scapegoat for the Confederacy's military defeat. In North Carolina, the state legislature had grudgingly rescinded limits on Jews' voting or holding elected office only after forced to do so by the radical Republican constitution during Reconstruction in 1868. The region's war-wracked economy and the humiliating Reconstruction increased tensions between Jewish peddlers and storekeepers and their rural customers. Farmers often perceived Jewish merchants as exploitative and held them responsible for the farmers' indebtedness. In the last quarter of the nineteenth century, angry mobs forced Jewish storekeepers to flee towns in Tennessee, Louisiana, and Georgia. At the time of the Jaffes' arrival in Durham, therefore, numerous exceptions

59. Howard N. Rabinowitz, "Nativism, Bigotry, and Anti-Semitism in the South," *American Jewish History* 77, no. 3 (March 1988): 441–4, 446–9; Thomas Clark, "The Post–Civil War Economy in the South," *American Jewish Historical Quarterly* 55, no. 4 (1966): 430; John Higham, "Social Discrimination Against Jews in America, 1830–1930," *Publications of the American Jewish Historical Society* 47, no. 1 (1957): 23.

existed to the frequently harmonious relations between Jews and Gentiles in the South, and some of the most odious anti-Semitic incidents in the region were yet to come.[60]

Clearly, Louis's Jewish heritage marked him as an outsider. Religiously, the southern states comprised by far the nation's most homogeneous area; only Mississippi had fewer Jewish inhabitants than North Carolina. Baptists and Methodists made up over 75 percent of the Tarheel State's population. Children of eastern European Jewish heritage differed from their Christian peers and must have felt painfully isolated at times.[61]

Louis stood apart racially as well as religiously. During the 1890s, theories of Anglo-Saxon superiority and concerns about racial pollution swept through the United States. Particularly in the isolated and economically depressed South, where many poor whites had little in which to take pride other than the color of their skin and their Anglo-Saxon ancestry, concerns about "mongrelization" intensified. Many poor whites regarded Jews as racially different, and some regarded them as inferior. As a young man, Louis would write, "I am always conscious that racially a fine but unmistakable line separates me from my non-Jewish friends."[62]

This "fine but unmistakable line" may have helped sow the seeds of editor Louis Jaffé's lifelong tendency to empathize with underdogs. Some of the editor's outrage over mob justice, the propensity for violence in the South, and the intimidation of minorities may also have stemmed from his boyhood observations and experiences in North Carolina. As his parents learned to negotiate the alien folkways and mores of the South, they always

60. Rabinowitz, "Nativism, Bigotry, and Anti-Semitism in the South," 441; Leonard Dinnerstein, "A Neglected Aspect of Southern Jewish History," *American Jewish Historical Quarterly* 61, no. 1 (1971): 56–7.

61. Howard W. Odum, *Southern Regions of the United States* (Chapel Hill: University of North Carolina Press, 1936), 140; Jaffé family tree, Louis Jaffé Jr.; Louis Jaffé to Alice Rice, 23 August 1939, Louis Jaffé Jr.; Louis Jaffé war diary, 26 July 1918, Jaffé Papers.

62. William Ripley, *The Races of Europe: A Sociological Study* (New York: D. Appleton, 1910); Madison Grant, *The Passing of the Great Race* (New York: Charles Scribner's Sons, 1916); Charles Regan Wilson and William Ferris, eds., *Encyclopedia of Southern Culture*, vol. 4 (New York: Anchor Books, 1991), 158–61; Louis Jaffé war diary, 26 July 1918, Jaffé Papers.

had to exercise caution lest an unintended slight come across as an infringe-ment of honor.[63]

Although such an incident would less likely have triggered a clash in Durham than in many places, stories of quick-tempered and hot-blooded southerners abounded. Murders took place much more often in the state than they had in Michigan. And lynchings, which must have evoked for eastern European Jews memories of the pogroms, occurred with alarming frequency in the South, albeit with less regularity in the upper southern states. Mob violence peaked in North Carolina in the 1890s.[64]

The acrimonious state election of 1898, in which the Democratic Party wrested control of the legislature from the "fusion" alliance of Repub-licans and Populists, and the Wilmington race riot of that same year revealed the precariousness of law and order in North Carolina. As red-shirted bands of whites armed with rifles cowed and bullied blacks in an effort to stymie their participation in the election, Democrats conducted a viciously racist campaign by appealing to "men of Anglo-Saxon blood" to end "Negro domination." White supremacy triumphed as the fusionists were swept from power.[65]

It was in this context that what one scholar has called "perhaps the bloodiest white supremacist coup d'état in North Carolina history" tran-spired. The mulatto editor of the black *Wilmington (N.C.) Daily Record*, Alexander Manly, responding to Democratic charges that fusion rule had led to black men's taking liberties with white women, editorialized that some white women were as attracted to black men as white men were to black women. This claim stimulated a ferocious outcry in the white commu-nity and increased Red Shirt activity. Authorities ordered Manly to leave the city immediately. Although the editor escaped, a mob of four hundred smashed his press and burned the newspaper office. In the ensuing violence,

63. Stephen J. Whitfield, "Jews and Other Southerners: Counterpoint and Para-dox," in *"Turn to the South"*, ed. Nathan M. Kaganoff and Melvin I. Urofsky (Charlottesville: University Press of Virginia, 1979), 79–80; Eli N. Evans, "Southern-Jewish History: Alive and Unfolding," in *"Turn to the South"*, 161.

64. Odum, *Southern Regions*, 146; Powell, *North Carolina Through Four Centu-ries*, 448.

65. Powell, *North Carolina Through Four Centuries*, 433–8.

three whites were wounded, but eleven blacks were killed and twenty-five wounded. Large numbers of blacks fled the city.[66]

The family's finances caused the Jaffes additional chronic concern. Their meager resources contrasted sharply with Durham's prosperous merchant class and the ostentatious wealth of the tobacco and mill barons. The Jaffes' marginal existence in the years immediately following their arrival in North Carolina probably explains their omission from the Durham Directory until 1902. By this date, Louis, who a few years earlier had performed odd jobs in a Durham china store, was clerking for his father in the family's small grocery store on East Ramseur Street, a block removed from the town's choice business location on Main Street. The Jaffes lived in the rear of the building or just above the store.[67]

For the next three or four years, Louis clerked at clothing stores on East Main Street. An honor student at Durham High School, he had begun an ambitious savings program to fund his college education. He was a gifted student, to whom his classmates looked for help with their lessons. His propensity toward journalism and literature, not commerce, likely disappointed Philip and Lotta, who by now had experienced modest success and had opened a second store, a confectionary on East Main. The sons of Jewish merchants, particularly in the South, often went into partnerships with their fathers. As Hyman grew older, he took over his brother's responsibilities in the family business. More conventional than his older brother, Hyman lacked Louis's academic inclination and would choose to follow in his father's footsteps.[68]

Louis's indifference toward his parents' religion probably also displeased them. Philip and Lotta governed their lives according to their traditional Jewish beliefs; and the fact that Durham had a synagogue—one of a very few in small southern cities—may well have figured in their decision to

66. Ibid., 436–7.

67. 1900 federal population census for Philip Jaffe's household, Durham Township, Durham Co., N.C.; *Durham Directory,* 1902.

68. *Durham Directory,* 1903–1904; Alonzo Dill, "A Glimpse of Parnassus: Travels of Louis I. Jaffé" (author, n.d.), 2; Jaffé family tree, Louis Jaffé Jr.; Evans, "Southern-Jewish History," 159; Golden, *Jewish Roots in the Carolinas,* 47–8.

locate there. They practiced Jewish Orthodoxy in their home. However, the demands of their business and the need to operate it on their Sabbath would have made it difficult to avail their young sons of structured synagogue training.[69]

Other duties and interests appear to have taken precedence over organized religion early in Louis's life. Some Jewish dogma may also have been diluted for him by the Christian prayer and Scripture readings that served as opening exercises in many public schools in the South, by the schools' observance of Christmas and Easter, and by discussion—even debate—with peers over religious differences. The dearth of same-faith contemporaries in southern schools magnified the likelihood of erosion of Jewish students' traditional faith. Late in life, Louis would write that he had received little formal Jewish religious training as a child.

The unsystematic nature of his exposure to the Torah notwithstanding, his religious background undoubtedly helped shape his ethical and moral framework. Judaism urges *Zedakah*—charity and social justice—and affirms human dignity. Jewish religious teachings stress intellectual freedom and strongly emphasize learning and scholarship. Such values served to orient and motivate Louis throughout his life. References in his writings confirm an enduring faith in the Almighty.[70]

At Durham High School, Louis worked on the school paper, the *Messenger,* serving as its editor-in-chief in his senior year. Here appear some of the earliest examples of his writing. Bemoaning the football team's lack of success in previous seasons, he waxed poetic: "Far too often in past years has the chronicle of our football doings taken unto itself the form of an elegy; far too often in past years have our soaring September hopes turned traitor moons and moons before Thanksgiving." Happily for Louis and his schoolmates, the team improved and posted a winning record that year.[71]

In his editorial farewell, the youthful journalist sounded world-

69. *Halifax (Va.) Gazette,* 23 March 1933; Gruber, "From Pine Street to Watts Street," 15; Jaffé family tree, Louis Jaffé Jr.

70. Milton R. Konvitz, ed., *Judaism and Human Rights* (New York: W. W. Norton, 1972), 190–1; Louis Jacobs, *What Does Judaism Say About . . . ?* (Jersualem: Keter, 1973), 109–10; Abraham D. Lavender, "Jewish Values in the Southern Milieu," in *"Turn to the South",* 128–9.

71. Durham High School *Messenger,* November 1907.

weary as he bade his classmates adieu. In "The World's a Stage," he called his graduation the "last rehearsal" before he and his classmates entered adulthood. At the ceremony the "footlights will glare and the orchestra will play with the same intense disinterestedness with which they glared and played at numerous other last rehearsals whose erstwhile splendor is now a dim speck in the vista of years," he wrote. "The players will enact their pathetic little parts in the same prescribed way and with the same apparent *sang froid* that characterized the players in other last rehearsals. Everyone will smile; it is the proper thing to do—every player at every last rehearsal since the memory of man runneth not to the contrary has smiled. Who shall ever know how much have been the trials, the joys, the pleasures and the heartaches concealed beneath the tinsel and powder of smiles and laughter."[72]

But if Jaffé assumed a somewhat cynical posture toward the capstone experience of his high school years, his depiction of the colleges and universities he and some of his classmates would soon be attending was decidedly romantic: "College with its shady campus, its sequestered nooks, its libraries, its erudition, and its fine old traditions. College with its hundred and one opportunities for broadening out and developing those God-given faculties which were meant by our Creator to be developed. Here they will meet with men who have drunk deep in the fountain of learning, and whose broader views of humanity shall help them towards the emancipation of the soul from the gross and the material, and send them out better men and women." Almost certainly Jaffé had Trinity in mind as he developed this description. The controversial little college on the outskirts of Durham had earned a reputation as a bastion of liberalism, as one of the few southern institutions of higher education that zealously protected academic freedom.[73]

To Philip and Lotta their sons owed not only indoctrination in traditional Jewish morality but encouragement to learn and examples of fortitude. By settling in Durham, the elder Jaffes propitiously enabled Louis to attend one of the South's best high schools, enjoy the cultural privileges provided by city leaders for the townspeople, and grow up in the shadow of an excellent liberal-arts college destined to mark his future indelibly.

72. Ibid., June 1907.
73. Ibid.

3   GREAT EXPECTATIONS

Louis Jaffé's arrival at Trinity College in 1907 coincided with his family's launch of a new business venture. For twenty years, under difficult circumstances, Philip had supported his wife and children. Doubtless it was a proud and wonderful day when the Jaffes closed their grocery shop on Ramseur Street and transformed the confectionery on East Main into a clothing store, rechristening it "P. Jaffe and Son." The family surely celebrated, believing that they had turned the corner financially.[1]

Their commercial ascent was typical among southern Jews: small-goods-stand operator, owner of a mom-and-pop shop, proprietor of a dry-goods store. But even though Jaffe and Son stood alongside many of the town's more prosperous retail businesses, it would have compared poorly to them, as it specialized in cheaper goods and catered primarily to blacks and poor whites.

Closing down their grocery shop required the family to vacate their Ramseur Street living space. They rented a house on North Roxboro Street, a few blocks from their new store. For the Jaffes, the privacy and quiet of their new home contrasted sharply to living in the commercial district. Louis lived at home with his parents for the first part of his college career.[2]

Trinity stood on the outskirts of town. Louis might already have familiarized himself with the campus and perhaps could have recognized by sight a number of the more prominent faculty and administrators, many of whom participated actively in Durham's civic and educational affairs. Like nearly every citizen in the state, he would have known of the little college's reputation for critical examination of southern shibboleths.

In 1902 the first edition of the college's *South Atlantic Quarterly*

1. *Durham Directory*, 1907–1908.
2. Ibid.

had carried as its opening essay a treatise entitled "An Inquiry Concerning Lynchings," written by Trinity president John Kilgo. In it, Kilgo urged politicians to end their incendiary exploitation of racial issues and called for a concerted educational campaign. He directed particular criticism at the southern press. "Crimes have been portrayed in the most glaring manner, while headlines have appealed to passions. 'A Subject for the Stake,' 'Burning is too Good for the Brute,' 'Lynch the Wretch' are headlines that aid mob law, and a recklessness quite as blame-worthy as lynching," he charged. The article typified a spirit shared by nearly all within the college.[3]

Louis Jaffé would almost certainly have attended to a particularly notorious incident at Trinity involving race, academic freedom, and journalistic responsibility. Just four years before he began his freshman year, a mighty uproar had ensued when mild-countenanced Professor John Spencer Bassett—a native North Carolinian and one of the South's handful of academically trained historians—inflamed the passions of whites who embraced the traditional racial attitudes of Dixie. His "Stirring Up the Fires of Racial Antipathy," published in the *South Atlantic Quarterly,* which he edited, sparked the greatest controversy in the college's history. Although Bassett unquestionably intended his article to be provocative and to stimulate reflection and discussion, he could never have foreseen the furor it would arouse. Certainly he could not have anticipated the sheer vindictiveness with which he and the college would be attacked by Josephus Daniels, editor of the state's leading newspaper, the *Raleigh News and Observer.* The "Bassett affair" is regarded today as one the country's most significant cases involving academic freedom.[4]

In "Stirring Up the Fires of Racial Antipathy," Bassett charged that the exploitation of racial prejudice by southern politicians and "political editors" had resulted in "more hatred of whites for blacks and blacks for whites than ever before, . . . leading the country to an end which I dare not name." Bassett urged an objective and reasoned analysis of the "negro problem" and a realistic assessment of the condition and capabilities of

3. John Carlisle Kilgo, "An Inquiry Regarding Lynching," *South Atlantic Quarterly* 1, no.1 (1902): 13.
4. Porter, *Trinity and Duke,* 120; Powell, *North Carolina Through Four Centuries,* 408–9.

blacks. Whites who pointed to the most deprived class of blacks as representative of the race as a whole were wrong, as were "well intentioned people" who viewed black intellectuals and leaders as typical.[5]

One of Bassett's examples for the latter point provided Democratic Party stalwart Daniels with the words that he wrenched out of context to hammer away at the professor and Trinity. "A man whose mind runs away into baseless optimism is apt to point to Booker T. Washington as a product of the negro race," Bassett wrote. "Now Washington is a great and good man, a Christian statesman, and take him all in all the greatest man, save General Lee, born in the South in a hundred years; but he is not a typical negro."[6]

One of the three hundred copies of the *South Atlantic Quarterly* found its way into Daniels's hands, and the November 1, 1903, edition of the *News and Observer* featured the blaring headline "PROF. BASSETT SAYS NEGRO WILL WIN EQUALITY." Underneath it, subheads read, "He also says Booker Washington is 'The Greatest Man, Save General Lee, Born in the South in a Hundred Years,'" "SOUTHERN LEADERS SLANDERED," and "Dire Predictions of a Coming Conflict Between the Races— Struggle Will Go on as Long as One Race Contends for Absolute Inferiority of the Other. 'Dares Not Name the End.'" On his editorial page, Daniels called "bASSett" a "freak," whose "absurd statements . . . Damn the State of North Carolina" and whose "dangerous doctrines . . . would destroy the civilization of the South." Daniels then reprinted the full text of the article, although few subscribers probably bothered to read through it.[7]

The vehemence of Daniels's attack almost certainly stemmed from a thinly veiled reference in Bassett's article, charging that a "certain emotional and 'yellow' newspaper" had printed "lurid descriptions" and misrepresented a recent incident involving Washington. Bassett had asserted that this press had irresponsibly and falsely accused a group accompanying Washington of contravening Jim Crow laws and behaving rudely to whites in the dining room of a North Carolina hotel. The allusion to the *News*

5. John Spencer Bassett, "Stirring Up the Fires of Racial Antipathy," *South Atlantic Quarterly* 2, no.4 (1903): 304.

6. Ibid., 299.

7. *Raleigh News and Observer*, 1 November 1903.

and Observer would have been clear to all of the *South Atlantic Quarterly*'s readers.[8]

Washington had previously aroused the ire of Daniels and other white southerners by accepting an invitation to dine with President Theodore Roosevelt and his family in the White House. The *Richmond Times* had purported that the dinner underscored the president's desire that "negroes shall mingle freely with whites in the social circle [and] that white women may receive attentions from negro men." The accommodationist Washington was a popular figure at Trinity, which was the first white southern college to invite him to speak. He had addressed its students and faculty in 1896, and they had cheered him as he left.[9]

For over a month Daniels delivered a dizzying array of punches at Bassett and Trinity. The *News and Observer*'s attacks bloodied the waters and initiated a journalistic feeding frenzy among the state's newspapers. The Raleigh editor gleefully excerpted and reprinted his colleagues' editorials. Bassett's hometown paper, the *Goldsboro Argus,* accused him of "out-RooseveIting Roosevelt [whose dinner with Washington had] outraged the sentiments of the white people of the South beyond any racial incident in all history in this country." Bassett's article had caused the "white people of this State to stand aghast, as if coming suddenly upon a vicious, deadly reptile ready to strike where they were wont to gather flowers and drink from pure fountains of refreshing water." In "The Freak Disease Coming South," the *Charlotte News* called the professor's views "clotted nonsense." The *Wilson Times* portrayed Bassett as "simply a species of fungous growth that periodically springs up in the South."[10]

The fiery editorial response of North Carolina's newspapers to Bassett's article was especially withering, though not untypical of the highly personalized and partisan journalism practiced by most of the southern press of the era. But even in this heady and charged environment, Josephus Daniels remained North Carolina's acknowledged expert at attack-dog newspapering, violently denouncing any deviation from Democratic Party

8. Bassett, "Stirring Up the Fires," 303.

9. Lewis L. Gould, *The Presidency of Theodore Roosevelt* (Lawrence: University Press of Kansas, 1991), 22–4; Anderson, *Durham County,* 235.

10. *Raleigh News and Observer,* 3–5 November 1903.

orthodoxy. The *News and Observer* functioned more as a party organ and vehicle of political persuasion than as a newspaper in its modern sense. Daniels had more resources and more of an appetite for editorial violence than his small-town peers. In addition, because of its location in the state's capital city, his paper exerted a tremendous influence on politicians and policy makers. As Daniels battled fusionists, the Republican Party, and the minutest step toward equality between blacks and whites, he did much to facilitate the conditions in which lynchings and racial violence could flourish.[11]

For many years the *Raleigh News and Observer* had prominently displayed reports detailing alleged rapes and molestations of white women by black men throughout the South. "Gashed and Bleeding She Fought for Honor Against a Negro's Brutal and Merciless Might," a representative headline read. The newspaper frequently referred to blacks as "coons." It printed bigoted letters that fueled racial hatred and provided intellectual justification for lynching. "The influence of morality and intelligence dominate the conduct of the lighter races," wrote one medical authority, "and therefore the dominion is essentially pshychic [*sic*]. In the negro the psychic differentiation is withheld, while the organic sex-development continues. . . . A perversion from which most races are exempt, prompts the negro's inclinations towards the white woman; whereas other races incline toward the females of their own. . . . Some self-constituted philosophers have threatened to take the negro by cross cut over the centuries which have been necessary to the evolution of the white race, and place him in power and position for which he will not be qualified in a thousand years. This is a wrong which cannot be condoned." While Daniels never condoned lynching in his editorials, he nonetheless maintained that sexual assaults committed by blacks against white women served as the underlying cause for mob violence.[12]

Only in the most isolated parts of North Carolina could newspaper readers of any age or the public in general have escaped the white-supremacist agitprop circulated by Daniels and most of his editorial peers. A youth of Louis Jaffé's precocity would have weighed and digested all that he heard and read on the subject. Given also his dream of attending Trinity College

11. Porter, *Trinity and Duke*, 110–5.
12. *Raleigh News and Observer*, 8, 11 November 1903; Porter, *Trinity and Duke*, 113–4.

and his literary inclination, he undoubtedly followed the Bassett furor assiduously. Factoring in the passion for social justice that would later characterize his editorship, one can safely deduce his position on the case at the time and his opinion even then of the likes of Josephus Daniels.

The Bassett affair came to a head on December 1, 1903, at a special meeting of Trinity's board of trustees. Despite the support of the Dukes, the faculty (who threatened to quit en masse should the administration accept Bassett's proffered letter of resignation), and the students, the situation looked grim. It appeared inevitable that the *South Atlantic Quarterly*'s editor would be forced out. In a similar incident, Emory College had dismissed Professor Andrew Sledd the previous year after he had written "The Negro: Another View" for *Atlantic Monthly*. The southern press termed the Virginia-born Sledd a "Boston nigger-equality citizen" and threatened him with a tarring and feathering.[13]

The meeting began that evening in the faculty room. Students crowded into the adjoining halls and rooms and into the basement to eavesdrop. Outside in the cold they peered through the window, straining to hear the proceedings. Trinity alumnus and trustee Furnifold Simmons led the charge for Bassett's dismissal, and a number of Methodist clergymen on the board sided with him. Simmons reportedly had said that he came to the meeting intending to win his "last fight for white supremacy."[14]

Josephus Daniels's agitation had been effective, but Trinity president John Kilgo's impassioned oratory more than matched the editor's rhetoric. Fortunately for history, one student, Eber Perrow, carefully recorded the proceedings in his diary:

> All around sat solemn-faced trustees and our old Doctor standing in their midst, with his arms out-stretched, a look of heaven on his face, pleading with the dignity of an old Roman senator for the teacher whom he trusted, and for the institution he loved.
>
> ". . . He has committed no crime. He has done injury to no one. He has violated no law. He has simply spoken his honest opinion.

13. Porter, *Trinity and Duke*, 130–1; Mims, *The Advancing South*, 153–4; A. Sledd, "The Negro: Another View," *Atlantic Monthly*, July 1902, 65–73; Dabney, *Liberalism in the South*, 338–9.
14. Porter, *Trinity and Duke*, 132–3.

He is not responsible for the furor into which the state has been thrown. . . . This furor has been incited by one man who has twisted the article out of shape, and with it stirred the entire state into a whirlpool of passion. You might as well hang the man who made the revolver and let go free the assassin who pulled the trigger as to punish Dr. Bassett and let this man go free. You might as well execute the man who made the match and let the incendiary go free, as to punish Dr. Bassett and let this man go free.

"It is one of the inalienable rights of an educational institution and of its teachers to express honest thought. It is this freedom from bondage that has made Trinity College what it is. I beg of you, gentlemen, do not tear out the heart of Trinity College and leave standing there only the carcass of an institution!"

Then Dr. Kilgo pictured Trinity as a virgin about to be spoiled of her virtue: "I stand here tonight to plead for the virtue of Trinity as I would plead for the chastity of my mother and the purity of my wife!"[15]

Other Bassett supporters who spoke eloquently after Kilgo, most notably board chairman James Southgate, turned the tide and stymied the parliamentary maneuvers of Simmons's faction. At three o'clock that morning, the trustees voted eighteen to seven in favor of Bassett.

The students celebrated boisterously. As Perrow wrote, "Trinity was free! The boys at the doors and windows began to cheer and soon woke up the few who had gone back to their rooms. Someone suggested that we climb the tower and ring the college bell. I went with them, and soon we had the old bell ringing out the good news, while students from every point of vantage were crying out 'Trinity free! Trinity free!' There were no recitations in Trinity that day!"[16]

Perrow neglected to mention that the students' revelry also included hanging two effigies of the editor of what they termed the "*News and Disturber.*" For a hard-bitten newspaperman, Daniels displayed a curious sensi-

15. Eber C. Perrow, "Trinity College (N.C.) and Academic Freedom: A Report on the Meeting of the Board of Trustees, on December 1, 1903" (Duke University Archives, 1958).

16. Ibid.

tivity toward the incident, titling a chapter of his memoirs, "I Am Hung in Effigy," and portraying himself as the aggrieved party. In an ironical choice of words, the editor—who had done so much to create in North Carolina a climate conducive to mob violence—called the students' actions a "lynching."[17]

The *News and Observer* treated the mock hanging with great seriousness, reporting that "all through the hours of the early morning the figure swung from the limb over the race track. The grey dawn came and found it still hanging there. . . . This was a fitting close of the triumph of 'liberality of thought and freedom of speech' as seen in the Kilgo policy of 'rule or ruin.'" Shortly thereafter the North Carolina Press Association, meeting in the nation's capital, solemnly condemned the students' actions in a formal resolution, claiming that it constituted an "attempt to abridge the freedom of the press."[18]

The incident had shaken Bassett, but he must have felt completely vindicated when two years later President Theodore Roosevelt, speaking from an old flatbed railway car covered with a fine Persian carpet and trimmed with bunting, addressed a crowd of fifteen thousand in front of Trinity's gates. The town's leaders declared a holiday, and nearly everyone in Durham turned out. Louis would not have missed it for the world. Had any of the significance of the Bassett Affair been lost on him earlier, Roosevelt underscored for him the need for academic freedom and tolerance of unpopular ideas. The president read aloud Trinity's mission statement and lauded the little college: "I know of no other college which has so nobly set forth as the object of its being the principles to which every college should be devoted, in whatever portion of this union it may be placed. . . . You stand for academic freedom, for the right of private judgment, for the duty more incumbent on the scholar than upon any other man, to tell the truth as he sees it, to claim for himself and to give to others the largest liberty in seeking after the truth."[19]

A quarter of a century later, Jaffé, looking back on the Bassett

17. Ibid.; Porter, *Trinity and Duke,* 134; Josephus Daniels, *Editor in Politics* (Chapel Hill: University of North Carolina Press, 1941), 427–37.

18. *Raleigh News and Observer,* 3 and 4 December 1903.

19. Porter, *Trinity and Duke,* 142–3; Anderson, *Durham County,* 291; Mims, *The Advancing South,* 156–7.

affair, would focus on the injustice done Bassett and the misrepresentation of the professor's ideas by sons of the South and his own journalistic ancestors: "When the patriots of that day got through distorting what Professor Bassett had written, and when editorial writers had finished pointing out how he had out-Yankeed the Yankees in doing violence to sacred Southern tradition, some of the more influential clients of Trinity College began calling for the professor's head. . . . What its faculty and president and trustees did . . . when the issue of academic liberty hung in the balance remains to this day [the college's] most precious possession."[20]

This heady atmosphere, which still prevailed at Trinity when Louis arrived in the fall of 1907, made it an exciting time to attend the little college. The administration had expanded course offerings and increased the size of the faculty. Nearly all the professors were comparatively young; many had received their training at major northern universities. The college boasted a number of new buildings, and the endowment had soared. Buck Duke had funded the construction of a new library and a major acquisition of books. Women made up an increasing percentage of the student body, and a law school had recently opened. Trinity's standards for admission, although lagging behind those of the more prestigious eastern colleges and universities, now ranked among the most rigorous in the South.[21]

Much of Louis's study consisted of a standard curriculum: four years of English; a one-credit Bible course; two years of history, mathematics, philosophy, and economics; and one year each of biology and chemistry. In the area of languages, however, he pursued a particularly ambitious course of study, far exceeding the college's requirement. Having presented Greek for admission, Louis mastered German VI by his sophomore year and by graduation had completed Latin II and French III. From his parents and others in Durham's Jewish community, he also had gained a fair amount of Yiddish and a smattering of Hebrew. This foreign language concentration, which promoted the expansion of his cultural as well as linguistic horizons, would serve him well in his travels and in the mechanics and substance of his life's work.[22]

20. *Pilot*, 31 January 1928.
21. Porter, *Trinity and Duke*, 88–91, 143–9.
22. Louis Jaffé transcript (Duke University Archives); Louis Jaffé to E. Jacob Londow, 3 April 1920, Jaffé Papers.

Durham's fine public school system had prepared him well; Louis excelled in the classroom. He would graduate magna cum laude, with honors in German. When Trinity acquired a Phi Beta Kappa chapter nearly a decade after his graduation, the honor society elected him a member.[23]

Louis exuberantly involved himself in writing and publishing during his collegiate years. He served as associate editor and then editor-in-chief of the student newspaper, the *Trinity Chronicle*—irreverently dubbed by its staff the "Chronic-ill"—and as an associate editor of the *Trinity Archive,* the college literary magazine. He also contributed occasional reports to newspapers in North Carolina and Virginia.[24]

By all accounts he made a cracking good editor, confident of himself and his abilities. "Few college weeklies have so able an editor as Mr. Jaffé," a reporter for the student paper wrote. "[Jaffé], a gentleman of the tribe of Judah, uses English with a familiarity that amounts almost to contempt. [He] has put brightness into every issue of the *Chronicle.*" For many years afterward, student editors exhorted their reporters to devote more time to their journalistic duties than they could afford, in order to rise to the standard set by Louis. Several decades later, one of his successors as editor reflected on his apprenticeship "served under that to-me-then-genius Louis I. Jaffé. He had a corner room in the old rambling firetrap, the Inn, where he smoked a rank pipe and wrote editorials after midnight in his shirtsleeves, and criticized my efforts with good-natured superiority. . . . I worshipped [his] style."[25]

A representative editorial by Jaffé provides an example of his choice of subject matter and his writing style during this period. Focusing on the antagonism that existed between students at Trinity and the nearby University of North Carolina, he pointed out the irrationality of the bitter rivalry:

23. Louis Jaffé transcript (Duke University Archives); *Durham Sun,* 7 June 1911; William Wannamaker to Louis Jaffé, 11 April 1922, Wannamaker Papers, Duke University Archives; "Deaths," *Duke Alumni Register,* April 1950, 103–4.

24. Daniel Daily, letter to author, 26 January 1996; *Duke Chronicle,* 5 October 1937; Everett Ewing, "Romances of American Journalism," *Editor & Publisher,* 1 June 1929, 14.

25. "Louis Isaac Jaffé, '11, Honored," *Trinity Alumni Register,* January 1920, 295–6; "Louis I. Jaffé Gets Pulitzer Award for Best Editorial," *Duke University Alumni Register,* June 1929, 200–1; *Trinity Chronicle,* [September 1912?]; M. Bradshaw to Louis Jaffé, 2 January 1937, Jaffé Papers; *Duke Chronicle,* 5 October 1937.

"Now tell us all about the war. And what they fought each other for," vainly asks little Wilhelmine of Kaspar. But Kaspar, good old soul, can make but one reply: "It was a famous victory." What it was all about and why it was at all is a closed book to him. . . . What is it that causes the unsisterly attitude between Trinity and Carolina?

One cannot help regretting that the two leading educational institutions of the state are not on more cordial terms. Any evidence of jealousy on the part of one institution with regard to another is usually inspired by fear, and nothing is more likely to impair the usefulness of a college or university than a spirit of unfriendly rivalry. The proximity of the two colleges should make for friendly and mutually beneficial intercourse. . . . Surely North Carolina is big enough, and individual tastes and preferences diverse enough, to afford both colleges wide fields of activity free from friction with one another.[26]

Trinity's interactions with other North Carolina colleges furnished frequent grist for Louis's editorials. When neighboring Wake Forest hosted a baseball game between the two schools, some of its students had painted "To Hell With Trinity" on the grandstand. Despite an attempt to paint over it, the epithet was visible to the spectators. Louis denounced the "few hoodlooms" [sic] responsible for the prank. This brought a spirited response from his counterpart at the little Baptist college, Gerald Johnson, years later to become the most influential editorial writer on southern affairs. Johnson felt that Jaffé should have given more credit for the attempt to mask the statement. Louis printed the letter but stood by his position, declaring, "The grievance . . . has scant justification. . . . The fact that an attempt was made by the better students to render the inscription illegible . . . hardly palliates the intent of those who painted it." Despite this inauspicious early exchange, the two editors would become good friends and share virtually identical views throughout their professional careers.[27]

Only a few of Louis's editorials foreshadowed the stances the *Virginian-Pilot* would take on crucial southern issues such as sectionalism. One

26. *Trinity Chronicle* [September 1912?].
27. Ibid., 12 April 1911.

of these editorials criticized a contest sponsored by a chapter of the United Daughters of the Confederacy at one of the region's colleges. That organization offered a gold medal to the student who wrote the best essay on "The Right of Secession." "No doubt, there will be many able responses to the offer made by these good ladies, the noble daughters of Confederate heroes," the college's newspaper predicted.

The contest elicited a biting editorial response from Louis: "We cannot help reading into this incident a belated spirit of sectionalism and almost mawkish sentimentality which the progressive South has abjured these many years. Secession may or may not be a right of the individual states. The best political scientists of the nation have differed on this point time and time again. The solution may be properly left with the jurists and economists who have made the question of states' rights the study of a lifetime. To look for light on the secession doctrine from youthful undergraduates of Southern colleges is little less than folly."[28]

Louis's widely acknowledged academic abilities and his success as a budding journalist aside, one wonders what sort of reception the son of poor Jewish parents would have received at Trinity, a mighty bastion of Protestant Christianity. Did the "gentleman of the tribe of Judah" encounter religious bias and snobbery? Trinity's student body consisted of no more than 350 students, overwhelmingly Methodist, with a sprinkling of Baptists and Episcopalians. Louis was one of a handful of Jewish students that included his friends Jacob Londow and "Goldy." He and Fanny Gladstein were almost certainly the only Jewish members of his graduating class.[29]

Only one professor of Jewish ancestry served on the faculty—the recently hired dean of the law school, Samuel Mordecai. Sensitive to his religious heritage, which he thought would set him apart from the college's teaching staff, Mordecai had felt obligated to make clear to President Kilgo during his hiring process that he was an "Episcopal Jew." Kilgo's response provides a heartening indication of the administration's tolerance toward religious minorities at Trinity. "I am not hunting for a churchman, but for a lawyer," he told Mordecai. One might wonder whether an actively prac-

28. Ibid., 15 March 1911.
29. Robert Roy, "Reminiscences of Trinity" (Duke University Archives, January 1939); Louis Jaffé to E. Jacob Londow, 3 April 1920, Jaffé Papers; *Durham Sun,* 7 June 1911.

ticing Jew, particularly a Russian émigré, would have been as zealously recruited as Mordecai. But Trinity operated "without regard to religious creeds, political faiths, or social castes," its president claimed, and "no attempt to proselyte students would be tolerated for a moment." If anyone was in the position to engage in evangelism, it was Kilgo. He taught the required Bible course that students took each and every year. He treated it nonchalantly, frequently canceling class when away from campus on college or church business. When he did "teach," he nearly always preached a sermon.[30]

Despite the best efforts of Trinity's president, on a number of occasions Louis must have felt the sting resulting from the "fine but unmistakable line" he perceived as separating him from his non-Jewish friends. What characterized the college more than anything else, according to one of his fellow students, was "without doubt the religious teachings and influences of [the students'] simple Christian homes."[31]

Trinity's students and faculty may have accepted Jaffé's religious distinctiveness, but southerners largely refused to accept Jewish cultural separatism. This may have helped diminish Louis's Jewish identity. Louis Schmier writes, "As Gentiles beckoned the Jews to become a part of southern society, they exerted a pressure upon the Jews to forego their old ways and adopt southern lifestyles. . . . Though the forces of acculturation that were at work were not uniquely southern, the pressure imposed on the Jews was greater in the South." Louis's comparative religious isolation at Trinity may have intensified this process somewhat.[32]

However, he does not seem to have experienced much, if any, overt or even tacit anti-Semitism at Trinity. His senior class elected him vice-president, and he was a popular figure on campus. Kilgo's successor as president, William Few, remarked on Louis's ability to attract companions, and Professor William Wannamaker observed that he left many friends behind after

30. Porter, *Trinity and Duke*, 144–5, 165; Eber C. Perrow to H. Jackson, 25 October 1965, Duke University Archives.

31. Louis Jaffé war diary, 26 July 1918, Jaffé Papers; Roy, "Reminiscences of Trinity."

32. Wilson and Ferris, eds., *Encyclopedia of Southern Culture*, vol. 4, 40–3.

he graduated. Years after his graduation, he remained an eagerly sought-after speaker there.[33]

It is difficult to assess the degree of classism Louis confronted. He worked his way through college, holding jobs as a clothing-store clerk, a student instructor, and perhaps also a dentist's assistant. Many of his class-mates knew that his family operated an unpretentious business a short walk away in Durham. But few students at the little college came from wealthy families, and some came from poor ones. Most were the sons and daughters of farmers and merchants. Nearly half the students at Trinity worked, either to earn spending money or to finance their educations. Although one student from this period recalled an egalitarian atmosphere, a classmate of Louis's charged that a social hierarchy existed on campus. Jacob London perceived Trinity's fraternities—"organizations of wealthy or make-believe aristocratic students for snobbish purposes"—as "clannish to an obnoxious degree." A contemporary article in the *Archive* also suggests a patronizing relationship between students from families of means and their less affluent counterparts. "More than all the rest, the wealthy, aristocratic students admire and encourage the working student," effused the writer.[34]

As editor of the *Chronicle*, Louis addressed the issue of class in his first editorial. He belittled the "'college man' of vociferous clothes one used to meet with in the advertising pages of the magazines" whose "college life is a happy, tripping, irresponsible drinking-song ground out by a hectic hurdy-gurdy whose motive power is periodically renewed by checks from home." "Young man," he lectured the freshman reader, "you may not know it, but you are one of the world's princelings about to be fed with a golden spoon. A far-fetched metaphor? Not at all. Most young men of your age have to toil for their daily bread. The world does not owe you a living, much less a college education. Ethically, there is no reason why you should

---

33. *Trinity Chronicle*, 28 September 1910; Dill, "Glimpse of Parnassus," 5; William Wannamaker to Louis Jaffé, 22 November 1919, Wannamaker Papers, Duke University Archives; *Duke Chronicle*, 10 February 1926.

34. Roy, "Reminiscences of Trinity"; Pleasants, "How Trinity Students Help Themselves," *Trinity Archive* 27 (December 1913): 111; E. Jacob London, "Some College Questions," *Trinity Archive* 24 (February 1911): 175; Ewing, "Romances of American Journalism," 14; Dill, "Glimpse of Parnassus," 2.

sojourn pleasantly for four years at the feet of Wisdom, while your fellow man labors in the field or mart for bare sustenance. Only a maladjustment of the social fabric, with a gentle lift from that institution known as Private Property, has made possible this advantage which you enjoy over your less fortunate brother."[35]

Wishing to explore other cultures and practice his German, Louis arranged to work his passage abroad to Europe in the summer following his sophomore year. A friend, upperclassman Gilmer Siler, accompanied him. They sailed from Philadelphia aboard the SS *Merion* on June 20, 1908, in the company of 600 cattle, 330 paying passengers, and 20 other college students serving as "cattlemen." Chronicling his adventures in four articles he wrote for the *Archive,* Louis called the trip the greatest experience of his life. One of his future *Virginian-Pilot* associate editors, Alonzo Dill, believed that the series may have represented his colleague's "first sustained journalistic effort."[36]

On the voyage to Europe, Louis proved himself resourceful by securing a job sweeping the cattlemen's cabin and bringing their food from the galley, thus avoiding the more onerous chore of tending to the animals. He also learned how to induce the ship's cooks to prepare better meals for himself and Siler. "It was bribery, pure and simple, but on shipboard no stigma is attached to the practice," he later wrote. "The gravity of our offense was lessened in our eyes by the sight of some edible food."[37]

He and the other student cattlemen passed some of their free time by flirting with young women traveling in passenger class. Louis's and another youth's dalliance earned the ire of the burly quartermaster when he caught them conducting a proscribed tour of the ship's nether regions. "'You d—— cattlemen think you run this boat, don't you?'" he hissed to them out of the girls' hearing range. He marched the pair of culprits unceremoniously to the deck and reported them to the captain as the other cattlemen chortled. "Two such humiliated would-be gallants . . . were never seen," Louis recalled with chagrin.[38]

35. *Trinity Chronicle,* 7 September 1910.

36. Louis I. Jaffé, "To Europe on a Cattle Steamer," *Trinity Archive* 22 (February 1909): 170; Dill, "Glimpse of Parnassus," 5.

37. Jaffé, "To Europe on a Cattle Steamer," 171.

38. Ibid., 173–4.

With modest pecuniary resources and a bulging suitcase apiece, he and Siler strode down the gangplank at Liverpool and began to negotiate the strange pronunciations, monetary systems, and customs of Europe. From Liverpool they traveled on third-class tickets to Stratford, where—like so many tourists before and after them—they found Shakespeare's house disappointing. "One would have preferred to associate the master poet of all mankind with a birthplace a little less prosaic," Louis admitted. In a small park on the Avon they lay on the grass, drinking in the atmosphere that had inspired the Bard and hoping that it might provoke in them similar sagacity. They came away discouraged by their "own innate inferiority."[39]

On they traveled to Oxford, where they closely observed their British counterparts. An incredulous Louis, who knew something about clothing, scrutinized their costumes: "They were dressed for the most part in flannels—tight-fitting trousers and absurdly short and ill-fitting coats . . . [that] seemed to fit nowhere in particular, but had the appearance rather of being hung up to dry." Regardless of the comical togs, the two Americans pronounced their English peers a fine-looking lot. Louis and his friend found the Bodelian Library, Christ Church, and Oriel College truly impressive.[40]

Arriving in London, they viewed the scenery from high atop a three-penny bus and took in *The Mikado* at the Savoy. They attended services at St. Paul's on Sunday morning and devoted the rest of the day to the British Museum. They would have liked to spend weeks there, and only the ringing of the gong signaling the museum's closing tore them away.

In Hyde Park, the public romancing mildly scandalized the "uncouth provincials." As Louis later wrote, "The English park lover loving his love on a green bench in Kensington Garden is without counterpart in America. No false modesty troubles him. He embraces his colleen in full view of the moon, the electric lights and the passing throng and seems to glory in so doing. As far as I could determine, by involuntary observation, the more his sylvan bower was exposed to the gaze of the curious, the more intent was he in his wooing and the more affectionate in his caresses. Nor

39. Louis I. Jaffé, "Two Trinity Men in England," *Trinity Archive* 22 (May/June 1909): 320–1.
40. Ibid., 322.

was Phoebe always passive. She, too, showed no embarrassment, but gave herself up to his kisses with utter abandon—as if she intended to wed him on the next Bank Holiday."[41]

Westminster Abbey interested the Americans greatly. Louis remarked on the incongruity of bitter rivals Queen Elizabeth I and Mary Queen of Scots having been buried almost side by side. At the Poets' Corner of the abbey, the two young men paid homage to great writers of English from Chaucer and Shakespeare to Tennyson and Browning, even the American Longfellow. Then they visited the Victoria and Albert Museum, the Albert Memorial, and the National Gallery, where Louis appreciated the treasures but not, he later confessed, with the expert eye of an art "connoisseur."[42]

The young tourists crossed the North Sea to Holland by ferry and journeyed by train to Dusseldorf and Cologne. In Germany, Louis observed the militancy and aggressiveness of the people and the "contempt that the wearer of any kind of a uniform . . . bestows on those in civilian garb." He and Siler immediately acquired a taste for the strong, dark beer, and they stayed up until midnight on a park bench watching the Rhine, "which next to God and the Kaiser, is most holy in the heart of every German." They watched the water's movement in awe. Although they had planned to visit Berlin, time ran short; in August, with great regret, they sailed back to the United States.[43]

Taking into account the exuberance of a young man overseas for the first time, one finds Louis's writing undeniably impressive. The gestation of a professional writer appears unmistakably in the *Archive* series. The editor-to-be displayed sensitivity, a strong curiosity, and an eye for detail; he expressed himself with economy, precision, and an occasional flash of humor. These attributes would characterize his later writing.[44]

Around the time of Louis's European trip, the Jaffe family closed down P. Jaffe and Son and moved to South Boston, Virginia, where they opened

41. Ibid., 330.
42. Ibid., 334.
43. Louis I. Jaffé, "A Glimpse of Holland," *Trinity Archive* 23 (October 1909): 20; Louis I. Jaffé, "First Impressions of Germany," *Trinity Archive* 23 (December 1909): 139, 146.
44. Dill, "Glimpse of Parnassus," 9.

another clothing store. Precisely what precipitated their relocation remains unclear, but probably their business had fared poorly, given the steep competition they faced from Durham's well-developed merchant community.

A local historian of the era touted South Boston as a "good place to live in, to be sick in and to die in, since the cemetery stock has been bought up by public subscription." In addition to this morbid enticement, the town had much that attracted entrepreneurs. It had become a booming tobacco center; American Tobacco, Liggett & Myers, R. J. Reynolds, Imperial, and a number of other major tobacco companies had substantial business presences there. Importantly for the Jaffes, the town's mercantile infrastructure had not yet firmly established itself. In many ways South Boston resembled an earlier version of Durham.[45]

While the town's economic climate may have attracted them, the Jaffes' religious faith would isolate them in South Boston even more than in Durham. South Boston's Jewish community included only about ten families. The county was almost exclusively Protestant, "99 and 44/100 percent" to be exact, according to a local history. Newspapers, magazines, and billboards proudly extolled this figure throughout the region. The author reported that the few Jews and Catholics who lived there had "entered into and identified themselves with our life and institutions in a noble fashion." Regardless of the patronizing tone, the description was not inaccurate. South Boston's Jews—in much the same fashion that Harry Golden described—embedded themselves in the community and played a notable role in the town's affairs.[46]

Although the Jaffes' business did not prosper there greatly, the family became well known and well liked. Hyman involved himself in civic affairs, helping to found the town's highly successful Tobacco Festival. These activities generated friendly relationships such as the one he shared with future governor William Tuck, a South Boston native.[47]

* * *

45. Wirt Johnson Carrington, *A History of Halifax County, Virginia* (Richmond: Appeals Press, 1924), 60.

46. Alvin Silverman, interview by author, 8 July 1996; Barbour, *"Halifacts"*, 169.

47. Silverman, interview, 8 July 1996; William Tuck to Louis Jaffé, 20 December 1940, Jaffé Papers; William Tuck to Hyman Jaffé, 28 June 1934, Tuck Papers.

Louis's graduation ceremony in June 1911 provided a fitting conclusion to his college career. Trinity pulled out all the stops for its graduates. Automobiles and carriages decorated with navy blue Trinity banners streamed out to the college, and the streetcar company ran double-headers.[48]

Jacob Riis—journalist, author, and the nation's most famous social reformer—delivered the commencement address. Under Louis's editorship, the *Chronicle* had called Riis "one of the very few men who have accomplished lasting good with their pens. With absolutely no other resources than his active mind, his wide sympathy, and his reporter's pencil, he began and waged an untiring war against human misery until the public conscience was awakened and reforms put under way."[49]

Riis's personal experiences informed his writing. After his emigration from Denmark in 1870, he had endured a hardscrabble existence, at times literally starving as he worked through a succession of jobs— roustabout, laborer, salesman—before becoming a reporter. His books, which included *How the Other Half Lives, The Children of the Poor, The Battle with the Slum,* and *The Peril and Preservation of the Home,* had focused national attention on the urban poor and had served as the impetus for a host of important reforms. Many Jews from Eastern Europe counted the muckraking author as a knowledgeable and sympathetic advocate, well versed in the immigrant experience. (Probably unknown to most Jews outside New York, however, Riis had aroused controversy as a result of his settlement house's Christian tenor, which had alienated a faction of that city's Jewish community.) In Riis, Louis encountered a very different type of newspaperman than the partisan Josephus Daniels. Riis's reporting and photojournalism had made an important difference in the lives of New York's poor and had influenced social policy. His efforts had earned him the title "The Most Useful Man in New York" and had won him the respect and friendship of Theodore Roosevelt.[50]

Riis entitled his commencement address at Trinity "The Problem of Social Amelioration and Civic Betterment." His Danish accent perceptible

48. *Durham Sun,* 7 June 1911.

49. *Trinity Chronicle,* 22 March 1911.

50. Lewis Fried, *Makers of the City* (Amherst: University of Massachusetts Press, 1990), 11, 19; Jeffrey S. Gurock, "Jacob A. Riis: Christian Friend or Missionary Foe? Two Jewish Views," *American Jewish History* 71, no. 1 (1981): 29–47.

at times, he implored the graduating seniors to use their idealism, talents, and energy to mitigate pressing social ills. He saw no "little problems" in the world around them. "Righteousness counts as it never did before, and he who lives it wins," he told his audience. Those who felt that there existed "no dragons to be slain" in the modern age erred. He identified monsters that needed slaying: infant mortality, tenements and slums, tuberculosis, and child labor. No record of Louis's impression of his commencement speaker's speech survives, but Riis's audience received the speech enthusiastically.[51]

The newly minted college graduate went straight to work for the *Durham Sun,* where he had held a job the previous summer as circulation manager. He began in the circulation department but soon transferred to news. Despite the claim of his alma mater's alumni magazine that he "contributed a large measure of success" to the *Sun,* it hardly seems likely that he did much more than get his feet wet there.[52]

Meanwhile, Trinity president William Few had recommended Jaffé to John Stewart Bryan, publisher of the *Richmond News Leader* and the *Richmond Times-Dispatch.* Few described Jaffé as a "man who has more demonstrative ability to do newspaper writing than any student who has ever been in this College during my connection with it. . . . He would be glad to have a position, and if you are in need of a man who can write, I am confident you will make no mistake in getting him." Few enclosed a clipping from the *Chronicle.*[53]

Few's high opinion of his student may have diminished slightly when the cap-and-gown rental service that had furnished the graduation attire for the recent commencement notified the college that "Mr. L. I. Jaffé," who had coordinated the order, had bounced a check for $56.25. This probably resulted in a call from Trinity's administrative offices to the *Sun.* The embarrassed cub reporter must have made good, because Few's papers contain no further mention of the incident.[54]

In late July 1911 Jaffé received a letter from the *Times-Dispatch's*

51. *Durham Sun,* 7 June 1911.
52. *Trinity Chronicle,* 7 September 1910; "Deaths," 103–4.
53. William Few to John Stewart Bryan, 22 May 1911, Few Papers; Earle Dunford, *Richmond Times-Dispatch: The Story of a Newspaper* (Richmond: Cadmus, 1995), 38–9.
54. Cotrell & Leonard to F. Brown, 23 June 1911, Few Papers.

city editor, R. W. Simpson, who urgently needed help. Simpson, however, viewed Few's praise of Jaffé with skepticism. In the past month the *Times-Dispatch* had had to discharge a succession of three young reporters, each of whom had come with similarly strong references and had lasted no more than a week. He requested a frank description of Jaffé's journalistic experience and samples of his work. Should Jaffé pass muster, he would receive a weekly salary of eighteen dollars and rapid promotions. But Simpson cautioned the young reporter, "If you drink at all, I would advise you not to apply for the position. . . . I will give you a full and fair chance, but if I see from your copy that you do not come up to the standard, then we might as well understand the situation, for it would not be possible to keep you."[55]

Jaffé's response obviously satisfied the editor, who three days later cabled his offer of a probationary job and requested that Jaffé begin immediately. Three days after receiving the cable, Jaffé reported for work in the *Times-Dispatch*'s city room. He did not disappoint the city editor, whose brusque and intimidating manner proved to be a bluff. A few days after Jaffé began work, Trinity's president received a letter from his former student, thanking him for the recommendation and informing him that the *Times-Dispatch* had printed one of its new reporter's stories "with very little editorial emendation so I take it there is no objection to my style." Simpson, Jaffé confided, had "been rather kind."[56]

Over the next two years Jaffé earned several small raises and took on increased responsibilities, including coverage of the prestigious city hall/politics beat. He apprised Few that regardless of the salary increases, the "emolument" continued to be "disturbingly modest—a fault of the newspaper business."[57]

Jaffé's new base displayed many of the characteristics of the New South. Richmond functioned as an important railroad hub and the country's leading manufacturer of cigarettes. The city, then in the process of greatly increasing its size and population through annexation, contained a major iron industry and granite quarry. The Kline Motor Car Company began to

55. R. W. Simpson to Louis Jaffé, 20 July 1911, Jaffé Papers.
56. Ibid.; Louis Jaffé to William Few, 27 July 1911, Few Papers.
57. Louis Jaffé to William Few, 7 June 1913, Few Papers.

produce automobiles there in 1912, and they sold well. Richmond boasted a lively shopping quarter on Broad Street and a bustling financial district three blocks over, on Main Street. Virginia's capital also had achieved a reputation for its arts. In 1913 audiences could attend a wide range of plays, concerts, musicals, vaudeville shows, and movies in the city's thirty-four theaters. Resident novelists Ellen Glasgow and James Branch Cabell wrote satirically and critically about their southern homeland.[58]

Regardless of these cosmopolitan features, Richmond bore the indelible stamp of its past. The city devoted an inordinate amount of energy to romanticizing and sentimentalizing the antebellum South and the former Confederacy. Richmond served as the capital of rebel nostalgia, as exemplified by the imposing statues of the icons of the Lost Cause—Robert E. Lee, J. E. B. Stuart, and Jefferson Davis—which towered over Monument Avenue.

Race relations in Richmond had deteriorated significantly in the several decades preceding Jaffé's arrival. Segregation had become so widespread that strict separation governed nearly every interaction between the races. With an eye on the South's long tradition of miscegenation between white men and black women, black leader John Mitchell Jr., who published the *Richmond Planet,* caustically observed that "Jim Crow beds are more necessary in the Southland than Jim Crow cars."[59]

Virginia's Constitution of 1902 had almost completely eliminated the black vote through a pastiche of obstructionist devices, including literacy tests and the restoration of poll taxes. By these stratagems, Virginia's legislators had succeeded in slashing the state's roster of black voters from a pre-Constitution count of 147,000 to fewer than 10,000. In Richmond's Jackson Ward, the black electorate had declined in size from 2,983 to 33. Many blacks turned away from the polls had furnished proof of having been sired by Confederate veterans.[60]

58. Virginius Dabney, *Richmond: The Story of a City* (Garden City, N.Y.: Doubleday, 1976), 267, 282–3, 285–6, 287; Berman, *Richmond's Jewry,* 278.

59. Dabney, *Richmond,* 258.

60. Ibid., 270; Virginius Dabney, *Virginia: The New Dominion* (Charlottesville: University Press of Virginia, 1971), 436–7; Emily J. Salmon and Edward D. C. Campbell Jr., eds., *The Hornbook of Virginia History: A Ready-Reference Guide to the Old Dominion's People, Places, and Past* (Richmond: Library of Virginia, 1994), 63–4.

The pervasiveness and degree of disease and substandard housing shocked the white altruists who ventured into the city's impoverished black neighborhoods. An array of progressive white churchwomen and club women attempted through various organizations to abate the social, educational, and health problems they had encountered in these areas.[61]

Richmond had an entrenched and well-organized Jewish community. Rabbi Edward Calisch, who headed the largest and most prosperous synagogue in the city, Beth Ahabah, had earned the respect of the city's Gentile leaders. The scholarly and progressive Calisch espoused a brand of Reform Judaism that subordinated tradition and ceremony to Americanism and public relations. He foresaw a day when "progress" would eliminate the religious differences between Jews and Christians, and the two religions would merge "into the great temple of the brotherhood of man." German Jews had established Beth Ahabah in 1841. It had absorbed Beth Shalome, one of the oldest Jewish congregations in the United States, which dated from 1789. Kenesseth Israel, the "Polish Synagogue," and Sir Moses Montefiore, the "Russian Synagogue," served Orthodox and more traditional worshipers.[62]

At the time of Jaffé's arrival in Richmond, 2,844 Jews lived there, slightly over 2 percent of the city's population. For many years they had played important roles in municipal and economic affairs. Some indication of their social acceptance by the Gentile community is evinced by the fact that prior to the turn of the century Jews had belonged to the city's most exclusive social organizations, the Richmond, Westmoreland, and Commonwealth clubs. Jews also had affiliated with the Masons, Elks, and Knights of Pythias.[63]

Richmond's Jews had not faced the violence that some of their Deep South brethren had encountered in isolated communities in Mississippi and Louisiana, when hard times had encouraged scapegoating. The

61. Salmon and Campbell, *Hornbook of Virginia History,* 61–2.

62. Myron Berman, *Richmond's Jewry, 1769–1976: Shabbat in Shockoe* (Charlottesville: University Press of Virginia), 154, 242–9; David Bernstein and Adele Bernstein, "Slow Revolution in Richmond, Va.: A New Pattern in the Making," in *Jews in the South,* ed. Leonard Dinnerstein and Mary Dale Palsson (Baton Rouge: Louisiana State University Press, 1973), 254–5; Salmon and Campbell, *Hornbook of Virginia History,* 206.

63. Berman, *Richmond's Jewry,* 234, 261, 275.

Virginia capital city's Hebrew community never experienced the terror and degradation Atlanta's Jewry would endure as a result of the Leo Frank trial and lynching in 1915. Nor had Jaffé's Richmond coreligionists ever confronted the manifest anti-Semitism that characterized many regions of the North.[64]

But during the 1890s, the city's newspapers began to provoke a downturn in inter-religious relations. With increasing frequency, press reports characterized Jews in unflattering terms. The front page of the *Richmond Dispatch* described one wife beater as a "Russian Jew." In his book on the city's Jewish population, Rabbi Myron Berman writes, "Although a Jew could serve as president of the prestigious Westmoreland Club in the 1880s, a sharp social demarcation between Jew and Gentile had been drawn in Richmond by the turn of the century." Five years into Jaffé's tenure as a reporter for the *Times-Dispatch,* the paper printed a story highlighting a rebuke delivered by a Protestant minister to the city's Gentiles: "I should like . . . to know what is in the heart of this Christian woman that prompts her the moment she enters a social club to turn and slam the door in the face of the sister of her Christ?"[65]

During the seven years Jaffé resided in Richmond, he affiliated himself with the city's Jewish community. Perhaps as a result of the vigorous recruiting efforts of Beth Ahabah's Young Men's Committee, he joined the congregation there as a "seatholder." While this stratum lay beneath "member," it suggested an appropriate level of tithing for a young man beginning his career. He developed a close friendship with Mrs. Henry Wallerstein, a member of Beth Ahabah's congregation, and her two sons, Emanuel and Henry. During Jaffé's overseas experiences during and immediately following World War I, he would correspond frequently with Mrs. Wallerstein, calling her "Mutterchen." Jaffé also joined the Jefferson Club, which drew its membership from the city's wealthier Jews. By way of recommendation, President Few informed the organization's board of directors that his former student had "left behind him an excellent name and a brilliant record."[66]

64. Ibid., 246–7.

65. Ibid., 247.

66. Shirley Belkowitz, interview by author, 4 August 1997; *Congregation Beth Ahabah Yearbooks, 1915–1917,* Richmond, Va.; Edna Sara Lazaron, interview by author, 19

Periodically the young reporter ventured to South Boston to visit his family. While there he became romantically involved with a young woman named Ida Greenberg, whose father owned a butcher shop in nearby Danville. The Jaffes likely had become acquainted with the Greenbergs from attending religious services in that town, whose Jewish community exceeded that of South Boston. Ida had graduated from Randolph-Macon Woman's College in Lynchburg, Virginia, and had taught school in Mississippi. She had earned a reputation in Danville for her intelligence. She later married a physician, and Jaffé directed his attentions elsewhere.[67]

At the *Times-Dispatch* Jaffé continued to earn promotions, eventually rising to become a political writer and assistant city editor. His years in the state's capital provided him with invaluable training in Virginia government and politics. He covered several sessions of the legislature and established contacts with political and business leaders. Upon his departure from Richmond in 1918, his paper would refer to him as a "well-known newspaperman."[68]

In Richmond, Jaffé became friends with Douglas Southall Freeman, a young editorial writer at the *Times-Dispatch*, who would one day earn Pulitzer Prizes for his meticulously researched and carefully written biographies of George Washington and Robert E. Lee. When Bryan sold his interest in the paper in 1914, Freeman followed him to the afternoon *News Leader* and became its editor one year later. Freeman, who had earned a doctoral degree from Johns Hopkins University, would acquire a widespread reputation for his liberal viewpoint, expertise in military history, and prodigious literary output (as well as his rigidly controlled schedule and his condescension). He became an inveterate Baptist preacher as well, broadcasting Sunday inspirational talks from his study.[69]

August 1997; Berman, *Richmond's Jewry*, 287; William Few to J. Jonesoff, 22 May 1911, Few Papers.

    67. Silverman, interview by author, 8 July 1996.

    68. Ewing, "Romances of American Journalism," 14; *Richmond Times-Dispatch*, 3 May 1918.

    69. Louis Jaffé to Douglas Southall Freeman, 7 June 1949, Jaffé Papers; Dunford, *Richmond Times-Dispatch: The Story of a Newspaper*, 307–13; Mims, *The Advancing South*. 189–96; *Pilot*, 26 June 1949; Parke Rouse, *We Happy Wasps: Virginia in the Days of Jim Crow and Harry Byrd* (Richmond: Dietz Press, 1996), 59–60, 155–6.

Jaffé also developed a friendship with Alexander Forward, the *Times-Dispatch*'s political expert. The English-born Forward provided the paper with astute analyses of state politics. He enjoyed a close relationship with Virginia governor Henry Stuart (1914–1918), for whom he had worked as an assistant and advisor. In 1917 Stuart appointed Forward a commissioner of the newly developed State Corporation Commission, which oversaw the rates and public service responsibilities of utilities, railroads, and other common carriers.[70]

In addition to publisher John Stewart Bryan, Jaffé met other powerful older men in Richmond. Precisely how he got to know Thomas Wheelwright remains unclear; perhaps the two became acquainted through Jaffé's work as a reporter. As president of both the Virginia Railway and Power Company and Old Dominion Iron and Steel Works, Wheelwright was one of Virginia's most significant business leaders. He had begun his career in Norfolk, where his brother-in-law, attorney and banker Hugh C. Davis, served as a member of the *Virginian-Pilot*'s executive committee and the paper's board of directors.[71]

Jaffé also met Henry W. Anderson, a prominent corporate attorney, then engaged to Ellen Glasgow. Anderson would shortly head the American Red Cross's war relief efforts in the Balkans. Smitten by Romania's beautiful English-born Queen Marie, who had just conferred three decorations upon him, he allegedly fell to his knees and kissed the hem of her dress. Learning of this by reading the queen's autobiography, Glasgow terminated the engagement and nearly her life by taking an overdose of sleeping pills. Fortunately for belles lettres, she recovered, earning the Pulitzer Prize for literature in 1942 for her novel *In This Our Life*. Anderson ran for governor of Virginia on the Republican ticket in 1921, exposing Democratic corruption and inefficiency in state government.[72]

The growing progressivism that characterized American social pol-

70. *Pilot,* 25 July 1920.

71. Richard L. Morton, *History of Virginia,* vol. 2 (Chicago: American Historical Society, 1924), 240–1; Joseph Shank, comp., *Raw Materials on the History of Norfolk-Portsmouth Newspapers* (Norfolk: Norfolk Public Library, Sargeant Memorial Room, n.d.), 1469, 2331.

72. Dabney, *Richmond,* 299–303; Salmon and Campbell, *Hornbook of Virginia History,* 76.

icy, literature, art, and journalism during the first decades of the twentieth century also marked the tenor of Virginia politics during Jaffé's tenure with the *Times-Dispatch*. The General Assembly allocated more funding for education and legislated a host of reforms and innovations: increased regulation of railroads and natural monopolies; construction of hospitals, asylums, prisons, reformatories, and a highway network; and enactment of pure-food-and-drug standards and child-labor laws. The legislature created an assortment of agencies to oversee these programs. On both state and national levels, prohibition and women's suffrage—outgrowths of the progressive movement—became two of the most significant and controversial issues of this period, and undoubtedly Jaffé's political reporting exposed him to both.[73]

Methodist Bishop James Cannon Jr. headed Virginia's Anti-Saloon League and prohibitionist movement with tireless energy, strong organizational abilities, and a Machiavellian sensibility. He directed the daily *Richmond Virginian,* the pages of which he used to champion temperance and other moral causes. By the time of Jaffé's arrival in Richmond, Cannon had dried up most of the state's rural counties and towns and many of its smaller cities and had become one of the dominant figures in Virginia politics. In 1914 Cannon successfully rammed through the Assembly an enabling act for a statewide referendum on prohibition. Later that year Virginia's electorate voted three to two for state prohibition.[74]

One might expect that Cannon would have aligned himself with Virginia's suffrage movement (many observers believed that women voters would support prohibition), but he did not. The Equal Suffrage League of Virginia—formed in Richmond in 1909 by reformer Lila Meade Valentine and prominent women writers and artists such as Ellen Glasgow—met with Cannon's disdain and the open animosity of the liquor and saloon industry. Three times between 1912 and 1916 the League succeeded in bringing the

73. Louis D. Rubin, *Virginia: A History* (New York: W. W. Norton, 1984), 159–60.

74. Virginius Dabney, *Dry Messiah: The Life of Bishop James Cannon, Jr.* (New York: Alfred A. Knopf, 1949), 59–70; Cappon, *Virginia Newspapers,* 191; Rubin, *Virginia: A History,* 159–60; Lenoir Chambers, Joseph Shank, and Harold Sugg, *Salt Water & Printer's Ink: Norfolk and Its Newspapers, 1865–1965* (Chapel Hill: University of North Carolina Press, 1967), 283–4.

suffrage issue to the floor of the General Assembly; three times the organization experienced overwhelming defeat. Not until 1952 would the Virginia General Assembly acknowledge the right of women to vote.[75]

The *Times-Dispatch* opposed both prohibition and women's suffrage. For their support of local option, Cannon dubbed the newspaper and other wet leaders the "Bold Brave Boys of the Bottle." The paper's editorials strongly opposed extending the ballot to women, asserting that their vote would pose a threat to white supremacy. Suffrage for women, the paper declaimed, "would double the number of uncertain and dangerous votes and put the balance of political power in the hands of 165,000 colored women, only to gratify the whims of a small group of women who don't really know what they are about." No one bothered to explain why the provisions of the Constitution of 1902 that prevented black men from voting would not do the same for black women.[76]

Jaffé's views on these two key issues at the time can only be surmised from his previously demonstrated liberality and the positions he would later support as an editor. At the *Virginian-Pilot,* he would urge repeal of the Eighteenth Amendment and ratification of the Nineteenth. He would term prohibition a "political and social nightmare" and acknowledge the courage of suffragists who "fought on and won—with the aid of a belated national recognition of the preposterousness, in modern times, of disenfranchisement based on sex."[77]

A preponderance of particularly newsworthy events marked the year 1914 for Jaffé. In addition to the referendum for state prohibition and the Equal Suffrage League's agitation, that spring saw the assassination of the Archduke Franz Ferdinand in Sarajevo by Serbian terrorists and the outbreak of World War I in Europe.

75. Marjorie Spruill Wheeler, *New Women of the New South: The Leaders in the Woman Suffrage Movement in the Southern States* (New York: Oxford University Press, 1993), 11; Salmon and Campbell, *Hornbook of Virginia History,* 64–6; Elna C. Green, *Southern Strategies: Southern Women and the Woman Suffrage Question* (Chapel Hill: University of North Carolina Press, 1997), 157–77.

76. Dabney, *Virginia: The New Dominion,* 461–2; Wheeler, *New Women of the New South,* 26.

77. *Pilot,* 30 August 1920; Louis Jaffé, "The Brave New Century" [1940], Jaffé Papers; Dill, "Glimpse of Parnassus," 21.

The *Times-Dispatch* joined a national newspaper campaign urging a new trial for Leo Frank, the Jewish manager of an Atlanta pencil factory, who had been convicted of the murder of thirteen-year-old Mary Phagan the previous year. Frank's arrest and trial, the concomitant publicity, and his lynching in 1915 comprised the worst single case of anti-Semitism in United States history. The Atlanta police department had conducted an inept investigation, and a grandstanding prosecutor with political ambitions had asked a jury to convict Frank on the basis of flimsy circumstantial evidence. The city's newspapers fueled the hothouse atmosphere and vastly increased their circulation by devoting hundreds of pages to the murder, which one paper called the "greatest news story in the history of the state, if not of the South."[78]

As the jurors deliberated, they could hear through the open courthouse windows a mob of two thousand milling outside in the Georgia heat, chanting, "Kill the Jew." The crowd ignored the mounted policemen ordering them to disperse. During the trial, the judge, defense attorneys, and by some accounts the jury itself had received threats that they would not leave the courtroom alive if that "damned Jew" walked away a free man.[79]

Fearing a lynching if the jury exonerated Frank, Governor John Slaton ordered the readiness of Atlanta's National Guard. Slaton acted wisely; seven years earlier one of the bloodiest race riots in the history of the South had torn the city apart. (Nobel Prize winner Gunnar Myrdal more accurately described it as a "one-way terrorization" of the black community.) When it all ended, ten blacks and two whites lay dead, and a teenaged Walter White, future secretary of the NAACP, had been forever radicalized by the violence he and his family had narrowly escaped. The jury's verdict in the Frank case did not disappoint the mob, who hoisted the sobbing prosecutor on their shoulders and danced in the streets. The next day the judge passed down a death sentence.[80]

78. Leonard Dinnerstein, *The Leo Frank Case* (Athens: University of Georgia Press, 1987), 93, 13; Leonard Dinnerstein, "Atlanta in the Progressive Era: A Dreyfus Affair in Georgia," in *Jews in the South*, 187–8.

79. *Richmond Times-Dispatch*, 17 August 1915, 26 August 1913; *Washington Post*, 20 December 1983; Dinnerstein, *Leo Frank Case*, 60–1.

80. Gunnar Myrdal, *An American Dilemma*, 567; Walter White, *A Man Called White: The Autobiography of Walter White* (New York: Viking, 1948), 5–12; John Egerton, *Speak Now Against the Day: The Generation Before the Civil Rights Movement* (New York:

Frank's conviction and the mob's behavior horrified Atlanta's Jews in particular and southern Jews in general. The crux of the issue for Jews was that the word of a black man, Jim Conley, had convicted Frank. This transgressed a sacrosanct Old South precept previously assumed to be inviolable. Conley, a janitor at the factory, was a petty thief, a known liar, and in all likelihood Mary Phagan's murderer. Yet his bizarre and sordid narrative had transfixed the all-white, all-male, all-Gentile jury and persuaded them of another white man's guilt. Regardless of Frank's quiet dignity and eloquent testimony, his high-powered defense team, the many witnesses who attested to his unimpeachable character, and the national sentiment for his acquittal, the court had convicted him and sentenced him to hang. The Frank case profoundly underscored for southern Jews the fragile nature of the harmony that existed between them and Gentiles.[81]

The agitation that followed Frank's trial had even more dire consequences for Jews. Former congressman and Populist Party leader Tom Watson, capitalizing on the controversy in the pages of his weekly newspaper, *The Jeffersonian,* and his monthly periodical, *Watson's Magazine,* conducted a vicious anti-Semitic campaign that played to poor and uneducated white farmers and factory workers. Circulation of the *"Jeff"* skyrocketed from 25,000 to 87,000.[82]

Meanwhile, the courts rejected Frank's many appeals, and ultimately his life rested in the hands of popular Governor Slaton, whose term expired the day before the execution date. After studying the case exhaustively, Slaton, in an act of enormous courage, commuted the sentence to life imprisonment. He had become convinced of Frank's innocence and believed that he would eventually be freed.[83]

News of Slaton's action raced through the city, and a five-thousand-person mob stoked white hot by Watson's diatribes quickly assembled in

Alfred A. Knopf, 1994), 42; *Richmond Times-Dispatch,* 26 August 1913; *Washington Post,* 20 December 1983.

    81. *Washington Post,* 20 December 1983; Eli N. Evans, *The Lonely Days Were Sundays: Reflections of a Jewish Southerner* (Jackson: University Press of Mississippi, 1993), 30–1.

    82. C. Vann Woodward, *Tom Watson: Agrarian Rebel* (New York: Macmillan, 1938), 442.

    83. Dinnerstein, *Leo Frank Case,* 127–9.

Atlanta's downtown. Chanting, "We want John M. Slaton, Georgia's traitor governor," and armed with a wide range of firearms and other implements of mayhem—everything from brass knuckles to dynamite—they marched the six miles to the governor's mansion. Slaton had declared martial law, and a full battalion of bayoneted state militia had erected a cordon around the mansion. Members of the rabble never reached the governor, but they wounded or disabled sixteen soldiers charged with protecting him.[84]

In the wake of the commutation of Frank's sentence, Watson helped establish the Knights of Mary Phagan, an anti-Semitic order that conducted a boycott of Jewish businesses throughout Georgia. The state had one of the largest Jewish populations in the South, and nearly every town had small Jewish-owned stores like the one the Jaffes operated in South Boston. Boycott organizers distributed flyers that asked, "Can't you buy Clothing from an American?" Marietta's Jewish merchants received an edict to shut down their businesses and leave town. "We intend to rid Marietta of all Jews," the notice cautioned. "You can heed this warning or stand the punishment the committee may see fit to deal out to you." In another town, residents warned Jews to leave within twenty-four hours or face "summary justice." Many communities hanged and burned effigies of Frank and Slaton. The anti-Semitic threats had the desired effect. Many of Georgia's Jews armed themselves and fled Atlanta for Birmingham and other destinations. When the furor ended, three thousand Jews had left the state.[85]

Certain that a mob would attempt to lynch Frank, the governor had with lightning speed and near-total secrecy transferred the prisoner from Atlanta's jail to the state prison farm in Milledgeville, some eighty miles southeast of the capital. Anticipating trouble, Slaton ordered the prison warden to double the guard.[86]

Slaton's precautions were to no avail. One night shortly thereafter, twenty-five of the leading citizens from Mary Phagan's hometown of Marietta appeared before Frank as he lay in a prison hospital bed, his slit throat

84. Ibid., 132–3; Woodward, *Tom Watson: Agrarian Rebel*, 440.

85. *Encyclopaedia Judaica*, s.v. "Frank, Leo Max"; Woodward, *Tom Watson: Agrarian Rebel*, 442; Dinnerstein, *Leo Frank Case*, 130–1; *Washington Post*, 20 December 1983; Mary Phagan, *The Murder of Little Mary Phagan* (Far Hills, N.J.: New Horizon, 1987), 236.

86. Dinnerstein, *Leo Frank Case*, 126.

sutured, recovering from a near-fatal knife attack by a deranged inmate. The intruders, members of the Knights of Mary Phagan, had clipped the telephone and telegraph lines leading to the prison, overpowered the two guards on duty, and handcuffed the warden and superintendent. Adhering to the ritual of lynching, Frank's abductors planned to hang him near Phagan's grave in Marietta.[87]

On the seven-hour trip back, they repeatedly asked Frank to confess, but he refused to do so, even when his kidnappers promised to spare his life if he owned up to Phagan's murder. Frank's dignity and sincerity so impressed his kidnappers that most expressed the desire to return their hostage to Milledgeville. But when they considered that the sun would soon rise and that law authorities would be scouring the state en masse for their captive, they went forward with their plans. Unable to reach Phagan's grave, they stopped in a grove outside Marietta, took Frank to a large oak tree, hanged him, and quickly departed.[88]

Although the posses combing the region found no trace of Frank, Mariettans almost immediately determined the location of the lynching and flocked to the site. By mid-morning the crowd numbered around a thousand. Some milled about festively as if on a holiday, taking snapshots, snipping pieces of the rope, and tearing off scraps of Frank's clothing. Women and children examined the body swaying in the breeze. One man angrily demanded that the mob burn the corpse. When undertakers cut the body down, he rushed to it, stamped on its head, and ground his heel into the face of the corpse. According to a special report for the *Times-Dispatch*, members of the crowd cried, "Don't move the Jew's body until we shoot it full of holes."[89]

Jaffé's paper, which had reported extensively on the Frank case, asserted that the "lynching constitutes the most vicious blow that has been struck at organized government in this country in a century, and the South, in particular must suffer its effects. The circumstances of the case, the condition of the man, wounded and barely escaped from the jaws of death, make

87. *Richmond Times-Dispatch*, 17 and 23 August 1915.
88. Dinnerstein, *Leo Frank Case*, 139–41.
89. *Richmond Times-Dispatch*, 18 August 1915; Dinnerstein, *Leo Frank Case*, 143–4.

the crime more atrocious in its utter inhumanity, but even they could not increase the fearsomeness of the act itself." The *Times-Dispatch* wrote that it had repeatedly expressed "with all the force at its command . . . that Frank's conviction was the result of a prejudice against the prisoner, [and it had] urged the people of Georgia to save themselves from the blood guilt of legalized murder."[90]

Within the South, Frank's lynching intensified Jews' already considerable reluctance to challenge the region's injustices. Fearful of calling attention to themselves, southern Jews maintained a conspicuous silence regarding Jim Crow laws and customs. Malcolm Stern, an eminent Jewish historian and longtime rabbi of Norfolk's Congregation Ohef Sholom, writes that "in the decades between the Civil War and World War II, no Southern rabbi seems to have made any attempt to deal with the race question. The fear of anti-Semitism, which reached its peak with the trial of Leo Frank . . . remained so pervasive throughout the South, that few (if any) Jewish laymen or rabbis would have had the courage to speak out on so unpopular an issue as the rights of blacks."[91]

But the mob violence galvanized northern Jewish activism. Out of the firestorm surrounding Frank's case grew the Anti-Defamation League of B'nai B'rith. "The story of Leo Frank struck the American Jewish community like nothing before," recalled one of the league's chairmen. "It was Frank's destiny to give the League a sense of urgency that characterizes its operations to this day." The organization battled lynchings and mob justice from the outset.[92]

Out of the Knights of Mary Phagan grew what its first public announcement described as "A High Class Order for Men of Intelligence and Character"—the Knights of the Ku Klux Klan. The notice appeared in the *Atlanta Journal* in the winter following Frank's lynching, next to an advertisement for D. W. Griffith's *Birth of a Nation*. Griffith's groundbreaking film, perhaps the most incendiary racist propaganda ever produced,

90. *Richmond Times-Dispatch*, 18 and 25 August 1915.

91. Malcolm M. Stern, "The Role of the Rabbi in the South," in *"Turn to the South,"* 29–30; *New York Times*, 7 January 1994; Leonard Dinnerstein, *Uneasy at Home: Antisemitism and the American Jewish Experience* (New York: Columbia University Press, 1987), 136–7.

92. Phagan, *Murder of Little Mary Phagan*, 236–7.

combined with Watson's hate-mongering to create a fertile environment in which the new fraternal organization could flourish. Its organizers resurrected the name of a white underground resistance organization that had operated in the South after the Civil War.[93]

Under the visionary leadership of defrocked Methodist minister and failed garter salesman Colonel William J. Simmons (whose rank stemmed not from military service but from his command of five regiments of the Woodmen of the World), within a decade the nascent Klan would boast a membership of over two million. With a small group of the Knights of Mary Phagan, Simmons climbed to the bald top of Stone Mountain and heralded the second coming of the Klan by lighting a kerosene-drenched cross visible sixteen miles away in Atlanta.[94]

As Jaffé honed his journalistic skills on affairs closer to home, the social and political crises occurring regionally and worldwide stoked his inner fire. The quality of his reportage—and indeed the young journalist himself—did not go unnoticed, and important personal and professional connections were forged both at the *Times-Dispatch* and in the city of Richmond at large.

93. *Atlanta Journal,* 7 December 1915; Stephen J. Whitfield, "Jews and Other Southerners: Counterpoint and Paradox," in *"Turn to the South,"* 87.

94. Chalmers, *Hooded Americanism,* 28–38, 71; Phagan, *Murder of Little Mary Phagan,* 234; Dinnerstein, *Leo Frank Case,* 150.

4 A War Up Close

The name Louis I. Jaffé does not appear in the pantheon of American heroes of World War I alongside the likes of Rickenbacker, York, and Frank Luke, the moody Arizona balloon-buster. Stuck in a supply depot well behind the front, working as what he termed a "glorified shipping clerk," Jaffé cursed the gods of fate who had conspired to put him there.[1]

He had volunteered for military service a little more than a month following the United States' entry into the hostilities on April 6, 1917. Verdun, the Somme, and Ypres had with horrifying clarity shown that the Great War was to be an artillerymen's war, belonging to the German 105- and 150-mm. howitzers and the much lighter but tremendously efficient French 75s. Perhaps this explains Jaffé's decision to pursue training in field artillery at Fort Myer in Arlington, Virginia. The fortifications there, originally constructed to protect the nation's capital from British invaders, dated back almost to the Revolutionary War. Jaffé's class of nine hundred officer trainees, the first to graduate from the historic facility, drew President Woodrow Wilson, his wife Edith, and Secretary of War Newton Baker to the ceremonies. Jaffé graduated on November 26, 1917, receiving a commission as a second lieutenant. Pushing thirty, he was likely one of the older members of his class.[2]

Despite his decision to join up immediately following Wilson's declaration of war, Jaffé does not appear to have succumbed to the tide of flag-waving fervor that seized the United States. In his diary he expressed a dislike of patriotic and martial music, particularly "Over There"; he confided

---

1. Louis Jaffé war diary, 20 July 1918, Jaffé Papers.

2. S. L. A. Marshall, *World War I* (Boston: Houghton Mifflin, 1992), 45; James Cooke, *The U.S Air Service in the Great War, 1917–1919* (Westport, Conn.: Praeger, 1996), 24; *Air House: A History* (Washington, D.C.: Center for Air Force History, 1994), 3–4; *Richmond Times-Dispatch*, 26 November 1917; Dill, "Glimpse of Parnassus," 5.

that although he hoped for "at least one chance to get in real danger," he was "no blood thirsty hero."[3]

After earning his bars, Jaffé received further training—probably also in artillery—at Leon Springs Military Reservation, just north of San Antonio. But the Army had a surplus of officers in field artillery and urgently needed specialists in other areas, particularly in supply. The War Department scrambled to outfit the waves of American Expeditionary Forces spilling into Europe to spell the exhausted and decimated poilus and Tommies. The Service of Supply (SOS) struggled with the difficult logistical problems associated with creating an infrastructure and organizational system to transport 25,000 tons of equipment each day through the French ports of St. Nazaire, Bordeaux, Nantes, La Pallice, Le Havre, Brest, and Marseille on to the front.[4]

The newly formed Air Service, equipped for the most part with French and British airplanes and French observation balloons, especially suffered for want of supplies. It desperately required engines, parts, and maintenance and repair equipment. War materiel for the Air Service moved by rail from French ports via the centrally located hub of Romorantin to supply dumps in the advance section. The principal advance support depot was being constructed in the village of Is-sur-Tille, about seventy miles from the fighting.[5]

Jaffé apparently found Service of Supply's recruitment assurances, which included early embarkation to France, persuasive. Duly recommissioned in the Air Service, he underwent training at Kelly Field, on the southern fringes of San Antonio, with the 649th Aero Squadron. Pilot training was not an option; he had passed the cutoff age of twenty-five.[6]

3. Jaffé war diary, "rest of month of May 1918," 20 July 1918, Jaffé Papers.

4. *Camp Bullis: A History of the Leon Springs Military Reservation, 1890–1990* (Fort Sam Houston, Tex.: Fort Sam Houston Museum, 1990), 23–42.

5. Cooke, *U.S Air Service*, 127; Maurer Maurer, ed. *The Final Report and a Tactical History*, vol. 1, *The U.S. Air Service in World War I* (Maxwell AFB, Ala.: Albert F. Simpson Historical Research Center, 1978), 25, 70, 123–4, 126, 129; Johnson Hagood, *The Services of Supply: A Memoir of the Great War* (New York: Houghton Mifflin, 1927), 158–62.

6. Dill, "Glimpse of Parnassus," 6; Ann Krueger Hussey et al., *A Heritage of Service: Seventy-Five Years of Military Aviation at Kelly Air Force Base, 1916–1991* (Kelly Air Force Base, Tex.: Office of History, 1991), 15.

The desolate terrain and harsh conditions at Texas military bases were bleakness itself. Surrounded by sagebrush and cactus, exposed to violent dust storms and whirlwinds, sweltering hot in the daytime and freezing cold at night, billeted in tents and hastily erected crude wooden barracks, and subsisting on a diet consisting almost exclusively of beans and "monkey meat," many of the new recruits stationed there surely recalled civilian life with nostalgia. By the time Jaffé arrived at Kelly Field for indoctrination, 39,000 soldiers lived crammed together on the base. The SOS and the Air Service had just begun to develop cooperative procedures for training, and whatever makeshift instruction Jaffé received probably did not tax his intellectual abilities.[7]

San Antonio's nightlife contrasted garishly with the military regimen on the base and provided the editor-to-be with a wealth of observations and experiences from which he could one day draw when he wrestled with Norfolk's considerable public-health and safety problems stemming from the many military bases surrounding it. As a young reporter in Richmond, he doubtless had encountered vice aplenty. But his exposure to human weakness in the capital of the Confederacy could hardly have prepared him for the sheer enormity of what he would see deep in the heart of Texas. The influx of soldiers and government money into San Antonio attracted legions of prostitutes from destitute areas in the Mississippi Delta and the Plains, some just girls barely into their teens. Many had followed their new husbands there and found themselves stranded or abandoned without support when their spouses shipped out overseas. Some women worked as gold diggers and chiselers, marrying repeatedly and attempting to draw multiple allotments from the War Department. Sexually transmitted diseases ran rampant among the troops and their consorts. The situation deteriorated to such a degree that military authorities placed a moratorium on liberty for troops and fenced in a section of the base to quarantine the diseased soldiers. However, the town's merchants exerted political pressure, and soon soldiers again flooded the bars, dance halls, and pickup joints.[8]

7. Michael Lobb, *A Brief History of Early Kelly Field, 1916–1918,* ed. Ann Krueger Hussey, Robert S. Browning III, and Thomas M. O'Donoghue (Kelly Air Force Base, Tex.: Office of History, 1988), 42; Hussey et al., *Heritage of Service,* 15.

8. Lobb, *Brief History of Early Kelly Field,* 46–7.

Kelly's officers and chaplaincy wisely developed a range of more wholesome activities for the troops. Instead of visiting the "young locals," whom one soldier described as "cute as buttons but as mischievous as little imps of Satan," the airmen could now while away their off-duty hours in woodshops, orchestras, and theatrical troupes. Friday and Saturday nights were reserved for base dances, which the enlisted men and officers alike anticipated eagerly. Women—but not men—with questionable morals were barred, so that "nice girls" would consent to attend. Watchful chaperones accompanied young Hispanic-American women (a cultural practice not without justification).[9]

Early in the spring of 1918, Jaffé boarded the *Prinz Eitel Friederich*, an interned German commerce raider reoutfitted as the transport ship *De Kalb*. Sailing under strict secrecy, the camouflaged vessel quietly set sail from Newport News, Virginia. The drab departure impressed Jaffé as a "trifle sad and foreboding." That night the *De Kalb* anchored within view of the Chamberlin Hotel at Old Point Comfort. The festive resort, which he had visited many times during his years in Richmond, glowed with lights, and the sounds of its music drifted out to the ship. Jaffé wondered whether he would return from the war to dine and dance at the hotel again.[10]

Submarines prowled the ocean, and the troops practiced abandon-ship and lifeboat drills repeatedly. Jaffé, who had been assigned to command whaleboat no. 8, was vexed to discover one of the soldiers in his party missing during a drill. Finding him in his bunk, the second lieutenant remained unmoved by the man's excuse. "I raise particular & extended hell," Jaffé wrote in his diary, "reminding him he would be SOL if he followed such a course when the real alarm came." From that point on, the soldier performed flawlessly in drills.[11]

The 649th disembarked in St. Nazaire on April 14, and Jaffé without hesitation began a program to improve his French, which suffered in comparison to his German. He and another young officer noticed two young French women, "both rather good looking," glancing back at them.

9. Ibid., 43–8.

10. Thomas C. Parramore, Peter C. Stewart, and Tommy L. Bogger, *Norfolk: The First Four Centuries* (Charlottesville: University Press of Virginia, 1994), 289; Jaffé war diary, 29 March 1918, Jaffé Papers.

11. Jaffé war diary, 3 April 1918, Jaffé Papers.

Jaffé's companion did not speak a word of French, so the burden of translation fell upon Jaffé. His suggestion that the two couples take a walk was at first rejected out of hand. "You have not been introduced," Marie exclaimed. "Mama would be so angry." After a few minutes of additional conversation, the mademoiselles allowed the two officers to accompany them, but only to church for evening prayers. Afterwards Marie and her friend bade their momentary suitors adieu.[12]

A few days later Jaffé's squadron was routed through Romorantin to Is-sur-Tille. The village, located in the foothills of the French Alps, looked to Jaffé "exactly like a thousand other French villages [with] crooked streets, bedraggled shops, a church, a square with a . . . well, [a town hall], and chickens and children." The enormous military depot contained warehouses and sheds with over two million square feet of storage space and almost a hundred miles of railway track. Dijon, the closest city, was about eighteen miles away.[13]

Jaffé and another lieutenant shared a comfortable room with a stove. The officers took their meals at a well-equipped mess and relaxed during their off-duty hours in a rustic club with a thatched roof, baked clay walls, and enormous fireplaces. These amenities and the supply dump's pastoral setting notwithstanding, harsh reminders on all sides bespoke the ever-present danger of attack and the urgency of the encampment's mission. The warehouses were camouflaged to conceal them from German Gotha bombers and ringed with anti-aircraft guns, dubbed "Archie" by the Allied forces.[14]

Jaffé arrived at his new post having been exposed to the influenza virus, and almost immediately became ill. A "cold" turned into bronchitis, and his temperature soared to nearly 105 degrees. Medical personnel deemed him sick enough to transport him by ambulance to the military hospital in Dijon. Although he began to recover there, his ordeal was just beginning. An American doctor decided his tonsils should come out, and a botched operation resulted in Jaffé's nearly bleeding to death. Having lost two quarts of blood, he was anesthetized with gas, and the hole in his throat

12. Ibid., 17 April 1918.
13. Dill, "Glimpse of Parnassus," 7; Hagood, *Services of Supply*, 161–2.
14. Jaffé war diary, 25 April 1918, Jaffé Papers.

was sewn shut with five stitches. He awoke violently ill. Weakened by the surgery, he suffered a relapse of the chest infection, which was diagnosed as bronchial pneumonia. The physician considered Jaffé's condition sufficiently serious that he initially dissembled, trying to conceal from his patient the nature of the illness.[15]

For the final three weeks of May, Jaffé recuperated in Dijon. He occupied himself by reading newspapers, magazines, and his mail. The *Chicago Tribune,* called by its editor and publisher Robert McCormick the "World's Greatest Newspaper," did not appeal to Jaffé's taste. He much preferred the *New York Herald,* which he regarded as "newsy and interesting," and the American edition of the *London Daily Mail,* which—despite its "saccharine American flattery, so palpably propagandist"—devoted much attention to stateside doings. Of the magazines he read, he appreciated *London By-Stander* the most; but he devoured even months-old copies of *Literary Digest* and *Atlantic Monthly* voraciously. During his military service in France he also enjoyed a wide range of literature in French and English, including Voltaire, Maupassant, Cellini's *Autobiography,* and Savinien's *Cyrano de Bergerac.*[16]

Jaffé relished his mail and reread letters time and again. Lotta Jaffe wrote English poorly, and family correspondence usually came via Hyman. Mrs. Wallerstein was a loyal and charming correspondent. And letters from "Horty," probably Hortense Whitehill, with whom he conducted an on-again, off-again romance, alternately elated and demoralized him.[17]

Once a week a military band came to play for the ill and wounded soldiers. Patients hobbled into the courtyard, and those too infirm to walk were carried out underneath the trees and placed on cots. Jaffé, despite professing little ear for music, looked forward to the concerts, favoring the classical and popular tunes over the patriotic music.[18]

In early June, Jaffé was sent to a Vichy hospital for respiratory cases. Doctors there inspected him thoroughly and pronounced him much improved. They ordered him to exercise; though wobbly at first from his

15. Ibid., May 2, 7–18, "rest of the month of May 1918."

16. Ibid., "rest of the month of May 1918"; Dill, "Glimpse of Parnassus," 9.

17. Dill, "Glimpse of Parnassus," 12, 26; Jaffé war diary, "rest of the month of May 1918," 26 July 1918, 22 August 1918, 2 September 1918, 30 October 1918, Jaffé Papers.

18. Jaffé war diary, "rest of the month of May 1918," Jaffé Papers.

month-long confinement, he began to go on hikes. A few days later, nearly fully recovered, he had put on five or six pounds.[19]

Parisians fleeing Big Bertha's shelling had poured into Vichy. The medical staff allowed Jaffé the run of the city, and after exercising during the daytime, he and other convalescing officers gravitated to the cafes and restaurants during the evenings. Jaffé met the Picard family, with whose young daughter, Yolande, he developed a friendship. He and the seventeen-year-old Mademoiselle Picard took walks and played tennis together. She quickly grew infatuated with the American officer, but he did not reciprocate the attraction. For Jaffé she was "just . . . a kid," who still wore "shoe-top dresses." (Soldiers serving in the AEF had happily discovered that many French women, unlike their American counterparts, wore skirts that fell considerably above the tops of their shoes.)[20]

Not all of the city's young women boasted spotless reputations. The German artillery bombardment had driven "ladies of easy morals" from Paris to Vichy. While seated with Jaffé at a cafe, another American lieutenant spied one such woman with "whom he had an acquaintance." He invited her to join the two officers at their table. She accepted, and Jaffé studied her carefully. Yvette was not of the flashy Parisian demimonde, "silk-stockinged, arrogant, rouged & crepe de chined, glittering with cheap jewelry, odorous of good perfume . . . looking searchingly into the eye of each [man] with a look half-smiling, 1/4 inviting, 1/4 appraising." Jaffé described Yvette as an elegant courtesan, whom he found attractive and witty. Americans back home would have considered the cafe a "pretty fast joint" and the circumstances in which he found himself scandalous. But here the "honest bourgeois" and the "virtuous dames" seated at nearby tables raised nary an eyebrow over the two officers and their companion. As many a doughboy observed, France was different from the United States.[21]

Jaffé remarked in his diary that he "didn't come to France to stay in a hospital," and he happily returned to duty at Is-sur-Tille in late June. Upon returning to the depot, however, he found discipline "all shot to hell." A new detachment of green soldiers had arrived, and two of his sergeants

19. Ibid., 1, 6 June 1918.
20. Ibid., 19 June 1918; Cooke, *U.S Air Service*, 83.
21. Jaffé war diary, 19 June 1918, Jaffé Papers.

were quarreling. Worse, several of his men had returned to the post liquored up. Jaffé marched his detachment out to a field and read them the riot act.[22]

Shipping supplies was monotonous and mundane work, and he grew increasingly dissatisfied with his duties. "I'm weary of signing orders . . . and messing with shipments of wire, wheelbarrows, small parts, and airplane [supplies]," he wrote in his diary. "I wish to God I were back in the artillery. Now I'm in the blessed SOS. I'll never hear a gun fired except in practice. My loaded Colt mocks me with its useless six rounds gathering dust in the holster."[23]

He saw his supply-officer billet as "utterly unwarlike." The only thing preventing him from seeking a transfer to artillery or intelligence was his recent application for a promotion that would become sidetracked if he left the SOS. Jaffé had remained a second lieutenant for nearly a year, and many of his friends commissioned at the same time as he was had long since advanced to higher ranks. "Is it unpatriotic to want a promotion as badly as this?" he asked in his diary. "I know I am keeping abreast of my job, but it is only a clerkship." Jaffé drolly observed that a "fatal affinity existed between being in the SOS & S.O.L."[24]

Most officers routinely received promotions during the war, and the Army's failure to promote Jaffé is puzzling. No evidence exists linking this omission to anti-Semitism, and he apparently did not consider this a possibility, at least at the time. No scholarship has focused on prejudice encountered during World War I by American Jewish soldiers and sailors, whose numbers in proportion to their ethnic population far exceeded those of Gentiles serving in the armed forces. But anecdotal accounts of Jews such as David Sarnoff, whom the Navy refused to commission despite his mastery of communication technology, invite suspicion.[25]

Jaffé's diary does not reveal whether he commanded black troops, but blacks were stationed at Is-sur-Tille, where under the supervision of

22. Ibid., 26 June 1918.
23. Ibid., 29 August 1918.
24. Ibid., 21 October 1918, 6 April 1919.
25. J. George Fredman and Louis A. Falk, *Jews in American Wars* (New York: Jewish War Veterans of the U.S., 1942), 78; Carl Dreher, *Sarnoff: An American Success* (New York: Quadrangle/New York Times, 1977), 52; Sandor Cohen, interview by author, 20 May 2000.

white officers they unloaded and loaded supplies. An encounter with black officers transiting through the depot provides some indication of Jaffé's racial views at the time. "Colored officers are a problem," he wrote in his diary in 1918.

> I am not a negro hater and I admire many of the traits of the negro race, but I am not cheered by the increasing number of negro officers by those that I have seen over here. Most of them seem to lack balance, and nearly all of them are lacking in good taste. Many of them to-day were strutting around station with exaggerated pose & others carried crops & walking sticks. It's incongruous. They seldom salute you first unless outranked, and somehow it doesn't feel natural to salute them even if they are clothed in my country's uniform. So I avoid looking their way & get out of it that way. I suppose some [integration] of the [Army] was imperative, but I hope the [War Department] will not make too many officers of them. They make good soldiers: Perhaps they are too young in racial development to make good officers. They cause friction wherever they go, & it is not practicable to keep them at the same military post with white officers. The War Department has a knotty problem to solve here, complicated by race prejudices based on color & race which are infinitely more hard to overcome than prejudices based on national and religious grounds.[26]

Jaffé's racial consciousness at this juncture clearly lacked the development and sophistication that later would characterize it. Regardless of the non-discriminatory military code of conduct, the mores of the South and popular "scientific" thinking of the time still exerted a powerful influence on him. He found it difficult to salute black officers, in effect to acknowledge their equality. Though conceding that the officer corps should be desegregated to a degree, he placed the onus of any discord between white and black officers on the latter.

Viewed in light of his prior experience with blacks, Jaffé's mindset comes as no surprise. He had spent all but the first seven years of his life in the South. His interaction with blacks had been confined almost exclusively

---

26. Jaffé war diary, 23 September 1918, Jaffé Papers; Dill, "Glimpse of Parnassus," 7.

to menials and the poor and undereducated customers he had served as a sales clerk. His observations had confirmed for him the region's prevailing concept of blacks' innate lack of intellectual potential. A Booker T. Washington or a John Mitchell Jr. was an anomaly. By 1918 Jaffé had seen no reason to question this perception.

Consequently, he did not apply his demonstrated analytic ability to examination of the black officers' behavior from the standpoints of cultural patterns and blacks' experience with whites. The black officers observed swaggering at Is-sur-Tille that day likely were feeling acutely the critical scrutiny of their white counterparts. (It bears mention that nearly every American soldier in France carried a spiked ash walking stick for marching.) Nevertheless, Jaffé's observation that racial prejudices based on nationality and religion could be more easily surmounted than those rooted in race and skin color showed insight and implicitly conceded that the "knotty problem" resulted to a considerable extent from the bigotry of whites.[27]

Jaffé's conjecture that blacks were "too young in their racial development to make good officers" evokes the theories of scientific racism that dominated anthropological discourse at the time and for some years afterward. Popularizations of scientific racism—such as William Z. Ripley's *The Races of Europe* (1910) and Madison Grant's *The Passing of the Great Race* (1916)—influenced public attitudes strongly. Grant argued that "negroes have demonstrated throughout recorded time that they are a stationary species, and that they do not possess the potential of progress or initiative from within." Although these social scientists could not say definitively how many races existed or point to a single living example of a pure type, their work shaped the thinking of many intellectuals and filtered down in various forms to lay audiences, particularly in the South, where it served to legitimize Jim Crow. Various influential and highly respected authorities would subscribe to some of these theories for decades to come. As late as the 1920s the celebrated humanitarian and physician Albert Schweitzer, who devoted his life to the care of blacks in Africa, stated that the "negro is a child, and with children nothing can be done without the use of authority."[28]

27. Marshall, *World War I*, 314.
28. Ripley, *Races of Europe*; Grant, *Passing of the Great Race*, 69; Wilson and Fer-

As white southern legislatures disenfranchised blacks and institutionalized white supremacy, scientific racism shifted toward a new threat: the mass migration of eastern Europeans, particularly into the United States. Grant warned against the dangers of extending citizenship to Russian and Polish Jews, "whose dwarf stature, peculiar mentality, and ruthless concentration on self interest are being engrafted upon the stock of the nation."[29]

Jaffé's ruminations on the difficulty of overcoming racial prejudices are particularly significant because he believed that Jews, too, constituted a separate race. "What of the Jews?" he had asked two months earlier in his diary. "Are they nation, race, religious sect or persistent strain? I started out in college days with a pretty theory that there was nothing national or racial implied nowadays in the proper definition of 'Jew.' I have withdrawn from that view. As long as there is no intermarriage we must remain a people apart 'racially' not nationally."[30]

Jaffé wondered if what he perceived as the racial integrity of Jews warranted preservation. Influenced by assimilationist thinking similar to that of Rabbi Calish, he maintained that intermarriage between Jews and Gentiles would eliminate racial differences between the two groups. Genuinely worthwhile aspects of Jewish culture and religious teachings would be preserved and become the "property of civilization," which would survive well after Judaism, Christianity, and other present-day faiths had been supervened by new religions better suited to meet the needs of successive generations.[31]

Jaffé's Judaism presented him with many moral and ethical conflicts. He had, for instance, attended social functions at the Chamberlin Hotel, which probably discriminated against Jewish guests during that era. Throughout the South many other resorts, hotels, and clubs practiced similar policies. Few clues exist regarding Jaffé's thoughts on "restricted" environments, but reflecting on his Jewish roots many years later, he recalled

---

ris, *Encyclopedia of Southern Culture*, vol. 4, 158–61; Albert Schweitzer, *On the Edge of the Primeval Forest* (New York: Macmillan, 1931), 130–1.

29. Grant, *Passing of the Great Race*, 14.

30. Jaffé war diary, 26 July 1918, Jaffé Papers.

31. Ibid.

that he had "made compromises" as his "social and philosophic predilections" increasingly drew him to Christianity and Christian society.[32]

Operating under the false hope that participation in the military would result in major strides toward racial justice and equality after the Great War, American blacks had responded in large numbers to the call to arms. The NAACP lobbied the War Department for the commissioning of black officers and the establishment of black combat units, in an ambitious public relations campaign to refute stereotypes of racial inferiority and demonstrate to the American public that blacks possessed both the patriotism and the courage to put their lives on the line for their country. Repeated efforts to integrate officers' training camps proved unsuccessful, however, and the NAACP settled eventually for the establishment of a separate facility in Des Moines, Iowa. Grudgingly and belatedly, the Army granted blacks commissions.[33]

The issue remained a sensitive one. Southerners made up a disproportionate percentage of the officer corps, and many policy makers insisted that commissioning blacks would cause racial tensions that would harm the American war effort. Many whites from states north of the Mason-Dixon line also believed that blacks were intellectually inferior and therefore incapable of serving in leadership positions in the military.

At President Wilson's behest, Dr. Robert Moton—Booker T. Washington's successor as principal of Tuskegee Institute—embarked on a fact-finding tour to assess the performance and morale of black troops in France. Moton had been commissioned a major in the Army. Speaking with large numbers of black and white soldiers and examining written records, he gathered evidence to refute racist rumors that circulated widely among white American troops and filtered back to the States. Within what Moton termed a "whispering gallery," two charges against black soldiers prevailed: that they had committed large numbers of what he termed the "unmention-

32. David J. Johnson, interview by author, 23 May 2000; Louis Jaffé to Alice Rice, 23 August 1939, 20 August 1941, both Louis Jaffé Jr.

33. Herbert Aptheker, ed., *A Documentary History of the Negro People in the United States, From the N.A.A.C.P to the New Deal* (New York: Citadel Press, 1973), 207, 210; White, *Man Called White*, 36.

able crime" and that their officer corps had behaved in a cowardly manner under fire.[34]

Moton's well-supported findings were eye-opening. Within the black 92nd Division, which consisted of over twelve thousand men, only two soldiers had been convicted of rape. Furthermore, only a small number of officers leading a single battalion had been charged with cowardice. A subsequent investigation exonerated the officers, determining that intense fire, heavy fortifications, and inadequate supplies had resulted in the unit's failure to take its objective. General Pershing himself confided to Moton that white officers facing the same challenges would likely have failed.[35]

Whatever inroads blacks made in the American armed forces were short-lived. The undisputed courage of the 369th, 370th, 371st, and 372nd Negro regiments, which had performed magnificently in the bloody Meuse-Argonne offensive, earning high praise from their officers (most of whom were white) and the French who fought alongside them, was quickly forgotten. As late as 1940 the Army would have but two black officers, the Navy none. Genuine steps toward eliminating racism in the military would begin only upon President Harry Truman's order desegregating the armed forces in 1948.[36]

Encapsulating the heady expectations some black soldiers had held regarding the post–World War I world and their subsequent disappointment, General S. L. A. "Slam" Marshall wrote, "At the base ports . . . Negroes, serving with the Army stevedore units, had married French women. When it came time for the unit to ship out, they were given the choice of being discharged and staying with their wives or returning home alone. They couldn't understand it; they thought the war had made all men brothers. In this they were no more naive than the wise men of the world, who thought that the armistice would be followed by peace eternal."[37]

34. Aptheker, ed., *Negro People, From the N.A.A.C.P to the New Deal*, 296–7.

35. Ibid., 297; Robert Russa Moton, *Finding a Way Out: An Autobiography* (College Park, Md.: McGrath, 1969), 234–65; John Keegan, *The First World War* (New York: Alfred A. Knopf, 1999), 374.

36. William Manchester, *The Glory and the Dream: A Narrative History of America, 1932–1972*, vol. 1 (Boston: Little, Brown, 1974), 294; Marshall, *World War I*, 458–9.

37. Marshall, *World War I*, 459.

Any illusion that the peace would usher in a bright new fellowship of man was dashed during the "Red Summer" of 1919, when racist mobs attacked blacks in urban and rural areas across the United States. (This violence differed in one important respect from previous incidents: blacks— many of them veterans—armed themselves and fought back determinedly, inflicting much bloodshed on their assailants.) In Norfolk, an elaborate ceremony intended to welcome home black troops devolved into a riot. When it ended, five blacks and two white policemen lay wounded.[38]

If Jaffé's tedious duties in the Service of Supply provided him with little adventure, the befuddling signals Horty sent him in her letters offered little certainty regarding the couple's romance. "Comes a letter from Horty which leaves me puzzled," he wrote in his diary. "Warm and all that can be wished for in spots and yet uncertain. *Uncertain,* that is the word." Perhaps her mother's ambivalence toward Jaffé had created the problem: "Her mother seems to have no love for me, which does not worry me too much for I haven't much love for her either. All I want is her respect. More if possible, if not, well and good."[39]

In spite of Jaffé's customary reserve, a tender letter from Horty could fill him with emotions he had previously thought himself incapable of possessing. "Today, Monday, goes down in history as a most exciting day on account of a letter from Horty in which she is supremely dear." In her letter, she had confessed for the first time that she loved him, and Jaffé "treaded on air" for most of the afternoon and could barely eat. "I didn't know I could be affected like that," he marveled. He read the letter over and over. Despite the fact that his heart did not "lend itself to love," she had moved him deeply. "I wonder," he pondered, "I wonder, if she is really destined to be mine. . . . It is only a little short letter, but it is most satisfying." In more dispassionate moments, Jaffé suspected that regardless of Horty's occasionally encouraging letters, the relationship would not blossom. "Don't believe that girl is for me," he wrote. "Just have a hunch." (Jaffé's

38. Herbert Shapiro, *White Violence and Black Response: From Reconstruction to Montgomery* (Amherst: University of Massachusetts Press, 1988), 146–57; Henry Lewis Suggs, *P. B. Young, Newspaperman: Race, Politics, and Journalism in the New South, 1910–1962* (Charlottesville: University Press of Virginia, 1988), 41.

39. Jaffé war diary, 30 October 1918, Jaffé Papers.

intuition would prove correct; apparently his involvement with Horty soon ended.)[40]

Shortly after disembarking in France, he had expressed in his diary the desire "to see different people, different outlooks on life," and he took every advantage of opportunities to acquaint himself with the French. In Dijon, he regularly visited the Regents, teachers in the city's public schools. Taking tea in elegant Limoges cups, he practiced his French and delighted in his hosts and the other guests whom they invited. The younger sister of one of the Regents' colleagues, perhaps not even into her teens, shocked Jaffé by cadging cigarettes from the adults and smoking a Lucky Strike "with all the nonchalance and placid enjoyment of a deep-sea sailor, blowing the smoke from her nostrils in jets of white."[41]

The arrival of Rosh Hashanah caught Jaffé unawares. In spite of the suffering and destruction wrought by the war, he confided in his diary that he continued to feel little attraction to organized religion: "My religious consciousness, I am more sorry than ever to confess, is still far from where it should be." Soldiers in the AEF had been given passes to attend services at synagogues in nearby towns, but Jaffé did not plan to go: "I have little desire to go to Dijon. If I went I should not pray. I can pray best at night in my own room, or in the fields or in the woods—when I am alone. I cannot, absolutely cannot, pray by rote and I find it difficult to pray in concert."[42]

As the Allied offenses began to break the stalemate, the SOS made plans to move the depot from Is-sur-Tille to Clichy, near Paris. Jaffé's duties grew less demanding, and his diary entries focused more on the war and the great powers' diplomatic maneuverings than on local subjects. On two occasions, with special permission as a noncombatant, he traveled to the front. On these trips he examined battlefields recently retaken from the Germans. His exposure to the destruction wrought by the conflict impressed him deeply. "War reads heroic in the newspaper," he wrote, "but a 'close up' of it is infinitely disgusting and repulsive. Mangled men, human filth, stench, vermin, disease—all these things meet the eye and the mind loses sight for the moment of the principles for which these things must be."[43]

40. Ibid., 22 August 1918, 2 September 1918.

41. Ibid., 19 April 1918, 20 October 1918; Dill, "Glimpse of Parnassus," 8.

42. Jaffé war diary, 7 September 1918, Jaffé Papers.

43. Dill, "Glimpse of Parnassus," 9–10; Jaffé war diary, 8 November 1918, Jaffé Papers; Louis Jaffé to William Wannamaker, 18 November 1919, Jaffé Papers.

Although Jaffé held Germany responsible for the initiation of the hostilities, he fixed blame for the war on the belligerency of the country's leaders and people, not on German culture per se. As the Central Powers retreated in disarray, he thought back on his tour of Europe during his Trinity years: "When I recall the proud and imperial Germany that so impressed me during my pilgrimage through that country with Gilmer Siler in college days, and think of her now, fallen and destitute, even robbed of honor and made a byword by her ruthless rulers, I am more than ever impressed by the absolute vanity and fragility of human institutions that are not founded in right and honor."[44]

Jaffé managed to visit Paris half a dozen times during his military service. War had marked the magnificent city. Sandbags ringed Notre Dame, the military displayed captured German weapons in public squares, and Big Bertha's enormous shells had damaged a number of buildings. Many of the city's museums and attractions remained closed. But the spirit of Paris prevailed, even in the midst of the conflict. Not even war could dampen Parisian commerce and nightlife.[45]

Jaffé reveled in the city and recorded his impressions. The grand boulevards lined with small shops and lively sidewalk cafes delighted him. The reporter-turned-soldier also relished the foment and excesses of the city's journalism. *La Vie Parisienne,* with its spicy illustrations, would have scandalized American readers, he noted. Dozens of one- and two-sheet dailies filled the little newspaper and magazine stands at the corners. From a business standpoint, the newspaper competition made no sense, but what wonderful journalistic exuberance![46]

One needed not have developed finely honed linguistic abilities to understand the meaning of the "frothy" burlesque shows at the Folies Bergere, Jaffé wrote— "just a good pair of eyes." Audiences back in the States would have deemed the suggestive material far too risqué, but the French did not consider it the least bit coarse. During breaks in the show, "young ladies of joy," speaking only a few words of English, attempted to strike up conversations with American and British soldiers, calling out, "Hello dearie,

---

44. Jaffé war diary, 9 November 1918, Jaffé Papers; Dill, "Glimpse of Parnassus," 10.

45. Dill, "Glimpse of Parnassus," 11.

46. Jaffé war diary, 15 August 1918, Jaffé Papers.

where are you going?" or "Hello, mon cheri." "C'est la vie intense Paris,"
Jaffé exclaimed in his diary.[47]

When at precisely 11:00 A.M. on the eleventh day of the eleventh
month of the year, hostilities ceased, American and German troops rose
from the trenches, stood mute, and warily ventured out into the no-man's-
land that had divided them. After Allied soldiers had traded soap, cigarettes,
and rations for war souvenirs, doughboys played hopscotch between the
shell holes and amidst the barbed wire. Later, dice rolled and liquor flowed,
as all over the world, combatants and noncombatants alike breathed an
exquisite sigh of relief.[48]

With the cessation of hostilities, Jaffé turned his attention to his postwar
career. He contacted John Stewart Bryan, publisher of the *Richmond News
Leader,* and offered to cover the Paris Peace Conference for that paper.
Jaffé, with some justification, called the conference the "greatest congress of
nations since the Lord finished his labors on that memorable sixth day and
rested." In a detailed letter, Jaffé informed Bryan that the *Norfolk Virginian-Pilot* had a correspondent on the scene. Should the preeminent paper in
Virginia's capital allow her "seaside rival" the prestige of having a special
correspondent in Paris and rely solely on Associated Press reports? For one
hundred dollars a week, he could cover the conference, which he surmised
with considerable accuracy would last for six months.[49]

Jaffé's proposal contained a confident listing of his qualifications to
cover such a complex and historic event. He cited his command of both German and French, which few of the American correspondents assembling in
Paris could claim. Jaffé had followed the war closely, and he knew the major
ethnic and nationalistic questions that the delegates would need to address.
His college training at Trinity had provided him with a firm enough grounding in economics and theories of government for him to deal with these complicated subjects in some detail. Finally, his knowledge of Paris enabled him
to work productively there from the outset. Jaffé did not consider his proposed salary—twice what he had received in Richmond—excessive, given

47. Ibid., 10 August 1918.
48. Marshall, *World War I,* 451–3.
49. Louis Jaffé to John Stewart Bryan, 1 January 1919, Jaffé Papers.

the high cost of living in post-Armistice Paris. Besides, his Army experience had served to make him a "better newspaper man."[50]

The letter's tone bordered on brashness, and Jaffé apologized to the dean of Virginia journalism: "If I have had to be a shade argumentative in this letter, you will pardon me. I had to tell you what I could do in order to give you something on which to base a judgment." Bryan's response does not survive, but he must have discussed his rationale for rejecting Jaffé's proposal three weeks later when the two men met in Paris. Jaffé's postwar future remained hazy. He toyed with the idea of staying in France to find work or enroll in a university.[51]

A two-week leave early in February 1919 offered a distraction from these serious considerations. He boarded a train in Dijon for a trip to Rome by way of Genoa. In Rome he met Alexander Forward, his old friend from the *Richmond Times-Dispatch,* who now held the rank of major in the Balkan commission of the American Red Cross. Working as Colonel Henry Anderson's assistant, Forward oversaw the transportation of relief supplies throughout the shattered region. Jaffé, as a result of his tenure in the Service of Supply, knew something of the challenges his friend faced in provisioning the Red Cross's many aid stations via mined harbors and the broken-down Balkan transportation system. Doubtless informed of Jaffé's stillborn deal with Bryan and desiring to help his friend, Forward arranged a meeting with his boss.[52]

Colonel Anderson had commanded the American Red Cross's relief efforts in unoccupied Romania in 1917 and 1918, where he had met the brave and compassionate Queen Marie. Through those dark days Marie, tirelessly and with no regard for her safety, had ministered to her people, visiting hospitals filled with patients suffering from typhus and smallpox and personally delivering food and medical supplies to refugees. Anderson's vanity and dreams of a romance with the queen may have made him a slightly comic figure, but he and his staff had displayed great initiative and organizational ability under exceedingly difficult circumstances in attempt-

50. Ibid.

51. Dill, "Glimpse of Parnassus," 12.

52. *Pilot,* 25 July 1920; *American National Red Cross Annual Report,* 30 June 1919, 124.

ing to feed, clothe, and provide medical care to thousands of Romanians. He now headed the American Red Cross's work throughout the region. Forward respected the colonel despite his foibles and explained to Jaffé that Anderson grew more likable with time. "Perhaps," remarked Jaffé.[53]

At their meeting, Jaffé found Anderson in "fine fettle." Wearing a medal awarded him by Queen Marie, he read "with relish" to Jaffé and Forward a letter from her highness commending him. With Forward's encouragement, Anderson offered Jaffé an appointment as a captain in the paramilitary service. Working out of the Department of Public Information in Paris, he would join the Balkan commission and, traveling with inspection teams, would author articles and reports on the Red Cross's activities.[54]

Jaffé had not yet been discharged from the Army, and since it would take time to process the paperwork for his new job, he turned his attention to the original purpose of his trip—sightseeing. He visited the galleries of the Vatican, the Sistine Chapel, the catacombs, the Appian Way, the Coliseum, and many other sites. With what he considered much creativity but little regard for veracity, guides at the Chapel of Quo Vadis (where allegedly the crucified Jesus had spoken to St. Peter) showed the dubious Jaffé Christ's footprints in the stone.[55]

From Naples, Jaffé fulfilled a lifelong ambition by visiting Vesuvius and Pompeii. In Florence, although he found the Uffizi Gallery closed, he visited the Pitti Gallery twice. "My art education is progressing," he wrote. "I can tell a saint from a satyr at sight now." He disliked Botticelli's women "with their pasty oval faces" but greatly appreciated Titian, whom he regarded as the most "human" of the old masters. Touring the Medici Chapel evoked reflection on the legacy of the great family: "What people these Medicis! Heroes, tyrants, scholars, prisoners, conquerors, patrons of art. Their record is bloodstained, but one must admit they had taste."[56]

53. Alice Gall, *In Peace and War: A Story of Human Service* (New York: Thomas Y. Crowell, 1942), 155–65; *American National Red Cross Annual Report*, 30 June 1918, 133–6; Jaffé war diary, 10 February 1919, Jaffé Papers.

54. Jaffé war diary, 10 February 1919, Jaffé Papers; Dill, "Glimpse of Parnassus," 14.

55. "The Titulus Fasciolae" [cited 3 October 1997], available from http://pub.xplore.it/nerone/nerone/ARCHIVIO/arch10.htm; Dill, "Glimpse of Parnassus," 14; Jaffé war diary, 5, 7 February 1919, Jaffé Papers.

56. Jaffé war diary, 12 February 1919, Jaffé Papers.

In Venice, he saw the Basilica of St. Mark with its Byzantine gilded domes. With other sightseers there he laughingly turned down a gondolier's offer to show them Shylock's home. At his last major stopping point, Milan, he found Leonardo da Vinci's *Last Supper* at the Santa Maria delle Grazie disappointing. A flawed attempt at restoration had left the remarkable painting looking "moldy and moth-eaten."[57]

Back in Is-sur-Tille, Jaffé said good-bye to the French families he had known, "charming, simple people," whom he pledged never to forget. He passed through Paris to deliver to Red Cross headquarters Colonel Anderson's request for his commissioning. He then traveled to St. Nazaire for temporary duty while the Army processed his demobilization papers. The military tried to discourage servicemen from mustering out in France, and Jaffé's discharge required many visits to authorities to cut through the red tape.[58]

For nearly a month, Jaffé worked at the Quarter Master Corps' effects depot in St. Nazaire, biding his time while waiting for his paperwork. His morbid duties—filling out casualty cards for dead soldiers, "gravely recording [each] man's name, number, organization, date of death, etc."—darkened his outlook regarding his own future. He began to question the wisdom of his service in the Red Cross: "I am debating with myself now whether it would not be better to throw up the whole thing and ask to be put on a sailing list for the states as soon as possible. . . . When Col. Anderson broached the Balkan business, it looked like a good chance to step out of the Army and get my hand back to writing, writing of a rather modest character requiring not too much imagination, but yet writing which I haven't done for nearly two years. Now I ask myself if it is worthwhile."[59]

Jaffé grew increasingly disenchanted with the idea of returning to his pre-war profession, which he considered a "beggar's life at best." At thirty, his life lacked stability. His younger brother, Hyman, had been married for several years and had two little girls. "Little by little I grow to dislike the idea of going back to newspaperwork," Jaffé wrote. "I need money to put it brutally—need it not to get me glory or power, but to obtain for

57. Ibid., 15 February 1919.
58. Dill, "Glimpse of Parnassus," 15.
59. Jaffé war diary, 23 March 1919, Jaffé Papers.

me the books, the pictures, the house, the surroundings that my heart craves for—that and the means to give a life worth living to the girl who in my dreams is to share my life someday." The solution to the "toughest problem I have faced in a long time" might involve embarking on a totally new career: "It must be back to newspaper work and the precarious future it has in store for a man not over-gifted and without many means, or something else—business. It is one or the other and right now I don't know which I shall choose."[60]

Late in March 1919, having at last received his discharge papers, Jaffé traveled to Red Cross headquarters in Paris, where he met that organization's leadership and endured another lengthy round of bureaucratic folderol to obtain his passport, visas, and orders for the Balkans. A sighting of Queen Marie at a distance, surrounded by admirers as she left the opera, brought to mind another of her ardent fans, Colonel Anderson.[61]

From Paris Jaffé traveled by rail to Rome, where he ping-ponged from embassy to embassy—American, Greek, Serbian, Romanian—attempting to secure the many stamps his passport required. The frustrations he faced did not bother him. No longer troubled by the melancholy he had felt in St. Nazaire, he now looked forward to his new job as "something of a lark." In Taranto he boarded the SS *Campinas* for a voyage across the Ionian Sea, through the Gulf of Corinth, to Itea at the foot of Mount Parnassus. Future *Virginian-Pilot* colleague Alonzo Dill would later write that when the editor-to-be glimpsed the summit, sacred to the nine Muses and the Oracle of Apollo, "it must have seemed a good omen for his future as a man of letters."[62]

At Salonica, in northern Greece, where the Red Cross had its headquarters for the Balkan relief mission, he rendezvoused with Anderson and Forward. After a two-year hiatus, Jaffé now resumed his peacetime profession, writing a news dispatch for the Associated Press on the colonel's arrival in Greece and beginning work on a magazine article on Balkan relief. Anderson assigned him to an inspection team assessing the activities at the

60. Ibid.
61. Ibid., 27, 31 March 1919; Dill, "Glimpse of Parnassus," 16.
62. Jaffé war diary, 9 April 1919, Jaffé Papers; Dill, "Glimpse of Parnassus," 16.

many relief stations scattered throughout the region. Jaffé regarded the barrister-turned-commissioner irreverently, mentioning in his diary the "may it please your honor style" with which Anderson dealt with subordinates.[63]

The three-month inspection trip, which took Jaffé to some of the most remote reaches of the Balkan Peninsula, proved a remarkable adventure. It required him to traverse primitive transportation routes—which included flooded and shot-up roads and blown bridges—via what he described as "every kind of conveyance, railway, boat, wagon, ox-cart, pack-mule and my own feet." Leaving Salonica, the party traveled in a temperamental Fiat and a Ford into Serbia, which had lost a quarter of its population to the war. Past Lake Doiran they drove through eerie landscapes littered with weapons, helmets, and horses' skeletons.[64]

Shelling and bombing had left Monastir a shadow of what it had been. Before the war one hundred thousand Serbs, Turks, and a hodgepodge of other ethnic groups had lived in the thriving city. Fewer than a third of its residents remained. Here the Red Cross maintained a base with a hospital, bacteriological laboratory, disinfection center, and public bathhouse, as well as a flour mill and bakery. During the war, typhus and Spanish influenza had swept across Serbia, killing hundreds of thousands. The Red Cross struggled to prevent the recurrence of such epidemics. Working with sparse resources, it also attempted to clothe and feed the returning refugees and to minister to the ill and the many children orphaned by the fighting.[65]

Jaffé inspected the Red Cross's facilities, interviewed the prefect, and toured the marketplace, where he found women selling Macedonian costumes. Later he met some of his Old World co-religionists when he visited a Jewish boys' school, which he found clean and well-maintained. The Jewish War Relief in America had created a special fund for Monastir's Jews, and the Red Cross had used the money well.[66]

A few short months ago, Jaffé's diary entries had revealed a simplis-

63. Dill, "Glimpse of Parnassus," 17; Jaffé war diary, 17 April 1919, Jaffé Papers.

64. Louis Jaffé to William Wannamaker, 18 November 1919, Jaffé Papers; Jaffé war diary, 21, 22 April 1919, Jaffé Papers.

65. Ibid., 26 April 1919; *American National Red Cross Annual Report,* 30 June 1919, 135–40.

66. Jaffé war diary, 29 April 1919, Jaffé Papers; *American National Red Cross Annual Report,* 30 June 1919, 134.

tic and naive view of racial and ethnic identities. But his exposure to Monastir's Jewish community made plain the crucial role of environmental factors in shaping identity. In an article for *American Israelite* on Serbia's Jews and the special relief fund, Jaffé conveyed a more nuanced attitude. Of the Jewish schoolchildren he encountered, he wrote:

> It is idle to assert the oneness racially between these children and their brothers and sisters in America. If they are of common origin, drastic centuries under far different character-forming conditions and climes have made of them a different race. On their young faces is stamped the cast of generations of living in the East, and there are signs of mingled strains from lands still further towards the rising sun. The unconscious influence of the Turk and successive Balkan dynasties have altered the very countenances of these young people. Many of the faces are more characteristically Turkish than Jewish. Here is a youngster with the skull and cheekbones of the Bulgar—almost a Mongolian type. Another is so dark in complexion as to startle one with a suspicion of negro blood, although a closer look shows the utter absence of the African's broad nose and crinkled hair. There are children with the well defined face lines of the Serb. Only a few are purely Jewish in type, if such a thing as a purely Jewish type exists, and of these the greater number by far are girls. In all, it is a heterogeneous collection of youngsters who impress one with their reserved bearing. One looks in vain in their faces for the inquisitive, alert, sparkling qualities that mark the school child in America.[67]

Traveling north through Serbia, the inspection team examined aid stations at Gostivar and Skopje, stopping for several days in Vranje, where the Red Cross distributed food and farming tools and maintained an orphanage and school. The British—who impressed Jaffé greatly throughout his journey with their can-do attitude, efficiency, and cordiality— operated a hospital there. Unlike other Serbian cities, Vranje had few Muslims, but Gypsies filled the streets. In the hospital Jaffé observed many cases of typhus and advanced gangrene. At the crowded orphanage the chil-

67. Louis Jaffé, "Serbia and Its Jews," *American Israelite* 65 (1919): 1.

dren flocked to him and kissed his hand, grateful for the shelter and the bean soup and bread the Red Cross provided them. At night, he attended a dance hosted by the British, where a Scottish nurse entertained the revelers with a lively Highland fling and sword dance.[68]

Along the Morava River, on nearly impassable roads, his party traveled north to Leskovatz in a cold rain. There they inspected a hospital filled with Bulgarian, Austrian, and German prisoners of war. Many of these patients suffered from typhus; some had the "stamp of death on them." Although the American nurses kept the facility clean, they lacked the staffing to provide their patients with the care they required. Nor did the bread and soup the defeated soldiers received provide them with adequate nutrition. With Serbian authorities watching over his shoulder, Jaffé questioned the German patients regarding their treatment. "It is good," they replied in German, looking nervously at the Serbs. Some indication of Serbia's backward condition and its devastated infrastructure can be ascertained from the fact that in Leskovatz Jaffé found electric lights (albeit poorly functioning ones) for the first time since he had crossed over from Greece. After inspecting dispensaries, hospitals, and distribution centers in Pirot and Cuprija, the party arrived in the capital, Belgrade. Jaffé witnessed the parliament in action and learned of its plans for agrarian reform.[69]

Crossing the border into the Austro-Hungarian province of Bosnia, Jaffé struck out by himself for Sarajevo, where the Red Cross had established a station to provide food and medical care for the city's starving children. After interviewing aid workers, Jaffé visited the downtown site of Archduke Ferdinand's assassination, which had precipitated so much carnage. In the Turkish quarter, wearing slippers, he entered an ancient mosque. The synagogues and churches of Jaffé's previous experience prepared him little for what he found. Fine carpets covered the floor of the enormous prayer room, but the temple contained no pictures, stained glass, windows, or seats. A large pulpit extended from the eastern wall, in the symbolic direction of Mecca, toward which the congregation faced. Only

68. Jaffé war diary, 1, 2, 5 May 1919, Jaffé Papers; *American National Red Cross Annual Report*, 30 June 1919, 139; Dill, "Glimpse of Parnassus," 17.

69. Jaffé war diary, 8–15, 17, 20 May 1919; *American National Red Cross Annual Report*, 30 June 1919, 139.

men worshipped in this building; women prayed in a separate sanctum. On the streets, afterwards, he passed many heavily veiled Islamic women.[70]

Jews, too, lived in the multicultural city. Austrian Jews attended services in an impressive temple with large conical domes; Sephardis, less prosperous, worshipped in a rundown synagogue in a poor neighborhood. Jaffé carefully studied a "Spanish Jewess," who wore, in keeping with custom, a "peculiar tall white headdress."[71]

Traveling by rail along the Neretva River, he came within view of the Adriatic and welcomed the sight of its blue waters after "weeks of gorges and mountains." Then he headed south into primitive Montenegro and its capital city, Centinje, and west to Podgorica, visiting hospitals and food distribution centers along the way. At the jury-rigged hospital in Niksic, he observed three operations. The last patient, an elderly woman with a gangrenous foot, died shortly following the surgery. Journeying to the aid station in Niksic, he met numerous bands of armed men ostensibly searching for bandits. One of these gun-toting men, "his chest festooned with bandoliers of cartridges," demanded a ride. "It is advisable not to refuse & we carry him," Jaffé wrote in his diary. The country seethed with political factions and ethnic groups, each harboring a different grievance. Jaffé, with his reporter's curiosity, tried mightily to make sense of the Balkan complexities.[72]

After waiting on the Montenegrin side of Lake Scatter with a "miscellaneous lot of vagabonds all carrying ugly guns," Jaffé boarded a little steamer flying a French flag and sailed for Albania. A several-hour voyage took him to the "many-minareted" city of Scutari. The Red Cross faced tremendous difficulties in Albania, then the most primitive European nation. The country lacked a railroad system, and transportation depended on crude roadways, many of which had been damaged by the war. For nearly four years Austria had occupied Albania and cruelly exploited its resources, almost obliterating its livestock. Italy's territorial ambitions made matters worse. Resentful of President Wilson's desire that Albania maintain its inde-

70. *American National Red Cross Annual Report,* 30 June 1919, 144; Dill, "Glimpse of Parnassus," 18; Jaffé war diary, 23, 24 May 1919.

71. Jaffé war diary, 24 May 1919.

72. Ibid., 25–7 May 1919.

pendence, the Italians, who now controlled transportation there, worked to stymie the shipment of supplies to Red Cross bases. The religious customs of the sizable Muslim population further diminished the effectiveness of the Red Cross. Ramadan, the holy month of fasting, limited male participation in relief efforts during Jaffé's visit. Religious and cultural strictures greatly constrained women's activities.[73]

In Scutari the Red Cross operated a dispensary and washed, deloused, fed, and clothed many children orphaned by the war. The organization also served meals at schools in an attempt to attract truants. A lack of supplies, however, limited the success of the American workers' efforts and demoralized them. At night, a muezzin's call to prayers awakened Jaffé. He found the summons "mysteriously beautiful and thrilling."[74]

In Tiranë, Jaffé observed the Ramadan services of a primitive Islamic sect through a latticed window in an anteroom. As the imam led the ceremony, the congregation moved about the prayer room in a slow dance. Drummers beat a progressively more rapid rhythm, and the worshipers circled the room faster and faster. On some occasions, Jaffé learned, the congregants pierced their cheeks with pins "in an excess of emotionalism." "For twentieth-century [Muslims]," he wrote, "it is a benighted performance, about on the level with the 'religion getting' antics of the negroes in the South."[75]

He needed to report his findings to Colonel Anderson in Bucharest, where the colonel had established new headquarters. Rather than make a grueling overland journey, Jaffé elected to travel partially by sea. From the Albanian port of Durazzo he returned to Taranto, where he boarded a Constantinople-bound steamship; and in late June a French military ship took him from the ancient city to the "Paris of the East," the capital of Queen Marie's country. There he found Anderson in the process of reducing his headquarters staff to a cadre of essential personnel that included Jaffé. The

73. Ibid., 2, 8 June 1919; *American National Red Cross Annual Report*, 30 June 1919, 142; Joseph Held, ed., *Columbia History of Eastern Europe in the Twentieth Century* (New York: Columbia University Press, 1992), 21.

74. *American National Red Cross Annual Report*, 30 June 1919, 142–3; Jaffé war diary, 2 June 1919, Jaffé Papers.

75. Jaffé war diary, 8 June 1919, Jaffé Papers.

colonel sent Jaffé to Paris, where he would shortly be named director of the American Red Cross News Service's European bureau.[76]

Jaffé's Balkan journey had precluded his witnessing the signing of the Treaty of Versailles in late June, but he arrived in the capital in time to observe the greatest military parade ever, the victory parade of the Allies on July 14, 1919. Shortly afterward, he took leave and traveled into defeated Germany, returning to Cologne more than a decade after his collegiate trek. From there he went to Berlin and north to the now-Polish city of Stettin (Szczecin). No account of Jaffé's trip survives, but it must have been an extraordinary experience for him. Proud and bellicose Germany lay humbled, her people half starving, her economy in ruins. Six million of the nation's soldiers had been killed or wounded in the war, and the social structure had collapsed. Young toughs wearing red armbands tore medals from the uniforms worn by officers returning from the front. A weak social democratic government administered the democratic republic that had been established under the new constitution drawn up at Weimar. Fearful of German militarism, the Allies had almost entirely eliminated her air force and navy and sharply reduced her army. The victors had demanded thirty billion dollars in war reparations and stripped the country of many of its natural resources, its colonies, and much of its territory.[77]

In his new post, Jaffé served as news editor and chief copy reader of the field reports written throughout Europe. He supervised a staff of writers from ten countries. Working long hours, he whipped his department into shape and instilled professionalism into the news service's reports. In return, he received by Red Cross standards a very generous salary of over five thousand dollars.[78]

Jaffé's superiors within the Department of Public Information viewed his job as one of the organization's most important. Having suffered through a "continual stream of ex-advertising men, magazine people, college journalists, broken-downs, used-to-be's, has-beens, and never-wases,"

76. Dill, "Glimpse of Parnassus," 19; Louis Jaffé to William Wannamaker, 18 November 1919, Jaffé Papers.

77. Jaffé to Wannamaker, 18 November 1919, Jaffé Papers; Marshall, *World War I*, 453, 467, 471, 474.

78. C. Morris to M. Scheitlin, 30 September 1919, Louis Jaffé to Thomas Wheelwright, 13 September 1919, both Louis Jaffé Jr.

his supervisor, Major C. D. Morris, expressed his pleasure at having found a "newspaperman of more than ordinary ability and experience, a man with first-class desk experience." Jaffé "filled the bill in 100 percent fashion."[79]

Jaffé's salary enabled him to live comfortably, even taking postwar inflation into account. By now he had polished his French and knew the city well. His directorship of the News Service placed him in a marvelous position to observe the historic international events swirling around him as David Lloyd George, Georges Clemenceau, and Woodrow Wilson advanced competing visions of the peacetime world.

With an eye toward his future, Jaffé began to investigate several promising opportunities in other fields in Paris, probably in business. He must have been dumbfounded that August, when with little if any advance notice, he received from Norfolk a cablegram offering him sight unseen the editorship of the *Virginian-Pilot* at thirty-six hundred dollars a year. The terse message, signed just "*Virginian-Pilot*," bore no company officer's identification. Unbeknownst to Jaffé at the time, Thomas Wheelwright, the Richmond businessman and a *Virginian-Pilot* stockholder, had enthusiastically recommended him for the job. Wheelwright may have approached his brother-in-law, Hugh C. Davis, who served on the paper's executive committee and board of directors, on Jaffé's behalf.[80]

Back in 1917, on the day prior to the United States' declaration of war on Germany, Jaffé had discussed his future with Wheelwright in the latter's office. The two had had several such talks before. Wheelwright discerned in Jaffé intelligence and ambition, qualities by which the self-made industrialist set great store. He liked to mentor men with the right stuff, "to give them a shove up when I can." In the pre–Newspaper Guild era, particularly in the South, reporters' salaries remained discouragingly low, despite the long hours of a six-day workweek. Although the three-thousand-dollar salary Jaffé received from the *Times-Dispatch* enabled him to live in modest comfort as a bachelor in Richmond, the poor renumeration had dis-

79. C. Morris to M. Scheitlin, 30 September 1919, ibid.

80. Jaffé to Wheelwright, 13 September 1919, ibid.; Louis Jaffé to *Virginian-Pilot*, 12 September 1919, Jaffé Papers; Dill, "Glimpse of Parnassus," 20; Shank, *History of Norfolk-Portsmouth Newspapers*, 2331.

illusioned him with his profession. That day, when he met with Wheelwright, he had asked the older man to keep him "in mind for something
bigger" than the work he was then doing.[81]

For a day after he received the cablegram, Jaffé considered his
options. The prestigious editorial position with the *Virginian-Pilot* tempted
him greatly. He would succeed a venerated editor, William Cameron, now
elderly and ill. From Jaffé's six years with the *Richmond Times-Dispatch*,
he knew Virginia and its history and politics. He could land on his feet in
Norfolk and make a go of it. An opportunity like this might never come his
way again. But the salary—much smaller than his present one—diminished
the offer's appeal. Furthermore, Jaffé's superiors at the Red Cross lobbied
him powerfully to stay on.

The next day he cabled his response: "ACCEPT YOUR OFFER EDITOR-
SHIP VIRGINIAN PILOT [*SIC*] SALARY THIRTY-SIX HUNDRED PER YEAR STOP
SAIL IN TEN DAYS LOUIS I. JAFFE."[82]

81. Jaffé to Wheelwright, 13 September 1919, Louis Jaffé Jr.; Richard Morton, *History of Virginia Biography*, vol. 2 (New York: American Historical Society, 1924), 240–1; Virginius Dabney, *Across the Years: Memories of a Virginian* (Garden City, N.Y.: Doubleday, 1978), 105, 112.

82. Louis Jaffé to *Virginian-Pilot*, 12 September 1919, Louis Jaffé Jr.

5 Accepting the Helm

The lead editorial in the September 2, 1919, edition of the *Virginian-Pilot,* titled simply "Notice," had sounded the impending retirement of the newspaper's editor, ex-governor William Cameron. Signed by the "*Virginian-Pilot* Publishing Company," the strangely worded announcement assured readers that Cameron's "relinquishment of the laboring oar to other hands will not involve any change in the principles and policies heretofore steadfastly maintained and stoutly advocated." The company did not name a successor.[1]

Cameron's storied career had involved him intimately in nearly every important historic episode in Virginia from the Civil War to the Great War. The hotheaded native of Petersburg enlisted as a private and fought with Lee's Army of Northern Virginia in all but one of its major engagements. (Wounded at Second Manassas, he lay recuperating during the bloody battle of Antietam.) By the war's end he had been promoted to colonel.[2]

At twenty-three he edited the *Virginian,* one of the *Virginian-Pilot*'s journalistic ancestors. In Petersburg he associated himself with the *Index* and the *Progress* and in the state capital with the *Enquirer.* A scar precariously near his heart bore testimony to the violence—both editorial and physical—that characterized his craft in that era of personal journalism. On the banks of the Dismal Swamp Canal, in North Carolina just across the Virginia line and out of reach of the commonwealth's legal authorities, a rival editorial writer had shot him in a duel.[3]

As a politician—Democrat, Republican, Readjustor, Democrat—he

1. *Pilot,* 2 September 1919.
2. Chambers, Shank, and Sugg, *Salt Water & Printer's Ink,* 21–2; Dill, "Glimpse of Parnassus," 1.
3. Chambers, Shank, and Sugg, *Salt Water & Printer's Ink,* 48–52.

alienated the Virginia gentry by aligning himself with William Mahone's political machine. Progressivism marked Cameron's gubernatorial tenure (1882-1886). Under his leadership, Virginia's legislature increased expenditures for black and white schools and colleges, abolished the whipping post (which served primarily to punish and intimidate blacks) and the one-dollar poll tax, and raised taxes on corporations. He later regained the aristocracy's good graces by publicly breaking with Republican kingpin Mahone and attacking him ferociously.[4]

In 1906 Cameron returned to Norfolk to live in the socially prestigious Virginia Club and edit the *Virginian-Pilot*. In many ways the colonel belonged to the previous century. By the time of his retirement, Cameron, still mobile and alert although ill, was near eighty. Publisher Lucien Starke Jr. developed emotional attachments to his colleagues, and his farewell editorial revealed both sadness over Cameron's retirement and indecision regarding his replacement.[5]

In the nine days that passed between Starke's announcement and his offer to Jaffé via cablegram, the publisher must have been a busy man. Starke consulted with his board and its executive committee, weighing the merits of other potential successors in addition to the little-known Red Cross captain. In the end, the publisher made a bold but risky decision. By placing young, energetic, and cosmopolitan Louis Jaffé at the helm of his newspaper, Starke—regardless of his assurance to readers that the paper's editorial stance would remain fixed—sent an unmistakable message that the *Virginian-Pilot* would advance a modern viewpoint and examine issues critically and independently.[6]

Having reached the difficult decision to leave Paris behind, Jaffé traveled to London for four days of sightseeing. A railway strike nearly caused him to miss the passage he had booked on the SS *La France*. Landing in New York on October 8, he returned to Virginia for the first time in nearly two years and spent time with his family in South Boston. He

4. Dabney, *Virginia: The New Dominion*, 387–8.

5. Chambers, Shank, and Sugg, *Salt Water & Printer's Ink*, 261–3; Dill, "Glimpse of Parnassus," 1.

6. Chambers, Shank, and Sugg, *Salt Water & Printer's Ink*, 312.

reported for work at the editorial suite on the third floor of the *Virginian-Pilot* building on October 25, intending "to make good on my new job."[7]

When and why Jaffé assumed the henceforth-standard pronunciation of his surname—the Gallic "J" and accented second syllable—make for interesting speculation. A Jewish senior citizen of South Boston, Virginia, remembering the family emporium there, called it "Jaffies'" and smiled at Louis Jaffé's interpretation of the spelling as an affectation. Perhaps Jaffé's pronunciation represented the family's preference all along, approximating a European version that had been corrupted by clumsy Americans. (Indeed, one of Louis's uncles consistently called himself by the accented form of the name.) Many if not most acquaintances in France would naturally have applied French phonetics to a name so spelled, with or without an accent symbol. Whatever its basis, Jaffé arrived in Norfolk with a gallicized version of his surname, rhyming with "away," permanently attached. It would become a colophon so distinctive as to provide, without appendage, instant recognition in a conversational reference or on the telephone.[8]

The first few months in his new position, Jaffé confided to Major Morris of the Red Cross, involved some "pretty hard sledding." Jaffé's overseas service had precluded his following Virginia politics. He was also well aware that management and Cameron, who was convalescing in Louisa, Virginia, and Tallahassee, Florida, were carefully monitoring the new editor's performance during his probationary period.[9]

Jaffé dealt with his predecessor deftly. Because of Cameron's illness, Starke had not consulted him regarding the choice of his replacement. Indeed, Cameron only learned Jaffé's full name several weeks after the latter had assumed the editorship. Nevertheless from the first, Jaffé's work impressed the former governor, who expressed to Starke his approval of his replacement. On *Virginian-Pilot* letterhead still bearing Cameron's name as editor, Jaffé had introduced himself to his predecessor and confessed that he

7. William Wannamaker to Louis Jaffé, 11 April 1922, Wannamaker Papers; Louis Jaffé to Thomas Wheelwright, 13 September 1919, Louis Jaffé Jr.; Dill, "Glimpse of Parnassus," 21; *Pilot,* 17 July 1952; Cappon, *Virginia Newspapers,* 143.

8. Raynell Lantor, interview by author, 8 July 1996; Jaffé family tree, Louis Jaffé Jr.; Mason, *One of the Neighbors' Children,* 151.

9. Louis Jaffé to C. D. Morris, 18 November 1920, Jaffé Papers.

"had bequeathed to his successor a disconcertingly large pair of shoes." The ex-governor responded by pronouncing his satisfaction that Jaffé's "convictions and sympathies are in accord with the principles and policies of which the V. P. has been a consistent advocate."[10]

Starke desired that Cameron continue to contribute to the editorial page, and this arrangement required the new editor to exercise both tact and firmness. Jaffé ran many of Cameron's occasional editorials, publishing them over Cameron's initials. But Jaffé evaluated them carefully in regard to timeliness and consistency with his own editorial views, and he filed some of them away without printing them. Although Cameron would live for another eight years, his editorial participation rapidly waned. Under Jaffé's leadership, one of his future associate editors later wrote, the *Virginian-Pilot's* "editorial page [quickly took on] a freshness of approach, crispness of style and a new breadth of outlook on both foreign and domestic affairs."[11]

Jaffé's old friend Alexander Forward, who had returned to his post as a commissioner on the State Corporation Commission, contributed immeasurably to his early success. Writing as often as twice a day to Forward, who possessed both a reporter's nose for news and splendid connections to powerful politicians and public servants, Jaffé gained an insider's perspective of the legislative maneuverings in Richmond.[12]

"You're a brick," Jaffé wrote to Forward, with whom he had shared much in their Balkan relief work. "I don't know what I would do without the direct touch your letters give me on developments at the capitol." Forward—as did many of the state's political leaders—read Jaffé's editorials every day. He believed that his friend's work, which he had considered impressive from the outset, grew even stronger as Jaffé settled into his position. Yet Forward did not hesitate to pass on criticism, confiding that Governor Westmoreland Davis felt the *Pilot's* editorials could be

10. Louis Jaffé to William Cameron, 4 November 1919, William Cameron to Louis Jaffé, 6 November 1919, both ibid.

11. Jaffé to Cameron, 4 November 1919, ibid.; Chambers, Shank, and Sugg, *Salt Water & Printer's Ink,* 312; Dill, "Glimpse of Parnassus," 21.

12. *Pilot,* 25 July 1920; Dill, "Glimpse of Parnassus," 22; Louis Jaffé to Alexander Forward, 29 November 1919, Jaffé Papers.

shortened. Jaffé seconded the governor's judgment: "I think most of our editorials are too long and we are bending our efforts to cure this defect."[13]

Although Forward's reports and Jaffé's own pre-war stint in Richmond provided him with the background required to write incisive editorials about state politics, Jaffé had come to Norfolk with only the most
cursory knowledge of his new city. Unquestionably this deficiency
accounted for some of the "hard sledding" he faced at first. Jaffé steeped
himself in the history and workings of the seaport city and labored to understand the many problems that confronted it.

The Great War had transformed Norfolk, turning it into a modern
city and a modern port. Conflicts in previous centuries had not been so kind
to the city. The Revolutionary and Civil Wars both had ravaged Norfolk.
On New Year's Day 1776, British men-of-war had drawn up abreast the
Town Point wharves and proceeded to shell the city methodically and at
length. Patriot soldiers—demoralized and poorly disciplined (many drunk
on rum)—looted homes and businesses and put them to the torch. Flames
shot up into the sky and lit the countryside for miles around as terrified residents fled the city. The walls of St. Paul's Church and little else had survived
the conflagration.[14]

In the following century, Union general George McClellan's Penin-
sular campaign had doomed Norfolk. Withdrawing Confederate troops
burned the navy yard and the redoubtable *Merrimack*. According to a
recent history of the port, the Union blockade and subsequent occupation
turned Norfolk "into a city mainly of paupers as whites lost their means of
livelihood and slaves sought refuge from nearby North Carolina and Virginia counties." A succession of Union generals, most notably Benjamin
"Beast" Butler, oversaw the city's occupation. Whites were forced to sign
oaths of allegiance to the federal government, while black troops and police
guards drilled in the streets and patrolled the city. Another epochal New
Year's Day in Norfolk's history occurred in 1863, when blacks paraded

13. Louis Jaffé to Alexander Forward, 23 January 1920, 1 December 1920, Alexander Forward to Louis Jaffé, 8 September 1920, all in Jaffé Papers.

14. Parramore, Stewart, and Bogger, *Norfolk: The First Four Centuries*, 94–6;
Thomas J. Wertenbaker, *Norfolk: Historic Southern Port*, 2d ed., ed. Marvin W. Schlegel (Durham: Duke University Press, 1962), 62–3; *Hill's Norfolk-Portsmouth City Directory*, 1931.

down Main Street, shredding and trampling Confederate flags in celebration of the Emancipation Proclamation.[15]

World War I altered the character of the city irrevocably. As vessels taking on cargoes of supplies and armaments clogged the harbors of New York and Philadelphia, industry and government turned their gaze south to Norfolk. Much to the jealousy of its Piedmont rival Richmond, situated where the James River grows shallow, Norfolk boasted one of the world's finest natural harbors. In the waning years of the nineteenth century, an industrial-age marvel—the Norfolk and Portsmouth Beltline—further enhanced the city's geographical advantages. The mammoth beltline allowed interconnectibility between the many railroad companies that served the region and enabled them to transport goods and produce to Norfolk's numerous warehouses, terminals, and piers with modern efficiency.[16]

As the Allies' supplies of resources dipped perilously low, seemingly endless trains streamed into Hampton Roads from the Appalachian coal fields, bearing fuel for war-torn Europe. Energy-hungry American war industries, now shifting into high gear, also looked to Norfolk; colliers in increasing numbers steamed out of the port, bound for the northeast seaboard. Other cargoes filled the holds of merchant vessels that sailed from Norfolk and the surrounding cities: fruits and vegetables, tobacco, and petroleum. Ships bearing exported goods from the world over charted courses for Hampton Roads.[17]

Military planners, too, fixed their vision on Norfolk. On the grounds of the Jamestown Exposition, where the tricentennial of the nation's first permanent English colony had been celebrated a decade earlier, construction began on naval training camps, a supply facility, an aviation station, and a submarine base. Great piers suddenly jutted out into the Elizabeth River. Engineers dredged thirty-five-foot channels, deep enough to accommodate the most massive dreadnought. Hundreds of buildings and

---

15. Parramore, Stewart, and Bogger, *Norfolk: The First Four Centuries,* 209–18; Wertenbaker, *Norfolk: Historic Southern Port,* 217–20; *Hill's Norfolk-Portsmouth City Directory,* 1931.

16. *Hill's Norfolk-Portsmouth City Directory,* 1931; Workers of the Writers' Program of the Work Projects Administration in the State of Virginia, *Virginia: A Guide to the Old Dominion* (Richmond: Virginia State Library and Archives, 1992), 241.

17. Wertenbaker, *Norfolk: Historic Southern Port,* 304–5.

miles of streets, railroads, and bulkheads materialized almost overnight. Hordes of "gobs" reported for sea and shore duty. Many of them sized up Norfolk and made liberty plans for activities not entirely restricted to church attendance and closely supervised YMCA dances.[18]

Nearby, the War Department constructed a thirty-million-dollar Army supply base with gargantuan piers and warehouses. Two million tons of supplies and a quarter million mules and horses would be shipped overseas to the Allied Expeditionary Force via this depot. Industries not directly associated with the war effort also recognized Norfolk's commercial promise. The British American Tobacco Company established four new factories there. Texas Oil expanded its facility, and Dupont created a storage warehouse.[19]

Just across the Elizabeth River in Portsmouth, the historic Norfolk navy yard underwent a tremendous expansion. Soon it boasted the country's greatest concentration of naval dry-docks, including one that could accommodate the fleet's largest battle wagon. The Navy built more piers there and equipped them with tracks, trolleys, and cranes. Anticipating casualties and illnesses, the War Department remade the naval hospital next door into the largest such facility on the East Coast.[20]

From across the country soldiers, sailors, clerks, and laborers— black and white—formed a human tide, flooding the city and swamping its antiquated municipal services. Labor contractors scoured the country, attempting to entice workers to Norfolk. Hundreds of young white women from rural areas arrived, eager to work as clerks or stenographers. Young black women from farms in eastern North Carolina and the Virginia Piedmont surged in, seeking jobs as domestics and as workers in tobacco, textile, and furniture factories. The city's population doubled, and the outlanders

18. Chambers, Shank, and Sugg, *Salt Water & Printer's Ink*, 296–8; Wertenbaker, *Norfolk: Historic Southern Port*, 308; Parramore, Stewart, and Bogger, *Norfolk: The First Four Centuries*, 288.

19. *Hill's Norfolk-Portsmouth City Directory*, 1931; Earl Lewis, *In Their Own Interests: Race, Class, and Power in Twentieth-Century Norfolk, Virginia* (Berkeley: University of California Press, 1991), 48.

20. Chambers, Shank, and Sugg, *Salt Water & Printer's Ink*, 296; Wertenbaker, *Norfolk: Historic Southern Port*, 308–9; Parramore, Stewart, and Bogger, *Norfolk: The First Four Centuries*, 288–9.

engulfed every nook and cranny of housing. Norfolk creaked, strained at the seams, and nearly burst.[21]

Vast numbers of men and women with less savory ambitions—hustlers, con artists, and prostitutes—also spilled into the city, attracted by the quick money and easy marks. In one two-month period, the police arrested five hundred prostitutes and B-girls—many under eighteen years old or infected with venereal diseases—and locked them away in the city's dilapidated and crowded jails. Lenoir Chambers, Jaffé's successor as editor of the *Virginian-Pilot,* wrote that the town was aghast when in 1918, "Dr. F. C. Steinmetz, rector of the dignified Christ Episcopal Church, . . . [proclaimed] that 'immoral indulgences' were rendering a third of certain groups of the armed forces in Norfolk 'incapable of properly serving their country.'"[22]

In spite of the influx of workers, labor shortages developed, providing unions with increased leverage to lobby for improved employment conditions and better pay. During World War I, Norfolk endured at least eight strikes and threats of many more. Management, long used to compliant southern labor, regarded any attempt at collective bargaining with concern. Nonetheless, the Coal Trimmers Union and the Transportation Workers Association, which represented black longshoremen and female cigar stemmers respectively, successfully gained concessions. Despite some small victories for labor, the dual pay scale for white and black workers remained intact, and blacks labored in working conditions more onerous and dangerous than those of their white counterparts.[23]

Black dissatisfaction was not confined to employment grievances. The deplorable state of housing, roads, sanitation, and police protection in the Huntersville and Barboursville sections, to which Jim Crow had relegated most of the city's blacks, vexed the community's leaders. Violence in particular concerned blacks. Some white soldiers and sailors passing through Norfolk bullied blacks and picked fights with them. And the lax

21. Chambers, Shank, and Sugg, *Salt Water & Printer's Ink,* 297; Wertenbaker, *Norfolk: Historic Southern Port,* 309; Workers of the Writers' Program of the Work Projects Administration in the State of Virginia, comps., *The Negro in Virginia* (Winston-Salem, N.C.: John F. Blair, 1994), 370; Suggs, *P. B. Young, Newspaperman,* 38.

22. Chambers, Shank, and Sugg, *Salt Water & Printer's Ink,* 297.

23. Lewis, *In Their Own Interests,* 48–56; Suggs, *P. B. Young, Newspaperman,* 38.

police presence and economic deprivation in black neighborhoods allowed the prevalence of diversions that frequently attracted raucous and inebriated military men, whose tempers flared and fists flew with little provocation.[24]

These conditions exacerbated racial tensions and set black nerves on edge. In East St. Louis, similar dynamics had resulted in a race riot in 1917. Police, militia, and white civilians there had killed forty blacks and wounded many others. One resident heard a soldier instructing a white man to "kill all the niggers he could." A Russian-Jewish immigrant who had observed the tumult concluded that the "makers of Russian pogroms could learn a great deal from the American rioters." Russians allowed Jews to escape from their burning homes before attempting to murder them, he noted. In East St. Louis whites gunned down blacks fleeing blazing buildings.[25]

In Norfolk, blacks' fears of rampaging and rioting sailors and doughboys stemmed from reality. In 1918, Halloween and New Year's Eve festivities downtown had ended in the deaths of a sailor and a policeman and in the injury of many others. Sailors had smashed store windows, and a detachment of Marines, armed with Springfields, had cleared the streets. Outraged municipal authorities demanded and secured a permanent Navy shore-patrol unit.[26]

The nation's preeminent black civil rights organization mined black Norfolkians' trepidation and anger. James Weldon Johnson—schoolteacher, lawyer, composer, diplomat, author, newspaperman, and future executive secretary of the National Association for the Advancement of Colored People—visited Norfolk and organized an NAACP chapter there in 1917. The membership elected the editor of the black *Norfolk Journal and Guide* newspaper, thirty-three-year-old Plummer Bernard "P. B." Young, president.[27]

The problems Norfolk faced during the war years underscored for residents the need for a radically new administrative system. The explosive growth of the city starkly revealed the shaky nature of its municipal infra-

24. Suggs, *P. B. Young, Newspaperman*, 38–9.

25. Shapiro, *White Violence and Black Response*, 115–7.

26. Chambers, Shank, and Sugg, *Salt Water & Printer's Ink*, 298–9; Suggs, *P. B. Young, Newspaperman*, 38–9.

27. Suggs, *P. B. Young, Newspaperman*, 31.

structure. Over half of the streets remained unpaved. Natural gas and water shortages—combined with electrical shortages and blackouts—paralyzed the city. Authorities asked civilians to forgo electricity for three and a half hours every afternoon.[28]

On September 1, 1918, as a result of a referendum overwhelmingly approved by the city's voters, a commission-manager system replaced the unwieldy council-mayor form of administration that had governed Norfolk for nearly two hundred years. A five-man council selected as city manager capable and energetic Charles E. Ashburner, an engineer who had pioneered the position of city manager in Staunton, Virginia, and Springfield, Ohio.[29]

Thus Louis Jaffé's return to the United States and his assumption of the *Virginian-Pilot*'s helm coincided with a turning point in Norfolk's history. Fed up with the status quo, the citizenry—black and white—were crying out for solutions to the ills that plagued the city. With a level of humanity, acumen, and vigor rare among his peers in the southern press, Jaffé began to attack the many problems that confronted the city and its environs and to inform his readers about the larger world into which the war had drawn them.

Jaffé's new job provided him with an exceptional level of autonomy and enabled him to focus almost solely on editorial writing and the makeup of the other elements of his page: political and literary columns, book reviews, letters to the editor, cartoons, and the like. Typically, an edition of the *Virginian-Pilot* contained four original editorials. During an informal morning conference, Jaffé and his associate discussed the news and its significance, determined writing responsibilities, and reached decisions regarding the treatment and conclusions of the editorials. In the event of disagreement, the editor's views prevailed. Jaffé wrote the lead piece and often one or two others and devoted the remainder of his attention to managing the editorial page. The associate editor usually wrote two or three editorials and assisted

28. Parramore, Stewart, and Bogger, *Norfolk: The First Four Centuries*, 293–4; Chambers, Shank, and Sugg, *Salt Water & Printer's Ink*, 298.

29. Wertenbaker, *Norfolk: Historic Southern Port*, 318–20; *Hill's Norfolk-Portsmouth City Directory*, 1931.

Jaffé in his other duties. Each day they produced three columns of double-leaded material.[30]

Early in his tenure Jaffé developed what admiring colleagues would one day refer to as the "Jaffé editorial formula." As Lenoir Chambers described it: "The subject had to be absorbed, the attitude toward it had to be made clear, and the conclusion had to be to the point." To this methodology Jaffé brought prodigious daily reading, a growing sensitivity, and an extraordinary editorial gift.[31]

Lore has it that he could "work miracles" with a copy pencil and transform an associate's flawed effort into a crisp and polished editorial. Sometimes he would rewrite the piece so thoroughly that when it ran, almost none of it could be recognized. Then he would compliment the writer on his work. But not everyone saw Jaffé this way. Robert Mason, who wrote editorials for Jaffé and who succeeded Chambers as the *Pilot*'s editor in 1962, believed that Jaffé surrounded himself with talented writers who could write as well as he could, but that not having recently spent time at a newsroom desk, he assessed other writers' efforts impatiently. Jaffé, as Mason recalled, would glance over his work and tell him that surely he could do better. He would return to his desk, wait, and resubmit the same work, "maybe retyped, maybe not." This time the editor attended more carefully to the editorial. "After reading it then, Mr. Jaffé would say, 'That's much better; fine.'"[32]

Jaffé worked hard but did not consider his responsibilities overly taxing. The workday, which began at 9:00 A.M. and usually concluded at 6:00 or 6:30 P.M. unless pressing news required evening and night work, occasionally allowed him and his associate editor the time for independent writing.[33]

Although Lucien Starke Jr. sought his editor's advice regarding general questions of management and news coverage, tradition confined Jaffé's

30. Louis Jaffé to L. Whipple, 4 October 1922, Jaffé Papers.

31. Mason, *One of the Neighbors' Children*, 152; Chambers, Shank, and Sugg, *Salt Water & Printer's Ink*, 315.

32. Chambers, Shank, and Sugg, *Salt Water & Printer's Ink*, 382; Mason, *One of the Neighbors' Children*, 152.

33. Jaffé to Whipple, 4 October 1922, Jaffé Papers.

influence principally to the editorial page. A managing editor, Keville Glennan, whose reporting on the Paris peace conference Jaffé had called to the attention of John Stewart Bryan, oversaw the paper's news coverage. Jaffé admired Glennan, whose "brilliant mind" and nearly three decades of reporting and editorial experience with the old *Virginian* and then the *Virginian-Pilot* qualified him highly for his job.[34]

Starke, an attorney and businessman first and foremost, had little talent or inclination for editorial work. He had built a successful law practice in Norfolk and had come to journalism indirectly, almost reluctantly. As a young man, he had skillfully negotiated the purchase of one of the *Virginian-Pilot*'s ancestors, the *Pilot,* for Albert H. Grandy in 1898. Grandy had pressed Starke to devote his attentions entirely to managing the newly acquired paper, but Starke resisted, believing that newspapering offered too precarious a future. Upon Grandy's death, however, Starke gradually abandoned his law practice for journalism.[35]

Starke, who bore the title of colonel as a result of his appointment to the staff of one of Virginia's governors, oversaw the transformation of the *Virginian-Pilot* from a small-town paper into a metropolitan daily. Although the staff knew that Starke was in command, he ran the paper almost democratically, placing great faith in his department heads. He did not stand on ceremony and visited the members of his staff at their work sites as frequently as they met with him in his office. Starke set great stock in hiring able employees and then allowing them a generous measure of freedom in their work. Nevertheless, he did not countenance sensational treatment of the news, and he insisted that his editorial page speak independently and remain free from political entanglements. In an era of heated newspaper competition, when many of the region's presses practiced highly partisan journalism, the *Virginian-Pilot* stood out as a modern and progressive paper.[36]

Jaffé relished his new job and the platform it provided him. "The job is very much to my liking," he wrote to a friend. "Everybody from the

34. Ibid.; Mason, *One of the Neighbors' Children,* 151; Chambers, Shank, and Sugg, *Salt Water & Printer's Ink,* 323–4; *Pilot,* 29 September 1921.

35. Mason, *One of the Neighbors' Children,* 148.

36. *Pilot,* 1 August 1931.

Big High Chief down has been most cordial and have made me feel welcome and at home. . . . Best of all is the complete freedom that they have given me to say what I dam [sic] please every morning—which suits my didactic temperament down to the ground."[37]

Still, Jaffé, like other editors, wrote within constraints and took care not to alienate himself too much from his readers. In the same letter, he confided that it was breaking his heart not to be able to say what he thought of flamboyant evangelist and former baseball star Billy Sunday, who shortly would begin a six-week crusade in Norfolk. As he traveled to Virginia, Sunday applauded the Justice Department's crackdown on radicals. "I would stand everyone [sic] of the ornery, wild-eyed I.W.W.'s, anarchists, crazy Socialists, and other types of Reds up before a firing squad," the preacher declaimed.[38]

Sunday, then at the pinnacle of his phenomenal popularity, attacked science and political liberalism in his sermons and preached a fundamentalist message that stuck in Jaffé's craw. But Jaffé's discretion proved wise. At the revival's kickoff, Sunday's disciples implored him to end a prolonged drought. The evangelist prayed for rain, and a torrential downpour ensued. After the storm had destroyed several seashore cottages, his nervous devotees again asked for his intervention, and Sunday received widespread credit and adulation for the prompt ending of the squall.[39]

Sunday's Norfolk crusade preceded by one day the implementation of the Volstead Act, and Prohibition's chief cheerleader savored his victory. Twenty costumed pallbearers accompanied a carriage bearing a twenty-foot casket in a downtown parade to ring in the temperate twenties. In the coffin lay the corpse of John Barleycorn. Mourning the death of his kinsman, a masked devil in a red costume followed sorrowfully behind the hearse. Cheering crowds lined the streets as the procession made its way to the 15,000-seat tabernacle constructed for the revival. Congregants greeted the arrival of the cortege with earsplitting huzzahs, and a band struck up a funeral dirge. To roars of approval, Sunday administered last rites to the

37. Louis Jaffé to "Matt," 1 January 1920, Jaffé Papers.

38. Louis Jaffé to Grover Hall, 16 October 1929, ibid.; Louis Jaffé to "Matt," 1 January 1920, ibid.; Roger A. Bruns, *Preacher: Billy Sunday and Big-Time Evangelism* (New York: W. W. Norton, 1992), 266.

39. Parramore, Stewart, and Bogger, *Norfolk: The First Four Centuries*, 299.

Old Enemy. As the crowd sang the doxology, the nimble evangelist waved the Stars and Stripes from atop the pulpit. His voice rose above all others.[40]

Well before Jaffé took over the editorship, the *Pilot* had battled the drys. Cameron had fought statewide prohibition, which had come to Virginia in 1916. His young successor followed suit by lamenting the ratification of the Eighteenth Amendment, which had occurred slightly before his arrival in Norfolk. Two days after Billy Sunday's giddy celebration of Prohibition, Jaffé wryly observed that the United States had become the only civilized nation of the first rank to impose on its people a strict regime of prohibition. Although the great experiment might "prove to be the outstanding moral-economic reform of the century," he warned, "it may engender an unrest that may entrain disorders not now foreseen." Nevertheless, Jaffé urged lawfulness: "This newspaper has not in the past been a subscriber to the belief that rigid Statewide or nation-wide prohibition is the best way to deal with the appetite for stimulants. It does believe, however, and has from the beginning believed, that the law once put on the statute books, should be enforced."[41]

The postwar "Red scare" perhaps constituted the most significant issue with which Jaffé grappled early in his editorial career. The war, labor shortages, the booming economy, and inflation had energized and strengthened unions in Norfolk and across the country. By the decade's end, four million workers had participated in over two and a half thousand strikes. In Seattle, for example, unions shut down the city in 1919 in support of a shipyard workers' strike; in Boston, police struck for the right to organize. Mine, steel, and garment workers flexed their powerful muscles. Threatened by labor militancy, politicians sided with management and intervened to restore the status quo. Federal and state troops, police, the courts, and politically ambitious Attorney General A. Mitchell Palmer (known as the "Fighting Quaker") broke the strikes. Business and conservative leaders succeeded in portraying labor organizers as foreign radicals working in league with Russian revolutionaries. Very quickly, the anti-German hysteria of the war years turned into anticommunist paranoia.[42]

40. Bruns, *Preacher,* 266–7.
41. *Pilot,* 1 August 1914, 18 January 1920.
42. Bruce Levine et al. *Who Built America? Working People & The Nation's Economy, Politics, Culture & Society,* vol. 2 (New York: Pantheon, 1992), 259–64.

Jaffé's position on the Red scare soon conflicted unmistakably with the views expressed on his predecessor's editorial page. William Cameron, despite the many progressive stands he had taken throughout his career, had not preached tolerance for radicals. "Agitators who seek to substitute Anarchy for Democracy in America and to poison the minds of the citizenship against American institutions and ideals are entitled to no more consideration than that accorded a mad dog in full career," he had exhorted. Hanging comprised the only effective way of dealing with Bolshevism, a "serpent that has already dragged its slimy trail across the country's borders."[43]

Although in the first months of his new job Jaffé had defended the government's attempts to "crush out this menace," he almost immediately reversed his position and began to defend the civil liberties of anarchists, communists, and socialists. The Palmer raids in January 1920 shocked Jaffé and led him to rethink his views. The Red-hunting attorney general, assisted by young J. Edgar Hoover, rounded up six thousand alleged communists in cities across the country. Law authorities had not obtained warrants for many of the arrests. Prisoners languished in their cells uncharged, incommunicado, and without benefit of counsel while federal agents coerced confessions. The government made plans for mass deportations. (The previous month, Palmer had deported anarchist Emma Goldman—born, like Jaffé's parents, in Kovno—to the Soviet Union.)[44]

"Is there not a real danger that we are seeing red?" Jaffé asked. Perhaps reflecting on an editorial he had written less than a week earlier urging the ferreting out of radicals, Jaffé wrote: "Being ourselves the actors in the present Red drama, we do not realize how far we have traveled along the road of intolerance." The Palmer raids had set a frightening precedent. "Nothing like this wholesale round-up and expulsion of anarchists has ever happened in this country. . . . The fear is more than idle that we are in danger of destroying the Reds and liberty of thought and speech at the same time."[45]

A few days later, the New York State Assembly suspended five duly elected Socialist Party representatives. The assembly described the party's principles and platform as "inimical to the best interests of the United States

43. *Pilot,* 31 January 1919.
44. Ibid., 2, 8 January 1920; Levine et al., *Who Built America?* 265.
45. *Pilot,* 8 January 1920.

and the State of New York." Jaffé's editorial response would have raised the eyebrows of many of his readers. Southerners historically viewed "foreign" and "Yankee" ideas with suspicion. They reserved particular contempt—indeed, hostility—for what they saw as socialism and communism.[46]

"The Socialist Party has long held a respectable position in America," Jaffé declared in a lead editorial. "For many years there have been Socialist members in Congress and in various State legislatures." The assembly's actions, he continued, "evidence a spirit of intolerance wholly out of keeping with fundamental ideas of Democracy. . . . To hold socialistic doctrines is not a crime and is not to be regarded as constituting a substantial reason for exclusion so long as those doctrines are not incompatible with good citizenship and so long as those who hold them do not attempt to resort to unlawful means in applying them." The legislature's actions would only "add fuel to the fire it aimed to put out."[47]

Jaffé hammered on throughout January. When Palmer and Hoover trampled the civil rights of alleged Reds by denying them bail and holding them on Ellis Island in preparation for their deportation, Jaffé spoke out again: "It should not be lost to sight that the best interest of the Government is promoted by jealously guarding American institutions and ideals from perversion. The day of the 'third degree' has passed. It was but a modern edition of the torture chamber at best. Mere suspicion of wrongdoing is not sufficient to justify continued imprisonment—at least not in America."[48]

Not all agreed with Jaffé's views. His former paper, the *Times-Dispatch*, under the direction of still another journalistic colonel, editor and publisher Charles E. Hasbrook, expressed great confidence in Palmer and his "diligent investigation." "[Radicals] are being proceeded against as they ought to be," one of its editorials concluded. "The government is absolutely justified in deporting such aliens and would be derelict in its duty to the nation if it did not resort to the use of ruthless methods . . . to rid the country of such a danger." Bryan had sold the paper to Hasbrook in 1914. The

46. Levine et al., *Who Built America?* 265; *Pilot,* 12 January 1920; Wilson and Ferris, eds., *Encyclopedia of Southern Culture,* vol. 4, 246.

47. *Pilot,* 12 January 1920.

48. Ibid., 19 January 1920.

new publisher did not share his predecessor's commitment to liberalism and tolerance.[49]

Yet Jaffé did not stand alone in his crusade for tolerance. The *Richmond News Leader,* its editorial page directed by Douglas Southall Freeman, conducted a tedious civics lesson: "Democracy postulates increasing needs, broader knowledge and loftier aspirations on the part of its members and growing utility, larger service and more complete plasticity on the part of its instruments." Unless New York's Socialist assemblymen espoused overthrow of the government, the *News Leader* counseled, they should retain their seats.[50]

The objections of Jaffé, Freeman, and other like-minded editorial writers notwithstanding, New York's State Assembly expelled its Socialist members later that spring. In "Inviting Dynamite," Jaffé warned that the action set a frightening precedent, undermined fundamental concepts of political liberty, and could incite violence: "America is confronted with the choice of repudiating the action of the New York Assembly or confessing itself politically less tolerant than any modern state, with the possible exception of Japan. Nothing is better designed . . . to stimulate anti-government lawlessness. [The assembly] has closed its doors to the change of government by constitutional means and opened wide the cellar door to reform by dynamite."[51]

Although Jaffé termed communism a "stupendous failure," believing that it worked counter to human nature by denying property rights, he mocked xenophobes and right wingers who sought to bar ties and cultural exchanges between the Soviet Union and the United States. A warning by the American Defense Society that a series of performances and exhibits by the Moscow Art League had sinister ulterior motives triggered a sarcastic response from him: "If we hadn't been warned . . . we might have thought the object of the American tour was to give this country some excellent Russian ballet and to reap a harvest of good American dollars in return." The Moscow Art League had recently visited France but, Jaffé continued, "so

49. *Richmond Times-Dispatch,* 13, 23 January 1920; Dunford, *Richmond Times-Dispatch: The Story of a Newspaper,* 38–9.

50. *Richmond News Leader,* 13 January 1920.

51. *Pilot,* 2 April 1920.

subtle was the poisonous propaganda which they spread that its effect has not yet been felt, and Paris does not even at this late date suspect that it was spread at all." Jaffé thanked the American Defense Society for its vigilance in protecting Americans from "Rooshian Bullsheviks" and "furrin propagander." He commended the organization's leadership, particularly its secretary, who, he said, "must be paid, . . . must find something to justify his official existence, and . . . can be depended upon at all times to be 100 per cent, if not more, for the American people and against all 'furriners.'"[52]

Palmer's popularity waned in the wake of congressional hearings into his methods, in addition to his false prophecy that communists planned violent riots in major cities across the country on May Day 1920. Police and legal authorities had braced for the Bolshevik onslaught, patrolling buildings and guarding political leaders, but the day came and went and nothing happened. The discredited attorney general had hoped to ride the hysteria into the White House, but James M. Cox won the Democratic nomination later that year.[53]

Jaffé's editorial voice had grown strong and confident during his campaign defending due process and the civil liberties of socialists and communists. He believed his journalistic peers—particularly in Virginia—had behaved with "reticence" and "timidity" while the government made a "mockery of the personal sanctities guaranteed by the Bill of Rights." But as the Red scare faded, a fringe group to the south was mushrooming into another sweeping issue for the *Virginian-Pilot*'s editor.[54]

In the five years since Colonel Simmons and his band of followers had scaled Georgia's Stone Mountain and ignited their torch atop the granite butte to herald the second coming of the Ku Klux Klan, the secret society's potential had remained unrealized. The colonel earned a comfortable living by garnering a percentage of each new recruit's membership fee, but the organization had plateaued at several thousand members. Despite Simmons's mastery of the masculine ritualism of fraternities and his unrivaled network of contacts with the legion of other orders that pervaded a nation

52. Ibid., 5 August 1921, 29 December 1922.
53. Levine et al., *Who Built America?* 265.
54. "Reticence, Timidity Hamper Press Jaffé Tells Virginia Editors," *Editor & Publisher*, 27 July 1929, 20.

of joiners, the new Knights of the Ku Klux Klan remained a bright idea in need of advertising.[55]

Simmons knew his limitations as a chief executive officer. In June 1920, he struck a contract with the Southern Publicity Association to provide the Klan with the boost it needed. Benefiting from the modern sciences of public relations and marketing, in a few short years the Klan would drive its membership to five million "one-hundred-percent Americans"—men, women, and children alike.[56]

55. Chalmers, *Hooded Americanism*, 30–1; Nancy McClean, *Behind the Mask of Chivalry: The Making of the Second Ku Klux Klan* (New York: Oxford University Press, 1994), 5.

56. Chalmers, *Hooded Americanism*, 32; McClean, *Behind the Mask of Chivalry*, 10.

6   SETTING A COURSE

Margaret Davis was not the boss's daughter, but she was close to it. Her father, banker and prominent attorney Hugh C. Davis, had served as secretary of the *Virginian-Pilot* Publishing Company years earlier, and he now sat on the newspaper's powerful executive committee. Davis, his wife, Margaret (Thomas Wheelwright's sister), and their children, attorney Hugh W. Davis and Margaret, comprised one of Norfolk's "best and oldest families."[1]

The younger Margaret worked as a Sunday feature writer for the *Virginian-Pilot*. The war effort had depleted the paper's male reporting staff, and some women had achieved success as replacements. Jaffé found Margaret attractive, bright, and engaging. The two soon learned they held similar perspectives on many issues.[2]

The Davises had displayed great courtesy to Jaffé upon his arrival in town, and provided him with an entrée into Norfolk society. Hugh Jr., two years older than Jaffé, helped him find an apartment and sponsored his membership in the Princess Anne Country Club in nearby Virginia Beach. Both young men had served overseas in the Army. In fact, Jaffé may have met Davis at officers' training school at Fort Myer; they graduated as members of the same class. Davis had stuck it out in field artillery and attained the rank of major. Before the war, he had earned a law degree at the University of Virginia and worked for several years in business in Florida and New York before joining his father's law firm. Jaffé regarded his contemporary, who displayed a confident manner born of his long Virginia ancestry and

1. Shank, *History of Norfolk-Portsmouth Newspapers,* 1469, 2331; Samuel Slover to Frederick Thompson, 7 September 1925, Louis Jaffé Jr.
2. Jaffé family tree, Louis Jaffé Jr.; Louis Jaffé to J. J. Lankes, December 1935, Jaffé Papers; Chambers, Shank, and Sugg, *Salt Water & Printer's Ink,* 300.

membership in exclusive organizations such as Norfolk's German Club, as "sophisticated."[3]

Margaret and the other Davises thought highly of Jaffé's work on the paper, and they praised his performance to Wheelwright. The influential Richmond businessman relayed their approbation to the *Pilot*'s new editor, who found the positive evaluation of his writing and management of the editorial page gratifying.[4]

As Jaffé's attraction to Margaret developed, he attended closely to her feature writing, which in retrospect reads as somewhat trite. One lengthy piece concerned a young Canadian officer with the improbable name of Coningsby Dawson. "Tall and spare and vigorous, notwithstanding the fact that he still bears the marks of physical hardening that stamp him as a soldier, Lieutenant Dawson seems to have cast from him the outlook engendered through military experience," she wrote. (The description matched not at all the accompanying photograph of a prim-looking young man seated at a table and staring up at the camera.) Although Dawson apparently had done or seen little of importance during the war, he tediously discussed his "peace-time philosophy." Margaret quoted and paraphrased him, devoting an entire page of the newspaper to a story with little point. In a note to "Miss Davis," Jaffé evaluated the article—not the pontificating lieutenant—generously: "After reading your story in to-day's paper I have a somewhat better opinion than I had before of Coningsby Dawson. I congratulate you on the story. It was interestingly and professionally done."[5]

Although Jaffé saw himself as a realist, Margaret could inspire him to wax sentimental. From his office window he looked out at a magnolia tree growing in a dreary well formed by four tall buildings. Throughout the

3. Louis Jaffé to Thomas Wheelwright, 29 November 1919, Jaffé Papers; Hugh W. Davis to Louis Jaffé, 23 March 1920, 7 September 1920, Jaffé Papers; Helena Lefroy Caperton, ed., *Social Record of Virginia* (Richmond: Garret & Massie, 1937), 74; *Who's Who in the South,* 1927, 207; Henry Clarkson Meredith, *The Norfolk German Club* (Richmond: Whitlet & Shepperson, 1961), 46; Louis Jaffé to Sherwood Anderson, 3 February 1931, Jaffé Papers.

4. Thomas Wheelwright to Louis Jaffé, 3 March 1920, Jaffé Papers.

5. *Pilot,* 1 February 1920; Louis Jaffé to Margaret Davis, 1 February 1920, Jaffé Papers.

winter, Jaffé wrote, the "sad magnolia tree has looked in the third-story window of the Temple of Wisdom. The longer it looked the sadder it got. Its glossy leaves drooped and many of them turned yellow and fell to the macadamized ground. What was the use of being a perfumed magnolia tree if it was only to be kept awake all night by a pounding composing room and to look all day upon the window of a Heathen Temple? The sadder the magnolia got the sadder became the high priests at the Altar, and the sadder became their sermons to the people. It was very sad." But that day in late spring, Jaffé informed his readers, "everything . . . changed. The magnolia tree is still espaliered against the perpendicular wall of the Temple of Omniscience, but it looks upon the one window which is its world and smiles. For just out of reach from the window there rocks gently the pale ivory youngster that came in the night. The magnolia tree that was forgotten of Man was not forgotten of God."[6]

Margaret liked the story but thought it uncharacteristic of Jaffé, who she felt did not "believe in fairy-tales." She advised him to write a sequel more in keeping with his temperament, one in which the "bloom withered in the blighting atmosphere of the Temple of Omniscience, or was forever lost because the vandal hand of the copy-boy plucked it and cast it to the pavement to be trampled underfoot." Jaffé replied that Margaret had helped inspire him to write the story by egging him on to "excursions in metaphysics," when his natural impulses were "all in the direction of a very plebeian pragmatism." He reported regretfully that the magnolia blossom had withered but that the tree, "like Lady Astor," had not finished yet.[7]

Margaret had shown an aptitude for writing and had proven her worth in a male-dominated profession; with Jaffé's encouragement she now began to tackle subjects more substantial than Coningsby Dawson. Noticing a picture of Alexander Forward in Jaffé's office and hearing about his exploits, she decided the commissioner would make a good subject for a feature. Jaffé coordinated the interview, in which Forward found Margaret "capable and businesslike." The resulting article focused on Forward's background, his tenure on the State Corporation Commission, and his

6. *Pilot*, 23 May 1920.

7. Margaret Davis to Louis Jaffé, 23 May 1920, Louis Jaffé to Margaret Davis, 24 May 1920, both in Jaffé Papers.

groundbreaking work in regulating utilities and natural monopolies. Business and political leaders commended Margaret on a good story. Jaffé had played a role in shaping the piece, but Margaret had demonstrated an ability to deal with serious subject matter.[8]

In the summer of 1920, the two attended a newspaper convention in Asheville, North Carolina. Jaffé extended "many kindnesses to her" there, probably by introducing her to other reporters and editors and speaking favorably of her feature writing. Their romantic relationship began to blossom at this time. Shortly after the Asheville trip, Jaffé began addressing Margaret in their correspondence as "Petite" and expressed a preference for writing to her in longhand rather than by typewriter.[9]

In early December 1920 they were married in Wheelwright's country home in Buckhead Springs, just outside Richmond. Margaret's immediate family, a few of her relatives, publishers John Stewart Bryan and Lucien Starke Jr., and Forward and another of Louis's friends attended the intimate ceremony. Although the wedding announcement in the *Virginian-Pilot* stated that a few additional guests attended the reception that followed, none of the stories in the Norfolk or Richmond papers mentioned the presence of Jaffé's family.[10]

It is not known whether his family boycotted the wedding or if Louis and Margaret discouraged their attendance, believing that the presence of his conspicuously Orthodox Jewish parents would disrupt the Episcopal ceremony. Louis's marriage to a "goy" displeased his family, particularly his mother. A scathing letter he received from Hyman during the honeymoon wounded Louis deeply and made it difficult for him to call his brother by his first name for several years thereafter.[11]

Beyond a doubt his parents' attendance would have distracted and discomfited the Gentile guests. Many of Virginia's clubs and resorts, such as

8. Louis Jaffé to Alexander Forward, 16 June 1920, Alexander Forward to Louis Jaffé, 10 July 1920, both ibid.; *Pilot,* 25 July 1920; Thomas Wheelwright to Louis Jaffé, 29 July 1920, Jaffé Papers.

9. Thomas Wheelwright to Louis Jaffé, 29 July 1920, Louis Jaffé to Margaret Davis, 25 October 1920, both in Jaffé Papers.

10. *Pilot,* 9 December 1920; *Richmond News Leader,* 9 December 1920; *Richmond Times-Dispatch,* 8 December 1920.

11. Louis Jaffé to Hyman Jaffe, 4 July 1921, 20 February 1942, Louis Jaffé Jr.

the Chamberlin Hotel at Old Point Comfort and the Martha Washington Hotel in Virginia Beach, advertised the fact that they catered to "carefully Restricted Clientele." As late as 1963, 20 percent of Virginia's resorts still barred Jews. Only the state of Arizona exceeded this figure.[12]

Louis and Margaret would have discussed their divergent religious backgrounds and the strains this difference could pose. Obviously, they had decided that their love for each other could surmount any prejudice they might face. They likely also downplayed the potential for marital discord. A growing number of interfaith marriages were taking place. Louis's own religious beliefs—or lack of them—created no conflict.

He did not attempt to construct a new identity for himself by hiding his Jewish roots; he merely entered into a life unconstrained by his parents' religion, which from an early age he had regarded ambivalently. The reform Temple Ohef Sholom in Norfolk had a capable and progressive leader, Dr. Louis Mendoza, who embraced an assimilationist philosophy similar to that of Richmond's Rabbi Edward Calisch. Christian ministers welcomed Dr. Mendoza into their pulpits. But Jaffé's interactions with his almost exclusively Gentile newspaper colleagues and his new social acquaintances provided little time or incentive for entry into Norfolk's Jewish community. Consequently, having critically evaluated his tenuous ties to Judaism during his military and Red Cross service, he chose to lead a secular existence in his new city.[13]

After a brief honeymoon trip north, he and Margaret returned to Norfolk. They set up housekeeping in an apartment in the Ghent residential area, a few blocks away from the *Pilot*'s offices. Jaffé's marriage represented the fulfillment of the dream he had so poignantly expressed in his war diary—his wish for a family. Margaret was loving, and she doted on him. From time to time he found her enigmatic—impulsive and emotional; but he had never before lived in intimacy with a woman, and he attributed her

12. *Southern Progress: A Magazine of Opportunity and Patriotism,* July 1935, 8; *Richmond Times-Dispatch,* 29 October 1934; Dinnerstein, "Neglected Aspect of Southern Jewish History," 67.

13. *Pilot,* 6 September 1925; Stern, "Role of the Rabbi in the South," 27; Parramore, Stewart, and Bogger, *Norfolk: The First Four Centuries,* 276–7; Jaffé family tree, Louis Jaffé Jr.

occasionally puzzling behavior to her artistic temperament, genteel upbringing, and femininity.[14]

Jaffé also relished the professional success he was experiencing. Magazines,
such as the *Literary Digest,* and other newspapers quoted him and reprinted
his editorials with increasing frequency. His reputation had begun to extend
beyond his paper's immediate sphere of readership. In particular, his forceful attacks on the metastasizing Ku Klux Klan began to arouse national
attention. The Klan's invasion of Virginia and its rapid expansion there
stepped up Jaffé's assault. In 1920 the fraternal organization established its
headquarters in Richmond, where it sponsored speeches and parades and
recruited with great success. Richmond and Roanoke would soon be home
to the state's largest and best-organized klaverns.[15]

Imperial Wizard William Simmons's recently hired public relations
experts, Edward Young Clarke and Elizabeth Tyler, convincingly cloaked
the Klan in patriotism and fellowship, but the order's menacing purpose
would soon emerge. A running series in the *New York World*—then under
the leadership of master editor Frank Cobb, whom Jaffé regarded highly—
revealed to many the true aims of the secret society but did nothing to stymie
its frenzied growth. (The *Virginian-Pilot* would augment its Associated
Press coverage with the *New York World*'s wire service in 1926.)[16]

In his seminal book on the Klan, *Hooded Americanism,* David
Chalmers contrasted the activism with which the *Virginian-Pilot* denounced
the secret society to the passivity of the *Times-Dispatch* and *News Leader.*
Jaffé's Richmond peers had determined that editorial exclusion would deny
the imperial order publicity and result in its eventual entropy. Jaffé took the

14. *Pilot,* 9 December 1920; *Norfolk Telephone Directory* (Chesapeake and Potomac Telephone Co., 1921); Louis Jaffé to Lucien Starke, 27 June 1923, Jaffé Papers; Margaret
Jaffé to Louis Jaffé, 22 August 1921, Louis Jaffé Jr.

15. Louis Jaffé to Lucien Starke, 27 June 1923, Jaffé Papers; Chalmers, *Hooded
Americanism,* 330; Kenneth T. Jackson, *The Ku Klux Klan in the City, 1915–1930* (Chicago:
Ivan R. Dee, 1992), 81.

16. *Pilot,* 6 October 1920, 23 May 1926; Chalmers, *Hooded Americanism,* 35–8;
Michael Emery, Edwin Emery, and Nancy Roberts, *The Press in America: An Interpretive His-
tory of the Mass Media* (Boston: Allyn & Bacon, 2000), 214–5; Frank Luther Mott, *American
Journalism: A History, 1690–1960* (New York: Macmillan, 1962), 643; Louis Jaffé to Walter
Lippmann, 31 December 1924, Jaffé Papers.

opposite approach. He censured, disparaged, and mocked the Klan "from the moment it sprang like Minerva, full panoplied, from the head of Emperor Simmons, to embark on a celebrated mission of hate." He decried the "editorial reticence alternating with gentle wrist-slappings" with which Virginia's press in general greeted the order's appearance and spread. Reflecting on the press's lack of courage in confronting the Klan, he wrote, "Here was an anti-social development promising nothing but violence, bigotry and disorder, but months and years passed before editors brought themselves to call the new terror by its right name. The prelude to this final buckling on of the sword of condemnation and ridicule, was a disheartening period of fearfulness, of timid deprecation, of euphemistic allusions to 'masked mobs' and 'hooded orders' and worse than that of pained silence."[17]

Jaffé did not entirely lack for company in his early assault on the Klan. A handful of other southern editors displayed similar courage. Julian Harris, general manager of the *Columbus (Ga.) Enquirer-Sun,* bought into the paper in 1920 after having lived in the Northeast and in Europe. He and his wife, Julia, battled the Klan almost from the moment the journalistic couple arrived. (Columbus and the surrounding area had become a hotbed of Klan activity.) Several years later the associate editor of the *Montgomery (Ala.) Advertiser,* Grover Hall, inspired by his correspondence with H. L. Mencken, mounted a similar attack on the Klan. Upon becoming editor of the *Advertiser* in 1926, Hall assailed the hooded order with ever-increasing vigor.[18]

Jaffé's opening shots came in the fall of 1920. In October, he challenged Simmons's right to exhume the Ku Klux Klan. In "The New Ku-Kluxers," he acknowledged that the excesses of Reconstruction may have necessitated the original Klan's formation, but he denied that the present era required such a society: "The new Ku-Kluxers are to defend Americanism.

17. Chalmers, *Hooded Americanism,* 230; "Reticence, Timidity Hamper Press," *Editor & Publisher,* 20.

18. Gregory C. Lisby, "Julian Harris and the *Columbus Enquirer-Sun*: The Consequences of Winning the Pulitzer Prize," *Journalism Monographs,* no. 105 (April 1988): 4–8; Daniel Webster Hollis III, *An Alabama Newspaper Tradition: Grover C. Hall and the Hall Family* (Tuscaloosa: University of Alabama Press, 1983), 29, 32–40; James Goodman, *Stories of Scottsboro* (New York: Vintage, 1995), 296.

If they are to defend anything else they are keeping it dark. It is not clear just how Southern Americanism is in peril and from what source the attack is to be feared, but we have a valiant organization of 100 per-centers who are ready to rush to its defense on white chargers, appropriately disguised to prevent their being recognized by the grateful populace and overwhelmed with bravos." After taking a swipe at Thomas Dixon's *The Clansman* and by inference the film *Birth of a Nation,* which, he said, "traffic in the passions of America's tragic hours," Jaffé concluded his editorial: "There is no law against men banding themselves together for any uncriminal purpose, however destitute of sense. If they find pleasure in midnight mummery they can unite for that purpose with impunity. But all men are under obligation to preserve a decent regard for the past."[19]

Apparently "The New Ku-Kluxers" displeased Virginia's King Kleagle, who clipped the editorial and forwarded it to the Imperial Palace in Atlanta. Two weeks later Jaffé received a letter from the Klan's Department of Propagation. Imperial Kleagle Edward Young Clarke himself appealed to the editor's "sense of fair play" and sought to correct his "misperceptions" regarding the hooded order's mission. Clarke's professional background included newspaper work in an indeterminate capacity (presumably not reporting, editorial writing, or desk work), and he did not lack confidence in his ability to spin the fourth estate: "I am sure that your criticism is based upon ignorance of the facts and a notation from an article in your paper, which has been called to my attention, is an injustice to our organization. I am sure the *Virginian-Pilot* does not wish to be in the attitude of being unfair or unjust to any individual or organization."[20]

Clarke obligingly elucidated for Jaffé the relationship between the original Klan and its offspring: "The old Klan disbanded voluntarily for just reasons of which the public had no knowledge and in disbanding it accomplished certain purposes which were worth the disbanding of the organization temporarily. The organization was revived and reorganized in 1915 by a sufficient number of members of the old order to make the new organization THE Ku Klux Klan." Apparently deciding that Jaffé might require fur-

19. *Pilot,* 6 October 1920.
20. E. Y. Clarke to Louis Jaffé, 19 October 1920, Jaffé Papers; Chalmers, *Hooded Americanism,* 31.

ther tutoring, the Imperial Kleagle informed the editor that he was enclosing "A.B.C. of the Knights of the Ku Klux Klan," which he asked Jaffé to "read and make to me a comment on same." The Department of Propagation's clerical staff neglected to include the pamphlet.[21]

Jaffé probably did not know whether to laugh or cry. The hooded order's rattle-brained leadership, alliterative mumbo jumbo, and ridiculous ritualism would provide a rich vein of material for mocking and scoffing editorials. And how dire a threat could the fraternal society pose? But even then, Jaffé sensed the Klan's sinister purposes and the threat that it posed to religious and ethnic minorities. He knew that the anti-Semitism, mob hysteria, and terrorism surrounding the Frank trial and lynching had helped Simmons resurrect the Klan and that some former Knights of Mary Phagan had aided and abetted Simmons in the founding ceremony.[22]

Early reports on the secret society confirmed Jaffé's suspicions. Introduced to a Georgia audience, Simmons had silently drawn two handguns from his pockets and placed them on a table. After draping a cartridge belt over them, he produced a Bowie knife, which he plunged into the table. Then he broke his silence: "Now let all the Niggers, Catholics, Jews, and all others who disdain my imperial wizardry, come on." As word of showstopping introductions such as this and of the Klan's real agenda—which included a boycott of Jewish businesses—leaked out to the press, Jaffé's concern grew.[23]

A month after his first letter to Jaffé, Clarke expressed dismay upon learning from the *Pilot*'s editor that he still awaited arrival of the clandestine order's primer. Despite the embarrassing faux pas, the Imperial Kleagle sought to clinch the "sale": "I feel confident that . . . if I could step into your office and we could have a personal conversation of about an hour that you and I both will agree on the need and value of this organization and that there will be no word of criticism in your heart." Clarke expressed the "greatest sympathy" for the reservations Jaffé had stated regarding the need for the "most secret of secret organizations." The Klansman confided, "If I were not on the inside and knew the real facts, I might be in the same atti-

21. Clarke to Jaffé, 19 October 1920, 15 November 1920, Jaffé Papers.
22. Chambers, Shank, and Sugg, *Salt Water & Printer's Ink*, 315.
23. Chalmers, *Hooded Americanism*, 32–3.

tude." Warming to his subject, Clarke attempted to clarify the Klan's raison d'être: "[The] problem of the control of this country by the brains of the country, which largely rest in the white man's head, is not the only problem that faces America. If I could talk to you I'm sure you would agree with me that there are problems in this country today—North, South, East and West—which are just as much an emergency to meet as was the situation in the South at the close of the [Civil] War."[24]

In Danville, Virginia, the Klan—with the help of a recruiter from Atlanta—began to organize ominously close to Jaffé's family in South Boston. The *Virginian-Pilot* reported that Danville's white ministers, after "heated debate," had collectively refused to support a petition by the town's black clergy to join them in condemning the Klan. The vote had taken place in an anxious atmosphere, and the participants had pledged not to divulge information regarding the discussion.[25]

Jaffé's parents and brother traveled frequently to Danville to attend religious services at the Orthodox synagogue there. Jaffé knew the town well. When he had lived in Richmond, he had visited Danville with his family and when he called on Ida Greenberg. His family must have seemed to him vulnerable and isolated. A South Boston resident of this period recalled that the ten or so Jewish families who operated stores there stood out sharply because of their distinctive dress and religious customs. South Boston did not have a large Klan membership in this era, he said, but Yanceyville—just across the North Carolina border—earned renown as an organization stronghold.[26]

Klan activities in Norfolk first attracted public attention in the summer of 1921, when signs appearing on telephone poles in the Ocean View area advised "all undesirables" to leave town. Norfolk had a storied reputation for iniquity, and the fiat was intended to clean up licentiousness: "The eye of the unknown has been and is constantly observing. Gamblers, bootleggers, high speeders, thieves, crooks, grafters, houses of ill-fame and proprietors—this is their last warning. Beware." Had all the culprits obeyed the

24. Clarke to Jaffé, 15 November 1920, Jaffé Papers.

25. *Pilot*, 5 May 1921.

26. L. Beatrice W. Hairston, *A Brief History of Danville, Virginia: 1728–1954* (Richmond: Dietz Press, 1955), 54; Silverman, interview by author, 8 July 1996; Stevens, interview by author, 10 July 1996.

edict, the population of the city would have dropped considerably. Another sign solicited members: "If you are a man, we respect you. If you are 100 per cent American, we want you. . . . Do you believe in the tenets of the Christian religion, free schools, free speech, free press, law enforcement, liberty and white supremacy? Can you take a man's oath?"[27]

A Klan rally at the Norfolk Armory later that summer filled every seat and left almost no standing room. Surrounded by robed Knights, Colonel J. Q. Nolan from Atlanta explained that the secret society sought "to preserve racial integrity and white supremacy, assuring for unborn generations in its pristine purity that heritage bequeathed by the founders of the nation." Nolan viewed non-Anglo Saxon immigration as particularly menacing. The *Virginian-Pilot* reported that he believed that "old world tendencies have seeped into all parts of this country with the spread of polyglot races." Ironically, an adjoining story announced the arrival from New York of two rabbis seeking to raise funds for the Hebrew Sheltering and Immigration Aid Society.[28]

Shortly thereafter, local members of the Klan held their first public rally. Following a torch-bearing leader, one hundred knights filed with ghostly stealthiness down the main thoroughfare in the Ocean View district. Navy-issue bell-bottomed trousers peeked out beneath many of the robes.[29]

Regardless of the Klan's avowed reverence for the Constitution's First Amendment, underscored in the Ku Klux Kreed, Jaffé began to receive warnings to tread carefully in his editorials. Imperial Kleagle Clarke's soft sell having failed, the Klan had adopted a new rhetorical strategy. In the "Disillusioned Dragon," Jaffé signaled his intention to continue his criticism: "Anonymous warnings signed 'K.K.K.' have been received by the *Virginian-Pilot*. Neither these warnings nor any others will in the minutest degree divert this newspaper from its intention to treat illegal acts as illegal acts or from calling criminals by their right name."[30]

Back in Durham, faculty members at Jaffé's alma mater approvingly followed their prominent graduate's editorial attacks on the hooded

27. *Pilot*, 24 June 1921.
28. Ibid., 20 July 1921.
29. Ibid., 31 July 1921.
30. Ibid., 8 August 1921.

order. Their support meant much to the Trinity alumnus. Jaffé wrote to R. L. Flowers, "It is especially gratifying to me to find you in agreement with the very decided views I hold in respect to so reprehensible an organization as the Ku Klux Klan as it is at present conceived and directed."[31]

The summer of 1921 was notable, too, in that notorious polemicist H. L. Mencken's disparaging attack on the South finally penetrated the Magnolia Curtain and hit home with the sleepy southern press. The journalist and coeditor of the witty and urbane *Smart Set* had fired his first volley on southern *Kultur* in 1917 in a *New York Evening Mail* article entitled "The Sahara of the Bozart," a play on the French words "*beaux arts.*" In November 1920, Mencken's diatribe in expanded and more devastating form had filtered down to a few southern bookstores, with the publication of *Prejudices: Second Series.* But it was the reprinting of the much milder and more constructive "The South Begins to Mutter," in the summer 1921 *Current Opinion* magazine, that finally roused the region's newspaper editors. Belatedly they awoke to the damage Mencken's earlier broadsides had wrought to the region's reputation.[32]

In the expanded "Sahara of the Bozart," Mencken had argued that the South, which had at one time nurtured the nation's greatest thinkers and statesmen, had grown as desolate and lifeless as the great African desert. With characteristic panache and great exuberance, he lampooned the region and its inhabitants. "There are single acres in Europe that house more first-rate men than all the states south of the Potomac; there are probably single square miles in America," he wrote.[33]

Although Mencken regarded Virginia as the most advanced southern state, he pummeled unmercifully what had once been the "arbiter elegantiarum of the Western World." In an earlier era, the commonwealth had nurtured presidents and statesmen. Now, he wrote, "politics in Virginia are cheap, ignorant, parochial, idiotic; there is scarcely a man in office above the rank of professional job seeker. . . . A Washington or Jefferson dumped there by some act of God, would be denounced a scoundrel and jailed over-

31. Louis Jaffé to R. L. Flowers, 25 August 1921, Jaffé Papers.

32. Fred C. Hobson, *Mencken: A Life* (Baltimore: Johns Hopkins University Press, 1994), 213; Fred C. Hobson, *Serpent in Eden: H. L. Mencken and the South* (Chapel Hill: University of North Carolina Press, 1974), 24, 27, 193.

33. H. L. Mencken, *A Mencken Chrestomathy* (New York: Vintage, 1982), 186.

night." Mencken also heaped scorn on Virginia's thinkers and artists. "Elegance, *esprit,* culture? Virginia has no art, no literature, no philosophy, no mind or aspiration of her own. Her education has sunk to the Baptist seminary level; not a single contribution to human knowledge has come out of her colleges in twenty-five years; she spends less than half upon her common schools *per capita,* than any Northern state spends. In brief, an intellectual Gobi or Lapland."[34]

Mencken was an elitist. A lifelong resident of Baltimore, who had grown up in a German-American culture, he considered himself a southerner of sorts by virtue of his border-state upbringing and his reverence for a romanticized Old South. Mencken maintained that antebellum Dixie had been led by an aristocracy superior to the country's other social groups. He clung to a delusion that the nineteenth-century South had been ruled by a gentry akin to the Virginia gentlemen of the eighteenth century. Subsequent scholars and observers such as W. J. Cash would reveal the flaws in Mencken's thinking but would not effectively challenge the essential truth of his devastating critique.[35]

Defenders of the region's culture—southern newspaper editors in particular—conducted a furious counteroffensive in the summer of 1921. In *Serpent in Eden,* Mencken scholar and biographer Fred C. Hobson detailed the reactions to the Sage's assault. The Arkansas press led the attack. Mencken had mocked the Razorback State and its residents mercilessly. The *Arkansas Democrat* and the *Little Rock Trade Record* now questioned his patriotism and accused him of having close ties to Germany. "A man signing his name Menneken has been defaming the good people of the South," the editor of the *Little Rock Daily News* charged. He labeled Mencken an "infernal and ignorant mountebank" and a "miserable, uninformed wretch." Closer to Norfolk, Richmond editor Douglas Southall Freeman assailed Mencken for "his sad lack of historical perspective and positive knowledge." The *Danville (Va.) Register* called him a "bitterly prejudiced and ignorant critic of a great people." Richmond author James Branch Cabell, whom Mencken had cited in his essay as the only southern writer worth reading, warned his friend—only partly in jest—that a "lynching party

34. Ibid.
35. Hobson, *Serpent in Eden,* 18.

awaited H. L. Mencken at all points south of Maryland." Certainly, some of the anger in the southern response to "Sahara" resulted from the article's claim that many southern whites concealed black ancestry and that mulattos exhibited a clear superiority to the region's whites intellectually and artistically.[36]

Looking back on that summer, Mencken wrote that his criticism had "made a dreadful pother in the South, and brought me a great deal of violent denunciation, but all [of] the more enlightened Southerners had to admit its truth." Many did. Much to his surprise, he found the role of advisor and spiritual leader of the southern renaissance thrust on his shoulders. "Dazed at first and incredulous for some time," wrote his colleague Gerald Johnson, Mencken began to direct his attention to nurturing a generation of young southern writers, artists, scholars, and journalists. In stark contrast to the earlier attacks on him in the southern press, admiring letters from the South's young intelligentsia began to trickle northward, expressing approval of the clobbering that Mencken had dealt their region.[37]

Mencken inspired, counseled, promoted, and helped many individuals in Jaffé's professional network, including journalists whom the *Pilot*'s editor held in high regard, such as Grover Hall, Julian and Julia Harris, and Gerald Johnson. Mencken endorsed other editors and social critics whom Jaffé read appreciatively, including Virginius Dabney, W. J. Cash, Nell Battle Lewis, and Howard Odum. Critic Addison Hibbard, whose literary column would soon appear on Jaffé's editorial page, received encouragement from the Sage. Playwright Paul Green, a favorite of Jaffé's, also looked to Baltimore for support.[38]

As other southern editors swarmed to the region's defense, stinging Mencken with what he called "many waspish paragraphs," Jaffé kept his own counsel. A close reading of the newspaper's editorial page in the months following publication of Mencken's incendiary essays reveals not a single mention of Mencken or the journalistic ruckus he fomented. Jaffé knew of the uproar. He voraciously consumed opinion writing, considering

36. Ibid., 27–8; Mencken, *Mencken Chrestomathy,* 190–3.
37. Mencken, *Thirty-Five Years of Newspaper Work,* 151; Gerald W. Johnson, foreword to *Serpent in Eden,* by Fred C. Hobson.
38. Egerton, *Speak Now Against the Day,* 60–1.

this monitoring an editorial writer's duty. He had followed Mencken's work in the *Baltimore Sunpapers,* the *Smart Set,* and the other national publications that published and reprinted his work. Jaffé had also read the first two volumes of the *Prejudices* series. He may simply have considered "Sahara of the Bozart" too hot a potato for his readership's consumption. Mencken's howling jihad differed drastically from the "level-headed liberal" editorial writing of the *Virginian-Pilot.* Unlike Mencken, Jaffé had to pick and choose his battles. His attacks on the Klan soon would begin to reduce the *Pilot*'s circulation.[39]

According to one of his future associate editors, Jaffé admired Mencken and occasionally corresponded with him. (Neither the Jaffé nor the Mencken papers contain any letters exchanged between the two men.) But he did not require inspiration or mentoring from Mencken. Jaffé was older and more fully formed than Mencken devotees such as W. J. Cash and Virginius Dabney. Jaffé's upbringing and experience assured that he would not want for motivation for his editorial stances, and his editorial pulpit was a daily outlet for his opinions. The reprinting of his editorials in regional and national journals was enlarging his readership and may have diminished any desire on his part to publish in the *Smart Set* and later the tremendously influential *American Mercury,* which Mencken and George Nathan would found in 1924.[40]

Jaffé viewed Mencken with greater detachment than did many of his younger journalistic colleagues. "It is always to be borne in mind," Jaffé wrote to P. B. Young, editor of the black *Norfolk Journal and Guide,* "that Mencken is essentially a bold caricaturist and draws his pictures always in bold, crude lines—a legitimate form of art—but always to be interpreted with the limitations of that style in mind." To a former professor at Trinity, Edwin Mims, Jaffé wrote that Mencken "sometimes strikes out without verifying all of his assumptions." As a veteran, Jaffé also must have found Mencken's defense of Germany during the war troubling. Mencken maintained an abiding identification with that nation, rationalizing its militancy and aggressiveness and minimizing its role in initiating the conflict.[41]

39. Hobson, *Serpent in Eden,* 35; Louis Jaffé to Grover Hall, 22 April 1927, 16 October 1929, Jaffé Papers.

40. Alonzo Dill, interview by author, 20 November 1992.

41. Louis Jaffé to P. B. Young, 1 October 1927, Louis Jaffé to Edwin Mims, 9 Sep-

A mountain vacation in late August 1921 distracted Jaffé from his editorial duties. Margaret had fallen ill earlier in the summer. Still weary and listless, she looked forward to spending time at the Old Sweet Springs resort in West Virginia. After a sojourn there, Louis returned to Norfolk, leaving Margaret behind. She soon began to feel a "lifting of the miserable lethargy" that had plagued her and wrote that she hoped to return "well enough to be some use and not a dead weight, draining you of any tenderness and patience." Margaret enclosed a piece of goldenrod to remind him of their happy times together. She signed her letter with a series of Xs, which she indicated would one day soon come also from "Christopher and Agatha," children's names the newly married couple had chosen.[42]

Margaret extended her stay at Old Sweet Springs, and her correspondence to Louis displayed a preoccupation with illness. Although she had no fever, she monitored her temperature. She helped administer "treatments" to a sick child staying at the resort. She cautioned Louis not to become ill through overwork. Golf and hiking distracted her during the day, but at night she missed Louis "with aching." She affectionately and playfully signed her letter, "Je t'aime, je vous adore; that's me all over, Mabel; Sweetheart, MD."[43]

Louis returned to Old Sweet Springs some time later, intending apparently to surprise Margaret. He discovered instead that she had left the resort. In a letter, she wrote him of her plans to do more "flitting," and suggested that he stay there without her for a week of "frivolous vacationing." This page of the letter she signed "SWAK," which she felt her husband, with his lack of understanding of women and "their caprices," would not know meant "sealed with a kiss." On the second page, however, Margaret's tone suddenly turned angry. Possibly referring to Louis's surprise visit, she wrote, "Don't take it for granted that I understand your thoughts and plans to take

tember 1926, both in Jaffé Papers; Carl Bode, *Mencken* (Carbondale: Southern Illinois University Press, 1969), 111–5; Mencken, *Thirty-Five Years of Newspaper Work*, 52–74.

42. Louis Jaffé to Hyman Jaffe, 4 July 1921, Louis Jaffé Jr.; Louis Jaffé to Alexander Forward, 29 June 1921, Jaffé Papers; Margaret Jaffé to Louis Jaffé, 22 August 1921, Louis Jaffé Jr.; Edward Alfred Pollard, *The Virginia Tourist* (Philadelphia: J. B. Lippincott, 1870), 239–41; Perceval Reniers, *The Springs of Virginia: Life, Love, and Death at the Waters, 1775–1900* (Chapel Hill: University of North Carolina Press, 1941), 277.

43. Margaret Jaffé to Louis Jaffé, [August 1921], Louis Jaffé Jr.

care of me and help me unless you tell them to me. That's masculine and artless and stupid, and it hurts." Perhaps regarding an interaction the two had had during his earlier trip to Old Sweet Springs, she warned him to "always keep away from me when I have such headaches."[44]

Upon his return to Norfolk, Jaffé learned of an assertion by Imperial Kleagle Clarke in a Klan newsletter that the secret society counted Norfolk's police chief as a member. According to Clarke, the chief had developed a secret plan to arm local Klan members, should racial tension give way to rioting. Jaffé responded by declaring that the mayor and law authorities should investigate the organization at once.[45]

This censure prompted a lengthy letter in which an anonymous writer obliquely explained the reasons for the order's discriminatory criteria for membership: "The K.K.K. do not take Catholics into this organization, because they believe that every Catholic recognizes the POPE as the Sovereign power of this World. . . . Jews are not taken in because most of the foreign population of the big cities of this Country are of a type that does not represent the ideals and principles for which this country was established." Jews and Catholics, the letter continued, had conspired to remove the Bible from the classroom; the Klan, although it believed strongly in separation of church and state, nonetheless intended to reintroduce the teaching of Protestantism in public schools. Jaffé's editorial had insulted the "100% Native Born, White American Anglo-Saxons" who comprised the secret society.[46]

As the number of anonymous communications Jaffé received from the Klan increased, he urged the society to end its secretiveness. In "Why Not Unmask?" the editor stated that before he would cease his criticism of the order, he needed to know that its mission and methods did not violate the law. He also needed to know the identity of the many correspondents who protested his reproachful editorials and who "labor pathetically to defend the Klan's case." Were these authors honest or were they the "Devil quoting scripture for his purpose?" If the Klan truly stood for high-minded

44. Margaret Jaffé to Louis Jaffé, [August/September 1921], ibid.
45. *Pilot*, 17, 18 September 1921; Jackson, *Ku Klux Klan in the City*, 81–2.
46. KKK to Louis Jaffé, 18 September 1921.

and noble principles, its members should proudly announce their affiliation with it. This would only increase their standing in the community. Let the Klansman "be a 100 per cent American in the open instead of in the dark," he concluded.[47]

Just across the Elizabeth River the next day, Portsmouth resident M. Cohen received his second threatening letter from writers who claimed to represent the Klan: "We ride by night, we move by day. We hear such words that you may say. Your number now we won't forget and will call around to see you yet." Refusing to believe that a klavern existed in his city, Cohen attributed the letters to children; but Klan recruiters experienced considerable success in Portsmouth and elsewhere in the Hampton Roads region throughout the decade.[48]

It would be hard to fault Jaffé if he derived some pleasure from a story that broke that week, linking Klan publicists E. Y. Clarke and Elizabeth Tyler in an embarrassing scandal. Two years earlier Clarke's wife, May, had directed Atlanta police to a house of questionable repute, where they had discovered the founders of the Southern Publicity Association not quite sober and not quite clothed. Their nearly forgotten conviction for "disorderly conduct" now surfaced in September 1921 as a result of inspired investigative reporting by the *New York World*'s Rowland Thomas. In a futile attempt to suppress the exposé, Atlanta Klansmen purchased all three thousand copies of the newspaper available in the state. Although the court records pertaining to the arrest and trial had mysteriously disappeared, the incident tarnished the reputations of Clarke and Tyler and greatly impaired their ability to represent an organization purporting to espouse high-minded goals of decency and morality. Clarke later confessed to having been arrested many times and to having been jailed in Indiana for possession of alcohol shortly after delivering a speech on law enforcement. Revelations concerning the couple's excessive profiteering earned them more notoriety.[49]

The Klan's leadership suffered another setback in October when its hard-drinking, visionary kingpin, Imperial Wizard William Simmons,

47. *Pilot*, 22 September 1921.
48. Ibid., 24 September 1921; Chalmers, *Hooded Americanism*, 231.
49. *Pilot*, 22, 25 September 1921; *New York World*, 19 September 1921; Jackson, *Ku Klux Klan in the City*, 11; Chalmers, *Hooded Americanism*, 36–8.

keeled over on the third day of his testimony before the Rules Committee of the U.S. House of Representatives during hearings regarding the secret society. Until that point, Simmons had comported himself reasonably well before the committee, but a new generation of Klan leaders lurking in the wings stood ready to depose the order's upper echelon. Simmons, Clarke, and Tyler soon faded into obscurity. Hiram W. Evans, a Texas dentist, would preside over the Klan during its period of greatest power.[50]

As Congress conducted its week-long investigation of the Klan, Jaffé kept up the heat at the *Pilot,* publishing three anti-Klan editorials in six days. In "Time to Unwrap," he marveled at the Klan's appeal: "It was always more or less of a mystery how even congenital joiners could fall for Klancraft with its shoddy sentiment, its blathering ritual and its desecrated English—how Americans of normal intelligence could be induced to part with $10 apiece to test the truth of the promise that 'he who explores the Dismal Depths of the Mystic Cave and from thence attains the lofty heights of Superior Knighthood may sit among the gods in the Empire Invisible.'" But the central problem with the Klan, as Jaffé saw it, lay in its secrecy. "If the Ku Klux Klan aspires to a respected place in American society it must divest itself of its false-faces and its cerements," Jaffé urged. "It must unwrap and be identified."[51]

On October 17, in "The Pretenders," he returned to the theme of his very first editorial attack on the clandestine order. Simmons had no right to revive the Klan and appropriate its name. In "Merci," two days later, Jaffé relished the rich irony of the Klan's having extended to Marshal Ferdinand Foch, the former generalissimo of the Allied armies, an invitation to meet with the secret society during a planned visit to the United States. Jaffé wondered how the Klan would explain to "France's most conspicuous Catholic layman" its policy of excluding the marshal's coreligionists from membership.[52]

Jaffé may have believed at this juncture that Klan scandals and internecine struggles, the congressional inquiry, the *World's* investigative reporting, and the stiffening backbone some of his editorial peers had begun

50. Chalmers, *Hooded Americanism,* 100–7.
51. *Pilot,* 15 October 1921.
52. Ibid., 17, 19 October 1921.

to display had put the hooded order on the ropes. Indeed, it is difficult to understand how the organization weathered the crisis. The commotion died down in the spring of 1922, and for a brief period the press directed its attention elsewhere. It may have seemed to many outsiders that the order was waning. Nothing could have been further from the truth. Even observers as astute as Jaffé underestimated the tremendous appeal of the Klan and the powerful undercurrents of fraternalism, anomie, religious fundamentalism, xenophobia, and vigilantism it tapped.

Late in 1921 Louis and Margaret learned that she was pregnant. Both yearned for children. That summer at Old Sweet Springs, when asked by a young boy if she had children, Margaret replied that she had none but wished she had ten. Throughout the fall and winter, she stayed busy reading and writing; her book reviews appeared regularly on the *Virginian-Pilot*'s editorial page.[53]

Margaret aspired to a literary career, although precisely in what capacity is not clear. The success she had experienced as a reporter and Sunday feature writer probably whetted her appetite for a larger audience for her work. Throughout the decade she would continue her feature writing and contribute occasional articles to magazines. She also discussed with her husband the possibility that the couple might purchase and edit a newspaper of their own. Inconsequential as Margaret's work as a book reviewer for the *Pilot* may seem, Emily Clark, who held the same position at the less-literary *Richmond News Leader*, had with almost no experience co-founded and edited the small but tremendously influential *Reviewer*. Mencken would help guide the fledgling journal and came to see it as the principal outlet for southern authors and critics.[54]

Jaffé, too, lauded the formation of the *Reviewer*; his support for what would become a pioneering vehicle for southern literature appears to have predated Mencken's involvement in the venture. "The attempt to

53. Margaret Jaffé to Louis Jaffé, [August/September 1921], Louis Jaffé Jr.; see *Pilot*, 9, 16 October 1921, 1 November 1921, 1 December 1921.

54. Louis Jaffé to Harry Byrd, 7 May 1930, Jaffé Papers; Louis Jaffé to J. J. Lankes, 22 March 1930, Jaffé Papers; Margaret Jaffé to Louis Jaffé, [August/September 1921], Louis Jaffé Jr.; Emily Clark to Louis Jaffé, 25 July 1922, Jaffé Papers; Hobson, *Serpent in Eden*, 36–41.

found in Richmond a self-sustaining magazine shows at once high hope and surpassing courage," Jaffé wrote. "The quality of this courage may be better appreciated from the fact that 'The Reviewer,' whose first issue appears in a few days, is to offer no sops to circulation in the form of sepia half-tones of movie vamps. It purposes to live or die by its high literary standard." He conceded that the magazine faced an uphill climb, but he implored his readers to "help and hope."[55]

A second editorial urging support for the "South's one and only magazine of discriminating literary quality," published in a "city that still manages, despite its material prosperity and absence of a public library, to retain its primacy in the South as a center of literary endeavor," brought a letter of gratitude from Emily Clark. The *Reviewer*'s editor disclosed that she admired the *Pilot*'s editorial page and felt that it had the "best literary quality of any of the southern papers." Clark confided that a member of her board of directors shared this view.[56]

Since assuming his position at the *Pilot,* Jaffé had greatly magnified the editorial page's focus on the arts. He felt he had a role to play in furthering the southern cultural renaissance by helping to "establish on a firmer footing the nurture and enjoyment of the fine arts." As a young reporter at the *Richmond Times-Dispatch,* he had contributed occasional book reviews to that paper, and he now sought to expand the *Pilot*'s treatment of literature. In his "Books and Letters" column, he featured reviews by local critics. He exposed the *Pilot*'s readers to belles lettres in the "Literary Lantern," a feature contributed by distinguished University of North Carolina academics Addison Hibbard and Howard Mumford Jones, both supporters of Mencken's campaign to revive southern letters. The paper's "Contemporary Poets" column brought modern poetry to Norfolk and promoted local writers such as Mary Sinton Leitch as well as Norfolk's own literary magazine, the *Lyric.*[57]

In 1924 Jaffé began to run Mencken's new column in the *Pilot*'s Sunday edition. Mencken began by dealing with noncontroversial literary criticism but soon enlarged his scope to include hot-button political and social

55. *Pilot,* 19 January 1921.

56. Ibid., 24 July 1922; Emily Clark to Louis Jaffé, 25 July 1922, Jaffé Papers.

57. *Pilot,* 1 January 1940; see *Richmond Times-Dispatch,* 15 February 1914; *Montgomery News Messenger,* 30 May 1957; Hobson, *Serpent in Eden,* 54.

issues. The *Chicago Tribune,* which syndicated the series, found the material difficult to place once Mencken began to "take . . . hack[s] at the Methodists, the American Legion, or any of the other inhabitants of [his] menagerie of hobgoblins." Most papers dropped the series, and Mencken ended it in 1927. Jaffé ran the column continuously throughout its short life.[58]

An emphasis on international politics also characterized Jaffé's editorial page. For a southern paper, it devoted an uncommon degree of attention to foreign affairs, even taking into account postwar Norfolk's heightened interaction with other parts of the world. In a single edition of the *Virginian-Pilot* in the early 1920s, a reader might find editorials dealing with the American occupation of Haiti, labor activism in England, and political upheaval in Germany. In retrospect, one wonders how many bleary-eyed subscribers opening the paper at breakfast tables could have persevered through nuanced discussions—no matter how skillfully written—of Albanian politics, the Kemalist revolution in Turkey, and Chinese nationalism. Jaffé's editorial page reflected his abiding interest in other cultures and peoples.[59]

As Jaffé directed his attention to the Klan, he began—slowly at first—to shape his attack on lynching. Interestingly, given the intensity of his editorial assault on the practice as the decade wore on, he did not respond directly to specific lynchings that occurred in Virginia early in his tenure as editor.

The first of these lynchings took place in the early morning hours of November 14, 1920, in the little southwestern Virginia town of Wise. A black man, twenty-five-year-old David Hunt, who had recently arrived in the area to work in a coal mine, had been accused of raping an "aged" white woman. The Associated Press reported that the crew of a passenger train had pursued Hunt via locomotive and captured him after an "exciting chase." The next morning a seventy-five-man mob battered down the jail door, dragged Hunt from his cell, strung him up by his ankles from a bridge near the site of his alleged crime, and riddled him with bullets. Douglas

58. Louis Jaffé to Arthur Crawford, 5 December 1924, Jaffé Papers; Mencken, *Thirty-Five Years of Newspaper Work,* 135; see *Pilot,* 5, 14 May 1925, 17 April 1927.

59. Chambers, Shank, and Sugg, *Salt Water & Printer's Ink,* 314; *Pilot,* 17 October 1920, 13 January 1921, 3 December 1927, 17 April 1927.

Southall Freeman of the *Richmond News Leader* and John Mitchell, editor of the black *Richmond Planet,* lobbied Governor Westmoreland Davis to conduct an investigation. Jaffé did not comment on the lynching.[60]

Wise and the surrounding area had a long tradition of backwardness, vigilantism, and frontier justice. The influx of black laborers into the mountainous county to work in the mines had exacerbated racial tensions. Whites—unaccustomed to living in proximity with large numbers of blacks—used violence as a means of defining racial boundaries and venting their frustration over their rapidly changing social order and their exploitation at the hands of distant capitalists.[61]

Law authorities in Wise comported themselves much better three weeks later, when thirty-five men from the neighboring mining town of Appalachia rushed the jail in an attempt to administer a similar brand of justice to another black man, whom press accounts identified only as the "negro named Williams." This time, however, the mob had telegraphed its intentions, allowing the constabulary time to prepare a defense. As the vigilantes fired into the building, Sheriff A. L. Corder and five heavily armed deputies shot back. The mob retreated, leaving two dead behind. The would-be lynch mob then regrouped and obtained reinforcements—by one account they now numbered six hundred—and prepared to dynamite the jail. In the nick of time, two Virginia National Guard companies under Governor Davis's orders arrived and whisked the prisoner to Roanoke. "Bully for Corder," a local branch of the NAACP exulted in a letter to the sheriff.[62]

This time Jaffé spoke out, applauding the actions of Wise's law authorities, the citizens who stood behind them, and the governor: "The garrison that held the jail at Wise very properly met force with force. And the State authorities very properly sent troops to the scene. Force is an argument that violence can understand. Those who are inclined to lawlessness

60. *Pilot,* 15 November 1920; *Lynchburg (Va.) News,* 16 November 1920; *Guide,* 16 January 1923; *Richmond News Leader,* 15 November 1920; *Richmond Planet,* 20 November 1920.

61. Workers of the Writers' Program, *Virginia: A Guide to the Old Dominion,* 538; *Looking Back: Wise County in the Early Years* (Wise, Va.: Lonesome Pine Office on Youth, 1992), 227–34; Brundage, *Lynching in the New South,* 143–5.

62. *Bluefield (W.Va.) Daily Telegraph,* 7 December 1920; *Lynchburg (Va.) News,* 7 December 1920; W. G. Young to A. L. Corder, 7 December 1920, NAACP Papers.

have a high regard for the arm of the law when it displays real strength. The surest way of crushing violence is to give its votaries to understand that they can not defy the law with impunity, that the hand of all good citizens will be raised against them should they break bounds, and that the State is determined to maintain order at all costs."[63]

Surprisingly, Wise's commonwealth's attorney indicted many members of the mob that had lynched Hunt, and won convictions of two of them in early 1923. The Virginia Supreme Court of Appeals refused to hear the men's appeals, and Governor Elbert Lee Trinkle declined clemency. Both men served two-year sentences. The *Norfolk Journal and Guide* celebrated, claiming this constituted the first sentencing of whites for lynching blacks in the state's history.[64]

The next Virginia lynching occurred in Tobacco on August 3, 1921. The little village was located in the rural Southside, in the middle of the state's "black belt," where the number of blacks equaled or exceeded that of whites. Although lynchings had occurred in the region before, the entrenched social order, established system of labor relations, and accepted racial hierarchy created a stability that contrasted strongly with the edginess in parts of southwestern Virginia. What transpired in Tobacco revealed simmering tensions just beneath the placid surface.[65]

A two-thousand-person mob waylaid three law officers transporting Lem Johnson, a black man accused of murdering the village postmaster in his store. According to the deputy sheriff in charge of the party, the masked men who crowded around the vehicle worked efficiently and left no clues as to their identities. A "reliable source," however, informed the press that "included in the mob were [some of the region's] most prominent citizens." The horde transported Johnson to the scene of the alleged crime, forced him to confess, and hanged him from a tree. The next morning the funeral procession for the murdered postmaster passed almost directly underneath Johnson's swaying body.[66]

Fearing that another black accused of complicity in the murder

63. *Pilot,* 7 December 1920.

64. *Guide,* 6 January 1923, 17 March 1923.

65. Workers of the Writers' Program, *Virginia: A Guide to the Old Dominion,* 474; Odum, *Southern Regions,* 134; Brundage, *Lynching in the New South,* 150–4.

66. *Pilot,* 6 August 1921; *Richmond Planet,* 6 August 1921.

would be lynched, law authorities rushed him from the jail in the county seat of Lawrenceville and traveled a circuitous route of more than 150 miles to reach nearby Petersburg. Drivers passing through the region reported seeing dozens of automobiles ominously parked alongside the roads. The governor ordered the city's entire police force to guard the jail until the prisoner could be sped to the state capital.[67]

Editor John Mitchell decried Johnson's lynching: "Notwithstanding the integrity and adequacy of our courts, the mob spirit prevailed in the usually quiet, law-abiding community, the law was robbed of its functioning and the tree and rope were exalted above the judge and the jury. . . . This example of outlawry must not be permitted to stand as a precedent." Jaffé did not join Mitchell in speaking out against the Johnson lynching.[68]

Jaffé's response to an early federal antilynching bill introduced into the House of Representatives later in the year by Missourian Leonides C. Dyer may partially explain his reticence and defines the limits to which the editor felt he could go in opposition to mob violence at this time. Dyer sought to employ the equal protection clause of the Fourteenth Amendment to make lynching a federal offense and to hold local law authorities responsible for preventing mob violence. The Dyer bill also would have fined a county in which a lynching occurred ten thousand dollars to compensate victims' families.[69]

Although Jaffé termed lynching an "abomination that cannot be too severely dealt with," he did not support the passage of a federal antilynching bill. He objected—as did virtually all of his peers in the southern press—to the numerous antilynching bills that wended their way through Congress, on the grounds that they undermined state sovereignty. "While [the Dyer bill] is deliberately aimed at the South," he wrote, "its most baleful effect . . . will be on the sovereign status of the States. It would clear the way for Federal assumption of authority on an unlimited scale. For, if the central government has the authority to interfere with the States in the case

67. *Pilot,* 4 August 1921.

68. *Richmond Planet,* 6 August 1921.

69. Roy Wilkins, *Standing Fast: The Autobiography of Roy Wilkins* (New York: Da Capo Press, 1994), 51; "Editorial Paragraphs," *Nation,* 4 January 1922, 3; "The Federal Anti-Lynching Bill," *Outlook,* 11 January 1922, 46–7.

of lynching, it has the authority to interfere in all other criminal matters affecting life, liberty and property."[70]

Jaffé believed that lynchers engaged in murder both individually and collectively and that states already had an adequate body of law to deal with the crime. "Lynching is an evil that calls for an unsparing suppressive effort," he asserted. "But the suppression should be applied by the States and their officials—not by the Federal Government." Jaffé did not broach the obvious question his argument begged: What would spur inert state law authorities to action? The fact that an intellectual of Jaffé's caliber, liberal leanings, and cosmopolitan experience so ardently defended the rights of the states in light of those entities' long record of lethargy in dealing with lynchings is telling. It bespeaks the powerful influence his southern upbringing exerted upon him.[71]

When the Republican-dominated House easily passed the Dyer bill, Jaffé expressed the hope that the Senate would act to kill the proposed legislation. Late in 1922, southern senators did just that in a blustering filibuster. Although the leadership of the Republican majority in the Senate made a face-saving display of support for the bill to curry favor with their black constituents, a widespread rumor accused them of having struck a sub rosa bargain with southern Democratic colleagues not to challenge their obstructive tactics aggressively. Supporters of the legislation sought comfort in the fact that the graphic congressional testimony about lynchings had underscored for the American people the horrors of the crime. Never again, however, would a federal antilynching bill come so close to passage.[72]

Jaffé resented the intrusion into the South's affairs by "so-called friends of the colored people [such] as champions of antilynching legislation who are proceeding on the false assumption that the whites and the blacks are natural enemies." He argued that this meddling worsened race relations

---

70. *Pilot*, 19 December 1921, 28 January 1922.

71. Ibid., 19 December 1921.

72. Ibid., 28 January 1922; *Nation*, 13 December 1922, 650; Robert L. Zangrando, *The NAACP Crusade Against Lynching, 1909–1950* (Philadelphia: Temple University Press, 1980), 69–70; Myrdal, *An American Dilemma*, 565; Albert P. Blaustein and Robert L. Zangrando, eds., *Civil Rights and African Americans: A Documentary History* (Evanston, Ill.: Northwestern University Press, 1991), 350–1; W. Augustus Low and Virgil A. Clift, eds., *Encyclopedia of Black America* (New York: Da Capo Press, 1984), 619.

by stirring up prejudice. "Racial adjustment" would be best served by cooperation between the region's liberal leaders, both black and white. He lauded the recent Tuskegee Negro Conference, hosted by the institute's principal, Robert Moton. Pointing to enhanced funding for black schools and what he perceived as a greater degree of legal justice for blacks, Moton saw evidence of improved racial understanding. "The wise leadership of both races is working along lines that promise solution," Jaffé wrote. "The clear-sighted colored people know that the white people of the South are their true friends and that this friendship, coupled with mutuality of interests, promises fair dealing."[73]

Jaffé believed that liberal southerners—black and white—working in concert could do much to improve racial relations, particularly to eliminate lynchings. He saw evidence of the formation of a "new public temper," characterized by respect for the law and abhorrence of mob justice. Schoolteachers, college professors, the clergy, authors, and playwrights all had roles to play in educating the public and advocating this new view. He charged journalists with special responsibility. Newspapers had to report crimes committed by blacks against whites, but stories did not have to sensationalize events and inflame passions, Jaffé cautioned. Such cases created the most severe tensions between the races and could easily spark lawlessness. He cited the *Virginian-Pilot*'s coverage in August 1922 of a black man's murder of two whites. The paper and the city's other presses had "handled this difficult class of news" in a restrained and responsible manner. The media, working in conjunction with law authorities, had succeeded in defusing the incident.[74]

Jaffé appreciated the fact that P. B. Young, his counterpart at the black *Norfolk Journal and Guide,* had commended the *Pilot*'s handling of the murder. Jaffé had attended carefully to the *Journal*'s news and editorial coverage, specifically "its carefully considered opinions on the many-sided race question." He praised the paper as representing the "best that Southern negro journalism has so far produced." Jaffé believed that the *Journal* and the *Pilot* shared a "high duty in the service of justice and inter-racial understanding."[75]

That summer a joyous event occurred in his life, distracting him from weighty editorial issues. In Norfolk's Sarah Leigh Hospital, Margaret gave birth to Louis Christopher Jaffé.

73. *Pilot,* 31 January 1922.
74. Ibid., 11 August 1922.
75. Ibid.

7   THE ROARING TWENTIES

The bullish economy of the Roaring Twenties changed the lives of many Americans for the better. Growing salaries and a reduction in the workweek spurred consumerism and participation in leisure activities. An increased percentage of the population found it possible to purchase automobiles and electrical appliances, previously considered toys for the rich. Americans worshiped at the altar of free enterprise and capitalism. One best-selling book went so far as to portray Jesus as a successful businessman and joiner and Christianity as a sales organization.[1]

New communication technologies brought glamorous media personalities and their worldly attitudes to all corners of America. Hollywood studios sought to produce a picture a week for the twenty-two thousand theaters that had sprung up by the decade's end. Eight years after the first commercial radio station began broadcasting in 1920, fifty million listeners tuned in.[2]

The Jazz Age and the concomitant changes in the social order provided the Ku Klux Klan and moral reformers with a legion of hobgoblins to demonize. Evolving religious, social, and sexual mores—in short, the waning of many traditional values—triggered a backlash that reinvigorated old prejudices. Some influential figures such as Henry Ford, perceiving Jews as the enemy on several domestic fronts, fanned the anti-Semitic sentiment that flourished in the postwar period. Jews pulled the strings behind the scenes and undermined American institutions, Ford's *Dearborn Independent* claimed; Jewish gamblers corrupted baseball, a Hebrew song trust made jazz the national music, and Hollywood studio heads churned out Jewish

---

1. David H. Bennett, *The Party of Fear: The American Far Right from Nativism to the Militia Movement* (New York: Vintage, 1995), 199–201.

2. Ibid., 200.

propaganda. The Detroit inventor and philanthropist painted Jews as a cultural menace even more dire than the harrowing political and economic threat he believed they posed. Ford's accusations resonated with many Americans. In the early years of the decade, a Chicago employment agency reported that two-thirds of its clients specified they did not want Jewish applicants.[3]

Of the large percentage of American families—particularly those residing in rural areas—who remained poor, unaffected by the booming economy, thousands flocked to the industrial cities in search of work. Throughout the 1920s urban migration continued unabated, but the new city dwellers often found themselves adrift, without benefit of kinship and friendship ties or the social and religious institutions that played such an important role in small-town life. Anomie fueled a search for community.

A plethora of service clubs and social fraternities filled the void for many people. Others found comfort and validation of their beliefs in religion. Most of the joiners and believers intended no malevolence. The danger developed when the rabble-rousing leaders of some of these organizations scapegoated minorities. The complementary appeals of fundamentalism and nativism exerted a powerful appeal for millions of white Protestant Americans, while intimidating Jews, Catholics, blacks, immigrants, and freethinkers.

Jaffé battled against these narrow-minded and exclusionary forces by challenging their assumptions and refuting their hypotheses. In "Are We Better or Worse?" written early in the 1920s, he asked his readers: "Virtue for virtue and vice for vice, is it not true that we are a better and more moral people than we were, say a generation ago?" He methodically punctured the moral reformers' rhetoric by contrasting the present to the past. "On every corner to-day there is a movie," he conceded. "But in the good old days on every corner there was a saloon. We have less respect for hell and damnation but we don't work little children in coal mines. We talk somewhat freely about sex but we don't allow girls and boys to grow up in criminal ignorance. A generation ago we were more given to uttering loud Amens but we looked on with cheerful indifference while cotton mills depopulated the kindergartens. There were longer skirts those days—yes, and longer hours

3. Ibid., 205–6.

for shop girls. Public opinion did not tolerate toddling but it did tolerate police-protected red light districts, combinations in restraint of trade, railroad passes for members of the Legislature and a chattel status for women." He clinched his argument with the observation that "short skirts will follow long skirts and long skirts will follow short skirts in dreary cycles and jazz will go the way of the tom-tom and something else will take its place, but Morality will climb on and on. We must hold to this faith or acknowledge that civilization is a failure."[4]

Billy Sunday's return to the area at the decade's midpoint evoked from Jaffé a variation on this theme. The aging Sunday's influence began to decline as the 1920s wore on, and his message grew more extremist. He blamed "foreigners" and "modernists"—terms he defined poorly or not at all—for most of the nation's problems. On the opening night of his six-week engagement in nearby Newport News, Sunday assailed immigrants who "bring their damnable continental customs with them" and arrive without "an American hair in their heads nor an American thought in their old brains."[5]

Jaffé struck back forcefully at the confluence of old-fashioned religion and nativism. He termed the evangelist's sermon, which a trombone-twirling musical director had introduced, the "kind of stuff which, fed to the patriots with selections from the Scriptures and . . . the trombone, breeds a generation of kluxers, chauvinists and witch-hunters. . . . It is a dreary business—this reviving of the people's flagging religious spirits with large intravenous injections of prejudice. We wish Billy Sunday would have done with it. Perhaps there are no human emotions less in need of religious stimulation than the emotions of prejudice, suspicion and hate. We seem to come by these virtues naturally and without need of external assistance. The function of the religion of Christ, it would seem, is to abate their intensity instead of to whip them up."[6]

In the summer of 1922, the resignation of his associate editor forced Jaffé to search for a replacement. Fortunately for Jaffé and the *Pilot,* John New-

4. *Pilot,* 19 June 1921.

5. William G. McLoughlin Jr., *Billy Sunday Was His Real Name* (Chicago: University of Chicago Press, 1955), 276–7; *Pilot,* 3 March 1925.

6. Ibid.; Bruns, *Preacher,* 103–4.

ton Aiken, a feature writer and business reporter for the *Pilot*'s afternoon competitor, the *Norfolk Ledger-Dispatch,* applied for the job. The two newspapermen already knew each other well. Aiken had been a fellow student at Trinity College and had succeeded Jaffé as editor of the *Chronicle.* With Jaffé's support, Aiken had secured his first real newspaper job at the *Richmond Times-Dispatch.* The two men even had shared an apartment in Virginia's capital for several years before Aiken returned to his home state of Tennessee to clerk for a judge. Although Aiken had seen no action during the war, he had earned a captaincy in the Allied Expeditionary Force.[7]

The new associate editor began work in February 1923, earning the same fifty-dollar-a-week salary he had drawn at the *Ledger.* Jaffé made the deal more palatable with a promise of raises to come. In the interim, Aiken supplemented his wages by freelancing for trade papers, particularly those connected with the coal industry. The armistice had done nothing to diminish Norfolk's standing as a coal center; at times hundreds of colliers lay anchored in its harbors, lined up to receive cargoes bound for Europe. Aiken had excelled as a business reporter and had developed useful industry contacts. He quickly proved his worth as an associate editor, and his writing attracted attention throughout the region.[8]

Aiken analyzed editorial topics dispassionately and logically. He did not approve of flair in editorials. In his history of the *Baltimore Sun,* where Aiken later was employed, Harold Williams wrote that Aiken's subordinates there, believing that his editor's pencil frequently bled the life from their copy, declared that he "had an instinct for the telling word and apt phrase and would delete them." On the matters of Aiken's humanitarianism and progressive beliefs, however, his colleagues maintained that he "brought to his work a political liberalism as firm as the generosity with which he defended it."[9]

Jaffé retained command of the editorial page, but he delegated work responsibilities fairly. Each day he and Aiken wrote two editorials

---

7. Chambers, Shank, and Sugg, *Salt Water & Printer's Ink,* 313; Newton Aiken, *Newton Aiken Autobiography* (Baltimore: Baltimore Sun Library, 1979), V-9, II-16, II-3, II-4, III-8; Louis Jaffé to Lucien Starke, 27 June 1923, Jaffé Papers.

8. Aiken, *Newton Aiken Autobiography,* V-3–V-5.

9. Harold A. Williams, *The Baltimore Sun, 1837–1987* (Baltimore: Johns Hopkins University Press, 1987), 303.

apiece. With over three years of experience behind him as the *Pilot*'s editor, Jaffé had developed a strong understanding of local issues and had regained his grasp of state politics. He authored most of the editorials that focused on these topics, as well as on international relations. Aiken wrote primarily on national affairs and politics. He would later describe the *Pilot*'s editorial duo as perfectionists, who worked harder and longer hours than the reporting staff. With Aiken at his side, Jaffé accomplished some of his most impressive work.[10]

Throughout the 1920s, the *Virginian-Pilot*'s editorial page featured a number of political columns in addition to Mencken's. The commentary of Mark Sullivan, who had earned renown earlier in life as a muckraking journalist for *Ladies Home Journal, McClure's,* and *Collier's,* appeared in the *Pilot* three times a week for part of the decade. When Sullivan grew more conservative as he aged, Jaffé replaced him with Charles Michelson, head of the *New York World*'s Washington bureau. The *London Times*'s erudite and eccentric Washington correspondent, Willmott Lewis, followed Michelson. A medical article authored by a physician and a Monday-morning sermon contributed by a Methodist minister supplemented the political columns and the literary features and book reviews.[11]

Winsor McCay, whose *New York Herald* Syndicate–distributed comic strip, "Little Nemo," had achieved great popularity, drew many of the *Pilot*'s political cartoons. Jay Norwood "Ding" Darling, whose work combined deep affection for the democratic process with a healthy skepticism regarding its excesses, drew others. After two years with the *New York Herald,* Darling returned to his home in Des Moines, where he eventually earned a million dollars and two Pulitzer Prizes for his cartoons. Jaffé also optioned the McClure Newspaper Syndicate's "The Young Lady Across the Way," which portrayed a young woman who, without the benefit of masculine guidance, reached mistaken conclusions about the world around her.[12]

10. Aiken, *Newton Aiken Autobiography,* V-10, V-11.

11. Charles Fisher, *The Columnists* (New York: Howell, Soskin, 1944), 136–50; Sam G. Riley, *Biographical Dictionary of American Newspaper Columnists* (Westport, Conn.: Greenwood, 1995), 317–8; Cabell Phillips, ed., *Dateline: Washington, The Story of National Affairs Journalism in the Life and Times of the National Press Club* (Garden City, N.Y.: Doubleday, 1949), 64; *Struggles in War and Peace, 1939–1966,* vol. 5, *The History of the Times* (London: Time Books, 1984), 151–2; Aiken, *Newton Aiken Autobiography,* V-10, V-11.

12. Elmo Scott Watson, *A History of Newspaper Syndicates in the United States,*

Jaffé regularly headed the editorial page with four short quips, a sentence or two in length, that cleverly summarized news and social trends: "How soon France gets out of Germany will have something to do with how much" and "Naturally, La Follette figured that if he accepted nomination from the Reds his candidacy would be marooned." Jaffé and Aiken labored over even this minor feature of their page. *Literary Digest,* which summarized opinion writing, compiled a full page of the best of these quotations from newspapers around the country in its "Topics in Brief" section. In 1924, the *Pilot* averaged well over one quotation per issue of the weekly magazine. With ever-increasing frequency, the *Digest* and other publications also excerpted and reprinted the *Pilot*'s editorials, making it the most widely quoted paper in the South and among the top in the nation.[13]

Jaffé's editorial page especially attracted the attention of his editorial peers at the *Baltimore Sunpapers,* which throughout the 1920s ranked among the country's great newspapers. Baltimore had many historic ties to the Old South, and the *Sunpapers* turned their attention with great frequency in that direction. The *Evening Sun*'s editorial page in particular, under editor Hamilton Owens, vigorously attended to southern issues. Drawing upon some of the South's best journalistic talent, Owens developed a network of special correspondents throughout the region. Mencken's "Sahara of the Bozart" essay in its earliest form first appeared in the *Evening Sun.* Jaffé's approval by the editors of the *Sunpapers* signified his arrival as a major force in southern journalism.[14]

Jaffé had likely come to Owens's notice prior to 1924, but at the urging of his boss, J. Edwin Murphy, the *Evening Sun*'s crusty managing

---

1865–1935 (Chicago: n.p., 1936), 55, 59; Charles Press, *The Political Cartoon* (Rutherford, N.J.: Farleigh Dickinson University Press, 1981), 60–1, 277; Emery, Emery, and Roberts, *Press in America,* 441; Roger A. Fischer, *Them Damned Pictures: Explorations in American Political Art* (North Haven, Conn.: Archon, 1996), 189; Gerald W. Johnson, *The Lines are Drawn: American Life Since the First World War as Reflected in the Pulitzer Prize Cartoons* (Philadelphia: J. B. Lippincott, 1958), 30–5, 134–9.

13. "Topics in Brief," *Literary Digest,* 19 July 1924, 17; "Topics in Brief," *Literary Digest,*16 August 1924, 15; Emery, Emery, and Roberts, *Press in America,* 160; Louis Jaffé to Lucien Starke, 27 June 1923, Jaffé Papers.

14. Gerald W. Johnson et al., *The Sunpapers of Baltimore, 1837–1937* (New York: Alfred A. Knopf, 1937), 366–82, 384–5, 395; Williams, *Baltimore Sun,* 164–88.

editor, Owens established formal contact with the *Pilot*'s editor that fall. The demanding Murphy commanded respect from his subordinates. According to one awestruck colleague, he "ruled the premises with thunder and lightning." Compliments from this newspaperman's newspaperman did not come gratuitously.[15]

In a letter, Owens informed Jaffé that Murphy had gone down to Virginia Beach to do some golfing; "but," said Owens, "so far as I can discover he spent most of his time reading your editorial page." Murphy had complimented Jaffé's work so glowingly that Owens wished to develop an exchange whereby the two editors would receive copies of each other's papers. Owens ended his letter graciously: "I don't know that reading the *Evening Sun* would do you as much good as Mr. Murphy seems to think reading your paper will do us, but perhaps you will be willing to take the chance."[16]

Jaffé did not shrink from apprising management of the accolades his editorial page had earned as he pressed for raises for his associate and himself. In June Jaffé reported to publisher Lucien Starke that Aiken had made "steady progress" but that his salary "embarrasses him." Aiken would seek work at another paper if he did not receive a fifteen-dollar increase, the editor warned. Jaffé also made clear that he too deserved a raise: "I am doing as effective work on the *Virginian-Pilot* as any editor is doing on any paper anywhere in the South—not excepting the largest dailies of Atlanta and New Orleans. I am surely doing as effective work as is being done by any editor in Virginia. Yet I fall short by at least $3,000 a year of what the best paper in Richmond is paying its editor [Douglas Southall Freeman of the *News Leader*]. The *Virginian-Pilot* can afford to pay its editor as much as any paper in Virginia. I think it ought to."[17]

Starke had increased Jaffé's salary from $3,600 to $6,000 in 1920. But Jaffé emphasized that his marriage and Christopher's birth had tripled his living expenses, and he had received no raises in the past three years. He explained that "in spite of every reasonable economy I can practice . . . it is

15. Williams, *Baltimore Sun*, 221.
16. Hamilton Owens to Louis Jaffé, 30 October 1924, Jaffé Papers.
17. Jaffé to Starke, 27 June 1923, ibid.; Cappon, *Virginia Newspapers*, 180; Dunford, *Richmond Times-Dispatch: The Story of a Newspaper*, 307–13.

practically impossible for me to lay aside $1,000 a year toward the purchase of a home." Jaffé disclosed that he had become "somewhat discouraged" as a result of his economic situation. The *Pilot*'s publisher and editor soon came to terms regarding salary, and Jaffé expressed delight that his "carefully considered estimate of what I should . . . be making is acceptable" to management.[18]

The bad press generated by the antics of Klan leaders Simmons, Clarke, and Tyler may have influenced Norfolk's Klan to adopt a low profile temporarily. Its activities attracted little public attention in late 1922 and in 1923. Preoccupied with internecine feuding and wishing to avoid negative publicity, the Klan's high command issued an unmasking directive in the summer of 1922, effective "until further orders."[19]

Jaffé guardedly approved of the hooded order's new policy, while pointing out to his readers the impermanent nature of the Klan's proscription and the fact that it did not bar masking within the confines of its lodges. "Sufficient unto the day are the victories thereof," he wrote. "In view of the change for the better one is disposed to patience." But he urged more sweeping changes: "The Klan has decided to meet [the public's suspicions] not . . . by permitting its members to come out into the open and hold their assemblages unmasked, but by forbidding parades and public assemblages. The next step is to make a bonfire of the whole dreary paraphernalia of disguise and bring the Klan truly into the light of day. Nothing will do it more good than a thorough sun bath."[20]

Jaffé particularly welcomed any steps that would end the Klan's "church and graveside performances." With or without church authorities' prior knowledge, throngs of masked Klansmen would appear in churches' vestibules during services and silently file forward in ghostly columns to the pulpit to present ministers with purses of thirty-five or forty dollars. At funerals, robed and masked members—often bearing flower arrangements in the shape of a cross—would assemble in formation alongside the grave.

18. Jaffé to Starke, 27 June 1923, 15 October 1925, Jaffé Papers.
19. Jackson, *Ku Klux Klan in the City*, 12–4; Bennett, *Party of Fear*, 212; *Pilot*, 24 July 1922.
20. *Pilot*, 24 July 1922.

Jaffé denounced the first practice as "crude and ostentatious" and the second as "heartless and distasteful."[21]

Klan violence in Louisiana served as the impetus for a series of *Pilot* editorials. In Mer Rouge, near the Arkansas border, black-hooded Klansmen abducted and flogged five men in August 1922. The "wrecking crew" released three of its hostages but drove a road-grading tractor over the other two, later decapitating and dismembering the corpses. In late fall, after the Klan dynamited a ferry wharf across which rumrunners allegedly transported their wares, two torsos bubbled to the surface of Lake Lafourche. Louisiana governor John M. Parker pledged to "tear the mask off of the Klan," but violence escalated in the Klan-controlled northern part of the state and created a situation so explosive that he sent an emissary to the Justice Department in Washington, D.C., to plead for federal assistance. In a dispatch from Baton Rouge, one Washington correspondent claimed that the secret society had "reduced the sovereign state of Louisiana to the vassalage of the Invisible Empire."[22]

Jaffé expressed consternation that the situation in the Pelican State had deteriorated to such a degree: "The spectacle of the Governor of a sovereign state appealing to the federal government for help in curbing the operations of an organization professed to be dedicated to the purposes of high patriotism is without parallel in American history." Jaffé, who had so ardently defended states' rights the previous year, urged that federal authorities investigate the hooded order: "It is easily to be seen that if the Klan extends to the States generally the plan of action that has made it odious in Louisiana, government action will be needed to choke off the stream of money and organizers at the Atlanta fountain-head. If the government now lacks the power to do this, it will have to be given that power by new legislation. We have elaborate laws making the central government the watch-dog of interstate trade. It will hardly be illogical to add a new law empowering the government to restrain an organization engaged among other things in the interstate dissemination of law defiance."[23]

21. Chalmers, *Hooded Americanism,* 34; Jackson, *Ku Klux Klan in the City,* 149; *Pilot,* 24 July 1922.

22. *Pilot,* 22 November 1922, 30 December 1922; Chalmers, *Hooded Americanism,* 59–65.

23. *Pilot,* 22 November 1922.

At the Governor's Conference in Hot Springs, Virginia, that fall, Parker denounced the Klan, and Jaffé informed his readers that events had overtaken the "gentlemanly council of elders." Previously the conclave had culminated in a "number of gently phrased resolutions"; the current session, to the contrary, had the states' chief executives agonizing Hamlet-like over "whether it is nobler in the mind to suffer the tar and feathers of the night-shirted fascisti or to take arms against a sea of kluxers and by opposing end them." Jaffé advised the governors to wrestle in unison with the difficult problems posed by the rise of the Klan rather than face them alone when they returned to their home states.[24]

Parker's gubernatorial peer in nearby Oklahoma, Jack Walton, faced an even more dire situation. Turbulent social and economic forces, a long history of frontier justice, and a Klan recruiting drive—which resulted in ninety thousand Sooners joining the order—threatened the social structure and resulted in a total breakdown of the criminal justice system. Klan activities in the state included sponsoring "whipping parties" in the hundreds, perhaps thousands; kidnapping a newspaper editor and instructing him to use his pages to espouse the society's agenda; and flogging a Jew and mutilating his genitals. The last incident spurred Governor Walton to declare martial law in Tulsa and soon thereafter throughout the state.[25]

In "The Klan Unmasked in Oklahoma," Jaffé attacked the "menace which an organization surrounded by concealment holds against the security of Oklahoma or any other commonwealth." While conceding that the First Amendment protected the Klan's rights to free speech and assembly, he argued that "secrecy and disguise are contrary to the spirit of American institutions and an organization sheltered behind such practices invites not only its own unruly members but others to resort to violence."[26]

The Klan's hiatus in Norfolk coincided with the genesis in Richmond of the Anglo-Saxon Clubs of America, an organization kindred in spirit to the Ku Klux Klan but with none of its rough edges. John Powell and Major Ernest Sevier Cox served as the principal founders of the organi-

24. Ibid., 16 December 1922.
25. Chalmers, *Hooded Americanism*, 49–55.
26. *Pilot,* 12 September 1923.

zation. Powell, an internationally acclaimed concert pianist, composer, and ethnomusicologist, who drew inspiration for his most renowned work from African-American music, had absorbed the teachings of eugenicists Lothrop Stoddard and Madison Grant. Powell lent the organization an aura of cultural and social elitism. Cox, an ethnologist, explorer, and author who had journeyed around the globe to study what he perceived as "race problems," vested it with scientific authority. Within a year's time eleven other states claimed chapters; the Old Dominion boasted twenty-five posts, including a particularly strong affiliate at the University of Virginia, Powell's alma mater.[27]

The Anglo-Saxon Clubs espoused goals nearly identical to those of the Klan, while eschewing its violence and secrecy. In lengthy articles that Powell wrote for the *Richmond News Leader* and *Richmond Times-Dispatch* in the summer of 1923, he outlined his organization's purposes: "strengthening of Anglo-Saxon instincts, traditions, and principles among representatives of our original American stock, . . . intelligent selection and exclusion of immigrants, and [enacting] fundamental . . . solutions of our racial problems in general, most especially of the negro problem." The new organization's creed stated somewhat contradictorily, "I believe in the supremacy of the white race in the United Sates of America, without racial prejudices or hatreds."[28]

Despite Powell's Virginia niceties, his rhetoric bore an eerie resemblance to that of another artist, Adolf Hitler, then hacking away at *Mein Kampf* in a Bavarian prison. "The survival of civilization in America is dependent upon the preservation of racial integrity," Powell wrote. "The impossibility of an immediate final solution of the negro problem necessitates legislation which will insure us a breathing space pending the final solution." Powell, whom Virginia would later honor by declaring Novem-

27. Pocahontas Wight Edmunds, *Virginians Out Front* (Richmond: Whittet & Shepperson, 1972), 354–5; Madison Grant to John Powell, 1 February 1924, Powell Papers; John Powell to Stone Deavours, 20 April 1925, Powell Papers; W. A. Plecker to W. B. Hesseltine, 21 August 1924, Powell Papers; *Richmond News Leader*, 6 June 1923; *Richmond Times-Dispatch*, 22 July 1923.

28. *Richmond News Leader*, 6 June 1923; *Richmond Times-Dispatch*, 22 July 1923; *Newport News (Va.) Daily Press*, 15 March 1925.

ber 5 John Powell Day, ushered in one of the most shameful periods in the state's history.[29]

Through petitions, lobbying, and an energetic public relations campaign, the Anglo-Saxon Clubs pressed the General Assembly to pass legislation empowering the state registrar of vital statistics to develop and maintain a system documenting the racial composition of every Virginian—man, woman, and child. The law would allow whites, defined as persons of exclusively Caucasian ancestry, to marry only among themselves. With the *Richmond Times-Dispatch*'s editorial page in the vanguard, Powell and his followers generated a groundswell of support for the adoption of a racial integrity law. The Assembly, convening in Richmond in the winter of 1924 for its biennial session, began to debate the merits of a bill patterned along the lines suggested by the Anglo-Saxon Clubs.[30]

Jaffé advocated that the bill "be killed as obnoxious legislation." The state "can have nothing to do with this preposterous scheme to force the whole population, those already married, those not married as well as those past the age of marriage, to take out passports attesting their racial composition, in order that a documentary check may be had on the 1 or 2 percent of the population so indefinitely blooded and pigmented as to need registration." He sardonically suggested that such a scheme of racial registration might have served a purpose during the antebellum era when "white masters . . . became the fathers of a mixed race," but that it would do nothing to discourage intermarriage in the present era. Persons who wished to pass as white could easily provide false documentation or bribe enterprising local registrars.[31]

Jaffé waxed philosophic on the subject, pointing out the cultural relativism of various systems of racial hierarchy and the primal forces that led to interracial unions proscribed by both society and law: "Given one setting and it produces a sensational liaison between a lowly English Nordic and the brown-skinned heir to an Indian throne. Given another setting and it weds a scion of the Knickerbockers to the tinted daughter of a drayman.

29. *Richmond News Leader*, 6 June 1923; *Richmond Times-Dispatch*, 16 August 1963.
30. *Richmond Times-Dispatch*, 22 July 1923.
31. *Pilot*, 19 February 1924, 3 December 1924.

Given still another and continental setting, and it produces the great race problem of the Southern States. Whoever knows how to curb human love and extirpate human lust, has the key to racial integrity. All others have only theories."[32]

Jaffé's criticism of the bill notwithstanding, in late March 1924 the General Assembly passed the Racial Integrity Act. The law mandated that local registrars maintain "registration certificates" documenting the race of residents in their districts and forward copies of the form to Dr. W. A. Plecker, the state registrar of vital statistics in Richmond. The law required authorities to scrutinize the race of couples wishing to marry. Should any suspicions exist regarding the racial purity of individuals declaring themselves as white, the certificates provided a means of ascertaining "that the statements as to color of both man and woman are correct." The law defined whites as persons having "no trace whatsoever of any blood other than Caucasian."[33]

Sensitive to the fact that a number of socially prominent residents claimed descent from Pocahontas, who had married John Rolfe in Jamestown in 1614 with the unqualified support of Virginia's governor, the legislature built in an exemption. The law declared as white persons individuals with one-sixteenth or less American Indian ancestry as long as they possessed "no other non-Caucasic blood." (Curiously, in her laudatory chapter on John Powell in *Virginians Out Front,* biographer Pocahontas Wight Edmunds, an Old Dominion native who claimed lineal descent in two lines from her namesake, mentioned the composer's leadership of the Anglo-Saxon Clubs movement only inconspicuously in a chapter endnote. Edmunds, who knew Powell personally, avoided entirely any treatment of the state's racial integrity movement and its various manifestations.)[34]

Registrar Plecker enthusiastically implemented and administered the racial integrity act. Unconcerned with privacy rights, for many years he obligingly shared with private citizen Powell the details of many of the cases crossing his desk, and he briefed the renowned musician on the state's prog-

32. Ibid.
33. Ibid., 11 February 1926; *Acts and Joint Resolutions of the General Assembly of the State of Virginia* (Richmond: Division of Purchase and Printing, 1924), 534–5.
34. Edmunds, *Virginians Out Front,* 378.

ress in ensuring the purity of the white race. "We have a report of the birth of your child," Plecker wrote to one mother soon after the law's passage. The midwife who delivered the baby certified "that you are white and that the father of the child is white. We have a correction to this certificate sent to us from the City Health Department at Lynchburg, in which they say that the father of this child is a negro. This is to give you warning that this is a mulatto child and you cannot pass it off as white. A new law passed by the last Legislature says that if a child has one drop of negro blood in it, it cannot be counted as white. You will have to do something about this matter and see that this child is not allowed to mix with white children. It cannot go to white schools and can never marry a white person in Virginia. It is an awful thing."[35]

The Klan ended its low profile in Norfolk with a sensational public event whose success must have underscored for Jaffé the limits of his ability to influence opinion and behavior. Despite his nearly four-year campaign against the order, approximately thirty thousand spectators swarmed through the main gate of Norfolk's fairgrounds in 1924 to witness the Klan's co-opting of Independence Day in a celebration extraordinaire. Perched high atop the gateway, the *Virginian-Pilot* reported, "towered a cross throbbing with ruby and opalescent electric bulbs and surmounted by the Stars and Stripes."[36]

Having determined that the crowd had exceeded maximum capacity, the fire department ordered the gate closed, leaving many crestfallen ticket holders locked out. A flute sounded the eerie rallying call of the Klan; and from around a bend in the track, the order's drum and fife corps, resplendent in white silken robes and purple capes lined with gold, stepped into view. The cadre marched behind, set off by its scarlet finery. Then came the women's contingent and behind it the rank and file. Seven hundred novitiates brought up the rear. Flanking the procession, mounted knights rode back and forth on prancing and snorting hooded steeds. The masked three-thousand-person cavalcade wended its way around the track to an altar beneath a huge flaming cross. Smoke from red flares and the fiery crucifix ringed the glowing tableau and its American flag backdrop. The collapse of

35. W. A. Plecker to Mrs. Robert Cheatham, 30 April 1924, Powell Papers.
36. *Pilot,* 4 July 1924.

the cross at the very moment the advance guard reached it provided the single faux pas of the night's elaborately choreographed ritual, but the showmen pressed on with the induction ceremony.

Afterward, a "hooded individual" introduced the evening's featured speaker. From the judges' stand, C. I. Hoy—like Imperial Wizard Hiram Evans, a resident of Dallas—addressed the crowd through a megaphone. Hoy predicted a national membership of fifteen million "white, Protestant, native born Americans" by the year's end. He saw the Klan's greatest accomplishment as the passage of anti-immigration legislation that "put up bars at Ellis Island." (Congress had passed these laws with the express intent of limiting immigration from eastern and southern Europe.) The *Pilot*'s news staff wrote that "frequent outbursts of applause, not from the hooded hordes, but from the grandstand," interrupted the speaker. An elaborate fireworks display capped the evening's festivities.[37]

In a lead editorial, "Our Own Klan Show," Jaffé alternated sarcasm with the detached tone of a social scientist in his analysis of the "truly imposing Klan rodeo." He conceded that the order had behaved and provided viewers with a "good show." But other klonvocations, held contemporaneously with Norfolk's, he pointed out, had displayed a more malevolent quality. In Montgomery, Alabama, a Klan keynote speaker had threatened the state's popular and respected senator, Oscar Underwood, and the state's delegation to the Democratic National Convention in New York with "political death" because of their anti-Klan plank. In Pennsylvania, which contained a sizable population of Roman Catholics (including men and women of Irish descent who did not shrink from physical confrontation), a Klan rally had triggered a riot and four deaths in the little mining town of Lilly.[38]

Nothing like that had occurred in Norfolk, Jaffé conceded. "Nobody was threatened with death, political or otherwise, and no harsh words were said concerning anybody but a few million foreigners who, the orator of the evening believed, would either have to be assimilated or sent back home. One did not get the impression that it was advisable for any of these, as yet, to begin arranging for passage."[39]

37. Ibid.
38. Ibid., 5 July 1924; Chalmers, *Hooded Americanism*, 79, 239–40.
39. *Pilot*, 5 July 1924.

For Jaffé, the "depressing consideration was that so much human energy and so much human ingenuity could be conjured up in the name of so spurious a cause as the defense of imperilled native, white Protestant Americanism." He pointed out to his readers the irony that "when a few years ago, the nation called for volunteers to defend wife, child and fireside against the enemy, the call was answered by only a few tens of thousands. How different with the call to defend imperilled, native white Protestant Americanism. Not tens of thousands responded, but millions. What is one to make out of a citizenship that waits to be conscripted to defend kith, kin and country, but joins up by the million in a fight to preserve in that country the permanent hegemony of a certain religious element?"[40]

He thought it possible that little of substance lay behind the secret society. "The closer one studies the psychology of the Klan movement the more likely one is to be convinced that here we have nothing more than our old friend human gregariousness preened out in new feathers and as usual fitted out with a 'cause.' The 'cause' happens to be spurious, but the simple-hearted folk who are buying hoods and nightshirts at $10 an outfit have not yet discovered it. Until they discover it, the financiers who are exploiting the business will not enlighten them."[41]

Jaffé likely had mixed feelings when less than two weeks later thousands of men and women packed the armory in nearby Newport News, a hive of Klan activity, to hear a KKK lecturer preach a white supremacist sermon and deplore past immigration policies, which he declared had nearly turned the United States into a European nation. "Virginia is menaced; you can't erect a wall around it," he fumed. Although the speaker's nativist message remained consistent with the order's talking points, none of the attendees concealed their identity behind masks. Perhaps Jaffé's relentless reiteration of his message had had some effect.[42]

Any satisfaction Jaffé may have derived from the Newport News unmasking did not last long. In late 1924 the Reverend Dr. C. S. Coggins of South Norfolk, addressing an audience of twelve hundred, portrayed the

40. Ibid.
41. Ibid.
42. Andrew Buni, *The Negro in Virginia Politics, 1902–1965* (Charlottesville: University Press of Virginia, 1967), 72; *Pilot,* 17 July 1924.

secret society as no more of a threat than the Odd Fellows. Coggins claimed that he had conducted a "thorough investigation" before reaching his conclusion. He also asserted indignantly that recent immigrants and their children committed a disproportionate percentage of crimes. Undoubtedly the 150 masked and robed Klansmen in attendance expressed enthusiastic approval of the clergyman's message.[43]

Jaffé sarcastically dissected Coggins's study. "How 'thorough' was this research?" he asked. Fraternal organizations such as the Odd Fellows had never tarred and feathered anyone. They had incited no riots nor committed any murders. These organizations did not conceal the names of their members or hide the locations of their meeting places. As Jaffé wrote:

> One suspects that the research was as thorough as that which led Dr. Coggins to view with alarm the fact that 'eight per cent of the criminals of this land are of foreign birth and extraction,' and to suggest that if the country is to stand it must keep itself pure. Since 36,000,000 of America's 106,000,000 population in 1920 were either foreign born or of half or whole foreign extraction, it appears that while the 66 per cent native element furnished 92 per cent of the criminals, the 34 per cent foreign born or foreign-descended element furnished 8 per cent. Accepting Dr. Coggins' figures, it appears that if the native element were as law abiding as the alien element, it would have furnished 15 percent of the nation's criminals instead of 92 per cent. From this it follows—still working with Dr. Coggins' figures—that the native element is six times as criminal as the alien! At this rate how law abiding would be a nation composed entirely of indigenous klansmen, cyclops and kleagles?[44]

Jaffé saved the best for last: "Nineteen and a quarter centuries ago about this time, in honor of a babe wrapped in swaddling clothes, a heavenly host praised God saying 'Glory to God in the highest, and on earth peace, good will toward men.' Happily that was before the Ku Klux Klan and some of its evangelical protagonists cornered the truth and put a night

43. *Pilot*, 16 December 1924.
44. Ibid.

gown on it. Otherwise Luke the physician might have recorded that the heavenly host praised God saying: 'On earth peace, good will toward the white Protestant and native born.'"[45]

As might be expected, the editorial displeased Norfolk's Klansmen. That same day an anonymous letter writer penned a response to Jaffé, which contained both creative punctuation, spelling, and capitalization and an unmistakably persuasive appeal:

> Sir—
>
> This—is—just—to—Let—you—know.—That—there—are approx.—10,000 men—strong—In the—City—of—Norfolk— standing behind—Dr. Coggin's (of—So. Norfolk—Va.) Sermon, on—Sun. Dec 14—1924. Why—Don't you Print—the—Principals of the Klan (outlined—by—Mr. Coggin's)—We—understand— why—you Don't do this—Remember—We know—all—see— All—& Hear—All A—Citizen.[46]

Precisely what the correspondent and his brethren "understood" cannot be inferred with certainty, but the editor's Jewish roots and ethnic origin probably had become a point of discussion in the city's klaverns. To a greater degree than his Gentile peers who attacked the Ku Klux Klan, Jaffé's vehement, unwavering, and high-profile criticism of the secret society placed him at risk. In his seminal book *The Southerner and World Affairs*, Alfred Hero Jr. concluded that Jews who challenged intolerance in the region "needed considerably more courage and less sensitivity to probable public reactions" than did Gentiles who embraced similar positions. One of Jaffé's former associate editors, Alonzo Dill, recalled that Jaffé knew that his controversial stands made some of his readers mutter behind his back, "That's what you get from a Jew editor."[47]

Jaffé's editorial stance jeopardized his family in rural South Boston. Virginia's hooded order never displayed the predilection for violence that plagued Louisiana or Oklahoma, but Klan "wrecking crews" operated in

45. Ibid.
46. "A Citizen" to Louis Jaffé, 16 December 1924, Jaffé Papers.
47. Alfred O. Hero Jr., *The Southerner and World Affairs* (Baton Rouge: Louisiana State University Press, 1965), 499; Dill, interview by author.

the Old Dominion throughout the decade. Additionally, the Klan's Realm of Virginia smeared and attempted to intimidate public officials and conducted boycotts. Philip, Lotta, Hyman, and Hyman's wife, Hattie, eked out a marginal existence near a center of Klan strength. The organization might easily have orchestrated a boycott against their store or directed "poison squads" to develop a whispering campaign of lies against the family. Perhaps it did.[48]

In her examination of the Women of the Ku Klux Klan in Indiana in the 1920s, Kathleen Blee observed that nearly all of her many WKKK informants recalled specific economic boycotts and organized gossip campaigns against Jewish and Catholic stores. She wrote that "tales about the personal lives, merchandise, and political allegiances of the town's outsiders destroyed the Klan's enemies without a trace." One could never determine with certainty whether an invisible boycott bankrupted a business. Even Jews apparently successfully integrated into their small towns suffered. One interviewee mentioned such a family who even attended dinners at Protestant churches. Nevertheless, the woman recalled that she and other klanswomen refused to shop at their store. Blee maintained that the pattern of out migration of Jews and the closing of their businesses in Indiana indelibly underscored the effectiveness of the Klan's perfidiousness.[49]

Nancy MacLean's exploration of the Klan in Athens, Georgia, identified similar activities engaged in by the local klavern. She cited one local lecturer who exhorted klansmen to determine the religion of their grocers and clothing and shoe merchants, boycott Jewish and Catholic business, and encourage others to do the same.[50]

Beyond a doubt, Jaffé knew that his editorial campaign placed him and his family in harm's way. Nevertheless, he blasted away.

The Klan's scrutiny did not influence Jaffé's decision to convert to Episcopalianism in the early summer of 1925, but it likely contributed to the secrecy surrounding his baptism and confirmation. For this delicate matter Jaffé sought out the Reverend Dr. Walter Russell Bowie, the minister who had

48. Chalmers, *Hooded Americanism*, 233–4.
49. Kathleen M. Blee, *Women of the Klan: Racism and Gender in the 1920s* (Berkeley: University of California Press, 1991), 149–50.
50. MacLean, *Behind the Mask of Chivalry*, 78.

officiated at his marriage ceremony. "I have a personal problem, which I feel you of all the men I know can best help me to solve," Jaffé wrote. The liberal-minded clergyman had displayed compassion and sensitivity in conducting Jaffé's wedding. Although no canon proscribed Louis's marriage to Margaret and despite the fact that the Episcopal Church included more progressives than the leadership of other southern churches, some of its clergy restricted the performance of nuptial rites to baptized Christians.[51]

Bowie had served as rector of aristocratic and historic St. Paul's Church in Richmond at the time of Jaffé's marriage. In Virginia's capital the Harvard-educated Bowie had edited the *Southern Churchman,* an Episcopal weekly, and had energetically participated in a range of progressive causes. From his pulpit and the pages of the *Churchman,* Bowie had opposed intolerance in general and the Klan in particular. He now headed prominent Grace Church in New York City.[52]

Although Jaffé had abandoned his tenuous ties to Judaism upon volunteering for military service, reaching the decision to convert anguished him. His marriage to Margaret had distressed his parents enormously. Another two generations would pass before Jewish-Christian mixed marriages would become relatively widespread. In the 1920s, the Jewish community still regarded marriage to Gentiles as crass opportunism, a self-serving ploy to avoid discrimination and prejudice. Jews and Christians alike frequently ostracized interreligious couples.[53]

Their oldest son's apostasy would have shamed and pained Philip and Lotta further. Jews viewed voluntary conversion as betrayal of their

51. Louis Jaffé to Walter Russell Bowie, 14 May 1925, Jaffé Papers.

52. Julia Randle, letter to author, 27 March 1998; *General Convention of the Protestant Episcopal Church, Constitution and Canons for the Government of the Protestant Episcopal Church in the United States of America* (New York: General Convention of the Protestant Episcopal Church, 1919), 122–3; William B. Williamson, *A Handbook for Episcopalians* (New York: Morehouse-Barlow, 1961), 120; Mims, *The Advancing South,* 297–8; Dabney, *Liberalism in the South,* 305; Salmon and Campbell, *Hornbook of Virginia History,* 215; Emory M. Thomas, *Robert E. Lee: A Biography* (New York: W. W. Norton, 1995), 372; Dabney, *Richmond,* 296; Julia Randle, interview by author, 24 March 1998; Walter Russell Bowie, *Learning to Live* (New York: Abingdon Press, 1969), 129.

53. Egon Mayer, *Love & Tradition: Marriage Between Jews and Christians* (New York: Plenum Press, 1985), 48–9, 53; Judy Petsonk and Jim Remsen, *The Inter-Marriage Handbook: A Guide for Jews & Christians* (New York: William Morrow, 1988), 27–8.

people, who had suffered terribly at the hands of Christians in the Pale of Eastern Europe and throughout that continent. Although religious law dictated that a born Jew never lost his or her membership in the Hebrew community, the majority of Jews at the time regarded converts to Christianity as dead, irrevocably cut asunder from their former coreligionists.[54]

For some time Louis and Margaret had attended services without formally joining the congregation at Norfolk's storied St. Paul's Church, the city's oldest building and the only structure to survive the 1776 bombardment and conflagration. Its south wall remained pocked with an embedded British cannonball. Jaffé might easily have had his baptism and confirmation performed there. No doctrine blocked his conversion. But the Episcopal Church regarded baptism as a public rite, to be performed before the entire congregation. Some clergy viewed private ceremonies as abuses of the Sacrament of Holy Baptism and permitted their administration only under exceptional conditions.[55]

Many factors likely contributed to Jaffé's decision to travel to New York, where Bowie would perform the ceremony discreetly. Given his reclusive nature, Jaffé would not have welcomed a public airing of so personal a decision. He may also have wished to spare his parents embarrassment and to avoid estranging them further. Word of his baptism and confirmation in Norfolk would have spread rapidly among Virginia's Jewry. He may have planned never to inform Philip and Lotta of his conversion. After all, what purpose would it serve?

He surely also took into account the many proponents of "100 per cent Americanism" whose displeasure he had incurred. In light of the Ku Klux Klan's assault on Jews and immigrants and his critical editorial stands, undoubtedly he preferred not to advertise his Jewish heritage. Although he had not attempted to conceal his roots, to have publicized his ethnic background might have exposed him and his family to serious repercussions not excluding violence.

Margaret also strongly preferred to avoid public discussion of her

54. Petsonk and Remsen, *Inter-Marriage Handbook*, 27–8.

55. Salmon and Campbell, *Hornbook of Virginia History*, 215; Wertenbaker, *Norfolk: Historic Southern Port*, 135; Randle, interview by author, 24 March 1998; Williamson, *Handbook for Episcopalians*, 88–9.

husband's lineage. She fretted about the harmful effects of gossip on Louis Jr.—"Chris" or "Kit." Jews faced widespread prejudice not only from members of nativist organizations such as the Klan but from rank-and-file Americans as well. A large segment of the general population favored limiting the influx of Jewish immigrants, viewing them as radicals and squalid misers. The racist and anti-Semitic theories of Madison Grant and his peers had trickled down to the mainstream, providing validation for such views. "The cross between any of the three European races and a Jew is a Jew," the influential anthropologist had written. Margaret wished to shield her child from hurtful discussion of his Jewish heritage. She had never felt at ease with her in-laws. Despite her outward liberalism, their appearance, customs, and social class embarrassed and discomforted her. Philip's and Lotta's lives and culture lay far beyond her realm of experience and well outside her ken. She discouraged their visitation, referring to them as "those people."[56]

So in late May 1925, Jaffé traveled to New York, where Bowie performed the baptism and confirmation ceremonies in the Cathedral of St. John the Divine. The Reverend Herbert Shipman, the suffragan bishop of New York, served as a witness. Jaffé thanked Bowie profusely: "I wish I could adequately express to you my feeling of gratitude for the understanding, sympathy and liberalism with which you received me and my problem. Be assured that I shall always hold you in grateful remembrance for the peace of spirit which you have helped me to enter, and that my abiding interest and friendship shall attend you in your fine, courageous ministry as long as I live." A few days later, Bowie completed the conversion procedure by effecting a membership transfer from Grace to St. Paul's in Norfolk. "I shall always like to remember that you turned to me in a time like that," he wrote to Jaffé.[57]

Despite Jaffé's ambivalence toward organized religion, his conversion and the formal severance of his ties to Judaism liberated him. From

56. Paul Cowan and Rachel Cowan, *Mixed Blessings: Marriage Between Jews and Christians* (New York: Doubleday, 1987), 90; Louis Jaffé to Margaret Jaffé, 5 October 1936, Louis Jaffé to Margaret Jaffé, 6 March 1933, both Louis Jaffé Jr.

57. Louis Jaffé to Eliot White, 10 November 1925, Louis Jaffé Jr.; Louis Jaffé to Walter Russell Bowie, 29 May 1925, Walter Russell Bowie to Louis Jaffé, 1 June 1925, both in Jaffé Papers.

early on, he had found the "conventions and tabus" of his parents' religion "appall[ing]." He divulged to one of Bowie's colleagues at Grace Church that he was "happy in the fellowship of Christ's church," and admitted feeling "more at peace in spirit" than ever before in his life.[58]

Jaffé's newfound spiritual serenity did not lead him to become an active churchman. Soon thereafter he declined an invitation to attend a supper at St. Paul's parish house and participate in an after-dinner discussion of religion. To the Reverend H. H. Covington, he wrote, "It would have been a pleasure to meet with you and the men who will be there, even though I must confess myself temperamentally unsuited to the task of stimulating others to a livelier interest in religion. Perhaps it is my daily exhortings in matters profane that leaves me thus sapped of the strength to exhort in matters sacred. Whatever the reason for my shortcomings in this respect, I must frankly confess them and at the same time express the hope that I may be able to serve you and the Church in some other way."[59]

That summer, Jaffé wrestled with religion professionally as well as personally. Earlier in the year Tennessee's General Assembly had enacted House Bill 185, which had made it unlawful for any teacher or professor in its public schools or state-supported colleges and universities "to teach any theory that denies the story of the Divine Creation of man as taught in the Bible, and to teach instead that man has descended from a lower order of animals." Governor Austin Peay had signed the bill into law. Searching for a case to test the legality of the new statute, the American Civil Liberties Union advertised for a Tennessee teacher willing to serve as a defendant.[60]

In little Dayton, fifty miles from Chattanooga, a few townspeople, at the instigation of an outsider, cooked up the idea of putting the town on the map by having young John Scopes arrested for violating the new law. Scopes, a science teacher at Dayton High School, had used the official textbook, *A Civic Biology*, for a review session he had conducted for a sick colleague. The text and a score of other biology books used in the state

58. Louis Jaffé to Alice Rice, 23 August 1939, Louis Jaffé to Eliot White, 10 November, 1925, both Louis Jaffé Jr.

59. Louis Jaffé to H. H. Covington, 16 November 1926, Jaffé Papers.

60. Sheldon Norman Grebstein, ed., *Monkey Trial: The State of Tennessee vs. John Thomas Scopes* (Boston: Houghton Mifflin, 1960), 3.

discussed evolution. It took some convincing, but Scopes agreed to play along.[61]

When three-time presidential candidate and creationist William Jennings Bryan—the "Great Commoner"—announced he would assist in the prosecution of Scopes, the media stirred to life and began to attend to what had previously amounted to a minor story. In reality, the press and intelligentsia to a large extent constructed what one contemporary book would term the "world's most famous court trial." Novelist Joseph Hergesheimer suggested to Clarence Darrow that he enter the fray as Bryan's antagonist. Darrow assembled a defense team and sought Mencken's advice regarding possible legal strategies. The Sage recommended that Darrow sacrifice his client, "who was a nobody," and lure Bryan to the stand "to state his barbaric credo in plain English." "Getting Scopes acquitted," Mencken predicted, "would be worth a day's headlines in the newspapers, and then no more, but smearing Bryan would be good for a long while . . . and make Tennessee forever infamous." The Great Commoner would in fact become Darrow's sole defense witness.[62]

Baltimore Sun publisher Paul Patterson sprang Scopes from jail by posting five hundred dollars for his bail and sent Mencken, three other reporters, and a cartoonist to Tennessee. All in all, over 120 journalists representing New York's *Times, Herald Tribune,* and *World,* the Associated Press, and large and small newspapers and magazines from around the country—indeed, around the world—descended on Dayton.[63]

From the beginning of his editorial tenure, Jaffé had attacked obscurantism and attempts by fundamentalists to constrain scientific inquiry. Two and a half years earlier he had written, "If religion and science are incompatible, and if religion cannot hold its own against science, then it is not the fault of science, but of religion. There are thousands of religions, but science is one and universal. It has no prejudices, but only seeks the truth. With theologians at loggerheads with one another over mere creeds

---

61. L. Sprague de Camp, *The Great Monkey Trial* (New York: Doubleday, 1968), 1–16.

62. Mencken, *Thirty-Five Years of Newspaper Work,* 137–8; Leonard W. Levy, ed., *The World's Most Famous Court Trial: State of Tennessee v. John Thomas Scopes* (New York: Da Capo Press, 1971).

63. De Camp, *Great Monkey Trial,* 147–8, 160–5.

and dogmas, it is at least an act of considerable presumption for any of them to read out of the body of truth a naturalistic doctrine concerning which scientists of all religions are in substantial agreement."[64]

Jaffé dubbed the anti-evolutionist fervor that had led to the Scopes trial the "American revival of medievalism." "If these things can come to pass in the realm of pedagogy," he wrote, "may we not confidently look forward to the day when a medievalized public opinion will demand conformity to Genesis as a condition of eligibility for public office, and will perhaps impose the same compulsion on soda-dispensers, vestrymen and shoe-clerks?"[65]

The editor favored a legal strategy that would circumvent the comic drama Mencken ardently desired. Jaffé foresaw only one action to forestall a "State-by-State spread of the particular kind of medievalism represented by the Tennessee statute." He advised the defense to seek an injunction to initiate an examination of the constitutionality of Tennessee's anti-evolution statute in the federal courts: "If the law could be invalidated by reference to the . . . 'due process' clause of the Fourteenth Amendment to the Federal Constitution . . . all attempts to dominate education in the interest of particular religious beliefs would be at an end. A test of the law in this respect is especially to be desired. No court ruling can permanently determine the moral issues involved in the case, but court rulings on fundamental legal points will facilitate a better understanding of these issues."[66]

Despite the carnival-like environment surrounding the trial, Jaffé discerned that powerful forces vied with one another in Dayton. "The prosecution is no mere circus ballyhoo to gain publicity as many have contended," he wrote, "but is a real conflict over so-called religious issues in which the people concerned are moved to their depths. . . . They are animated by the . . . desire to protect their fundamentalist faith against the inroads of modernism."[67]

Scopes's conviction ended what Jaffé called the "most famous heresy case since the trial of Galileo." He welcomed the verdict, believing the

64. *Pilot*, 30 December 1922.
65. Ibid., 4 July 1925.
66. Ibid., 8, 16 July 1925.
67. Ibid., 14 July 1925.

appeal would remove the case from the "ruck and noise of lemonade-stand oratory and revival tent hymn shouting" and place the issue before "tribunals quieter, more urbane, and more learned."[68]

A few days after Darrow humiliated Bryan on the witness stand, the "Great Commoner" died suddenly of what doctors diagnosed as "apoplexy." "Well, we killed the son of a bitch," Mencken commented. A year and a half later, Tennessee's Supreme Court overturned Scopes's conviction. Wishing to end the public humiliation of their state, the justices—while upholding the constitutionality of the anti-evolution law—ruled that the trial judge had exceeded his authority by fining Scopes one hundred dollars. Tennessee's constitution stipulated that only juries could levy fines in excess of fifty dollars. This technicality enabled the justices to short-circuit the appeal process. Tennessee's law would remain intact—although unenforced—until 1968.[69]

The Klan continued to sponsor high-profile activities throughout the mid-twenties. The 1925 Independence Day klonvocation at Norfolk's fairgrounds attracted an even larger crowd than the previous year's had drawn, and spectators witnessed the initiation of an even larger number of novitiates into the order. The all-day festivities included a performance by a Klan band, boxing and wrestling matches, and cabaret-style performances. The *Pilot* reported that the event, which many women and children attended, had a "picnic atmosphere." A Norfolk minister's prayer, a patriotic recitation by a robed Klansman, and the presentation of the American flag preceded the evening's induction ceremonies. Then an unidentified speaker from the organization's national headquarters, addressing the crowd, stressed the importance of "keeping America safe for Americans, keeping America safe for the Protestant church, and making America safe for Jesus and his church."[70]

Soon the speaker fixed on his principal theme: "inter-racial" marriage. "In my traveling about the country," he declaimed, "I have found that

68. Ibid., 22 July 1925.

69. Bruns, *Preacher,* 282; De Camp, *Great Monkey Trial,* 469–72; Eric Foner and John A. Garraty, eds., *The Reader's Companion to American History* (Boston: Houghton Mifflin, 1991), 971.

70. *Pilot,* 4 July 1925.

in Virginia less than one-half of one percent of the American men marry foreign-born wives, but that the percentage of American women who marry foreigners is much larger." He vowed that soon Congress would enact a deportation act that would ship back to Europe the "scum" that had polluted American ideals and undermined its racial integrity. When a large crowd gathered at Norfolk's armory to witness still another induction ceremony late that summer, anonymous Klan speakers denounced the "rapid birthrate among foreigners" and urged that the Bible serve as the foundation for public school instruction.[71]

In the spring of 1926, pointing up Norfolk's increasing prominence as a recruiting ground, pudgy and bespectacled Imperial Wizard Hiram Evans journeyed to the city for consultations with local Klan officials and a speech before a capacity crowd at the armory. Fledgling WTAR radio station broadcast Evans's message through the ether. The *Pilot* reported that throngs of knights clustered around radio receivers set up at Klan halls throughout the area. Although he was not above employing incendiary rhetoric, the Imperial Wizard took the high ground for this auspicious occasion and limited his remarks to espousing isolationism and assailing the World Court.[72]

The secret society's presence in Norfolk reached its apex a few months later in the form of the musical extravaganza *The Awakening* and a big parade celebrating its opening. Behind a police motorcycle escort and a fifty-piece Klan band and drum corps, sixteen hundred robed and masked knights marched along the major downtown thoroughfares—Granby, Main, and Bank Streets and City Hall Avenue—then down Boush and Tazewell Streets, before dispersing at the Puritan Club. The spring rain did not dampen the cavalcade's enthusiasm.[73]

According to *The Awakening*'s reviewers, only the director's inspired blocking enabled the city's best playhouse, the Norfolk Academy of Music, to accommodate the "miles of bare knees" and "acres of shimmering shoulders" in the "hippodramatic" Klan melodrama. (Competing diversions such as the nearby Majestic Theater's "Aviation Girls," replete with a

71. Ibid., 4 July 1925, 6 September 1925.
72. Ibid., 19 March 1926; Chalmers, *Hooded Americanism*, 238–9.
73. *Pilot*, 3, 4 May 1926.

"fast-stepping beauty chorus" and the "shortest petticoat ever seen in Seville," likely accounted in part for *The Awakening*'s frisky staging.)[74]

Featuring a cast of over six hundred amateur actors and actresses— "tiny but distinctively talented tots" to "oldtime darkey-dancing . . . mammies"—the historical drama chronicled the birth of the Ku Klux Klan. "Virginia Here I Come," the most extravagantly staged number of the twenty-three-scene review, deployed one hundred fifty boys and girls in "open order, platoons, in single, double, triple numbers and double sextettes [which] then massed and dissolved again." The dancers—tap, strut, toe, ballet, oriental, Charleston, and cakewalk—performed with such vigor and enthusiasm as to "make a paralytic throw away his crutches and join in." A peppery jazz band provided the music.[75]

From the moving battlefield tableaux of "On the Front Line Trenches" to the uproariously funny "Daddy Swiped Our Last Clean Sheet and Joined the Ku Klux Klan" to the presentation of the lovely Klan queen and her beguiling court, audiences found the extravaganza "dazzling" and "astounding." Many of the wide-eyed spectators who motored in for the show from their homes in rural Virginia and North Carolina had never before seen a professionally staged play. *The Awakening* shattered all attendance records for local theater during its initial run, and the producers scheduled another week of performances. The box office proceeds went to a building fund to construct a Klan temple in Norfolk.[76]

The success of *The Awakening* did not dispirit Jaffé. To the contrary, he regarded the public nature of the performance and its employment of so many elements of popular culture as a positive occurrence. In "Klan Evolution," he subjected the secret society to his closest historical and sociological scrutiny thus far in his five-year editorial campaign. "The Klan is not what it used to be," he asserted. He traced the development of the modern Ku Klux Klan, the social forces its leadership had exploited, and the scapegoats they had created. After the Red scare had fizzled, the "most inviting object for nationalist attack was not the native stock liberals and radical elements of which there were few, but the minority racial and religious

74. Ibid., 11, 16 May 1926.
75. Ibid., 5, 16 May 1926.
76. Ibid., 4, 5, 11 May 1926.

groups of which there were many, and a large proportion of which was alien or of alien parentage." Madison Grant and other scientific racists had aided the flourishing of nativism by inventing the "theory of imminent Nordic engulfment." Into this fertile soil the "Georgia mystic" Simmons had transplanted his Klan seedling.[77]

But, the editorial continued, the postwar unease faded away as Republican Party candidates Warren Harding and Calvin Coolidge overwhelmingly defeated radical Democrats and Progressive and Socialist Party candidates. The fears the Klan had mined no longer existed. This led the hooded order, which had begun "heroically by riding radicals on rails, by tarring and feathering some people, by frightening others out of town, by beating still others black and blue and, occasionally, as at Mer Rouge, by executing a few disciplinary murders . . . to change its tactics. The Klan is passing . . . from the cavern of secrecy to the openness of the market place. . . . [It] is moving toward the day when it will take off its mask, make public its membership and lay its cards on the table. What will happen to the Klan after that does not much matter. It may follow the Know-Nothing party into oblivion or it may continue to attach itself to those who find spiritual sustenance in a brotherhood dedicated to keeping that part of the population which is not native, white, Protestant America in its place. American civilization will be safe in either case. The important gain will be the passing of a force that worked secretly—masked—in the dark."[78]

As the 1920s progressed Jaffé began to direct an increasing amount of attention to the *Norfolk Journal and Guide,* the city's black weekly. Its editor, Plummer Bernard "P. B." Young Sr., a contemporary of Jaffé's, had grown up in Littleton in central North Carolina, near the Virginia border. His storekeeper father had edited the weekly *True Reformer.* Young attended grades one through twelve at a Baptist-sponsored academy, one of the few schools in the state that offered more than a cursory education for black children. As a child he had run errands for a white daily and delivered his father's paper. The Young family's attendance of services at a black Episcopal church marked them as members of Littleton's black "aristocracy."[79]

77. Ibid., 4 May 1926.
78. Ibid.
79. Suggs, *P. B. Young, Newspaperman,* 6–8; James D. Anderson, *The Education*

Young furthered his education in Raleigh at black St. Augustine's Normal School and Collegiate Institute. After marrying the adopted daughter of the institute's president, Young with his bride boarded a train for Norfolk, where he began his professional career in 1907 as plant foreman for the *Journal and Guide,* a lodge newspaper. Two years later Young became its editor. In 1910 he purchased the paper, renaming it the *Norfolk Journal and Guide* and adopting for it the motto "Build Up, Don't Tear Down."[80]

Like many of Norfolk's black elites at the time, Young advanced Booker T. Washington's conservative self-help philosophy, emphasizing economic advancement over civil rights. He met Washington—who assiduously courted editors of black newspapers—a number of times and corresponded with him until the influential leader's death in 1915. Young believed that he and his paper could help facilitate communication between blacks and whites, and he rapidly became an articulate and respected spokesperson for the black community. Whites regarded him as an "able and safe leader."[81]

Soon after Washington's death, Young associated himself with the nascent NAACP, his former mentor's antagonists. He understood the limitations of the "Wizard of Tuskegee's" accommodationist philosophy—that it had done little to address the disenfranchisement of his people, the racial violence that plagued the South, and the sham of "separate but equal." In 1917 Young became president of the new Norfolk chapter of the NAACP. Over the next four decades, however, the NAACP's national leadership and Young would frequently regard each other with ambivalence, at times even distrust. The editor's penchant for freelancing placed him at odds with the organization on a number of occasions. He often preferred to accomplish his goals by using his personal power with the white establishment rather than by following the NAACP's game plan. Despite his fundamental conservatism, over his long career Young would make many significant contributions to improving the condition of blacks in his city and throughout the

---

of Blacks in the South, 1860–1935 (Chapel Hill: University of North Carolina Press, 1988), 203–4.

80. Suggs, *P. B. Young, Newspaperman,* 9–10, 20, 22–3.

81. Ibid., 24–5, 29, 32; Lewis, *In Their Own Interests,* 25–6.

region. He focused on reforms that would not estrange the liberal whites in Norfolk and throughout the South who helped form his power base.[82]

Under Young's leadership the *Journal and Guide* greatly increased its circulation, from five hundred in 1910 to twenty-nine thousand in 1935. Its readership spread throughout the East and into the Midwest. It became the most widely distributed black newspaper in the South and the fourth in the nation. Young's well-written, persuasive, and thought-provoking editorials, which earned him a national reputation as a "race man," played an important role in educating his black readers, as well as the whites who turned to the *Journal and Guide* to learn more about the views of Norfolk's "37 percent." Gunnar Myrdal would term the paper "highly respected and respectable." In 1925, judges in a national newspaper competition awarded the *Journal and Guide*'s editorial page first place among black newspapers. The award pleased Jaffé, who applauded the "intelligence, discrimination and fine restraint" of the black weekly's editorials. He devoted an editorial to the subject.[83]

Having established with his readers the *Journal and Guide*'s credentials, Jaffé reprinted its concerns regarding the white presses' racial news values. "Why is it," he paraphrased the black weekly, "that the same white newspaper that dismissed with a few lines and a small caption the death of Henry Lincoln Johnson, one of the most eminent political leaders of the colored race, gave liberal space and bold black head to the news of the arrest of a 'colored alleged burglar'?" According to Young, this was "another phase of Southern psychology which Negroes do not comprehend." Jaffé considered the question and attempted a response: "The problem here is an old one and we do not pretend to have the complete answer." But, he pre-

82. Suggs, *P. B. Young, Newspaperman*, 32, 58–9, 160–3; Alexander S. Leidholdt, *Standing Before the Shouting Mob: Lenoir Chambers and Virginia's Massive Resistance to Public School Integration* (Tuscaloosa: University of Alabama Press, 1997), 56; Armistead S. Pride and Clint C. Wilson II, *A History of the Black Press* (Washington, D.C.: Howard University Press, 1997), 141–2.

83. Henry Lewis Suggs, *The Black Press in the South, 1865–1979* (Westport, Conn.: Greenwood, 1983), 140; Suggs, *P. B. Young, Newspaperman*, 45–7; Workers of the Writers' Program, *The Negro in Virginia*, 315; Egerton, *Speak Now Against the Day*, 252; Myrdal, *An American Dilemma*, 917.

dicted, the development would "unquestionably be in the direction of less exploitation of negro crime and greater publicity for negro achievement."[84]

However, he did not censure the white southern press for fostering stereotypes and fueling racial violence. He pointed instead to the "circumstance that in the South colored readers form a very small proportion of a [white] newspaper's total circulation. Since the general rule holds that a story is worth for the newspaper what it is worth for its readers, it is to be expected that the obituaries of negro politicians, eminent and worthy though they may have been, will not be gone into at length for a body of readers for whom he holds only casual interest. Crime, of course, has a direct human appeal, regardless of color, nativity, or origin." Jaffé suggested that blacks could help address the problem by bringing economic pressure to bear on the white press: "Let the negroes of a community begin to figure in force as a body of advertisement and news readers, and economic law will see to it that the newspapers will not unduly slight the legitimate news in which they are interested."[85]

Although Jaffé's response likely frustrated and displeased Young, the *Journal and Guide*'s editor did not publicly respond. Young almost certainly would have felt that Jaffé's insight into racial problems required considerable refinement. Although Norfolk housed a number of comparatively prosperous black businesses, they lacked by far the financial clout necessary to change editorial policies. The city's predominantly poor black population could not afford to buy white newspapers in effectively large numbers. Moreover, the state of black schools in Norfolk and the surrounding areas in Virginia and North Carolina that fed the black population of the city did little to promote literacy.

Jaffé's editorial fell further short in that it completely skirted the issue of journalistic responsibility. Two decades later, the Southern Regional Council would chastise the southern press for portraying the "Negro [as] either an entertaining fool, a dangerous animal, or (on the comparatively rare occasions when a Negro's achievements are applauded) a prodigy of astonishing attainments, considering his race." According to the SRC, the region's newspapers constituted the most significant influence in perpetuat-

84. *Pilot,* 5 October 1925.
85. Ibid.

ing demeaning stereotypes of blacks and had historically served to exacerbate racial tensions.[86]

Jaffé's commentary must have irked Young on a business level, too. Young zealously promoted the circulation of his paper and tried to stave off any attempts by the white press to cut into his readership. Many years later he would protest in strong terms the publishing of black obituaries in the *Virginian-Pilot*, claiming that it drew readers from his newspaper.

86. Southern Regional Council, *Race in the News: Usage in Southern Newspapers* (Atlanta: Southern Regional Council, n.d.), 2–3.

8 MOBS IN HIS CROSS HAIRS

The lynching of Raymond Bird in 1926 served as the impetus for Jaffé to intensify his examination of mob violence and invested the issue with new urgency on his editorial agenda. He had vigorously protested previous mob atrocities, but his editorial responses had not been sustained and had lacked concrete policy recommendations. Certainly earlier crimes had not sparked the personal advocacy that characterized his reaction to the Bird lynching.

Just two weeks after the mob violence in Wytheville—with Jaffé's antilynching campaign well under way—a mob armed with heavy switches flogged two young women in nearby Bristol. The Ku Klux Klan almost certainly planned and committed the crime in an effort to clean up moral transgressions in the city, which the Virginia-Tennessee border bisected. Railroads had made Bristol relatively prosperous, and the influx of railroad workers with steady paychecks had attracted a legion of black and white prostitutes. Large brothels did a booming business, as did independent streetwalkers. Black prostitutes serviced clients of both races. Most of their white counterparts refused black customers, but the truly desperate turned away no one.[1]

The two Bristol flogging victims' social status remains uncertain, but in all likelihood they did not boast reputations as paragons of rectitude. In late August, they made the mistake of accepting a ride with two strangers who promised to drive them home but instead headed out of of town and down a deserted road. This seems to have aroused the women's suspicions, for they asked to return to town. As the driver stopped to turn around, however, a mob of twenty men rushed forward and pulled the women from the

---

1. Chalmers, *Hooded Americanism,* 234; Workers of the Writers' Program, *Virginia: A Guide to the Old Dominion,* 440–1; Bud Phillips, interview by author, 17 July 1995.

car, whipping one woman until she fainted. When the victim regained consciousness, they resumed beating her with even greater force. The two women nursed their wounds for a day before filing a complaint at the Tennessee police station, where they presented as evidence scars and large welts. The chief of police refused to investigate, claiming the alleged beating had occurred outside the city limits. "Little attention is being paid by the local officers" to the case, the *Bristol News Bulletin* reported.[2]

Nonetheless, the publicity generated by the incident elicited a complaint from another pair of local young women regarding a similar attack several months earlier. Two strangers in a car had approached the women while they walked on the Virginia side of State Street. "We had not flirted with the men," one woman asserted, saying that "it was at their solicitation that we got into their car."[3]

The men drove the women across the Tennessee border and stopped the vehicle. A masked mob rushed forward and surrounded the car. Mob members made a show of dragging the two men away deep into the woods, and the sounds of a terrible whipping resounded throughout the area. "We could hear the licks and we did not expect the men to be able to stand if they ever returned to the car," one woman recalled. Members of the mob told the women a harrowing story of how they had previously stripped female victims completely naked, flogged them, and poured salt on their wounds. The women begged for mercy and concocted a story that they recently had been discharged from the hospital and could not withstand a severe beating. Perhaps the ruse worked; their abductors administered only ten blows to their fully clothed victims. Soon the women's escorts returned, seeming none the worse for the experience, and drove them back to town.[4]

The disclosure of the second flogging did nothing to rouse Bristol's law authorities. "Although the affair seems to have been a bold one," the *Bristol Herald Courier* reported, "no investigation has been started in connection with either occurrence." In the *Virginian-Pilot,* Jaffé reprinted the

2. *Bristol (Va.) Herald Courier,* 4 September 1926; *Bristol (Va.) News Bulletin,* 21 September 1926.

3. *Bristol (Va.) Herald Courier,* 18 September 1926.

4. *Bristol (Va.) News Bulletin,* 18 September 1926.

Baltimore Evening Sun's charge that the "only evidence produced against the whippers is, that judging by the welts on the girls' backs, they must have been pretty strong."[5]

Klan "wrecking crews" ran amok that August, on at least two occasions in Jaffé's own backyard. In Norfolk County a grocer reported that a group of Klansmen had visited his store and flogged a Catholic customer. At a filling station in the Wards Corner section of the city, a band of hooded pistol-wielding men piled out of a truck and searched the premises. After claiming to have found a large quantity of liquor there, they dragged four of the attendants into the nearby woods, stripped off their clothing, and beat them with heavy leather straps. The vigilantes warned their victims that they would kill them if they reported the attack to the police. Later that night a group of robed and hooded Klansmen, presumably the assailants of the service station attendants, flagged down a policeman in Ocean View and surrendered to him eight gallons of liquor.[6]

As Jaffé observed the lethargy with which many of Virginia's law authorities pursued their investigations into Klan terrorism and violence, he began to doubt their integrity and loyalty. He did not limit his concern to county sheriffs and small-town police officers. His research had led him to conclude that the majority of Norfolk's police department belonged to the secret society. He studied police mortuary records and notified his readers that a "very large proportion of the policemen who died in the last few years . . . were buried with Klan ceremonial. If the affiliation of policemen as disclosed by death is an approximately correct index to their affiliation in life, the Norfolk police force is from 50 to 75 percent kluxized."[7]

In a lead editorial, "A Dangerous Affiliation," he warned of the consequences of this state of affairs: "The only way to ferret out the perpetrators of atrocities committed under cover of the mask is through the police and detective force. But this force is itself to a very large extent affiliated with a masked order and is, practically speaking, paralyzed and worthless as a detector of this type of crime." "Why should the facts be blinked?" he asked. "The facts are that no genuine, sincere and honest-to-God police ser-

5. *Bristol (Va.) Herald Courier,* 18 September 1926; *Pilot,* 8 September 1926.
6. *Pilot,* 22 August 1926, 8, 16 September 1926.
7. Ibid., 23 September 1926.

vice as against masked mobbery is available in Norfolk." He called for an immediate investigation by the city manager and the police chief.[8]

The *Pilot*'s obituaries of police officers buttressed Jaffé's findings. A cross-shaped formation of police motorcycles covered with red crepe streamers had escorted a hearse bearing one police sergeant to his final resting place the previous spring. At the cemetery the cortege passed between two lines comprised of over a hundred Klansmen, who then formed a circle surrounding the mourners. As the last notes of "Lead, Kindly Light" faded away, the Klan leader, dressed in red and bearing an American flag and a burning cross, stepped forth from a patch of woods nearby. Behind him filed ten robed followers. The Klan party then administered rites to the deceased policeman.[9]

Jaffé's reservations regarding the police department's integrity paralleled his concern over the Klan's tenuous foray into Virginia politics. The Richmond papers sought to contain the issue by avoiding it. Jaffé, who regarded "'playing down' certain types of news . . . to be a dubious procedure," spelled out for his readers the secret society's attempts to influence electoral outcomes.[10]

The Klan focused its principal efforts at the state level on defeating John Purcell, a Roman Catholic running for state treasurer. In the 1925 Democratic primary, which for all intents and purposes would determine the final election, the KKK had supported Purcell's opponent, who had conducted an ineffectual campaign and seemed to stand little chance of receiving his party's nomination. Incumbent Purcell prevailed, but by the slimmest of margins. Jaffé promptly charged the Klan with subjecting Purcell to a "political knifing," and he castigated Virginia's leaders for ducking the issue. "Our public men will not begin discussing it until the business of proscribing public servants on account of their religious faith has assumed the proportions of a statewide scandal," he wrote. "Then there will be a great public awakening accompanied by public statements and editorials."[11]

He fired an early editorial salvo: "The *Virginian-Pilot* has no hesi-

8. Ibid.

9. Ibid., 26 March 1926.

10. Chalmers, *Hooded Americanism,* 233; Louis Jaffé to Douglas Southall Freeman, 19 July 1932, Jaffé Papers.

11. *Pilot,* 10 August 1925.

tancy in condemning such a development as contrary to public policy and violative of an underlying principle of American government. A duty is laid on all fair-minded, liberty-loving and justice-seeking citizens to employ their votes as well as all the influence they can command to defeat so clear a perversion of the purpose of free elections."[12]

The editorial refrainment of Richmond's *News Leader* and *Times-Dispatch* did nothing to stymie the Klan's politicking. Furniture magnate John David Bassett—who hailed from the Martinsville area of southwestern Virginia, a bastion of Klan activity—faced Purcell in the general election. Bassett sidestepped questions regarding whether he belonged to the order, but posters circulated throughout the state lauded him as the "100 per cent candidate." Upon the disclosure of Klan dirty tricks, which included forging a circular on Knights of Columbus letterhead instructing Catholics to vote for Bassett, Virginia's Republican Party, to its great credit, denounced the scheming. Purcell eked out another narrow victory. Belatedly Jaffé's Richmond peers decried the anti-Catholicism directed at Purcell.[13]

Jaffé had predicted that the Klan's heightened level of activity in Norfolk would lead to the order's involvement in local politics. In the summer of 1926, rumors circulated widely that several of the candidates in the forthcoming city council election had joined the order. Although he lacked evidence regarding which of the eight prospective councilmen belonged to the Klan, Jaffé endorsed candidates who did not truck with the organization. "We need no kluxery in the Council," he wrote. "We need a Council representative of the whole citizenship and not especially representative of any part of it secretly banded together for the advantage of bitterly controversial causes. It is sufficient for the present to take note of the Klan rumor and to remind the voters that a Klan candidate will be more useful outside the Council than in it. Government is difficult enough without being bedeviled by religious and racial rivalries."[14]

The Klan's kidnapping of the Reverend Vincent J. Warren in neighboring Princess Anne County in early September 1926 and the lethargic and inept investigation launched by the county's law authorities infuriated Jaffé.

12. Ibid.
13. Chalmers, *Hooded Americanism*, 232–3.
14. *Pilot*, 10 August 1925, 31 May 1926.

Warren, a Catholic priest described as "cheerful and cherubic," served as pastor of Norfolk's black St. Joseph's Church and directed St. Joseph's Academy for black children. Beyond a doubt the editor's and the priest's paths had crossed many times prior to the kidnapping. Their common commitment to advancing race relations would have brought them together, and both belonged to the Norfolk Civitan Club, a service organization. If they did not share a warm friendship prior to the kidnapping, they soon would.[15]

Warren, along with white Norfolk businessman Belford Emanuelson and an elderly white man, had accompanied the academy's boys' band on a trip to Princess Anne County to present a concert for the children's relatives. Before the trip the priest had received several "missives" from the Klan warning him to stay away from the county, one of the order's strongholds. He took the threats seriously and had consulted with a prominent lawyer from the area and the county's commonwealth's attorney. They anticipated no problems. Despite these assurances, on the night of the performance a service station operator reportedly observed a suspicious convoy of automobiles from Norfolk headed in the direction of the concert.[16]

In order to avoid charges that he had organized an integrated event, Warren and his white companions waited in their parked car while the students performed nearby in a black farmer's yard. The concert proceeded smoothly for two hours. As the band began its last number at 9:15 P.M., a caravan of seven cars containing nearly thirty Klansmen arrived. The music ended abruptly as the students and guests spotted the intruders, who began at once to search with flashlights through the crowd and cars until they located Warren. They responded with silence to his questions regarding their intentions and dragged him from his car. Thinking his abductors would beat him, he removed his glasses and passed them to his companions.[17]

The Klansmen pushed the priest into one of their cars. Some of the mob struck the white men accompanying Warren when they attempted to

15. *Pilot*, 2 March 1975; *Baltimore Sun*, 4 September 1926; Louis Jaffé to Daily Walsh, 15 September 1926, Jaffé Papers; Louis Jaffé, "Father Warren" (speech presented at Knights of Columbus tribute to Vincent Warren, Norfolk, Virginia, 1936), Jaffé Papers.

16. *Richmond Planet*, 11 September 1926; Chalmers, *Hooded Americanism*, 230; *Pilot*, 30 May 1965; *Baltimore Sun*, 14 September 1926.

17. *Pilot*, 2 September 1926, 30 May 1965.

come to his aid. Emanuelson succeeded in tearing the hood from one of the men and recognized him as a Norfolk resident. As the kidnappers drove off, Emanuelson leapt on the running board, vowing to stick close to Warren's side. A Klansman drew a pistol, pressed it to the businessman's chest, and forced him from the car.[18]

The Klansmen kept their silence as the convoy sped toward a far corner of the rural county. Seated between two of his abductors, Warren prayed his rosary as his captors trained pistols on him. They parked along-side a dark woods, exited their cars, and circled around the priest. While the mob's leader interrogated him, the rest of the band uttered threats and suggested punishments. "What is your purpose down here?" the spokesman asked. "I am trying to train these young people to be good law-abiding citizens," Warren replied. During a lull in the interrogation, he overheard a conversation between several of the Klansmen, in which one mentioned that they had "plenty of gasoline." "I was afraid for a time they might try to brand me," Warren later recalled.[19]

The spokesman interrogated Warren at length. But after learning that the captive did not intend to open a Catholic school for blacks in the county and had not advocated interracial association or encouraged blacks and whites to mix for immoral purposes, the Klansmen admitted they had made a mistake. They drove Warren to a site a mile from a church, and their leader bade him good night.[20]

Without his glasses and in the dark, the priest could barely see, but he soon came upon the house of a black man who had attended the concert. He directed Warren to the home of a white man who lived nearby, but the white man refused to help. After a long walk Warren met a black family, who in the early morning hours drove him back to Norfolk in their truck. They displayed considerable bravery in assisting the priest. The Klan operated virtually without challenge in the county. A few days prior to the kid-napping, hooded terrorists had dragged two blacks away from their homes and flogged them in a secluded area. Earlier a masked mob had broken up

18. Ibid., 2 September 1926; *Baltimore Sun,* 8 September 1926.

19. *Guide,* 4 September 1926; *Richmond Planet,* 11 September 1926; *Pilot,* 2 September 1926, 30 May 1965.

20. *Guide,* 4 September 1926; *Pilot,* 2 September 1926.

a party given by a black woman in her home and warned her against hosting such events in the future. "A reign of terror among the Negro residents has been existing several months," P. B. Young's *Journal and Guide* reported.[21]

Immediately after Warren's kidnapping, Emanuelson attempted to summon aid from Princess Anne County's principal law authority, Sheriff John C. Litchfield. Finding him away from his home at that late hour, Emanuelson rushed to the police station in little Virginia Beach. The town's mayor refused to provide assistance, explaining that strained relations existed between the resort town and the county and that sending his police out of their jurisdiction might be construed by county officials as "interference." Norfolk's police had no such compunctions. Late that night, after word reached the city regarding what had transpired, the head of Norfolk's police department dispatched a detective accompanied by three newspaper reporters to track down the missing priest. In the meantime the intrepid Emanuelson traveled back to Litchfield's home and found that the sheriff had returned but that he displayed no inclination to carry out his duties. "I wouldn't go out with you at this time of night to look for anybody," he declared. Asked the following day why he had refused to conduct a search, he snapped, "That's my business."[22]

Jaffé had no patience with the euphemistic allusions to "masked gangs" and "masked mobs" that county and state authorities and the region's white press used to describe Warren's kidnappers. The *Pilot*'s editor did not mince words. "It is stultification," he raged, "to pretend that the abductors were innocent of Klan gospel and had no connection with kluxery. All the facts point the other way. There will be a gain all around in frankly recognizing the facts. These are that kluxery has treated this community to a brazen, contemptible and high-handed piece of violence, and that the authorities sworn to enforce the law and preserve the peace are to an alarming degree indifferent about it. A Christian minister of the highest standing in the community is abducted by a band of masked hooligans armed with revolvers and the authorities do not even turn a finger to discover the identity of the criminals. Could anything be more humiliating?"

21. *Pilot*, 2 September 1926; *New York World*, 6 September 1926; *Guide*, 11 September 1926.
22. *Pilot*, 2, 3 September 1926.

The *Baltimore Sun* reprinted the editorial, as did many other newspapers from around the country.[23]

Sheriff Litchfield grew less aggressive and more apologetic throughout the week as the *Virginian-Pilot* and many other state and national presses—including the *New York World* and the *Baltimore Sunpapers*—brought pressure to bear on the county and castigated his investigation. "What can I do?" he asked. "Where would I start?"[24]

Warren's kidnapping and the national exposure it received occurred at an inopportune time for the Klan. The bad publicity coincided with the hooded order's annual parade in the nation's capital. The previous year 35,000 gowned knights had marched thirty abreast down Pennsylvania Avenue. Blacks and Catholics pointing to the priest's abduction urged the District of Columbia's police department to revoke the secret society's parade permit for that year. Half as many Klansmen assembled in the capital that September, and the spectacle paled in comparison to the previous year's. Only Virginia's delegation, estimated at over one thousand, appeared to have grown larger.[25]

In all likelihood Jaffé attended the Civitan Club's weekly meeting the Friday after Warren's encounter with the Klan. Members gave the priest a standing ovation and adopted a resolution condemning the kidnapping and urging authorities to conduct a vigorous investigation. Two days later Father Warren preached before a packed Sunday morning congregation at St. Joseph's Church. Many whites attended the service, and the two races sat on opposite sides of the church. The *Journal and Guide* described the priest's sermon as "fervent." He referred to his abduction only once, imploring his parishioners, "Don't do like the mob did. Don't violate the law. You remember how Christ was dragged down the highways by a mob and how, when he was dying on the cross he lifted his eyes toward heaven and prayed for his persecutors in this manner, 'Father forgive them for they do not know what they do.'"[26]

The formal investigation of Warren's kidnapping followed a pre-

23. Ibid., 3 September 1926; *Baltimore Sun,* 4 September 1926.

24. *Pilot,* 3 September 1926.

25. Ibid.; *Baltimore Sun,* 14 September 1926; Chalmers, *Hooded Americanism,* 289.

26. *Baltimore Sun,* 4 September 1926; *Guide,* 11 September 1926.

dictable course, paralleling in many ways the Raymond Bird inquiry. In the wake of widespread and embarrassing press attention, Judge B. D. White of Princess Anne County Circuit Court summoned a grand jury. Court officers swore in an all-white, all-male jury. Despite the judge's best efforts and his eloquent charging of the jurors, in which he asked them whether they wished to have a "government of law and order . . . or a government of a self-constituted invisible organization whose only law is that of a mob," authorities seemed unlikely to incriminate any of the mob members.[27]

Jaffé placed no great hope in the grand jury, but he did applaud the county's stirring from its slumber and launching an investigation: "The sound of the law enforcement machinery at work, creaking and rusty though it be, is comforting. We may not be able to lay hands on the criminals who stuck up Father Warren, but at least we shall serve notice to the organization from which this choice piece of villainy sprang that it was wholeheartedly condemned and that only the success of the criminals in preserving their anonymity protects them from a room in the penitentiary."[28]

Warren himself feared the entry of outside parties into the investigation, believing it might worsen the already precarious conditions in the county. The American Civil Liberties Union wired the priest, volunteering its assistance: "We gladly offer our legal resources and the influence of our friends in bringing these idiotic cowards to book and giving publicity to the facts." He declined the offer, but for several days New York detectives employed by the organization gathered evidence in the county.[29]

In part, the investigation failed because Warren wished to protect his students' families and relatives from further harm. Although he had learned from blacks who had attended the concert the identity of several of the mob members, he refused to reveal the names of his abductors or to pressure his understandably nervous black witnesses to testify before the grand jury. "If they tell the names of these men they are certain to be subjected to rough treatment at the hands of hooded mobs," he explained to the *New York World*. "For that reason I am not going to make public at this time the information I have about some of the men who composed the

27. *Baltimore Sun,* 14 September 1926.
28. *Pilot,* 7 September 1926.
29. Ibid., 5 September 1926; *Baltimore Sun,* 8 September 1926.

mob." In the end, as Jaffé had predicted, Judge White's grand jury indicted no one.[30]

Although Warren's kidnappers escaped justice, their abduction of the priest, in conjunction with the summer's Klan terrorism and racial violence, spurred Norfolk's city council in early September to enact an anti-mask ordinance. Jaffé's unrelenting editorial campaign against Klan masking had helped lay the groundwork for the council's action, and served to rally support for the law. The ordinance made it illegal to wear in public places masks or hoods that concealed the identity of wearers. Jaffé endorsed the new policy without reservation and urged the General Assembly to pass a statute along the same lines: "The law that has just been adopted by the council of the city of Norfolk may be recommended for adoption by the legislature. If it is good for masking in the holy cause of kluxery, it is also good for masking in the sacred cause of lynching and in the holy cause of beating young girls with straps. Within a month we have had in Virginia examples of all three abominations—to the permanent damage of the state's good name."[31]

In response to the bad publicity their night riding had created, the Klan in late September organized a spectacular public relations event in historic Williamsburg, wrapping itself almost literally in the Stars and Stripes. The secret society announced it would confer upon the College of William and Mary an American flag and a flagpole. The college, the nation's second oldest, counted three United States presidents—including Thomas Jefferson—among its many distinguished alumni. Imperial Wizard Hiram Evans planned to deliver the keynote speech and then to present the flag to Dr. J. A. C. Chandler, the college's president. Klan officials had agreed that members would attend the ceremony unmasked. Clearly the event would constitute a marvelous photo op.[32]

In an editorial, Jaffé, who would have preferred that the college decline the gift, offered advice to President Chandler. He predicted that Evans would warn attendees "to beware of popery, to be on guard against

30. *New York World,* 6 September 1926.
31. *Pilot,* 8, 9 September 1926.
32. Salmon and Campbell, *Hornbook of Virginia History,* 259–60; *Pilot,* 25 September 1926.

furiners, to keep a baleful eye on the Negroes, and to cultivate all the other discriminatory graces comprehended in the Klan's definition of 100 per cent Americanism." Jaffé believed that Chandler should accept the Klan's gift and should return the favor by presenting the imperial wizard with an engrossed copy of the college's citizenship creed, which counseled readers "to seek to promote good feeling between all groups of . . . fellow citizens and to resist as inimical to public welfare, all partisan efforts to excite race, religious, class and sectional prejudice."[33]

Five thousand Klan devotees accompanied by their families traveled by car from all over Virginia and eastern North Carolina to Williamsburg to witness the occasion. Virginia's grand dragon, his three great titans, and a Baptist minister seated themselves alongside Evans and Chandler on the speakers' platform, where Evans, speaking without notes, began his talk by lauding the college. He toned down his rhetoric for the public audience, and he embraced lofty principles. "All people have the right to life, liberty and the pursuit of happiness," he asserted. The Klan's leader then turned his attention to mob violence. He claimed the South enjoyed a racial climate superior to that of the North: "More colored people have been killed in two race riots [there] than in all the lynchings in the South. They kill them by the hundreds up there, while the South kills them only one at a time." The secret society had served as a positive influence in this regard, he said; since its rebirth in 1921, lynchings had declined by a third. "Let's make the condition of the other race as happy as possible without crossing the boundary line of social equality," he exhorted his audience. After touching on foreign affairs and extolling nonsectarian education, he presented Chandler with the flag.[34]

William and Mary's president had faced considerable criticism over his decision to accept the gift; but as Jaffé had urged him, he used the occasion to turn the tables on the secret society. Chandler applauded the Klan's avowed reverence for the Declaration of Independence. "Would that every American would hold to this view," he told the crowd, "and in holding this view, would not be content with the mere expression of this view, but would put into practice this ideal, not only as an individual but in all his group

33. *Pilot*, 25 September 1926.
34. Ibid., 27 September 1926.

connections, for sometimes men declare one thing and practice another." He reviewed the meaning of the Constitution and the Virginia Bill of Rights, and he lectured his audience on tolerance. Chandler's irony may have gone over the heads of many of the Klansmen, but more astute listeners could not have missed his meaning.[35]

Jaffé termed Evans's remarks the "usual abracadabra of [the Klan's] fake 100 per cent Americanism with the more blatant hokum deleted, out of consideration for the inability of the academic mind to contemplate this kind of guff with a straight face." Despite the "definite sensation of nausea" the event had created in him, Jaffé relished the college president's "first rate dressing down of the Klan's acts as distinguished from its professions." Much to the editor's liking, Chandler had "showed himself to be a diplomat wholly lacking in the bowels of mercy."[36]

As autumn arrived, Klan activity and racial violence in the state momentarily subsided. Jaffé increasingly directed his attention to Virginia's young governor, Harry F. Byrd Sr. Byrd's work as a state senator had come to Jaffé's attention during his days as a reporter in Richmond, but the two first met formally in May 1925, in the midst of the heated gubernatorial primary campaign. Their relationship began inauspiciously; Jaffé endorsed Byrd's opponent in that year's Democratic primary. When Byrd won his party's nomination, Jaffé congratulated him in a personal letter and expressed his confidence that the nominee would, after the anticlimactic general election, serve as an "effective and progressive" administrator. The *Pilot*'s editor had begun to see potential in the Old Dominion's future chief executive.[37]

Byrd zealously attended to and courted Virginia's journalists. Complimentary reports and editorials pleased him enormously; critical coverage, however, wounded him personally. His experience as publisher and editor of the *Winchester Evening Star* may have created in him an appreciation for the influence of the fourth estate, but curiously, his journalistic background had not toughened his skin for the inevitable criticism he would face as a

35. Ibid.
36. Ibid., 28 September 1926.
37. Harry Byrd to Louis Jaffé, 22 May 1925, Louis Jaffé to Harry Byrd, 7 August 1925, both in Jaffé Papers.

public official. He regarded newspapers as businesses primarily, political vehicles on occasion. He never grew to accept the idea that a responsible press should challenge elected officials and at times question their policies. Although he would spend most of his life in public service, Byrd, a successful apple grower and publisher, would remain a business owner at heart, more comfortable with executive responsibilities than with the give and take of the democratic process.[38]

Byrd valued loyalty above all else and demonstrated an elephantine memory for criticism by his detractors, but he had too much political acumen to feud needlessly with one of the state's most prominent newspapermen. While acknowledging that Jaffé had written the most effective editorials against him in the Democratic primary, the governor-elect conceded that the editor had been "fair and courteous." Jaffé's insight into "State questions" had impressed Byrd, who expressed the hope that he would be able to consult with Jaffé throughout his gubernatorial tenure.[39]

Virginia's new chief executive hit the ground running. In his inaugural speech in February 1926 and in two addresses to the General Assembly over the next two days, the progressive young governor laid out in clear terms his plans for a badly needed reform of Virginia's antiquated and unwieldy state bureaucracy. Byrd biographer Ronald Heinemann described the new governor as a "businessman who wanted a businesslike government." Byrd proposed shortening the state ballot from seven to three positions: governor, lieutenant governor, and attorney general. The state's chief executive would function like the head of a modern corporation, appointing and supervising the heads of administrative departments that previously had been independent of the governor. This arrangement would make government much more efficient (and greatly strengthen gubernatorial power). Byrd advocated eliminating many bureaus, boards, and departments and consolidating nearly one hundred agencies into a manageable number of departments. A single budget, controlled by the governor, would fund all state agencies, and local governments would standardize their accounting systems with the commonwealth's.[40]

38. Heinemann, *Harry Byrd of Virginia*, 50–1, 59.
39. Harry Byrd to Louis Jaffé, 28 August 1925, Jaffé Papers.
40. Heinemann, *Harry Byrd of Virginia*, 58, 60–1; Rubin, *Virginia: A History*,

Byrd's bold agenda met with the support of most of the state's press and business community. Jaffé called the proposals "thrilling" and described the plan as the "most promising that the political thought of the day offers." "A public espousal of it in a State dominated by one political party and exclusively officered by that party's retainers," he informed his readers, "is an act of high political courage." "The *Virginian-Pilot* will let no good opportunity pass to advance the cause," he wrote to Byrd.[41]

Jaffé's support gratified Virginia's governor, who expressed concern over a rumor that an out-of-state press had made the editor an offer. Byrd read the *Pilot*'s editorials "every day with the utmost interest" and hoped Jaffé—"one of the best editorial writers in the South"—would stay put. Some months earlier Frederick Thompson, publisher of the *Birmingham (Ala.) Age-Herald,* had made confidential inquiries to Colonel Samuel Slover, publisher of the *Norfolk Ledger-Dispatch,* regarding the identity of the editor of his paper's morning rival. The two powerful newspaper executives likely knew each other well from Southern Newspaper Publishers Association conferences and their work as members of its executive committee. Slover informed Thompson that Jaffé was "not only the best editorial writer in Virginia but in the South." Had an informal agreement against bidding wars not existed between the owners of the local papers, Slover said he would long ago have stolen Jaffé away from the *Pilot.* Thompson would encounter difficulty enticing the editor away from Norfolk, Slover warned, but if he succeeded, Jaffé "would be a wonder for you." To Governor Byrd's satisfaction, Thompson did not succeed in luring Jaffé to the booming industrial city. It appears likely, however, that the editor used the offer as leverage for a salary increase with publisher Lucien Starke Jr., who awarded him a raise the very next month.[42]

164–5; Wilkinson, *Harry Byrd and Virginia Politics,* 7; Guy Friddell, *What Is It About Virginia?* (Richmond: Dietz Press, 1966), 74; *Pilot,* 7 February 1926.

41. *Pilot,* 7 February 1926; Louis Jaffé to Harry Byrd, 29 April 1926, Jaffé Papers.

42. Harry Byrd to Louis Jaffé, 24 March 1926, 30 April 1926, Jaffé Papers; Walter C. Johnson and Arthur T. Robb, *The South and Its Newspapers, 1903–1953: The Story of the Southern Newspaper Publishers Association and Its Part in the South's Economic Rebirth* (Chattanooga: Southern Newspaper Publishers Association, 1954), 77, 88; Samuel Slover to Frederick Thompson, 7 September 1925, Jaffé Papers; Louis Jaffé to Lucien Starke, 15 October 1925, Jaffé Papers.

It is interesting to imagine Jaffé's role had he assumed the helm of the *Birmingham Age-Herald*. Exploitation of labor by absentee northern owners and racial and ethnic conflict between workers would have provided him with a rich lode of material to mine throughout the twenties and thirties. Might his intercession have helped mitigate any of these ills?[43]

Byrd's activities during his first weeks in office may have filled Jaffé with optimism, but the General Assembly's demagoguery in February 1926 touched off a series of critical editorials. Hampton representative George Alvin Massenburg, building on Virginia's racial integrity act, introduced a bill separating blacks and whites in public areas. Adoption of the law would have the demeaning effect of forcing nearly two generations of black Virginians to file upstairs for balcony seating after purchasing tickets for concerts, plays, and movies.[44]

Massenburg's bill gained momentum as a result of the controversy started in 1925 by Walter Copeland, the elderly publisher and editor of Newport News's *Daily Press* and *Times-Herald* newspapers and a well-respected figure in the state's white journalistic community. Copeland's extensive newspaper experience included editorial stints in nearly all of Virginia's major cities, including Norfolk, where prior to Jaffé's birth he had served as city editor of the *Virginian,* one of the *Virginian-Pilot*'s ancestors. Copeland complained that the seating arrangements for a modern dance recital at Hampton Institute's Ogden Hall had compelled him and his wife, Grace, to sit next to blacks. (Perhaps adding to the Copelands' mortification, the dancers, another white later reported, had appeared "almost nude.") For years the two races had attended public events together at the private black college's auditorium, with no reported friction. Much of Grace Copeland's concern regarding matters of racial integrity resulted from her friendship with John Powell, the guiding spirit behind the formation of the Anglo-Saxon Clubs.[45]

43. Wilson and Ferris, eds., *Encyclopedia of Southern Culture,* vol. 4, 318–20; W. T. Couch, ed., *Culture in the South* (Chapel Hill: University of North Carolina Press, 1934), 63; Thomas A Krueger, *And Promises to Keep: The Southern Conference for Human Welfare, 1938–1948* (Nashville: Vanderbilt University Press, 1967), 7–11.

44. Workers of the Writers' Program, *The Negro in Virginia,* 270–1.

45. Richard B. Sherman, "'The Last Stand': The Fight for Racial Integrity in Virginia in the 1920s," *Journal of Southern History* 54, no. 1 (February 1988): 82; Richard B.

Copeland's first of many editorials on the subject—"Integrity of the Anglo-Saxon Race"—warned that the "cherished ambition of the negro race is to use the blood of the Anglo-Saxon race to rid the negro race of objectionable characteristics in their forms and features." The editor claimed that Hampton Institute's teaching of "social equality between the white and negro races" would lead to "racial amalgamation." He would rather that "every white child in the United States were sterilized and the Anglo-Saxon race left to perish in its purity." The *Richmond Times-Dispatch,* which for years had expressed sympathy with the goals of the Anglo-Saxon Clubs, echoed his refrain.[46]

When the University of North Carolina glee club performed at Hampton Institute later in 1925, the local Anglo-Saxon Club vigorously protested, because the event's organizers had made no arrangements for separate seating. Club officers demanded that the state erect a legal barrier that would end interracial seating once and for all. As racial purists voiced their outrage over the glee club commotion, Jaffé weighed in with an editorial in which he offered a simple solution to the predicament: "Instead of making no end of unpleasantness to induce a negro college to provide them with special seating accommodations for spectacles they are under no compulsion to attend, why do not these white people who object to mixed seating stay away?"[47]

Three months later, as the General Assembly debated the Massenburg bill, Jaffé lobbied against what he termed "fiat ethnology." "At this particular moment in our communal thinking we are obsessed with the fear that the white race will be mongrelized and its culture lost to the world," he wrote. "The pseudo-scientific alarums of our Lothrop Stoddards and Madison Grants have, with the lumbering assistance of the Ku Klux Klan

Sherman, "'The Teachings at Hampton Institute': Social Equality, Racial Integrity, and the Virginia Public Assemblage Act of 1926," *Virginia Magazine of History and Biography* 95, no. 3 (July 1987): 279–81, 291; Chambers, Shank, and Sugg, *Salt Water & Printer's Ink,* 292; Cappon, *Virginia Newspapers,* 79–80, 132–3, 151, 177, 188, 197.

46. *Newport News (Va.) Daily Press,* 15 March 1925; see also *Newport News (Va.) Daily Press,* 20, 27, 29 March 1925, 5 and 21 April 1925, 12, 13, 26, 27, 29 November 1925, 28 January 1926, and 2 February 1926; Sherman, "Last Stand," 76, 82; *Richmond Times-Dispatch,* 22 July 1923.

47. *Pilot,* 16 November 1925.

and, later, with the help of the refined casuistry of our Anglo-Saxon Clubs, been invested with apostolic authority." Jaffé implored, "May heaven preserve us from our present race of purifiers."[48]

The following week he expressed approval of "racial integrity" but argued against "Prussianized segregation enforced by the aid of a sheriff in a privately-owned assembly hall of a privately-endowed negro college." He greatly preferred voluntary segregation to separation mandated by law. "The more the Massenburg bill is studied the clearer it is seen that it is packed with mischief," he cautioned. "It has no business becoming law."[49]

Copeland professed astonishment over Jaffé's editorials. "We have seen strange things since the World War ended and we are prepared for more," the dean of Virginia journalism wrote, "but we did not believe we should live to see in a white man's newspaper in Virginia, especially in this section of Virginia, an editorial article in opposition to a legislative enactment 'requiring the separation of white and colored persons in public halls, theatres, opera houses, motion picture shows and places of public entertainment.'"[50]

To Jaffé's chagrin the bill sailed through the General Assembly, nearly unanimously. Byrd privately expressed his disapproval, telling James Gregg, the Harvard-educated white principal of Hampton Institute, he would not have voted for it. Because of the overwhelming support for the legislation, however, the new governor did not attempt a veto. The Massenburg Public Assemblage Act passed into law without his signature.[51]

Virginia's white leadership often boasted that a superior racial climate in the state elevated it above its Deep South brethren. But scholar Richard B. Sherman has rebutted this contention, noting that none of the South's other legislatures adopted so draconian a law. Combined with the Racial Integrity Act, state laws proscribing integrated schools and mandating racial separation on public conveyances, and local ordinances ensuring

48. Ibid., 8 February 1926.

49. Ibid., 15 February 1926.

50. *Newport News (Va.) Daily Press*, 2 February 1926.

51. *Acts and Joint Resolutions of the General Assembly of the State of Virginia* (Richmond: Division of Purchase and Printing, 1926), 945–6; Sherman, "Last Stand," 83–4; *Newport News (Va.) Daily Press*, 6 February 1926.

segregation in residential neighborhoods, the Public Assemblage Act completed a formidable system of apartheid.[52]

Massenburg would remain in effect until overturned by the courts in 1963. John Powell died a month before the Virginia Supreme Court of Appeals ruled the legislation unconstitutional. The *Richmond Times-Dispatch,* then under the leadership of Pulitzer Prize–winning editor Virginius Dabney, devoted an editorial and article to the passing of Virginia's most famous musical son. Dabney lauded Powell as a man of "intense feelings, great emotional depth and complete integrity." Neither the article nor the editorial mentioned Powell's leadership in the racial integrity movement or the editorial support the *Richmond Times-Dispatch* had lent him.[53]

As passage of the Massenburg bill seemed certain, Jaffé had written to James Gregg, conceding defeat and acknowledging the legislation's popularity with the General Assembly. "More is the pity," he lamented. Jaffé revealed to Gregg that he had researched the relationship between state-enforced segregation and racial purity, and he asked to borrow any books the college might have on the subject. The attacks on Hampton Institute stimulated the editor's support for the college, and he began to attend events hosted at Ogden Hall frequently.[54]

Copeland took another jab at Jaffé that summer over his opposition to the Massenburg law and his advocacy for fairer treatment for blacks. The Reverend Richard H. Bowling, pastor of Norfolk's black First Baptist Church and a regular contributor to P. B. Young's *Journal and Guide,* had devoted one of his "Guide Post" columns to Virginia's new public assemblage law. While traveling throughout the Deep South, Bowling had noticed that even in areas with much greater racial animosity than Norfolk, public transportation companies did not subject blacks to the same indignities they suffered on Norfolk's streetcars and buses. He entitled his editorial "Why? Norfolk, Why?" One of the *Journal and Guide's* readers, undoubtedly aware of Copeland's racist editorial campaign, sent a copy of the paper to the *Newport News Daily Press.* In an editorial of his own—"Referred to the

52. Sherman, "Last Stand," 84.
53. *Richmond Times-Dispatch,* 16, 17 August 1963.
54. Louis Jaffé to James Gregg, 26 February 1926, James Gregg to Louis Jaffé, 5 January 1927, 19 October 1927, all in Jaffé Papers.

Virginian-Pilot"—Copeland feigned puzzlement as to why he had received Bowling's column. "We hold no brief for Norfolk," he wrote, "so we pass the complaint on to that bright and particular champion of Negro rights, the *Virginian-Pilot*."[55]

The needling rankled P. B. Young, who deftly expanded the elderly editor's portrayal of the *Pilot*. "By denominating the *Virginian-Pilot* a *bright and particular* champion of Negro rights," Young editorialized, "the *Daily Press* fails to apply to the Norfolk paper the full appellation that it deserves and by the omission gives a misleading cognomen. We have not heretofore known the *Virginian-Pilot* to be, nor have we heard it said that it was a bright and particular champion of Negro rights, nor for the sake of ourselves are we able to define any such thing as 'Negro rights.' We readily confess, however, that we regard the *Virginian-Pilot* as and have heard it widely declared to be not only a bright and particular but a vigorous and uncompromising champion of human rights. Incidentally, in these days the Negro is regarded as at least human. . . . We base our hope for a larger life and fuller opportunity in this noble land upon the increasing tribe of champions of the rights of man and we are not at all reluctant to admit that we have found the *Virginian-Pilot* playing in that role."[56]

In a personal letter to Young, Jaffé expressed his gratitude. He conceded that Copeland's gibe had placed him in an awkward position; the most effective rejoinders came from others, such as Young, rising to his defense. "To be a 'vigorous and uncompromising champion of human rights' as you say the *Virginian-Pilot* is [is] to be something truly thrilling," he wrote. "However short we may fall of being that, we shall at least strive toward that high distinction, and shall always remember your generous words."[57]

Shortly thereafter members of Norfolk's black Grace Episcopal Church extracted from Jaffé an agreement to address the group's annual Men's Day meeting. Young figured as one of the most prominent members of the congregation, and undoubtedly his lobbying had helped persuade Jaffé to accept an invitation to speak before a group. Jaffé suffered an aver-

55. *Guide*, 24 July 1926.
56. Ibid.
57. Louis Jaffé to P. B. Young, 26 July 1926, Jaffé Papers.

sion to the oratorical duties that his editorial post occasionally demanded, and he did his best to wriggle out of them. In a letter to a future associate editor, he would write, "There is certainly no worse public speaker in the United States than myself. I do not go in for that sort of thing, never having learned the art, and being too old to learn."[58]

Giving a speech to blacks generated additional anxiety. Despite his liberalism on racial issues, Jaffé had no experience speaking before such an audience. Expressing uncertainty regarding his subject matter, he sought out the counsel of Gregg. The editor explained that although he wished to avoid highly controversial topics, he did not want his talk to consist merely of trite remarks. Gregg, an experienced speaker to black audiences, advised him to give the same speech he would to a white audience of "more or less comparable intelligence."[59]

A near lynching in Smithfield, a short distance from Norfolk, distracted Jaffé from his speech writing. In mid-October 1927, Isle of Wight County law authorities arrested Shirley Winnegan, a twenty-five-year-old black man with a history of mental instability, and charged him with the rape and murder of Hilda Barlow, a white girl fourteen years of age. The volatile incident contained all of the ingredients necessary for a lynching.[60]

As white tempers seethed and a mob formed, county commonwealth's attorney George Whitley and Sheriff W. H. Chapman rushed Winnegan to a neighboring county's jail and then secretly on to Petersburg. Removing the suspect from the area infuriated the area's residents. The night following the murder, a mob of several hundred convened at the sheriff's home, demanding to know Winnegan's whereabouts. Under severe pressure Chapman revealed the information, and the mob, greatly swelling in size, started out for Petersburg. Whitley warned that city's police of the violence brewing, and they sped the prisoner to Richmond.[61]

58. Suggs, *P. B. Young, Newspaperman,* 139; Louis Jaffé to William Meacham, 2 July 1929, Jaffé Papers.

59. Louis Jaffé to James Gregg, 25 October 1927, James Gregg to Louis Jaffé, 2 November 1927, both in Jaffé Papers.

60. *Richmond Planet,* 22 October 1927.

61. *Pilot,* 29 November 1927; *Guide,* 22 October 1927; *Richmond Planet,* 3 December 1927.

As the early November trial date grew closer, twelve hundred men and women gathered in the county high school's auditorium to denounce Whitley and Chapman. In the recent Democratic party primary, the county's electorate had by wide margins nominated both officials to succeed themselves. The many speakers at the mass meeting encountered difficulty expressing in clear terms what the two men had done wrong. One participant informed the *Pilot*'s reporter lamely, "If there is a citizen of this county who does not understand the circumstances, he is hopelessly behind the times and it would do no good to explain."[62]

The crowd shouted down many of the more responsible speakers, urged the return of Winnegan to the county's jail, and—at the behest of the murdered girl's father—agreed to scratch Whitley's and Chapman's names from their ballots for the next week's general election and write in the names of two new candidates. "We don't want to get cold feet," Hunter Barlow exhorted the audience. "We won't, don't worry," the crowd roared back.[63]

In a lead editorial on October 26, Jaffé called the "political violence" directed at Whitley and Chapman "an ill-considered act of retaliation for their activity in preventing a lynching." He cautioned the meeting's participants, "Isle of Wight County can not permit such an ill-conceived act of reprisal. It could never be explained to Virginia. It could never be explained to the world." He enclosed a copy of the editorial in a confidential report he sent to Governor Byrd regarding the incendiary situation. He emphasized his uneasiness to Byrd further via telephone. Mob violence might erupt if authorities returned Winnegan to Isle of Wight County for trial without an extensive militia or police escort, Jaffé warned the governor. He also expressed his concern regarding the price paid by Whitley and Chapman for thwarting the lynching, and the message this telegraphed to law officers throughout the state. "I want very much to see this case disposed of without a disgraceful lynching and without a disgraceful political head-chopping," he wrote. "I have the feeling that a quieting word from you passed along to a few influential leaders . . . might ease the situation and deprive it of much of its menace. At any rate I am hoping that . . . you

62. *Pilot*, 25 October 1927.
63. Ibid.

will not permit the Negro to [*sic*] brought into Isle of Wight save under heavy guard."[64]

Byrd hurried an emissary to the rural county and learned that Jaffé had not exaggerated the seriousness of the situation. Local sources, believing county residents would resent any outside interference, cautioned the governor not to make a public comment on the political aspects of the case. In an effort to calm tempers, however, Byrd reprinted Jaffé's editorial and mailed it by way of the local Democratic committee to every voter in the area. The governor encouraged the *Pilot*'s editor to continue to advise him on the situation.[65]

The Winnegan incident highlighted the substandard condition of the state's mental health system. A lunacy commission of two physicians had declared Winnegan insane a few months prior to the murder, but because of overcrowding at Central State Hospital in Petersburg, authorities had allowed him to stay at large under the supervision of Sheriff Chapman. The initial diagnosis of Winnegan notwithstanding, a panel of three physicians examining him in the heady atmosphere following the murder judged him sane and fit for trial. Many whites in the county had feared he would escape prosecution, and the panel's decision helped defuse the explosive atmosphere. Nevertheless both Chapman and Whitley suffered defeats to the write-in candidates in the general election.[66]

The circuit court judge with jurisdiction over the case further averted the potential for mob violence by postponing the trial and transferring its venue to the Richmond Hustings Court. None of Isle of Wight's bar would consent to defend Winnegan, and the hustings court judge appointed a prominent Norfolk attorney to serve as a defense counsel. Although no one saw Winnegan commit the rape and murder, physical and circumstantial evidence—much of it provided by blacks—pointed to his guilt, and the judge sentenced him to die in Richmond's electric chair. "You are killing an honest man," Winnegan protested.[67]

Jaffé found no fault with the trial's conduct. "A jury of a vicinage

64. Ibid., 26 October 1927; Louis Jaffé to Harry Byrd, 26 October 1927, Byrd Executive Papers.

65. Harry Byrd to Louis Jaffé, 31 October 1927, Byrd Executive Papers.

66. *Guide,* 12 November 1927; *Richmond Planet,* 3 December 1927.

67. *Richmond Planet,* 3 December 1927.

far removed from the scene of the crime was convinced of [Winnegan's] guilt," he editorialized. "An impartial judge presided over the case and safeguarded all the proceedings. The verdict produced by such a trial must be accepted as a just one. We have no more exact means of determining innocence or guilt." But the issue of Winnegan's sanity nagged at him and cast doubt on the appropriateness of the sentence. He attacked the "system which provides machinery for adjudging persons insane and ordering their confinement, but which does not at the same time provide adequate complementary asylum facilities for the reception of persons ordered into custody."[68]

In late November 1927, a capacity audience of the area's black elite assembled in Norfolk's black-built and -operated Attucks Theater to hear Jaffé. P. B. Young introduced the *Pilot*'s editor, calling him a "true exponent of the New South."[69]

Jaffé's talk focused on race relations in Norfolk and the South. He began by saying that although he did not like the term "race problem," he could think of no better way to describe the suspicion and fear that often existed between the two races. Regardless of pronouncements by northern critics that prejudice alone accounted for the racial difficulties in the South, Jaffé distrusted such a simplistic analysis. Education might cure prejudice, but psychological, sociological, and experiential dimensions complicated the problem and would not easily yield to pat solutions. Despite this, Jaffé viewed the future optimistically. He pointed to W. E. B. Du Bois, James Weldon Johnson, Langston Hughes, Walter White, and many other eminent figures as evidence of blacks' cultural and intellectual abilities. Emancipation—"white America's bitter and belated atonement for the Seventeenth and Eighteenth Century debauch in criminal avarice"—had ended slavery, and through slow and deliberate progress southerners could achieve racial harmony. "The ultimate and happiest goal may be shrouded in distant mists," he said, "but there are important nearer goals which are in sight and toward which we may work with every confidence of early attainment."[70]

68. *Pilot*, 1 December 1927.
69. *Guide*, 3 December 1927.
70. Ibid.

Jaffé named economic inequality as the most pressing aspect of the "race problem." He set an admittedly ambitious and perhaps unrealistic goal: a single pay standard. "I never traverse the streets inhabited by our Negro population without sensing its implied indictment of an economic system cruelly distorted," he declared. "Wretched housing, squalid alleys, unkempt roadways, unclean pavements—there is something monstrously wrong with an economic system that makes these conditions so unfailingly and so exclusively the reward of Negro labor."[71]

Some of the blame for the economic situation rested with blacks, he argued; they lacked work and organizational skills, had little capital, and sometimes acted improvidently. Jaffé believed that the current generation of blacks, better educated and more politically aware, had begun to accumulate economic power by spending less on hair straighteners, membership in secret fraternal orders, and burial societies and by husbanding their resources instead. The editor pointed to the racism of white labor unions and the exploitation by white employers of their black employees, which thwarted their upward mobility. White southerners, he said, needed to realize "they could not permanently hold the Negro workman down in the economic gutter without staying there with him."[72]

Jaffé advocated that municipalities provide blacks with a more equal allocation of resources. Norfolk had taken its first few steps in this direction. It had completed construction of perhaps the finest black secondary school in the state, Booker T. Washington High School. The city's leadership had recently admitted the inadequacy of Norfolk's recreational facilities for blacks, who had access to no beach resort and almost entirely lacked children's playgrounds. Jaffé urged the city to act to remedy these deficiencies, and he recommended the building of a modern hospital for black patients.

He believed the South had made great progress in the area of administration of justice and foresaw the day when the region would celebrate a lynchless year. Blacks, he predicted, would begin to vote with greater regularity. The extent to which whites would tolerate large numbers of blacks participating in the electoral process would depend on their willing-

71. Ibid.
72. Ibid.

ness to rise above political compacts based on racial considerations alone. Southern whites viewed with alarm black suffrage that threatened to undermine social mores. Jaffé proposed convening an interracial panel of men and women, patterned after Will Alexander's Commission on Interracial Cooperation, to provide leadership in improving relations between blacks and whites in Norfolk.

He concluded his talk by chiding his white editorial peers: "The newspapers of the country, those of the North no less than those of the South, are not yet living up to their duty in respect of racial fairness. . . . They are still too prone to exploit Negro crime, too much disposed to give a racial identification to criminal acts charged against unidentified Negroes on insufficient evidences of probability, too indifferent to the demands of the self-respecting Negro world for the elimination of stereotyped terms and useages that give it offense, too timid about giving space and attention to those aspects of Negro life that bear witness to its dignity and to its finer aspirations."[73]

His own paper, he said, had given serious thought to its portrayal of blacks and had endeavored to correct shortcomings in this regard. (Interestingly, Jaffé's recently adopted policy of capitalizing the word "Negro" on his editorial page placed him at odds with managing editor Winder R. Harris's practice of spelling the word with a lowercase "n." The opposing policies created an awkward moment when the *Pilot*'s news coverage of Jaffé's speech, which contained many lengthy quotations using the word "Negro," did not capitalize the common noun. Nearly all white southern papers at the time adhered to Harris's practice. Journalism historians David Sloan and Laird B. Anderson credit the *Atlanta Constitution,* which under editor Ralph McGill's leadership began capitalizing "Negro" eleven years after Jaffé's speech, as having been "perhaps" the first white newspaper in the region to do so.)[74]

The *Journal and Guide* reported that after Jaffé completed his talk, the audience "with overwhelming sincerity prolonged its ovation for several seconds, a fact forcefully attesting its appreciation of Mr. Jaffé's speech and his work as editor of the local morning paper." Young devoted an editorial

73. Ibid.
74. *Pilot,* 28 November 1927; Sloan and Anderson, *Pulitzer Prize Editorials,* 144.

to the speech, drawing its title—"A True Exponent of the New South"—from his introductory remarks. Jaffé's talk clearly had cemented their relationship. Young placed the *Pilot's* editor in the top tier of liberal white southern journalists, alongside Julian Harris, the courageous editor of the *Columbus (Ga.) Enquirer-Sun,* and Earle Godbey, editor of the highly literate *Greensboro (N.C.) Daily News.* For years, Young maintained, the *Virginian-Pilot* had worked with success to establish better race relations in the region. The willingness of its white editor to speak frankly to a black audience had strengthened the paper's advocacy manifoldly. The editorial, Jaffé confessed to Young, left him "with a sense of unworthiness," by saying "kinder things about my work and . . . place among the South's liberals than I would care to admit to myself."[75]

The upper echelon of Norfolk's black community attending the Attucks Theater speech may have viewed Jaffé as a visionary leader, but his optimistic prognostication regarding the waning of racial violence proved incorrect. On November 30, 1927, less than three days after his talk, Virginia was shaken by a lynching of unimaginable horror. Even today, elderly black residents who live near the lynching site recall the event fearfully and will not discuss it in any detail with outsiders. The incident took place in Pound Gap, Virginia, just a few yards from the Kentucky line, on a speakers' platform that local Kiwanians had constructed for ceremonies dedicating a new highway connecting the two states. Ten days prior to the mob violence, former Virginia governor Elbert Lee Trinkle and Kentucky governor William J. Fields, standing upon the platform to address a crowd from the mountainous region, had expounded the merits of interstate cooperation as local bands played "My Old Kentucky Home" and "Carry Me Back to Old Virginia."[76]

The lynching had its origins in the murder of Hershel Deaton, a resident of Wise County, Virginia, who worked for a coal company in Fleming, Kentucky. According to white press reports, as Deaton and two co-

75. *Guide,* 3 December 1927; Louis Jaffé to P. B. Young, 3 December 1927, Jaffé Papers.
    76. Confidential interview, 25 September 1996; *Norton (Va.) Crawford's Weekly,* 19 November 1927.

workers drove back to work together after spending the weekend with their families, a black man—thirty-five-year-old Leonard Woods—and two black women hailed them and climbed onto the car's running boards without permission, demanding a ride to a mine tipple. "This is not a taxi, and we're full up," Deaton reportedly explained as he stepped out of his Chrysler coupe to put them off. One of Woods's companions, described by one black newspaper as "attractive Race women," allegedly thrust a revolver into Woods's hands, and he fatally wounded the popular mine foreman. Deaton collapsed, gasping, "He's killed me."[77]

Law officers and deputies scoured the area that night, searching for Woods. They found the women, one of whom reportedly confessed to the crime. Just after dawn, authorities apprehended Woods and jailed him, along with the two women, in nearby Jenkins, Kentucky. When the mood among the area's white residents grew volatile, officials hastily transferred the three prisoners to Whitesburg, the seat of Kentucky's Letcher County.[78]

Deaton's family, friends, and lodge brothers packed the Methodist church in Coeburn, Virginia, for the funeral services the next afternoon. No one could remember a larger gathering in the little town. The ministers praised the young foreman and deplored the tragedy. The sight of Deaton's grieving widow, his bride of only a few weeks, undoubtedly moved the many mourners at the emotional ceremony. Although the black *St. Louis Argus* suspected Deaton of belonging to the Ku Klux Klan, local newspaper coverage of his funeral did not mention any presence of the order at the ceremony.[79]

Across the Kentucky border, in the area surrounding Whitesburg, a lynch mob began to form. Its leaders passed word back to Wise County, extending an invitation to residents there to join in. The discussion in the county's barber shops that day, according to one local newspaper, centered on the impending "neck-tie party in Kentucky." That night a convoy of over

---

77. Ibid., 3 December 1927; *Pilot,* 1 December 1927; *Bristol (Va.) Herald Courier,* 30 November 1927; Lina Tindal, letter to author, 10 April 1996; *St. Louis Argus,* [December 1927?]; *Louisville Courier-Journal,* 3 December 1927.

78. *Norton (Va.) Crawford's Weekly,* 3 December 1927; *Louisville Courier-Journal,* 3 December 1927.

79. *Norton (Va.) Crawford's Weekly,* 3 December 1927; *St. Louis Argus,* [December 1927?].

thirty-five automobiles with Virginia license plates headed across the border. One automobile broke down on the trip, delaying the contingent and spoiling the rendezvous with the Kentuckians. The group's leaders decided to wait in Fleming—just to the northeast of Whitesburg—knowing that the Bluegrass State mob intended to lynch Woods nearby.[80]

Whitesburg's jailer, warned in the early morning hours of the vigilantes' approach, scooped up her children (who lived with her at the jail) and placed them in a neighbor's care. When she returned, a swarm of five hundred people had seized control of the streets. She refused demands for the building's keys. The crowd then broke down the high iron fence that surrounded the jail, and after attempting unsuccessfully to shoot off the exterior door's lock with high-powered rifles, prepared to blast its way inside with dynamite. White prisoners, fearing for their lives, volunteered the information that the roof could be broken through with comparative ease. Members of the rabble went to a hardware store, roused the owner at gunpoint, and returned with wrecking tools. Equipped with hacksaws, railroad cross ties, and sledgehammers, they hacked through the roof. The white prisoners fingered Woods, and the attackers sawed through the bars separating them from their intended victim and the two black women.[81]

As members of the mob placed a chain around Woods's neck and pulled him from his cell, he reportedly took sole responsibility for Deaton's murder and implored them to leave the women behind. His confession persuaded his captors, who locked the alleged accomplices back up. Belatedly, the county's sheriff, Morgan T. Reynolds, appeared on the scene to give an ineffectual talk on law and order. No law officers offered any resistance or attempted to stop the abduction of Woods. When some of the region's residents later asked why the sheriff and his deputies had not done more to protect their prisoner, one observer replied, "Foolish questions. The mobbing was a popular movement. Everybody wanted the nigger taken by the mob."[82]

80. *Norton (Va.) Crawford's Weekly,* 3 December 1927.

81. Ibid.; *St. Louis Argus,* [December 1927?]; Roy L. Sturgill, *Nostalgic Narratives and Historical Events of Southwest Virginia* (Bristol, Va.: R. L. Sturgill, 1991), 44–6; *Louisville Courier-Journal,* 3 December 1927; *Whitesburg (Ky.) Mountain Eagle,* 1 December 1927; *Baltimore Afro-American,* 3 December 1927.

82. *Norton (Va.) Crawford's Weekly,* 3 December 1927.

The Kentuckians drove out of town shooting and headed with their prisoner for Fleming, where the Virginia contingent waited. The two groups merged, proceeded to the site of Deaton's murder, and surveyed the area for a lynching spot. Law officers arriving from Fleming informed the mob that the surrounding land belonged to a coal company that employed many black miners, whom a lynching might scare off or lead to protest. These authorities—implicitly condoning the planned mayhem but perhaps seeking to move it across the state line—suggested the mob take their victim to Pound Gap. Carrying Woods back to old Virginia, the convoy proceeded up the new highway to the platform upon which the two governors, both of whom abhorred such violence, had stood. The structure symbolically marked the border, but the Kiwanians had constructed it on the flatter land just over the Virginia side.[83]

According to some newspaper accounts, Woods remained defiant to the end. Asked if he had any last words, he expressed no remorse over having murdered Deaton. The mob, now swollen to a thousand, proceeded to hang him, and gunmen standing across the Kentucky line fired into their victim. Over six hundred bullets ricocheted off the stone cliff that lay behind Woods. The fusillade shredded the rope and cut him down. "Let's burn the black bastard," one person suggested. A woman—one of many on the scene—announced she had a fuel can in her car. The crowd broke down the platform and doused it with gasoline. The smell of burning flesh soon filled the air. Flames cast light on the mob and revealed that few of its members wore masks.[84]

The next morning, souvenir seekers combed through the debris. Some pried bullets from the charred corpse. Some carved out blood-stained shavings from the wreckage. Others picked up cartridge shells. Later that day, road workers buried what remained of the body in a shallow grave just to the side of the highway. Visitors to the grave site poked sticks through the mound above it to determine how far underneath the wooden casket lay.

Bruce Crawford, the stalwart editor of little *Crawford's Weekly,*

83. Ibid.; *Baltimore Afro-American,* 3 December 1927; Wright, *Racial Violence in Kentucky,* 196–7; *Richmond Times-Dispatch,* 22 March 1925.

84. *Pilot,* 1 December 1927; *Norton (Va.) Crawford's Weekly,* 3 December 1927; Sturgill, *Nostalgic Narratives,* 44–6; *New York Times,* 1 December 1927; *St. Louis Argus,* [December 1927?].

published in the Wise County town of Norton, provided the most accurate and detailed account of the lynching. But even Crawford, who fearlessly battled the Klan and mine owners throughout the decade, placing himself directly in harm's way, could only hint that the story he printed in his paper flaying the mob did not include crucial information regarding Woods's motive for shooting Deaton. In a cryptic aside pasted awkwardly underneath his article's headline, Crawford wrote, "Since the following story was put in type, rumors have been heard to the effect that there might have been more provocation for the shooting than was originally reported." Subsequent editions of the weekly, however, provided no further details regarding the foreman's murder.[85]

A sentence tucked into one of P. B. Young's editorials may shed light on Crawford's puzzling statement and may explain why aged blacks in Wise County still recall the lynching as particularly unjustified. Dismissing a white newspaper's claim that black men raping white women served as the principal cause for mob violence, Young wrote, "The Negro that was lynched on the Virginia-Kentucky border a few weeks ago came to his death because he first resented, then resisted, physical intimacy between the white man he killed and the black woman he loved."[86]

A confidential report to the NAACP's James Weldon Johnson from Lawrence D. Kellis, a Letcher County black schoolteacher, likely served as the basis for Young's claim. The *Baltimore Afro-American* also had obtained access to Kellis's letter and had reprinted it while withholding his identity. In his account, entitled "The Cause of the Lynching of Leonard Wood," Kellis furnished a more plausible explanation for the bold presence of Leonard Woods and the two black women in and on Deaton's automobile than the one the foreman's two white companions provided. "Two colored women . . . who were intimate with Hershel Deaton and another white man started on an automobile ride Sunday night, Nov. 27 at eleven o'clock in Jenkins, Ky. Leonard Wood [*sic*], a negro, a friend of the colored women objected to the women going out on this wild joy ride with the white men. . . . Wood jumped on the running board of the car . . . and attempted to make the women get out. . . . Deaton then jumped out of the car and beat

---

85. *Norton (Va.) Crawford's Weekly*, 3 December 1927.
86. *Guide*, 31 December 1927.

and kicked Wood. . . . Wood then pulled out a revolver and shot and killed Deaton."[87]

Kellis also alleged that after breaking into Whitesburg's jail, the mob had not harmed the two black women because the "white man who was with Deaton when he was killed pleaded [with them] not to harm his woman." The schoolteacher further reported that Letcher County sheriff Reynolds had received a clear warning that the mob intended to lynch Woods and that, despite having at his disposal a force of deputies and two machine guns, he had done nothing to prevent the murder. Kellis stated that Reynolds, who later claimed he could not identify a single member of the mob, had mingled with it for an hour.[88]

In "Virginia Again Disgraced," written the day after Woods's lynching, Jaffé reprinted a vivid account of the violence as reported by the Associated Press. He also excerpted quotes from Governor Byrd's strong denunciation of the incident, as well as the governor's offer to dispatch state investigators to Wise County if officials there requested his assistance. Despite Byrd's forceful statement, Jaffé predicted that nothing would come of the inquiry. He urged the General Assembly to enact a statute that would provide for state intervention in lynching investigations. "The lynching cancer appears to be beyond adequate treatment by local authorities," he wrote. "To the *Virginian-Pilot* it seems more and more clear that there will be no adequate grappling with this form of savagery until the punishment of lynchers is made a primary obligation of the State and legislation is enacted to that end." That same day he bolstered his editorial advocacy with a personal letter to the governor. Jaffé appealed to both the governor's state pride and his moral instincts: "I hope you will find the means of forcing a showdown on this outrage—in the name of Virginia and in the name of decency."[89]

In "What to Do About Lynching," a lead editorial published a few days later, Jaffé cut to the core of the issue. He expressed his certainty that

87. *Baltimore Afro-American*, 24 December 1927; Lawrence D. Kellis to James Weldon Johnson, 13 December 1927, NAACP Papers.

88. Lawrence D. Kellis to James Weldon Johnson, 13 December 1927, NAACP Papers.

89. *Pilot*, 2 December 1927; Louis Jaffé to Harry Byrd, 1 December 1927, Jaffé Papers.

the morning-after denunciations of the lynching by the "publicists and politicians of the State" would have absolutely no effect in preventing future incidents. Some of Virginia's officials claimed that Kentucky had jurisdiction over the crime, but Jaffé derived no solace from the geographic ambiguity surrounding the lynching and gave no quarter on that account. "The disgrace stinks across the boundary line," he wrote. He urged Byrd to move beyond his condemnation and offer of state assistance. "The tragedy of the whole business is that these moral revulsions are never supported by action. The coroners' juries enter their usual finding of 'death at the hands of persons unknown,' perfunctory investigations are instituted, on rare occasions a few arrests are made, but invariably the books are closed without any of the lynchers feeling the wrath of the law. Why is it that murders committed by individuals are usually punished in Virginia, while murders committed by mobs are never punished in Virginia? It is not because the law draws any distinction between individual murder and mob murder, but because the State has never, in any effective manner, recognized the social and legal enormity of mob murder and singled it out for the attention it deserves."[90]

Jaffé's incisive analysis of the state's lynchings likely vexed many Virginians who believed their state's rich history and genteel manners entitled them to look down their noses at their southern neighbors. "Lynching goes unpunished in Virginia because, deny it as one will, it commands a certain social sanction," he wrote. "An unwritten code is invoked to give the color of social necessity to a crime which is plainly destructive of guarantees which have been regarded as inviolate in Anglo-Saxon thinking and jurisprudence since Runnymede. The main task of those who look at lynching as something monstrous and foul is to stamp the unwritten code from which it draws its sanction as loathsome and poisonous."[91]

He cited the state action that in the previous century had effectively eradicated another social malady, dueling. "Today [it] is as extinct as the dodo," he wrote. "Participation in a lynching, either as principal or accessory, must be made punishable by the same forfeiture of citizenship rights that applies to participation in a duel. Strict laws must be incorporated in the code providing fines and punishments for members of a lynching party,

90. *Pilot,* 4 December 1927.
91. Ibid.

. . . apart from the question of additional liability on the charge of attempted murder. Finally, the barriers must be swept away which at present prevent the State, as the parent law enforcing agency, from assisting the local authorities in the pursuit and punishment of lynchers, unless these authorities invite such assistance. In short, lynching must be recognized as a State cancer, requiring direct State action. It must be rid of its social cachet and stamped with the State's curse."[92]

Although constrained by Virginia's antiquated laws, Governor Byrd attempted to facilitate the investigation of Woods's murder. Without delay he had wired Wise County's sheriff, in an attempt to determine whether the lynching had occurred within state boundaries. The sheriff asserted that Kentuckians had lynched Woods on their state's soil. Not unexpectedly, Kentucky law officials disagreed, notifying Governor Fields that a Virginia mob had conducted the lynching in the Old Dominion. In the wake of contradictory reports, Byrd wired Fields, urging that the two states work cooperatively to prosecute the mob. Fields informed him that Letcher County authorities were "exerting their efforts to develop facts necessary to prosecution."[93]

The degree of exertion expended by Letcher County's officials in pursuing the investigation did not impress Kellis, who informed Johnson, "If you want the names conclusive and definite just send some person to me who can pass for white . . . [such as] a Mr. Walter White type . . . and I can show him where & who to see & get all the names & evidence you need." According to Kellis, all of the county's residents knew that "Deaton Father member of Mob & father fired the first shot in Wood body." The schoolteacher apprised the NAACP that he intended to leave his post soon because he could not "stand the K.K.K. condition in Letcher County any longer."[94]

Johnson sent letters to the editors of the South's leading dailies, asking them to put to rest the myth that rapes of white women served as the

92. Ibid.
93. Harry Byrd to P. H. Kennedy, 1 December 1927, P. H. Kennedy to Harry Byrd, 1 December 1927, both in Byrd Executive Papers; *New York Times*, 1 December 1927; Harry Byrd to W. J. Fields, 1 December 1927, W. J. Fields to Harry Byrd, 2 December 1927, both in Byrd Executive Papers.
94. Lawrence D. Kellis to James Weldon Johnson, 14 December 1927, NAACP Papers.

impetus for lynchings. He informed them that accused rapists accounted for only 20 percent of the victims of mob violence. In addition, terming the Woods lynching the "most recent American atrocity in the forty-year series of more than 4,000 unpunished outrages," Johnson telegraphed President Calvin Coolidge on December 6 and asked him "as head of the armed forces of the United States to take cognizance of the break-down of orderly government upon the border of the states of Kentucky and Virginia."[95]

Assistant Attorney General C. R. Luhring replied that because Woods was a "state prisoner, there would be no action which [the Department of Justice] could take against those implicated in [the] affair." He advised the executive secretary that "redress should be sought through the authorities of the state in which the alleged offense was committed." Nonetheless, in an address to Congress on December 7, Coolidge deplored lynching and urged his audience to enact legislation that would make participation in the crime a federal offense. Sage observers, however, such as P. B. Young, accurately predicted that Congress would respond to the president's prompting with nothing but "dodging and hedging."[96]

In the aftermath of the lynching, Byrd wrote to Jaffé and suggested that the two meet privately a few days later, immediately following a previously scheduled meeting in Richmond at which the governor planned to communicate his "Program of Progress" initiatives to Jaffé and other newspaper editors. "I hope we will have an opportunity to discuss [state intervention in lynching investigations] after our conference," he wrote. "This is a most difficult matter to handle in view of the constitutional requirements in Virginia." Jaffé undoubtedly welcomed this opportunity for a private meeting with Byrd to press his ideas about state antilynching legislation.[97]

Meanwhile, disgusted by the authorities' lethargic investigation and the presses' wringing of hands and pro forma remonstrations of the lynching, Bruce Crawford took action. He began a fifty-dollar fund to encourage witnesses to come forward with information leading to the prosecution and conviction of the lynch mob's members. Crawford challenged the state's

---

95. *Guide*, 31 December 1927.

96. *Norton (Va.) Crawford's Weekly*, 17 December 1927; C. R. Luhring to James Weldon Johnson, 6 December 1927, NAACP Papers; *Guide*, 10 December 1927.

97. Harry Byrd to Louis Jaffé, 2 December 1927, Jaffé Papers; Heinemann, *Harry Byrd of Virginia*, 76.

other newspapers to contribute. Virginia's press had always deplored mob violence, he wrote. Yet their protests had done nothing to deal with the problem. In the aftermath of the Raymond Bird lynching in Wytheville, the "editorial guns fired long and loud, but accomplished nothing." The editor also solicited donations from residents of Wise County and the surrounding area.[98]

Crawford's stance outraged many of his readers, and he received a number of hostile letters and telephone calls. Some adversaries circulated a petition in which signers pledged to cancel their subscriptions to his weekly paper. The criticism and financial pressure only steeled Crawford's resolve. "Not only is this paper heartily ashamed of that lynching," he wrote, "but it is saddened to know that many people of seeming enlightenment seek openly and frankly to justify the revolting crime. Our fund stands."[99]

Even though Crawford lived in close proximity to many who had participated in Woods's lynching, he taunted the mob (and parodied his own profession of small-town journalism). Alongside stories with headings like "Hoke I. Horne on Honeymoon" and "Visiting in Kingsport," which detailed Norton's social events and the townspeople's comings and goings, he printed a piece entitled "Attend Lynching." Crawford drolly informed his readers that a "number of Coeburn, Toms Creek, and Wise people, accompanied by a few from Norton and other parts of Wise County, were at Pound Gap Tuesday night attending the lynching. Names of those present were unobtainable at the time of going to press."[100]

Crawford's gadfly advocacy offended some of his peers in the state's press, who accused him of making a "more or less permanent issue of the . . . lynching." He responded with an editorial entitled "Are Virginia Editors Superficial?" "For obvious reasons," he wrote, "the majority of Virginia dailies shy away from [lynching] . . . , yet they gird themselves for a mighty demonstration of moral concern and strain at a gnat." He excepted only Jaffé and Douglas Southall Freeman from his indictment.[101]

98. *Norton (Va.) Crawford's Weekly,* 3 December 1927.

99. *Guide,* 24 December 1927; *Norton (Va.) Crawford's Weekly,* 17 December 1927.

100. Roy L. Sturgill, *Crimes, Criminals, and Characters of the Cumberlands and Southwest Virginia* (Bristol, Va.: Quality Printers, 1970); *Norton (Va.) Crawford's Weekly,* 3 December 1927.

101. *Guide,* 4 February 1927.

Jaffé reciprocated Crawford's admiration and appreciated his courage. The two editors followed each other's work closely; probably they had developed an agreement whereby they exchanged newspapers. In 1935, when Crawford finally succumbed to financial pressure and sold his paper, Jaffé eulogized the editor and the independent weekly. He recapitulated Crawford's early stands against "kluxery, political clericalism, obscurantist anti-evolution laws, evangelistic mountebankery and the assorted banalities of high-pressure Babbitry." When the weekly's editor had thrown in his lot with miners "in an environment dominated by the barons of the soft coal industry and their commercial and spiritual retainers," the paper had teetered on the verge of insolvency. "The more red blood he shed for the underdogs the nearer his paper moved toward the red ink. . . . No more consecrated soldier in the war of human rights was ever graduated from the training school of Virginia journalism," the *Pilot*'s editor wrote.[102]

Despite Jaffé's and Crawford's editorial and personal advocacy, the NAACP's activism, and Byrd's outrage, law authorities charged no members of the mob that lynched Leonard Woods.[103]

In August 1926, in the wake of the Raymond Bird lynching in Wytheville, Jaffé at Governor Byrd's request had formulated for him the key provisions of a state antilynching statute. The proposed law required that local law officers rush suspects "charged with specific provocative offenses" to the nearest city jail. The proposal also mandated that state law authorities vigorously intervene in lynching investigations and trials when the governor determined that local officials had behaved irresponsibly. The implementation of such a law—coupled with a strong gubernatorial antilynching statement and a concerted public education campaign—would in Jaffé's "humble opinion rid Virginia of the lynching evil in a few years."[104]

Now nearly a year and a half had passed, and nothing had come of Jaffé's plan. In a letter to Byrd immediately following the Woods lynching, he reminded the governor of his earlier proposal: "A long time ago I made bold to urge upon you the advisability of making mob violence a primary

---

102. *Pilot,* 13 February 1935.
103. Wright, *Racial Violence in Kentucky,* 205.
104. Louis Jaffé to Harry Byrd, 30 August 1926, Jaffé Papers.

concern of the State law enforcement agencies, by means of appropriate legislation, and I am still of the view that that would be the most effective approach to this problem." The next month, Byrd would preside over the final legislative session of his term. "Would it not be possible to take a step in this direction at the next General Assembly?" Jaffé asked.[105]

On a personal level the governor needed little if any convincing; mob violence tarnished Virginia's luster and scared outside investors away. But Byrd, a savvy politician, preferred to avoid risk by keeping his thumb on the pulse of the assembly and the state's intentionally restricted electorate, initiating only action that would receive overwhelming support.[106]

At their meeting in early December 1927, following the press conference with the state's editors, Jaffé likely underscored for Byrd the near-providential timing for the introduction of a state antilynching bill and the extent to which its passage would burnish his gubernatorial legacy. Jaffé's solid grounding in state politics enabled him to discuss knowledgeably any realpolitik issues of concern to Byrd. The two men probably also fine-tuned the key provisions of the statute Jaffé had outlined.

The *Pilot*'s editor perceived in the 1928 General Assembly session a unique opportunity for enactment of an antilynching law. Jaffé's long and consistent editorial campaign had laid the groundwork for the introduction of a bill. His personal connection to Virginia's young and popular reform-minded governor—in Byrd's view the two men had developed a warm friendship—provided a powerful entree into the legislative process. The Woods lynching had received widespread coverage in the regional and national press, and the drubbing the Old Dominion's reputation had taken over the incident mortified the state's lawmakers. Moreover, President Coolidge's support for federal antilynching legislation foreshadowed the possibility of another go-round similar to that over the Dyer bill. Virginia's solons might see the adoption of a strong state antilynching statute as a means of staving off federal encroachment and Dixie-embarrassing testimony at congressional hearings.[107]

Indeed, at the very moment the General Assembly prepared to meet,

105. Louis Jaffé to Harry Byrd, 26 October 1927, ibid.
106. Heinemann, *Harry Byrd of Virginia*, 77–8.
107. Ibid., 51; Buni, *Negro in Virginia Politics*, 102.

the NAACP's leadership was strategizing with Congressman Dyer to seek the House's approval of antilynching legislation. Although Dyer believed his colleagues might pass the bill (as they had five years earlier), he felt certain the Senate would kill it again. Nevertheless the congressman debated the possibility of having a powerful senator introduce the measure to bring about hearings that would stimulate public examination of lynching.[108]

Despite his liberality and racial activism, Jaffé still opposed federal antilynching legislation and continued to embrace states' rights dogma. The previous year, when the Senate Judiciary Committee had failed to report an antilynching bill, the editor had welcomed its demise. Such legislation "would only delay the process of reform [by] attempt[ing] to accomplish by Federal force what the people of the States are themselves unwilling to undertake," he had written.[109]

On January 11, 1928, Byrd delivered for the General Assembly's biennial session his opening address, suitably dubbed "Virginia's Business Government." He reviewed the successes of the first half of his administration, focusing on economic development, the cost savings of his administrative reorganization, and the state's healthy economy. Speaking to the legislature five days later, he conveyed his "Plan for Progress" for the final two years of his tenure. The second installment of his address centered to a large extent on taxation and education. He proposed cutting taxes for stocks and bonds and businesses and upping them slightly for gasoline. He called also for an increase in educational funding—too modest an increase in light of a recent federal report that had classified Virginia's schools among the nation's very worst. (Having left school at fifteen to run his father's newspaper, self-made Byrd valued practical education more highly than formal schooling. Unlike Jaffé, who retained a lifelong interest in fine arts and world affairs, Byrd's horizons never extended much beyond balance sheets and voting returns. Conversations between the two men during their occasional social visits with one another must have focused almost exclusively on politics and public policy.)[110]

Byrd inserted two additional items into his address. He proposed

108. Zangrando, *NAACP Crusade Against Lynching,* 85.
109. *Pilot,* 20 May 1926; Zangrando, *NAACP Crusade Against Lynching,* 84.
110. Ibid., 5–6, 78.

that the state solicit private donations for a statue of one of his heroes, Robert E. Lee, for the capital. He also recommended that Virginia adopt an antilynching law. In his high-pitched, flat voice and in characteristically plain language, he informed the General Assembly, "Virginia is the last State in the Union where lynching should be tolerated, for Virginia contributed to America the leaders who taught that this was a government of laws." "Mob law is anarchy," he asserted, "and it is the duty of the Governor to see that the laws are enforced. I intend to discharge this duty to the extent of the resources of the State, and to seek out the identity of those who take the law into their own hands and cause them to be prosecuted . But the law is now insufficient; it must be made more drastic in order that it may be dreaded by those who permit their inflamed passions to drive them into crimes of mob violence."[111]

Byrd outlined the proposed bill's three key provisions. First, lynching would become a state offense; the attorney general and state prosecutors, along with local officials, would pursue investigations. Second, the law would mandate that the county or city where the lynching occurred would pay a settlement of $2,500 to a victim's heirs. Finally, the governor would have access to unlimited discretionary funding to support his inquiry. Byrd made clear that the new law would in no way affect the constitutionally guaranteed rights of the accused to obtain trial in the localities where the lynching occurred.

The next day Jaffé began an editorial campaign to build public support for the resolution. He told his readers he could think of no objections to the proposal "that can compare in seriousness with the gravity of the lynching evil itself and the duty of an enlightened State to stamp it out." While he conceded that the fining provision might unfairly punish taxpayers who had not engaged in mob violence, he maintained it would significantly help "stimulate the growth of antilynching sentiment." Richmond's *News Leader* and *Times-Dispatch* also supported the measure.[112]

P. B. Young, too, lobbied vigorously for the proposal, which he observed "follows very closely along the lines previously advanced by the

111. *Guide,* 21 January 1928.
112. *Pilot,* 17 January 1928; *Richmond News Leader,* 18 February 1928; *Richmond Times-Dispatch,* 9 March 1928.

Virginian-Pilot." He expressed the desire that "Virginia . . . become among the first states of the nation to place specific outlawry upon this crime." The influential black editor reprinted Jaffé's editorials on the subject in his weekly paper. Young, like Jaffé, still preferred state rather than federal anti-lynching legislation. He believed southern whites would view a national law as an unwarranted interference into their affairs and work to stymie the statute's enforcement. States' rights arguments also influenced him.[113]

Several weeks passed without the assembly's taking action on the antilynching proposal. Any representative introducing a bill mandating state responsibility in lynching investigations risked offending the large section of the electorate who embraced the tenets of localism. Jaffé, growing increasingly anxious, prodded Byrd: "Is it possible that after your courageous pronouncement, the whole matter will come to nothing in default of a lawmaker brave enough to follow you?" He reminded the governor that an antilynching law would constitute a vital part of his political legacy. It would, he said, "contribute importantly to freeing Virginia from the recurring lynching disgrace, and would at the same time bring our State and our Governor the homage of every thoughtful student of public affairs in the United States." Jaffé had carefully monitored the press reaction to the proposed law, and he reported that he had found no criticism of it from any newspaper of merit. He emphasized his concern that the session would soon adjourn.[114]

That same day state senators James S. Barron of Norfolk and Cecil Connor of Leesburg, after careful deliberation with Byrd, formally introduced the bill into the General Assembly. The governor wired Jaffé the good news. Barron, the bill's principal sponsor, and Jaffé had already established a close friendship. As it had for Byrd, Jaffé's unremitting antilynching advocacy had acted as a prime influence in persuading Barron to take action. According to the state senator, his "first thoughts on the subject came from [Jaffé]." The editor had acted as a "pioneer," shaping public opinion and supplying the data and arguments in support of the measure.[115]

113. *Guide,* 21, 28 January 1928; Suggs, *P. B. Young, Newspaperman,* 60.
114. Brundage, *Lynching in the New South,* 161; Louis Jaffé to Harry Byrd, 3 February 1928, Jaffé Papers.
115. Harry Byrd to Louis Jaffé, 6 February 1928, James Barron to Edwin Alderman, 25 January 1929, Louis Jaffé to Sally Barron, 24 January 1933, all in Jaffé Papers.

Differing from Byrd's proposal only slightly, the bill Barron sponsored mandated that all members of a lynch mob and any accessories to the crime would receive murder sentences. Mob participants perpetrating assault and/or battery would receive penitentiary sentences of one to ten years. The bill ordered commonwealth's attorneys throughout the state to track down and prosecute lynch mobs vigorously. To supplement local investigations, the attorney general and state prosecutors, acting under the governor's direction and supported by whatever funding he required, would seek out and apprehend mob participants. The legislators weakened the fining provision. In order to receive payment, heirs would have to initiate action in the county or city where the lynching occurred. The localities would then recover whatever payments they had made by fining mob members.[116]

Jaffé redoubled his efforts to push the bill through. He evaluated the Barron bill highly, despite the fact that he preferred the fining provision proposed by the governor. He believed that "juries drawn from the tax lists" would never levy fines against their own localities. In late February the state senate unanimously passed the bill with one small modification. Victims' heirs seeking damages would have to undertake law action against mob participants—not the localities where the lynching had taken place.[117]

Jaffé reiterated for his readers the bill's many strengths and the fact that its passage would provide the state with a powerful weapon to eliminate not just lynchings, but all mob violence. He wrote:

> Had this law been in effect at the time of the Wytheville lynching, the State would have been spared the hemming and hawing that took place over the question of whether it was proper for the State to take notice of a mob murder that the local authorities were disposed to accept with considerable indifference. Had it been in effect when a Princess Anne County band wearing robes and hoods and armed with pistols, kidnapped a Catholic priest, this little adventure in banditry might have escaped the swift oblivion that overtook it. For the new law takes cognizance not only of lynchers and lynching mobs, but also of all criminal acts performed by

116. *Pilot,* 10 February 1928.
117. Ibid.; *Richmond News Leader,* 17 February 1928.

groups conspiring for this purpose. The unanimous vote cast by the Senate suggests that the kidnapping, flogging and lynching business is in for some long-delayed State regulation. With the help of the localities and an alert, supporting public opinion, it is easily within the State's power to stamp this business out.[118]

The General Assembly approved the bill on March 14, 1928, and Byrd signed it into law. The legislation's enactment marked one of the high points of Jaffé's career.[119]

The incidence of lynching had declined in Virginia over the last several decades. The number of instances (six) that had occurred in the first seven years of the 1920s paled in comparison to the over thirty cases in the 1890s. Mob violence had never flourished in Virginia to the extent that it had in the Deep South. But as Jaffé had emphasized, the new law put not only lynch mobs but all night riders, whipping parties, and wrecking crews on notice that their lawlessness would incur the state's wrath. The Old Dominion had seen plenty of this sort of mayhem since Jaffé had assumed the helm of the *Virginian-Pilot*.[120]

Would the law that Jaffé had so ardently promoted make a difference? In 1933, University of North Carolina law professor James Harmon Chadbourn, working in conjunction with the Southern Commission on the Study of Lynching, published *Lynching and the Law*, which contained an analysis of antilynching provisions and a description of existing state laws pertaining to mob violence. Formed in 1930 under the auspices of Will Alexander's Commission on Interracial Cooperation, the SCSL endeavored, by sponsoring research and disseminating findings, to build public support for measures that would end lynching. Chaired by George Fort Milton, the progressive young editor of the *Chattanooga News*, the commission included in its membership Julian Harris; Howard W. Odum, the South's

118. *Pilot*, 21 February 1928.

119. *Acts and Joint Resolutions of the General Assembly of the State of Virginia* (Richmond: Division of Purchase and Printing, 1928), 715–6; *Richmond News Leader*, 8 March 1928.

120. Brundage, *Lynching in the New South*, 281–3; Commission on the Study of Lynching, *Lynchings and What They Mean: General Findings of the Southern Commission on the Study of Lynching* (Atlanta: Commission on Interracial Cooperation, 1931), 74.

most prominent social scientist; Robert R. Moton and Monroe N. Work of Tuskegee Institute; and a number of other black and white southern luminaries.[121]

Chadbourn directly and indirectly pointed to the effectiveness of certain provisions of Virginia's law. Its constitution of lynching and mob violence as crimes, *sui generis,* placed it in the forefront of antilynching legislation thus far enacted by states. Definitions, the law professor declared, counted for nothing if laws went unenforced, but they provided useful starting points for legislation and added rhetorical unity to antilynching laws. Virginia's clear and concise definitions of mobs, lynchings, and mob assaults and batteries matched in substance if not in exact wording the corresponding definitions in the law professor's model acts.[122]

By making the punishment of lynchers, in Jaffé's words, a "primary obligation of the State," the commonwealth's new law met with Chadbourn's approval. He referred disparagingly to Virginia governor James Hoge Tyler's failure to intervene in a 1900 Newport News lynching and his explanation later that the whole matter "lay with local authorities." Chadbourn stressed the importance of investing state officials with the power to investigate lynchings. Local law authorities for reasons of complicity, incompetence, and fear often shirked their responsibilities. Virginia's antilynching law's provision expanding the powers of the attorney general and other state law authorities closely paralleled the corresponding section in the model acts. Jaffé considered this facet of the law—the first of its kind in southern antilynching legislation—to be its hallmark.[123]

The Commission on Interracial Cooperation later would emphasize in a report the indispensability of "applying in the local community the standards of the wider community which does not countenance lynching." "Lynchers," it explained, "go unpunished because punishment of their crime depends upon the same police officers and court officials whose impotence they demonstrated when they lynched. . . . Expecting these officers

121. Commission on Lynching, *Lynchings and What They Mean,* 6–7; Wilma Dykeman and James Stokely, *Seeds of Change: The Life of Will Alexander* (Chicago: University of Chicago Press, 1962), 137–41.

122. James Harmon Chadbourn, *Lynching and the Law* (Chapel Hill: University of North Carolina Press, 1931), 29–31, 134, 208–10.

123. Ibid., 80–1, 136, 208–10; *Pilot,* 13 May 1929.

and courts to arrest and punish lynchers is like expecting a dethroned government to punish those who overthrew it. . . . [Mobs] and their sympathizers constitute the effective majority in the community where a lynching occurs."[124]

The General Assembly might have gone further. It could have included provisions fining localities where lynchings occurred, ousting peace officers who failed to protect prisoners, and ordering jail transfers and changes of venue for crimes likely to provoke mob violence. Most significantly, it also might have mandated changes of venue for those accused of mob violence. Jaffé supported many if not all of these measures, but the assembly lacked the political will to adopt such ambitious legislation. Nevertheless, from the perspectives of southern liberals like Chadbourn, Virginia's new law had significant preventive and punitive effects. Other states in the region—Georgia and South Carolina, for example—had previously passed antilynching legislation; but by failing to empower state authorities to pursue lynching investigations, their statutes lacked the potency of Virginia's.[125]

Virginia's law in some respects exceeded in strength the federal antilynching bills championed by the NAACP in the 1920s and 1930s. These proposed laws mandated no direct federal action against lynchers, concentrating instead on authorities who shirked their duty and counties and cities where mob violence occurred. Virginia's statute, although it stipulated no sentences for law officers or fines for localities, telegraphed a clear message to mobs and their accessories that they risked murder sentences for lynchings and lengthy prison terms for assaults and/or batteries.[126]

Walter White, who succeeded James Weldon Johnson as executive

124. Commission on Interracial Cooperation, *The Mob Still Rides: A Review of the Lynching Record, 1931–1935* (Atlanta: Commission on Interracial Cooperation, 1936), 11, 19.

125. "Summary of Laws Relating to Lynching in the States (Except Texas) Having More Than 25 Lynchings in Past Thirty Years," May 1919, NAACP Papers; Chadbourn, *Lynching and the Law*, 154–6, 201–3; Stewart E. Tolnay and E. M. Beck, *A Festival of Violence: An Analysis of Southern Lynchings, 1882–1930* (Urbana: University of Illinois Press, 1995), 212–3.

126. Zangrando, *NAACP Crusade Against Lynching*, 43, 114–5.

secretary of the NAACP in 1929, authored another contemporary work on the efficacy of state antilynching laws. As Jaffé's advocacy bore fruit in the General Assembly, White—in France on a Guggenheim fellowship—completed *Rope and Faggot,* a seminal study of lynching. (NAACP correspondence during White's absence describes but does not appraise the statute.) Although White's reaction to the Virginia antilynching law is unknown, he likely would have conceded that the law had merit, and that in an Upper South state such as Virginia or North Carolina, where public sentiment militated against mob justice, a statute administered by a committed state government backed by the press, educational institutions, and organizations such as the NAACP and the soon-to-be-formed Association of Southern Women for the Prevention of Lynching and Southern Commission on the Study of Lynching could significantly deter mob violence.[127]

Generally speaking, however, White, an inveterate proponent of federal antilynching legislation, believed that state laws lacked the power to prevent lynching and punish mobs. "State anti-lynching laws are valuable and effective in an inverse ratio to the need for them," he wrote. "Unsentimental examination . . . causes one to conclude . . . that for such states as Mississippi, Arkansas, Florida, and others of the lower South there is little hope of effective action against lynchers through this channel. Until the lyncher of any person, regardless of the colour of the victim's skin or the offense with which he is charged, can be promptly indicted, tried, and convicted, state laws in such states are an illusion—and no honest citizen can assert that they will not continue to be in this generation and in several to come."[128]

White and his allies likely viewed Virginia's law as a distraction or an attempt to stave off national legislation. The *Literary Digest* regarded the statute this way, writing in the wake of the law's passage, "Virginia has forestalled the movement for a Federal anti-lynching law." W. Fitzhugh Brundage, who has authoritatively examined mob violence in Virginia and

127. White, *Man Called White,* 92–8; "Lynching," 4 April 1928, NAACP Papers; Kathleen Atkinson Miller, "The Ladies and the Lynchers: A Look at the Association of Southern Women for the Prevention of Lynching," *Southern Studies* 2, nos. 2–4 (1991): 261–80.

128. Walter White, *Rope and Faggot: A Biography of Judge Lynch* (New York: Alfred A. Knopf, 1929), 206–7.

traced the history of antilynching efforts in the state, has credited this inducement partially for the law's passage.[129]

But Jaffé did not dissemble; he genuinely objected to a federal law on the grounds that it would usurp the rights of the states. Nearly all editors of major southern dailies had joined Jaffé in urging the defeat of the Dyer bill, insisting that the states could put an end to lynching. To Jaffé's credit, he realized that his stand obliged him to advance a state remedy for mob justice. Indeed, no confirmed lynchings took place in Virginia after the enactment of the bill he had largely devised and so ardently promoted.[130]

The *Charleston (W.Va.) Gazette* encapsulated and endorsed this policy: "Virginia is to be commended for her consistency. She has insisted that this is a State matter with which Congress has nothing to do, and now she has recognized the truth that States must exercise this power. Virginia's example regarding lynching should be followed by all the States that have not strict anti-lynching laws."[131]

Hindsight confirms that White, who would greatly have preferred a powerful federal antilynching law over a hodgepodge of forty-eight statutes of varying strength, stood on the correct side of the issue. Virginia's law served the Old Dominion well, but it did not inspire emulation by her neighbors in the Deep South, where racial violence continued unchecked.

129. "Virginia's Anti-Lynching Law," *Literary Digest*, 10 March 1928, 14; Brundage, *Lynching in the New South*, 189–90; Brundage, "To Howl Loudly."
130. Rable, "South and Antilynching Legislation," 207.
131. "Virginia's Anti-Lynching Law," 14.

Philip Jaffe, Louis's father, with granddaughter Margie and son Hyman (Margie's father and Louis's brother). The image is undated, but judging from Margie's age it was taken about 1917.

Lotta Maria Jaffe, Louis's mother, date unknown.

Louis in 1907, the year he graduated from Durham High School and entered Trinity College.

Durham High School fraternity group, 1907, Louis's graduation year. The young men all wear the same silver-skull lapel pin visible in Louis's formal portrait of the same year.

While a student at Trinity College, Louis traveled to Europe as a deckhand on a cattle transport bound for Germany. He is seen in white cap, front row, second from left. June, 1908.

Louis in his dormitory room at Trinity College.

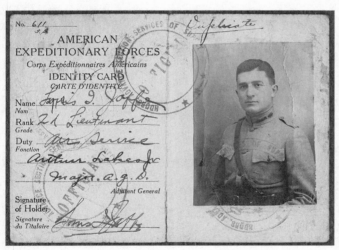

Identity card as a second lieutenant in the American Expeditionary Forces, 1918.

Celebrating the armistice, Is-sur-Tille village hotel, France, November 11, 1918. In the first photo, Jaffé is standing third from left, hand raised in toast. In the second, he is second from right, between Mme and M. Victor Régert, with Mme wearing Louis's cap. M. Régert was manager of the P.L.M. freight station.

With French officers at Itea, Greece, April 1919, after disembarking from the steamer that carried him from Taranto, Italy. Jaffé was on his way to Salonika to begin his tour of the postwar Balkans, reporting on conditions to the American Red Cross.

In the summer of 1920, six months after assuming editorship of the *Norfolk Virginian-Pilot,* age thirty-two. Taken in the Tazewell Street building at his desk.

Margaret Davis Jaffé with Louis Christopher Jaffé, born 1922. From his age in this photo, it appears to have been taken around 1925. Margaret and Louis were divorced when their son was fourteen; she retained custody and legally changed his name to Christopher Wheelright Davis.

Christopher Davis in his teens. He died of heart failure in 1974, aged fifty-two.

Guests at a luncheon given by Douglas Freeman in honor of John Stewart Bryan in 1936. All present had served under Bryan on the *Richmond Times-Dispatch* (except his brother), and all became editors of Virginia newspapers. Left to right: Douglas Southall Freeman, J. St. George Bryan, Jaffé, John Stewart Bryan, Douglas Gordon, Virginius Dabney, William B. Smith, Robert Glass.

Jaffé and Lenoir Chambers in Jaffé's office, 1937.

Jaffé, third from left, on a visit to the salt mines near Salzburg, Austria, July 25, 1937. Tourists donned special coveralls to enter the mine with a guide. Jaffé toured Europe with a friend on the eve of WWII, observing the increasingly tense situation, while trying to distance himself from his failed first marriage.

Louis weds Alice Cohn Rice in Norfolk, May 14, 1942.

Louis in his office in 1944. Alice Jaffé wrote: "A grim picture. But these were grim times."

Louis, Alice, and Louis Jr., born October 12, 1946.

Jaffé photographed by Ralph T. K. Larson in 1949.

9 THE WANING TWENTIES

Jaffé's zealous and unremitting campaign for human rights was all the more remarkable in light of the pressures he was facing in his personal life. As the 1920s wore on, his relationship with his wife, Margaret, began to unravel.

Her concern over the health of their son, Christopher, must have seemed justified at first. At age three the boy had developed a temperature that mysteriously hovered at one hundred degrees for a prolonged period, and local doctors had removed his tonsils. The diagnosis shifted to a glandular problem when the elevated temperature persisted. Apparently dissatisfied with the quality of local physicians, Margaret consulted a Washington, D.C., pediatrician, Dr. John Foote. In late 1926 she and Jaffé made the four-hundred-mile round trip to the capital with Christopher for the first time. Back in Norfolk, Christopher's temperature returned to normal for a few days and then again rose slightly. Margaret grew anxious, and Jaffé, not overly alarmed, wrote to Foote asking him to reassure her. Later in the year, Jaffé wrote again to Foote—at his wife's "insistence"—to express her concern over the child's constipation and the condition of his heart.[1]

The Jaffés' appointment with Foote began a pattern of Margaret's traveling away from Norfolk with her child to seek help from a range of doctors and from more healthful environments at resorts and spas. Sometimes Jaffé accompanied her; more often he did not. The frequency and duration of her absences increased, as did the expense of Christopher's many medical treatments in Washington, D.C., and his mother's lengthy stays with him in luxury hotels there. Adding to the cost, Margaret engaged a private nurse to attend to her son. The two women and Christopher lodged in the capital's expensive Martinique Hotel and then traveled back

1. Louis Jaffé to John Foote, 15 December 1926, 29 January 1927, 2 September 1927, Louis Jaffé Jr.

to Norfolk together. Jaffé may have tried to convince his wife that Norfolk's comparatively large medical community could adequately care for their son. By and large, however, throughout the latter half of the 1920s, he indulged her. In order to finance her trips, he dipped deeply into his savings and the careful investments he had made in preparation for retirement.[2]

Margaret's brother, prominent Norfolk lawyer Hugh W. Davis, noticed his sister's preoccupation with her child's health. He had called on the three Jaffés during one of their medical trips to Washington, but Margaret, worried that Davis might infect Christopher, "bounced" him off quickly because she was "afraid of 'bugs.'" Christopher did have less than robust health, but his mother's overprotectiveness, her restrictions, and her fixation on minor ailments undoubtedly impaired his development. Her constant uprooting of her son militated further against his prospects for any semblance of a normal childhood.[3]

Medicine provided Margaret with a theme for her story "Shut In," which *Catholic World* magazine published in 1926. She considered publication of the story, parts of which may have been suggested by her own perceived experience, one of the major successes of her literary career. Two collections of short stories, while not reprinting the piece, mentioned it in their appendices along with hundreds of other stories.[4]

Sylvia Calhoun, the heroine of "Shut In," shares the lonely life of her physician husband in eastern Kentucky. Selfless Robert Calhoun has devoted his career to ministering to poor mountain people in an isolated community. Lacking companionship, the genteel and cultured Sylvia has wasted away emotionally and physically. A friend of the couple, acclaimed surgeon Edward Garth, who shares Robert's passionate love for his wife, arrives to perform a difficult obstetrical procedure involving the Calhouns' unborn child. They have lost two children previously.

Sylvia gives birth to a son but teeters on the verge of death. Her heart stops beating, and Robert is unable to revive her through hypodermic

2. Peggy Johnston to Louis Jaffé, 1928, Louis Jaffé to Margaret Jaffé, 22 March 1931, both ibid.

3. Hugh W. Davis to Louis Jaffé, 12 October 1928, Jaffé Papers.

4. Margaret Davis Jaffé, "Shut In," *Catholic World*, October 1926, 75–87; *Catholic World*, June 1933, 367; Blanche Colton Williams, ed., *O. Henry Memorial Award Prize Stories of 1927* (Garden City, N.Y.: Doubleday, Doran, 1928), xx.

injection, artificial respiration, and external heart massage. He pledges he will leave his mountain clinic and accept a post in the city if she lives. Failed by the science of medicine, he intuitively places their child in bed beside her. The story continues:

> He took his wife's thin, unresisting hand and placed it against the soft body. His finger rested on her wrist. He called her name again, drew the child more closely into the circle of her arm. And strangely, it was as if something in the contact penetrated to her, recalling her from the peace in far-off places where she had withdrawn. Slowly, imperceptibly, the thread of her pulse fluttered. Life trembled its way into her face, stirred it to expression, to remembrance—to a whole shimmering aura of emotion that he did not understand—as a chance stone stirs widening circles in the still waters of a pool. Her breast heaved. One hand flew out in sudden fear and hunger toward her son. Then the long bronze lashes fluttered down over the violet eyes in deep content. Her breath began to come and go unevenly. And the will to live came back.[5]

Sylvia recovers and, filled with maternal bliss, implores her husband to retract his desperate promise to move them to the city. She vows to help him bear the burden of his humanitarian work in the mountains.

Margaret did not limit her preoccupation with illness to her son and short story themes; the state of her own health also frequently absorbed her attention. Throughout the 1920s she sought treatment for a range of medical and dental concerns. Her complaints of illness would grow more frequent in the following decade.[6]

Jaffé's relationship with his parents placed him under additional strain. His workload and the demands of real and imagined sickness in his household left little time for visiting with the elder Jaffes, and he seldom traveled to South Boston. That his wife and son ever accompanied him seems unlikely. Margaret's concern over Christopher's health would have

5. Margaret Davis Jaffé, "Shut In," 85.

6. See Louis Jaffé to Hyman Jaffe, 4 July 1921, Margaret Jaffé to Louis Jaffé, 22 August 1921, Louis Jaffé to Mrs. Ruffer, 8 January 1929, [March 1929], 11 March 1929, 2 May 1929, all Louis Jaffé Jr.; Louis Jaffé to Lucien Starke, 8 October 1929, Jaffé Papers.

provided a rationale for limiting—probably excluding entirely—their presence on such trips. She distanced herself and her son from her in-laws as completely as she could, regarding them with disdain and wishing, above all, to shield the boy from his Jewish ancestry. Her attitude would certainly have discouraged Jaffé from inviting his Orthodox parents for stays in his home.[7]

A letter to Louis Jaffé dictated in the mid-1920s by Lotta, who spoke but did not write English, deplores his alienation from his parents and implicates Margaret in the estrangement: "It has been eleven months since we have seen each other, and I am certain you can imagine how I feel about it. Last summer when I was in Norfolk, I brought a little present from home to give your baby. After hearing about your people, I was certain your wife would not accept it or either would throw it out and very disappointed I took it back home with me. Dear son, why is it that you do not write me more often? Have I wronged against you? I can't think of any time in which I have. . . . I hope you will come to see me. If you can't come yourself, come with your family."[8]

Another letter to Jaffé at the decade's end, as cataracts blurred Lotta's vision, suggested that relations had improved little: "In your last letter to me, you said that you would be here shortly. We have waited & waited, but as yet, have seen nothing of you. What's the trouble? Guess you think I am trying to repay you by waiting so long to answer, but really it's very hard for me to get someone to write. I would write in Jewish, although it is hard on my eyes, but I am afraid you won't be able to read it."[9]

Philip, too, now suffered poor health. In 1920 he had undergone a serious operation in Baltimore, perhaps related to the "spells" that would plague him until his death in 1933. The elder Jaffes and their son Hyman, who lived in South Boston with his wife, Hattie, and their two young daughters, Gladys and Margie, undoubtedly experienced occasional prosperity, particularly following bountiful growing seasons when the fall tobacco sales at the warehouses—Planters, Edmondson's, and the Independent—brought customers into their store. Nevertheless Jaffes' Dry Goods fared poorly in

7. Louis Jaffé to Margaret Jaffé, 6 March 1933, 22 March 1931, Louis Jaffé Jr.
8. Lotta Jaffe to Louis Jaffé, n.d., ibid.
9. Lotta Jaffe to Louis Jaffé, 6 March 1929, ibid.

comparison to other local clothing stores. It lacked the resources to weather severe economic downturns and competition from the chain stores that had begun to make inroads across the South.[10]

In 1926 the inaugural edition of the *Astonisher,* a monthly business magazine published in South Boston, promoted in editorial form the wares of various merchants in an attempt to stimulate sales. It highlighted Raiff's and Glasers Department Stores' inventories of Prince of Wales sport coats and silk crepe dresses, and announced the arrival at Jewish-owned Lantor's and Bermann Brothers of "celebrated gold-stripe hose" and "English prints in new patterns." The less glamorous "Happy Home Dresses . . . represent[ing] an unusual value in house dresses" available at Jaffes' seemingly placed the store a tier or more beneath rival businesses. Unlike nearly all of the town's other dry goods merchants, Hyman and Philip—perhaps for economic reasons—did not advertise in the *Astonisher.*[11]

Elderly residents of South Boston recall the town's boom-and-bust economy of the 1920s. A bumper crop of tobacco in 1927 brought good times, but droughts and hailstorms during several of the decade's growing seasons spelled hard times for merchants, farmers, and warehouse workers alike. South Boston's cotton mill and trade in mules, fertilizer, and lumber provided too little economic diversity to cushion the town from a failed crop. By all accounts "tobacco was king."[12]

In the late 1920s, as he vigorously prodded Byrd to introduce an anti-lynching bill, Louis Jaffé became one of the first southern editors to endorse New York governor Alfred E. Smith's presidential candidacy. By most objective measures the pinstripe-suited, cigar-chomping, nasal-accented Tammany politician offered the best credentials and the most charisma to give the Republicans, who had annihilated the Democrats in the two previous elections, a run for their money.[13]

10. Louis Jaffé to Alexander Forward, 27 August 1920, Jaffé Papers; Stevens, interview by author, 10 July 1996.

11. "Glad Rags," *The Astonisher: A Magazine of Facts and Near-Facts about South Boston and Halifax* (March 1926), 16–7.

12. Carol Headspeth, interview by author, 1 April 1996; Stevens, interview by author, 10 July 1996.

13. John Kneebone, *Southern Liberal Journalists and the Issue of Race, 1920–1944* (Chapel Hill: University of North Carolina Press, 1985), 44.

At the 1924 Democratic National Convention, party kingmakers had recognized the governor's presidential timber; however, after much hand-wringing they had anointed a compromise candidate with less skill but with fewer perceived liabilities than the New Yorker. Nearly all informed observers had surmised that Dixie would serve as the national election's decisive battleground. The conventional wisdom of the day had divined that Smith—a Roman Catholic, a "wet," and the son of poor Irish immigrants—would split the so-called "Solid South" in half. One hundred three ballots later, the Democrats sent neither Al Smith nor native southerner William G. McAdoo forth to do battle with Calvin Coolidge, but the prosaic corporate lawyer, John W. Davis. Coolidge received nearly twice as many popular votes in the general election that fall.[14]

The Democratic Party picked itself up off the mat and made plans for the next election. Virginius Dabney in *Dry Messiah,* arguably his finest book, writes that as the 1928 Democratic convention neared, the "drys were strong enough in the South to stifle Smith sentiment in almost all political circles, but in the rest of the country hardly anyone but Smith was in the running." The election—Al Smith's front-running candidacy for his party's nomination in particular—galvanized a formidable host of opponents: Herbert Hoover and the Republicans; the pro-Prohibition forces marshaled in the South by Methodist bishop James Cannon Jr.; and the Ku Klux Klan, reinvigorated, albeit briefly, by its demagogic evocation of a Catholic chief executive allegiant to Rome. From within his own party, too, the governor faced much opposition.[15]

Smith's candidacy spawned one of Jaffé's few editorial excursions into magazine and journal writing. "The Democracy and Al Smith" appeared in the *Virginia Quarterly Review* in the summer of 1927. The piece is useful in understanding the editor's lifelong affinity for the Democratic Party and his penchant for Smith. Jaffé expressed both a clear vision of what the party should stand for and an abhorrence of what it had become in his region. "Outside the South," he wrote, "the Democratic party retains some of the old Jeffersonian affections for individualism and the concerns

14. Henry F. Pringle, *Alfred E. Smith: A Critical Study* (New York: Macy-Masius, 1927), 291–314.

15. Dabney, *Dry Messiah*, 176.

of the plain people. . . . Jefferson's Democracy was compounded of freedom of religion, freedom of the press, freedom of the person, equal and exact justice to all men, of whatever state or persuasion, religious or political, absolute separation of church and State, local and State self-government, the completest measure of personal liberty consonant with effective co-operation in government, and the arraignment of all abuses at the bar of public reason."[16]

Few vestiges of this, Jaffé lamented, endured in the party's Dixie component, which he accused of having become "essentially Bourbon." He cataloged the liberties on which the ruling Democrats tacitly condoned restrictions: "Of freedom of the press, individual liberty, and separation of church and State there is less in the Southern citadel of Democracy than in any other section in the country. It is here, in the shelter of all-Democratic Legislatures, that we have the most successful ecclesiastical inroads on the processes of lay education and the most effective evangelical control of tests for public office." He pointed out the pressures these restrictions exerted on his own profession: "It is here that newspapers that venture to question the godliness of prohibition and the decency of its enforcement are punished by the largest number of cancellations, and it is here, too, that the heaviest reprisals are carried out against newspapers that make bold to denounce the assassination of the religious equality principle by the Ku Klux Klan. It is here that the freedom of the press is curtailed by the strictest libel laws."[17]

Jaffé urged the Democrats to reject their previous focus on realpolitik, which had led them to cater to the sectional interests of a southern elite, and instead to construct their campaign on the beliefs that had historically and sharply differentiated their party from the Republicans. "Nothing has been done to make the party representative of progress and liberal thought, nothing has been done toward tying the party to principles rather than personalities," he wrote. He urged the Democrats to serve as the voice of the common people and to champion fairness.[18]

He especially deplored the attacks on the New York governor from

16. Louis I. Jaffé, "The Democracy and Al Smith," *Virginia Quarterly Review* 3, no. 3 (1927): 326–7.
17. Ibid.
18. Ibid., 325.

within his own party. "For the first time in the history of American politics," Jaffé wrote, "there is heading up within the Democratic Party an evangelical crusade openly and unashamedly dedicated to the proposition that this is a government of the Protestants, by the Protestants, for the Protestants, and that Catholics have no political rights under the Constitution save those meted out to them by the religious majority in the exercise of its all-enfolding mercy."[19]

In Al Smith he saw exceptional potential. The governor's commitment to liberalism, his common touch, and his leadership and political skills qualified him well to serve as the Democratic candidate for the presidency. Jaffé conceded Smith's comparative weakness in the South but believed voters there would cast their ballots for him in large numbers should he earn the nomination. Even if Smith divided the electorate, so much the better in the long run. Jaffé protested the "political one-sidedness" he saw as his region's "baneful inheritance from Carpetbagger days." A genuine two-party system in the South would purge the party of Jefferson and Jackson of "its political amphibians," Democrats who embraced Republican ideals. It would stimulate the political participation of the white masses—theretofore compliant with or manipulated by the ruling oligarchy—for the purpose of advancing their own interests.[20]

But far and away the greatest benefit rendered by Smith's nomination would be to "confront this serpent of religious recrimination and defang it." Jaffé sounded a hopeful call: "An opportunity, wholly fortuitous, is offered the party to perform a distinguished national service—to import into the management of the nation's highest public trust that complete religious equality, unto this very day denied, that is the last command of our Constitution and the first concern of our Bill of Rights."[21]

Jaffé's defense of religious freedom and other civil liberties and his advocacy for the common man stopped short in one crucial respect: it did not contest white supremacy. Although he advocated a Democratic Party that would champion "equal and exact justice to all men," he felt it essential to emphasize that the development of a genuine two-party system in the

19. Ibid., 323.
20. Ibid., 339.
21. Ibid., 341.

South would not lead to an increase in black political power that could challenge Jim Crow. "No racial complications would follow this bi-partisan revolution because the Caucasian instinct, immeasurably deeper rooted than the partisan instinct, would command a common racial policy," he wrote. He catalogued many problems that plagued the Democratic Party in the South but chose not to examine race, the mainspring of politics in the Solid South.[22]

Jaffé lent Smith the full support of the *Pilot*'s editorial page, and newspaper peers disseminated his views on the election in areas far away from Norfolk. The *Danville (Va.) Register,* commenting on Jaffé's unequivocal endorsement of Smith in a guest editorial in the *Baltimore Sun,* stated that the Norfolk editor's views had "attracted national attention not only because of their literary robustness, but also because of their always certain ring of sincerity." Future *Richmond Times-Dispatch* editor Virginius Dabney found Jaffé's arguments for Smith compelling; two years after the publication of the *Virginia Quarterly Review* essay, Dabney remarked that it "gave me a bigger kick than any magazine article I have ever read."[23]

Jaffé's *Virginia Quarterly* essay initiated an exchange of letters with Julian Harris, editor of the *Columbus (Ga.) Enquirer-Sun* and the son of newspaperman and folklorist Joel Chandler Harris of Uncle Remus fame. Until that time, Jaffé's most noteworthy connections with journalists elsewhere had consisted of contacts with the editorial staff and publisher of the *Baltimore Sunpapers.* Harris, who later reprinted Jaffé's pro-Smith article in installments in the *Enquirer-Sun,* wrote to the *Pilot*'s editor in the summer of 1927, congratulating him and expressing his approbation of the piece.[24]

In 1920 Harris, the former managing editor of the *Atlanta Constitution,* had come home to Georgia from Europe, where during the war he had served as editor of the *New York Herald*'s Paris edition. (Jaffé's and Harris's journalistic experiences in the French capital at roughly the same time had apparently not led to their introduction.) In Columbus, Harris pur-

22. Ibid., 339.
23. *Danville (Va.) Register* [March 1928]; Kneebone, *Southern Liberal Journalists,* 44–5.
24. Louis Jaffé to Julian Harris, 2 July 1927, Jaffé papers.

chased half ownership of the *Enquirer-Sun,* the smallest daily in Georgia. Two years later, after assuming full control of the paper, he and his erudite wife, Julia—whose journalistic talents equaled if not exceeded her husband's—proceeded to campaign against not only the Ku Klux Klan but also lynch mobs, religious fundamentalists who sought to outlaw the teaching of evolution, and the suppression of free speech at the University of Georgia. Columbus lay in the heartland of Klan territory, and the Harrises' work there exposed them to the danger of arrest, bombing threats, physical intimidation, and bankruptcy. One thousand subscribers, nearly 20 percent of their readership, boycotted the paper after one series of anti-Klan editorials. Other campaigns attacking Prohibition's excesses and the proscription of the teaching of evolution lost another seven hundred readers.[25]

While the *Enquirer-Sun*'s controversial stands alienated many local subscribers, journalists in the national press and around the country followed the Harrises' struggle and applauded their courage. In 1925 the paper earned the Pulitzer Prize for public service. Jaffé praised the judges' choice. "Among the newspaper fraternity," he wrote, "this award will be recognized as particularly well-deserved. The *Columbus Enquirer-Sun* has been a fearless and hard-hitting enemy of obscurantism, intolerance, and cant in all its forms, and in a State where and at a time when, the service of such journalism was badly needed."[26]

With a letter of appreciation, Harris enclosed many of the *Enquirer-Sun*'s editorials, and Jaffé spent an entire evening reading them. He replied to his Georgia colleague that while the *Pilot* battled similar foes, it practiced a more mannered style of journalism: "The antics and attitudes you assail afflict us down here too, and we do our best to damn them but the frontal-attack-stink-bomb method you use would get us in endless trouble. We have to be several degrees more urbane about the business in these parts, but we try to pack the wallop nevertheless."[27]

25. Lisby, "Julian Harris and the *Columbus Enquirer-Sun,*" 4, 8; Kenneth Coleman and Charles Stephen Gurr, eds., *Dictionary of Georgia Biography,* vol. 1 (Athens: University of Georgia Press, 1983), 403–5; Charles Pekor Jr., "An Adventure in Georgia," *American Mercury* 8, no. 32 (August 1926): 410.

26. *Pilot,* 6 May 1924.

27. Louis Jaffé to Julian Harris, 2 July 1927, Jaffé Papers.

The next year Jaffé, at Harris's request, contributed a statement for use in a special edition of the *Enquirer-Sun* celebrating the paper's centennial. Jaffé's remarks provide insight into his views regarding the mission of the fourth estate. The Georgia paper's age mattered little to him, but he prized the *Enquirer*'s courage in having placed itself in the forefront in the battle against intolerance, nativism, and mob violence. "The great public service," he wrote, "is performed by individuals and newspapers who assail these and kindred abominations before the people have come to know them as abominable, who let fly boldly and unremittingly in the face of private and official hostility, in spite of accusations of treason, irreligion and degeneracy, in spite of sullen advertisers, fiery crosses and cancelled subscriptions, who are trailblazers in making their communities safe for the decencies of civilized living and not merely followers."[28]

Grover C. Hall, another southern editor, initiated a correspondence with Jaffé at approximately the same time Harris first wrote to the Norfolk editor. After having labored as the *Montgomery Advertiser*'s associate editor for over a dozen years, Hall took the helm of the paper in the summer of 1926. In 1924, he had written to H. L. Mencken and had received encouragement to confront vexing southern problems head-on in his editorials. Mencken brought Hall to the notice of *Baltimore Evening Sun* editor Hamilton Owens, who urged the Alabamian to contribute to the *Evening Sun* and employ his journalistic platform to illuminate the dark side of the Klan, religious fundamentalism, and anti-intellectualism.[29]

Although as yet Hall had achieved little prominence outside Alabama, Mencken had burnished the new editor's reputation in an *American Mercury* book review of Edwin Mims's *Advancing South*, which chronicled the growth of southern liberalism. (Mims, who headed the English department at Vanderbilt University, had previously taught at Trinity College, where he was one of Jaffé's professors.) Believing that Mims had given short shrift to a cadre of promising young southern journalists, Mencken chastised the professor for omitting Hall, as well as others such as Jaffé and the *Richmond News Leader*'s Virginius Dabney. Both Hall and Dabney basked

28. Louis Jaffé to Julian Harris, 19 April 1928, ibid.
29. Hollis, *Alabama Newspaper Tradition*, 29, 31–2.

in the attention Mencken's acknowledgment earned them, and it seems safe to assume that Jaffé, too, enjoyed his momentary celebrity.[30]

In Hall's first letter to Jaffé, written in the spring of 1927 as he awaited management's approval for an editorial campaign against the Klan, he sounded out his more senior colleague regarding the effect of controversial editorials on the *Pilot*'s circulation. "We have had but few cancellations on account of our prohibition policy," Jaffé wrote back, "nothing to be concerned about. Our sharpest reaction has been in connection with our anti-Klan policy, but even this has caused us no particular alarm. Many who have left us on account of the Klan business have come back and the Klan itself, I am glad to see, is gradually losing out." The Virginia editor went on to express his high regard for the *Advertiser*'s editorial page—"one of those the South can take pride in"—and his desire to make Hall's acquaintance.[31]

Hall replied that he greatly admired the *Pilot*'s editorial page. The two papers had recently established an exchange agreement; previously, he had known of Jaffé only by reputation. His reading of the Norfolk newspaper had confirmed the "good reports" he had received. "Your stuff frequently is nothing less than majestic," Hall wrote, and he extended to Jaffé a standing invitation to visit him in Montgomery. He mentioned that H. L. Mencken and publisher Paul Patterson of the *Baltimore Sunpapers* had sojourned there the previous fall and had taught him all the words to "I Am a One Hundred Percent American."[32]

Mencken's whistle-stop journey from Baltimore to Montgomery (the home of one of his inamoratas, novelist Sara Powell Haardt) had attracted the attention of southern politicians. Despite Mencken's well-known animus towards the South, they attended closely to the Sage's electoral prognostications. With characteristic deviltry, Mencken had publicly dubbed a favorite son of each state he passed through as Calvin Coolidge's

---

30. H. L. Mencken, "The Library," *American Mercury* 8, no. 32 (1926): 506; Louis Jaffé to Edwin Mims, 15 May 1926, Jaffé Papers; Michael O'Brien, *Rethinking the South: Essays in Intellectual History* (Athens: University of Georgia Press, 1993), 147; Fred Hobson, *Tell About the South: The Southern Rage to Explain* (Baton Rouge: Louisiana State University Press, 1983), 187–9; Dabney, *Across the Years*, 116; Hollis, *Alabama Newspaper Tradition*, 30.

31. Louis Jaffé to Grover Hall, 22 April 1927, Jaffé Papers.

32. Grover Hall to Louis Jaffé, 25 April 1927, ibid.

heir apparent. The anointed politicians wallowed in the publicity until they figured out the caper.[33]

Hall also shared with Jaffé the *Advertiser*'s strategy for deflecting criticism of its often unpopular positions: "We try to keep the public reconciled to our editorial policy by means of fair news and an open forum column that is really open. In our letter column contributors have denied everything from the Virgin Birth to the infallibility of [Anti-Saloon League leader] Wayne Wheeler." Hall closed his letter by revealing that he had a standing bet of $1.00 that the Democratic party would nominate Al Smith, and a subsequent wager of $1.25 against $1.00 that if nominated the New Yorker would win the general election that fall. Hall's assault on the Klan would earn him a Pulitzer Prize.[34]

As a Trinity alumnus, Jaffé might have been expected to tread lightly when Buck Duke's forty-million-dollar bequest in 1924 transformed the small college into a major institution (Duke University) with an endowment placing it among the nation's half-dozen wealthiest. He did not. In "Duke University's Bid for Greatness," published in *McNaught's Monthly*, Jaffé minced no words and vexed Duke president William Few, who may have regretted writing John Stewart Bryan the laudatory letter of recommendation that sent young Louis off to his first real newspaper job. Jaffé believed the constraints that Buck Duke had placed on the university—that it conduct "sane and practical" education—consigned to the institution a "somewhat pedestrian mandate . . . in the luncheon club tradition of ruthless service." The university's inclination to avoid contention also troubled him. Despite the courageous stand Trinity had taken in upholding academic freedom in the Bassett affair two decades earlier, Few had not spoken out forcefully when in 1925 North Carolina fundamentalists had nearly passed an anti-evolution law. William Poteat, president of Baptist-funded Wake Forest College, and the University of North Carolina's president Harry Chase had bravely opposed the measure and figured prominently in its defeat. (President Few comported himself better two years later at a conference of Methodist educators when he sponsored a resolution opposing legislation that would

33. Mencken, *Thirty-Five Years of Newspaper Work,* 160.
34. Grover Hall to Louis Jaffé, 25 April 1927, Jaffé Papers.

"interfere with the proper teaching of Scientific subjects in American Schools and Colleges.")[35]

Jaffé insinuated that the Duke administration's earlier failure to speak out reflected the powerful influence North Carolina's Methodist conferences exerted over the university's trustees. In the present era, he wrote, the university "extols free speech but its leading intellects find it convenient and comfortable to practice the fine art of reticence. There are no sacred cows ostentatiously belled, but . . . there has been perfected at Duke an attitude of pietistic restraint, a disposition to avoid grappling with social controversy and intellectual unrest, and to stick to the unadventuring muttons of polite learning."[36]

Few could hardly ignore Jaffé's criticisms, since the *Duke Chronicle* reprinted the entire piece. The following Saturday, he informed a senior class assembly that "every false notion and every idle rumor concerning Duke University has been gathered together and put into one article." He did not identify specific errors, and the students puzzled over what he meant. The *Chronicle* reported that their president's attitude disturbed many of the students, who despite supporting their administration "thought Mr. Jaffé to be one of the best friends of the institution." The members of the senior class who knew the *Pilot*'s editor liked him very much and did not believe he had intended to attack the university.[37]

The incident inspired an exchange of polite but terse letters between the two protagonists. Few drew a distinction between the "creative" role he had to play as Duke's president and the "critical" attitude his former student had to adopt as an editor. The difference between the two eluded Jaffé, who concluded his rejoinder, "I am hoping that when the last balance is

35. Willard B. Gatewood Jr., *Preachers, Pedagogues, & Politicians: The Evolution Controversy in North Carolina, 1920–1927* (Chapel Hill: University of North Carolina Press, 1966), 76–9, 124–7; Gerald Johnson, *South-Watching*, ed. Fred Hobson (Chapel Hill: University of North Carolina Press, 1983), 177–8, 197–8; Louis I. Jaffé, "Duke University's Bid for Greatness," *McNaught's Monthly*, February 1926, 43–6; William D. Snider, *Light on the Hill: A History of the University of North Carolina at Chapel Hill* (Chapel Hill: University of North Carolina Press, 1992), 189; "Educational Association of the Methodist Episcopal Church, South, Resolution," 10 February 1927, Few Papers.

36. Jaffé, "Duke University's Bid for Greatness," 43–6.

37. *Duke Chronicle*, 3, 10 February 1926.

struck the critics of this world will be found to have been also the creators. Unless I believed this I should be very unhappy."[38]

In 1928, as the national presidential election neared, Jaffé took Few and Duke to task again, this time claiming that the institution's president had politicized the campus. Earlier in the year, John Bassett's death in a streetcar accident had prompted a *Pilot* editorial recalling the controversy surrounding his notorious article and Trinity's defense of academic freedom. Ten days later, however, Jaffé chided Few for a speech he reportedly had given to religious leaders, declaring his opposition to separation of church and state. Few's remarks must have seemed to fly in the face of Bassett's legacy.[39]

Jaffé accused the university of spearheading the formation of an anti-Smith organization in Durham. Smith's candidacy had spawned frenzied resistance to him throughout the region. Bishop James Cannon headed the ecclesiastical campaign against the New Yorker south of the Potomac, publicly attacking Smith for his opposition to Prohibition and privately fanning the flames of anti-Catholicism. Many Baptist and Methodist leaders followed Cannon's example; the Ku Klux Klan also demonized Smith. Anti-Smith forces—including many clergymen—spread false rumors and innuendo about his personal life. Virginius Dabney called what ensued a "campaign of vilification and misrepresentation such as had not been seen since reconstruction."[40]

Jaffé based his critical editorial on press reports that Few had attended an organizational meeting of the Durham Anti-Smith Club, where he had informed its membership that another Duke administrator had agreed to serve as the group's chairman. Few, an ardent Prohibitionist, regarded New York's "wet" governor unfavorably. The thought of his alma mater ganging up against Smith disturbed Jaffé greatly. He consulted another source to confirm the newspaper accounts and went on the attack. He claimed that Few's anti-Smith stand and the trustees' ties to the Method-

38. William Few to Louis Jaffé, 11 February 1926, Louis Jaffé to William Few, 22 February 1926, both in Jaffé Papers.

39. *Pilot,* 10 February 1928.

40. Alfred E. Smith, *Up to Now: An Autobiography* (New York: Viking, 1929), 395–6; Frank Graham, *Al Smith: American* (New York: G. P. Putnam's Sons, 1945), 198–201, Dabney, *Liberalism in the South,* 283.

ist Church had cowed many of the professors, who feared to express their own views. He alleged that only "at Duke University . . . among the larger North Carolina institutions of learning have prominent members of the faculty lent themselves to political belligerency."[41]

Several days later, however, Jaffé learned that he had based his censure on false information. Dean William Wannamaker, his old German teacher, wrote his former pupil a devastating critique of his editorial, pointing out many factual errors. The two men shared an affection for each other, and the rebuke stung Jaffé.[42]

Few had not told the Anti-Smith Club that one of his colleagues would serve as its chairman; he had not even been in Durham that day. True, several of the faculty had joined the club, but Few had voiced his concern over their assumption of leadership roles. Wannamaker expressed astonishment that Jaffé really believed that the faculty would not vote according to their own convictions. He found the notion that Duke's Methodist connections had intimidated academic staff into joining the anti-Smith Club preposterous: "When men like you, a son of the house, publish such raw insinuations . . . you surely do the University . . . immeasurable harm."[43]

Wannamaker administered a harsh scolding, but he knew Jaffé would wish to correct his error: "My feeling is just what it would be if you back in college should have published what I considered an inaccurate interpretation of . . . Faust. Anyway we shall always understand each other. I know you would rather present the truth with no reward than to attain fame by brilliant editorials . . . at the expense of anyone or any institution, however great or small."[44]

Jaffé apologized and published an editorial retraction entitled "In Justice to Dr. Few." Nevertheless the "son of the house" undoubtedly remained in the university administration's doghouse for the next several years.[45]

41. Louis Jaffé to William Wannamaker, 10 August 1928, William Wannamaker to Louis Jaffé, 16 August 1928, both in Jaffé Papers; Robert F. Durden, *The Launching of Duke University, 1924–1949* (Durham: Duke University Press, 1993), 207.

42. Louis Jaffé to William Wannamaker, 10 August 1928, 2 December 1938, Wannamaker Papers.

43. William Wannamaker to Louis Jaffé, 16 August 1928, Jaffé Papers.

44. Ibid.

45. *Pilot*, 7 September 1928.

* * *

The *Virginian-Pilot* maintained its editorial stance throughout the 1928 presidential election. In the face of what W. J. Cash termed the "militant Protestantism" that permeated the South, particularly its rural areas, Jaffé battled for Smith, whose candidacy confirmed for many in the region their belief that the Vatican schemed to seize the White House.[46]

Jaffé conducted a detailed examination of every attack made on Smith—his religion, views on Prohibition, working class roots, lack of formal education, Tammany connections, New York accent, and even his wife's appearance, clothing, and manners—and exposed their pettiness, meanspiritedness, and falsity. In the process, he challenged the claims of clerical politicians such as Bishop Cannon, who presented themselves as the sole arbiters of morality. Jaffé's successor, Lenoir Chambers, appraised his predecessor's unrelenting campaign as the "finest example of editorial political fighting in his career."[47]

In the end, of course, Jaffé lost his fight—gloriously and totally. Hoover carried the day in a landslide and swept the electoral college overwhelmingly. The Democrats prevailed in the largest cities, but Jaffé's efforts notwithstanding, Norfolk voted for Hoover 8,300 to 5,800. Despite all the talk about the Solid South, the states of Virginia, Florida, North Carolina, Tennessee, and Texas bolted the Democratic Party. Only the Deep South states, where whites felt even more threatened by high percentages of blacks than by the specter of a papist president, remained loyal to the historic party of Jim Crow.[48]

Herbert Clark Hoover—engineer, statesman, and humanitarian—assumed the presidency in a period of unrivaled prosperity. During his inaugural address in March 1929, a chilly rain spattered his face while he confidently declared that "in no nation are the fruits of accomplishment more secure" than in the United States. Many indicators seemed to support his assertion. Throughout the decade the national income had increased by

46. W. J. Cash, *The Mind of the South* (New York: Vintage, 1991), 334.
47. See *Pilot*, 19 April 1927, 28 and 29 June 1928; Chambers, Shank, and Sugg, *Salt Water & Printer's Ink*, 339.
48. Chambers, Shank, and Sugg, *Salt Water & Printer's Ink*, 339–40; V. O. Key Jr., *Southern Politics in State and Nation* (Knoxville: University of Tennessee Press, 1984), 318–9; J. S. Reed and D. V. Reed, *1001 Things*, 119.

45 percent. Builders had constructed three and a half million new homes, and the American people had engaged in an orgy of consumption, purchasing a dizzying amount of communication and transportation technology—six million telephones, seven million wireless sets, and fourteen million automobiles. A skyrocketing percentage of young people attended grade and high schools, colleges, and universities. "I have no fears for the future of our country," the new president proclaimed. "It is bright with hope." Hoover possessed a matchless reputation for efficiency and idealism, and the American public blithely looked forward to the good times that lay ahead.[49]

In late June 1928, a few days prior to the opening ceremonies of the Democratic convention in Houston, Jaffé had directed his attention to the booming oil metropolis for reasons other than politics. A gang of unmasked white men with revolvers in hand had abducted a black patient from a Houston hospital and hanged him from a bridge. If the vigilantes had simply wanted Robert Powell dead, they might have saved themselves the trouble; the wound he had suffered in a shoot-out with police probably would have killed him anyway. Plainly blood lust and a desire to terrorize the area's blacks figured prominently in the killers' motivation.[50]

The Advisory Board of the School of Journalism at Columbia University would soon cite Jaffé's response to the lynching, "An Unspeakable Act of Savagery," as an exemplar of superior editorial writing, worthy of the Pulitzer Prize. But in truth the piece—while certainly conforming to the tenets of the "Jaffé editorial formula"—displayed no greater command of his craft than scores of others he had authored.

"As the Democratic hosts prepare to rededicate themselves anew to fairness and justice," he wrote,

> the bustling Southern city in which they are to meet is disgraced by an unspeakable act of savagery. There is no other way to describe the performance of the eight armed white men who yanked Robert Powell, 24-year-old Negro, from a hospital cot on which he lay with a bullet in his stomach, and hanged him from a bridge just

49. *New York Times*, 5 March 1929.
50. *Pilot*, 21 June 1928.

outside the city. Powell was under the charge of killing a detective in a shooting match from which he himself emerged with an apparently mortal wound. In the event of his recovery, he was headed for the courts. But to this Texas mob neither Death nor Justice was an acceptable arbiter. Nothing would satisfy them but a loathsome act of murder carried out against a human being while he lay in agony with a bullet in his entrails.[51]

Jaffé conjectured that the national attention focused on Houston had led state law authorities to pursue the investigation with uncharacteristic energy. "Ordinarily," he observed,

Texas Justice proceeds in these matters with considerably less dispatch and excitement. But this is no time to inquire too closely into motives. One of the proudest cities of Texas has been polluted by one of the foulest forms of mob murder, and it is a matter for general satisfaction that the authorities are moving so energetically to repair the damage to Texas' good name. If the perseverance of the authorities is in keeping with their initial burst of energy, one or more of the group that bravely did to death a crippled man lying on a hospital cot, may see the inside of the Texas penitentiary.[52]

Probably the Advisory Board at Columbia—as Robert Mason, one of Jaffé's editorial successors at the *Virginian-Pilot,* surmised—detected in the final paragraph evidence that the writer had mastered his subject through painstaking study:

The year that saw four months pass without a single lynching, has now accumulated five of them. Five lynchings in six months represents a proportional reduction in savagery from last year's record of 16 lynchings in 12 months, but the year is only half gone and no one may be too confident. We have come a long way from the dark days of 1892 when America celebrated the 400th anniversary of its discovery with 255 lynchings, but we have not yet arrived at that social abhorrence of this crime that must precede its practi-

51. Ibid., 22 June 1928.
52. Ibid.

cal extinction. When eight presumably decent and rational beings can gain the consent of their conscience to rob a hospital bed for the purpose of executing summary vengeance, and when, as was the case a few days ago in Louisiana, two Negroes are torn from their guards and lynched because they were brothers of another Negro who was accused of murder, it must be recognized that the rise and fall of the lynching curve is governed by racial passions that remain still to be brought under civilized control.[53]

For three years—1925, 1926, and 1927—Jaffé had submitted applications for the Pulitzer Prize for Distinguished Editorial Writing. Each time, in his own words, he had lost to "abler and more deserving competitors." Good sportsmanship aside, he knew that his work, 1927's in particular, placed him in a league with the winners.[54]

Despite the straightforward criterion that the winner receive the award "for the best editorial article written during the year, the test of excellence being clearness of style, moral purpose, sound reasoning and power to influence public opinion in what the writer conceives to be the right direction," the judging process could hardly be construed as a dispassionate and objective evaluation of a single editorial's merits. The Advisory Board gave "due account [to] the whole volume of the editorial writer's work during the year." Subject matter, the entrant's record of achievement, and his or her network of friends and colleagues also influenced decisions. For the 1928 competition, Jaffé determined to maximize his chances of winning by putting together an unbeatable portfolio.[55]

He thus sought advice from Grover Hall, the previous year's winner. Jaffé intended to structure his application around his advocacy for Virginia's antilynching law, and he queried the Montgomery editor regarding

53. Ibid.; Mason, *One of the Neighbors' Children*, 150.

54. Louis Jaffé to Grover Hall, 7 January 1928, Jaffé Papers.

55. Sloan and Anderson, *Pulitzer Prize Editorials*, xiii, xviii; John Hohenberg, *The Pulitzer Prize Story: News Stories, Editorials, Cartoons, and Pictures from the Pulitzer Prize Collection at Columbia University* (New York: Columbia University Press, 1959), 334; Richard Terrill Baker, *A History of the Graduate School of Journalism, Columbia University* (New York: Columbia University Press, 1954), 91.

the advisability of including in his materials letters from Governor Byrd, P. B. Young, and State Senator Barron attesting to the *Virginian-Pilot*'s role in shaping the legislation and securing its passage. Although Jaffé did not believe that the rules prohibited the submission of such documents, he asked whether Hall thought that some judges might regard it as an "effort to dragoon a decision."[56]

The *Advertiser*'s editor wasted no time in responding. He contended that Jaffé had deserved a Pulitzer several times in the past and confided that he had come "within an ace of getting it" the previous year. Hall revealed that he had not entered the contest and presumed that Julian Harris or Sara Haardt had taken it upon themselves to nominate him for the award and prepare an exhibit. (Mencken, in his memoirs, revealed that he had "pulled the wires" to see that both Harris and Hall won their Pulitzer awards.) Hall suggested that a respected intermediary—such as the president of the University of Virginia, Edwin Alderman—could nominate Jaffé and include letters of support without any appearance of impropriety. Hall knew that Harris, who served on the committee, appreciated the "high character of [Jaffé's] editorial work," but feared that he might lack a comprehensive understanding of the *Pilot*'s campaign for Virginia's antilynching law. The materials submitted by Alderman should include adequate background information to ensure that the Advisory Board knew the breadth of Jaffé's work. Hall volunteered to contact several committee members and urge them to give special attention to the *Pilot*'s exhibit.[57]

Alderman agreed to sponsor Jaffé's nomination, and the editor began to compile his application materials. Byrd, Barron, and Young, as well as James Gregg, principal of Hampton Institute, wrote letters of support. John M. Gandy, the black president of Virginia Normal and Industrial Institute in Petersburg, may also have written a letter, but no record of it survives. Jaffé included a five-page review of his advocacy for the antilynching bill, a transcript of the law, two editorials from the *Baltimore Evening Sun* and the *Norfolk Journal and Guide* highlighting the *Pilot*'s fight

56. Louis Jaffé to Grover Hall, 7 January 1929, Jaffé Papers.
57. Grover Hall to Louis Jaffé, 10 January 1929, ibid.; Mencken, *Thirty-Five Years of Newspaper Work*, 158.

against mob justice, and six of his editorials focusing on lynchings and the bill. He selected "Byrd's Anti-Lynching Proposals"—not "An Unspeakable Act of Savagery"—as his entry for the award.[58]

Byrd wrote to Alderman that Jaffé's "editorials over a long period in advocacy of making the punishment of lynchers a State responsibility supplemented by his personal representations" had figured more prominently than any other outside pressure in persuading Byrd to make the "passage of a drastic anti-lynching law" a legislative priority. Jaffé's role in the law's formulation and passage, the governor continued, represented "but a fractional part of the work accomplished by him for liberalization of thought in connection with many matters looking to the progress and the advancement of the people."[59]

Barron's letter stressed the fact that Jaffé's editorials had laid the groundwork for the bill's enactment: "Mr. Jaffe's unremitting war against the spirit of the mob, kluxery, racial prejudices and injustice created an atmosphere and public sentiment without which . . . the anti-lynching Law would not have been passed. His editorials have created a spirit of liberality and tolerance in many quarters, and made people and public men afraid and ashamed to oppose [progressive] measures."[60]

But it remained for P. B. Young to write the most eloquent and knowledgeable testimonial. For a decade he had observed Jaffé's work on a daily basis. The two editors, whose views coincided on so many matters, had by that time formed an exceptional relationship predicated on a mutual respect that transcended Jim Crow. Excepting only associate editor Newton Aiken, no other journalist knew Jaffé's editorial achievements better. "I doubt if 'disadvantaged groups' without regard to class or race, have a warmer or more effective advocate in America than Mr. Jaffé," Young wrote. The *Virginian-Pilot* had become "one of the most able and consistent exponents of liberal thought in the United States" under its editor's leadership.

> His treatment during the past year of the problems of labor has been consistently constructive; his advocacy of educational opportunity and of health and recreational facilities has been productive

58. Louis Jaffé to Edwin Alderman, 25 January 1929, Jaffé Papers.
59. Harry Byrd to Edwin Alderman, 28 January 1929, ibid.
60. James Barron to Edwin Alderman, 25 January 1929, ibid.

of substantial benefits to those in need of them. He has made an effective contribution to the movement to suppress organized forces of sinister purpose like the Ku Klux Klan. But his most outstanding achievement was his antilynching law. His was the first paper in the State to propose an antilynching law, the first to submit a tentative outline of such a measure—his being substantially the measure as adopted after passing through tedious objections and prunings by legislators—and it was his courageous and convincing advocacy of the bill after it was introduced that aided most in bringing to Virginia the distinction of being the first Southern State to adopt an antilynching law. [Young's lack of knowledge regarding other southern states' antilynching laws provided some indication of their effectiveness.] Before approaching the definite task of securing the adoption of [the] law . . . , he had, over a period of several years, made the reception of such a movement possible by building up through convincing editorial treatment an invulnerable case against this particular social cancer.[61]

Late in January 1928, Alderman drafted a letter nominating Jaffé for the Pulitzer Prize, and he forwarded the completed exhibit to the Office of the Secretary of Columbia University.

Notwithstanding his impressive editorials in 1928, Jaffé believed that he had delivered his "heaviest licks for the antilynching law" in December 1927, in the wake of the Leonard Woods lynching. One of the rules for the Pulitzer contest specified that competition for a prize would be limited to work done within the calendar year. On the surface it appeared that the Advisory Board could not take into account Jaffé's groundbreaking work completed in the final month of the preceding year. Jaffé had treated that advocacy in the historical summary he had written reviewing the *Pilot*'s sustained championship of the law. Another contest rule, however, gave him hope that the judges might evaluate his 1928 work within the context of his entire antilynching campaign. If a member of the Advisory Board requested it, the guidelines allowed the introduction of collateral material such as Jaffé's summary.[62]

61. P. B. Young to Edwin Alderman, 22 January 1929, ibid.
62. Louis Jaffé to Grover Hall, 9 February 1929, ibid.

Jaffé accepted Hall's offer to contact "one or more members of the committee" on his behalf. He hoped that Harris might request that the jury consider the entire story of the Norfolk newspaper's antilynching advocacy. In addition to Harris, who had begun his tenure on the Board in 1927, Hall may have lobbied Frank R. Kent, a *Baltimore Sun* executive and columnist and a newcomer to the Advisory Board. Hall, like Jaffé, enjoyed excellent relations with the *Sunpapers*. Coincidentally Kent had begun his newspaper career over three decades earlier at the *Columbus Enquirer Sun,* which Harris now edited.[63]

Jaffé's hour had struck. On May 12, 1929, Columbia University's Board of Trustees announced the winners of the 1928 Pulitzer competition. The next day a photograph of Jaffé, looking a little tired and more than a little intimidating, appeared in the *New York Times* alongside those of other literary and fourth-estate luminaries such as poet Stephen Vincent Benét, novelist Julia Peterkin, *Chicago Daily News* war correspondent Paul Scott Mowrer, cartoonist Rollin Kirby, and reporter Paul Anderson of the *St. Louis Post-Dispatch.* Inside, the *Times* reprinted the entire text of Jaffé's winning editorial, "An Unspeakable Act of Savagery."[64]

Why the Advisory Board based its selection on this editorial and not the one Jaffé himself had chosen remains unclear. Certainly the winning piece carried a more striking title. The immediacy of the subject, too, may have affected the board's decision. A discussion of the merits of Governor Byrd's antilynching recommendations may have seemed less compelling than Jaffé's vivid description of the Houston lynching. The judges may have attributed more power to influence public opinion to "An Unspeakable Act of Savagery," which required no special knowledge to understand, than to "Byrd's Anti-Lynching Proposals," which could best be appreciated as a part of a long-running campaign.

In accordance with tradition, the committee had assembled at Columbia University the month prior to the announcement of the awards.

---

63. Grover Hall to Louis Jaffé, 10 January 1929, Jaffé to Hall, 9 February 1929, both ibid.; *Pilot,* 13 May 1929; Robert B. Downs and Jane B. Downs, *Journalists of the United States: Biographical Sketches of Print and Broadcast News Shapers from the Late 17th Century to the Present* (Jefferson, N.C.: McFarland, 1991), 196; Hohenberg, *Pulitzer Prize Story,* 364–5.

64. *New York Times,* 13 May 1929.

Although it had conducted its deliberations in secrecy, some clues regarding its discussions and its rationale for awarding Jaffé a prize appear in an editorial initiated by his principal advocate on the board, Julian Harris, and written by Julia Collier Harris. On May 13, the *Columbus (Ga.) Enquirer-Sun* lauded the recipient of the year's Pulitzer Prize for Distinguished Editorial Writing, while making no mention of the specific merits of "An Unspeakable Act of Savagery." "That Louis Jaffé [has] been cited is something for which every patriotic Southerner will rejoice," Julia Harris wrote. "Mr. Jaffé is not only one of the most courageous and straight-thinking editors in the United States but one of the most intelligent and cultivated. His paper stands for everything that fearless and honorable men respect. His attitude toward lynching, toward religious bigotry, toward oppression of helpless and humble citizens has been outspoken and persistent and his denunciations of this kind of lawlessness and cowardice have been couched in terms that were as high-toned and intelligent as they were bold and unequivocal."[65]

The board had awarded Jaffé his prize not for his winning editorial alone but for a "series of articles written on the lynching evil and in successful advocacy of legislation to prevent it." But more broadly, the honor spoke to the body of Jaffé's work over the past decade, as described to the board in recommendations such as Byrd's and Young's. Douglas Gordon, the editor of the *Virginian-Pilot*'s afternoon rival, the *Ledger-Dispatch*, underscored this point when he wrote that "An Unspeakable Act of Savagery" served as but one example "of a large number of able, thoughtful and powerfully written editorials produced" by Jaffé, not just during 1928 but "during many another year."[66]

Jaffé shared credit for the award with publisher Lucien Starke, writing that "everyone familiar with the making of newspapers and the defining of news and editorial policies, knows that a paper's liberalism and independence never rise higher than their source—the seat of final executive authority. That may be said to be a publishing axiom. . . . The newspaper is to

---

65. Hohenberg, *Pulitzer Prize Story,* 331, 333; Louis Jaffé to Julian Harris, [May 1929], Jaffé Papers; *Columbus (Ga.) Enquirer-Sun,* 14 May 1929.

66. Hohenberg, *Pulitzer Prize Story,* 349; *Norfolk Ledger-Dispatch* (hereafter cited as *Ledger*), [May 1929].

[Starke] not only a private and corporate responsibility but also, in a real sense, a public trust—its influence and power to be exerted uncompromisingly in the interest of social and economic justice. In his own unostentatious way, Colonel Starke strikes every day the keynote of liberalism, urbanity, fairness and deep human understanding that inspires the *Virginian-Pilot*'s editorial and news policies and keeps them on their course." Although the occasion called for such a statement, Jaffé did not make these assertions merely as a courtesy. Starke afforded his editor an unusual level of autonomy and backed him unfailingly, whatever controversy Jaffé's editorials raised. The support of his publisher vastly amplified Jaffé's effectiveness.[67]

Jaffé also acknowledged that he had served as but one soldier in the battle against mob justice: "The fight against lynching and the social outlook in which it shelters itself has been waged so long by so many newspapers and so many individuals and agencies not connected with newspapers that there can be no such thing as an unshared honor for service in this cause. I cannot but feel honored that my own efforts in this cause last year should have been singled out as deserving of the Pulitzer Foundation's editorial award, but a knowledge of the extent and fighting quality of the antilynching battle line counsels one to humility. The fact known to all informed persons is that the press of the South, practically as a unit has for many years denounced this venomous perversion of the race-preservation instinct and joined in the demand for its extirpation."[68]

Jaffé emphasized the crucial roles played by Byrd and Barron in the passage of the commonwealth's new antilynching law. He also reminded readers that Virginia journalists, educators, and public leaders in particular had long excoriated lynching. Although he mentioned no names, Jaffé likely alluded to black editor John Mitchell and former governor Charles T. O'Ferrall, whose advocacy thirty-five years earlier had reduced mob violence in Virginia but had failed to result in the passage of antilynching legislation.[69]

From around the country congratulatory letters and complimentary

67. *Elizabeth City (N.C.) Independent,* 24 May 1929.
68. *Pilot,* 13 May 1929.
69. Ibid.; Brundage, "To Howl Loudly," 325–41.

newspaper stories and editorials poured in to the *Pilot*'s mailroom. In "The Desert Blossoms," *Baltimore Evening Sun* editor Hamilton Owens lauded the selection of southerners Jaffé and Peterkin, whose work in large part focused on their region's problems and themes. "The South has an indisputable right to point to these thorough Southerners as two of its writing people who are among the best," Owens wrote, "not merely in the South, but in the country. And this must be peculiarly satisfying to the erstwhile 'Sahara of the Bozart.'"[70]

A reading of the coverage of Jaffé's Pulitzer by peers who knew his work intimately provides insight into his stature in the region's press. In the words of Earle Godbey, editor of the *Greensboro (N.C.) News* and arguably the South's finest newspaper stylist, "Jaffé has demonstrated a fine and balanced liberalism, a broad and catholic knowledge and a craftsmanship which is at all times skillful and on occasion . . . brilliant." The *News*'s editor also stressed the *Pilot*'s influence throughout the Tarheel State due to both its circulation in the state and the extensive reprinting of *Pilot* editorials.[71]

Future two-time Pulitzer Prize winner for history, Dr. Douglas Southall Freeman, who edited the *Richmond News Leader* and had cut his teeth along with Jaffé at John Stewart Bryan's *Richmond Times-Dispatch,* pointed to Jaffé's erudition and analytical mind. "When [he] sits down to write his daily editorials," Freeman wrote, "he does not rely on his stored knowledge, great as that is. He brings that knowledge down to the hour and he refurbishes it with sound reflection." Freeman described Jaffé as a "scholar without pedantry, an editor without cant."[72]

Robert Lathan, editor of the *Asheville (N.C.) Citizen,* who in 1925 as editor of the *Charleston (S.C.) News & Courier* had brought to America's Dixie the region's first Pulitzer Prize for Distinguished Editorial Writing, had long followed Jaffé's work on a daily basis. Endorsing the Pulitzer board's selection, he called the *Pilot*'s editorial page a "force for straight thinking and clean progress."[73]

70. *Baltimore Evening Sun,* 13 May 1929.
71. *Greensboro (N.C.) News,* [May 1929].
72. *Richmond News Leader,* 13 May 1929.
73. *Asheville (N.C.) Citizen,* 13 May 1929.

Charlottesville (Va.) Progress editor J. H. Lindsay, who had known Jaffé since his early days at the *Times-Dispatch,* attributed his success to "cleancut thinking . . . ; the ability to put it in direct, incisive English; [and] courage." "The career of Mr. Jaffé has been remarkable without ever having approached the spectacular," Lindsay observed.

> In the first place, he seemed naturally cut out for newspaper work. He started young and stuck to it; perhaps he knew he was right. If he did he was naturally luckier or smarter than most of the others. He started at the bottom and went through the mill but he went at a higher rate of speed than the majority of his fellow tradesmen, and according to the Pulitzer commission, he is a good deal better than they are, which probably accounts for the ease with which he climbed the ladder.
>
> Those who were with him on the *Times-Dispatch* in years gone by are not at all surprised that he has achieved this uncommon distinction. They remember his excellent grasp of every situation, his faculty for obtaining and then analyzing news and then a more than usual talent for reducing it to readable and understandable words. None of these men has any doubt that the Pulitzer commission has placed its prize where it is richly deserved.[74]

Two months later Jaffé, unquestionably then the leading figure in the commonwealth's journalistic community, stood before the Virginia Press Association in Danville to deliver the keynote speech at the organization's annual dinner. Given his distaste for public speaking, the association must have conducted a formidable lobbying campaign to persuade the state's first Pulitzer Prize winner to accept its invitation. Many of the editors assembled in the dining room likely anticipated an innocuous speech that would kick off a jolly and lubricated evening of fellowship.

Although Jaffé did not cite by title *Near v. Minnesota,* a landmark First Amendment case then making its way toward the Supreme Court, the case nevertheless formed part of the text of his speech. The rabble-rousing publishers of a Twin Cities weekly, the *Saturday Press,* had scapegoated Jews for the gambling, bootlegging, and racketeering problems of Minneap-

---

74. *Charlottesville (Va.) Progress,* [May 1929].

olis and St. Paul and claimed that public officials had turned blind eyes to crime. "Practically every vendor of vile hooch, every owner of a moonshine still, every snake-faced gangster and embryonic yegg in the Twin Cities is a JEW," the paper had fulminated.[75]

Invoking a state statute that enabled them to declare the paper a public nuisance, local authorities had enjoined *Saturday Press* from further publication and distribution. In 1928 Minnesota's supreme court had upheld the law's constitutionality. Three years later, however, the U.S. Supreme Court in a five-to-four ruling would determine that the state statute constituted prior restraint and thus violated the First Amendment. The decision—that government censorship is permissible only under very exceptional circumstances—would receive prominent treatment in journalism and law schools for the next seven decades.[76]

Jaffé could have structured his remarks around *Near v. Minnesota* and its ramifications for the editors seated around him in the room that night. Certainly it presented the most obvious topic for his talk; the American Newspaper Publishers Association would soon issue a statement denouncing the Minnesota statute as "one of the gravest assaults upon the liberties of the people that has been attempted since the adoption of the Constitution." But Jaffé chose to refer to the case only in passing and to focus instead on a threat that many contemporary media critics argue constitutes a greater peril than government interference: the press's abdication of its historic responsibility to adhere to the intent of the First Amendment.[77]

The title Jaffé had chosen for his talk, "The Press and Virginia's

75. Fred W. Friendly, *Minnesota Rag: The Dramatic Story of the Landmark Supreme Court Case That Gave Meaning to Freedom of the Press* (New York: Random House, 1981), 46.

76. *Near v. Minnesota*, 383 US 697 (1931); Robert J. Wagman, *The First Amendment Book* (New York: Pharos, 1991), 11–8; Don R. Pember, *Mass Media Law* (Boston: McGraw-Hill, 1998), 62–3.

77. Friendly, *Minnesota Rag*, 90; Louis Jaffé, "The Press and Virginia's Coming of Age," 19 July 1929, Jaffé Papers; James Fallows, *Breaking the News: How the Media Undermine American Democracy* (New York: Pantheon, 1996), 267–70; Robert W. McChesney, *Corporate Media and the Threat to Democracy* (New York: Seven Stories Press, 1997), 22–9; Newton N. Minow and Craig L. Lamay, *Abandoned in the Wasteland: Children, Television, and the First Amendment* (New York: Hill and Wang, 1995), 6–7; Owen M. Fiss, *The Irony*

Coming of Age," provided little indication of the speech's contents. The next week, *Editor & Publisher* published a transcript of the speech under a headline and subhead that more accurately reflected the substance of Jaffé's remarks: "Reticence, Timidity Hamper Press Jaffé Tells Virginia Editors; Lack of Courage Greater Menace Than Threats of Statutory Action Against Press Freedom, Editors Told—Cites Examples of Complacency of Newspapers."[78]

"I make bold to suggest," Jaffé ventured, "that what we need in Virginia and elsewhere in the South is not newspapers freer from legal restrictions imposed by law, but newspapers freer from self-imposed inhibitions." Quoting the Duke of Albany, he challenged his colleagues: "If we Virginia newspapermen are to continue to qualify as the 'unconvenanted servants on the whole progress and civilization' of our state, it behooves us, I think, to subject ourselves to a continuous and critical self-examination directed to seeing that we remain the servants of the whole people and not merely special groups of them. . . . Only as unfailing and alert tribunes of the people, as defenders of their rights and liberties and as spokesmen of their grievances, can we realize our highest mission." He continued, "Such a self examination, if we conduct it honestly and fearlessly, will show, I believe, that statutory threats against the freedom of the press, notwithstanding that we make much noise about them, constitute a negligible danger compared with the creeping paralysis of our own lack of courage—our own reticence and timidity."[79]

Jaffé proceeded to cite specific cases. Although his use of a first-person pronoun may have softened his criticism somewhat, undoubtedly his speech reddened the faces of many in the audience. He deplored the "gentle wrist-slappings" with which most Virginia newspapers had treated the resurgence of the Ku Klux Klan. The state's journalists in reporting on Klan violence had made euphemistic allusions to masked mobs and whipping parties and had lacked the courage to "call the new terror by its right name. . . . No law of God or man," he declared, "prevented us from dipping

---

of Free Speech (Cambridge: Harvard University Press, 1996), 52; Cass R. Sunstein, *Democracy and the Problem of Free Speech* (New York: Free Press, 1995), 58–62.

78. "Reticence, Timidity Hamper Press," *Editor & Publisher*, 20.

79. Jaffé, "Press and Virginia's Coming of Age," Jaffé Papers.

our pens in vitriol and cauterizing this infamy from the first day of its public appearance, but timid inhibitions held us in check."[80]

Creationists had not threatened academic freedom in the commonwealth as severely as they had in the neighboring states of Tennessee and North Carolina; but, he said, "it was a discouragingly long time before the press of Virginia joined without reservation in the fight against an obscurantism that threatens any day to cross our own frontiers." Jaffé marveled at the fact that one of his colleagues at a major and respected daily had supported William Jennings Bryan's assertion that taxpayers had a right to censor curricula at public colleges and universities.[81]

He asked the members of the Press Association if they believed they had comported themselves courageously when the Red scare swept through the nation, making a "mockery of the personal sanctities guaranteed by the Bill of Rights." Had they softened their criticism of Prohibition and its excesses, fearing advertising and circulation boycotts by Bishop Cannon and his followers? Had they accurately portrayed the causes for the South's growing labor problems—"underpaid workers struggling with mounting living costs"—or had they acted as the mouthpieces for industrialists by maintaining that "alien propaganda" had poisoned the minds of a previously contented workforce and stoked unrest and activism? Finally he asked whether Virginia's press had spoken "with the voice of old ancestral fear or with the voice of confident humanitarianism" in regard to racial issues.[82]

Looking toward the future, Jaffé predicted that the warnings of the Nashville Agrarians about the steep price the South would pay for unrestrained exploitation of its resources and an unquestioning embrace of dehumanizing industrialization would fuel a debate in which the press would play a major role. (The Agrarians' publication of *I'll Take My Stand* the following year did in fact stimulate further heated discussion.)[83]

80. Ibid.
81. Ibid.
82. Ibid.
83. Louis D. Rubin Jr., introduction to *I'll Take My Stand: The South and the Agrarian Tradition,* by Twelve Southerners (Baton Rouge: Louisiana State University Press, 1977), xix-xxii; Robert B. Downs, *Books that Changed the South* (Chapel Hill: University of North Carolina Press, 1977), 229–36.

The press itself served as a part of the "commercial fabric" and by its very nature, Jaffé said, "echoes the cry for more industries, larger payrolls, bigger cities, better roads, more airports, better transportation systems, more traffic and greater wealth." Jaffé exhorted his colleagues to fulfill their "social mission" and examine critically the human consequences of development and industrialization. "It will not make for a happier Virginia," he cautioned, "if we build here an industrial order founded on pauper wages. It will not make for a more civilized Virginia if we crystallize here a social order pyramided on a hope-abandoned peasantry. It will not make for a sweeter Virginia if we seal here a covenant of convenience with a priestly dictatorship. It will not make for a more enlightened Virginia if we allow our pursuit of material aggrandizement to deflect us from the cultivation of the arts and sciences, or make us intolerant of social experiment and intellectual curiosity."[84]

Once again Louis Jaffé had laid it on the line. He had this night informed yet another establishment that he pulled no punches. He had made it abundantly clear that neither personal nor professional ties or obligations could stay his unrelenting drive for justice and fair play.

84. Jaffé, "Press and Virginia's Coming of Age," Jaffé Papers.

10 THE AVANT-GARDE

An even blacker Tuesday followed Black Thursday—October 24, 1929—
and the value of American securities plummeted by a total of more than
twenty-six billion dollars. "Stock Market Prices Dive Down Again at
Alarming Rate," read a *Virginian-Pilot* front-page headline that day. By the
end of November, investors' losses would quadruple. Financiers, government officials, and editorialists struggled to understand what seemed to
make no sense at all. "Emotion has usurped the place of reason and . . .
what is taking place can not be related to any normal laws of business,"
Jaffé wrote. That much he stated accurately, but he would prove no more
prescient than his newspaper peers across the country with respect to the
economic crisis. Who could have imagined the catastrophe that lay ahead?
Norfolk, with its port and its government salaries, had as yet barely felt the
depression.[1]

By the beginning of 1930, Jaffé would express guarded optimism:
"One finds American business . . . embarking on the new year free of . . .
misgivings, but with a certain wariness that was born of the stock market
collapse and which the presidential pulmotor has not yet succeeded in
entirely eliminating. . . . Perhaps it is just as well that the business year opens
with the accent on caution. The country has just passed through a disturb-
ing experience and, everything considered, has kept its head remarkably
well. . . . At the turn of the year the prevailing view is one of confidence
tempered by caution."[2]

Breaking economic news in the fall of 1929 would demand the concerted efforts of the *Pilot*'s editorial duo; but that dark October Jaffé and

1. *Pilot*, 29 October 1929, 30 October 1929; Ronald L. Heinemann, *Depression
and New Deal in Virginia: The Enduring Dominion* (Charlottesville: University Press of Virginia, 1983), 8; Chambers, Shank, and Sugg, *Salt Water & Printer's Ink*, 344.

2. *Pilot*, 2 January 1930.

Aiken's seven years of teamwork, which had made the Norfolk newspaper's editorial page among the South's best, came to an end, and on a sour note. Jaffé's wife, Margaret, figured prominently in the discord.

From Washington, D.C., where she had traveled with Christopher for medical care, Margaret cabled Jaffé at work on October 8: "Need you very urgently. Please come at once." Aiken had planned to travel out of town for a "business engagement," and Jaffé asked him to reschedule his appointment. Aiken acquiesced and left for lunch. But when he returned to the office he had changed his mind, explaining that he could not possibly delay his meeting. He asked Jaffé to describe the predicament to Margaret and to postpone his own trip. The two men had a "very plain and animated argument." Jaffé telephoned Margaret long distance and told her he would arrive that night. Then he informed Aiken that if he did not remain on the job while Jaffé was away, it would no longer be possible for the two to work together. Aiken threatened to take the matter to Starke.[3]

Before departing, Jaffé left Starke a letter explaining his side of the imbroglio: "My present feeling is that Mr. Aiken's usefulness as a collaborator with me . . . is at an end. I feel all the more keenly about this because when Margaret was sick at home with two nurses and I had to be by her side, he declined to leave his wife's side when she was ill. . . . I feel that in this emergency my place is with Margaret in Washington, and I do not desire to be longer associated with an assistant-editor who absolutely refuses to recognize my urgency to the extent of postponing . . . a purely business engagement."[4]

Aiken and his wife, also named Margaret, had socialized with Louis and Margaret Jaffé and counted them as good friends, but Jaffé's absences resulting from his family's many illnesses had worn on his subordinate. Aiken later recalled that when one of the two men did not report to work, the "other had a very burdensome life." He had stood up to Jaffé previously when he felt he had been treated unfairly. Years earlier he had "rebelled" when the editor had attempted to establish a work schedule requiring both of them to return to the office after dinner to read proof. Aiken had probably observed at close quarters Margaret Jaffé's hypochondria and may have

3. Louis Jaffé to Lucien Starke, 8 October 1929, Jaffé Papers.
4. Ibid.

believed that her insistence that her husband rush to her side on this occasion had little justification.[5]

The unspecified "business appointment" that Aiken could not postpone consisted of a job interview at the *Baltimore Sun*. While making no mention of the office imbroglio in his unpublished memoirs, Aiken wrote that he had traveled to the nation's capital exactly at that time to interview with J. Fred Essary, the *Sun*'s Washington bureau chief. Essary had worked as a cub reporter in Norfolk many years earlier, and the two men—both native Tennesseans and former economics reporters—had formed a congenial relationship. Later on the day of the interview, Aiken journeyed on to Baltimore and met with managing editor William Moore, who wanted him to start work at once in order to cover the Virginia gubernatorial election. A few days after his argument with Jaffé, Aiken resigned his post at the *Pilot*. He would serve the prestigious *Sun* successively as Washington reporter, London correspondent, an editorial writer, and finally editor of its editorial page.[6]

Aiken's departure placed Jaffé in a serious bind, and the editor began at once the onerous process of finding a competent associate who shared his liberal perspective. Stringfellow "Winkie" Barr, who taught modern European history at the University of Virginia, came to Jaffé's mind immediately. With time out for war service, Barr had earned degrees from the University of Virginia, the University of Paris, and Oxford University, which he had attended on a Rhodes Scholarship. He would in the future edit the *Virginia Quarterly Review*, publicly debate the Agrarians regarding their romantic prescription for the South, and lead St. John's College in Annapolis, where he would scrap the existing curriculum in favor of a program of study based solely on one hundred great books. Barr also would achieve a reputation as a prolific author, publishing an eclectic body of work that included histories of Europe and Greece, a novel, a cookbook, and a children's book.[7]

The previous year, Jaffé had recruited the erudite Barr to write

5. Aiken, *Newton Aiken Autobiography*, V-10.

6. Ibid., V-14; Williams, *Baltimore Sun*, 303, 371; Johnson et al., *Sunpapers of Baltimore*, 373, 421–2; Chambers, Shank, and Sugg, *Salt Water & Printer's Ink*, 313.

7. *Pilot*, 5 February 1982; Kneebone, *Southern Liberal Journalists*, 60–1.

occasional editorials and fill in as a substitute when either he or Aiken vacationed. Summarizing the *Pilot*'s stance for Barr, Jaffé had written, "Our general editorial trend may be described as liberal. We go as far toward the Left as is safe for the country and are as radical as a right-thinking, Christian community will permit us to be without canceling their subscriptions. When it is necessary to allude to these things, we do not use euphemisms for rape, adultery, birth control, prostitution or [referring to the Teapot Dome scandal] naval oil thieveries."[8]

Jaffé made a discreet inquiry regarding Barr's salary and then attempted to woo him away from the University of Virginia. "There are certain intellectual, polemic and stylistic traits about you," he wrote, "which have led me to the belief that liberal journalism would be quite as satisfying a career for you as liberal teaching." Barr replied that if he had two lives to live, he would consider living one of them at the *Pilot,* but that he loved teaching and intended to stay in Charlottesville.[9]

Jaffé then turned to his professional network, which included Gerald Johnson, Grover Hall, and Douglas Southall Freeman. "I am looking for a budding Gerald Johnson-Grover Hall-Julian Harris," he wrote to Hall, "a well-educated, level-headed liberal who can write intelligently, vigorously and attractively about the things that the editorial page holds out to discuss and illumine, and can do it without alienating the customers. That, as you know, is no mean trick."[10]

No name came to Hall's mind immediately; he would "have to scratch [his] head and think." But in the meantime, the *Montgomery (Ala.) Advertiser*'s editor directed Jaffé toward an unknown editorial writer at the *Greensboro (N.C.) Daily News*. "It strikes me that whoever is helping Godbey . . . is fit to be on any paper." In a second letter Hall again suggested that Jaffé focus his efforts on Godbey's anonymous assistant. He also recommended W. J. "Sleepy" Cash, who had worked one summer as a reporter for the *Charlotte Observer* and intermittently for a few years as a reporter

8. Louis Jaffé to Stringfellow Barr, 31 October 1928, Louis Jaffé to Robert Tunstall, 12 October 1929, Louis Jaffé to Stringfellow Barr, 3 November 1928, all in Jaffé Papers.

9. Louis Jaffé to Stringfellow Barr, 12 October 1929, Stringfellow Barr to Louis Jaffé, 14 October 1929, both ibid.

10. Louis Jaffé to Douglas Southall Freeman, 12 October 1929, Louis Jaffé to Grover Hall, 16 October 1929, Gerald Johnson to Louis Jaffé, 14 October 1929, all ibid.

and editorial writer at the more liberal *Charlotte News*. Cash's most recent newspaper experience had consisted of editing for one year a clamorous country semiweekly in Shelby, North Carolina, the birthplace of *Clansman* author Thomas Dixon. Repeated bouts of debilitating physical and mental illness had punctuated both Cash's fledgling journalistic career and a short stint as a college instructor.[11]

Despite his checkered employment record, Cash had earlier in 1929 burst on the national scene as a freelance magazine writer. He made his debut in the *American Mercury* that summer with "Jehovah of the Tar Heels." As Jaffé began his search for a replacement for Aiken, Mencken published Cash's "The Mind of the South," the nucleus for its subsequent classic namesake book. Still hungry for southern fare, the Sage of Baltimore featured the young Carolinian again a few months later with "The War in the South." Cash would contribute regularly to the periodical for the next several years.[12]

Cash's considerable talents aside, it is difficult to imagine a journalist less suited to serve as Jaffé's associate. The *Pilot*'s editor had his hands full with illnesses, real and imagined, at home. He needed a stable, dependable associate. The *American Mercury* had brought Cash to Jaffé's attention prior to Hall's letter, and Jaffé appreciated Cash's acumen and his flamboyant and hyperbolic prose, so derivative of Mencken's. But Jaffé would have deemed Cash's style incompatible with the more judicious brand of journalism practiced at the *Virginian-Pilot* and unsuitable for the paper's readership.

Jaffé also considered as a possible replacement for Aiken—"not as first choice but somewhere down the line"—another young Mencken devotee, *Richmond Times-Dispatch* reporter and future Pulitzer Prize winner Virginius Dabney. Only three years after Dabney had started work at the *Richmond News Leader* in 1922, Hamilton Owens, the editor of the *Baltimore Evening Sun*, had tapped him as a contributor to the paper's editorial page. This marked a watershed in the reporter's professional life. He was exhilarated to find himself mentioned in Mencken's *American Mercury*

11. Grover Hall to Louis Jaffé, 18, 19 October 1929, ibid.; Bruce Clayton, *W. J. Cash, A Life* (Baton Rouge: Louisiana State University Press, 1991), 41–78.

12. Clayton, *W. J. Cash, A Life*, 79; Hobson, *Serpent in Eden*, 111–6.

review of *The Advancing South.* A few months later, Mencken published in the *Mercury* an article Dabney had written about Virginia; and for days after, Dabney recalled in his memoirs, he "was walking on air." The star of the editor-to-be was ascending.[13]

Despite this initial success, Dabney's style in future submissions never fully satisfied Mencken. "I can't get rid of the feeling that the tone is wrong for us," the *Mercury*'s editor wrote back, rejecting an article criticizing a group of now-forgotten mountebanks. "You are too indignant. We ought to deal with such frauds in a more satirical fashion, praising them as 100% Americans and revealing their imbecility more artfully. At times you actually denounce them. We never do that to Christian men." Other editors appreciated Dabney's talents, however, and his name began to appear with increasing frequency in *Scribner's*, the *Nation*, and other national journals. Dabney later acknowledged Mencken's powerful influence on him during this period. "[His] questioning of many accepted beliefs appealed to my youthful mind," he recalled. "I had no idea of following him blindly, but he made me think."[14]

Although Dabney may have appreciated Mencken's fulminations, the scholarly and reserved Douglas Southall Freeman was less enamored of the Baltimore journalist and deplored his influence on impressionable young reporters. Despite professing a great fondness for Dabney, Freeman advised Jaffé against hiring him. "He has been badly infected with the germ of Menckenism and sometimes has seizures that carry him to extremes of statement," the Richmond editor warned, adding that he had never considered placing Dabney in a position of responsibility. He believed that Dabney lacked originality and judgment. While not sharing Freeman's distaste for Mencken, Jaffé also expressed reservations regarding Dabney's "judicial balance, his analyzing and synthesizing talents and his interest in the more serious social, economic, political and international questions that our editorial pages hold out to discuss and illumine." (Dabney would one day regard this exchange of letters between the state's principal editors as so

13. *Pilot,* 12 October 1929; Mencken, "Library," 506; Virginius Dabney, "Virginia," *American Mercury* 9, no. 35 (1926): 349–56; Dabney, *Across the Years,* 116.

14. H. L. Mencken to Virginius Dabney, 8 August 1927, Dabney Papers; Dabney, *Across the Years,* 118, 120; Virginius Dabney, "Reflections," *Virginia Magazine of History and Biography* 93, no. 3 (1985): 286–7.

embarrassing that he would take the extraordinary step of having the correspondence withdrawn from the Jaffé papers at the University of Virginia,
where it remained inaccessible to scholars until his death in 1995.)[15]

Hall could not identify the *Greensboro Daily News* editorial writer
whom he recommended, but Jaffé's editorial rival from student days, Gerald
Johnson, knew him well. Lenoir Chambers had replaced Johnson as associate editor when the latter left that paper for a short stint as a journalism
professor at the University of North Carolina in 1924. In 1926 H. L.
Mencken and the *Sunpapers* had enticed Johnson north to Maryland, where
for the next seventeen years he wrote a weekly column, frequently devoted
to the South. In Baltimore he earned an appellation as the city's "second
sage."[16]

Jaffé and Johnson first met in person in 1925; and ever since, Johnson had helped spell the *Pilot*'s editorial team during summer vacations.
Johnson endorsed Chambers in the highest terms but believed it unlikely
that anyone could ever pry him away from Greensboro. "Lenoir Chambers
is exactly the man you want," Johnson wrote. Chambers had the "stuff—
education, intelligence, a graceful style, intellectual balance, liberal spirit,
and as for personality he [was] simply marvelously equipped." Johnson
expressed puzzlement over why his replacement had stayed in North Carolina so long: "What's the matter with the damn fool I don't know—too
much married, I fear—but he seems to be afflicted with an inertia that will
hold him in Greensboro the rest of his days." Johnson had "done [his]
damnedest to drag [Chambers] up to Baltimore" without success.[17]

Chambers, born in Charlotte in 1891 into a family of means,
attended high school at the prestigious Woodberry Forest School in Orange,

15. Douglas Southall Freeman to Louis Jaffé, 15 October 1929, Jaffé Papers; Louis
Jaffé to Douglas Southall Freeman, 12 October 1929, Jaffé Papers; *New York Times*, 29
December 1995.

16. Lenoir Chambers to Morrow, 20 August 1959, Chambers Papers; Leidholdt,
Standing Before the Shouting Mob, 18–9; Kneebone, *Southern Liberal Journalists*, 28–9;
Mencken, *Thirty-Five Years of Newspaper Work*, 118; Downs and Downs, *Journalists of the
United States*, 190.

17. Louis Jaffé to Gerald Johnson, 15 September 1925, Jaffé Papers; Chambers,
Shank, and Sugg, *Salt Water & Printer's Ink*, 321; Gerald Johnson to Louis Jaffé, 14 October
1929, Jaffé Papers.

Virginia. As a student at the University of North Carolina, he edited the campus newspaper, the *Tar Heel,* and played varsity football, basketball, and tennis. A talented student, he graduated third in his class and Phi Beta Kappa. A year's additional study at Columbia University's School of Journalism in 1916–1917 exposed Chambers not only to the urban Northeast but also to a broad spectrum of literary and political thought. Columbia's journalism students at that time acquired a reputation for rebelliousness and provided the university's Anti-Militarism League with its most strident members. Some of the period's leading activists—including Max Eastman and John Reed—propounded their radical views at Columbia. No record of Chambers's reactions has survived, but a young intellectual of his caliber would certainly have evaluated the ferment of doctrines there, weighing them against the mores of his region.[18]

Like Jaffé and Johnson, Chambers served in France during the war. He briefly commanded a company in trench combat with German troops in Alsace, where his unit was shelled and repelled an enemy advance. Later in his life, he recalled the war with revulsion, blaming it on "human stupidity and blindness and cruelty and the arrogant ordering of men's lives." Even in wartime, however, Chambers found Europe more sophisticated than New York and especially his native North Carolina. He described France as the "most civilized and cared-for country" he had ever seen. He observed that blacks there enjoyed privileges denied them in the segregated American South. "In my hotel lives an American Negro prize-fighter, a fine-looking figure of a man, very well dressed. He eats . . . where I eat sometimes, and he talks very pleasurably and intimately with the French." Chambers also was impressed by the multinational and multiracial composition of the Allied forces: "Great numbers of them. Every nationality, race, color, and variety of uniform."[19]

When he returned to Chapel Hill after the armistice to serve as director of the University of North Carolina News Bureau, he found his for-

---

18. Alex Leidholdt, "Virginius Dabney and Lenoir Chambers: Two Southern Liberal Newspaper Editors Face Virginia's Massive Resistance to Public School Integration," *American Journalism* 15, no. 4 (fall 1998): 38–9.

19. *Stars and Stripes,* 7 May 1919; Lenoir Chambers to Max Schuster, 15 April 1933, Chambers Papers; Lenoir Chambers to Grace Chambers, 19 March 1919, 19 July 1918, Chambers Papers.

merly unexceptional alma mater transforming itself into an institution of national prominence, well on its way to becoming the South's preeminent university—a phenomenon within the mediocrity that characterized southern higher education at the time. Newly appointed university president Harry Woodburn Chase, described by Gerald Johnson as a "damnyankee, a genuine, blown-in-the-bottle Massachusetts bluebelly," quickly selected Chambers to serve on a special committee alongside future president Frank Porter Graham and Louis Round Wilson, director of the University of North Carolina Press, to organize an ambitious funding campaign that would enable the university to stimulate a social and cultural renaissance in North Carolina and throughout the South.[20]

The committee succeeded beyond all expectations. Soon Wilson's press was pioneering publication in the South of books on contemporary political, economic, and racial topics. His successor, William T. Couch, would build on this foundation, bringing out a much more provocative list, including many books authored by blacks. Sociologist Howard W. Odum arrived at the university in 1920 and launched the Institute for Research in Social Science and the *Journal of Social Forces,* which would fearlessly and systematically investigate southern society and culture. The university expanded its graduate school, developed a school of engineering, and invigorated its theater and journalism programs. Louis Graves, Chambers's replacement as news director, who also taught journalism in the English department, left the university after just a few years but stayed to found the *Chapel Hill Weekly,* which reflected the town's progressive spirit and served as a meeting place for liberal journalists throughout the region. Under President Chase's leadership, the university had become a fertile oasis in the Sahara of the Bozart. Chambers maintained a lifelong close association with his alma mater.[21]

In 1921 Chambers joined the staff of the *Greensboro Daily News.* He had conducted a thorough and critical search for his first real newspaper job and chosen the *News* because of its reputation as a highly literate and nonpartisan paper. He worked briefly as a reporter before rising to the posi-

20. Snider, *Light on the Hill,* 169, 173.

21. Ibid., 176–81; Egerton, *Speak Now Against the Day,* 129–34; Dabney, *Liberalism in the South,* 349–51, 408; Couch, *Culture in the South,* 155.

tion of city editor, and then associate editor. Johnson, upon reading Chambers's first editorial, offered only faint praise but strongly worded advice: "You are under the most solemn obligation to speak as much of the truth as you are able to speak . . . [and] to use all of the brains God gave you all the time, even when it is likely to be highly unpleasant and even dangerous to use them. . . . The newspaper editor who is afraid to stand up to be laughed at, or sworn at, is . . . a slacker." Johnson enjoined Chambers to sit at Godbey's feet and drink in his wisdom.[22]

For five years Chambers had done just that, and he had begun to establish a reputation of his own as an important liberal journalist. Clearly he possessed the talent and maturity Jaffé was seeking. Johnson advised Jaffé to write to Chambers but warned that it would take a "miracle" to budge him. Remarkably, on the day after Johnson mailed his letter to Jaffé, the "miracle" occurred. Johnson received a letter from Chambers in which—"yelling bloody murder"—he expressed revulsion regarding a turn in his paper's politics. He perceived liberal editor Godbey's influence as waning and the power of managing editor A. L. Stockton as rising with the *News*'s owner.[23]

Chambers's fears stemmed from his paper's coverage of an ugly episode of labor violence. Early in the morning of October 2, 1929, outside the gate of the Marion Manufacturing Company's textile mill in western North Carolina, a local sheriff and his heavily armed, heavily drinking, and hastily sworn-in deputies had fired into the backs of a crowd of unarmed strikers, killing six and seriously wounding twenty-five. The sheriff served as a patsy for the mill manager, who, instead of protesting the violence, complimented the shooters on their aim. "I think the officers are damned good marksmen," he told Robert Lathan's *Asheville Citizen*. "If I ever organize an army they can have jobs with me." He had read that in the World War it had taken five tons of lead to kill a soldier; law authorities in Marion had used less than five pounds in the melee outside the mill.[24]

22. Leidholdt, *Standing Before the Shouting Mob*, 18; *Greensboro (N.C.) Daily News*, 21 October 1941; Gerald Johnson to Lenoir Chambers, 13 September 1924, Chambers Papers; Gerald Johnson, *South-Watching: Selected Essays by Gerald Johnson*, ed. Fred Hobson (Chapel Hill: University of North Carolina Press, 1983), 78–9.

23. Gerald Johnson to Louis Jaffé, 14, 16 October 1929, Jaffé Papers.

24. *Asheville (N.C.) Citizen*, 4 October 1929; Benjamin Stolberg, "Madness in Marion," *Nation*, 23 October 1929, 462–4.

Labor unrest threatened the textile industries that anchored Greensboro's economy, and Stockton's front-page story the day after the massacre had exonerated Marion's law authorities and blatantly sided with the mill's owners. Stockton maintained that in the confusion, some of the protesters had been shot by pistol-wielding strikers—not by the sheriff and his deputies. His lead sentence set the tone for his report: "The community building erected by the Marion Manufacturing Company for the pleasure and comfort of its . . . workers was tonight an armed camp."[25]

The managing editor's story did not divulge that the mill workers toiled in appalling conditions, commonly receiving wages of less than ten dollars for a workweek of fifty-five to sixty hours, or that in the mill village, families of eight to ten people lived crowded into three-room houses with cracked paint and leaking roofs. He further neglected to mention that workers were charged ten cents—a substantial sum, given their low salaries— each time they bathed, swam in the pool, or bowled in the community center, and that they too frequently had to spend tomorrow's wages for today's provisions at the company store.[26]

The *News*'s editorial page contravened Stockton's stance. Referring to a spate of recent incidents of violence directed at organized labor, Chambers wrote, "Surely it must have sunk into the state . . . that in no instance of disorder anywhere in the state these months has any sheriff, deputy sheriff or policeman handled any situation confronting him in a manner to create confidence in him or what he stands for. The state has little truth about this Marion killing; perhaps it will never have the full truth. But it knows that a squad of officers thrown face to face with a real problem not only did not solve it but so acted that the end was tragedy. That is failure—and it is a failure which has been multiplied many times in North Carolina this year."[27]

The Greensboro editorial team chided its peers in the Tarheel press who sided with irresponsible mill owners: "To glorify the fraternity of the manufacturers and to 'put down' the brotherhood of workers is tyranny too

25. *Greensboro (N.C.) Daily News*, 3 October 1929; Powell, *North Carolina Through Four Centuries*, 488.

26. Stolberg, "Madness in Marion," 462–4; Marion Bonner, "Behind the Southern Textile Strikes," *Nation*, 2 October 1929, 351–2; Hall et al., *Like a Family*, 119, 215–6.

27. *Greensboro (N.C.) Daily News*, 4 October 1929.

stupid to be tolerated a day. But that's just what has been going on in this state. The preposterous unfairness of a group of mighty millionaires combining for their own profit, then blithely discouraging the organization of the union for the purpose of trading with them on something like even terms! Yet, you can't read the papers a week without seeing this thing sticking in your eyes. . . . The sheriff's firing squad in Marion won't stop [union activity], no matter how fine the aim or how broad the backs of the victims."[28]

The labor unrest in Marion followed on the heels of strikes in a rayon-spinning plant in Elizabethton in eastern Tennessee and in the "South's City of Spindles"—Gastonia, North Carolina—in early 1929. In Elizabethton a young woman fresh from the marginal farms in the surrounding hills had organized a walkout that spread to the mill's entire work force. Low wages, stepped-up quotas, and inhumane policies served as the impetus for the walkout. The anticommunist United Textile Workers of America, affiliated with the American Federation of Labor, represented workers. Dispensing with any pretense of impartiality, the Tennessee National Guard stationed machine guns on the plant's roofs and escorted scabs through the town. Goons sworn in as "special policemen" by law authorities intimidated union organizers and engaged in night riding. Despite the union's heroic resistance, the strike crumbled.[29]

In Gaston County, North Carolina, workers at the Loray Mill had walked out, calling for a minimum wage of twenty dollars a week, equal pay for women and children, an end to the stretch-out, and union recognition. Management evicted the protesters and their families from the mill village. When the police chief tried to break up the tent city the strikers had constructed, a gunfight broke out, killing him. The violence rapidly escalated. Men firing into a truck carrying union members murdered organizer Ella May Wiggins, whose songs had inspired the strikers, then raided the procommunist National Textile Workers Union headquarters and kidnapped and beat members. "We're all 100 percent Americans and anybody that don't like it can go back to Russia," members of the rabble shouted. Law authorities and the state militia refused to act, giving tacit permission to

28. Ibid., 6 October 1929.
29. Hall et al., *Like a Family*, 213–4.

rioters and vigilantes to continue their campaign of violence and intimidation. Juries convicted the police chief's murderers but turned Wiggins's killers free.[30]

The courts would ultimately acquit Marion's trigger-happy lawmen. In the wake of the shootings, Johnson reported to Jaffé that Stockton, who had "always believed in more and better murders," had given Chambers a "sharp case of spiritual and damn nigh physical vomiting." He advised Jaffé to tender an offer at once. The *Pilot* and *News* exchanged papers, and Jaffé probably had already observed the schizophrenia in the Greensboro paper. He put out a feeler to Chambers, emphasizing the "broader future" an associate editor would enjoy working for a larger newspaper in a major city and pointing out the similarities between the two papers' editorial perspectives.[31]

Jaffé had not exaggerated the similarities between the two papers. The *Pilot,* like the *News,* had stood up for fairer and more humane treatment of workers. In "Mythical Anglo-Saxon Docility" and "Industrial Genetics," Jaffé warned that exploitative industries should think twice before locating in the South. Chamber of commerce claims of submissive and compliant labor pools to the contrary, the rash of worker unrest signified that the region's workers would no longer kowtow to irresponsible managers and owners. Future strikes could be averted only by "consideration and kindness."[32]

Jaffé dismissed arguments that radicals had fomented the labor unrest: "It is interesting to reflect that the strikers in Elizabethton, . . . free from any taint of Communism, would seem to be just as enthusiastic in their desire to attain their ends as the strikers in Gastonia, where the Communist influence is supposed to be present. It is also to be noted that the employers at Elizabethton are just as stubborn and that the authorities there would

30. Ibid., 214–5; Nell Battle Lewis, "Anarchy vs. Communism in Gastonia," *Nation,* 25 September 1929, 321–2; John A. Salmond, *Gastonia 1929: The Story of the Loray Mill Strike* (Chapel Hill: University of North Carolina, 1995), 23–166.

31. Hugh Talmage Lefler and Albert Ray Newsome, *North Carolina: The History of a Southern State* (Chapel Hill: University of North Carolina Press, 1973), 640–1; Gerald Johnson to Louis Jaffé, 16 October 1929, Jaffé Papers; Louis Jaffé to Lenoir Chambers, 15 October 1929, Jaffé Papers.

32. *Pilot,* 15 April 1929, 2 May 1929.

seem to have been just as harsh in their dealings with the strikers as has been the case in Gastonia. It appears from these comparisons that the economic theories held by the leaders of a strike are of relatively little consequence and that the presence of a few Communist agitators at the North Carolina textile center has not made the course of events there different in any material respect from that in the Tennessee community." Jaffé advocated neutral federal and state inquiries into labor practices, which he believed constituted a "festering sore." The South's economic welfare depended to a large measure "on a frank effort to face distasteful problems" as they arose.[33]

Later that month, Chambers traveled to Norfolk, where Jaffé conducted the interview—in reality, more of a sales pitch. The interaction included a game of golf at Princess Anne Country Club near Virginia Beach, after which the two men—both of whom liked an occasional drink—enjoyed violating the Volstead Act. Chambers pronounced the cache of booze to which Jaffé had obtained access "excellent."[34]

Jaffé rarely engaged in flattery, but he pulled out all the stops for his recruitment of Chambers. "I am enormously attracted to you," he declared in a letter after the interview, "both as a person and an intellect. . . . We have the makings of a great team. . . . This team, for the good of both of us, ought to be consummated." Jaffé went on to quote Shakespeare and to implore Chambers to join him: "There is a tide in the affairs of men, which taken at flood leads on to fortune." These lines, he said, had been stirring in his mind all morning. "I do powerfully believe that this tide now waits on you. Don't let it give you the slip! Cast out fear. Come. The time will come, I do believe, when you will regard this as a historic letter." Chambers accepted the position, largely because of his high regard for Jaffé's ability as an editor.[35]

With the entire responsibility of the editorial page on his shoulders, Jaffé prodded his new associate to start work at once. Chambers, however, bargained for more money, negotiating a yearly salary of $5,200 with a promise of a small raise within a year. His search for an apartment, coupled

33. Ibid., 16 May 1929.
34. Louis Jaffé to John Gordan, 25 November 1929, Jaffé Papers.
35. Louis Jaffé to Lenoir Chambers, 24 October, 1929, ibid.; Lenoir Chambers to E. Roberts, 17 February 1937, Chambers Papers.

with his desire not to leave Godbey in the lurch, further delayed Chambers's arrival. Jaffé grew increasingly frustrated over the delays.[36]

Before Chambers reported for work at the *Pilot* in December, Johnson warned the brusque Jaffé to go easy at first. "Handle [Chambers] with kid gloves for the first couple of weeks," he cautioned. "Under his surface enamel, the fellow is shy. But under that is a substratum of hard common sense, which is the real Lenoir. Once he has got his feet under him and knows where he stands, you can give it to him straight and as hot as you know how, and he won't bat an eye." Jaffé thanked Johnson for the insight into his "new coadjutor's sensibilities." After observing Chambers's personality, Jaffé had "ordered [his own] deportment accordingly." He reported that "everything [was] running smoothly." Chambers met all of Jaffé's expectations. He expressed his gratitude to Johnson for the assistance in recruiting Chambers but warned, "This will not prevent me from being mad as hell if the *Sunpapers* should lay violent hands on him." The Baltimore journalist should "pass this word down the line."[37]

For the next decade and a half, Chambers served as Jaffé's associate editor. Chambers reported to Johnson that his new editor was a "tip-top" colleague, whom he respected and liked "immensely." Jaffé frequently visited the Chambers home, and the children would grow up calling him "Uncle Louis." As different in physical appearance, background, and temperament as the proverbial chalk and cheese, the two newspapermen would develop such a close relationship that Chambers would later joke that he knew Jaffé better than he knew his wife, Roberta.[38]

Chambers, taller than the stocky and dark Jaffé and losing his hair, still sported the thin mustache he had grown as a company commander in France ten years earlier. Neither man cut a natty figure, but both kept up dignified appearances. They wore flannel or tweed in the cooler months and linen or seersucker during Norfolk's hot and humid summers. Depending

36. Louis Jaffé to Lenoir Chambers, 29 October 1929, Jaffé Papers; Leidholdt, *Standing Before the Shouting Mob,* 23.

37. Gerald Johnson to Louis Jaffé, 4 December 1929, Louis Jaffé to Gerald Johnson, 31 December 1929, both in Jaffé Papers.

38. Lenoir Chambers to Gerald Johnson, 11 March 1935, Chambers Papers; Elisabeth Burgess, interview by author, 25 September 1990; Lenoir Chambers to J. E. Dowd, 7 May 1950, Chambers Papers.

on the season, Jaffé wore a wide-brimmed felt or a panama hat. For formal occasions he wore conservative suits purchased from Brooks Brothers in New York.[39]

The courtly and mannered Chambers, whose rapid promotions at the *Greensboro Daily News* had precluded lengthy exposure to coarse and combative newsroom culture, preferred to avoid personal conflict and displays of unpleasantness. Jaffé, much to the contrary, did not stand on ceremony. Robert Mason, a future *Virginian-Pilot* editor, described Jaffé's approach as "direct and a little frightening." One longtime Norfolk political figure confided to Mason that whenever he answered his telephone to "This is Jaffé," whatever information was being requested immediately vanished from his mind. Future associate editor Alonzo Dill recalled that many people were "put off" by Jaffé. "He was rough. He could not suffer fools, [but] if you knew him, he was very, very warm." Mason remembered Jaffé similarly, noting his essential reticence but his affability with trusted friends and colleagues.[40]

Jaffé's humble roots and upbringing had afforded him no entree into the privileged world he now occupied by virtue of his editorship, Pulitzer Prize, and marriage into a socially prominent family. He functioned as a respected member of Tidewater's social and professional communities and an honorary member of the Norfolk Bar Association and the Norfolk Medical Association. He received invitations to naval ceremonies and civic gatherings as a matter of course. Despite his intellect and innate confidence in his abilities, however, he may have felt occasional insecurity in these unaccustomed milieus. Conversely, Chambers, born into southern gentility, moved confidently and comfortably among Norfolk's social and official elite. According to Mason, he could blend "into a clubroom like walnut and leather." "Lenoir came from the gentlemanly precincts of Woodberry Forest and the gentle atmosphere of the University of North Carolina, and Louis probably wouldn't have gone to a fine college unless he'd lived in the shadow of one," explained Dill.[41]

39. Mason, *One of the Neighbors' Children,* 151, 155; Louis Jaffé to Brooks Brothers, 6 October 1947, Louis Jaffé Jr.

40. Mason, *One of the Neighbors' Children,* 151; Dill, interview by author; Robert Mason, interview by author, 18 September 1995.

41. Robert Mason, interviews by author, 10 April 1989, 17 July 1990; Mason, *One of the Neighbors' Children,* 153; Dill, interview by author.

Chambers, only a few years younger than his new superior, came to Norfolk fully formed as an editorial writer. He had turned down offers to assume editorships of other newspapers, including Lathan's *Asheville Citizen*. Despite the extensive experience he had acquired in Greensboro, Chambers perceived that he could still learn a great deal from Jaffé. The senior editor divided the writing duties evenly between Chambers and himself. The two men occupied adjoining offices and consulted each other frequently throughout the day. Although both felt capable of dealing with virtually any subject matter, Jaffé, because of his familiarity with local issues and Virginia politics, chose to author many editorials on these topics and on labor, industrialization, and race. Chambers and Jaffé both wrote extensively on southern, national, and international issues.[42]

Throughout his career Jaffé insisted that his associates keep abreast of a broad spectrum of opinion. Each morning he carried with him to work a dark-green linen book bag packed with reading material ranging from the arch-conservative to the ultra-liberal. "He took in the whole spectrum of opinion," recalled Dill. "He believed that was an editorial writer's duty."[43]

The editorial team worked in separate quarters from the *Pilot*'s reporting staff and displayed no interest in the production of the newspaper. Although the paper continued a long tradition of confining its editors' official responsibilities to the editorial page, Starke and succeeding publishers consulted with Jaffé on important policy matters.[44]

Soon after hiring Chambers, Jaffé, capitalizing on his lightened workload, began to develop close friendships with artist Julius John "J. J." Lankes and famed author Sherwood Anderson. That Jaffé found fraternity among such controversial nonconformists is significant. For several years he had felt increasingly alienated from traditionalist and non-intellectual members of his social circle. This feeling perhaps had accounted for his resignation a number of years earlier from Norfolk's Civitan Club. "I cannot convince myself any longer that my membership in the club has any meaning or purpose," he wrote. One should expect a "certain feeling of purposiveness, of

42. Lenoir Chambers to L. Penry, 6 February 1937, Chambers Papers; Dill, interview by author; Lenoir Chambers to John Curtis, 6 March 1935.

43. Dill, interview by author.

44. Mason, interview by author, 18 September 1995; Frank Batten, interview by author, 25 September 1990.

joy-in-fellowship, of spiritual satisfaction in a confraternity of good fellows," but for reasons he found difficult to explain to himself, Jaffé found "these satisfactions becoming fewer and fewer."[45]

Lankes, a competent painter and sculptor, would earn his principal renown for his woodcuts. His woodblock prints would grace books by Robert Frost and Sherwood Anderson and would hang in the Metropolitan and British Museums, the Bibliothèque Nationale, and the Library of Congress. Lankes had moved to Hilton Village, near Yorktown, in 1925. In his art and life, he celebrated the aesthetics and values of the preindustrial age. In the landscapes, dilapidated buildings, and rough, self-reliant county folk of rural Tidewater Virginia, the iconoclastic artist found ideal subject matter. Individualist, democrat, curmudgeon, bohemian, and skewerer of hypocrites and the pretentious, he eked out a marginal living with his wife, Edee, and their four children in the midst of the Depression.[46]

Lankes acknowledged he had derived much stimulation early in his career from the ideas advanced in the pages of *The Masses* by social critics and writers such as Max Eastman, Floyd Dell, John Reed, and Sherwood Anderson. (In 1917 the Post Office Department, by denying *The Masses* mailing privileges because of its pacifist and socialist ideology, had effectively suppressed its publication.) "I was an ardent Socialist at one time, and then a Communist," Lankes later wrote to Anderson.[47]

Lankes moved to Hilton Village because of its low cost of living as well as the surrounding area's rich subject matter. The thin, bespectacled

45. Louis Jaffé to Daily Walsh, 15 December 1926, Jaffé Papers.

46. *Pilot,* 6 April 1930; Mantle Fielding, *Mantle Fielding's Dictionary of American Painters, Sculptors & Engravers* (Poughkeepsie: Apollo, 1986), 519; Welford Dunaway Taylor and Richard Waller, *J. J. Lankes (1884–1960): Woodcuts of Rural America* (Richmond: University of Richmond Marsh Art Gallery and the Virginia Museum of Fine Arts, 1994); "A Preliminary and Sketchy Chronology of the Life of J. J. Lankes," 12 July 1978, Lankes Papers; Sherwood Anderson, "J. J. Lankes and His Woodcuts," *Virginia Quarterly Review* 7, no. 1 (1931): 18–26; J. J. Lankes, *Woodcut Manual* (New York: Crown, 1932), 88–92; Carl Zigrosser, *The Artist in America: Twenty-Four Close-Ups of Contemporary Printmakers* (New York: Alfred A. Knopf, 1942), 184–5; Welford Dunaway Taylor, *Robert Frost and J. J. Lankes: Riders on Pegasus* (Hanover, N.H.: Dartmouth College Library, 1996), 39.

47. *Pilot,* 6 April 1930; Wm. David Sloan and James D. Startt, eds., *The Media in America* (Northport, Ala.: Vision Press, 1996), 379, 393; Emery, Emery, and Roberts, *Press in America*, 226, 256; J. J. Lankes to Sherwood Anderson, 8 January 1929, Anderson Papers.

artist practiced his craft in a workshop in his modest home. He was an inveterate and witty correspondent; while living in Virginia, he had begun exchanges of letters with Mencken and Anderson.[48]

Jaffé first established contact with Lankes in March 1930 while attempting to secure an interview for Margaret for a *Pilot* Sunday feature article. "As an artist doing his work in Virginia, we feel our people ought to know about you," he wrote. "Needless to say, the article would be handled with appropriate restraint and discrimination." Lankes accepted the offer and complimented Jaffé, telling him he had often wished to write to him to praise his work: "I have never seen a better page than yours." A few days later, Lankes took the ferry across Hampton Roads to Willoughby Spit to visit the Jaffés at their home on the Chesapeake Bay. Margaret's piece— featuring five of Lankes's woodcuts and a photograph of the artist— appeared in early April.[49]

The next month Lankes sent Jaffé a letter to the editor. Of the many newspapers he had read, he would "place the editorial page of the *Virginian-Pilot* first," he wrote.

> It is a daily joy to me. It restores my faith in the press. I admire greatly the way you handle stupid congressmen and wishy washy senators, shoddy gambling bishops and all pestiferous meddlers in general.
>
> I make a boast of being a subscriber of the *Pilot,* and am constantly sending it to various parts of the country as a pattern of ideal journalism. May your pen bite even more trenchantly the hypocrisy, the rascality and especially the meddlesomeness which God in his infinite wisdom has inflicted on humanity—perhaps to develop our character, maybe to serve as limits to mortal aspirations, but most certainly to furnish amusement to the angels.[50]

Jaffé did not print the letter, explaining that "to use it as an advertisement to the generality would be somehow to profane it." As he wrote to

48. *Pilot,* 6 April 1930.
49. Louis Jaffé to J. J. Lankes, 22 March 1930, J. J. Lankes to Louis Jaffé, 24 March 1930, Louis Jaffé to J. J. Lankes, 27 March 1930, all in Jaffé Papers; *Pilot,* 6 April 1930.
50. J. J. Lankes to Louis Jaffé, 24 May 1930, Jaffé Papers.

Lankes, "I do not mind printing the most generous bouquets as long as they come from the Rotarians. It is part of the business. But a letter like this one from you is for the private refreshment of the editors and we shall not share it with a crowd that does not speak your language or think your thoughts. Be assured that it goes into my personal file—to be resorted to for spiritual fortification when I am more sorely beset than usual by the Brahmins, the right-thinkers and the luncheon clubs."[51]

Sherwood Anderson, an Ohio native twelve years senior to Jaffé, had led a restless and impulsive life. He had endured childhood poverty when modern mass production made his father's previously secure craft of harness-making obsolete. Anderson's father had moved from job to job, and the family had drifted with him through villages and small towns across Ohio before settling in Clyde, near Sandusky. As an author Sherwood would draw heavily upon his childhood experiences. The repressed desires of small-town residents and the machine age's impact on the lives of workers would appear as persistent themes in his short stories, novels, and essays.[52]

In 1919 Anderson published *Winesburg, Ohio*, the book that would earn him a lasting literary reputation. The collection of stories was written simply, without regard for formal literary devices, but it displayed keen psychological insight into the lives of a series of conflicted and defeated small-town characters sexually and spiritually repressed by convention. Anderson had transformed the American short story and would powerfully influence a generation of writers, including William Faulkner and Ernest Hemingway. Startlingly sexual for the era, *Winesburg, Ohio* evoked great controversy; many critics labeled it "nasty" and "dirty." Other books followed: *Poor White, The Triumph of the Egg, Many Marriages, A Storyteller's Story*, and *Dark Laughter*. Although Mencken had given some of the *Winesburg, Ohio* stories a chilly reception, Anderson became one of his favorite writers. In 1925 the Sage dubbed him "America's most distinctive novelist."[53]

51. Louis Jaffé to J. J. Lankes, 28 May 1930, ibid.

52. James Erwin Schevill, *Sherwood Anderson: His Life and Work* (Denver: University of Denver Press, 1951), 8–10, 14; Ray Lewis White, ed., *Sherwood Anderson's Memoirs: A Critical Edition* (Chapel Hill: University of North Carolina Press, 1969), 35–44.

53. Schevill, *Sherwood Anderson: His Life and Work*, 94–108; White, ed., *Sherwood Anderson's Memoirs*, 22; Welford Dunaway Taylor, *Sherwood Anderson* (New York:

Anderson visited southwest Virginia in the summer of that year to escape the heat of New Orleans. In Troutdale, a little lumber town near Marion, Virginia, he wrote an autobiographical novel, *Tar: A Midwest Childhood,* in a one-room cabin located in a cornfield. He fell in love with the area, and using the royalties from *Dark Laughter*—a popular success that Faulkner and F. Scott Fitzgerald derided and Hemingway publicly satirized—he built the house he had long dreamed of owning. But the energy he devoted to construction of his country home distracted him only temporarily from the knowledge that his writing had grown stale. He gave up temporarily on creative writing and, with the help of a loan, impetuously purchased two country weekly newspapers in Marion, the Republican *Smyth County News* and the *Marion Democrat.* Improbably, he made a success of both ventures. He enjoyed himself enormously, and his contacts with the townspeople reinvigorated him.[54]

In 1928 he met Eleanor Copenhaver, who was more than twenty years his junior, when she visited her family in Marion. Anderson and Eleanor, a brilliant social activist who worked as the secretary of the industrial division of the YWCA in New York, quickly developed an intellectual and physical attraction. Fearful of the effect of any hint of scandal upon Eleanor's career (Anderson and his third wife separated in late 1928 but the divorce would not become final for five years), he and Eleanor conducted their relationship in strict secrecy. He would accompany her as she traveled around the country in the course of her work, and through her passionate involvement in the labor movement, she directed the focus of Anderson's attention toward the social and economic problems that beset the country. She believed that America's great writers avoided themes that dealt with the exploitation of labor, and she challenged him to explore the subject.

Frederick Ungar, 1977), 36, 43; George Perkins, Barbara Perkins, and Phillip Leininger, eds., *Benét's Reader's Encyclopedia of American Literature* (New York: Harper Collins, 1991), 37.

54. White, ed., *Sherwood Anderson's Memoirs,* 23–4; Hobson, *Serpent in Eden,* 16, 133; Schevill, *Sherwood Anderson: His Life and Work,* 212–4; Kim Townsend, *Sherwood Anderson* (Boston: Houghton Mifflin, 1987), 227–9, 243; Sherwood Anderson to Horace Liveright, 15 January 1929, Anderson Papers; Schevill, *Sherwood Anderson: His Life and Work,* 243, 245; Charles E. Modlin, ed., *Sherwood Anderson's Love Letters to Eleanor Copenhaver Anderson* (Athens: University of Georgia Press, 1989), xiii; Sherwood Anderson, *The Buck Fever Papers,* ed. Welford Dunaway Taylor (Charlottesville: University Press of Virginia, 1971), xvi–xvii.

Together they visited Elizabethton during the strike and met with the mill-workers. The experience moved Anderson deeply. He journeyed throughout the South to factories and textile mills to learn more about the conditions in them and became increasingly radicalized. "I am getting nearer communism myself all the time," he wrote to Lankes. "I don't see how we can avoid it."[55]

Jaffé and Anderson appear to have met at a party in Charlottesville, perhaps following a speech that Anderson had delivered, entitled "The Newspaper and the Modern Age," at the University of Virginia's Public Affairs Institute in August 1929. Their mutual friendship with Lankes brought the two men closer together.[56]

The following August, Anderson visited with Jaffé for ten days at his house on Willoughby Spit while Margaret and Christopher were away. The boy had been ill earlier in the summer; and fretting over his health, Margaret had taken him for a prolonged stay at a resort in Pennsylvania. "I am lonesome and need some company," Jaffé wrote Anderson. The famous author spent the nights on his host's sleeping porch, and the two had many "interesting discussions 'about it and about,'" Jaffé reported to Lankes. Then Eleanor arrived, and the "literary feast was off." Anderson "was so busy courting her" that Jaffé saw little of him for the remainder of his visit. Jaffé did not mention and may not have known that his guests, perhaps negotiating their new love affair and sexual relationship, quarreled during their stay. The nature of the discord remains unknown, but Anderson referred to the incident in a letter to Eleanor immediately following their departure. "There is a new inner dignity to my life that I have wanted," he wrote. "It has come most fully since we went together into Jaffe's house. I am afraid I tried to be untrue to something there but couldn't." Six months later he returned to the episode in another letter to her: "I think of all the things I must have put you through—the record back of me—my failures

55. Modlin, ed., *Sherwood Anderson's Love Letters to Eleanor Copenhaver Anderson,* xiv; Ray Lewis White, ed., *Sherwood Anderson's Secret Love Letters* (Baton Rouge, Louisiana State University Press, 1991), 8–9; Townsend, *Sherwood Anderson,* 249, 255–63, 288; Sherwood Anderson, *Perhaps Women* (New York: Horace Liveright, 1931), 111–17; Sherwood Anderson to J. J. Lankes, 26 June 1931, Anderson Papers.

56. J. J. Lankes to Louis Jaffé, 27 July 1930, Anderson, "Newspaper and the Modern Age," both in Jaffé Papers.

. . . the state of mind I was in when you first knew me . . . that queer hour in the Jaffe house."[57]

That same month, the *Virginian-Pilot*'s editor met H. L. Mencken for the first time. Jaffé had traveled to Baltimore to see his friend John Owens, editor of the *Sun*. On a Saturday evening Paul Patterson, the *Sunpapers'* publisher, convened an informal meeting for his editorial principals, and Owens brought Jaffé along with him. The two editors joined Mencken and Patterson in front of the fireplace in Patterson's study. Gerald Johnson, Hamilton Owens, and Edwin Murphy, the *Evening Sun*'s crusty managing editor, who had first brought Jaffé to the *Sunpapers'* attention six years earlier, also joined the confab.

Many years later Johnson still remembered the evening clearly. Before the men turned their attention to business, Hamilton Owens related an amusing story. The previous weekend he had visited with writer Emily Clark and several other women who knew Mencken, and they had demanded to know when the Sage would marry author and critic Sara Powell Haardt. The newspapermen gathered in Patterson's study laughed over the idea of Mencken, fifty years old and long considered a confirmed bachelor, ever marrying.[58]

The first hour of the meeting focused on a policy question. Mencken debated Patterson and John Owens over the matter. After the discussion ended, Mencken glanced over at Patterson, who then drew a sheet of copy paper from his pocket and passed it to John Owens. "John, here is a thing we are going to run tomorrow morning," he said. "Read it aloud." Owens fumbled for his glasses and leaned back in his chair. "August 2, Montgomery, Alabama; special to the *Sun*," he read. "Mrs. John Anton Haardt, of this city, today announced the engagement of her daughter, Miss Sara Powell Haardt, to H. L. Mencken of Baltimore. The wedding will take place September 3."[59]

57. Louis Jaffé to Sherwood Anderson, 11 August 1930, Louis Jaffé to J. J. Lankes, 20 June 1930, 3 September 1930, all ibid.; Modlin, ed., *Sherwood Anderson's Love Letters*, 122, 152.

58. William Manchester, *Disturber of the Peace: The Life of H. L. Mencken* (New York: Harper & Brothers, 1951), 239.

59. Bode, *Mencken*, 290.

No one spoke. Then Murphy blurted out, "I don't get the catch in it. I don't think it's funny." "It's true," Patterson said. "We're running it tomorrow, the lead item on the Society Page." Another long silence followed. Mencken's friends and colleagues stared at him incredulously, still suspecting he had concocted a practical joke. Jaffé—the only outsider in the group—sized up the situation. He rose and said, "I understand, Mr. Patterson, this is a firm announcement of Mr. Mencken's engagement?" "It is," the publisher responded. Jaffé walked over to Mencken and said simply, "Then you are to be congratulated, sir." With the awkward quiet ended, the other guests rushed forward to congratulate the betrothed.[60]

Soon after this encounter, Jaffé shared with Lankes his impressions of Mencken: "It was my first meeting with the Editor of the *American Mercury,* and I was very much impressed with him. He seems to be an all-fired good scout, without any horns or tail, and with a discriminating taste for unconstitutional refreshments."[61]

A significant mention of Jaffé by Mencken surfaced in 1991 when the Enoch Pratt Free Library opened his sealed manuscript entitled *Thirty-five Years of Newspaper Work.* In one section Mencken recalled his discovery of many journalists throughout the country who became occasional correspondents for the *Sunpapers,* including Grover Hall and Gerald Johnson. He wrote that "[Hamilton] Owens also unearthed some competent ones on his own—for example, Louis Graves of Chapel Hill, N.C., Robert Lathan of Asheville, N.C., and Louis I. Jaffé of Norfolk, Va., the last-named one of the few Jews ever to work for the *Sunpapers.*"[62]

The notation of Jaffé's Jewishness by Mencken resurrected the long-running controversy over Mencken's possible anti-Semitism, invigorated most recently by Charles Fecher's publication in 1989 of Mencken's diary. After examining the diary thoroughly, Fecher regretfully labeled Mencken an anti-Semite. The love of America's then most prominent critic and journalist for colorful language and vernacular and his tendency to stereotype people according to their religion, race, ethnicity, social class, and gender provides evidence aplenty to bolster Fecher's accusation of bigotry.

60. Manchester, *Disturber of the Peace,* 240; Bode, *Mencken,* 290–1.
61. Jaffé to Lankes, 3 September 1930, Jaffé Papers.
62. Mencken, *Thirty-Five Years of Newspaper Work,* 118.

Many of Mencken's views on foreign affairs and domestic politics further buttress the charge that he was an anti-Semite. His identification with Germany—born of his own German-American background and affinity for that country's culture, coupled with the persecution he had faced for siding against the British early in World War I—bred in him a deep suspicion of detractors of Deutschland during Hitler's rise to power. Mencken's rabid hatred of Franklin Roosevelt, who had humiliated him at a Gridiron dinner for journalists early in his presidential tenure and whose New Deal flew in the face of Mencken's deeply held libertarianism, made him skeptical of America's involvement in World War II.[63]

But Mencken confounds easy categorization. Alistair Cooke has pointed out, exaggerating only slightly, that all of Mencken's best friends were Jewish. Despite his inexcusable failure to speak out against Germany, he loathed both Nazism and Hitler, likening the Führer to an imperial wizard. The Sage devoted his energy and finances to help Jews flee Europe and in strong terms attempted to shame the United States into granting refuge to German Jewry. Moreover, despite his use of offensive racial terms and his penchant for racial stereotyping, he damned lynchings and skewered the Klan, incurring death threats as a result. Throughout the 1920s he more than any other editor mentored and aided black authors, Walter White serving as a prime example. He often viewed individual blacks as superior to whites. Although he regarded himself as a southerner, he entertained blacks in his home, contravening the mores of his era.[64]

What then to make of Mencken's reference to Jaffé? While it can be interpreted as an affirmation of Mencken's anti-Semitism, it can also be read in an opposite light—as an implied criticism of the *Sunpapers*' exclusionary hiring practices. Perhaps the remark should be taken at face value: Jaffé—despite his conversion to Episcopalianism—was indeed one of the

63. H. L. Mencken, *The Diary of H. L. Mencken,* ed. Charles A. Fecher (New York: Vintage, 1991), xxiii-xxv, 76–7; Joseph Epstein, "Mencken on Trial," *Commentary* (April 1990): 31–9; Mencken, *Thirty-Five Years of Newspaper Work,* xiv-xviii; Charles Angoff, *H. L. Mencken: A Portrait from Memory* (New York: Thomas Yoseloff, 1956), 161–9.

64. Alistair Cooke, *Six Men* (New York: Alfred A. Knopf, 1977), 110; Epstein, "Mencken on Trial," 31–9; Mencken, *Thirty-Five Years of Newspaper Work,* xiv-xviii; White, *Man Called White,* 65–7; Williams, *Baltimore Sun,* 237; Zangrando, *NAACP Crusade Against Lynching,* 117.

few journalists of Jewish lineage to contribute to the influential Baltimore papers. Most significantly, however, Mencken's observation establishes the fact that Jaffé's ethnicity was common knowledge among a circle of influential journalists throughout the region, including the leadership of the Baltimore dailies. It also confirms that Mencken, although he lacked a personal relationship with the *Pilot*'s editor, regarded him highly.

Jaffé's description of his encounter with Mencken suggests that despite his perspicacity, he sensed nothing untoward during the meeting at Patterson's home and the evening of celebration that must have followed the engagement announcement. To the contrary, he found Mencken charming and personable. Jaffé's earlier evaluation of the Sage as a "bold caricaturist who draws his pictures always in bold, crude lines [and who] practices a legitimate form of art—but [one] always to be interpreted with the limitations of that style in mind" makes clear that while he often appreciated the spirit of Mencken's work, he took much of its content with more than a grain of salt.[65]

A few months after that evening in Baltimore, Jaffé, Mencken, and Anderson all played bit parts in a comic opera that nearly ended with the tarring and feathering of Lankes. In an attempt to try his hand at writing, the artist had completed a manuscript of a short story for the *American Mercury*. More an exercise in reporting than creative writing, Lankes's story, written in the first person, revolved around his encounters in nearby Yorktown over the course of an afternoon and evening.[66]

While sketching a church in the hot sun, the narrator meets Marcus, who dabbles in art and pontificates on free love, socialism, and other controversial ideas gleaned from superficial reading of the *New Masses*, *Winesburg, Ohio*, and other radical literature. Late in the day the narrator accompanies Marcus to a drugstore, where some rubes tell anti-Semitic jokes. Then the two men walk to a nearby dance hall. Outside, men furtively swig whiskey and neck with women on a lovers' lane. Inside, couples grope on the dance floor. Marcus tells how he once nearly persuaded a woman to

65. Louis Jaffé to P. B. Young, 1 October 1927, Jaffé Papers.
66. J. J. Lankes, "Afternoon and Evening," *American Mercury* 11, no. 82 (October 1930): 238–43.

engage in sexual relations with him by convincing her of his philosophy of living life fully. "To live splendidly—that's the thing," he tells his new friend. The narrator contemplates this advice and wonders aloud if the rabble-rousing dictator Benito Mussolini provided an example of living splendidly.[67]

At the request of Lankes, Jaffé and Anderson looked the story over and made various suggestions. Jaffé believed that the Marcus character required development and that Lankes should flesh out the setting's location and ambiance. "You don't have to identify Yorktown, but you DO have to give the smell and the contours of the Virginia scene," he wrote. "That will give your sketch the necessary third dimension." Mencken, however, rejected Jaffé's and Anderson's suggestions out of hand. "As for Sherwood's criticism," he wrote, "I refuse to heed it. As a critic, he is an excellent harness-maker."[68]

"Afternoon and Evening" appeared in the October 1930 issue of *American Mercury*. Inexplicably, none of the skilled writers and journalists advising Lankes had thought to warn him that the good burghers of Yorktown might acquire a copy of the *Mercury* and look askance at the artist's thinly veiled and scathing portrayal of their town. And of course that is precisely what happened.

Had he known of Lankes's predicament, Jaffé might to some extent have calmed tempers editorially and diffused the imbroglio. However, he had traveled with his wife and son to Miami to settle them for the winter in the resort city, whose climate Margaret believed would benefit the boy's health. The artist's many letters to his friend thus went unanswered. "The postmaster's assistant," Lankes wrote nervously in one letter, "informed me yesterday in a rather severe schoolma'am tone that Yorktown has ceased to be a healthy place for me. The druggist got wind of the story and was trying to get a *Mercury*. He is a kluxer type, the sort of feller that delights the heart of Comrade Mencken."[69]

The situation worsened when several days later Yorktown com-

67. Ibid., 242.

68. Louis Jaffé to J. J. Lankes, 20 June 1930, J. J. Lankes to Louis Jaffé, 24 September 1930, both in Jaffé Papers; H. L. Mencken to J. J. Lankes, 29 July 1930, Lankes Papers.

69. Unidentified Miami newspaper, 20 November 1930, J. J. Lankes to Louis Jaffé, 11 November 1930, both in Jaffé Papers.

monwealth's attorney W. E. Hogg appeared at Lankes's door in Hilton Village to warn him of impending libel suits. Hogg demanded that Lankes apologize to the individuals he had affronted and publish an apology in the *Virginian-Pilot*. "It is going to be up to you . . . newspapermen to educate some of these small town hicks against excessive zeal in punishing offenders," Lankes wrote to Jaffé. "I'm keen for this education, for I fear I may be a victim some day. . . . I am getting the lynching complex pretty badly."[70]

As passions began to cool in Yorktown, Lankes lamented the timing of Jaffé's departure and his advice to establish more clearly the setting of "Afternoon and Evening." "It was a right sad blow when I heard you had just set off for a week's absence," he wrote, "for I thought you of anybody else could calm the tempest. I took occasion to look up a letter you wrote concerning the story. You wrote, . . . 'the locale is too indeterminate.' I made too good a job of it for my comfort. I was told the various characters compared notes and decided the picture was perfect. I'd like to talk to you about it on your return."[71]

70. J. J. Lankes to Louis Jaffé, 13 November 1930, J. J. Lankes to Louis Jaffé, [November 1930], both ibid.

71. J. J. Lankes to Louis Jaffé, 16 November 1930, ibid.

11 A CRUSHING LOAD

Having made arrangements for Margaret and Christopher to winter in Miami, Jaffé resumed his editorial duties. Margaret, however, quickly concluded that the warm weather did not have the salubrious results she had anticipated, and she traveled with her son back to Virginia. "It happens that Mrs. Jaffé has become dissatisfied with the effect of the Florida climate on our little boy's health and is returning to Norfolk at an early date," an exasperated Jaffé wrote to John Owens of the *Baltimore Sun*. After a brief stay at home, she returned with Christopher to Washington to consult with the boy's physicians there. In the year between the summers of 1930 and 1931, Margaret and Christopher—residing in Washington, Blue Ridge Summit, Pennsylvania, Miami, and again the District of Columbia—spent no more than two months in Norfolk.[1]

Jaffé grew increasingly concerned over the effects that such a nomadic upbringing and his wife's now obvious instability were having upon Christopher, who was approaching ten years of age. But any suggestion that local doctors could tend competently to their son's medical care infuriated Margaret. Her impulsiveness and obsession with the boy's health, coupled with the heavy expense of out-of-town doctors and costly resorts and hotels, pushed Jaffé emotionally and economically nearly to the breaking point. Many of the places Margaret lodged undoubtedly catered to "restricted clienteles." Almost certainly Jaffé would have had access to their facilities, but their discriminatory policies must have affronted and vexed him.

As the Great Depression wore on, it began to sap his savings and deplete his investments; he had the "very devil of a time" staying solvent. It

---

1. Louis Jaffé to John Owens, 29 November 1930, Jaffé Papers; Louis Jaffé to Margaret Jaffé, 22 March 1931, Louis Jaffé Jr.

sometimes appeared to him that every security he possessed had "turned insecure." Bills poured into Jaffé's home and office throughout the early thirties. The debts incurred by Margaret, who blithely ignored the depression's effect on the family finances, imperiled them further. The exclusive Hay-Adams House hotel in Washington—where Margaret resided repeatedly and at length, attended by a private maid—requested for a single five-day stay a $91.00 payment that included charges for a broken lamp, cigarettes, and many telephone calls. A business billed him $69.50 for a bronze sunlamp shipped to her at the hotel. Portable x-rays accounted for a $75.00 expenditure. A range of physicians in Washington, treating both Margaret and Christopher, clamored for payment, as did a women's clothing store there. Her expenses for the year totaled considerably more than $7,000.[2]

Margaret's distress over Christopher's health did not completely account for her de facto desertion of her husband during this period; she also blamed Jaffé. In a letter written to him during her extended stay at Blue Ridge Summit in the summer of 1930, she outlined her reasons for absenting herself from him and informed him of the changes he would have to make to effect a reconciliation.

She alleged that he had failed to "establish the machinery" to realize the ideals he had set forth for his life. Given her earlier romantic love for him, she wrote, he could have ensured a harmonious marriage by simply giving her a "free hand in first securing and then preserving Christopher's health," granting her the right to pursue her "literary purposes," and defending her from the "most cruel tyranny" of her parents. This "would have made me happy," she continued, "made you deserve my love—added to your honorable name—produced security both for Christopher and for me—so that when summoned to judgment by God, you could have reported not only that you had cherished certain ideals—but had set in motion machinery to execute them—That is the only way I can help you—by showing you the way to win and preserve my love and respect."[3]

The charge by Margaret that Jaffé had thwarted her literary career

2. Louis Jaffé to James Barron, 18 September 1931, Hay-Adams House bill, July 1930, Jelleff's clothing shop to Louis Jaffé, 7 April 1931, Louis Jaffé to Margaret Jaffé, 22 March 1931, all Louis Jaffé Jr.

3. Margaret Jaffé to Louis Jaffé, 30 August 1930, Louis Jaffé Jr.

is singular in their existent correspondence; no mention of this issue surfaces elsewhere in Jaffé's records. In actuality, Jaffé frequently used his editorial power, personal connections, and prestige on her behalf. He regularly featured Margaret's book reviews in his "Books and Letters" column on the *Pilot*'s editorial page. He repeatedly secured interviews with subjects for his wife's *Virginian-Pilot* Sunday feature articles; interventions with Alexander Forward, Julius John Lankes, Governor Harry Byrd, and others provide evidence of his advocacy for her. Even after Margaret left the paper in the early 1930s to attempt a career as a freelance feature writer and short-story author, Jaffé obtained reference material for her and lent emotional support to her efforts.[4]

Most men of the era viewed women's roles and abilities chauvinistically. The hyper-masculine world of journalism greatly limited the number of women reporters and generally circumscribed their roles to duties on society and women's pages. Southern papers may well have been more narrow-minded in this respect than their northern counterparts. A full generation later the talented writer and witty cultural observer Florence King found herself relegated to the women's department at a North Carolina newspaper, covering the "bride and deb" beat.[5]

Within Jaffé's journalistic circle, however, considerable precedent existed for bucking this mindset. Men like Julian Harris and H. L. Mencken actively promoted their wives' reporting and literary efforts. Jaffé displayed his appreciation for the contributions of women writers and artists in his admiration for journalist and author Julia Harris and his interest in the literary theories of Gertrude Stein. Closer to home, he helped arrange the logistics for a visit of photographer Margaret Bourke-White to Norfolk, and he developed a lasting friendship with local poet Mary Sinton Leitch.[6]

Margaret surely faced challenges and experienced frustrations as

4. Louis Jaffé to Alexander Forward, 16 June 1920, Louis Jaffé to J. J. Lankes, 22 March 1930, Louis Jaffé to Harry Byrd, 7 May 1930, all in Jaffé Papers; Louis Jaffé to Margaret Jaffé, 12 February 1931, Louis Jaffé Jr.

5. Florence King, *Southern Ladies and Gentlemen* (New York: St. Martin's Press, 1975), 107–26.

6. Louis Jaffé to Stringfellow Barr, 22 November 1943, Eleanor Anderson to Louis Jaffé, 10 December 1935, Mary Sinton Leitch to Louis Jaffé, 28 October 1947, all in Jaffé Papers.

she began her new career as a freelance author, but the principal obstacle to her success lay in the quality of her work. Although a competent feature writer, she lacked creative talent. The most sympathetic of readers could not have discerned much merit in her short stories.[7]

Precisely what triggered Margaret's rift with her mother and father remains elusive. At her prompting, in 1927 they had purchased property and set aside twelve thousand dollars to fund the construction of a house for her. Since that time, however, she had quarreled with her parents, whom she perceived as meddling in her life and "talking about" her. Her behavior angered her father, and in 1929 he expressed his intention to sell the property and withdraw his offer to pay for the home. He informed his daughter in a letter that the "unkind spirit" she had displayed had caused "much unhappiness"; calling her attitude unreasonable, he expressed the hope that it "would not continue to cloud the evening" of her parents' lives. Margaret, however, had initiated the construction of the home before her father could rescind his offer. Jaffé also had made a sizable contribution to the building of the house. In the fall of 1930, with Margaret and Christopher away in Washington, he moved his family's possessions from their bayside bungalow on Willoughby Spit to the new home in Norfolk's fashionable Algonquin Park.[8]

The discord between Margaret and her parents worsened. A letter Mrs. Davis wrote to Margaret reveals the near-total breakdown of relations between the two: "I am sorry I cannot see and talk with you about several business matters. But it is only fair I should tell you that your present personal income is all that you need expect from me. I have changed my will in favor of other relatives." She warned Margaret that "Louis' salary is all you have to look to, and it is part of providence for you to conserve it. A salaried man's earnings depend upon his health. . .and they can fall *very flat.*" She

---

7. Margaret Davis Jaffé, "Shut In," 75–87; Margaret Davis Jaffé, "Kitchen Etchings," *Catholic World* (June 1933): 291–7; Margaret Davis, "A Hut With Wattles Made," *Catholic World* (February 1943): 581–8.

8. Margaret Wheelwright Davis to Margaret Jaffé, 6 November 1930, Louis Jaffé to Margaret Jaffé, 5 October 1936, Hugh C. Davis to Margaret Jaffé, 3 October 1929, all Louis Jaffé Jr.; *Norfolk Telephone Directory,* Chesapeake and Potomac Telephone Co., 1932–1934.

finished the letter on a frigid note: "Don't fear that I will interfere with you when you come home. You won't see or know that I am in the same town."[9]

Margaret's desertion of her husband sparked considerable discussion within her family. Hugh C. Davis told Jaffé that he had agonized over the situation and that his son-in-law had his "absolute confidence, admiration and affection." Davis disclosed the scope of his worries in a private communication to his wife's brother, Thomas Wheelwright. "None of us can do anything with Margaret," Davis wrote. "For some years she has been defying us and making life for Louis and ourselves unbearable. She first turned against her mother, then against me and now against Louis. I have long thought her mentally unbalanced but was unwilling to act without the approval of her mother and Louis. I would gladly put her in a sanitarium but she will never go to one except by force. . . . I know no other man who would have submitted to Margaret's tyranny but Louis, and before he notified her that he could no longer submit to her desertion and conduct in staying in Washington, he told me that he felt compelled to take this step for Margaret's protection as well as the child's. . . . Nothing will satisfy her but to have her own willful and cruel way." Wheelwright, who served as a mentor and counselor to Jaffé, showed him the letter in confidence.[10]

Alienated from her parents and husband, Margaret turned to Wheelwright for help, but she had exhausted her uncle's patience. "I must confess that your record does not appear to me to have been guided by . . . loyalty to your Mother and Father, to your Aunts, not to mention myself," he wrote. "The truth of the matter is as I see it that you have been guided consistently by your own whims regardless of whether or not it added to the burdens of others." Margaret had written a hurtful letter to her cousin Esther, Wheelwright's only child from his first marriage, and the powerful industrialist took his niece to task: "You wrote Esther the most disgustingly insulting and untrue letter I ever read, wounding her deeply and destroying every remnant of the affection which she had for you and showing yourself

9. Margaret Wheelwright Davis to Margaret Jaffé, 6 November 1930, Louis Jaffé Jr.

10. Hugh C. Davis to Louis Jaffé, 24 January 1931, Jaffé Papers; Hugh C. Davis to Thomas Wheelwright, 7 April 1931, Louis Jaffé to Thomas Wheelwright, 8 December 1935, both Louis Jaffé Jr.

entirely wanting in loyalty to her. For this I do not harbor in my heart anything but pity."[11]

Jaffé, like Davis, had long considered Margaret mentally ill. For
years he had observed the "subtle psychological decay" he saw as clouding
her "otherwise fine mind." He told his brother, Hyman, that she suffered
from a "case of neurosis prolonged over years and apparently beyond cure."
This statement suggests that physicians had been consulted but that, given
the primitive state of psychiatric care, they could not help. Her behavior
suggests conditions ranging from hypochondria and paranoia to manic
depression.[12]

Margaret apparently had periods of lucidity, and institutionaliza-
tion would have seemed excessive and inhumane. Her distrust of Jaffé and
her parents—and her self-imposed estrangement from them—compounded
the impossibility of influencing her behavior. The stigma attached to mental
illness worsened the problem. Wheelwright's disclosure of Davis's letter in
confidence suggests that the Davises never fully divulged to their son-in-law
their suspicions regarding their daughter's mental health.

Jaffé sought to deal with her mental illness and the disintegration
of their marriage by consulting the best psychological and marital-relations
literature of the day. His library contained many such books, which stood
out starkly from the volumes on journalism, southern politics, and domestic
and international affairs one would expect him to have owned. *Gestalt Psychology, Unmasking Our Minds, Why We Behave Like Human Beings,
Married Love,* and *Ideal Marriage: Its Physiology and Technique*—all with
publication dates in the mid-twenties and early thirties—testify to his search
for answers.[13]

11. Thomas Wheelwright to Margaret Jaffé, 4 April 1931, Louis Jaffé Jr.

12. Louis Jaffé to Thomas Wheelwright, 15 April 1931, Louis Jaffé to Hyman Jaffe,
10 April 1931, both ibid.

13. Wolfgang Köhler, *Gestalt Psychology* (New York: Horace Liveright, 1929);
David Seabury, *Unmasking Our Minds* (New York: Boni and Liveright, 1924); George A. Dorsey, *Why We Behave Like Human Beings* (New York: Harper & Brothers, 1925); Marie Carmichael Stopes, *Married Love, A New Contribution to the Solution of Sex Difficulties* (New
York: Eugenics, 1931); Theodoor H. van de Velde, *Ideal Marriage: Its Physiology and Technique* (London: William Heinemann, 1930).

In March 1931, the economic downturn led *Virginian-Pilot* publisher Lucien Starke, after consulting with his editor and other principal
employees, to adopt emergency measures and slash the payroll. Jaffé's salary soon fell from $12,500 to $10,000. "The long feared salary cut is upon
us," he wrote to Margaret at the Hay-Adams House. "Please write me
immediately how things stand with Christopher and yourself," he entreated
her, "for it is necessary to act promptly. The house and fence and grounds
are all in shape for Christopher's and your comfort and I hope you can come
back without delay. If Dr. Foote regards it as necessary that Christopher
remain in Washington a while longer, then the only thing left to do is to find
an apartment or good boarding house in a cheaper part of town and get rid
of the staggering Hay-Adams incubus which is beyond our means and
which we cannot keep up any longer without danger. In that case I shall do
my part, as I am doing now, by going servantless, cooking my own breakfast
and living on fifty-cent lunches and dinners."[14]

He dealt with her delicately. Despite the expenses she had accumulated, he did not accuse her of extravagance, and he expressed his understanding of the emotional toll wrought by the illnesses she believed that she
and Christopher had recently suffered. He attempted to explain the need for
economy: "What I am trying to do now is to take the necessary steps to
save all of us from going the way of hundreds who are being floored by an
unprecedented depression—to keep our expenses inside our income instead
of sinking deeper and deeper in debt at a time when sound businesses on
[all] sides are crashing and jobs along with them."[15]

Jaffé's remonstrations proved futile. For another six weeks Margaret and Christopher stayed on at the Hay-Adams House. Still Jaffé did not
accuse her of profligacy. He did, however, itemize the many expenses she
had amassed over the past year, as well as the fixed costs for their home in
Norfolk. He warned her that they had completely drained their checking
account. "The reason I didn't send you more money in the last letter is that
there is not one red cent in the bank and won't be until next Friday," he

14. Louis Jaffé to Paul Huber, 30 December 1939, Jaffé Papers; Louis Jaffé to Margaret Jaffé, 12 February 1931, Louis Jaffé Jr.
15. Louis Jaffé to Margaret Jaffé, 12 February 1931, Louis Jaffé Jr.

wrote. "I can't indefinitely be selling off securities and destroying the little pile I have saved up against old age or possible disaster. I am struggling to keep our expenses inside our income, but it is a losing game."[16]

Adding to Jaffé's desperation, a letter had arrived from his parents, describing a grim financial situation. "On top of it all," he reported to Margaret, "comes now a pitiful call from my old mother and father—the former just about blind and the latter gray and feeble—who have been practically deprived of their living by this prolonged and cruel depression, for help. And help them I must or condemn my soul to everlasting hell. Knowing how you feel about my father and mother, I have avoided telling you about this, but the truth must out."[17]

He revealed to Margaret that the pressures of the past year had affected both his physical and his mental health. At times he felt himself precariously near "cracking up," he told her, stressing that they must reach a resolution soon. "I do love you and Christopher more than anybody else in the world and want to make you both happy," he wrote. "But if my love and my honest effort is not enough, then we must find a new way out. You can have the house for yourself and Christopher. I will not bother you if you don't want me to. I will find myself some quarters elsewhere in town. It will not cause any more talk than I imagine is already going around. . . . We have to make a change. The present manner of living is destroying our capital and surely undermining my ability to keep on making a living for us."[18]

In late April 1931 Jaffé engaged his close friend, Norfolk lawyer James Barron, who had sponsored Virginia's antilynching legislation, to negotiate an agreement of separation from Margaret. She remained at the Hay-Adams House and retained Washington attorney Paul Rogers. At first she attempted to dictate terms, insisting on a clause that made divorce and her custody of Christopher conditions of the agreement. Jaffé told Barron that he had no desire to force Margaret to live with him if their relationship could not be repaired, but that in the event of divorce, he demanded custody of his son. "It is my determined intention to obtain possession of the child," Jaffé wrote, "as I regard his mother, in her present mental condition, to be danger-

16. Louis Jaffé to Margaret Jaffé, 22 March 1931, ibid.
17. Ibid.
18. Ibid.

ously incompetent to bring him up in a sane manner. . . . Let there be absolutely no misunderstanding on that point." At the end of his rope, Jaffé gave Barron permission to make clear to Margaret that she could no longer count on her husband to finance her "absentee residence in a Washington hotel."[19]

Christopher's well-being lay at the core of the settlement, and Barron implied to Paul Rogers that should the case go to court, Margaret would have to answer some difficult questions. "One might be pardoned for inquiring why a room in a hotel with her son is so superior to her own attractive home with her son," Barron wrote; "why under the laws of general average someone of the medical profession of this city is not competent to be physician to her son; why if a mother wants her son with her all the time a father should not want to have him with him sometimes. . . . I am afraid that the trouble is that Mrs. Jaffe sees nothing unusual in her attitude, and certainly there is nothing so far to indicate that she considers [her husband] has any rights."[20]

In the midst of the negotiations Mrs. Davis, growing distressed over Margaret's condition, rushed to her side, over Hugh Davis's protests. Mrs. Davis undoubtedly discussed with Jaffé her impressions of Margaret and how best to repair the situation. In an effort to break through the impasse, Jaffé traveled to Washington in early May in a last-ditch attempt to persuade Margaret to return home. He found her pale and ill in bed.[21]

The two had an emotional discussion of their life together. So desperate did Margaret seem regarding Christopher's medical care and so committed to ending his year-long absence from school, that Jaffé promised to consider allowing Christopher's new Washington physician, a Dr. O'Brien, to have overall responsibility for the boy's care. Margaret told him that in spite of the bitter events of the previous years, she knew in her heart that she still cared for him. If they could settle their differences, she pledged to come home in ten days. If not, she intended to travel to Reno, Nevada, and obtain a divorce.[22]

On the steamer trip home, Jaffé reflected on their marriage. Despite

19. Louis Jaffé to James Barron, 1 May 1931, ibid.

20. James Barron to Paul Rogers, 4 May 1931, ibid.

21. Louis Jaffé to James Barron, 1 May 1931, ibid.

22. Louis Jaffé to Margaret Jaffé, 9 May 1931, Louis Jaffé to James Barron, 11 May 1931, both ibid.

Margaret's instability and hurtful behavior, he loved her. "I have lain awake nights crazy with bitter thoughts over the months of emptiness and neglect and apparent indifference," he wrote her the next day, "only in the morning to see something that belongs to you, a dress hanging in the closet or a poor little shoe with a hole in it . . . and know that you are deep in my heart and that nothing that could happen could alter that fact." He acceded to her request that Dr. O'Brien would, in consultation with a panel of three other Washington physicians, attend to any major medical problems Christopher might have; a Norfolk doctor would oversee the boy's routine health needs. In return, he requested that she put an "end to her ruinous prolonged stays" away from Norfolk.[23]

Margaret agreed to these terms. She returned to Norfolk, and the couple attempted to rebuild their marriage. For the next several years they managed to restore a semblance of normalcy to their lives together. It could not have been easy; Margaret's mental illness remained untreated and undoubtedly strained their relationship. Her irrational behavior frequently mortified her husband.

Her reaction to the kidnapping of Charles and Anne Lindbergh's infant son on March 1, 1932, serves as a case in point. The nation's attention turned briefly to Norfolk when John Hughes Curtis, a local boatbuilder of high social standing, claimed to have made contact with intermediaries who knew the abductors. Curtis enlisted the help of two prominent Norfolk men who knew the Lindbergh family, and together they persuaded Lindbergh of the authenticity of the contacts. The famous aviator journeyed to the city several times, participating in long and fruitless searches for shady characters reportedly plying the waters in mysterious boats or hiding out in meandering inlets. Not wishing to obstruct the search, the local press placed a moratorium on news coverage, but the story soon leaked out, and media from all over the nation raced to Norfolk. In reaction to the frenzy, Margaret grew anxious that the kidnappers might attempt to abduct Christopher, and insisted that the *Virginian-Pilot* post an employee outside the Jaffé home to guard against such a possibility. Jaffé had no recourse but to accept this embarrassment.[24]

23. Louis Jaffé to Margaret Jaffé, 9 May 1931, ibid.

24. Chambers, Shank, and Sugg, *Salt Water & Printer's Ink*, 358–60; Ludovic Kennedy, *The Airman and the Carpenter: The Lindbergh Kidnapping and the Framing of Richard*

On May 12 authorities notified Curtis and Lindbergh aboard a yacht off Cape May, New Jersey, that police had found the baby's body in a ditch less than five miles from the aviator's New Jersey home. Curtis confessed to duping Lindbergh but then recanted. The courts later fined him and sentenced him to a one-year suspended prison sentence for failing to provide information to law enforcement officers. Whatever relief Margaret derived from this evidence that kidnappers had not targeted her son for abduction was short-lived; she soon refocused her anxiety on the threat that she believed germs and viruses posed to Christopher's health.[25]

Sherwood Anderson visited the Jaffés that summer and shared his impressions of the household with Eleanor Copenhaver: "Yesterday I drove from Richmond to Norfolk in a terrific heat. Saw Jaffé's wife. She flaps about more than any woman I have ever seen—all soft, too much yielding ass, hips, soft legs. I think she is probably a PEN [International Association of Poets, Playwrights, Editors, Essayists, and Novelists] Woman. There is something nasty, not enough mental, not enough physical. She smokes cigarettes all the time. Jaffé is as nice as ever. He is limited but straight. He will play it safe and succeed. There is tremendous vitality. When he walks across a room you think of a bear. He is stuck with this woman O.K."[26]

Anderson's impression of Jaffé as "limited" probably referred to his comportment. The iconoclasts and bohemians who comprised the tight circle of friends with whom he felt most comfortable—Anderson, Lankes, and local cotton broker and cultural authority Michael "Mickey" Agelastro, who had studied at Johns Hopkins, Cornell, and Columbia—appreciated Jaffé's authority on a catholic array of subjects, respected his intelligence, and enjoyed his company, but did not constrain themselves to his conventional brand of personal conduct. Robert Mason believed that Anderson may have regarded Jaffé as a "bit square," as exemplified by his commitment to Margaret. Anderson, who regarded monogamy as bourgeois, must have marveled at Jaffé's loyalty to his difficult spouse.[27]

Hauptmann (New York: Viking Penguin, 1985), 115–6; Mason, interview by author, 18 September 1995.

25. Chambers, Shank, and Sugg, *Salt Water & Printer's Ink,* 359–60; Kennedy, *Airman and the Carpenter,* 116–7.

26. White, ed., *Sherwood Anderson's Secret Love Letters,* 188.

27. Peter Agelastro, interview by author, 11 July 1996; *Pilot,* 29 April 1974; Robert Mason, letter to author, 5 May 1996.

* * *

Having dislodged Margaret and Christopher from the Hay-Adams House, Jaffé attempted to salvage his finances. Salary cuts and his parents' and Hyman's increasing reliance on his economic support made this virtually impossible.

The Great Depression devastated South Boston and all of Virginia's Southside. The 1930 drought—the worst local farmers could recall—had served as a harbinger of what the region's residents would endure for the remainder of the decade. The Southside's tobacco income had plummeted by 50 percent. Throughout the depression the crop fetched an abysmally low price, tumbling as low as ten cents a pound. One grower reported a profit of only $2.60 after selling over four hundred pounds of his harvest. "From what I can learn about the tobacco situation in some sections of Virginia, it looks like the crop . . . is absolutely the worst that ever came out of the ground," a buyer reported. Farmers closed out their savings accounts and defaulted on loans. As crowds milled around outside, officials at all of South Boston's banks posted closing signs on their doors and shut down. Children stayed home because they lacked clothing to attend school. Unable to afford fuel, farmers converted their cars and trucks into "Hoover carts" by harnessing mules and horses to them. Desperate merchants attempted to reclaim goods they had sold on time. Approximately a dozen of the town's shopkeepers declared bankruptcy.[28]

Jaffes' Dry Goods—like most of South Boston's businesses—relied overwhelmingly on tobacco money. Customers grew scarce as farmers curtailed their purchases and relied on what they could grow and make themselves. The Jaffes had survived economic crises and bad weather previously, but the chain stores that had recently set up business in town posed a grave and permanent threat to their livelihood. Despite these distressing conditions, Hyman, whose limited education restricted his career options, informed Jaffé of his intention to "stick it out."[29]

28. Stevens, interview by author, 10 July 1996; Evans, *Provincials,* 86; Heinemann, *Depression and New Deal,* 8; Charles Stebbins statement, March 1982, South Boston (Va.) Public Library.

29. Headspeth, interview by author, 1 April 1996; Silverman, interview by author, 8 July 1996; Hyman Jaffe to Louis Jaffé, 30 September [1930], Louis Jaffé Jr.; Stevens, interview by author, 10 July 1996.

Although Margaret had nearly exhausted Jaffé's savings, he sent every penny he could spare to prop up Hyman's business. Creditors had threatened to place the store in receivership; and in late March 1932, Jaffé rushed three hundred dollars to his brother, two-thirds of it obtained from a loan on his insurance policy. Jaffé requested that Hyman inform their parents of his financial assistance and his resolve to stand by them in their time of need. Hyman, however, humiliated by his bankruptcy, attempted to conceal his desperate financial condition and his brother's aid from the senior Jaffes and his wife, Hattie. Previous checks probably had preceded this one; many would follow it. In August Jaffé sent another hundred dollars, and he promised to send an equal amount the following month. "There is only one thing I want you to be careful to do," he wrote. "I want Father and Mother to know of every check I send you for it would hurt me very much if they felt I was deserting them in their old age and their hour of trial."[30]

Throughout the Great Depression, this intervention sustained the senior Jaffes and Hyman and his family; Jaffé referred to it as keeping the "wolf from the door." Later he would finance the college education of his niece Margaret at Duke University and mine his connections within the Byrd machine to obtain secure state jobs for both her and her sister, Gladys, in Richmond.[31]

Far-reaching changes in the *Pilot*'s management and ownership in 1931 and 1932 added to Jaffé's anxiety about his ability to provide for Margaret and Christopher and for his family in South Boston. Lucien Starke's death in August 1931 had created a vacuum in the *Pilot*'s leadership. For nearly thirty years Starke had led the paper, overseeing its evolution from a small-town daily into a major metropolitan newspaper, one of the South's best. With inexperienced management at the helm, the *Virginian-Pilot* began to founder in the dismal economy.[32]

Norfolk's afternoon paper, the *Ledger-Dispatch,* headed by Colo-

30. Louis Jaffé to Hyman Jaffe, 30 March 1932, 1 August 1932, Louis Jaffé Jr.

31. Louis Jaffé to William Tuck, 29 June 1934, Tuck Papers; William Tuck to Louis Jaffé, 2 July 1934, Tuck Papers; Louis Jaffé to William Prieur, 28 December 1936, Jaffé Papers.

32. *Pilot,* 1 August 1931; Newton Aiken, "Romances of American Journalism," *Editor & Publisher,* 3 March 1928, 10; Chambers, Shank, and Sugg, *Salt Water & Printer's Ink,* 350–1.

nel Samuel L. Slover, posed stiff competition. Although it lagged behind the *Pilot* in the quality of its editorial and news departments, it led its morning rival in circulation, advertising, and profit. Slover, vigorous and not yet sixty, provided the *Ledger-Dispatch* with astute and bold leadership. As a young advertising salesman at the turn of the century, he had impressed the *Richmond Times*'s publisher, Joseph Bryan, with his pluck and productivity. In Newport News six months later, he had quickly pulled the languishing *Evening Times* out of the red and earned half ownership in the paper. When the *Evening Times* merged in 1901 with that city's *Morning Herald,* Slover became publisher of the *Times-Herald.*[33]

In Norfolk in 1905, he and a partner had purchased the moribund *Public Ledger.* Stretched to the limit financially, Slover pawned his gold watch on more than one occasion to meet his payroll. Within four months, however, the *Ledger* was running neck and neck with the city's other afternoon paper, the *Norfolk Dispatch.* In 1906 the *Dispatch*'s owners ended the newspaper war by consenting to a merger and retiring from the publishing business. For the first time since the Civil War, Norfolk had only a single afternoon daily.[34]

By 1923 Slover held the reins not only of the *Ledger-Dispatch* and the *Times-Herald* but also of many other Virginia newspapers, including the *Portsmouth Star,* the *Petersburg Progress-Index,* and the *Richmond Times-Dispatch* and *Evening Dispatch.* Slover, who had acquired his colonelcy from his appointment to Governor Westmoreland Davis's staff, also sat on the boards of a number of the state's major businesses. He ranked among the region's most powerful publishers, as his peers in the Southern Newspaper Publishers Association confirmed by electing him to various positions of leadership.[35]

In 1929, at considerable financial loss, he had disposed of the majority of his stock in the highly profitable *Ledger-Dispatch* to a company made up of the newspaper's employees. *Editor and Publisher* declared such an occurrence unprecedented: "It is a new way of solving the much discussed problem of employee profit-sharing. It is one of the finest tributes an

33. Chambers, Shank, and Sugg, *Salt Water & Printer's Ink,* 350, 354.
34. Ibid., 248–59.
35. Ibid., 330–3; Johnson and Robb, *South and Its Newspapers,* 68, 168, 177.

American publisher has ever paid to a loyal and able staff. Fortunate these men." Slover, who served as chairman of the new *Ledger-Dispatch* Corporation, arranged for loans for his associates who lacked the means to purchase stock.[36]

Throughout 1932, at Slover's behest the owners of the *Virginian-Pilot* and the *Ledger-Dispatch* contemplated consolidation. He had executed such a strategy many times in his career, and from the business end it made great sense. Nevertheless such a move undoubtedly would generate criticism: one publishing company would control the city's only two newspapers. Might not the proposed merger signify an end to the independence of the two papers' news and editorial departments?[37]

Jaffé worried that the new owners of the combined newspapers would put an end to the editorial autonomy he enjoyed, and possibly even eliminate his position. "There is taking place . . . a consolidation of the *Virginian-Pilot* and the *Ledger-Dispatch* properties. The matter has weighed so heavily on my spirit and so bothered me, that I have allowed an unconscionably long time to go [in responding to your letter]," he wrote to Lankes.[38]

As the negotiations wound on, Jaffé traveled to Baltimore to talk with *Sunpapers* publisher Paul Patterson. Patterson gave an "interested and sympathetic hearing" to a proposal Jaffé presented. A follow-up letter does not define the overture, but Jaffé may have been attempting to secure a position with the Baltimore papers or even to interest them in purchasing the *Pilot.* "The situation [here] remains confused for the present," he reported to Patterson, "but I am still hoping that events will so shape themselves as to make it possible to preserve the *Virginian-Pilot*'s 'territorial and administrative' independence. That is the ideal solution."[39]

Conjecture that Jaffé may have attempted to broker the purchase of the *Pilot* by the *Sunpapers* is strengthened by the fact that he had established close ties not only to Patterson, the Owenses, Gerald Johnson, and Edwin Murphy, but also to members of a branch of the Abell family who owned sizable amounts of stock in both the *Virginian-Pilot* and the *Sunpap-*

36. Chambers, Shank, and Sugg, *Salt Water & Printer's Ink,* 345–9.
37. Ibid., 354.
38. Louis Jaffé to J. J. Lankes, 30 November 1932, Jaffé Papers.
39. Louis Jaffé to Paul Patterson, 17 August 1932, ibid.

ers. In 1910, after fifteen years' experience at the *Sun,* Charles S. Abell had purchased the *Virginian-Pilot*'s morning competitor, the *Norfolk Landmark.* Announcing that the *Landmark* would embrace the independent policy of the *Baltimore Sun,* he had hired a managing editor with *Sunpapers* experience and switched the local news to his paper's back page—long a hallmark of the *Sun*.[40]

Despite publishing a spirited paper, Abell could make little headway against the *Virginian-Pilot* or the afternoon *Ledger-Dispatch* in terms of circulation and advertising. In early 1912, he announced a merger in which he would hold nearly a quarter of the stock in the *Virginian* and *Pilot* Publishing Company. He served as an "officer without portfolio" in the *Pilot*'s business department throughout Jaffé's early editorial tenure. Jaffé would develop a strong friendship with Charles Abell's young son, William S. Abell, later a Washington attorney and member of the board of directors of the newspapers in Norfolk. Jaffé may have believed that a partnership between the *Sunpapers* and the *Pilot* would safeguard his editorial autonomy and protect his community from the potential harm of a newspaper monopoly.

The many weighty matters that burdened Jaffé personally during the early 1930s seemed at times to stoke his editorial fires. The precarious financial condition of his family personalized for him the suffering wrought by the depression, and it increased his outrage over the insensitivity of political leaders like Harry Byrd, who refused to take action to assist the many needy Virginians.[41]

One might imagine that Jaffé would have withheld or at least soft-pedaled his objections to Byrd's policies. After all, without Byrd's imprimatur Virginia's antilynching law would never have passed through the General Assembly. Furthermore, the former governor's letter to the Pulitzer Advisory Board had figured prominently in its decision to anoint Jaffé. Sheer pragmatism also suggested that a conciliatory relationship with Byrd

---

40. Chambers, Shank, and Sugg, *Salt Water & Printer's Ink,* 271–7; Williams, *Baltimore Sun,* 123–4, 320; Johnson et al., *Sunpapers of Baltimore,* 289; Robert Mason letter to author, 21 October 1995.

41. Heinemann, *Depression and New Deal,* 132–9.

would benefit a newspaperman's career. The Byrd machine would shrewdly run Virginia politics for the next three and a half decades, retaining power by constricting Virginia's electorate to such an extent that political scientist V. O. Key would remark that Mississippi seemed by comparison a "hotbed of democracy." Already Byrd had made it clear that he would not relinquish his hold on the state's politics. Jaffé foresaw better than most the continued rise of Byrd's political fortunes. In 1932 Byrd was making a run for his party's presidential nomination; the following year he would obtain the U.S. Senate seat he would not give up until his retirement in 1965. Jaffé, who enjoyed Byrd's good graces as evinced by occasional overnight stays in the executive mansion and the clockwork-like arrival of baskets of apples at Christmas, occasionally tore into Byrd with an acerbity that made him wince.[42]

In the early 1930s, Virginia's citizenry cried out for relief. Many questioned Byrd's wisdom in backing continued expenditures for the highway system at the expense of other services. Jaffé lobbied for tax reductions and a diversion of funding from road programs to schools, hospitals, and asylums. To placate rural taxpayers, Byrd—who maintained his iron grip on the state through his role as the principal advisor to his successor, Governor John Garland Pollard—pushed forward a bill advocating that the state assume responsibility for county roads, thus saving counties millions of dollars in expenditures. (The plan would have the added benefit of enhancing the Byrd machine's ability to consolidate its hegemony further, through patronage.) The bill mandated, however, that cities would retain financial responsibility for the construction of roads within their boundaries. Residents in urban areas and their representatives exploded over the unfairness of Byrd's proposals.[43]

Jaffé believed that Byrd's reverence for tax segregation—allocating gasoline taxes to highway construction and maintenance alone, for example—made no sense. The former governor's keen political antennae sensed impending disapproval from the *Virginian-Pilot,* and he wrote to Jaffé,

42. Key, *Southern Politics in State and Nation,* 20; Heinemann, *Harry Byrd of Virginia,* 90; Wilkinson, *Harry Byrd and Virginia Politics,* 7; Louis Jaffé to Harry Byrd, 30 January 1929, Jaffé Papers.

43. Heinemann, *Harry Byrd of Virginia,* 123–4; Heinemann, *Depression and New Deal,* 14–5.

attempting to persuade him of the soundness of his views. In early February 1932 the editor politely but firmly informed Byrd that he had considered the issue from all perspectives and he would protest the "vicious disproportion between what the state is spending for one activity—improved roads, and what it is spending for all other vital services."[44]

A few days later "Highwayolotry as a State Religion" appeared in the *Pilot,* denouncing Byrd's misplaced priorities. Jaffé delivered another blow two weeks later with "Unfair and Unsound": "The State road bill first proposed in Virginia by Harry Flood Byrd, of Winchester, 'a private citizen whose views are entitled to no more weight than those of any other private citizen,' has swept through the House of Delegates by a 90 to 7 vote and the ways are greased for its swift passage through the Senate. The most radical measure of the legislative session is receiving less consideration and less debate than was accorded the oleomargarine bill. Considering the fact that before Private Citizen Byrd proposed this measure and gave it its benediction, it had no part in the administration program and that the theory of such a sweeping absorption of local functions by the State was pointedly denounced by Governor Pollard, the question of who is running this General Assembly answers itself."[45]

Jaffé charged that the odd circumstances surrounding the bill placed on "Mr. Byrd" the heavy responsibility for the sponsorship of an official policy of discrimination against the commonwealth's cities. "Mr. Byrd" should not delude himself regarding the consequences. "Himself an apostle of a united Virginia and a frequent pleader for the abolition of sectionalism, he has reason to view with profound apprehension the enactment of a bill, born of his mind and enacted in response to his urging." The editor went on to assert that the "indefensible discrimination between two classes of citizens equally entitled to the benefits of Mr. Byrd's statesmanship . . . will not be forgotten by the citizens who are victimized. If Mr. Byrd thinks that this kind of discrimination can be legislated with impunity he is likely to find that he is mistaken. It is this kind of government for the special benefit of particular population elements that is undermining the faith of the

44. Harry Byrd to Louis Jaffé, 4 February 1932, Louis Jaffé to Harry Byrd, 8 February 1932, both in Jaffé Papers.
45. *Pilot,* 13, 28 February 1932.

people in the fairness of the Democratic monopoly of Virginia's public affairs and creating the demand for political competition that will give the people a fairer deal." Byrd wrote to Jaffé the next day, complaining that the editorial had contained very unfair "personal inferences." The two could "continue to be perfectly good friends" regardless of their differences, but he requested that Jaffé not question his "sincerity of purpose."[46]

Several days later, Jaffé traveled to Richmond to meet with Byrd to lobby for increased funding for city roads. He met with some success, although he believed that even the amended legislation shortchanged Virginia's metropolitan areas. As he had predicted, the bill sailed through the rural-dominated legislature with little resistance. Jaffé later apologized if "one or two of my editorials seemed to you unnecessarily sharp and personal," but he had put the state's dominant political figure on notice that the *Pilot* would speak out loud and clear, unconstrained by personal or political alliances.[47]

On the last day of 1932, the president of the newly formed Norfolk Newspapers, Paul Huber, announced the merger of the *Virginian-Pilot* and the *Ledger-Dispatch*. Although he stressed the economic benefits for the two papers, he stated emphatically that the changes in management would "in no way affect the editorial or news policies of the *Virginian-Pilot* or the *Ledger-Dispatch*. They will preserve their distinct personalities and characteristics unchanged, each independent of the other, and under the continued direction of the news and editorial executives who have guided them in the past."[48]

The leadership of the *Sunpapers,* whose own organizational structure resembled that of the consolidated Norfolk newspapers—although publisher Patterson had an impressive background as a reporter and editor, and Huber had none—observed the merger closely. Hamilton Owens, the *Evening Sun*'s editor, wrote to Jaffé, "I understand there have been big doings down your way, but that you, as usual, have come out near the top

46. Ibid., 28 February 1932; Harry Byrd to Louis Jaffé, 29 February 1929, Jaffé Papers.

47. Harry Byrd to Louis Jaffé, 4 March 1932, Louis Jaffé to Harry Byrd, 2 April 1932, both in Jaffé Papers; Heinemann, *Harry Byrd of Virginia,* 124.

48. Chambers, Shank, and Sugg, *Salt Water & Printer's Ink,* 354–5.

of the heap. Reverberations kept coming here while the negotiations were on, but at no time did it occur to anybody that it would be possible to make any deals which didn't include you." In his reply to Owens, Jaffé expressed his desire to discuss with him and the *Sun*'s editor, John Owens, the "problem of keeping the two papers as distinct as possible and yet have them feeding out of the same trough."[49]

Jaffé soon traveled to Baltimore for a consultation with the Owenses. They asserted that in matters of editorial policy the two co-owned papers should adopt similar positions. They nearly convinced Jaffé that his desire that the *Pilot* and *Ledger* speak with entirely independent voices was "several degrees too quixotic." Back in Norfolk, Jaffé met with Huber, who maintained that the two papers' editorial pages varied so greatly and readers so completely associated them with the personalities of their editors that for the foreseeable future the public would accept the differences between them as natural.[50]

Jaffé need not have feared that consolidation of the papers might eliminate his position. Slover had long regarded Jaffé as the South's premier editor and knew unequivocally how he had burnished the *Pilot*'s reputation. Jaffé's concern that Slover and Huber might rein in the editorial autonomy he had enjoyed from the start, while a more realistic possibility, also proved unjustified. With the possible exception of the endorsement of presidential candidates, Slover never intruded in editorial decisions at either the *Ledger* or the *Pilot,* and he apparently practiced an identical policy in Richmond. Near the end of his life in the early 1980s, renowned journalist Mark Ethridge, who had served as publisher of the *Times-Dispatch* between 1934 and 1936, expressed his gratitude that Slover had never interfered in any of that paper's editorial affairs.[51]

49. Williams, *Baltimore Sun,* 169; Johnson et al., *Sunpapers of Baltimore,* 324–6, 375–6; "Paul Huber Obituary," [September 1946], Jaffé Papers; Hamilton Owens to Louis Jaffé, 13 January 1933, Louis Jaffé to Hamilton Owens, 27 January 1933, both in Jaffé Papers.

50. Louis Jaffe to Hamilton Owens, 6 March 1933, Jaffé Papers.

51. Samuel Slover to Frederick Thompson, 7 September 1925, ibid.; Batten, interview by author, 25 September 1990; *New York Times,* 7 April 1981; Mark Ethridge to Harry Strozier, 1 April 1935, Ethridge Papers; Robert Mason, letter to author, 12 September 1996; Francis Pickens Miller, *Man from the Valley* (Chapel Hill: University of North Carolina Press, 1971), 172.

A keynote address that Jaffé delivered to the North Carolina Press Association at Duke University in January 1933 provides insight into his views regarding the tension between the economic forces that had led to the *Virginian-Pilot*'s merger and the press's vital role in advancing the public interest. His remarks received widespread attention in newspapers throughout the region. Given Jaffé's past criticism of his alma mater, President Few and the other Duke administrators who hosted the gathering must have felt some apprehension about the direction their prominent graduate's remarks would take.[52]

Jaffé first congratulated the association for choosing Duke as a meeting site. He believed that the press and institutions of higher learning shared the common purpose of expanding knowledge and educating the citizenry. No one in the South, he contended, upheld that mission more valiantly in the present era than the new president of the University of North Carolina, Frank Porter Graham. Nowhere in the South had commitment to these noble purposes been displayed with more courage than at Trinity College during the Bassett affair, when Kilgo and the faculty had stood behind their beleaguered colleague.

The Great Depression had generated tremendous ferment and initiated a national debate about the nature of American society. "Millions have come to believe," Jaffé declared, "and rightly I think, that certain growths in the present order must be killed that our industrial civilization shall continue usefully to live. There can be but little doubt that the western world will emerge from the present period of confusion markedly altered in its social philosophy and social practice. In venturing to subscribe to this view, we need not necessarily identify ourselves with the verdict of the Technocrats that unless our industrial civilization is completely and swiftly transmogrified on a techno-communistic basis and its compensation and exchange system reduced to the common denominator of energy, it will collapse into early chaos."

The tumultuous times, he said, demanded a daily press of the high-

52. *Duke Chronicle*, 18 January 1933, 1 February 1933; "Duke University is Host to the State Press Association," *Duke University Alumni Register*, January 1933, 22; *Durham Morning Herald*, 18 January 1933; *Chapel Hill Weekly*, 20 January 1933; *Danville (Va.) Register*, 20 January 1933; *Roanoke (Va.) Times*, 21 January 1933; *Petersburg (Va.) Progress-Index*, 22, 23 January 1933.

est quality. The overwhelming majority of the public derived their ideas and opinions not from books and magazines, but from their local papers. Jaffé directed his audience's attention to an industry trend that posed a threat to the integrity of his profession: the "steady reduction in the number of newspapers through mergers and the regimenting of competition between the newspapers that remain through the chaining up of papers published in far-separated localities, and through the unification of ownership of newspapers published in the same city." As a result of this phenomenon, he continued, "in many localities a state of alert intellectual competition between newspapers is giving way . . . to an uninspiring editorial uniformity, and it behooves the press more than ever in the face of these developments, to be on guard against bartering its birthright for a mess of profits. That is what it would do if it should fail the public in the service of information and leadership that has been its historic role."

The new medium of radio posed a challenge to newspapers and had begun to siphon off advertising revenue. Jaffé suggested that his peers avoid warring with radio on its own battlefield. Radio owed its popularity to its superior capability of providing entertainment; it lacked the ability to provide comprehensive news and opinion. "Would it not be a mistake of the first order if newspapers, in their confusion about radio competition should spend their energies in a futile effort to compete with radio entertainment features, and fail to develop to their fullest those daily services which are even more necessary to our civilization, and which only the newspaper can adequately perform?" he asked.

Jaffé deplored the "tendency of . . . newspapers in recent years [to] abdicate the responsibility of leadership." "Influences and compulsions have crept into the business of modern publishing that have blunted the edge of the newspaper as an instrument of reform," he declared. "It no longer cuts and penetrates with its old precision. The practically simultaneous development of mechanical typesetting, rotary printing, cheap transmission, cheap paper, low mailing charges and volume advertising has led to the saddling of the modern newspaper with an inexorable tyrant called Circulation. In order to succeed in a big way, materially speaking, the newspaper must attract and hold the largest possible volume of advertising; it must attract and hold the largest possible aggregation of readers. In order to attract and hold the largest possible group of readers it is under a relentless compulsion to popularize its appeal."

He questioned the "seductive doctrine that it is the paramount duty of the newspaper to give the public what it wants." "That role may be binding on the 5 and 10 cent store, and on the movies," he conceded,

> but a newspaper is differentiated from both of these by a social mission so important that it has been singled out for special immunity from interference, by the Constitution of the United States. The freedom of the press principle was not written into our basic law to protect the newspaper's right to give the public what it wants. It was written into our national charter to protect the newspaper's right to print and say what it conceives to be necessary to be said and printed, in order that our social and political arrangements may be kept decent, just and tolerable.
>
> ... It ought to be the ambition of ... [the] press to give the public not what is relished and smirked over by its shallowest readers, but what is enjoyed and welcomed by those of its readers who represent an intelligence and discrimination that is above the average. I intend here no absurd recommendation that newspapers address themselves exclusively to the tastes of the so-called Intelligentsia. The recommendation is that newspapers stop pandering to the fourteen-year-old mind and order their news, entertainment and illustrative material to the satisfaction of the adult intelligence. It is time for newspaper editors to take account of the progressive vulgarization to which their mediums have been subjected under the pressure of mass circulation and mass advertising, and to define a social and professional outlook that will emancipate them from the cult of the shoddy.

Just in case any of the members of the press assembled in Duke's auditorium needed clarification as to the issues that he believed required serious journalistic treatment, Jaffé provided them with a partial inventory:

> The minds of men are astir as never before, over the social value of Federal prohibition; over the stretch-out system and the right of underpaid textile workers to organize to improve their lot; over the ruthless resort to police tyranny to deny jobless and debt-ridden people the right of petition and peaceable assembly that is guaran-

teed to them in our Bill of Rights; over the economic tragedy of Southern farm tenantry and the usurious exploitation that is the cause of it; over the plight of 10,000,000 colored people caught in an economic vise not of their own making; over the clash of interests between war veterans demanding government benefits and taxpayers seeking relief from grinding imposts; over the deadly clash between a tariff system extolling the principle of a self-contained national economy and our desire to add to our national wealth by marketing vast export surpluses in foreign markets; over the larger implications of the war debt issue; [and] over the aggressions of fundamentalist theology on the fortresses of academia.

He ended his talk by reiterating that journalists and educators shared a common mission. He also expressed his approbation of a recent speech by President Few. Jaffé interpreted Few's remarks to mean that Duke—and other major southern universities—should promote a more cosmopolitan outlook and serve as centers for social science research to address the South's many problems. Duke had avoided entering the fray when Wake Forest and the University of North Carolina battled fundamentalists who sought to proscribe the teaching of evolution in the previous decade; and the moderate Few probably did not intend for his remarks to signify that Duke intended to adopt such an activist agenda. Jaffé may have hoped to prod Few in that direction.[53]

Over time, Jaffé had come to align himself more closely with the spirit of the University of North Carolina than with that of his alma mater. He had not overstated the role that Frank Porter Graham—a native Tarheel just three years into his presidential tenure—had begun to play in stimulating the spread of liberalism throughout the South.

On a fellowship in London in 1925 when North Carolina's legislature debated the anti-evolutionary Poole Bill, the young assistant professor of history had written a letter, which many of the state's newspapers had published, in support of academic freedom. Four years later, knowing that he would incur the wrath of powerful industrialists and risk being labeled a tool of the communists, Graham had nevertheless authored "An Industrial

---

53. Louis Jaffé, "What Role for the Newspaper?" 19 January 1933, Jaffé Papers.

Bill of Rights" in the wake of the Gastonia strike. Four hundred people, including some of the state's leading citizens, had signed the published statement, which urged labor reforms and protection of workers' rights. The next year, controversial appearances at the University of North Carolina by mathematician and philosopher Bertrand Russell (whose *Marriage and Morals* challenged predominant attitudes about sexuality) and black poet Langston Hughes (whose poem "Black Christ" had been reprinted by leftist students in Chapel Hill) had resulted in heated attacks against both Graham and his progressive institution. In 1933 he ended the quota system limiting the number of Jewish students who studied at the university's medical school. He also successfully defended one of his faculty who had contravened Jim Crow by dining with an interracial group that included the Communist Party's black nominee for vice president of the United States. By the decade's end, Walter White and other informed observers would justifiably regard Graham as the South's most notable liberal.[54]

Graham's unpopular stands and his support for unrestrained academic freedom placed the University of North Carolina in peril. Even in 1928–1929, at the height of the state legislature's support for the university, it had remained by a wide margin the most poorly supported of the twenty-nine American and Canadian institutions in the prestigious Association of American Universities. The next year the state slashed its appropriation by 25 percent. Another 20 percent cut followed in 1930–1931. Throughout the early 1930s the new president carried on a tireless public relations and lobbying campaign to keep Chapel Hill's bright light burning.[55]

Jaffé viewed his speech to the North Carolina Press Association not only as an occasion to exhort the state's journalists to live up to their historic mission but also as a fortuitous opportunity to come to the embattled Graham's aid. Four months earlier Graham had written to Jaffé to express his appreciation for the *Pilot*'s unwavering support when many powerful detractors had sought to vilify the university in the wake of the Hughes and

54. Warren Ashby, *Frank Porter Graham: A Southern Liberal* (Winston-Salem, N.C.: John F. Blair, 1980), 59–60, 77–81, 125–6; Snider, *Light on the Hill,* 204–19; Egerton, *Speak Now Against the Day,* 134; Walter White, "Decline of Southern Liberals," *Negro Digest,* January 1943, 43–6.

55. Ashby, *Frank Porter Graham,* 87; Morton Sosna, *In Search of the Silent South: Southern Liberals and the Race Issue* (New York: Columbia University Press, 1977), 83–7.

Russell talks. "You and other editors have reached out helpful hands from the nation to Chapel Hill, and believe me, we were glad to take hold of them," he wrote. "We . . . are not going to yield one inch on the essential issues involved. We will trust the people to know that this is a clean and wholesome place and that the implications of filth, and the rest, are outrageously twisted out of the context."[56]

On the evening before Jaffé's speech, Graham, along with North Carolina governor J. C. Blucher Ehringhaus, who assumed power that very month as economic conditions in the state hit rock bottom, had addressed the Press Association. "Press Institute Speakers Clash Over Funding," a *Durham Morning Herald* headline read, after Graham had informed the governor and audience that state legislature funding cuts would diminish the status of North Carolina's flagship university to that of a "prep school."[57]

The same day—possibly late in the evening after Graham's desperate appeal—Jaffé had written to him expressing his support and deploring the state budget bureau's draconian funding cuts. "I am one of innumerable thousands in the South and in the country at large, who have come to look upon the University of North Carolina as one of the great and moving educational forces of America," he wrote. "[The] university is to-day acclaimed the length and breadth of the land as one of the powerful and constructive educational forces of our time." Jaffé believed that the proposed reduction in funding would constitute both a "reproach to North Carolina statecraft and . . . an economic and social tragedy." It seems likely that Jaffé emended his speech after hearing Graham's, to make certain that he maximized his opportunity to be of service to the imperiled university.[58]

Fortified by the courage of Graham and other southern liberals who shared his progressive agenda, reconciled with Margaret for the present, relieved of much of her extravagance and of the distraction of the merger, Jaffé at the prime of his abilities seemed set to pursue his humanitarian goals relatively unencumbered.

56. Frank Porter Graham to Louis Jaffé, 26 September 1932, Jaffé Papers.

57. Hugh Talmage Lefler and Albert Ray Newsome, *North Carolina: The History of a Southern State* (Chapel Hill: University of North Carolina Press, 1954), 575–8; *Durham Morning Herald,* 19 January 1933.

58. Louis Jaffé to Frank Porter Graham, 18 January 1933, Jaffé Papers.

12   Two Faces of Intolerance

On March 4, 1933, Franklin Delano Roosevelt, standing on the main steps of the national Capitol, placed his left hand on the timeworn Bible of his Dutch ancestors, swore to protect and defend the Constitution, and became the thirty-second president of the United States. As he turned to face the crowd to deliver his terse inaugural address, the "laughing boy from Hyde Park," as one wag had dubbed him, lost for the moment his jaunty exuberance and grew uncharacteristically solemn. "First of all," he declared, "let me assert my firm belief that the only thing we have to fear is fear itself—nameless, unreasoning, unjustified terror which paralyzes needed efforts to convert retreat into advance." Over the next few minutes he sketched in vague terms his recovery plan, in which the federal government would play an unprecedented role in providing for the American people's welfare.[1]

Half a million sightseers lined both sides of Pennsylvania Avenue, perched on roofs, and even climbed trees, hoping to catch a glimpse of the new president as he was driven slowly in the back seat of an open car from the Capitol to the White House. The chilly and cloudy weather in Washington, D.C., matched perfectly the gloomy mood of the nation brought low by the Great Depression and the Hoover administration's inability to make meaningful headway toward ending the calamity. Not since the Civil War had an American president faced a more daunting task. But as Roosevelt traveled to his new quarters—stripped bare by his predecessor, who openly despised him—he regained his cocksure demeanor. "The new President's recurrent smile of confidence, his uplifted chin and the challenge of his voice did much to help the national sense of humor assert itself," the *New York Times* wrote.[2]

1. *New York Times,* 5 March 1933.
2. Ibid.; Manchester, *Glory and the Dream,* 92; Paul Johnson, *A History of the American People* (New York: HarperCollins, 1997), 747, 751.

Roosevelt's landslide victory had little to do with his platform; it resulted almost entirely from anti-Hoover sentiment. "Give me a ride—or I'll vote for Hoover," hitchhikers' signs had threatened prior to the election. Over the next one hundred days, Roosevelt would introduce into the Democratic Congress he convened in special session a dizzying array of acts intended to shore up the economy, create jobs, and bolster local relief efforts. Almost all passed, most with next to no debate. The whirl of activity, combined with Roosevelt's confidence, salesmanship, and artful use of the radio medium, began to lift the nation's spirits. That many of the programs in his New Deal owed their inspiration to initiatives already developed by his discredited predecessor went largely unreported and unrecognized.[3]

If Roosevelt's inauguration and the beginning of his presidency comprised the most important domestic story of the day, Adolf Hitler's rise to power constituted far and away the leading international news item. On March 5 a front-page *New York Times* report, adjacent to the coverage of the new American president's inaugural ceremonies, read, "Victory for Hitler is Expected Today." In the heady month preceding the German national elections, Hitler had engineered his appointment as chancellor, authorized his henchmen to contrive the destruction of the Reichstag by arson, and unleashed his storm battalions to suppress civil liberties and muzzle the opposing press. After describing the Nazi bonfires burning along Germany's borders and the countless parades of torch-wielding brownshirts snaking their way throughout the country, the *Times* quoted a statement released by the Federation of German Citizens of the Jewish Faith on the eve of the election: "We do not believe that our German fellow-citizens will let themselves be carried away into committing excesses against the Jews, but if, nevertheless, such were to happen, the power of the public authorities will protect the Jews. Such protection is the moral duty of the State. If it is not fulfilled, the fire will eat its way further, none knowing where it will end." The March 1933 vote marked the last democratic election for the German people during Hitler's lifetime. He immediately issued laws barring Jews from universities, public service, and the professions, and he proclaimed a boycott of Jewish businesses.[4]

3. Kenneth S. Davis, *FDR: The New Deal Years, 1933–1937* (New York: Random House, 1986), 77–81; Johnson, *History of the American People*, 740–1.

4. T. L. Jarman, *The Rise and Fall of Nazi Germany* (New York: New York University Press, 1956), 147–51; Jackson J. Spielvogel, *Hitler and Nazi Germany: A History* (Engle-

* * *

Franklin Roosevelt earned the support of only 41 percent of the nation's daily newspapers in the 1932 presidential election. The majority of leading southern liberal editors had remained unenthusiastic about his candidacy. Jaffé, however, had endorsed New York's two-term governor in no uncertain terms, writing the day before the election, "The *Virginian-Pilot* does believe that Roosevelt and his party offer a political program definitely more liberal and understanding as regards social problems, definitely more alert and constructive as regards our financial, transportation and utility problems, and decidedly less narrow and chauvinistic as regards our foreign relations and foreign trade perplexities, than the program of the Republican Party, and that the country's interests will be served by a Democratic victory." In the wake of Roosevelt's inauguration, Jaffé welcomed the outpouring of popular support the new president received, and he urged his readers to continue to rally behind their new leader. He called for patience, however; it would take time before new programs could noticeably improve the economy.[5]

He continued to cheer Roosevelt when the new president began to direct a steady stream of bills to Congress. Jaffé applauded the Emergency Banking Act, which assisted and regulated the nation's financial institutions. When Roosevelt—with limited support from his own party—faced down the powerful veterans' lobby and reduced the burgeoning deficit by cutting veterans' pensions and paring military, civil service and, congressional salaries, Jaffé celebrated his mettle. "President Roosevelt, in one forceful frontal assault, asks a grant of authority to end this fiscal and political cowardice," he wrote. As critics derided the president's launching of the Civilian Conservation Corps, Jaffé exulted over his boldness: "This is new. It is striking. It is Rooseveltian." The legislative branch should not flout the will of the public, he warned. "President Roosevelt, moving swifter than any national peace-time leader within memory, but on sure and certain paths, has laid down a challenge which a Congress pretending to be representative, can not

---

wood Cliffs, N.J.: Prentice Hall, 1988), 65–76; *New York Times,* 5 March 1933; William L. Shirer, *The Rise and Fall of the Third Reich: A History of Nazi Germany* (New York: Simon and Schuster, 1960), 177–95, 203.

5. Betty Houchin Winfield, *FDR and the News Media* (Urbana: University of Illinois Press, 1990), 127; Kneebone, *Southern Liberal Journalists,* 116–7; *Pilot,* 7 November 1932, 4 and 5 March 1933.

disregard. It should grant him the authority and cry Godspeed to a man of his determination and courage." Reversing their tepid initial support for Roosevelt, the region's liberal editors echoed Jaffé's enthusiasm for the energetic new president.[6]

Jaffé matched the ardor with which he defended the new president with his fierce suspicion of Hitler. Probably no other southern editor so clearly elucidated the dangers posed by the Führer and German nationalism. In the early 1930s, a distrustful Jaffé had in great detail apprised readers of Hitler's treacherous march to power. When evidence emerged regarding his systematic persecution of the Jews after the March 1933 Reichstag elections, Jaffé set about attacking Hitler and Nazism ceaselessly, in what would become the longest sustained editorial campaign of his career.

In her well-researched exposé, *Beyond Belief,* Deborah Lipstadt explores the role played by the American press in warning the public about the Holocaust. While Lipstadt identifies a number of foreign correspondents who reported accurately on Hitler's rise to power, she concludes that the U.S. press skirted the fact that persecution of the Jews was a bedrock tenet of Nazi ideology. She accuses publishers and editors in particular of irresponsibly ignoring or downplaying the early warning signs that portended the fate of European Jewry: "Rarely was news of the persecution of the Jews handled by journalists, particularly by those who viewed the situation from the safety of the United States, as an inherent expression of Nazism. . . . Those far from the scene and unfamiliar with Nazism discounted the news as exaggerated or dismissed it as not quite possible." In her conclusion, Lipstadt excoriates the American press for its "skepticism" and "indifference" regarding the Holocaust.[7]

Unlike the editors Lipstadt faulted, Jaffé recognized the threat Hitler posed to Germany and Europe from the outset. Jaffé had regarded the chancellor-to-be warily during the violence that marred an earlier national election in 1932. "If the campaign prelude to the Nazis' drive for power is of this deadliness," he asked, "what is to be expected in the way of rioting

6. *Pilot,* 4, 11, 22 March 1933; Kneebone, *Southern Liberal Journalists,* 118–9.
7. Deborah E. Lipstadt, *Beyond Belief: The American Press and the Coming of the Holocaust, 1933–1945* (New York: Free Press, 1986), 15, 27, 278.

and bloodshed if Hitler emerges from the election victorious?" Jaffé informed his readers that Hitler's appointment as chancellor constituted a dangerous victory for the Nazis: "The movement in Germany which found a symbol in a brown shirt, a leader in an Austrian and a program in belligerent nationalism, has achieved its greatest triumph in the selection of Adolph Hitler as Chancellor."[8]

The Nazi anti-Semitic brutality that followed Hitler's consolidation of power substantiated Jaffé's forebodings. A campaign to intimidate intellectuals and artists reached the height of preposterousness later that month when brownshirts searching the home of Jewish physicist and pacifist Albert Einstein, after accusing him of stockpiling arms and ammunition, emerged with only a bread knife. In a lead editorial entitled "Germany's Reign of Terror," Jaffé warned that "this kind of persecution . . . has been only a minor off-shoot of the main drive against members of the minorities, chiefly Jews. . . . The whispers of horror . . . just beginning to be heard through the German censorship indicate that these are mere incidents in a series of persecutions which take on the character of a reign of terror." The efforts of newly appointed minister of popular enlightenment and propaganda Joseph Goebbels notwithstanding, refugees had fled the Third Reich for other nations. "The tales they tell," Jaffé continued, "indicate a condition of affairs more serious than even a suspicious world had dreamed of. There appears no doubt now that in the days following the Nazi triumph, the brown-shirters ran wild, forcing their way into homes, damaging property, seriously injuring numerous innocent persons and probably murdering numbers of them."[9]

Speaking to a delegation of American Jewish leaders in late March, Secretary of State Cordell Hull implausibly maintained that Nazi thuggery had begun to wane. Though skeptical, Jaffé hoped that Hull might be proven correct. But even if the Nazis should order an end to the physical intimidation of Jews, Jaffé cautioned, other large issues must be addressed. "To be secure from pogroms or from being waylaid and beaten in a dark alley, is a pathetically bare boon," he wrote. "The important unanswered question is not whether Germany's citizens of the Jewish faith will hencefor-

8. *Pilot,* 20 July 1932, 31 January 1933.
9. Ibid., 24 March 1933.

ward be safe in limb and life, but whether they will be safe in their livelihood."[10]

Hitler answered this question a few days later when he announced a national boycott of Jewish stores. In "Germany's Hour of Fury," Jaffé protested the boycott as a breakdown of the "vaunted progress of civilization . . . at a crucial time and at a crucial place." The Nazis' economic attack on the Jews, he said, "reducing to beggary hundreds of thousands of innocent men and women . . . has not been attempted in this world since the Dark Ages. That it will be ruthlessly carried out in the Twentieth Century and by the government of an enlightened state, is beyond belief." The boycott would bring about a "moral stench so penetrating as to make the poisonous philosophy of its perpetrators disgusting to the whole of civilization."[11]

As he had with the Klan, the Nazi Party's spiritual kin, Jaffé employed sarcasm to mock the religious and philosophical contortions in which Hitlerists engaged to rationalize their actions and align them with current political policy. When the Protestant Nazi German Christian Movement, embarrassed by the prominent role Jews played in the Old Testament, advocated striking it from their canon and replacing it with native sagas and fairy tales, Jaffé weighed in. He professed sympathy for the movement's dilemma. The principal religions of the German people, Lutheranism and Roman Catholicism, he wrote, "both accord a place of honor and even a status of sanctity to an Old Testament regrettably peopled by non-Teutons like Abraham, Judah, Isaiah, Ezekiel and Habakkuk. Moreover, the Jehovah of the Old Testament chronicles is represented as harboring for these non-Teutonic worthies an affection not at all in harmony with the Nazi philosophy." Jaffé conceded that man had always made God in his own image but expressed doubt that the Nazis would ever "succeed in replacing Deborah with Brunhilde." Even if Hitler's followers were to divest the Bible of its Old Testament, many of whose great figures were "as unmistakably Hebraic as some of the department store owners on the Leipziger Strasse," Jews played an inextricable role in the New Testament. (Indeed, the Judaism

10. Ibid., 28 March 1933.
11. Ibid., 31 March 1933.

of Jesus, his disciples, and Paul would seem to have posed an insurmountable problem for the movement.)[12]

His correspondence with Virginius Dabney helps differentiate Jaffé from the many journalists who underestimated the Nazi threat in the early 1930s. In 1933 the Carl Schurz Memorial Foundation's Oberlander Trust awarded Dabney funding to travel to Germany. Despite his avowed purpose—to "study periodical literature"—he planned to use his trip to acquire an "objective view" of the Reich. He intended to write innocuous articles for the *Times-Dispatch* from Germany and, upon his return, to appraise the country more critically. Julian and Julia Harris and Mark Ethridge had traveled to Germany with the Oberlander Trust's support earlier in the decade, but Hitler's persecution of the Jews following his assumption of power had politicized perceptions regarding the trust, whose stated purpose was to "bring about a better understanding of German-speaking peoples by the American people, and vice versa."[13]

Dabney, who had just published *Liberalism in the South,* wrote to Jaffé in December 1933 to thank him for an editorial he had authored about the impending trip. Although Dabney would one day profess in his memoirs that "despite loud denials from certain quarters," it had been common knowledge at the time that Jews were being persecuted, he stressed in his letter to Jaffé his concern that the American reaction to Hitler had become overwrought. "While I need hardly say that I share your disgust with much that Hitler has done and is doing," he wrote, "I am frank to say that some of the comment on the Nazi movement seems to me to border on the hysterical. . . . Not only have the atrocities been over-emphasized, in my opinion, but they have been exaggerated. . . . I fail to understand why there is such a terrific howl every time the Nazis do something which some other government or party has done before without a comparable outcry." He went on to justify an assault on an American surgeon, Dr. Daniel Mulvihill, who had been struck violently behind the ear by a storm trooper. Mulvihill had failed

12. Ibid., 9 April 1933.
13. Virginius Dabney to Louis Jaffé, 3 December 1933, Jaffé Papers; Dabney, "Reflections," 281–3; Hans Gramm, *The Oberlaender Trust, 1931–1953* (Philadelphia: Carl Schurz Memorial Foundation, 1956), 48, 109; *New York Times,* 9 May 1933, 21 November 1934, 21 January 1935.

to give the Heil Hitler salute as a procession of brownshirts singing the Horst Wessel song marched past him in Berlin. Although Dabney did not believe the Nazis should have "swatted" the surgeon, he explained to Jaffé that they had been shooting a film and that Mulvihill had "spoil[ed] the effect for the screen."[14]

Dabney also claimed that an unnamed Jewish professor at the University of Marburg who had committed suicide had not done so to escape Nazi terrorism: "I am advised that the professor was treasurer of a student loan fund, that he made away with a large percentage of it, and that his peculation was discovered just before he killed himself. Of course this does not excuse the persecution of the Jews, and you know I have no patience whatever with such a policy. But I think you will agree with me that the press gave a distorted picture when it failed to say anything about the student loan fund." (The professor, Dr. Hermann Jacobsohn, a specialist in Indo-Germanic philology, had thrown himself in front of a moving train after authorities removed him from his academic post. Present faculty at the University of Marburg, who have studied the incident, dismiss out of hand the charge of embezzlement against Jacobsohn, for whom the city of Marburg recently named a street.)[15]

Dabney took particular offense at a recent *Nation* article's insinuation that the Nazis had co-opted the German branch of the Schurz Foundation, intending to employ it for propaganda purposes. He also complained about an editorial Oswald Garrison Villard, editor of the *Nation,* had written attacking Hitler's propagandists. "Machiavelli has been outdone," the German-born Villard had declared; "the Hitler technique surpasses his. Some day when Germany has worked out of its present insanity, there will be a marvelous opportunity for someone to write a book about the lie and its use under Hitler. Never has there been a national movement so entirely built upon falsehoods and never have there been people so eager to swallow them as the exhausted and ill-treated Germans." (Villard and other friends and relatives of German-American patriot Carl Schurz would later sign a

14. Dabney, *Across the Years,* 127; Virginius Dabney to Louis Jaffé, 3 December 1933, Jaffé Papers; *New York Times,* 18, 19 August 1933.

15. Dabney to Jaffé, 3 December 1933, Jaffé Papers; *New York Times,* 29 April 1933; Michael Haspel, letters to author, 26 March, 7 April 1999; Martin Schindel, letter to author, 26 March 1999; *Frankfurter Allgemeine Zeitung,* 3 February 1998.

statement protesting the use of his name in connection with organizations maintaining friendly relations with Nazi Germany.)[16]

As John Kneebone has observed in *Southern Liberal Journalists and the Issue of Race,* Dabney's major reason for downplaying Nazi atrocities during this period may have been his recollection of inaccurate press accounts of war crimes during World War I. Like Mencken—an early mentor and role model—Dabney expressed skepticism about the newspaper reports coming out of Germany.[17]

But the Sage of Baltimore's time was past; his voice would ring increasingly hollow throughout the decade. In his final edition of the *American Mercury,* which reached subscribers and distributors a few days prior to Dabney's writing to Jaffé, Mencken published his omnibus review of a group of books focusing on Nazi Germany under the title of "Hitlerismus." Displaying a woeful ignorance of Hitler and Nazism, he declared the Führer's ravings in *Mein Kampf* to be "often sensible enough" and his anti-Semitism "nothing to marvel over" because so many nations had exhibited anti-Jewish prejudice. "That a majority of Germans will go on yielding to Hitler ad infinitum is hard to believe, and in fact downright incredible," he wrote. "Either he will have to change his programme so that it comes into reasonable accord with German tradition and the hard-won principia of modern civilization, or they will rise against him and turn him out." Mencken had provided America with just the tonic it needed throughout the heady 1920s, but his bluster, iconoclasm, and libertarian and isolationist philosophy offered little of benefit to a nation mired in the Great Depression and soon to be thrust into world conflict.[18]

In his reply, Jaffé affirmed his confidence in Dabney as a "downright liberal," but he expressed concern that his colleague by way of a few

16. Ludwig Lore, "Nazi Politics in America," *Nation,* 29 November 1933, 615–7; Oswald Garrison Villard, "The Nazi Child-Mind," *Nation,* 29 November 1933, 614–5; *New York Times,* 21 January 1935.

17. Kneebone, *Southern Liberal Journalists,* 176; Dunford, *Richmond Times-Dispatch: The Story of a Newspaper,* 297; Dabney to Jaffé, 3 December 1933, Jaffé Papers; Mencken, *Thirty-Five Years of Newspaper Work,* 54, 65, 223, 309; Angoff, *H. L. Mencken,* 227; Dabney, "Reflections," 286–7; Dabney, *Across the Years,* 104, 116–7.

18. H. L. Mencken, "Library," *American Mercury* 30, no.120 (1933): 506–10; Angoff, *H. L. Mencken,* 63–169, 205–16, 226–7, 230, 236.

poorly substantiated anecdotes seemed to be rationalizing widespread Nazi brutality. His reasoning had left Jaffé feeling "vaguely troubled." "I could not make myself believe that the exculpatory analogies you suggest are in reality sound analogies," he wrote.[19]

Dabney's motivation for revealing his views on Nazism to Jaffé is perplexing. He certainly knew of Jaffé's Jewish roots and his vehement antipathy for Hitler. Jaffé must have puzzled over the curious letter. Worried that the Nazi handlers and propagandists might dupe the impressionable journalist, he dispatched a bon voyage message in which he expressed both confidence in Dabney's ability to know the truth if given a fair chance to see it and the expectation that he would live up to Jaffé's trust in him. Jaffé played to his role as an authority figure to the younger journalist, who valued his approval. "Should you ever fail my boundless faith in you," Jaffé wrote, "something I hold precious will die in me and I will be that much poorer the rest of my life."[20]

During his trip to Germany, Dabney appears to have displayed a surprising dearth of initiative for a seasoned reporter. Even considering his sub rosa agenda and the fact that he was accompanied by his family, he seems to have sleepwalked through one of the century's most significant stories, the "night of the long knives." On June 30, 1934, Hitler, having struck a devil's bargain with Germany's military and industrial leaders, drove with Joseph Goebbels and an SS detachment south from Munich to the resort of Bad Wiessee, where they arrested and summarily shot brownshirt minion Edmund Heines and his homosexual lover caught *in flagrante delicto*. Wielding a revolver, Hitler seized by the throat SA chief of staff Ernst Röhm, with whom he had launched the Third Reich, and packed him and his lieutenants off to Stadelheim prison in Munich to be executed by the SS. Hitler used the occasion to settle a series of old scores across the country, ordering the executions of as many as one thousand. Upon the death of elderly President Paul von Hindenburg later that summer, Hitler immediately consolidated absolute power in his new position as Führer.[21]

19. Louis Jaffé to Virginius Dabney, 7 December 1933, Jaffé Papers.
20. Ibid.
21. Max Gallo, *The Night of the Long Knives*, trans. Lily Emmet (New York: Harper & Row, 1972); Shirer, *Rise and Fall of the Third Reich*, 213–26; Spielvogel, *Hitler and Nazi Germany*, 76–80; *New York Times*, 1, 2 July 1934.

"NEWS IS AT A PREMIUM," a front-page *New York Times* subhead read the day following the bloody purge. Asked by the North American Newspaper Alliance to report on the purge, Dabney declined. He would seem to have been in an ideal position to provide an account of the massacre. He had been in the country for several months, and he spoke German fluently. Moreover he was staying in Berchtesgaden, the site of Hitler's Eagles Nest chalet, a short distance from both Munich and Bad Wiessee. His byline on such an important international news story would have burnished his reputation.[22]

"I was not in a position to [cover the event]," he later explained, "as I had no idea myself at that stage just what the inside story was. Furthermore, if I had tried to find out, given my altogether limited knowledge of the situation and my almost nonexistent contacts, I might have gotten myself shot, or at a minimum have been thrown out of Germany. I wanted to complete my six months in Central Europe, an invaluable experience for my future work, and then to express myself freely and frankly concerning the Nazi atrocities."[23]

In sharp contrast, William L. Shirer, then stationed in Paris, was champing at the bit, writing in his diary that summer: "What a story! . . . Wish I could get a post to Berlin. It's a story I'd like to cover." In his autobiography, he recalled that for a correspondent that summer, "Nazi Germany, as abhorrent as it was, was the place to be." Dabney had no grounds to fear for his safety; at worst he might have been ordered out of the country, but that unlikely occurrence would only have enhanced his stature. In August 1934 the Gestapo politely expelled prominent journalist Dorothy Thompson, who had offended Hitler by her unflattering portrayal of him in her book, *I Saw Hitler!* and by her criticism of his racial policies in articles she had published in the *Jewish Daily Bulletin* in New York. Her arms filled with American Beauty roses given to her in a tearful send-off by the American and British press corps, she boarded a train for Paris. German authorities had earlier coerced the *Baltimore Sun*'s Miles Bouton and Edgar Ansel Mowrer of the *Chicago Daily News* to leave the country. (Mowrer won a Pulitzer Prize in 1933 for his coverage of political turmoil in Germany; his

22. *New York Times*, 1 July 1934; Dabney, "Reflections," 280–2.
23. Dabney, *Across the Years*, 127.

older brother, Paul Scott Mowrer, had won the award along with Jaffé in 1929.) The Nazis would later expel many other American correspondents from Germany, including Edmond Taylor of the *Chicago Tribune,* Beach Conger of the *New York Herald Tribune,* and Otto Tolischus of the *New York Times.* (Tolischus would win a Pulitzer Prize in 1940 for his dispatches from Berlin.)[24]

Despite Dabney's earlier skepticism of press reports regarding the persecution of the Jews and his abdication of journalistic responsibility during his travels, his trip forever altered his perceptions of Nazism. During his stay in Berchtesgaden, he received a letter from the *Times-Dispatch*'s publisher appointing him chief editorial writer, with the promise of becoming the paper's editor if his work proved satisfactory. Immediately upon his return to Richmond in late September, Dabney, taking full advantage of his new editorial platform, published a series of three signed articles damning the Nazis and attesting to the truthfulness of accounts of their atrocities. He informed Jaffé that he had grown to despise Nazism.[25]

"The moment I read those three articles . . . I heaved a deep sigh of relief," Jaffé told Dabney. "It is good to know you are safely back and better to know that you have returned untouched at the core by political and social miasmas which you have had to inspect at close range." Jaffé added that although he had had faith in Dabney, he had suffered a "kind of troubled apprehension," after having seen so many liberals return from their exposure to Nazi Germany "with a lower blood count."[26]

Dabney discovered that the new general manager and soon-to-be

24. William L. Shirer, *Berlin Diary: The Journal of a Foreign Correspondent, 1934–1941* (New York: Alfred A. Knopf, 1941), 11, 249; William L. Shirer, *The Nightmare Years, 1930–1940,* vol. 2, *20th Century Journey: A Memoir of a Life and the Times* (Boston: Little, Brown, 1984), 108–9; Peter Kurth, *American Cassandra: The Life of Dorothy Thompson* (Boston: Little, Brown, 1990), 199–203; Dorothy Thompson, *I Saw Hitler!* (New York: Farrar & Rinehart, 1932), 13–4; Williams, *Baltimore Sun,* 237; Lipstadt, *Beyond Belief,* 14, 22; Hohenberg, *Pulitzer Prize Story,* 344; Howard K. Smith, *Last Train from Berlin* (New York: Alfred A. Knopf, 1942), 52.

25. Dunford, *Richmond Times-Dispatch: The Story of a Newspaper,* 297; Dabney, *Across the Years,* 130–1; Kneebone, *Southern Liberal Journalists,* 177; *Richmond Times-Dispatch,* 30 September 1934, 1, 2 October 1934; Virginius Dabney to Louis Jaffé, 7 October 1934, Jaffé Papers.

26. Louis Jaffé to Virginius Dabney, 11 October 1934, Jaffé Papers.

publisher of the *Times-Dispatch,* Mark Ethridge, shared his newly found desire to lambaste Hitler. Returning from Germany the previous year, Ethridge had resumed his position as managing editor of the theretofore liberal *Macon (Ga.) Telegraph* and from its pages vigorously defended the accuracy of American correspondents' reports of Hitlerian atrocities. Upon learning that his paper's politics had changed to conservatism during his absence, he had left and worked briefly for the Associated Press and the *Washington Post* before coming to Richmond to head the *Times-Dispatch.*[27]

Ethridge met Jaffé in Norfolk in December 1934 and afterward wrote him a letter containing a "somewhat fulsome" expression of admiration. Ethridge told Jaffé he had followed the *Pilot* for years and regarded Jaffé "as the ablest of southern editors." (Several years earlier Ethridge had attempted to persuade him to address the Georgia Press Association's annual meeting, but Jaffé had declined, citing family illness.) Jaffé reciprocated the admiration. He knew Ethridge's work at the *Telegraph*—which had attacked lynching, the Ku Klux Klan, and mill owners who exploited their labor forces—and he communicated to Slover his high esteem for Ethridge. During its new leader's tenure, the *Times-Dispatch* would adopt a more progressive posture and regain some of the luster it had enjoyed two decades earlier under the direction of John Stewart Bryan.[28]

The Nazis' persecution of Jews further honed Jaffé's longtime abhorrence of mob violence. In February 1935 he ended his long opposition to federal antilynching legislation and threw in his lot with the vanguard of southern liberals urging passage of the Costigan-Wagner bill. In "Pass the Anti-Lynching Bill," he explained his reversal: "To the *Virginian-Pilot,* which has in the past feared that the difficulties that would flow from a Federal anti-

27. Lipstadt, *Beyond Belief,* 26; *New York Times,* 7 April 1981; Couch, *Culture in the South,* 134; Harry Strozier to Mark Ethridge, 18 March 1933, Mark Ethridge to Harry Strozier, 30 March 1933, Mark Ethridge to W. T. Anderson, 20 March 1933, Samuel Slover to Mark Ethridge, 26 November 1934, all in Ethridge Papers.

28. Mark Ethridge to Louis Jaffé, January 1931, 7 December 1934, Jaffé Papers; Louis Jaffé to Mark Ethridge, 19 January 1931, Jaffé Papers; Dabney, *Liberalism in the South,* 402; Egerton, *Speak Now Against the Day,* 72; Louis Jaffé to Mark Ethridge, 6 December 1934, Ethridge Papers; Kneebone, *Southern Liberal Journalists,* 77–8; Couch, *Culture in the South,* 134; 139–40; Dunford, *Richmond Times-Dispatch: The Story of a Newspaper,* 207.

lynching law might outweigh its benefits, it no longer seems reasonable to entertain that view. It has become wholly illogical, it seems to us, to applaud the Federal Department of Justice for its effective pursuit of bank robbers, and at the same time to distrust a proposed Department of Justice pursuit of persons who, as members of orgiastic mobs, hang men to trees or burn them at the stake without benefit of judge or jury. [The Costigan-Wagner bill's] invasion of State's rights should cause no Southern heartburnings. There is no such thing, morally speaking, as a reserved right to deal in our own way with a form of collective murder which our own way has uniformly failed to punish."[29]

Southern editors took notice of Jaffé's endorsement of the bill. "No newspaper in America has more thoroughly studied lynching and its causes and effects than the *Norfolk Virginian-Pilot*," wrote the *Danville (Va.) Register*. "It long doubted the wisdom of a Federal anti-lynching bill. But it is now ready to throw the weight of its influence behind the [Costigan-Wagner] bill."[30]

The NAACP's secretary, publicist and lobbyist Walter White, whose childhood experiences at the hands of a white mob had forged in him a lifelong commitment to end lynching, heartily approved Jaffé's editorial: "We are delighted to learn of this action on the part of so influential a paper as the *Virginian-Pilot* though, since you are the editor, such action does not surprise us." Attempting to counter the Communist Party's successful recruiting efforts in the black community, White had staked the NAACP's prestige on a high-profile campaign to deliver a federal antilynching law.[31]

In January 1935, when White attempted to build momentum for the bill by printing a long list of pro-Costigan-Wagner associations with combined membership of more than forty-two million, the names of the South's principal white organizations fighting mob justice did not appear on the list. The region's preeminent antilynching organization, the Commission on Interracial Cooperation, viewed the bill ambivalently, preferring to focus its efforts on education and the passage and strengthening of state laws. Jes-

29. *Pilot,* 16 February 1934.

30. *Danville (Va.) Register,* 19 February 1935.

31. Walter White to Louis Jaffé, 19 March 1935, Jaffé Papers; White, *Man Called White,* 6–12; Shapiro, *White Violence and Black Response,* 96–103; Zangrando, *NAACP Crusade Against Lynching,* 100–1, 108.

sie Daniel Ames, who led the Association of Southern Women for the Prevention of Lynching, opposed the bill outright. Even George Fort Milton, the young and highly acclaimed editor of the *Chattanooga News,* who chaired the Southern Commission on the Study of Lynching, argued against federal legislation, on the grounds that southern efforts to eradicate lynching would prove more effective. Milton's position resembled that of most of the region's leading liberal journalists and many of the editors of the South's major newspapers.[32]

Jaffé helped lead the charge for Costigan-Wagner in the South. Sherwood Anderson joined him, writing in the pages of the NAACP's *Crisis,* "I do not see how any man can refuse to put in his word, for whatever it's worth, to any organized protest against lynching." Defying prediction, Mencken came out in support of the bill and testified in its favor before a Senate subcommittee alongside the NAACP's leadership. An especially horrifying mass mob lynching on Maryland's Eastern Shore had demonstrated to him the inadequacy of state laws. Clark Howell Sr., nearing the end of his long editorship of the *Atlanta Constitution,* had endorsed passage of a federal law in late 1933, and a few scattered papers such as the *Anniston (Ala.) Star* and the *Bristol (Va.) Herald Courier* soon followed his example.[33]

President Roosevelt, whose New Deal agenda lay at the mercy of powerful southern legislators occupying leadership positions on key congressional committees, neither endorsed nor opposed the bill. "If I come out for the anti-lynching bill now," he explained to White during a meeting

32. Walter White, "The Costigan-Wagner Bill," *Crisis,* January 1935, 10; Jacquelyn Dowd Hall, *Revolt Against Chivalry: Jessie Daniel Ames and the Women's Campaign Against Lynching* (New York: Columbia University Press, 1979), 237–48; Zangrando, *NAACP Crusade Against Lynching,* 104–5, 116, 126–7; Dykeman and Stokely, *Seeds of Southern Change,* 136; Rable, "South and Antilynching Legislation," 208; Miller, "Ladies and the Lynchers," 274, 277; "Public Enemy Number One!" *Crisis,* January 1935, 23; Kneebone, *Southern Liberal Journalists,* 105, 148.

33. "Public Enemy Number One!" 22; *New York Times,* 15 February 1935; Zangrando, *NAACP Crusade Against Lynching,* 104–5, 117; White, *Man Called White,* 140–1; Senate Subcommittee of the Committee on the Judiciary, *Punishment for the Crime of Lynching: Hearings on S. 24,* 74th Cong., 1st sess., 14 February 1935, 23–5,104–5; David C. Roller and Robert W. Twyman, eds., *Encyclopedia of Southern History* (Baton Rouge: Louisiana State University Press, 1979), 611–2; "Editorials," *Crisis,* May 1937, 145.

arranged by Eleanor Roosevelt, "they will block every bill I ask Congress to pass to keep America from collapsing. I just can't take that risk." (The president's pragmatism did not dissuade the First Lady from using her personal influence in an energetic attempt to secure the bill's passage.) Despite the Democratic Party's great victory in the 1934 congressional elections, the key legislation of Roosevelt's "Second Hundred Days" did indeed hang in the balance.[34]

In late April southern Democratic senators led by Ellison "Cotton Ed" Smith (S.C.), Richard Russell (Ga.), Tom Connally (Tex.), and Carter Glass (Va.) began a six-day filibuster. Tarheel senator Josiah Bailey, quoting an incongruous source, warned, "It shall not pass. 'We'll fight it out on this line,' as General Grant once said, 'if it takes all summer.' . . . We'll speak night and day if necessary." Jaffé took his state's senior senator to task, pointing out in "Rights Fail When Duties Falter" that Glass had misrepresented a speech Calvin Coolidge had given at the College of William and Mary, which the filibustering legislator cited to support his states' rights position. Jaffé clarified the record, informing his readers that the "burden of President Coolidge's argument was that the Federal Government would invade the sovereignty of the States if they persevered in a policy of indifference to the action required by 'the great body of public opinion of the nation.' The danger he pointed out was not—as Senator Glass recalled it— that of Federal usurpation encouraged by the failure of the states vigorously to assert their rights, but of Federal assumption of the policy of 'meting out justice between man and man' brought on by the failure of the States vigorously to do their duty." The diminutive but combative Glass, publisher of the *Lynchburg (Va.) Advance* and a caustic editorialist, undoubtedly made a mental record of Jaffé's embarrassing emendation.[35]

When maverick Republican senator William Borah, a widely

---

34. White, *Man Called White*, 169–70; Frank Freidel, *F.D.R. and the South* (Baton Rouge: Louisiana State University Press, 1965), 83–9; Tamara K. Hareven, *Eleanor Roosevelt: An American Conscience* (Chicago: Quadrangle Books, 1968), 119–23; Davis, *FDR: The New Deal Years*, 421–2; James R. McGovern, *Anatomy of a Lynching: The Killing of Claude Neal* (Baton Rouge: Louisiana State University Press, 1982), 124.

35. *New York Times*, 26 April 1935; *Nation*, 1 May 1935, 494; Tindall, *Emergence of the New South*, 552; *Pilot*, 1 May 1935; Rixey Smith and Norman Beasley, *Carter Glass, A Biography* (New York: Da Capo Press, 1972), 37–8, 56–8.

acknowledged constitutional law authority, joined his southern colleagues in opposing the bill, the upper house voted to move on to consideration of a veterans' bonus. One observer described the capitulation to the filibuster as "Appomattox in reverse." Jaffé again went on the offensive, maintaining that Borah's stance lacked consistency with a previous position he had taken: "This same Senator Borah who took up the cause of the Southern Senators with a denunciation of the spread of the Federal government and defense of the doctrine that the States alone have the authority to handle their lynchers, is the same Senator Borah who only a few years ago was stumping the South in behalf of a greater extension of Federal authority through the prohibition amendment than [Costigan-Wagner] contemplated." Jaffé predicted that antilynching legislation would come before Congress again "as surely as lynching remains a curse of Southern life. The best way to beat it is not to rely on a State rights standard in Washington which everyone knows is commonly used or discarded as circumstances dictate, but to get at the evil of lynching itself. There will be no anti-lynching bills if there are no lynchings."[36]

Throughout the 1930s Jaffé augmented his promotion of human rights on national and international levels with continued advocacy for Norfolk's black community, which made up over a third of the city's population. In early 1935, at the same time he declared his support for Costigan-Wagner, he redoubled his efforts to provide blacks with a beach-front park equipped with the necessary amenities. Along with P. B. Young and other black and progressive white community leaders, Jaffé had waged a relentless battle to provide blacks with access to the seashore. In an area bordered with beaches, Norfolk almost inconceivably had failed to furnish blacks with a recreational bathing facility. The city's negligence in this regard matched perfectly its irresponsibility in refusing to provide blacks with paved streets, functioning sewers, parks, adequate schools, police protection, and modern medical facilities.[37]

Jaffé had begun his campaign for a beach for blacks in the early

36. *New York Times*, 2 May 1935; *Pilot*, 3 May 1935.

37. Suggs, *P. B. Young, Newspaperman*, 91; P. B. Young to Louis Jaffé, 3 October 1927, Jaffé Papers; Lewis, *In Their Own Interests*, 81–5.

1920s. In 1926, urging support for purchasing the land that would become Barraud Park, Norfolk's first such facility for blacks, he stepped up his advocacy. "Not only is this neighborhood colored park needed," he wrote, "but there is needed in this community a large general park for the same purpose. Presumably such a park should have frontage on some body of water capable of providing a good bathing beach." He presciently warned that if the city did not act immediately to acquire such a site, "complications that might attack such an undertaking" would emerge, as the shorefront became more completely developed. Fundamental fairness dictated that the city act quickly: "A park policy supported by taxation that falls on both races but which benefits only one race alone, is unfair to the point of indecency. A beginning must be made in reducing the balance."[38]

Throughout the late 1920s and early 1930s, Jaffé employed both personal advocacy and a diverse range of rhetorical appeals to lobby for the resort. He persuaded Governor Byrd to serve on a foundation supporting the beach. Attempting to embarrass the city into acting, he drew an uncomplimentary comparison: "Other Southern cities far less generously endowed with good beaches have made provision for their colored populations. Norfolk, within a short distance of scores of miles of bay and ocean beaches, has made no provision at all. . . . The fact constitutes a damaging indictment against a city that is almost entirely surrounded by water." In "65,000 Norfolkians Without a Beach," he encouraged his white readers to imagine how they would feel if "by some malign miracle of industrialization all the available waterfront were preempted by commerce and shipping, and that this population of 115,000, denied the solace of nearby summer beaches, were left with the choice of journeying many miles to another city for this comfort, or steaming it out at home."[39]

After the Norfolk Interracial Commission, which counted Jaffé among its leaders, had identified a potential beach site at Little Creek in neighboring Princess Anne County, the issue stimulated a fierce debate. A vocal group of whites opposed acquiring the beach. Jaffé later catalogued the numerous obstacles the pro-beach forces had fought to overcome:

38. *Pilot,* 25 September 1927, 25 May 1926.

39. Louis Jaffé to Harry Byrd, 29 March 1929, Jaffé Papers; *Pilot,* 25 September 1927, 20 February 1929.

"immemorial prejudice, inertia, distrust of the untried, political timidity and vested selfishness."[40] Nevertheless, voters had defeated a city council ticket openly hostile to acquiring the beach in June 1930, and the city council had approved the purchase. Jaffé and *Ledger-Dispatch* editor Douglas Gordon then petitioned the State Corporation Commission to allow the Pennsylvania Railroad to relinquish the surplus property to the county. When the commission approved the transfer in late 1930, nearby property owners unsuccessfully appealed to the State Supreme Court.[41]

Amidst this rancor, the venerable *Philadelphia Tribune,* one of the country's major black weeklies, paid Jaffé and the *Virginian-Pilot* a remarkable tribute. "We have never done it before," editor Eugene W. Rhodes wrote, "but we permit . . . a white daily . . . to write our editorial. We consider this the finest expression of any we have seen in a white newspaper." The *Tribune* reprinted a Jaffé editorial, "A Plea for Justice," which deplored the "gross injustice involved in the complete denial of this community's extensive beach resources to the 70,000 residents of Norfolk who belong to the Negro race."[42]

These people suffer from the discomforts of hot weather even more acutely than the white population, because their living quarters are more congested. Their houses have fewer windows and fewer bathrooms. Their streets have poorer drains, fewer shade trees and more dust. They can not escape to the shade and solace of nearby parks, because the entire public park system, with negligible exceptions, although paid for and maintained by taxing both races, is reserved for the use of the white race alone. These are facts and however we may explain them we can not dispute them. The indisputable truth is that the very population element that is most cruelly in need of a means for escaping from the heated city to a cooling beach, has up to the present moment been denied any such means

40. Chambers, Shank, and Sugg, *Salt Water & Printer's Ink,* 366; H. G. Cochran to Louis Jaffé, 30 January 1933, Jaffé Papers.

41. Louis Jaffé and Douglas Gordon to State Corporation Commission, 25 September 1930, Jaffé Papers; *Pilot,* 8 March 1931, 18 February 1935; *Guide,* 16 February 1935.

42. Pride and Wilson, *History of the Black Press,* 132–3; R. B. Eleazer to Louis Jaffé, 19 March 1930, Jaffé Papers.

of recreation, whereas the population element whose need for this escape is less pressing has at its disposal private and public beaches without number. . . . The *Virginian-Pilot* affirms that there is injustice in such a state of affairs and that a commanding moral obligation rests on the government of the city of Norfolk and on the white population from which this government derives its mandate, to correct it.[43]

Throughout the early 1930s Jaffé relentlessly hammered away at the issue with editorials such as "Settle the Negro Beach Question" and "Colored Beach a Public Necessity." In 1932 the dispute reached a head when opponents of the beach obtained a temporary injunction barring local banks from cashing a $10,100 check Norfolk had issued to Princess Anne County to pay for the beach. In an end run around the injunction, pro-beach forces retained a prominent attorney, Colonel James Mann, and purchased the check from the county with cash. Mann refused to reveal the names of the benefactors, but the *Pilot* reported that "when asked if Douglas Gordon, editor of the *Ledger-Dispatch,* and Louis I. Jaffé, editor of the *Virginian-Pilot,* were among the group who obtained his services in the matter, Colonel Mann said they were." The legal wrangling came to a halt a few days later when the courts dissolved the injunction. "Let us write finis to the historic Negro beach controversy and begin a new chapter in civic helpfulness, simple fairness, and interracial harmony," Jaffé urged hopefully.[44]

Despite the editor's plea, whites telegraphed an unmistakable message to blacks that they had crossed a line with their bold advocacy. Celestyne Porter, the niece of black attorney J. Eugene Diggs, who along with P. B. Young had spearheaded the black community's activism for the beach, recalled that her uncle feared for his family's safety. After one crucial incident he returned home and took precautionary measures. "You all better turn out your lights and go to bed kind of early," he instructed the children, "and . . . by any means if you hear anything, don't get up. . . . Tensions are right high." Later that night whites burned a cross on Diggs's lawn.[45]

In 1935, as the Senate considered the Costigan-Wagner bill, the

43. *Philadelphia Tribune,* 23 January 1930.
44. *Pilot,* 3 February 1930, 8 March 1931, 6, 9 March 1932, 16 February 1935.
45. Celestyne Porter, interview by author, 18 May 1992.

Negro beach controversy rose again to the top of Jaffé's editorial agenda. The long and bitter fight Jaffé and others had waged to acquire the waterfront site notwithstanding, the modest resort they envisioned had remained barren and isolated for several years until the federal Civil Works Administration constructed an access road and built bathrooms and a keeper's house in 1934. But even then the city council refused to appropriate funding to hire a keeper and to provide shelter, water, and lighting for beachgoers.[46]

Jerry Gilliam, president of the local NAACP branch, would later tell a parable to illustrate white antipathy to blacks in matters such as the beach issue: "The whites deprive the Negro of privileges here like the mythical rat bites. I once slept in a back room in Washington, D.C., and big rats would run over me every night. A friend . . . told me to get out of there or rats would eat me to death. . . . 'The rat,' he said, 'will take a small bite off your toe, and then blow on it so you won't feel, then take another nibble and blow some more, until the blood starts flowing and you bleed to death in your sleep.' That's the way the white people lull Negroes to sleep in Norfolk and then bite them till they're bled dry."[47]

Doubtless many of the *Pilot*'s subscribers had tired of reading about the beach issue, but Jaffé refused to drop it. In one nine-day period he authored four editorials, two of them lead pieces, focusing on the beach. In "Indecent Exclusion," he castigated the city council for omitting improvements to the resort from a list of $16 million worth of projects it had identified for Public Works Administration funding. Calling the beach a "fraud," he shamed the city's leadership: "If human considerations have no appeal to those councilmen who have obstructed every move to make the Negro beach useable . . . it would seem that self-respect should. The present scheme of giving the colored people a beach with one hand and keeping it unusable with the other, is indecent. It is unworthy of responsible custodians of the common weal." In "Time for a Showdown," he threatened to fix blame on the specific council members who had undermined the project through their "under-cover opposition" and who made it a "pious fake."[48]

46. *Pilot*, 15 February 1935; *Guide*, 16 February 1935.
47. Lewis, *In Their Own Interests*, 147–8, 167.
48. *Pilot*, 11, 15, 23 February 1935.

In "The Beach Vendetta" he reviewed the affair's entire history, which had begun with a desire to provide blacks "with a secure bit of beach—one that was securely dedicated to their use and which would be proof against the mutations of the real estate market or the machinations of future Ku Klux Klans." Jaffé recounted and effectively dismissed the many "high-minded objections" that beach foes had used to mask their racism. He explained that he had detailed the "vicissitudes of the Negro beach . . . to exhibit to the fair-minded people of [Norfolk] the medieval ferocity with which the opposition has fought the rectification of an ancient injustice and has undertaken, by resort to one hollow argument after another, to hamstring, frustrate and nullify an elementary health and recreational project the soundness of which it professes to approve in principle."[49]

"This is the Record," the simplest editorial in the series, may have had the most devastating effect on the opposition. Jaffé began with two rhetorical questions: "Is it asking something unreasonable to ask the Council to install such modest improvements at the Negro bathing beach as will make it the bona fide recreational facility it was intended to be, instead of the mockery that it is at present? Is it asking for the colored population a recreational favor that has not been accorded the white population?" He proceeded to answer these questions by citing to the penny the city's investment costs for its various recreational assets. The Negro Bathing Beach and Barraud Park, the city's only two such facilities for blacks, and the thousand dollars it had devoted to acquiring playgrounds for black children had amounted to $30,379.13; the fourteen recreational facilities serving Norfolk's white population had totaled $1,212,575.10. "What is being asked of the Council now is not any redressing of this record," Jaffé wrote. "It is so fundamentally discriminatory that it is beyond all redressing." He calculated the effect of investing the several thousand dollars it would require to make the black beach an "honest source of recreation instead of a humiliating false-pretense": "The city's distribution of recreational facilities, as between the two races will become less discriminatory by something like eight-tenths of 1 per cent—instead of the recreational investment being divided 97.6 per cent for white use and 2.4 per cent for colored use, the division will be 96.8 per cent white and 3.2 per cent colored."[50]

49. Ibid., 18 February 1935.
50. Ibid., 19 February 1935.

In late February Jaffé spoke at a rancorous city council meeting that voted three to two against a plan he supported that would have granted a concession to develop the beach to a private company, which would recoup its investment by selling confections. A special provision would have barred the developer from charging access fees to bathers. City councilman John Gurkin explained that his vote against the proposal had nothing to do with the fact that he owned a home located close to the beach. "God knows the Niggers will never bother me," the *Journal and Guide* quoted him. "I have three houses in the city but I wish that the matter had not been brought up. I want the Niggers to have a beach as much as anybody." He claimed that he backed the use of another site—one much further removed from black population centers. But just one week later, wilting under the criticism directed at him by the *Virginian-Pilot*, the *Ledger-Dispatch,* and the *Journal and Guide,* Gurkin moved to reopen the matter. In early March he cast the deciding vote in favor of the development plan.[51]

That summer the *Journal and Guide* ran several series of photographs of large crowds of beachgoers enjoying the newly erected bathhouses, dance hall, and pavilion. Young could not resist plugging his paper to advertisers in a caption for a photograph showing a jammed parking lot at the beach: "Parking space at the Municipal beach was at a premium. It's pictures like this that give automobile, gas, tire and accessory dealers the idea that their advertisements in the *Journal and Guide* are reaching a receptive market."[52]

During this period Jaffé battled for fairer treatment for blacks in a host of other areas. Some of the issues, such as the barbering bill he helped torpedo through his editorials and personal intervention, have faded into near oblivion. Its passage would, in his words, have made barbering in Virginia "into a closed guild . . . that would have tended inevitably to make it a Caucasian monopoly." Other subjects, such as the Scottsboro trials, figure prominently in southern history. Along with leading southern liberal journalists Dabney, Freeman, Milton, and Jonathan Daniels, the novice editor of the *Raleigh News and Observer,* Jaffé conducted an editorial campaign urging Alabama to overturn the death penalty against the "Scottsboro

51. *Guide,* 23 February, 2, 9 March 1935.
52. Ibid., 22, 29 June 1935.

boys." He asserted that "if the prisoners were white instead of black [authorities] would not for a moment seriously argue that they ought to be executed."[53]

Norfolk contained some of the worst slums in the nation. Armed with information supplied by P. B. Young regarding the abysmal conditions in which many blacks lived, Jaffé urged federal intervention to wipe out the "jerry-built, packing box firetraps that infest several square miles" of Norfolk's black residential communities and replace them with "clean, modern and respectable shelter" affordable to "families of small means." Jaffé and Young also collaborated to demand more and better schools for blacks. When Young requested "editorial assistance" from Jaffé to urge that the city do something about overcrowding in black schools, Jaffé determined that behind-the-scenes advocacy would be more productive. "I am planning to have a talk with the City Manager . . . at an early date with a view of finding out what can be done by way of relieving the situation which you describe," he wrote back to Young.[54]

And when some of Roosevelt's initiatives had the unintended effect of forcing some local businesses to fire blacks, Jaffé protested that "it would be a grim and tragic commentary on the national recovery effort if a business and industrial regimentation directed to lifting the people out of a depression, should operate to plunge the most depressed of them in a worse depression still."[55]

His unrelenting advocacy earned him the respect and affection of Norfolk's blacks. "We are all very happy over the successful outcome of our beach matter, and I want to take this opportunity to personally thank you for your untiring efforts in our behalf," P. B. Young wrote. In a letter to the National Urban League's leadership, Young described Jaffé as the most

53. *Pilot*, 5 February 1930, 8 April 1933; L. R. Reynolds to Louis Jaffé, 3 February 1930, Jaffé Papers; Lewis, *In Their Own Interests*, 154; Goodman, *Stories of Scottsboro*, 163; Charles W. Eagles, *Jonathan Daniels and Race Relations: The Evolution of a Southern Liberal* (Knoxville: University of Tennessee Press, 1982), 3; Kneebone, *Southern Liberal Journalists*, 80–1.

54. *Pilot*, 2 August 1932; P. B. Young to Louis Jaffé, 17 November 1927, 13 November 1931, Jaffé Papers; Suggs, *P. B. Young, Newspaperman*, 87–8, 126; *Guide*, 14 November 1931; Louis Jaffé to P. B. Young, 2 December 1931, Jaffé Papers.

55. *Pilot*, 10 August 1933.

"out-standing figure" in the white southern press. J. Eugene Diggs, after serving with Jaffé on a special committee charged by the Norfolk Commission on Interracial Cooperation with resolving the beach issue, expressed deep appreciation for his contributions. Celestyne Porter, who would later play a prominent role in Norfolk's racial affairs, described Jaffé as the "moving force in stemming the tide of [racial] distrust [and] hatred." She recalled that the black community "loved" him. According to the Reverend Richard Bowling, pastor of Norfolk's prominent black First Baptist Church and a *Journal and Guide* columnist, blacks saw in Jaffé a "social seer, a friend of the oppressed, a fearless champion of deep and righteous convictions, a shining herald of that new day when America shall be truly a land of the free and when unhampered opportunity and mutual respect shall be the possession of her whole citizenry."[56]

Jaffé's activism for fairer treatment for blacks did not, however, extend at this time to questioning the larger doctrine of racial separation. In 1935, when Alice Jackson, an honor graduate of Virginia Union University, applied to the University of Virginia for graduate education, Jaffé defended the university's decision to "refuse respectfully" to accept her application. He conceded that the ruling had a "shaky foundation in law" but maintained that it had an "impregnable foundation in the kind of custom that law can not disregard without courting tension and disorder." He urged the state to begin to provide blacks with graduate and professional programs equivalent to those for whites or to develop scholarship arrangements for them to study at integrated programs in other states. Soon thereafter, responding to judicial pressure, Virginia expanded graduate program offerings at Virginia State College and established a scholarship fund to enable blacks to attend graduate and professional schools out of state.[57]

Jaffé's defense of segregated education, as demonstrated by his sup-

56. P. B. Young to Louis Jaffé, 10 March 1932, P. B. Young to Jesse Thomas, 17 November 1927, both in Jaffé Papers; Harold Sugg, letter to author, 12 October 1990; "Committee for the Norfolk Commission on Interracial Co-operation to Council of the City of Norfolk," 8 October 1934, Jaffé Papers; J. Eugene Diggs to Louis Jaffé, 17 May 1929, Jaffé Papers; Porter, interview by author, 18 May 1992; Richard Bowling to Louis Jaffé, 13 May 1929, Jaffé Papers.

57. *Pilot,* 21 September 1935; Suggs, *P. B. Young, Newspaperman,* 159–60; Workers of the Writers' Program, *The Negro in Virginia,* 304–5.

port for the University of Virginia's refusal to admit Jackson, should surprise no one. It placed him in accord with the unanimity of opinion on the
subject among white southern liberals. Throughout the 1930s and 1940s,
no white editor of a southern daily would argue for dismantlement of racial
separation. In the mid-thirties, with the exception of a few militant groups
such as the Fellowship of Southern Churchmen and the Southern Tenant
Farmers Union, no whites in the region publicly challenged Jim Crow. Even
writer and social activist Lillian Smith, one of the earliest native white
southerners to criticize segregation, focused her attention on literary matters
in her little magazine, *Pseudopodia,* and kept silent on the subject until early
in the next decade.[58]

Despite this liberal southern consensus, Jaffé's support for racial
segregation must have come at the price of considerable soul-searching. He
plainly discerned the fundamental inconsistency between his position on
this issue and his prolonged championship of civil and human rights. But he
believed that the region's whites would resist with all their might a fundamental shift in racial power relations. He had weighed the merits of integration against its inflammability, had made his decision, and could envision
no workable alternative in the racial climate of the South in the foreseeable
future. No evidence suggests ambivalence or self-reproach over his stand on
segregation.

In his decade-and-a-half stewardship of the *Virginian-Pilot,* Jaffé's
views on race had evolved considerably. He displayed a growing awareness
of the need for a role for the federal government in abating the racial injustices in the South and had begun to see himself clear of the states' rights
dogma that clouded the vision of his peers in the southern press. He recognized the economic infeasibility of the hard-pressed region's ever developing
genuinely "separate but equal" facilities. Over the next several years he
would become increasingly appreciative of the judicial and moral superiority of the arguments articulated by activists seeking to bring down the Jim
Crow system.

58. Egerton, *Speak Now Against the Day,* 154–8, 250; Anne C. Loveland, *Lillian
Smith: A Southerner Confronting the South* (Baton Rouge: Louisiana State University Press,
1986), 22, 43; Lillian Smith, *How Am I to Be?: Letters of Lillian Smith,* ed. Margaret Rose
Gladney (Chapel Hill: University of North Carolina Press, 1993), 52–60.

The national leadership of the NAACP, ever watchful for chinks in Jim Crow's armor, attended closely to the Jackson case. In 1935 Walter White persuaded Charles Houston, the stern taskmaster who had reformed Howard University's law school and trained a cadre of black attorneys who would prove capable of vying with the South's best white juristic minds, to direct the association's legal campaign against segregation. Working long hours, seven days a week, Houston began to challenge discriminatory education with a three-pronged attack that targeted segregated public graduate and professional programs, racial bias in teachers' salaries, and inequalities in the physical facilities of black and white elementary and high schools. Seeking to find a hot-button issue to jump-start the association's laggard recruiting efforts in Virginia, White, Houston, and Houston's young protégé, Thurgood Marshall, soon directed their gaze to Norfolk and its black schoolteachers.[59]

59. Genna Rae McNeil, *Groundwork: Charles Hamilton Houston and the Struggle for Civil Rights* (Philadelphia: University of Pennsylvania Press, 1983), 63–85; Juan Williams, *Eyes on the Prize: America's Civil Rights Years, 1954–1965* (New York: Viking, 1987), 10–4; Juan Williams, *Thurgood Marshall: An American Revolutionary* (New York: Times Books, 1998), 55–60; Mark V. Tushnet, *The NAACP's Legal Strategy against Segregated Education, 1925–1950* (Chapel Hill: University of North Carolina Press, 1987), 34; Buni, *Negro in Virginia Politics,* 127; Suggs, *P. B. Young, Newspaperman,* 160.

13 FROM BAD TO WORSE

In the late summer of 1935, as the new school year neared, rumors of a polio outbreak circulated throughout Norfolk. Ever vigilant to matters of health, Margaret, who had been vacationing with Christopher in Blue Ridge Summit for the past three months, postponed her return home. On September 9 she notified Jaffé in a postcard mailed from Washington, D.C., that she intended to stay away "for the time being" and that she would make "local arrangements" for Christopher's education.[1]

In his reply, Jaffé informed her that Norfolk's medical authorities had discovered no cases of polio and that all of the city's schoolchildren, including Christopher's classmates at Norfolk Academy, the selective private school he attended, had begun classes. Determined to head off another prolonged absence like the one he had endured several years earlier, Jaffé put Margaret on notice that he would not countenance her decision. "I will tolerate no repetition of what happened four and a half years ago . . . when a similar 'for the time being' absence from home led to a desertion of me," he told her. "I will not again be put in the equivocal position in which I was put then. I will amply provide for everything you and Christopher need provided it is here, at home. I will assume no responsibility whatever for maintaining you away from home. I have neither the means nor the strength. I have during the past three months been maintaining three establishments—in Norfolk, in Blue Ridge and in South Boston. It is beyond my means and will have to be terminated at once. . . . It was definitely understood between us that never again would I be subjected to a repetition of the Washington absenteeism with all its agony, expense and humiliation. That exploitation of me I shall never permit again.[2]

1. Margaret Jaffé to Louis Jaffé, 9 September 1935, Louis Jaffé Jr.
2. Alice Jaffé note, n.d., Louis Jaffé to Margaret Jaffé, 10 September 1935, 8 November 1935, all ibid.

Previously, in dealing with Margaret's irrational behavior, Jaffé could rely unquestioningly on his father-in-law's support. Together they had played the most prominent roles in persuading Margaret to end her earlier absence. But Hugh C. Davis had died the previous summer, and Jaffé now could depend only on Wheelwright, who could not exert on his niece the influence that had been her father's prerogative. In some ways the senior Davis had served as a paternal figure to Jaffé, whose own father had died in South Boston in early 1933. Jaffé had loved his father, but profound religious, cultural, and educational differences had precluded much real understanding between the two.[3]

Jaffé praised his father-in-law in a letter to Wheelwright, explaining that he would turn to Davis for advice were he still alive. Believing Wheelwright to be the one person in whom he could confide and who would best understand his predicament, Jaffé hoped to meet with him to discuss the new crisis but explained that he would understand if Wheelwright felt too close to Mrs. Davis and Margaret to play such a role. As always, Wheelwright remained sympathetic to Jaffé and constant in his support.[4]

In a four-sentence note in mid-October, Margaret at last responded to Jaffé's many letters and telegrams asking her to fix a date for her return. She denied that she had deserted him or planned to do so. "Are you going to take the position that you are not going to support me as long as I don't come home whenever you tell me?" she asked. She accused him of over-reacting to her extended absence. Jaffé made clear to her in his reply that he did not intend "to be treated as an inanimate drawing account to whom no explanations of an absenteeism now running into the fifth month are due." He wrote, "We are at a turning point. The decision rests with you. I ask you to do nothing you don't want to do about this. If you prefer to live your life without me from now on—with your mother, somebody else or alone, I do not raise a finger to stop you. . . . A frank, honest and definite statement of what you plan to do . . . is something I must have and something to which I am entitled."[5]

3. Louis Jaffé to Thomas Wheelwright, 9 October 1935, ibid.; *Halifax (Va.) Gazette*, 23 March 1933.

4. Louis Jaffé to Thomas Wheelwright, 9 October 1935, Louis Jaffé Jr.; Louis Jaffé to Laura Wheelwright, 31 December 1936, Jaffé Papers.

5. Louis Jaffé to Margaret Jaffé, 17 October 1935, Margaret Jaffé to Louis Jaffé, 14 October 1935, both Louis Jaffé Jr.

Margaret then resorted to a new tactic to force Jaffé to continue his financial support for her. In late October she accused her husband of cruelty in a series of postcards sent to him at work. "Are you going to send me some money or force me to file suit for separate maintenance?" she asked. "The child is ill. Would you like a doctor's certificate certifying this?" Two days later no funds had arrived, and on another postcard she informed Jaffé that both she and Christopher were ill with the flu. She had called in a second doctor, whom she claimed had ordered her to stay in bed. "It is incredible to me that you . . . are unwilling to send funds to tide through this emergency your wife and child!"[6]

"You have apparently embarked on a policy of washing our linen on postcards open to the inspection of everybody in the city room," Jaffé shot back. "It is too late, Margaret. Pride is dead, only justice remains." He had laid in a stock of postcards in "self defense"; if she continued her attempts to humiliate him, he warned, "I [will] set forth some of the accumulate wash I have been carrying around in my heart these many years—for the benefit of the Blue Ridge gossips."[7]

In the same letter Jaffé confronted Margaret with what he believed to be at the core of her estrangement from him: "I am too sick in spirit and tired in body to care what you do—sick unto death of the struggle to preserve my self-respect, my ability to work and therefore my ability to provide a home and living for all of us, against the implacable madness and cross-purposes that have dogged my hardest efforts and embittered them—sick unto worse than death of the subtle but relentless persecution of me because of my Jewish blood." Margaret's mother in a "burst of confidence" had informed him that that was the real reason for her daughter's unhappiness with her marriage and the disdain with which she treated Jaffé. "Perhaps she is right," he wrote. "But the time to hate me for that was before we married and brought a child in the world to share his father's blood-guilt. And yet Christ and his Disciples and Mary and Anne—all sprang from the same vile race. It is too much for me. But I am too sick to argue any more, even too sick to work. Do what you want to do—come back home or divorce me—but in God's name do it quick."[8]

6. Margaret Jaffé to Louis Jaffé, 23, 25 October 1935, ibid.
7. Louis Jaffé to Margaret Jaffé, 25 October 1935, ibid.
8. Ibid.

Throughout November Jaffé alternately attempted to reason with Margaret and threatened to end his support permanently. "As far as I am concerned this cruel racket is at an end," he wrote. "It is at an end now and forever in the future. We shall either live together on a sane, cooperative and mutually consultative basis, or you can go your way and I mine. I have told your mother how I feel about all this, and that I will not finance your abandonment of me any longer."[9]

Although Margaret had informed Jaffé that her physician had ordered her to stay in Blue Ridge Summit, she told her mother that she had driven to Washington for a blood test. Mrs. Davis shared the letter with Jaffé, who confronted his wife with his knowledge that she had driven one hundred miles to the nation's capital. While there she could have driven three miles to a Norfolk-bound steamer, but instead had chosen to make the long drive back to Blue Ridge Summit.[10]

Jaffé informed Margaret that her obsession with their child and the state of Christopher's health had atrophied their marriage and dehumanized him: "Since Christopher was born—and I say it, God knows, in no spirit of jealousy of my own child—I have been progressively relegated to a kind of helot's position—a person supposed to provide bread and meat and money, but otherwise with no particular rights that need to be respected. It began with my unceremonious ejection from the house when I was ailing with a cold and ended with a systematic ignoring of me as a man, as a husband, even as a social being entitled to a normal home." He believed it likely that Margaret held him entirely responsible for the condition of their marriage. If so, he told her, he had no hope that they could ever reconcile. He knew in his heart that he had acted as a "normal, well-intentioned husband and father, thwarted and embittered in all his efforts by an implacable irrationality." He no longer intended to struggle with her; the antagonism, he wrote, "has drained me and grayed my hair. But more important, it has worked a chemical change within me—within my innermost being." He continued poignantly, "Neither of us have too many years of life left. I do not propose to spend my remaining years apologizing to any living being for my blood or my child's blood, nor do I intend to spend them as a helot—an ass on a

9. Louis Jaffé to Margaret Jaffé, 1 November 1935, ibid.
10. Louis Jaffé to Margaret Jaffé, 8 November 1935, ibid.

treadmill—who can be deserted at will, who need not be consulted about anything, and who has no claim on anybody for home, companionship or social life."[11]

After visiting with Wheelwright in late November or early December, Jaffé reported to him that Mrs. Davis, expressing the belief that Margaret would return soon, had charged Jaffé with evading his responsibility in not providing for her. Although Mrs. Davis's shift of support must have demoralized him, he did "not blame her mother's heart for holding through thick and thin with her child." He confided to Wheelwright that he could not "continue this much longer without cracking up."[12]

Jaffé's grasp on his sanity must have been pushed to its limit on December 8, his fifteenth wedding anniversary, when his bitter struggle with Margaret threatened to assume a front-and-center position at the *Pilot*. Margaret's eccentricities, emotional outbursts at his office, and postcard-writing campaign had long generated newsroom gossip, which the intensely private Jaffé found mortifying. Throughout his ordeal, he must have felt grateful to Chambers, whom he could trust not to discuss the matter except possibly with Chambers's wife, Roberta (who had herself endured a painful previous marriage and would have empathized with Jaffé).[13]

On the morning of December 8, Margaret Davis, probably at her daughter's prompting, threatened to speak with Slover about Jaffé's refusal to finance his wife's absence. In a telephone conversation with her son-in-law, Mrs. Davis asked him if he would agree to a divorce. Jaffé replied that he would. She then asked him if he would relinquish all claim to Christopher. He rejected the idea out of hand but suggested that Margaret and he, with the help of their lawyers, could work out an arrangement for joint custody of their son. "That seemed to infuriate Mrs. Davis," Jaffé informed Wheelwright later that day. "She then said that if that is my attitude, she thinks she will go to see Colonel Slover. The implied threat here . . . is to blacken my character with the man who employs me in a position which requires above all that a man's ethics be above question. There seems to be

11. Ibid.

12. Louis Jaffé to Thomas Wheelwright, 5 December 1935, ibid.

13. Louis Jaffé Jr., interview by author, 7 February 1996; Mason, interview by author, 18 September 1995; Elisabeth Burgess, letter to author, 27 October 1992; Sally Abeles, letter to author, 24 November 1992; Leidholdt, *Standing Before the Shouting Mob*, 45–6.

a disposition between mother and daughter to force me to do something that no self-respecting man can do, or to destroy me. Can that be done in a civilized world?"[14]

Jaffé told Wheelwright that should Mrs. Davis meet with Slover, he would "have to tell him the whole story of [his] bitter tragedy." Although he had never discussed his personal affairs with Slover, he had to defend himself against "unjust accusations." Noting that Wheelwright had been familiar with the contretemps from its beginning, Jaffé asked the elder man to consider serving as a character witness for him. The editor referred to the letter that Hugh C. Davis had written to Wheelwright five years earlier, discussing Margaret's mental illness. "I don't want that letter ever to be known outside of those who know of it," Jaffé wrote, "but it is just possible, if I am forced to defend myself against the charge of inhuman treatment of my wife and child, that I would have to call upon a dead man in his grave to absolve me from that libel. Even then, I would not call upon this witness without your permission. . . . Should such an attack be made upon me, will you permit me to refer Col. Slover to you?"[15]

It seems probable that Wheelwright intervened to persuade his sister not to follow through with her threat. In the unlikely event Mrs. Davis ever confronted Slover—who surely had gotten wind of Jaffé's marital travails—her complaints undoubtedly would not have diminished the publisher's confidence in his nationally prominent editor. (Some indication of his trust in Jaffé and his desire to keep his star editor in his employ may be inferred from his loan of a sizable sum of money—apparently in the range of $30,000—to enable Jaffé to purchase stock in Norfolk Newspapers immediately following the merger of the *Virginian-Pilot* and the *Ledger Dispatch* in early 1933.)[16]

Margaret and Christopher returned to Norfolk for two weeks during the Christmas holiday but interacted minimally with Jaffé. Margaret also made it clear that she intended to alienate Christopher from him "as from something characterless and tainted," a program of subversion in

14. Louis Jaffé to Thomas Wheelwright, 8 December 1935, Louis Jaffé Jr.
15. Ibid.
16. Louis Jaffé to Samuel Slover, 1 March 1933, 2 July 1943, Jaffé Papers; Samuel Slover to Louis Jaffé, 1 July 1936, Jaffé Papers; Alice Jaffé to Louis Jaffé Jr., n.d., Louis Jaffé Jr.

which she had obviously engaged for many years. Jaffé wrote to her after her return to Blue Ridge Summit that he had given up his decade-long struggle to reconcile his self-respect with her conception of his "place in the domestic sphere." Upon her departure, she had told him that any "self-respecting man" would leave if he had been treated the way she had treated him. Jaffé informed her that he planned to do just that.[17]

Regardless of his threat, he stayed on, and the couple remained locked in their ravaged relationship throughout 1936. In October—after Margaret had spent ten of the previous seventeen months away with Christopher, ignoring Jaffé almost entirely during her infrequent sojourns at home except coldly to collect money to support her prolonged absences—Jaffé wrote her a four-page, single-spaced letter in which he raised again the issue of her anti-Semitism. Mrs. Davis had again told him that Margaret's animosity for him stemmed from what he described as "your inability to make your peace with the fact that I have Jewish blood in my veins . . . , a blood strain in me which you have come to regard as humiliating—something like a taint of syphilis." He continued,

> Why not face the fact this is the source of the difficulty and drop all pretense that the reason lies elsewhere? Let me then, for my part, make this statement. I am a man who has Jewish blood in his veins. That is known to *everybody* in Norfolk who has the slightest amount of curiosity about me. It is known to your best friends. I have made no concealment of it. Why should I? Even Christopher knows it, although by some inexplicable process of self-deception you seem to have arrived at the idea that by not mentioning it to Christopher you can conceal from him the fact that his father has Jewish blood and therefore he, too. The fearful tragedy of such a policy of self-deception and suppression of fact, is that while it can not hurt me—I am too old—it is virtually certain, if continued, to burden Christopher with a split and warring personality. How can he help looking with shame and self-pity on that ineradicable part of him which his own mother has subtly taught him to regard as humiliating? How can a child thus impregnated with self-depreca-

17. Louis Jaffé to Margaret Jaffé, 6 January 1936, Louis Jaffé Jr.

tion grow up as an integrated and self-reliant man? Don't turn aside from these questions, I beg of you.[18]

Jaffé presented a possible solution for their marital problems. She could quit the "futile and agonizing process of self-deception [and] recognize the Jewish question as just one of those things that exist in millions of families in this country and abroad that have been created by mixed marriages, and which makes no difference when it is not made the subject of poisonous concealment . . . [and] attempt a normal life again with all the facts faced honestly, with no fleeings to other parts of the United States to escape facts which cannot be escaped for they accompany one with the precision of a shadow cast by the sun." Such a course of action, he wrote, "would imply a normal relationship between you and me and a normal relationship between each of us and Christopher. No concealments. No false pretenses. A sympathetic camaraderie based on the assumption that all of us are decent and that all of our blood strains are decent, honorable and entitled to our own and the world's respect. No other kind of relationship is tolerable to me, for I intend neither to lie to my child about any part of my blood, nor to allow anybody to tell him that any part of his blood is less than honorable. That you may as well understand definitely."[19]

Should Margaret find herself unable to come to terms with his Jewish roots, Jaffé advocated a "clean and surgical" divorce. Although that would not protect Christopher from the psychological damage she would inflict on him by continuing to imprint on him the shameful nature of his ancestry, he declared, it would at least end their strife and allow them to get on with their lives.[20]

His candid analysis failed to sway Margaret, who stayed in Pennsylvania for much of the remainder of 1936 and returned home only for the Christmas holiday. She again left no doubt of her aversion to her husband and reiterated her intention to alienate their son from him. At long last, Jaffé gave up and notified her that he intended to move out at the beginning of the new year. He advised her that it would appear better for her if her lawyer took the initiative in arranging a separation agreement preliminary to

18. Louis Jaffé to Margaret Jaffé, 5 October 1936, ibid.
19. Ibid.
20. Ibid.

the actual divorce but that he would undertake the action if she preferred. He would take a few pieces of furniture and his books and move into a small apartment.[21]

Jaffé had labored mightily to hold his marriage together and fulfill his paternal responsibilities, but Margaret—her mental illness and blatant mistreatment of him notwithstanding—dealt from a position of power, leaving him few options. Her possession of Christopher proscribed a sustained severance of support. She had refused for many years to agree to a divorce, and any chance Jaffé had of convincing a court of her instability had evaporated several years earlier with Mr. Davis's death and Mrs. Davis's subsequent change of allegiance. Even if Jaffé had initiated formal divorce proceedings, a judge in that era would have granted Margaret custody of Christopher, barring proof of extraordinary maternal neglect. The best separation agreement Barron could broker gave Margaret custody of Christopher as long as they resided in Virginia, Washington, D.C., or Maryland, and she reared the boy in a "normal way." Jaffé could count on no support from his son; Margaret's influence had warped Christopher's view of his father.[22]

In the spring of 1936 Jaffé nearly left the *Pilot* to assume the editorship of the *Richmond Times-Dispatch* after its editor, Mark Ethridge, left for Louisville, where he would play a prominent role in building the *Courier-Journal* and the *Times* into nationally renowned papers. In his later career, Ethridge would place a premium on the skills editors like Jaffé brought to their newspapers. "I think there are good newspapers with poor editorial pages," he said, "but there is no great newspaper without a good editorial page." Jaffé found the proffered position appealing. He had cut his teeth on the *Times-Dispatch,* and he knew Richmond well. The editorship there would offer him a powerful platform in the state capital to influence policy and would afford him more direct access to the legislature and decision makers. Slover headed the paper and would not infringe on his editorial autonomy. He knew that Chambers—his obvious successor at the *Pilot*—deeply desired a promotion and would carry on the paper's liberal tradition.

21. Louis Jaffé to Margaret Jaffé, 21 December 1936, ibid.
22. Louis Jaffé/Margaret Jaffé separation agreement, [May? 1931], ibid.

And importantly, while the new position would remove him one hundred miles from Margaret, who would then reside in Norfolk, it would allow him to stay within easy visiting distance of Christopher.[23]

Only one matter troubled him. Simultaneously with the new editorial appointment, Slover intended to designate John Dana Wise as the *Times-Dispatch*'s publisher. Wise presently served as publisher of the *Columbia (S.C.) Record,* the *Augusta (Ga.) Chronicle,* and the *Spartanburg (S.C.) Herald-Journal* for representatives of the International Paper Company. Slover had promised Jaffé that he would have complete editorial authority and that Wise would have total responsibility for the business end of the paper. Jaffé had no doubts regarding the prospective publisher's administrative ability, but he had serious reservations regarding Wise's politics, racial outlook, and temperament, as well as the possibility that Wise would attempt to influence editorial policy.[24]

Before its purchase by International Paper, the *Record* under the editorial leadership of Charlton Wright had earned a reputation for its liberalism and independence. Jaffé had eulogized the paper in 1929 when its new ownership took over: "The most comfortable editorial path in the South, as elsewhere in the United States, is the path of unadventuring *laissez-faire.* The pressure on all sides is for conformity—toward an acceptance of what Is as Right, toward the uncritical testimonializing of the social, civic, industrial, and political environment. Mr. Wright was not one of the testimonial writers. On his editorial page one found a reasonable treatment of the solid affairs of business and industry, but also a forthright, critical and, at times, flaming treatment of the social and political obscenities that became the peculiar plague of the South with the rise of kluxery, Hefflinism, Bilboism and fiat theology." International Paper, interested in electrical power developments in South Carolina, had soon ended the *Record*'s editorial independence.[25]

Seeking to learn more about Wise, Jaffé wrote to an old friend from his days on the *Times-Dispatch,* University of South Carolina president J.

23. *New York Times,* 7 April 1981; Leidholdt, *Standing Before the Shouting Mob,* 24–5.

24. Johnson and Robb, *South and Its Newspapers,* 141–3; Dabney, *Across the Years,* 133.

25. Couch, *Culture in the South,* 133–4; *Pilot,* 18 May 1929.

Rion McKissick. Wise's "reputation as an alert, efficient, aggressive business man and newspaper publisher," McKissick reported, "is well deserved." But he also cautioned that Wise—a combative former boxing champion with a limited education—"is thoroughly conservative in his views and believes that the news and editorial departments should be subservient to the business interests of the paper." Wise had gone so far as to move his office into the *Record*'s editorial department to supervise its work. He had repeatedly expressed the sentiment that "nobody does anything without a selfish motive." McKissick warned Jaffé that his views would conflict strongly with Wise's: "From what I know of you and Wise, I believe that your social and intellectual outlook would differ widely from his."[26]

Jaffé turned the job down. Wise went to Richmond, where he promoted Virginius Dabney to editor and later became his nemesis. Wise orchestrated the merger of the *Times-Dispatch* and the *News Leader* in 1940, and in his capacity as vice president and general manager of Richmond Newspapers, used that organization to assail the Supreme Court's landmark 1954 *Brown v. Board* desegregation mandate. D. Tennant Bryan—who had inherited from his father, John Stewart Bryan, ownership of Richmond Newspapers but not his intellectual abilities or liberalism—fell under the sway of his dynamic hatchet man. After *News Leader* editor Douglas Southall Freeman retired in 1949, Wise replaced him with brash young James Jackson Kilpatrick.

Under Wise's tutelage Kilpatrick would earn the well-deserved reputation as massive resistance's foremost propagandist. In the explosive post-*Brown* years, Dabney, who had grown more conservative, acquiesced to what he later would protest was management's prerogative to set editorial policy. In the pages of the *Times-Dispatch* and in national news magazines, he insisted that racial justice could exist under a system of segregation, branded supporters of integration as irresponsible extremists, fanned the fear of "racial amalgamation," and expounded the racist arguments of northern segregationist writer Carleton Putnam. (Wise's death followed the pattern of his belligerent life; he shot himself to death in 1963.)[27]

26. Louis Jaffé to J. Rion McKissick, 6 April 1936, J. Rion McKissick to Louis Jaffé, 7 April 1936, both in Jaffé Papers; Dunford, *Richmond Times-Dispatch: The Story of a Newspaper*, 14, 322.

27. Leidholdt, "Virginius Dabney and Lenoir Chambers," 57–9; Dabney, *Across the Years*, 148, 232–3; Dunford, *Richmond Times-Dispatch: The Story of A Newspaper*, 14,

* * *

On the final day of 1936, certainly the bleakest year of Jaffé's life, he learned that Thomas Wheelwright had died. Jaffé had once described Wheelwright as the "patron saint of my postwar newspaper career," and Wheelwright's steadfast support of the editor in times of crisis had proved invaluable. "I went to him for counsel and I turned to him when I was sore in spirit," he wrote to Wheelwright's wife, Laura. "Never did I fail to find sympathy, understanding and encouragement." Wheelwright's death deprived Jaffé not only of a trusted confidante and mentor but of his last dependable support within Margaret's family. He must have suffered a sense of profound loss and aloneness.[28]

Although many in his small circle of close friends knew something of his marital problem and observed the toll it was taking on him, Jaffé tried mightily to conceal his pain. Eleanor King, who had grown close to him and gained entry to what he called "Norfolk's Little Group of Serious Thinkers," described him at this time as "secretive on principle," so much that he shut himself up "in a sort of shell." Even J. J. Lankes, who several years earlier had accepted a teaching post in New York State but returned during holidays to his home in Hilton Village, had been kept in the dark about the deterioration of Jaffé's marriage. "I am in a state of mental and spiritual distress and don't see daylight yet," Jaffé wrote in early 1937, finally informing Lankes of the breakup.[29]

As Jaffé ruminated over the circumstances that had combined to foment his private tragedy, he considered in exacting detail Hitler's persecution of German Jewry. With an insight informed by his sensitivity, European experi-

300–2, 321–2; Francis Pickens Miller, *Man from the Valley* (Chapel Hill: University of North Carolina Press, 1971), 172, 190–3; Egerton, *Speak Now Against the Day*, 254–6; Harry S. Ashmore, *Civil Rights and Wrongs: A Memoir of Race and Politics, 1944–1994* (New York: Pantheon, 1994), 62–3; Virginius Dabney, "Virginia's Peaceable, Honorable Stand," *Life*, 22 September 1958, 54–6; Virginius Dabney to Carleton Putnam, 22 July 1963, Dabney Papers; Carleton Putnam, *Race and Reason: A Yankee View* (Washington, D.C.: Public Affairs Press, 1961), 4–10.

28. Louis Jaffé to Thomas Wheelwright, 27 May 1929, Louis Jaffé to Laura Wheelwright, 31 December 1936, both in Jaffé Papers.

29. Eleanor King to Louis Jaffé, [October 1936], Louis Jaffé to Eleanor King, 15 October 1936, both ibid.; Taylor, *Robert Frost and J. J. Lankes*, 54, 70; J. J. Lankes to Sherwood Anderson, 21 August 1932, Anderson Papers; Sherwood Anderson, *The Sherwood*

ences, and fluency in German and French, Jaffé read a great deal and wrote with great frequency on the spread and growth of Nazism. Occasionally he confronted it personally.

When the French consul in Norfolk invited him in July 1936 to a dinner party that an ardent Nazi, a Fraulein Fortamann, would also attend, Jaffé felt obligated to mention that his antipathy for Hitler might make for some unpleasantness. "You are unaware perhaps, of a fact well known by most of my French friends that I have in my family tree . . . several living relatives who are Jews," he wrote in French. "From a Nazi perspective, this is a mortal stain, even for a Christian like myself. It's quite possible . . . that Fraulein Fortamann is such a maniacal Nazi that she would be embarrassed to find herself next to someone of such impure blood. Upon her return to Germany after such a nasty encounter she could be locked up in a concentration camp if this news got out to the Gestapo." Jaffé expressed in strong terms his hatred of Hitler and Nazi brutality. He would accept the dinner invitation happily, provided the consul understood that some tense moments might arise. "With this noted," he wrote, "I leave this diplomatic or should I say diabolical problem to you."[30]

Throughout the 1930s, Jaffé pounded Hitler in his editorials, broadcasting the torments suffered by Germany's Jews. In the final weeks of August 1935 he returned again and again to these subjects. "An Evening on the Kurfuerstendamm" deplored an anti-Jewish riot that reportedly had begun in Berlin's toniest theater, night club, and shopping district, when some viewers booed an anti-Semitic film. Storm troopers in and out of uniform had turned the area "into a hoodlum's paradise given over to the beating up of men and women, to the wrecking of restaurant interiors and to the messing up of the Kurfuerstendamm's proud pavements with non-Aryan blood." In "Repercussions of Overseas Agony," Jaffé obliquely raised for readers the specter of life in the United States under a Nazi-like regime in which "an American Fuehrer made use of the National Guard and the Ku Klux Klan to destroy the livelihoods of American minorities on the grounds of race, or to force millions of its people to abjure the religious forms in

Anderson Diaries, 1936–1941, ed. Hilbert H. Campbell (Athens: University of Georgia Press, 1987), 260; Louis Jaffé to J. J. Lankes, 12 January 1937, Jaffé Papers.

30. Louis Jaffé to Albert Olivier, 8 July 1936, Louis Jaffé Jr.

which they were brought up in favor of a State paganism conjured up by the Fuehrer's New Dealers." He warned, in "Reprieve from Terror," that a decision by Nazi leaders to soften their recently renewed vendetta against Jews amounted to a reprieve from Nazi persecution, not a discharge. "Only with the unhorsing of National Socialism or its radical redefinition," he declared, "will the terror that pursues the minority elements really be brought under check." Finally, in "The Flight From Hitler's Wrath," Jaffé urged the League of Nations to provide support to the private relief organizations swamped with Jewish refugees fleeing Germany.[31]

Jaffé reserved particular contempt for the Nazis' proclamation the next month of the Nuremberg laws, which forbade marriages and extramarital relations between Jews and Germans of Aryan descent and deprived Jews of German citizenship. Previous dictates had already excluded Jews from holding public office and from working in civil service, journalism, radio, farming, teaching, theater, motion pictures, and the stock exchange. He termed the laws "another turning of the screw on the rack of that medieval doctrine of racial nationalism," Nazism. "Nowhere else in all Christendom," he wrote, "not even in the countries where national totalitarianism is in other respects just as absolute, is the doctrine of the exclusive blood basis of nationality credited. But that means to the Nazis only that they alone have isolated the true secret of national salvation and that the remainder of the world is still in darkness. As long as that self assurance rules Germany's masters, the outlook for the victims of the medieval edicts issuing from it must remain desperate."[32]

Jaffé worried that his countrymen, casting about for explanations for the Great Depression and searching for simple solutions for their suffering, might fall prey to home-grown demagogues and xenophobes, many of whom scapegoated the usual suspects—including what he quoted French novelist Paul Morand as calling "that oldest of all foreigners, the Jew." The editor was justifiably worried. Throughout the 1930s a throng of prophets—ranging from the kindly but addlepated Francis ("Doc" or "Daddy") Townsend, unable to answer rudimentary questions about the workings of his old-age pension plan, to the menacing William Dudley Pelley, who

31. *Pilot*, 18, 20, 26, 31 July 1935.
32. Shirer, *Rise and Fall of the Third Reich*, 233; *Pilot*, 17 September 1935.

sought to become an "American Hitler" and modeled his Silver Shirt Legion on the Nazi SS—attracted millions of devotees. Huey Long proved to be the most gifted political organizer of these agitators, Father Charles Coughlin the most effective media propagandist, and the Reverend Gerald L. K. Smith the most spellbinding orator, stupefying even Mencken, a connoisseur of the noisy art.[33]

To Jaffé, the danger lay in the unpredictable nature of the disciples as much as in their leaders—in what he termed the "vulnerability of discouraged and hard-pressed people everywhere under the sun to the polemic onslaught of dynamic and half-mad Messiahs." The constituencies of many of the groups overlapped; should a fusion of these disaffected and wrought-up followers emerge, he warned, it might imperil the nation's democratic foundations.[34]

After Huey Long's assassination in 1935, Jaffé described his late regency over Louisiana's affairs as absolute to a degree rivaling that of the Mussolini and Hitler dictatorships. Long's reign had "been a tawdry compound of exploitation, rabble-rousing, panacea-peddling and political quackery." Jaffé conceded, however, that a fair appraisal of his legacy required cataloging his accomplishments: road building, support for education, reduction of illiteracy, implementation of a system of progressive taxation, and curbing the influence of powerful corporations. Jaffé perceived the Kingfish's political success as not having relied "wholly on selfishness, charlatanism and a phenomenal ability to mesmerize the public. . . . It rested also," the editor reflected, "on a passionate dedication to social justice— askew, superficial and unsound though much of his thinking on this subject was in the beginning and remained to the end—and on the conviction of the hill-billy masses over which he held sway that this dedication had borne fruit."[35]

In the spring and summer of 1935, newspapers across the country nearly every day augured the emergence of a new political party for the dis-

---

33. *Pilot*, 14 July 1935; Bennett, *Party of Fear*, 245–7; Alan Brinkley, *Voices of Protest: Huey Long, Father Coughlin, and the Great Depression* (New York: Vintage, 1983), 222–6, 275; Donald Warren, *Radio Priest: Charles Coughlin, the Father of Hate Radio* (New York: Free Press, 1996), 131; Mencken, *Thirty-Five Years of Newspaper Work*, 280–3.

34. *Pilot*, 11 September 1935.

35. Ibid.

contented. For advocates of a political upheaval, almost anything seemed possible. Roosevelt, stymied by the open warfare on his New Deal policies by what Drew Pearson and Robert Allen dubbed in their "Washington Merry-Go-Round" newspaper column the "nine old men" on the Supreme Court, appeared vulnerable. The overwhelming majority of the nation's newspapers opposed him, as did influential columnists Walter Lippmann, Dorothy Thompson, and Mark Sullivan. His campaign war chest for the upcoming election dipped perilously low. Former Democratic Party presidential candidates Al Smith and John Davis mocked his initiatives. The death of his closest friend, political guru Louis Howe, demoralized him and left him without an advisor with the courage to challenge his assumptions.[36]

Millionaire oilman and twice-elected Kansas governor Alf Landon, running as the Republican nominee on a platform of fiscal responsibility, promised to restore prosperity by way of free enterprise and the delegation of federal programs to state and local governments. His nondescript agenda, appearance, and personality made him the antithesis of Roosevelt.[37]

The nation's political climate grew volatile as the surviving kingpins of the "lunatic fringe"—Coughlin, Townsend, and Smith, who had attempted to position himself as Long's successor—circled each other and contemplated the transitory and dysfunctional marriage that would become the Union Party. They held their convention in Cleveland in the summer of 1936. Trying to top Smith, whom Mencken described as the "greatest rabble-rouser since Peter the Hermit," Coughlin peeled off his clerical collar and black coat and called Roosevelt a "great betrayer and liar." Jaffé described their convention as a "high mark in give 'em hell oratory."[38]

But the three messiahs linking arms on the convention rostrum proved themselves political bumblers when they nominated North Dakota congressman William Lemke, a stodgy rustic devoid of charisma. Worse, their convention came so late that Lemke failed to get on the ballot in fourteen states. To Jaffé, the Cleveland convention ended with a "curious anticlimax." Lemke had been completely upstaged; and, Jaffé opined, after

36. Brinkley, *Voices of Protest,* 241; Manchester, *Glory and the Dream,* 165–8; Davis, *FDR: The New Deal Years,* 311, 599–603.

37. Davis, *FDR: The New Deal Years,* 624–5.

38. Warren, *Radio Priest,* 89; Glen Jeansonne, *Gerald L. K. Smith: Minister of Hate* (New Haven: Yale University Press, 1988), 42–3, 52–4; *Pilot,* 21 July 1936.

Smith's and Coughlin's harangues, the crowd could not have worked itself up to a frenzy again if the Angel Gabriel himself had appeared. The unelectable Lemke was "plainly a sad substitute" to his patrons.[39]

The Union Party almost immediately self-destructed. Calling democracy a "lot of baloney," Smith defected and attempted to form a red-baiting "Committee of Ten Thousand," for which he envisioned backing by wealthy businessmen. In Jaffé's words, it combined the "best features of Nazism and the Ku Klux Klan." Townsend broke with Smith and withdrew his active support for the coalition. Coughlin drummed Smith out of the party and drained its finances on his own activities.[40]

As he had in 1932, Jaffé strongly supported Roosevelt. He had criticized a number of features of the president's first-term economic policies, such as the National Recovery Administration's "tendency to confer a government cachet upon a jungle of monopolies," but "checking accomplishments against failures," he recommended that the mandate of the Roosevelt administration be renewed. He dismissed "as preposterous all the Republican fear-bogies—that the Constitution is in danger, or that something dreadful is threatening 'the American way of life.'" Voters should understand the experimental nature of many of Roosevelt's policy initiatives and the inevitability that some of them would fail. The United States faced two supremely important challenges: the need for a "fairer, more enlightened and more responsible apportionment of the benefits and safeguards of our capitalistic economy [and a] new war threat engendered in the world by angrily antagonistic economic and social orders." Roosevelt, Jaffé insisted, offered by far the best leadership to solve these problems.[41]

The *Sunpapers,* with whose leadership Jaffé had for many years closely aligned himself, staked out an antithetical position. In an anxious war council, publisher Patterson dictated that his papers would speak with a concerted voice and oppose Roosevelt, whom they had endorsed in the previous election. Gerald Johnson made an understated but eloquent and reasoned argument in support of the president, but Patterson had made up

39. Manchester, *Glory and the Dream,* 140–1; Bennett, *Party of Fear,* 261; Warren, *Radio Priest,* 88; *Pilot,* 21 July 1936.

40. *Pilot,* 5 November 1936; Bennett, *Party of Fear,* 262–3; Warren, *Radio Priest,* 92–3; Jeansonne, *Gerald L. K. Smith,* 59, 61.

41. *Pilot,* 1 November 1936.

his mind. Johnson regretted the decision greatly, calling it late in his life the "most ghastly mistake" the *Sunpapers* had ever committed.[42]

Although Roosevelt obtained the support of only 37 percent of the nation's dailies in the 1936 election, most of the southern press endorsed him. The tremendous enthusiasm for the president among the South's rank and file—blacks and whites alike—and the "yellow-dog" Democrat sentiments of the region's publishers accounted for their nominal backing more than appreciation for the New Deal. Indeed, a large number of publishers directed that their papers subscribe to FDR-hating syndicated columnists. Like many of the region's newspaper owners, most southern political leaders—Virginia's in particular—endorsed the president although they could barely mask their antagonism for him. Jaffé's peers among liberal southern newspaper editors, however, genuinely supported Roosevelt.[43]

The president's overwhelming victory left only Maine and Vermont to Alf Landon. The Union Party claimed just 2 percent of the votes. Roosevelt had garnered the support of a patchwork of western and southern farmers, industrial workers, urbanites, and reform-minded intellectuals. Blacks had deserted the party of Lincoln and embraced the Democratic Party in record numbers. Jaffé wrote that the nation had given its chief executive a powerful mandate for "his doctrine of enlarged social responsibility."[44]

In the aftermath of the election, Jaffé breathed a sigh of relief over the Union Party's minuscule showing. He hoped that "one of the blessed gains" from Roosevelt's landslide reelection would be a "twilight period for such side-line hell-raisers as Father Coughlin, Daddy Townsend and the Rev. Gerald L. K. Smith, spiritual heir, at one or two removes, of the late Kingfish." He even believed it possible that dusk might "give way to an enshrouding night that will swallow up these prophets of cock-eyed systems of economic salvation for good." The president's victory had left them "at their microphones all dressed up and nowhere to go."[45]

42. Williams, *Baltimore Sun*, 241–2; Johnson et al., *Sunpapers of Baltimore*, 427–30.

43. Betty Houchin Winfield, *FDR and the News Media* (Urbana: University of Illinois Press, 1990), 127; Egerton, *Speak Now Against the Day*, 84–91, 137; Johnson and Robb, *South and Its Newspapers*, 184–5; Kneebone, *Southern Liberal Journalists*, 115–32.

44. *Pilot*, 4 November 1936.

45. Ibid., 5 November 1936.

Smith and Coughlin had passed their heyday, but they did not immediately fade into obscurity. Attracted to Detroit by Henry Ford's money, hatred of Jews, and union busting, Smith soon found a constituency there. The anti-Semitism he touted as divinely revealed grew more and more pronounced, until it assumed a dominant position in his Christian reactionary philosophy and earned him a dubious historical reputation as the nation's most successful anti-Jewish propagandist. Coughlin, who had promised to retire if Lemke lost, took only six weeks off and evolved into a mouthpiece for Nazism. With the support of Ford, Coughlin's private hatred of Jews became public. Like the automobile magnate and Smith, he reprinted and distributed the scurrilously anti-Semitic *Protocols of the Elders of Zion.* He termed the New Deal a "Jew Deal," and a faction of his supporters intimidated and roughed up pedestrians they perceived as Jewish-looking. In his publication *Social Justice* he reprinted Goebbels's speeches, and he became a sought-after speaker at German-American Bund meetings.[46]

In Jaffé's editorial career he had amassed a formidable record of battling nativist, red-baiting, racist, and anti-Semitic organizations indigenous to the United States, but in the Bund he confronted a conduit for a foreign cancer. Although its members professed to be good Americans, they were "at the same time industriously preaching anti-Semitism of the overseas Nazi order," he wrote. He traced for his readers the many similarities between the Bund and the Ku Klux Klan but underscored the First Amendment's protection of both organizations: "Drilling in dark uniforms is no more illegal than drilling in nightshirts. Greeting one another with the exclamation of 'Heil Hitler' is no more against our law than greeting one another with the secret passwords of native kluxery."[47]

Constitutional protections aside, he discerned in the Bund "bonds between some of their leaders and Berlin that need airing." He supported an ongoing probe of the organization by the Federal Bureau of Investigation and the convening of congressional hearings contingent on its findings. Beyond issues regarding the lawfulness of the Bund, he declared that "con-

46. Bennett, *Party of Fear,* 265–6; Jeansonne, *Gerald L. K. Smith,* 6, 8, 73–4, 105–14; Warren, *Radio Priest,* 132–60, 167–9.
47. *Pilot,* 11 September 1937.

cerning the perniciousness of the social and political poisons that the American-Nazi organizations are disseminating there is no question at all. What these organizations are doing is condemned by the principles of our democracy and destructive of the nation's peace."[48]

Like the Klan and the rest of its ilk, the Bund suffered from inept, egomaniacal, and less than circumspect leadership. Although married and the father of two children, Fritz Julius Kuhn, the jack-booted German army veteran who headed the organization, caroused in New York nightclubs with a bevy of girlfriends and later would receive a prison sentence for embezzling funds. But even if the Bund had boasted a preeminent field marshal, it could never have overcome the perception by most Americans that the league, with all its Nazi trappings, presented an alien and dangerous threat to democracy.[49]

Undoubtedly Jaffé cheered when Dorothy Thompson, an unimpeachable authority on Nazism, engaged in a form of highly personal journalism and belittled Bund leaders at a huge rally in Madison Square Garden. Dressed in an evening gown, she flashed her press pass and received a front-row seat. She then proceeded to interrupt and heckle speakers by laughing raucously throughout their speeches. As a squad of storm troopers hustled her out of the facility, she pronounced her judgment as to whether the Bund was, as its leaders claimed, an American patriotic organization and not a front for German Nazis. "Bunk, bunk, bunk!" she cried out. "*Mein Kampf,* word for word!"[50]

Antics like this, in addition to her unequivocal attacks on Hitler and American merchants of hate, provoked a whispering and letter-writing attack against Thompson. She would express to Jaffé her gratitude that in the wake of the criticism directed at her, he continued to feature her "On the Record" column on his editorial page. "I am assuming that you have been subjected to an organized barrage of letters fulminating against my column or in particular fulminating against me," she wrote. Many such letters, she informed him, accused her of being a communist or insinuated that either she or her husband, Sinclair Lewis, was Jewish.[51]

48. Ibid.
49. Bennett, *Party of Fear,* 248–9.
50. Kurth, *American Cassandra,* 287–9.
51. Dorothy Thompson to Louis Jaffé, 2 June 1939, Jaffé Papers.

She did not know how to respond to those who called her a Jew. "I don't consider it an insult to be called Jewish, but I am also perfectly well aware that if I protest that I am not Jewish my answer will be twisted around to mean that I consider Jewishness something shameful." Thompson believed that the letters were part of an organized campaign conducted against her by anti-Semitic organizations intending to undermine her credibility to speak out against Hitler's persecution of Jews.[52]

She had sent a similar if not identical missive to many editors of newspapers that carried her column. Jaffé, while obviously sensitive to the issues she raised and in accord with much of her editorial agenda, perceived her attempt to stake out the moral high ground as somewhat self-serving. He surmised that some of Thompson's motivation for sending the letters lay in the practical business of attracting and retaining subscribers. He had not yet seen evidence of the orchestrated campaign of hate mail that she reported.[53]

Jaffé may have had the opportunity to witness persecution of the Jews in central Europe firsthand. In the summer of 1937, dispirited and enervated by his long struggle with Margaret, he traveled to Europe with a friend, apparently Montgomery Osborne. The trip was "part of an escape idea—to find myself again," he wrote to Hamilton Owens in May of that year. Although he did not "approach it with a light heart," he said that he desperately needed a rest. During a *Sunpapers* party a few days earlier, he could not bring himself to tell Owens and his wife Olga about his separation from Margaret, but he now divulged that he had taken an apartment and that she and Christopher had moved back into the house.[54]

Although he traveled as a tourist, not as a journalist, he hoped to gain a better understanding of the European situation, which was growing more ominous daily. Writing to Assistant Secretary of State R. Walton Moore, a former Virginia congressman, Jaffé explained his intention to travel leisurely "through a few Central European countries in a Ford." He

52. Ibid.
53. Louis Jaffé to Alice Rice, 4 June 1939, Alice Rice to Louis Jaffé, June 1939, both Louis Jaffé Jr.
54. Louis Jaffé to Hamilton Owens, 12 May 1937, Jaffé Papers.

could speak French and German, he told Moore, and "to get some idea of what is stirring in those countries," he planned to interview a "few representative newspaper editors." He requested a letter of introduction written in English and translated into French and German.[55]

Jaffé sailed for Europe in early June and returned in late August. He sent no special dispatches to the *Virginian-Pilot* for publication, but some of the paper's editorials during this period featured a highly detailed analysis of central European affairs and probably were written by him. Although no account of his precise itinerary or his impressions during his trip has been uncovered, a few clues exist regarding his travels. Lankes received a postcard from Paris, and a telegram to the *Pilot* establishes that he visited Vienna and Budapest.[56]

He may have prearranged with Chambers a signal to confirm his safe transit through potentially hazardous areas. Using a Western Union traveler's telegraph code, he cabled from Vienna: "AB OZO FOURTEEN BUDA AMACO DOEKA NUXIL LOUIS." The decoded message reads: "Shall remain here until 14 and then go to Budapest. Hope you and your family are well. Inform friends of having heard NUXIL." Perhaps puzzled by the meaning of NUXIL, the Norfolk Western Union operator underlined it in both the coded message and his translation of it. (Dr. James A. Reeds, an authority on cryptography and telegraph codes, suggests that NUXIL may have been a "privately agreed on word, common newspaperman telegraphese or private slang.")[57]

As Jaffé traveled through Austria, Hungary, and possibly Germany, it would have been prudent for him to take precautions. His American passport notwithstanding, his surname might have elicited the close scrutiny of Nazi officials or sympathizers. He also had what one colleague and intimate believed that many people of the era regarded as a stereotypical Jewish appearance. Any conceivably non-Aryan physical feature or indication of refinement or intellect invited the attention of Fascist partisans. Had hostile

55. Louis Jaffé to R. Walton Moore, 22 May 1937, ibid.

56. See *Pilot,* 19 July 1937; Louis Jaffé to J. J. Lankes, [June/July 1937], Lankes Papers.

57. Louis Jaffé to Lenoir Chambers, 9 July 1937, Chambers Papers; *Western Union Traveler's Cable Code, Revised Edition* (n.p., n.d.); James A. Reeds, letters to author, 7 April 1999, 25 May 1999.

parties discovered his Jewish roots or learned of his long-running editorial campaign castigating Hitler, he could have found himself in menacing circumstances.[58]

At the time of Jaffé's visit, Europe hovered on the precipice of World War II. Just a year earlier, while France and Britain stood by fecklessly, Hitler had remilitarized the Rhineland, signaling to the eastern European nations that comprised *Mein Kampf*'s "living space" that German aggression would draw nothing but empty expressions of indignation from the great western European powers. The Spanish Civil War—the dress rehearsal for the impending world conflict—raged; with the help of German and Italian armaments and troops, Francisco Franco's Nationalists gained the upper hand. In the wake of the implementation of the Nuremberg laws, desperate Jews were attempting to flee Germany. Hitler was eyeing Austria and Czechoslovakia and finalizing plans for their imminent conquest. Throughout the year, in a precursor to the 1938 Anschluss, Austrian Nazi attacks, bombings, and street demonstrations were increasing in number and violence. In Hungary, Fascists were growing more powerful, and the government, hoping to expand its borders into Czechoslovakia, was establishing ever-closer ties to Germany. Jaffé traveled into this landscape with a prodigious curiosity, an avid interest in European geopolitics, compassion for human suffering, and more than a modicum of bravery.[59]

But if Jaffé saw similarities between the condition of Jews in Germany and that of blacks in the American South—and given the fact that the congruence between anti-Semitism and Jim Crow generated much discussion during the period, he must have reflected on it deeply—this perception still did not translate into a direct attack on racial segregation. Instead, like white liberal journalists throughout the region, he urged gradualism, a steady and concerted march toward racial progress within the context of separate but equal. He focused principally on attainable reforms for blacks in housing, employment, criminal justice, recreational facilities, and education. Although today such an approach seems anachronistic, Jaffé evaluated his

---

58. Dill, interview by author.

59. Jarman, *Rise and Fall of Nazi Germany*, 225–33; Spielvogel, *Hitler and Nazi Germany*, 198–205; Held, *Columbia History of Eastern Europe*, 182–4.

readers carefully and prodded them to the furthest reaches of their levels of tolerance and understanding. His editorial campaign to provide beach facilities for blacks and the NAACP's early attempts to secure equal educational opportunities for black students and equalize black and white teachers' salaries in Norfolk serve to delineate the boundaries of Jaffé's racial agenda in the immediate pre-war era.[60]

In 1936 the black Virginia State Teachers Association had begun contemplating legal action to challenge the state's dual salary scale for black and white teachers and raising funds to support litigants whom white school administrators might fire. The next year, in the wake of the NAACP's successful judicial efforts to equalize teachers' salaries in Montgomery County, Maryland, Thurgood Marshall expressed his intention to "get something started" in the Old Dominion. The NAACP had two objectives: to win a precedent-making decision and to galvanize recruiting efforts, particularly among teachers, who enjoyed elite status and exercised influence in the black community. After his success in Maryland, it seemed natural to Marshall to turn to Virginia; he had a strong network of colleagues in Washington, D.C., and believed he stood a better chance of earning favorable rulings in the less militantly racist Upper South.[61]

As the NAACP prepared its Virginia offensive in late 1938, it received a boost in morale when the Supreme Court, in *Gaines v. Missouri,* ordered that state either to enroll Lloyd Gaines in its university law school or to finance the development of a law program of comparable quality for blacks. The court determined that a state scholarship program that allowed Gaines to attend an integrated or black law school in another state would not afford him an equal educational opportunity. The decision set an important precedent; it required states maintaining segregated educational systems to integrate their graduate and professional programs or duplicate the facilities and instructional equipment and hire additional faculty, a high-priced if not prohibitively costly undertaking.[62]

Jaffé believed that a "strong argument of social expediency" could

60. Kneebone, *Southern Liberal Journalists,* 181–2.

61. Tushnet, *NAACP's Legal Strategy,* 60, 68, 77; Suggs, *P. B. Young, Newspaperman,* 160.

62. Tushnet, *NAACP's Legal Strategy,* 70–7.

be made against the Court's decision "but not . . . a good legal argument."
He previously had advised state leaders to establish and augment graduate
and professional programs at black Virginia State College—a policy backed
by numerous black leaders such as P. B. Young and Mordecai Johnson,
president of Howard University—but he conceded that the cost of replicat-
ing expensive courses of study such as medicine and dentistry might prove
preclusive. Some commentators and policy experts had urged that the
southern states develop regional centers for black graduate and professional
education, but Jaffé believed that the Supreme Court would regard them as
unconstitutional. A possible solution might lie in admitting blacks to select
programs at white institutions; Maryland had recently integrated its law
program. Nevertheless, Jaffé gauged public opinion south of that border
state as "not yet ready for such a step."[63]

P. B. Young initially served as a valuable ally to Marshall in Norfolk, and the NAACP's newly promoted chief legal counsel solicited the
publisher's help in the difficult job of securing plaintiffs. Eventually Aline
Black, a Booker T. Washington High School teacher with twelve years of
experience, stepped forward. Black could boast impressive qualifications,
including a graduate degree in chemistry from the University of Pennsylvania and course work toward her doctorate at New York University. She
involved herself in the case fully aware that white authorities might attempt
to retaliate. The Joint Committee on Equalization of Teachers' Salaries,
which the Virginia Conference of NAACP Branches and the Virginia State
Teachers Association had formed, backed her suit.[64]

In early March 1939 the Joint Committee filed in Norfolk Circuit
Court a petition for a peremptory writ of mandamus on Black's behalf to
compel the Norfolk school board to equalize white and black teachers' salaries. Marshall, Charles Houston (who had returned to private practice),
Howard University law professor Leon Ransom, and Richmond attorney J.
Thomas Hewin Jr. comprised Black's formidable legal team. No one could
dispute the fact that Norfolk paid black teachers substantially lower salaries

63. *Pilot*, 15 December 1938; Suggs, *P. B. Young, Newspaperman*, 164.
64. Aline Black press release, 17 June 1941, NAACP Papers; Tushnet, *NAACP's
Legal Strategy*, 78; *Guide*, 11 March 1939; Lyman Beecher Brooks, *Upward: A History of
Norfolk State University* (Washington, D.C.: Howard University Press, 1983), 36–7.

than it paid to equally qualified whites; even the white custodian at Booker T. Washington earned a higher salary than any black principal or teacher in the city.[65]

Jaffé understood well Black's motivation for bringing suit, and he attempted to defuse any hostility that whites might direct at her personally. "This is intended as a test case to obtain a judgment on an issue that has been agitating the Negro world for many years," he wrote. "The petitioner is not to be blamed for bringing it. It is human to resent economic discrimination not based on differences of qualification or responsibility. It is human to seek redress in the courts if such discrimination violates the law."[66]

But regardless of his defense of Black, his early editorial on the salary equalization case demonstrated the depth of Jim Crow's entrenchment in the South, even among liberal whites. Jaffé did not overtly denounce the practice of paying black teachers lower salaries. He perceived economic forces, supply and demand specifically, as lying at the core of the issue. Blaming the victim, he offered his assessment: "As long as qualified Negro teachers eagerly seek employment at the wages Southern school boards are willing to pay, the differential is likely to remain." He pointed out that no existing state law or city ordinance mandated discriminatory recompense and that the "whole South would be better off if Negro wages—public as well as private—were higher. It would result in a higher living standard all around, better health, less crime and better business. The effort must be toward that end." Incremental change, he wrote, not legal activism, offered the best solution to the South's racial problems. "The discrimination here complained of is rooted in a Southern economic and social system that can not be reformed overnight by a judicial finding."[67]

Norfolk's attorneys filed a demurrer and in the trial argued that the school board had the right to reach hiring and salary decisions without legal interference. No one had coerced Black to sign her salary-setting contract. "Take it or leave it," assistant city attorney Jonathan Old Jr. said with a rhetorical flourish. Marshall protested that this response placed his client in a catch-22 situation. She would not have legal standing if she did not enter

65. Lewis, *In Their Own Interests,* 156; *Guide,* 11 March 1939.
66. *Pilot,* 4 March 1939.
67. Ibid.

into a contract, but if she did so, she could not challenge her salary. He held that the city's undeniable right to determine teacher salaries did not allow it to violate the equal protection clause of the Fourteenth Amendment. Expressing his prescient belief that the case would ultimately be appealed to the U.S. Supreme Court, Judge Allan Hanckel ruled for the school board.[68]

Aline Black, who had listened to the proceedings with interest, learned within the week of her firing. Jaffé exploded: "The School Board may think it is equitable—this business of depriving a public employee of her bread because she invoked judicial process to obtain support for something to which the Board was opposed—but we don't." He termed the action "lamentable." Black collected a year's salary raised by the Virginia State Teachers Association and made plans to complete the residency requirement for her doctorate. Marshall pondered the sticky matter of engineering an appeal to the Virginia Supreme Court with a client of uncertain standing, and Norfolk's black community mounted a forceful protest.[69]

On June 25 hundreds of black Norfolk school students, led by a Boy Scout drum and bugle corps, marched through the center of the black district, beginning the largest mass racial demonstration in the city's recent history. Many children carried signs denouncing the firing. "Dictators—Hitler, Mussolini, and the School Board," "The School Board's Method of Dealing with Colored Teachers is Un-American," and "Qualify to Vote—The School Board Must Go," they read. Joining adults, the students filed into St. John's A.M.E. Church and filled it to the brim. P. B. Young, black and white religious leaders, the white secretary of the Norfolk Interracial Commission, and Jerry O. Gilliam, president of Norfolk's NAACP branch, all addressed the audience. Walter White and Thurgood Marshall also spoke. White made it clear that the NAACP had pushed its agenda well beyond "separate but equal." "Our goal is to smash every form of discrimination and separateness—no matter how long the battle," he declared.[70]

Jaffé implored the school board, whom he surmised had fired Black as a result of pressure exerted on it by state authorities, to reconsider its

<hr />

68. *Guide,* 3, 10 June 1939; Robert Mason, "Seeking to Undo Jim Crow," *Virginia Quarterly Review* 68, no. 2 (spring 1992): 385.

69. *Guide,* 10 June 1939; *Pilot,* 16 June 1939; Aline Black press release, 17 June 1941, NAACP Papers; Mason, "Seeking to Undo Jim Crow," 385–6.

70. *Guide,* 1 July 1939; *Pilot,* 27 June 1939.

action. He believed that Black's dismissal would do enormous harm to the city's racial climate: "The *Virginian-Pilot* hopes that the School Board will put an end to a group resentment that can do the city no good but which can do it a great deal of harm, by retiring from the business of pulling the State Education Board's chestnuts out of the fire, and returning to the business of dealing justly and magnanimously with a strictly local involvement."[71]

Jaffé's editorial prompted a response from Walter White. "OUR EARNEST THANKS FOR SUPERB EDITORIAL VIRGINIAN PILOT YESTERDAY ON TEACHING SALARY CASE," he cabled. "YOU HAVE TAKEN HIGHEST GROUND POSSIBLE HOPE NORFOLK SCHOOL BOARD WILL FOLLOW YOUR WISE ADVICE SO THAT ISSUE OF SALARY DIFFERENTIAL MAY BE SETTLED ON HIGH PLANE."[72]

In the wake of the fierce criticism directed at it, the school board wavered slightly; it issued a statement asserting that race had nothing to do with its decision and that it would consider rehiring Black upon the final resolution of her suit. Jaffé reminded his readers that when Norfolk firemen had undertaken legal action against the city over their right to unionize, authorities had not even threatened them with dismissal. "It has remained for the School Board to lay down the principle that a teacher's continuity of employment, regardless of his efficiency or previous tenure, depends on his refraining from testing his rights in a court of law," he wrote. "That, we think, is a thoroughly disquieting principle to be sponsored by the custodians of American education."[73]

In a move that demoralized Norfolk's black teachers, Marshall improvised a new strategy. He decided to drop Black's suit and pursue legal action with a new plaintiff in the federal courts. The black Norfolk Teachers Association (NTA) grew nervous and resentful; it had naively hoped for progress without personal risk. A fissure began to develop between the NAACP and accommodationist state and local black leaders.[74]

In September 1939 Marshall succeeded in enlisting Melvin Alston,

71. *Pilot,* 27 June 1939.
72. Walter White to Louis Jaffé, 28 June 1939, Jaffé Papers.
73. *Pilot,* 9, 13 July 1939; *Guide,* 15 July 1939.
74. Lewis, *In Their Own Interests,* 161; Tushnet, *NAACP's Legal Strategy,* 78–9; Robert Mason, letter to author, 24 August 1995.

another Booker T. Washington schoolteacher and the NTA's president, to serve as a plaintiff. Understandably anxious about the possibility of losing his comparatively well-paying position and being blacklisted in the midst of the Great Depression, Alston first secured a written promise that he would receive a thousand-dollar payment if the school board fired him.[75]

On February 12, 1940, U.S. District Court judge Luther B. Way issued a ruling virtually identical to that of the state court. In the *Virginian-Pilot*, Jaffé pointed out that the decision focused exclusively on the narrow matter of whether Alston had the right to raise the issue of unconstitutional discrimination after he had signed a contract, and that the courts had not yet ruled on the constitutionality of the practice of maintaining separate salary scales for black and white teachers. The NAACP, he stated, would without question continue its legal efforts.[76]

Marshall appealed, and the Fourth U.S. Circuit Court of Appeals assigned a three-judge panel—composed of John J. Parker of North Carolina, Armistead M. Dobie of Virginia, and Morris A. Soper of Maryland—to hear the case. Marshall and his legal team regarded Soper, a liberal on racial issues, as sympathetic, but they suspected the newly appointed Dobie, a native of Norfolk, and Parker of being unfriendly. In 1930 White and the NAACP had acquired a newspaper article reporting that Parker, running as the Republican candidate in North Carolina's gubernatorial election a decade earlier, had called black participation in politics a "source of evil and danger." White had skillfully used the clipping, which a young black man passing as white had purloined from the *Greensboro Daily News*'s offices, to help quash Parker's Supreme Court nomination.[77]

On June 18, 1940, Parker—who throughout his long career as a circuit court judge confounded predictions by compiling an impressive record of racial fairness—overturned Way's decision and remanded the case to his court for trial on its merits. He wrote that the school board's practice of paying blacks and whites different salaries was "as clear a discrimination

75. Lewis, *In Their Own Interests,* 161.
76. *Pilot,* 14 February 1940.
77. Lewis, *In Their Own Interests,* 162; Tushnet, *NAACP's Legal Strategy,* 59; Tindall, *Emergence of the New South,* 541–2; Kenneth Goings, *"The NAACP Comes of Age": The Defeat of Judge John J. Parker* (Bloomington: Indiana University Press, 1990), 24; *Greensboro (N.C.) Daily News,* 18, 19, 20 April 1930; White, *Man Called White,* 105–10.

on the ground of race as could well be imagined and [that it fell] squarely within the inhibition of both the due process clause and the equal protection clauses of the 14th Amendment." "Salary differentials based on color alone are on the way out," Jaffé wrote in response to this decision. "The governing authorities may as well realize that as inevitable and prepare for the new financial burdens it will impose." In late October the U.S. Supreme Court denied the school board's petition for a writ of certiorari. No other teachers' salary equalization case had yet risen to that level.[78]

Norfolk authorities who had adopted an obdurate position throughout the long struggle suddenly grew obliging and attempted to strike a bargain with the plaintiff's accommodationist and jittery allies. Exploiting the rift that divided the legal team and weak local branch of the NAACP from the conciliatory Young and conservative leadership of the black teachers, the city made overtures to the latter and portrayed itself as desirous of avoiding another district court trial. (A new trial would have postponed a settlement but inevitably have resulted in a judgment striking down Norfolk's dual-salary scale.) Jaffé applauded the city's new stance and urged compromise: "It would be the [better] part of wisdom . . . for the Norfolk authorities and the colored leaders of the salary-equalization effort to get together now on a practicable plan for settling this dispute without further litigation. . . . Both racial groups . . . will profit by a joint effort to reconcile the salary equalization burden with the city's financial position, and to effect the redressing not in a single oppressive act, but in several installments."[79]

Bypassing Marshall and his legal staff, a number of teachers' representatives, including Thomas Henderson, president of the Virginia State Teachers Association, and Booker T. Washington principal Winston Douglas, assembled in City Manager Charles B. Borland's office on November 4 to cut a deal. Young, who had no formal involvement in the case, attended the meeting at Borland's behest. Richmond attorney Oliver Hill, who had joined the NAACP's legal team on the case and tried mightily to preempt

78. Egerton, *Speak Now Against the Day,* 595; Wilkins, *Standing Fast,* 195; White, *Man Called White,* 114; *Alston v. School Board of City of Norfolk,* 112 F.2d 992 (1940); *Pilot,* 22 June 1940; *School Board of the City of Norfolk v. Melvin O. Alston,* 311 US 693 (1940); Williams, *Thurgood Marshall: American Revolutionary,* 91.

79. *Guide,* 2 November 1940; *Pilot,* 29 October 1940.

the meeting, later observed acidly to Marshall that "with upraised umbrellas the dear brethren sidled into the conference." Young, who hoped to secure a new black elementary school from the city, expressed his view that the school board should provide black teachers collectively with a series of annual raises of no less than $25,000 toward an eventual $129,000 settlement. Two days later Norfolk's city attorney proffered Marshall a first-year aggregate payment of $30,000 and full equalization of salaries over the following two years.[80]

Marshall, who had praised Young for his editorials and "splendid cooperation" in the case, had leaked information to him, and had withheld press releases from white newspapers until the *Journal and Guide*'s publication deadline, blew up over the publisher's "backdoor" tactics. The two black leaders had a series of angry confrontations, including one in which Marshall called Young a "liar." In his excellent biography of Young, Henry Lewis Suggs quoted an observer's recollection that the "NAACP met with the judge during the day, and Mr. P. B. met with the white folks at night, unraveled the agreement, and rewrote it to his own satisfaction."[81]

At a meeting in early November, members of the NTA unanimously agreed to settle the case out of court and ask for three yearly installments of $43,000 but to accept the city's offer if necessary. Marshall, who attended the meeting, called the decision the "most disgraceful termination of any case involving Negroes in recent years." He later informed Black that the "teachers have placed their heads in the lion's mouth and then proceeded to tickle the lion." The NAACP's leadership considered abandoning altogether their efforts to equalize teachers' salaries in Virginia. In February 1941, however, the NTA voted overwhelmingly to accept a consent decree that Marshall endorsed.[82]

The long court battle and the rancorous settlement process created

80. *Guide*, 16 November 1940; Oliver Hill to Thurgood Marshall, 6 November 1940, NAACP Papers; Alfred Anderson to Thurgood Marshall, 6 November 1940, NAACP Papers.

81. Suggs, *P. B. Young, Newspaperman*, 161–2.

82. *Guide*, 16 November 1940; Suggs, *P. B. Young, Newspaperman*, 162; Thurgood Marshall to Aline Black, 18 December 1941, NAACP Papers; Tushnet, *NAACP's Legal Strategy*, 80; Jerry O. Gilliam to Walter White, 8 March 1941, NAACP Papers; *Alston v. School Board of City of Norfolk*, consent decree (1941), NAACP Papers.

hard feelings and bruised egos that would linger for many years in Norfolk's black community. Fewer than seventy of the city's 240 black school teachers and principals attended a gathering in tribute to Black and Alston later that month. When White—suffering from a bad cold but with his healthy ego presumably intact—flew in through a snowstorm to represent the NAACP's national office, no one bothered to meet him at the airport, and he learned that a number of teachers opposed his presence at the affair.[83]

The denouement of Norfolk's salary-equalization dispute proved to be mixed. The city abided by the consent decree, and Black regained her job. But five years later, Young, who also had placed his head in the lion's mouth, would bemoan the fact that his school had not materialized.[84]

In the latter years of the decade, Jaffé, like nearly all his journalistic peers, remained focused most closely on the impending world conflict. He watched in horror as Europe quick-marched to war. He called Anschluss the "rape of Austria" and regarded the "ill-smelling peace" that emerged from the 1938 Munich conference with deep suspicion. By the time of Kristallnacht, British prime minister Neville Chamberlain's "peace in our time" had become in Jaffé's view "beastliness in our time." He compared Hitler's persecution of the Jews to the Russian pogroms and declared that the Nazis had committed "civilization's worst infamy." He dismissed far-fetched schemes to settle Jewish refugees in British Guiana and Tanganyika and implored the "civilized world" to offer sanctuary to a comparative "mere handful of people, all of them hard-working, industrious and prepared to enrich the nations that offer them hospice."[85]

When Hitler's troops marched into the divided Czechoslovakia, Jaffé warned that Romania, Hungary, and Poland would likely fall next. "It is just possible that Hitler's appetite will so expand after Czecho-Slovakia has been cut to pieces, cooked and digested," Jaffé wrote, "that he will at last bite off more than he can chew." He astutely predicted that in the end there would be the "Russian bear to deal with."[86]

83. Melvin O. Alston to Walter White, 16 March 1941, Walter White to Jerry Gilliam, 5 March 1941, Walter White to Melvin O. Alston, 3 March 1941, all in NAACP Papers.

84. Mason, "Seeking to Undo Jim Crow," 387.

85. *Pilot*, 12 March 1938, 30 September 1938, 15, 20, 13, 22 November 1938.

86. Ibid., 15 March 1939.

Well before Germany invaded Poland in early September 1939 and England and France belatedly declared war, Jaffé and Chambers buckled up for a long haul and intensified their vigil. As Jaffé strove also not to short-change Norfolk's black community, he confronted an agonizing problem in his private life. Under Margaret's manipulation, his relationship with his son, Christopher, was disintegrating, and he struggled to try to restore it.

14 A Light in the Tunnel

Jaffé had had so little contact with his son throughout the 1930s that as Christopher approached manhood late in the decade, the two were virtual strangers to each other. Margaret had preempted nearly all interaction between them and censored news about the boy to such a degree that Jaffé lacked even rudimentary knowledge regarding his son's upbringing and activities. He hoped that as Christopher began to escape his mother's influence, he might assess his relationship with his father independently. Jaffé knew that Margaret had damaged—perhaps irrevocably—his chances of rebuilding his relationship with Christopher, but he held out hope that with sensitivity and patience he might eventually become a part of his son's life.

Having long since given up on reconciliation with Margaret, Jaffé began a relationship in the summer of 1938 with Alice Cohn Rice, who edited the *Tidewater Arts Review* for the Norfolk Museum of Arts and Sciences. Alice had moved with her parents to Virginia Beach a few years earlier when her father, Colonel Henry Lawson Rice, retired from the Army. The Rices had built a home in Virginia Beach, then a quaint oceanfront village several miles away from Norfolk, and Montgomery Osborne took Jaffé there to meet Colonel Rice. After being introduced to Alice, Jaffé became a frequent visitor to the Rice residence. Over the course of a year, his relationship with her would grow from friendship into a love affair.

At the outset of the acquaintance, Alice was thirty-three years old. As a girl she had traveled widely throughout the United States when her father accepted engineering and management positions with a range of public utilities companies and later when he received postings to various military institutions. After completing four years at Holton Arms, a progressive private school for girls in Washington, D.C., she had graduated from Vassar

College in 1927 with a major in English literature and a serious interest in art history. She had visited Europe in 1927 and again in 1930.[1]

Although Alice did not flaunt her upbringing and academic achievements, her close friend, Sally Abeles, described her as "highly intelligent . . . and top-drawer socially." Virginia MacKethan, who knew Alice at Vassar, remembered, "You couldn't talk to her about any subject with which she wasn't familiar. She was extremely broad-minded, deeply informed." Abeles and MacKethan recalled her as attractive but not beautiful. Although Alice had had several beaux, she had never married and may have believed that she never would.[2]

Jaffé and Alice were well matched. Their interests in art, poetry, and literature brought them together, and he soon discovered that while she had a mind of her own, she shared many of his liberal views. Largely as a result of her involvement with him, she grew increasingly sensitive to the baneful effects of Jim Crow laws, which eroded blacks' dignity and limited their social and intellectual options. Without question Alice began to exert an influence on Jaffé, too. Robert Mason observed that Jaffé "profited from Alice's intelligence and ideas." But Mason emphasized that Jaffé "had long since set his [editorial] course [and] neither she nor anyone else could have steered his thinking."[3]

Alice and her parents belonged to the Episcopal Church, but her maternal grandfather, Rudolph Cohn, had practiced Judaism before converting to Presbyterianism when he emigrated from Austria to the United States as a young man. The Rices had a number of Jewish relatives still living in central Europe.[4]

Jaffé's marriage to Margaret had effectively ended a decade earlier, and his divorce would become final within the year. Nevertheless he conducted a decorous and deliberate courtship with Alice. More than fifteen years separated their ages, and many people of that era viewed divorce as

1. Jaffé family tree, Louis Jaffé Jr.; Louis Jaffé Jr., interview by author, 7 February 1996.

2. Louis Jaffé Jr., interview by author, 7 February 1996; Sally Abeles, letter to author, 21 September 1995; *Pilot*, December 1993.

3. Louis Jaffé Jr., letter to author, 7 June 2000; Robert Mason, letter to author, 12 June 2000.

4. Jaffé family tree, Louis Jaffé Jr.

scandalous. Perhaps he believed that these factors might cause her parents concern. Also, Margaret's anti-Semitism had disillusioned him and put him on guard. Accorded the respect of his journalistic colleagues and of Virginia's political leaders despite political differences, he nevertheless had found it impossible to overcome Margaret's intractable prejudice against his Jewish roots. He realized that Alice's attenuated connection to Judaism had not subjected her to a fraction of the discrimination he had suffered, and he wondered whether she fully grasped the subtle but painful harassment she might confront if they married. Her family's social status had shielded her from unpleasantness in general; did she have the courage and resolve to withstand the difficulties they might face? Did she understand that in the uncertain times in which they lived, she could encounter a fate much worse than snubs and slights? Irrespective of his conversion to Christianity, his ethnicity would mark them for a perilous fate if the world turned upside down and they fell into the hands of Hitlerists or their American disciples.[5]

Jaffé had felt an attraction to Alice soon after their introduction, but he had had little hope that their relationship would blossom until in late 1938 the Rices consulted him about the plight of their Jewish relatives in Czechoslovakia. Betrayed by Western appeasement, the Czech government had ceded the Sudetenland to the Nazis a few months earlier, and by March 1939 Germany occupied the entire nation. Jaffé briefed the Rices on the ominous situation in central Europe, and they attempted through their contacts within the government to secure passports.[6]

In all likelihood Alice's Jewish cousins in Prague did not live to see their country's liberation. Only 35,000 of Czechoslovakia's 190,000 Jews survived the Holocaust. The outrage and anguish that Alice felt in 1939 regarding her relatives' desperate condition signaled to Jaffé that she might after all comprehend some of what had scarred him, and that despite the tenuousness of her ties to Judaism, she also had felt the sting of anti-Semitism.[7]

*   *   *

5. Louis Jaffé to Alice Rice, 23 August 1939, Louis Jaffé Jr.
6. Ibid.; Alice Rice to Louis Jaffé, December 1938, ibid.
7. Spielvogel, *Hitler and Nazi Germany,* 291; Louis Jaffé to Alice Rice, 23 August 1939, Louis Jaffé Jr.

As the 1938–1939 winter holidays approached, Jaffé wrote to his sixteen-year-old son in Washington, D.C., where he and his mother had moved after having lived briefly in their Norfolk home. Jaffé asked Christopher what he would like for a Christmas present. A previous letter Jaffé had written asking him about his life and progress in school had elicited just a postcard. "You are a very bad letter-writer, my son," Jaffé wrote. "I want to know about you—what you are doing, how you are getting along in school—indeed, what school you are going to. Is that too much to ask? See if you can't do better by your old dad. You must know that means a whole lot in my bare life." Jaffé asked Christopher if he planned to come to Norfolk for the holidays. "I want very much to see you. It has been such a long time."[8]

The tempting opportunity to suggest a gift prompted a response, albeit in a decidedly cool tenor. Unwilling to call Jaffé "Father," Christopher began his letter with an impersonal "Hello." He told Jaffé that he attended "Friends." (Sidwell Friends School was an elite college-preparatory Quaker school, where many capital notables such as multimillionaire financier and *Washington Post* publisher Eugene Meyer educated their children.) He hoped that Jaffé would buy him a Hallicrafters Skyrider Diversity short-wave receiver. The radio cost between $425 and $550, about the price of an automobile—half a year's salary for many workers at that time. Christopher planned to be in Norfolk for several days in late December and said that he would visit then. Avoiding any term of endearment, he signed his letter "Merry Christmas, C."[9]

Christopher's tone must have disappointed Jaffé, but he continued to try to win his son's affection. He investigated the costly radio and, after having determined that he could not afford to purchase it outright, arranged to pay for it on credit. He sent Christopher a check for one hundred dollars and asked to be billed by the distributor for the balance. In Christopher's previous letter, he had sent a sketch he had written for one of his classes, and Jaffé complimented him on it, expressing the hope that he might keep it and that the boy would send him other samples of his writing. He

8. Louis Jaffé to Christopher Jaffé, 30 November 1938, Louis Jaffé Jr.

9. "Sidwell Friends" [cited 1 July 1999], available from http://www.sidwell.edu/admissions/first_look.html; "Hallicrafters Skyrider Diversity" [cited 1 July 1999], available from http://ww1.photomicrographics.com/webpages2/pmi/dd1/default.htm; Christopher Jaffé to Louis Jaffé, 5 December 1938, Louis Jaffé Jr.

requested a brochure from Sidwell Friends so that he could learn more about the school. Then he turned to the manner in which Christopher had begun his letter: "One more thing, Son—please don't just address me as Hello. That really isn't my name. You mean very much more than Hello to me." Christopher should telephone him the moment he returned to Norfolk, Jaffé wrote, and make plans to stay with him if at all possible.[10]

"Greetings, Your letter just received," Christopher replied. "Thank you very much for the check. Had I known that you were not able to get me the . . . receiver I certainly would not have asked for it." He suggested that his father not buy the radio on time; he would wait until he received the balance from him and buy it then. "The set won't exactly be a Christmas present but it will be appreciated just the same," he wrote. He planned to be in Norfolk for just a few days and would not have time to stay with Jaffé.[11]

This letter established the pattern of subsequent ones Christopher would write, in which he would wangle large sums of money or expensive gifts from his father. Margaret had not only indulged the boy completely; she had imparted to him the belief that he could treat Jaffé as she had. The selfishness Christopher displayed in his early letters could perhaps be excused by his youth, but as he grew older, he became by his own description "mercenary" in his insistent requests.[12]

In May 1939, as Jaffé's divorce became final, Christopher wrote again. The letter started abruptly, without a salutation and with no reference to his father. Margaret had just bought him a new Buick. The car had "cost quite a bit," and in an uncharacteristic act of economy, she had refused to pay for the special lights, radio, and exhaust system that Christopher wanted. He hoped that his father would send him one hundred dollars for accessories. Jaffé sent half that and promised to send more the next month. He again asked that Christopher begin his letters with a personal greeting to him: "I would like to have the letters addressed to Dad . . . or something, instead of to Blank. It makes me feel so dispensable and nobody-

10. Louis Jaffé to Christopher Jaffé, 9 December 1938, Louis Jaffé Jr.; Katharine Graham, *Personal History* (New York: Vintage, 1998), 41–2.

11. Christopher Jaffé to Louis Jaffé, 11 December 1938, Louis Jaffé Jr.

12. Christopher Jaffé to Louis Jaffé, 23 May 1939, ibid.

ish. After all, Kit—." He wanted to see Christopher as soon as he arrived in Norfolk that summer.[13]

In late June, Christopher wrote to request a birthday present—a $480 radio transmitter. In the fall he informed his father that the new equipment required additional components: "I need . . . to buy tubes and other incidentals for the transmitter you gave me for my birthday (expensive me)." He asked for a ninety-four-dollar check. In December he sent Jaffé an itemized Christmas wish list for an antenna system and other radio devices totaling just over $326.[14]

Margaret moved back to Norfolk, and Christopher spent at least part of the 1939–1940 school year attending Maury High School. Jaffé had moved into a small apartment in an elderly widow's home, about a mile from his old home. When the widow died, Jaffé purchased the house, which he called "as uninviting externally as an old shoe, but extremely comfortable." He soldiered on with his editorial responsibilities, but he informed Lankes that he experienced a "goshawful feeling of futility at the end of the day when I begin thinking about what is the purpose of all this sweating. To what end?" he asked.[15]

Thankfully his relationship with Alice, which by the summer of 1939 had grown into a romance, provided him with the first real happiness he had known in many years. It also generated additional stress. Alice had at last told him of her love, and he had kissed her. "The three tiny, so important words slipped out to you as naturally as if I'd said 'I'm sleepy' or 'I'm cold,'" she wrote to him. Although their feelings were now in the open, their new relationship put them both in a state of agitated confusion.[16]

"I ask myself what does this mean?" he wrote back. "There is deep inside me so much piled up winter Alice, my dear, that it *seems* the sun can never never reach it. Or is it my fifty-one gray years and their late bitterness? I have asked myself a hundred times and am just where I started. Maybe

13. Ibid.; Louis Jaffé to Christopher Jaffé, 4 June 1939, ibid.

14. Christopher Jaffé to Louis Jaffé, 26 June 1939, 2 November 1939, December 1939, ibid.

15. *Pilot,* 23 November 1938, 10 May 1940; Louis Jaffé to Hamilton Owens, 18 January 1938, Jaffé Papers; *Norfolk Telephone Directory,* Chesapeake and Potomac Telephone Co., 1939–40; Louis Jaffé to J. J. Lankes, 30 July 1938, Jaffé Papers.

16. Alice Rice to Louis Jaffé, [July/August 1939], Louis Jaffé Jr.

you have too. And yet I turn to the sun—hoping that something will sweep over me and make me certain and make you certain too. . . . This isn't at all the kind of letter that the Goose [one of Jaffé's pet names for Alice in addition to Gooseberry, Gosseberry, and Gosse], who calls me dearest deserves. How long has it been since I have been called that! But it is the only one I can write today and be honest. To pretend in a thing like this would be horrible. There are not enough years left to me to mistake again something that vanishes for the thing that stays. So please understand and help!"[17]

In late August Jaffé sent Alice the first of a series of letters in which he laid bare for the first time to anyone the struggle he had faced over his Jewish roots. He called the letters "De Profundis" ("Out of the Depths"), after the Latin title of the 130th Psalm. Germany had signed a non-aggression pact with the Soviet Union that very day; in a little over a week World War II would begin. The imminent cataclysm had made him return to the newspaper after work to read the cables, and he composed the letter in his office late that evening. "Tonight I am obsessed with a feeling of impending catastrophe in Europe," he wrote. "Not that a poor scrivener in Norfolk can do anything about it, but here I am. For that matter, our own problem—yours and mine—may before long shrink in the presence of something truly catastrophic, the end of which no living person can foresee. But tonight our problem is very near to me and so I begin. Just before we parted Sunday night you asked: 'Do you want me to love you? Do you want me to call you dearest?' And I said 'Yes.' But there was an unspoken reservation. Perhaps you knew it. This is the reservation: Yes, I want you to—ever so much—but only if you still want to after reading De Profundis."[18]

He revealed that he had begun to feel a fondness for her when she first came to talk to him about the dangers her Jewish cousins in Czechoslovakia faced. "Something deep in me told me that you might have the secret of bringing me release from a subtle tension with which I have struggled most of my adult life. This sounds selfish and self-centered, but it isn't really," he wrote.

> Oh I wish I could go on from this point in simple, one-syllable words. That is the way one should tell what is in one's heart to the

17. Louis Jaffé to Alice Rice, [July/August 1939], ibid.
18. Louis Jaffé to Alice Rice, 23 August 1939, ibid.

woman—for once I shall not call you Gosse—to whom it seems so worth telling, but it just can't be said that way for a damaged soul is a clinical case and I am that kind of soul and that kind of case. As I look back upon my years in review, I see the havoc wrought inside me by the passionate non-conformism which drove me from a judaistic frame whose conventions and tabus appalled me, to an irrevocable identification with a Christian ethic which satisfied my social and philosophic predilections, but which has left me particularly rootless—dogged by an introspective apartness (undoubtedly the atavistic compulsion of my mixed Jewish bloodstream) which can only be described by long hateful psychological words if it is to make any sense. [Jaffé's choice of the descriptor "mixed" perhaps referred to his separation from his religious heritage; he had no known Gentile ancestry. Or perhaps he alluded to suspected dilution of Jewish blood in his ancestral eastern Europe.]

Maybe this is all strange and forbidding to you. That would not surprise me. After all you are much further removed from this psychological dualism than I am—much more diluted into conformity perhaps. Yet it has seemed to me in brief exciting moments that you have gone through life with a little cross, have suffered a little Calvary of your own.

. . . All this it seems necessary for me to tell you, dear Girl, because you must know before you allow yourself to love me too much and before you allow me to love you too much, that life— surely through no one's fault but my own—has wounded me; that to be safe in the arms of Jesus does not mean being safe in the arms of his followers in name but not in love; and that dark and pervasive forces are at work in today's world that make it less safe than ever. How brave are you my love? Once when I came back from France, and held life in my hand like a cup, I dreamed that love could conquer all. I no longer believe it. I found that the world slays the love that seeks, unsupported by something with tougher fibre, to ignore its totems. Something more—something spiritually adventuresome and tough is needed in addition.[19]

19. Ibid.

Jaffé's heartfelt divulgence did not frighten Alice away. Instead, she sent him a photograph of herself. "Look well at this face & say where it could be at home if not in Zion," she wrote. She asked him if he could see any resemblance to her Protestant ancestors, who included New England preachers and Maryland farmers. She could not. When she viewed the picture and looked at her "curly mouth & droopy eyes and wide cheekbones," she said, "I see all the generations of Judaism behind my Bohemian grandfather." Alice believed they had to "speak and write of these things in order to come at last to the ultimate truth of each other." Clearly she did not flinch from self-scrutiny as Margaret had.[20]

The early Nazi successes in the war haunted Jaffé, and he focused on them obsessively. He regretted bitterly his powerlessness to take direct action against Hitler. "Your job is otherwise," Alice wrote, trying to comfort him, "and you're doing a swell one, darling, however impossible at times it must seem to you to bring something clear & level out of the emotions and anguish of the hour. And the pen is at least as mighty as the sword! All the same, you can't take the whole war on your back."[21]

Despite the many public obligations he incurred as an editor, Jaffé had grown reclusive in his personal life and wary of involvement in potentially hurtful social situations. He displayed little of the sociability and gregariousness that had marked him as a student at Trinity. He shared few if any details of his personal life; even close colleagues like Alonzo Dill knew little about him. When in late 1939 Alice invited him to dinner with a married couple with whom she was friendly, Jaffé requested that they be allowed to meet him informally before deciding whether they wished to spend the evening with him: "I *do* have some—no, a *great deal* of— hesitancy in accepting a dinner invitation from people who have never seen me, even though it is transmitted through the Gosse. Since they will be here some time, I would much prefer—if you sympathize with my prejudices in these matters—to meet them at your house and let them decide for themselves later if they want me for dinner. It is one of my peculiarities which you must try to understand."[22]

20. Alice Rice to Louis Jaffé, [August 1939], ibid.
21. Alice Rice to Louis Jaffé, [September 1939], ibid.
22. Dill, "Glimpse of Parnassus," 2; Louis Jaffé to Alice Rice, 10 January 1940, Louis Jaffé Jr.

His reclusiveness to the contrary, he interacted warmly among his intimates. Robert Mason recalled that Jaffé frequently joined his *Pilot* colleagues for after-work refreshments at Freddie Chinchilla's "blind pig," the Jefferson Ward Democratic Club, which in the 1940s operated across the street from the newspaper building. Although Virginia had outlawed liquor by the drink, Freddie, a "minor racketeer," kept a full-service bar. Mason wrote, "If Freddie anticipated the newspaper trade, he was not disappointed. . . . Jaffé . . . soon joined us, somewhat to our surprise but also to our delight."[23]

The divorce settlement between Jaffé and Margaret had specified that whenever Christopher was in Norfolk, he would visit his father. Jaffé had expressed to Margaret his hope that their post-divorce relations would be as amicable as possible, but she did her best to shut off his access to their son. She withheld her telephone number from Jaffé and through her attorney forbade him to enter her home. Only by writing to Christopher could he make arrangements for the two of them to meet. In spite of Margaret's restrictions, father and son spent occasional evenings together in early 1940, and Jaffé believed that he had begun to make inroads into building a relationship with Christopher. In the spring, however, his many letters to his son began to go unanswered.[24]

His failure to make headway with Christopher and the dismal news from the European front in May 1940 depressed him thoroughly. An article on the war in the *New York Tribune* written by French author and patriot Eve Denise Curie had brought tears to his eyes. As the Nazi army sliced effortlessly through the Netherlands, Belgium, and his beloved France, and British troops fell back to Dunkirk, he wrote to Alice: "I have quit trying to understand the fearful thing the war is doing to my spirit. . . . Something irreplaceably beautiful and precious seems to be perishing before my eyes. Can a just Omnipotence permit such a thing to come to pass?" He wrote in French, "I hold you and kiss you," and signed the letter.[25]

Two weeks later he sent Alice a second installment of "De Profun-

23. Dill, interview by author, 20 November 1992; Robert Mason, letter to author, 20 November 1992.

24. Louis Jaffé to Margaret Davis, 20 August 1940, Gardner L. Boothe to James Barron, 5 September 1940, both Louis Jaffé Jr.

25. Louis Jaffé to Alice Rice, 24 May 1940, ibid.

dis" and enclosed for her the letter he had written to the French consul four years earlier regarding his Jewish ancestry. He considered it to be a "part of De Profundis—the racial-cultural conflict" with which he had lived all his life. The clash, he wrote, "for reasons that run deeper even than Mendelianism, is the inescapable cross that all must carry—at least in the first generation—whose loves or compulsions drive them out of their ancestral grooves. In my early innocence, I dreamed that I could find peace that way. I know better now. It has not embittered me, but it has caused me to look the thing squarely in the face and adjust my philosophy to it."[26]

Thanks to Alice, he had at long last found a measure of serenity and begun to heal, but he feared that their relationship might also reopen his wounds. A year earlier, while driving with him, she had made a reference to a woman who had married a storekeeper—almost certainly a Jew—whose business catered to a primarily black clientele in a poor section of Washington, D.C., similar to Norfolk's Church Street. She had called the man an "impossible person." Jaffé did not believe she remembered saying it, but he had not forgotten. Those remarks, he wrote,

> reminded me that my only brother, after losing all that he had in the early years of the depression, is reduced to keeping a very much humbler shop, I imagine, in a Richmond equivalent of Church Street—a perfectly impossible sort of business, socially. [Hoping to make a new start, Hyman and Hattie had moved to Richmond to operate Arrow Cut Rate Store. The 1940 Richmond directory showed it surrounded by businesses such as the Prospect Social Club, the Casino Dancing Academy, and the Little Savoy Cafe, a "(c)"—indicating colored—following each of these listings.] . . . So, you see, I too am an "impossible" person by immediate derivation—only a bare generation or two removed from the Baltic ghettoes. No one can share my poor lot without, in a sense, sharing the burdens that go with it—not tangible burdens but intangible ones—the heaviest kind. It played a part in my most intimate disaster—in spite of an initial determination on the part of both to exclude it.
>
> From all this I have emerged on a kind of plateau of my own

26. Louis Jaffé to Alice Rice, 6 June 1940, ibid.

creation on which I have based my adjustments and compromises. It concerns me alone, and I have only so many more years to live it. What brings me up short and, at times frightens me, is the thought that I have no right to take anybody else out of secure and peaceful channels and make her share this plateau. It has its compensations—this plateau—but it also has its bleaknesses.[27]

While in New York in midsummer 1940 for the World's Fair and side trips to Gotham museums and bookstores, Jaffé traveled into the eastern European Jewish quarter. He sent Alice a letter on Bastille Day, just three weeks after the French surrender to the Nazis: "How I used to revel in New York in the old days!—before the ice stole in my veins & before a nameless dread stole in my heart. What has just happened in France fills me with foreboding for some 15,000,000 people—most of them sunk in nameless poverty as on the lower East Side of N.Y. which I saw today for the first time in 20 years. I took a cross-town bus into that tragic tawdriness this afternoon. . . . I could stand only an hour of it. I kept thinking of the European counterparts where terror stalks today—& quite beyond salvation in our lifetime."[28]

After four months of unsuccessful attempts to arrange a meeting with his son, Jaffé concluded by late August that Margaret had persuaded the boy to forgo all contact with him. At the same time he discovered by reading a *Ledger-Dispatch* article that Margaret had enrolled Christopher in Episcopal High School, an elite preparatory school in Alexandria, Virginia, under the name of Christopher Davis. The matter infuriated Jaffé. "Needless to say," he wrote to her, "I will resist in the courts, to the limit, any effort to bring me or my name into public contempt, or to put my son in the equivocal and humiliating position of becoming the instrument of such an act of contempt for his father, and take prompt steps to prevent his registration in any school or college under a patronymic that falsifies his birth and exposes both of us to humiliation."[29]

27. Amy Waters Yarsinske, *Norfolk's Church Street: Between Memory and Reality* (Charleston: Arcadia, 1999), 43–5; *Hill's Richmond City Telephone Directory,* 1940; Louis Jaffé to Alice Rice, 6 June 1940, Louis Jaffé Jr.

28. Louis Jaffé to Alice Rice, 15 July 1940, Louis Jaffé Jr.

29. Louis Jaffé to Margaret Davis, 20 August 1940, ibid.

Margaret did not answer the letter, and he wrote again a few days later. He approved of sending Christopher to Episcopal and would finance his education both there and throughout college, but he stressed again that he would oppose with every legal resource he could invoke, "regardless of publicity, any attempt to sail Christopher through school or college under an *assumed* name." "Never until a court of competent jurisdiction declares that *my* name denotes something shameful," he wrote, "will I consent to your stripping him of the name of his father—as you have already stripped him of the Louis that was given him, along with Christopher, at his christening. . . . Be assured that if necessary, I shall obtain a restraining order and bring into the open the whole miserable Hitlerian motivation of this attack on my honor and integrity, which is also an attack on the integrity of my son."[30]

A few days later he learned from Margaret's lawyer that Christopher himself—now eighteen years of age—had reached the decision to change his name. The attorney had attempted to persuade him to wait until he turned twenty-one, hoping he might change his mind. If Jaffé pressed the issue, Christopher could petition the courts for a change of name and would almost certainly prevail. In a subsequent letter to Jaffé, Christopher confirmed his desire to change his name to Christopher Wheelwright Davis. "I feel defeated and depleted," Jaffé wrote to Alice. "The trouble about Kit is working out the *worst* way. And that adds to my defeat."[31]

For several months Jaffé pondered his options and ruminated over his son's repudiation of his paternal name. In the end he decided not to contest the change. In November he wrote Christopher a remarkably forbearing letter, telling him that the decision had caused him "long pain and distress." After great deliberation, however, he had concluded that Christopher had the right to live his life as he saw fit. "No change of name alters the basic fact that you are my son, and I desire that that relationship remain unimpaired by what has passed," he wrote. "That episode is now closed. It will never be reopened by me." Jaffé expressed his wish that they would develop understanding and cordial relations, and his belief that with time their inter-

30. Louis Jaffé to Margaret Davis, August 1940, ibid.

31. Gardner L. Boothe to James Barron, 5 September 1940, Louis Jaffé to Christopher Davis, 19 November 1940, Louis Jaffé to Alice Rice, 25 September 1940, all ibid.

actions would become easier. He hoped that Christopher would write to him soon and tell him about his life at Episcopal. He enclosed one hundred dollars and sent his love and holiday greetings.[32]

Despite Jaffé's best efforts, Margaret's influence proved impossible to undo. In late August 1941 Jaffé asked Christopher to tell him forthrightly whether he wished to have contact with him. Jaffé had written his son four times over the previous half year and had enclosed checks in several of those letters. Christopher had not responded. "I think it would be fair and sporting to write me frankly whether you want to hear from me or not," he wrote. "I have been doing my best in a difficult situation to see you and keep in touch with you, but obviously unless you meet me half way, I cannot succeed." Jaffé told Christopher he was "building [his] hopes" on him and intended to leave him an inheritance if he wanted one. "It now depends on you and I shall be governed by your reply to this letter and by our future relations," he concluded.[33]

That same day, he sent Alice the third—apparently the final—installment of "De Profundis." He enclosed two letters from his brother, in which Hyman had described his desperate financial condition. Although Jaffé conceded it was an unfair thing to do to Hyman, he believed it was unfair not to let Alice see the whole picture. "Please guard this bit of my poor décor," Jaffé requested,

> and return it to me unseen by anyone else. It means, to speak brutally, that my nearest kith are "socially" nowhere at all and can be introduced in no clubs without shock. I make no apologies. I merely state a fact. And in a mystical sort of way, I am proud of them all for having moved from an ancient lineage to so humble a present estate without any compromise with their inner integrity. Myself, I have made compromises. There was no other way—[I had] to do what I had to do, or die. And if the war should bring disaster and I should be confronted with a choice between the blood that spawned me and the blood that drew me to mate outside the pale, I shall of course—by choice as well as by compulsion—share the bitter herbs that will be left to my old, old people. Either that, or

32. Louis Jaffé to Christopher Davis, 19 November 1940, ibid.
33. Louis Jaffé to Christopher Davis, 20 August 1941, ibid.

too old and brittle to make the readjustment, I shall seek a cowardly and swift way out.

I sometimes wonder whether, even in your most understanding moments, you had ever a real and downright understanding of the inner weight of all this on me and of its terrific possibilities for you.[34]

Alice was moved that he had sent her Hyman's letters. She did not care a whit about Hyman's financial condition or lack of social status, she replied, and would much rather have him for a brother-in-law than someone who moved in exclusive circles but who lacked character and honesty. She reproved Jaffé for having said he had compromised. She believed he had been as true to who he was as Hyman had been to himself. She had considered in detail the despairing scenarios in which their marriage might result. "As for the purely racial implication of your letter," she wrote, "I can only say again that I *have* grasped it and thought about it very deeply. I have questioned if for our children, if we should have them, and for my parents, if catastrophe should come, and for us. I have seen us living in a Ghetto and known that we could still make a life; I have seen us fleeing, and known that we would flee together; I have thought of the other way and known it was the one we'd never follow, nor you alone—for it would break my heart. Oh Louis, these things hurt to write about—but these are things I've truly thought and for a long time. Do they answer you?"[35]

As Jaffé's romance with Alice flowered, the war in Europe and its effect on Norfolk consumed much of his attention as a news analyst. Military preparations had drastically affected Norfolk and the lives of his readers. In 1938 President Roosevelt had appropriated a billion dollars for naval defense. Work had started at once on expanding the many military bases that surrounded the city and on improving their facilities. In nearby shipyards, workers feverishly began the construction of a fleet of warships, including the dreadnoughts *Alabama* and *Indiana,* whose sixteen-inch guns would soon be rushed to the Pacific theater to buttress the naval forces decimated by the Japanese attack on Pearl Harbor. The shipyards did not limit their

34. Louis Jaffé to Alice Rice, 20 August 1941, ibid.
35. Alice Rice to Louis Jaffé, 29 August 1941, ibid.

work to American vessels; British ships of war such as the battleship *Royal Sovereign* and the aircraft carrier *Illustrious,* terribly battered off Malta by German Junkers dive bombers, received repairs in Hampton Roads. Sailors, soldiers, military workers, and their families and sweethearts poured into town. By November 1941, the boom had effectively doubled the city's population.[36]

The build-up brought a welcome prosperity, but—as in World War I—Norfolk's resources and infrastructure proved hopelessly overextended. Lines of waiting people sprang up everywhere, housing grew impossibly scarce, and the streets became glutted with traffic. Norfolk's blacks suffered the most; a federal housing administrator during this period called the city's slums the "worst in the nation." Racial tensions increased as blacks and whites jammed together on streetcars and buses. Many whites had only recently moved to Norfolk from the rural South and expected black subservience and strict enforcement of Jim Crow ordinances. Many blacks, frustrated by the hypocrisy of their government, which expended seemingly limitless energy preparing to fight for democracy abroad while refusing to accord their race democratic privileges at home, asserted themselves with growing boldness. Local black militancy reflected the intention of the national black leadership not to subordinate its advocacy for increased rights and economic participation to the war effort, as it had done during World War I.[37]

These and other pressing developments, ranging from military campaigns to outbreaks of sexually transmitted disease (Norfolk was branded the nation's worst center of venereal disease during the war), demanded Jaffé's editorial attention. The strain of his long marital nightmare had eroded his vigor, and the increased workload tired him. The failure of most poten-

36. Wertenbaker, *Norfolk: Historic Southern Port,* 345, 347; Chambers, Shank, and Sugg, *Salt Water & Printer's Ink,* 368–9; *Jane's Fighting Ships of World War II* (Avenel, N.J.: Crescent Books, 1995), 260; Cesare Salmaggi and Alfredo Pallavisini, comps., *2194 Days of War* (New York: Windward, 1977), 95.

37. Suggs, *P. B. Young, Newspaperman,* 126; Marvin W. Schlegel, *Conscripted City: The Story of Norfolk in World War II* (Norfolk: Norfolk War History Commission, 1951), 31–8, 173–4; Patricia Sullivan, *Days of Hope: Race and Democracy in the New Deal Era* (Chapel Hill: University of North Carolina Press, 1996), 134–5; Lewis, *In Their Own Interests,* 173–5, 188–91.

tial contributors to meet his professional standards and the likelihood that seasoned *Pilot* reporters who might be groomed to help him would shortly be entering the armed forces added to his burden and fatigue. He began to experience painful arthritis, starting in a toe and soon spreading to his fingers, knees, wrists, and jaw. Typing became difficult, at times impossible.[38]

Although the national mood and the overwhelming majority of the country's presses favored American neutrality, Jaffé had long realized the folly of such a policy, as had most of his peers in the southern liberal press. When Pearl Harbor ended any discussion of continued American isolationism, Jaffé chided Charles Lindbergh and Senator Burton Wheeler for their advocacy of non-intervention. The Japanese air attack, he wrote, "proved that the Isolationists have not only grossly miscalculated the compass point from which the United States was most dangerously threatened by war, but also were grossly mistaken in assuming that if we but mounted guard on our own shoreline and our insular outposts, no power on earth would dare attack us. How many times have we been assured by our Wheelerghs that the Atlantic made us safe from any and all enemy air attack?" Jaffé believed the several wars raging constituted one world war, and he urged the United States to align itself "with those forces that are fighting for the only kind of world in which free institutions and live-and-let-die international intercourse can survive." Mussolini's and Hitler's declarations of war on the United States three days after Pearl Harbor settled the issue.[39]

As Jaffé and Alice decided to make their relationship permanent, he tried to prepare Lotta—who by that time had gone completely blind—for his marriage to another Gentile. He accordingly wrote to his brother to enlist Hyman's support. He believed that Hyman and Hattie would like Alice very much. "Unfortunately, from mother's viewpoint, [Alice] is only one-fourth Jewish by derivation and is an Episcopal in her church affiliation," he wrote. "That, as you know, doesn't make any difference to me, but I am afraid it

38. Chambers, Shank, and Sugg, *Salt Water & Printer's Ink*, 373; Louis Jaffé Jr., interview by author, 7 February 1996; Robert Mason, interview by author, 18 September 1995; Suggs, *P. B. Young, Newspaperman*, 128; *Pilot*, 13 April 1944; Lawrence H. Cotter, medical report, 15 May 1945, Louis Jaffé Jr.

39. *Pilot*, 3 September 1939; Chambers, Shank, and Sugg, *Salt Water & Printer's Ink*, 368; Kneebone, *Southern Liberal Journalists*, 183–4; *Pilot*, 8 December 1941.

will worry mother. For that reason, I hope you and Hattie will give me a hand with mother and help me reconcile her to another 'goye.'"[40]

Hyman and Hattie's living situation in Richmond had made it impossible for them to take in Lotta, and Jaffé had attempted unsuccessfully to locate an Orthodox Jewish family in Norfolk to care for her. Eventually Lotta would be moved to Baltimore, into an apartment near her widowed sister, Hennie Higger. Jaffé would pay her living and medical expenses. Unlike Margaret, who had assiduously shunned Jaffé's family, Alice would reach out to them, initiating a correspondence with Lotta and building a relationship with Hyman and Hattie, their daughters, and later the daughters' children.[41]

Jaffé and Alice were married on May 14, 1942. They had planned to have the wedding in Princess Anne, Maryland, where Alice's maternal grandparents had once lived, but Jaffé suffered a painful attack of arthritis in both knees, and they decided to conduct the service at the Rices' home instead. Only her immediate family attended. Jaffé and Alice preferred a simple ceremony, and he thought it best "to keep the whole affair as quiet as possible in view of my divorced status." Lankes sent his best wishes: "I wish you every happiness, Louis. You've been through the mill and are entitled to a peaceful and happy . . . afternoon of life." After the wedding, Jaffé and Alice traveled to New York for a short honeymoon.[42]

Alice had sent a wedding invitation to Christopher, then completing his freshman year at the University of Virginia. It evoked a formal response that conspicuously omitted the obligatory "regrets": "Mr. Christopher Davis declines the invitation of Miss Alice Rice for Thursday, May the fourteenth at four in the afternoon."[43]

*　*　*

40. Louis Jaffé to Hyman Jaffe, 20 February 1941, Louis Jaffé Jr.; Jaffé family tree, Louis Jaffé Jr.

41. Daniel Higger, interview by author, 4 February 1998; Louis Jaffé to Hyman Jaffe, 11 April 1942, Louis Jaffé Jr.; Louis Jaffé to Hattie Jaffe, 29 December 1942, Louis Jaffé Jr.; Louis Jaffé to Paul Huber, 30 December 1939, Jaffé Papers; Jaffé family tree, Louis Jaffé Jr.

42. Louis Jaffé to Hyman Jaffe, 11 April 1942, Jaffé Papers; *Pilot*, 15 May 1942; J. J. Lankes to Louis Jaffé, 11 May 1942, Jaffé Papers; Louis Jaffé to Alexander Forward, 12 May 1942, Jaffé Papers.

43. Christopher Davis to Alice Rice, 13 May 1942, Louis Jaffé Jr.

Jaffé's commitment to daily journalism, his reclusiveness, emerging health problems, and the many distractions he faced in his private life combined to militate against his direct personal involvement in the numerous organizations and conferences convened during this period by southern liberals—white and black—to chart strategies for dealing with their region's economic and racial problems. He did not attend the Southern Conference for Human Welfare, held in Birmingham in 1938, at which police commissioner Theophilus Eugene "Bull" Connor enforced the city's segregation ordinance at the Municipal Auditorium, to the dismay of Eleanor Roosevelt and other participants in the event. Nor did he take part in the Conference of White Southerners on Racial Relations, sponsored by the Commission on Interracial Cooperation in Atlanta in April 1943, which *Atlanta Constitution* editor Ralph McGill chaired. Liberals at the convocation responded to the "Durham Manifesto," issued by a working group of southern black leaders presided over by P. B. Young in October of the previous year. Young and the other black leaders had politely recorded their opposition to segregation but had emphasized the more immediate need for both races to solve the "current problems of racial discrimination and neglect." A biracial group from the two conferences met in Richmond in June 1943, and University of North Carolina social scientist Howard Odum deftly folded the Commission on Interracial Cooperation into what would soon become the Southern Regional Council.[44]

White southern liberal journalists such as Virginius Dabney, Mark Ethridge, George Fort Milton, Ralph McGill, and John Temple Graves II, editor of the *Birmingham Age-Herald,* provided leadership for many of these endeavors. But when they confronted the inevitable issue of segregation during the 1940s and early 1950s, they—like nearly all other southern white moderates and liberals—refused to consider in any meaningful way its dismantlement. When backed into a corner over the issue, some would lash out at their former allies.

Certainly this was the case with Virginius Dabney, who had forged

44. Egerton, *Speak Now Against the Day,* 190, 303–12; Dykeman and Stokely, *Seeds of Southern Change,* 283–4; Howard W. Odum, *Race and Rumors of Race* (Chapel Hill: University of North Carolina Press, 1943), 185–202; Neil McMillen, ed., *Remaking Dixie: The Impact of World War II on the American South* (Jackson: University Press of Mississippi, 1997), 79–81.

a partnership with Walter White in 1937 in an attempt to secure the passage of still another slate of antilynching bills under consideration by Congress. Although Jaffé had been one of the first white southern editors to endorse federal antilynching legislation, his support predating Dabney's by two years, his Richmond peer received conspicuous national attention for his stand. Capitalizing on his editorial vantage point and flawless southern credentials, Dabney had launched a sustained barrage of syndicated columns, articles in national opinion journals, and reprinted editorials calling for a national law. White in turn had exerted his influence as executive secretary of the NAACP to burnish Dabney's image and to lobby the Pulitzer Prize committee, albeit unsuccessfully, for an award for Dabney. White sought to establish Dabney as a model other southern editors would emulate.[45]

When, however, in the wake of the *Gaines v. Missouri* decision, White had in 1939 broached the possibility of integrated postgraduate education at Dabney's alma mater, the University of Virginia, the *Times-Dispatch*'s editor—while conceding that "logic is all on the side of admitting Negroes . . . on the same basis as whites"—objected strenuously to such a move, on the grounds that it would result in "much ill-feeling and trouble." Shortly thereafter, at the NAACP's convention in Richmond, Charles Houston angered Dabney by announcing that the organization would no longer content itself with "separate but equal" and intended instead to advocate the integration of the state's graduate and professional schools.[46]

Dabney withdrew his support for the NAACP altogether. In an editorial entitled "Far Too Radical for Us," he declared that if the NAACP was given an inch, it would take a mile. Warning that the organization sought to demolish the region's system of segregated education, he raised the specter of intermarriage. In the event of integration, he exhorted, "racial amalgamation would go forward at a greatly accelerated speed." In a 1943 *Atlantic Monthly* article, "Nearer and Nearer the Precipice," he would go so far as to claim that black extremists and white reactionaries had polarized race relations to the extent that a race war loomed large on the horizon.

45. *Richmond Times-Dispatch*, 2 February 1937; Virginius Dabney, "Dixie Rejects Lynching," *Nation*, 27 November 1937, 579–80; Walter White to Carl Ackerman, 26 April 1937, Walter White to Virginius Dabney, 26 April 1937, both in NAACP Papers.

46. Virginius Dabney to Walter White, 3 January 1939, NAACP Papers.

He blamed Philip Randolph's proposed march on Washington, NAACP demands for political and social equality, and the black press's focus on racial injustice for spawning the conditions in which racist demagogues like Mississippi congressman John Rankin could thrive. He accused activist black leadership of weakening blacks' commitment to the war effort and breeding disloyalty by pushing for immediate reforms. He especially objected to the increasing criticism of white southern moderates, among whom he still counted himself. If such criticism continued, he warned, the "white leaders in the South who have been responsible for much of the steady progress of the Negro in the past, and who can bring about a great deal more such progress in the future, will be driven into the opposition camp."[47]

Dabney did not overstate the last point. Black activism and criticism of the paternalistic approach of white southern liberals and their snail's-pace gradualism triggered a backlash in him. His writing on racial matters from this point on—particularly his support for massive resistance to public-school integration in the mid- to late 1950s—provide abundant evidence confirming his reversal of position. As John Kneebone has made clear in *Southern Liberal Journalists and the Issue of Race,* other prominent liberal editors in the region echoed Dabney's die-hard defense of segregation. Ethridge asserted that blacks "must recognize that there is no power in the world—not even in all the mechanized armies of the earth, Allied and Axis—which could now force the Southern white people to the abandonment of the principle of social segregation." John Temple Graves pronounced segregation "not an argument in the South [but] . . . a major premise."[48]

Would Jaffé's assumption of formal leadership roles in southern liberal organizations have changed their history? It seems highly unlikely. Jaffé, like his peers, embraced a policy of gradualism that stopped short of social integration. He genuinely did not believe that the region's whites could in the immediate future countenance an end to racial separation. This

47. *Richmond Times-Dispatch,* 17 July 1939; Virginius Dabney, "Nearer and Nearer the Precipice," *Atlantic Monthly,* January 1943, 98.

48. Leidholdt, "Virginius Dabney and Lenoir Chambers," 50–64; Kneebone, *Southern Liberal Journalists,* 198.

was a postulate that bore no dispute. Along with his white cohorts in the liberal press, he regarded segregation as so deeply woven into the fabric of the southern way of life that it might only be unraveled at some indeterminate time. No white journalist in the South in the 1940s pressed for ending Jim Crow. "Full-scale desegregation was not an issue in Mr. Jaffé's time," Robert Mason remembered. "He nor any of his bolder southern editorial brethren was moved to advocate it."[49]

Even Jaffé's successors in the liberal press, a generation younger than he, would need another ten years and the imprimatur of *Brown v. Board of Education,* a unanimous Supreme Court opinion, before they would advocate integration. Indeed, the handful of southern editors urging compliance with *Brown* in the tumultuous years that followed the landmark decision would base their lonely stands on the "law of the land," not on the iniquity of second-class citizenship. Reflecting on the immediate postwar period, editor Harry Ashmore of the *Little Rock Gazette* would recall, "You couldn't have stayed at home and had any influence at all if you openly opposed segregation."[50]

Jaffé and the other liberal editors were right; white southerners— egged on by their political leaders—were not ready for integration. It would require an activist Supreme Court, Martin Luther King Jr. and a mass protest movement comprised of demonstrators willing to put their lives on the line, the political machinations of Lyndon Johnson, and the television medium beaming the unfolding drama into the nation's living rooms to kill Jim Crow. An inescapable question remains, however: Could a concerted campaign by these influential molders of public opinion over the decade that preceded *Brown* have made the unthinkable thinkable and better prepared their region for the inevitability of integration?

Although they uniformly opposed ending racial separation, the South's liberal editors approached the subject with varying degrees of emotion and with differing rationales for their postures. Jaffé, while like Dabney preferring policies generated by southern whites and blacks for dealing with the region's racial problems, did not demagogue northern black leaders. He

49. Mason, letter to author, 12 June 2000.
50. Ashmore, *Civil Rights and Wrongs,* 84–5, 90, 97–100; Leidholdt, *Standing Before the Shouting Mob,* 96–7; Egerton, *Speak Now Against the Day,* 460–7, 616.

regarded blacks' struggle for equality as an understandable and natural impulse, not the result of manipulation by outside forces. He did not rule out integration at some future time. Importantly, he did not raise the inflammatory specter of "racial amalgamation." Young summarized this distinction best when he observed to White that "Editors like Dabney, who seem to be a little thin-skinned when it comes to according Negroes full civil liberties, are always dragging [intermarriage] as a red herring across the trail." Moreover, Jaffé never wounded black racial pride or distended whites' sense of superiority by alleging black inferiority, as the Richmond editor would later do. A close reading of *Pilot* editorials preceding and following news events that suggested increased black activism, such as Randolph's March on Washington movement (which would culminate in the formation of the Ethridge-led Fair Employment Practices Commission), establishes that Jaffé generally preferred to keep his own counsel on the growing black militancy that would alienate his Richmond peer.[51]

His standing as a racial leader under assault (some detractors went so far as to lump him alongside notoriously racist Georgia governor Eugene— "Farmer Gene"—Talmadge), Dabney in November 1943 authored two editorials urging Virginia to abandon its laws mandating segregation on public transportation. He argued that by making a symbolic gesture of their good will, southern whites could best preempt blacks' alignment with northern influences. Kneebone suggests two other possible motivations for Dabney's stand—to rehabilitate his tarnished reputation as a liberal and to evoke throughout the region a shattering explosion of white dissent that would telegraph an unmistakable message to impatient blacks to back off. Whatever his reasons, Dabney had made a bold proposal, albeit one strikingly inconsistent with his recent stands. He invited other editors in the region, including Jaffé, to consider his proposition.[52]

51. P. B. Young to Walter White, 26 July 1939, NAACP Papers; *Richmond Times-Dispatch,* 16 October 1958, 26 November 1958, 17, 22 January 1959; Putnam, *Race and Reason,* 4–12; Virginius Dabney to Carleton Putnam, 22 July 1963, Carleton Putnam to Lyndon Johnson, 6 May 1964, both in Dabney Papers.

52. *Richmond Times-Dispatch,* 13, 21 November 1943; "Virginians Speak on Jim Crow," *Crisis,* February 1944, 46–8; Kneebone, *Southern Liberal Journalists,* 209–13; Sosna, *In Search of the Silent South,* 134–6; Egerton, *Speak Now Against the Day,* 256; Louis Jaffé to Virginius Dabney, 15 November 1943, Virginius Dabney to Louis Jaffé, 16 November 1943, both in Jaffé Papers.

"You may be sure that your editorial . . . did not escape my attention," Jaffé wrote to Dabney. "I stewed over it all day yesterday and this morning talked it out with Chambers and [publisher Paul S.] Huber." Jaffé believed that segregation in public transportation "ought to be terminated as soon as practicable," but he feared that rather than defusing tensions between blacks and whites, immediate repeal of the ordinance might fuel racial violence in Norfolk. He met with Young to discuss the proposal, and the *Journal and Guide*'s editor mentioned in the postscript of a letter that he wrote to Dabney that Jaffé was "in sympathy with [Dabney's] position."[53]

Jaffé believed that Norfolk's streetcars and buses constituted the flashpoint most likely to trigger a race riot similar to those erupting throughout the country. White war workers and military men had inundated the city. Some of these young men, anxious to prove their masculinity during wartime, walked with swaggers and carried chips on their shoulders. How might they—particularly the many from the Deep South—react when blacks sat down beside them or a white woman? Compounding the danger, the quality and quantity of Norfolk's police force had diminished perceptibly as a result of military enlistments. When a marine and sailor beat a black man, a policeman had refused to intervene, explaining that he was not on duty. Incidents like this had led to the creation of a permanent shore patrol, but its formation did not make the city any less of an "armed camp," as the *Norfolk Ledger-Dispatch* described it.[54]

Young dispatched a reporter, whom he described as a "blue-eyed mulatto," to assess the white reception to Dabney's proposal. Assuming their questioner to be white, the interviewees did not censor their responses. "The stories [the journalist] brought back as to their reactions were for the most part terrifying," Young told Dabney. "He confined his inquiries chiefly to the working classes and among those he interviewed was a military policeman, who asserted that he would want nothing so much as a race riot

53. Jaffé to Dabney, 15 November 1943, Jaffé Papers; P. B. Young to Virginius Dabney, 2 December 1943, Dabney Papers.

54. Schlegel, *Conscripted City*, 194–5; Shapiro, *White Violence and Black Response*, 301–48; Chambers, Shank, and Sugg, *Salt Water & Printer's Ink*, 371; Suggs, *P. B. Young, Newspaperman*, 128.

in Norfolk, and that he would be one of the leaders in a general massacre of Negroes."[55]

Jaffé wrote to Dabney that the public transportation segregation ordinance should be repealed after the war build-up ended and Norfolk returned to normal but that he could not endorse it at present. Dabney would cease his advocacy on the matter when John Stewart Bryan, who had headed Richmond Newspapers, died in 1944 and John Dana Wise solidified his power at the *Times-Dispatch*.[56]

Jaffé evaluated Dabney's proposal on its merits, but *Pilot* insiders regarded Dabney's abrupt about-face as an attempt by the Richmond editor to restore his liberal renown. Robert Mason remembered that during Virginia's massive resistance to public-school integration in the 1950s, Chambers joked that Dabney's attack on segregated seating on public transportation "would be his ticket to heaven" and that Chambers delighted in repeating his wife Roberta's comment to the effect that "when racial decency was restored by the Good Lord, history would record that it began when Dabney got the jump on Rosa Parks."[57]

As Dabney recalled in his memoirs, only a small newspaper in North Carolina, the *Kinston Daily Free Press*, had the mettle to acknowledge his recommendation. Mason, familiar with small North Carolina papers including the *Free Press* and its editor at that time, believed that the Kinston paper's response had more to do with the pressure of finding an editorial topic—in this case one that could be easily written, as it would consist mostly of quotes—than with genuine support. Mason observed that because the little tobacco town had no public transportation anyway, reprinting Dabney's editorial would not generate distress among white readers.[58]

Jaffé did not shrink from weighing in on controversial events promptly and in no uncertain terms. Thus, given his passionate interest in race relations, his editorial silence on growing black militancy begs scrutiny.

55. Young to Dabney, 2 December 1943, Dabney Papers.
56. Egerton, *Speak Now Against the Day*, 256.
57. Robert Mason, letters to author, 12, 18 June 2000.
58. Dabney, *Across the Years*, 164; Mason, letter to author, 21 October 1995.

Jaffé had both championed redress for racial inequities and made clear the line beyond which his advocacy did not extend. Some *Virginian-Pilot* subscribers may now have looked to the paper's editor for elucidation of developments taking place at least partially in the gray area between these declared stances.

Jaffé's uncharacteristic refrainment from commentary represented a carefully considered strategy, probably arrived at jointly with Chambers. Impatient with whites' resistance to salary equalization and dubious that the state could equalize higher-education facilities, Jaffé surely sympathized with blacks' current initiatives toward these goals. But wary of white reaction to both the demands and the boldness of the tactics, he likely concluded that the less attention drawn to these matters in his volatile bailiwick, the less the danger of violent reaction. He may also have believed that his own apparent unconcern might help downplay their radicality. At any rate, he obviously saw restraint as the better part of diplomacy in these instances.

An editorial written in response to the Conference of White Southerners on Racial Relations in Atlanta made clear where Jaffé stood in his thinking on integration during the war. He applauded both the Durham and the Atlanta conferences. "Much has been said on the polemic front about the South's system of segregation," he wrote. "The Durham manifesto naturally recorded its opposition 'to the principle and practice of compulsory segregation in our American society, whether of races or classes or creeds,' but it recognized 'the strength and age' of the legal and customary patterns in which Southern race segregation is rooted." He then quoted the Atlanta manifesto, which attempted to skirt the issue of segregation but urged a more just apportionment of resources and fairer treatment for blacks: "The only justification offered for those laws which have for their purpose the separation of the races is that they are intended to minister to the welfare and the integrity of both races. There has been widespread and inexcusable discrimination in the administration of these laws."[59]

Jaffé maintained that both the Durham and the Atlanta statements appropriately dealt with the aspects of the "segregation question . . . that are within the range of present accommodation." He summarized the Atlanta group's recommendations, which matched in general terms his quarter cen-

59. *Pilot,* 14 April 1943.

tury of racial advocacy in Norfolk: equitable allocation of public utilities and benefits, an end to discriminatory treatment by police and courts, equal pay for equal work, and increased funding for black education. "One is struck," he wrote, "in considering the Durham and Atlanta proclamations, by the amplitude of their common ground—by the large number of correctives that can be applied without trespass on those very narrow precincts of the segregation question which raise issues too explosive to be tampered with." He ended his editorial by warning against "extremists on both sides who are the chief obstacles in the path of a rapprochement between the races that has very far to go."[60]

Perhaps the strongest example of Jaffé's continuous racial advocacy throughout the war years consisted of his detailed analyses of the many race riots that erupted across the United States during the period. More than 242 "racial battles" took place in forty-seven cities in 1943 alone, according to the count of black social scientist Charles Johnson. Jaffé rejected simplistic explanations and pat solutions for the lawlessness and refused to scapegoat blacks or impugn their patriotism. He focused instead on the roots of the disorders. "Straight thinking," he told his readers, "demands . . . a recognition of the fact that the war has aggravated pre-existing racial tensions; that these tensions spring from a natural desire of American Negroes to liberate themselves from the economic, political and governmental discriminations that prejudice their independence and security; and that permanent abatement of these tensions will require the abatement or abolition of their basic causes."[61]

In June 1943 he denounced the Los Angeles city council's prohibition against zoot suits in an attempt to end the zoot-suit riots. The ban, he wrote, "does not come within miles of getting at the basic causes of the riots between soldiers and sailors on the one hand and Los Angeles' youthful gangs (largely Mexican and occasionally Negro, in this instance) whose members happen to prefer just now the long draped coat, the pegged trousers full at the knees and narrow at the cuffs, and other zoot refinements." Jaffé informed his readers that the real reasons for the riots lay in "juvenile and recreational problems of ancient vintage, in the curse of poverty's con-

60. Ibid.
61. Shapiro, *White Violence and Black Response*, 337; *Pilot*, 27 June 1943.

gestion, in all the elements that make for junior hoodlumism. . . . Some of the zoot-suiters," he continued, "are undoubtedly tough babies, but maybe the Los Angeles policemen dealing with rebel youth don't know much more than toughness themselves. Toughness can crack a skull and break up a riot, but it does not often reach ultimate causes. Los Angeles has on its hands the responsibility of careful analysis and corrective policies as well as strong-arm tactics. It is no easy responsibility, but it cannot be avoided."[62]

A similar assessment followed the Beaumont, Texas, riot that occurred one week later. The military commander of the troops called in to stop the destruction, which was sparked by reports of black men molesting a white girl and woman, declared that the black section of the city was "literally stomped into the ground . . . , from a destructive standpoint [equaling] the Meuse-Argonne sector of the first World War." Jaffé called the origins of the riots breaking out across the country the "most difficult domestic issue in the United States today." Authorities across the country should "get at the causes of the discontent and deal with them before they grow beyond control," he wrote. "The call is for justice and fairness and patience and understanding and tolerance—the very qualities Americans like to think are typically American and therefore worth fighting for."[63]

A few days later a massive race riot broke out in Detroit, killing thirty-four, injuring hundreds, and disrupting crucial war production. President Roosevelt would soon appoint *Raleigh News and Observer* editor Jonathan Daniels to head a behind-the-scenes working group charged with identifying racially tense areas and defusing the conditions before violence broke out. Jaffé urged all municipalities to develop forceful efforts to prevent the mayhem borne "of desperate living conditions, of newly stimulated economic rivalries, of blind political leadership, of the recklessness of young men temporarily far away from their native surroundings and morally on the loose, of the fierceness of times which teach men to kill, of old and bitter racial emotions, and of all the hellish accompaniments of a people under the war strain and degenerating in an emergency to the primitivism that war inevitably engenders." He argued that slum clearance should take precedence over the construction of housing for Navy personnel. He joined

62. *Pilot,* 12 June 1943.
63. Ibid., 19 June 1943.

Young in campaigning for recreational activities for black servicemen and the inclusion of blacks on Norfolk's police force, and he urged an end to the discriminatory practices that impeded the employment of blacks in war industries.[64]

Jaffé believed that rumormongers had incited many of the riots with baseless claims of racial conflict. During the war, fantastic tales about race conspiracies circulated throughout Norfolk. Some whites claimed that blacks had purchased all of the available icepicks in the city and planned a bloody uprising. Others believed that insolent domestic workers had, at the First Lady's behest, formed "Order of Eleanor" and "Daughters of Eleanor" societies and intended to contravene Jim Crow by entering white homes through front doors and refusing to respond when addressed by their first names.[65]

Jaffé enlisted the help of Young, and the two editors—working hand in glove as they had throughout their careers—put an end to the rumors. Young assigned his reporters to run down the stories, which of course proved baseless, and the *Pilot* and the *Journal and Guide* denounced the reports as faked. Jaffé circulated his findings to other editors in the region. Elmer Davis, director of the Office of War Information, publicly commended Jaffé and Young, as well as Dabney and Josephus Daniels, who in his son's absence had resumed the editorship of the *Raleigh News and Observer*.[66]

During the war, Jaffé's advocacy for a black college in Norfolk bore fruit. He had long endorsed the establishment of such an institution in the city and, along with Winston Douglas, Young, and other black leaders, played an important role in encouraging sectarian black Virginia Union

64. Shapiro, *White Violence and Black Response*, 310–30; White, *Man Called White*, 224–32; Herbert Aptheker, ed., *A Documentary History of the Negro People in the United States: From the New Deal to the End of World War II* (New York: Citadel Press, 1974), 443–53; Eagles, *Jonathan Daniels and Race Relations*, 104–10; Suggs, *P. B. Young, Newspaperman*, 127–9; *Pilot*, 19, 28 June 1941, 23 June 1943.

65. *Pilot*, 27 June 1943; Lewis, *In Their Own Interests*, 191–2; Schlegel, *Conscripted City*, 193–4; Odum, *Race and Rumors of Race*, 73–89, 96–104.

66. *Pilot*, 20 August 1942; Louis Jaffé to T. R. Waring, 5 September 1942, Jaffé Papers; [*New York Herald Tribune?* 29 August 1942]; Suggs, *P. B. Young, Newspaperman*, 119.

University to open a small extension branch in Norfolk in 1935. Seven years later, with Jaffé serving on its board of trustees, the foundering college had restyled itself as independent Norfolk Polytechnic College, chartered by the state but totally reliant on tuition and city aid for its operating expenses.[67]

From early on, Jaffé and the institution's leadership, including President Lyman Beecher Brooks, aspired to obtain state support for the hard-pressed junior college. They hoped to incorporate Norfolk Polytechnic as an extension of non-sectarian black Virginia State College and thus qualify it for commonwealth aid. In *Upward: A History of Norfolk State University*, Brooks recalls that as a graduate student studying American history at the University of Michigan, he had first become aware of Jaffé's prominence. Lecturing on the rising influence of editorial writers, one of Brooks's professors had concluded that Jaffé "could well be the best and most powerful editorial writer in America." "As I sat there then," Brooks later wrote, "I had no idea that this same Louis I. Jaffé would become one of the strongest supporters of an institution to which I would dedicate the remainder of my career."[68]

When Norfolk native and former congressman Colgate Darden became governor of Virginia in 1942, the editor perceived a unique opportunity to place the college on secure footing. The two men enjoyed a warm friendship, and Jaffé knew that the new governor intended to make educational reform a centerpiece of his gubernatorial agenda. The preponderantly black Norfolk Joint Commission on the Negro Welfare Center, which the city had created to research and oversee the endeavor, elected Jaffé to chair the project. Certainly his personal relationship with Darden figured critically in the enterprise. In the numerous "Dear Colgate" and "My dear Louie" letters the two men exchanged, they acted expeditiously to cut through the many bureaucratic objections to the venture. Jaffé worked with dispatch to secure title to the buildings that had comprised an old hospital, which would serve as the new campus for the college. He faced many legal challenges as the deed moved from the hospital to the Federal Works

67. Lyman Beecher Brooks, *Upward: A History of Norfolk State University* (Washington, D.C.: Howard University Press, 1983), 31–54; Suggs, *P. B. Young, Newspaperman,* 157–8; Louis Jaffé to Colgate Darden, 8 April 1943, Jaffé Papers; Wertenbaker, *Norfolk: Historic Southern Port,* 385; *Pilot,* 26 October 1942.

68. Brooks, *History of Norfolk State University,* 64–5.

Agency to the city and finally to the state. Darden allocated $40,000 for renovations, and Jaffé and the other members of the commission oversaw the development of the plans for renovation of the facility.[69]

By 1946 more than eight hundred students had enrolled in the Norfolk Division of Virginia State College. Interestingly, Jaffé viewed the new facility as only a stopgap measure. He informed Darden that the tract of land that today comprises the grounds of predominantly black Norfolk State University would make an ideal location for a greatly expanded black college. Ironically, the property had previously served as a segregated golf course.[70]

Although Jaffé did not challenge segregation, his advocacy for blacks met with the often-strong disapproval of a large segment of his readership, apparently raising some hackles to the point of diminishing returns. Even his closest friends, members of Norfolk's avant-garde and liberal thinkers, believed that he went too far. A letter from one of his intimates, local poet Mary Sinton Leitch, speaks to this sentiment: "Louis, I hope you didn't think I was making any vicious attack on you about the negro question. Bless your dear heart, the thing your friends most love in you is your tenderness for the underdog. . . . But I feel that you are going too fast. . . . And I feel that PERHAPS the great editor doesn't give a hang for his public: he says what he thinks; he strikes out at all he thinks evil with a bludgeon that spares nothing and nobody. . . . Shall you accomplish more by not antagonizing people, by leading them more slowly along the path of reform? They are not ready for what you have to tell them. . . . You are putting the bristles up on a good many people who count."[71]

Despite Jaffé's failing health—in addition to his worsening arthritis, he had begun to suffer chest pains that his physician believed might signal

69. Ibid., 54–5; Louis Jaffé to Ellen Perry, 2 May 1949, P. B. Young to L. H. Foster, 11 February 1944, Louis Jaffé to Colgate Darden, 8 April 1943, 25 August 1944, 23 July 1945, Colgate Darden to Louis Jaffé, 9 April 1943, 31 August 1944, 14 July 1945, all in Jaffé Papers; Colgate Darden, Governor of Virginia, *Message of Colgate Darden, Jr., to the General Assembly of Virginia,* 12 January 1944 (Richmond, 1944), 6; C. A. Harrell to Louis Jaffé, 8 May 1947, Jaffé Papers; *Pilot,* 27 July 1945.

70. Louis Jaffé to Colgate Darden, 8 April 1943, Jaffé Papers; Brooks, *History of Norfolk State University,* 64–5.

71. Mary Sinton Leitch to Louis Jaffé, 11 September 1944, Jaffé Papers.

coronary vessel disease—he kept a relentless schedule. In his editorials he tracked the war in all of its complexity—the Japanese victories, Midway, the Battle of the Atlantic, the Soviet counterattacks, the island-hopping in the Pacific, the Italian campaign, Normandy, and finally the German and Japanese surrenders. On the home front, he continued his support for Roosevelt. In 1944, as in the previous election, Jaffé endorsed the president despite his opposition to the chief executive's unsuccessful attempts to pack a Supreme Court dominated by aging conservative Republicans, his efforts to purge Congress of the nominal Democrats from the South who opposed his New Deal programs, and the inefficiencies of his boondoggling National Industrial Recovery Act.[72]

When Roosevelt died in April 1945, Jaffé entitled his editorial eulogy "Roosevelt the Valiant." "None, viewing his role in the large, will deny that he played it valiantly and, with all allowances for mistakes, divagations and compromises, to the great good of the people of his day and time." Unlike his critics, Jaffé pointed out, Roosevelt had discerned that the Great Depression had not been a part of a business cycle, and he had acted with vigor and courage to attack it. He had exercised unprecedented powers and expanded the federal government to provide Americans with a permanent legacy of beneficial programs. In the case of the war, he had again seen what his detractors could not—the inevitability that the United States would one day enter the fray. "The rightness of this daring was being attested across the map of Germany at the very moment he died," Jaffé wrote. "The integrity of his belief in democracy and the incorrigible optimism of his hopes for the common man . . . fully as much as the record sheet of his achievements . . . will keep the name of Franklin Roosevelt high on America's roll of honor."[73]

72. Lawrence H. Cotter, medical report, 15 May 1945, Louis Jaffé Jr.; *Pilot,* 21 July 1944, 13 April 1945; Chambers, Shank, and Sugg, *Salt Water & Printer's Ink,* 363.
73. *Pilot,* 13 April 1945.

15 A FIGHT TO THE FINISH

As the 1940s progressed, Jaffé encountered change in many aspects of his life. He recast his private life with Alice, and they grew even closer. His working duties required adjustment; Lenoir Chambers, his longtime associate and close friend, left to head the *Ledger-Dispatch* after editor Douglas Gordon died in 1944. Not all of Jaffé's new associates over the years that followed satisfied him. A shift in the upper reaches of the *Pilot*'s management also affected him. The slow march of court cases and federal action on the racial front accelerated (although black leaders would still regard the pace as distressingly sluggish), requiring him to reconsider his support for segregation.[1]

No change, however, took place in Christopher's feelings for his father. The young man continued to reject Jaffé entirely. Christopher's decision to avoid all contact with him and Margaret's unwavering resolve that Jaffé receive no news whatsoever regarding their son reduced Jaffé to appealing to friends and acquaintances for reports of his progress.

After finishing his first year at the University of Virginia, Christopher transferred in 1942 to the University of the South in Sewanee, Tennessee. A sympathetic minister sent Jaffé a copy of a letter that he had written to Margaret (who had taken up residence in a Tennessee hotel near Sewanee), after she requested that he recommend Christopher for membership in a fraternity. Jaffé, in expressing his thanks for this gesture, added that it had conveyed "certain cheering information" withheld from him because of "unfortunate circumstances" beyond his control.[2]

Christopher's studies were interrupted when he enlisted or was

---

1. Leidholdt, *Standing Before the Shouting Mob*, 26.
2. *Ledger*, 1 August 1944; George Gunn to Margaret Davis, 9 October 1942, Louis Jaffé to George Gunn, 10 October 1942, both in Jaffé Papers.

drafted into the Army that October. Margaret joined him in New York in early 1943—apparently after he had completed basic training—while he awaited orders. He served briefly in the Signal Corps and then in the Air Transport Command before completing officers' training in 1944 and receiving a commission as a second lieutenant in the Army Air Forces, where he was assigned to duty as a communications officer.[3]

Uninvited to Mrs. Davis's funeral that year, Jaffé sent Hugh W. Davis a note of condolence expressing the wish that "happier circumstances might have permitted me the privilege of being near you and Margaret in an hour when I can remember only those many generous acts of Mrs. Davis with which I associate some of the happiest years of my life." Hugh appreciated the letter and expressed regret that he had been unable to intercede successfully with Margaret at Jaffé's behest on a matter regarding Christopher. "I did not get any satisfactory response," Davis wrote. "I am very sorry but, as you know, Margaret is just Margaret. I assure you that I have and have always had the highest regard and esteem for you."[4]

Christopher's maturing, undoubtedly augmented by his military experiences, did not lead to a reconciliation with his father. Three years later, Mary Sinton Leitch shared with Jaffé a report from friends regarding Christopher, possibly about his enrollment at Harvard College. Jaffé later met with the couple and requested that they attempt to find out more. "To these extremities I am driven by the unhappy fact that my son, though living, seems to have removed himself from my ebbing life," he wrote to Leitch.[5]

Jaffé's marriage to Alice could not erase the pain of his estrangement from Christopher but helped to palliate it. Jaffé and Alice enjoyed a closeness and an intellectual connectedness, and by all accounts their marriage brought both of them happiness. In 1944 they moved from the house Jaffé had purchased several years earlier to a graceful larger home that bordered on one of Norfolk's many inlets. Despite their love and their harmonious surroundings, they experienced much heartbreak during this period.

3. *Catholic World,* February 1943, 625; *Ledger,* 1 August 1944.

4. Louis Jaffé to Hugh W. Davis, 21 August 1944, Hugh W. Davis to Louis Jaffé, 25 August 1944, both in Jaffé Papers.

5. Louis Jaffé to Mary Sinton Leitch, 24 October 1947, ibid.; Lorain C. Davis to Alice Jaffé, 16 October 1974, Louis Jaffé Jr.

Louis Lawson Jaffé, born in October 1943 with a defective heart, lived only seven weeks. Colonel Rice died in the summer of 1945, and Alice's mother, Mary Cohn Rice, who had moved in with them, died after a long siege of cancer the following May. Several months later Lotta Jaffé died in Baltimore.[6]

Stress had exacted a heavy price from Jaffé; and in the era's ignorance of the consequences, he further aided and abetted the erosion of his health with a lifestyle that included a pack of cigarettes a day, no purposeful exercise, and a predilection for cholesterol-laden foods like short ribs. The medical treatments of the day for his debilitating arthritis—aspirin, serum injections, and colchicine pills—afforded him little relief; he walked with a limp. He continued to experience chest pain when he exerted himself, and his doctor prescribed nitroglycerin tablets, which along with rest and deep breathing helped somewhat. "My body has been very much with me of late—a painfully inflamed wrist (my cherished arthritis)—which has not only laid hold of my typewriting dexterity but invaded my wits, which is worse," he wrote to Mary Sinton Leitch. She deplored the intimation that his life was nearing its end but conceded that he was "far from well" and that for a long period he had "always been tired."[7]

Chambers later would recount for his associate editors a walk he took with Jaffé at this approximate time. It was a stormy day, and the men's ramble took them past a loading dock. In a dark mood, Jaffé pointed to the newspapers blowing through the parking lot. "This is what we write for— the wind," he said. "The wind. What we wrote yesterday is wasting down this alley, and what we wrote today will follow it tomorrow."[8]

In the fall of 1946, the birth of a healthy baby, Louis Isaac Jaffé Jr., elated Alice and Jaffé and brought them welcome relief from the sadnesses

6. Louis Jaffé Jr., interview by author, 7 February 1996; Sally Abeles, letter to author, 21 September 1995; Mason, interview by author, 18 September 1995; *Norfolk Telephone Directory,* Chesapeake and Potomac Telephone Co., 1940–42; Jaffé family tree, Louis Jaffé Jr.

7. Louis Jaffé Jr., interview by author, 7 February 1996; James F. Waddill, medical report, 6 February 1947, Lawrence H. Cotter, medical report, 15 May 1945, both Louis Jaffé Jr.; Louis Jaffé to Mary Sinton Leitch, 13 November 1947, Mary Sinton Leitch to Louis Jaffé, 28 October 1947, both in Jaffé Papers.

8. Mason, *One of the Neighbors' Children,* 151.

they had experienced. A photograph from this period pictures Jaffé—looking tired and ill but joyful—holding his son on his lap. Jaffé's colleagues shared in the high spirits. Chambers happily agreed to serve as godfather, and Harold Sugg, a reporter for political affairs and city government, expressed his delight to Robert Mason that the *Pilot*'s editor now had a namesake.[9]

When Chambers had moved next door to edit the *Ledger-Dispatch* in 1944, Jaffé brought in Jack W. Schaefer as a senior associate editor. Schaefer, aged thirty-seven and a native of Cleveland, Ohio, seemed impressively qualified. He held a degree from Oberlin College and had completed a year of graduate study in English at Columbia University. He had gained his entree to journalism as a United Press news service reporter and rewrite man. For a period, he had freelanced with theater and movie journals and as a book reviewer before accepting a position as the associate editor of the *New Haven Journal-Courier*. He had become editor of that paper in 1939 and after a few years had moved on to the *Baltimore Sun,* where he served as an associate editor. Schaefer came with outstanding recommendations; both Hamilton Owens and Gerald Johnson had rated him highly. In his off hours he wrote fiction about the American West, but nothing he had published on that subject had earned him any real recognition.[10]

Schaefer soon informed *Pilot* staffers that Jaffé had found him to be an "able substitute" for Chambers. In reality, he compared poorly to his predecessor. In his history of Norfolk's newspapers, *Salt Water & Printer's Ink,* Chambers described his replacement as an "intense and systematic editorial writer," but he told colleagues that he did not regard Schaefer as a strong writer. Robert Mason described him as "inexperienced" and felt that he "wrote too much."[11]

9. Jaffé family tree, Louis Jaffé Jr.; Lenoir Chambers to Louis Jaffé Jr., 9 February 1947, Chambers Papers; Harold Sugg, letter to author, 2 October 1990; Mason, interview by author, 18 September 1995.

10. Jack W. Schaefer to Louis Jaffé, 12 September 1944, Jaffé Papers; Chambers, Shank, and Sugg, *Salt Water & Printer's Ink,* 374; Jack Schaefer, *Shane: The Critical Edition,* ed. James C. Work (Lincoln: University of Nebraska Press, 1984), 16–8; *New York Times,* 27 January 1991; *London Independent,* 2 February 1991; *London Times,* 29 January 1991.

11. Chambers, Shank, and Sugg, *Salt Water & Printer's Ink,* 374; Mason, interview by author, 18 September 1995.

Beyond a doubt Jaffé regretted the departure of his longtime associate. Even if he allowed for Schaefer's newness on the job and did not evaluate his work censoriously, his behavior at work rankled. Schaefer had a puzzling and distressing habit of vanishing from his office for long periods of time. Jaffé may at first have believed that some of his new subordinate's after-hours writing had crept into the workday. Gradually, however, word began to circulate that the married Schaefer was carrying on an affair with a young reporter in the women's department. Warned by colleagues that this intrigue flouted standards for the comportment expected of an associate editor, he attributed their concern to jealousy and continued with his dalliance. After night watchmen reported that he had availed himself of the *Pilot*'s three-room editorial suite as a trysting place, word traveled around the newspaper with predictable speed.[12]

Jaffé had to have known. After numerous discussions with his subordinate regarding his truancy and perhaps even his licentiousness, he laid down the law in early 1948. Despite having informed Jaffé that he had performed a "surgical operation"—a reference to having ended either his marriage or the affair—Schaefer disappeared from his office one afternoon and failed to return. This absence, Jaffé wrote, had led him to conclude "that the operation had [not] been completed." He warned his associate editor that he had had enough: "Unless this apparently interminable complication can be disposed of in the manner which I outlined to you in our conversation of last month, we are back to the impasse which can have only one exit. I should like this letter to have your most serious consideration, for I do not intend to allow the situation here discussed to go uncorrected."[13]

Schaefer left the newspaper soon afterward, to Jaffé's great satisfaction and perhaps at his insistence. He also left Norfolk and his wife and children. In the North, nearly penniless and subsisting on Orange Juliuses, he put together enough money to stake a journey across the Mississippi and lived for a while with American Indians. In 1949 he published his first novel, *Shane,* which he had begun writing during his employment with the *Pilot.* Eminent director George Stevens soon turned *Shane* into a classic motion picture. (Late in his life Schaefer would reveal that he despised the film, par-

12. Mason, interview by author, 18 September 1995.
13. Louis Jaffé to Jack Schaefer, 12 February 1948, Jaffé Papers.

ticularly the performance of Alan Ladd, whom the diminutive novelist termed "that little shrimp." Asked whom he would have cast in the role of his protagonist, he suggested an improbable hero—the actor George Raft.) In his prolific career of writing Westerns, Schaefer would author over a dozen novels and volumes of short stories.[14]

Fortunately, throughout Jaffé's vexing association with Schaefer, which coincided with the rapid deterioration of the senior editor's health, he could count on the assistance of Alonzo Dill. Dill had moved into the editorial suite as a junior associate editor a few years before Chambers's departure and had proved both capable and reliable. A Tarheel native, Dill had graduated from the University of North Carolina in 1935 and worked briefly with the United Press news service in Chicago and Des Moines, as well as for the *Raleigh News and Observer*. After coming to the *Pilot* in 1937, he had quickly risen through the ranks to become one of the paper's star reporters and had caught Jaffé's eye. Aristocratic in taste and manners, Dill also could write superbly. He admired Jaffé and considered himself fortunate to work in close quarters with him, but wisely arranged to prevent editorial duties from usurping his private life entirely. Aware that Jaffé would call him frequently and at any hour, Dill refused to have a telephone installed in his apartment. He would later earn acclaim as an author for his exhaustively researched books, including *Governor Tyron and His Palace*.[15]

In the fall of 1946, in the midst of Jaffé's travails with Schaefer, Paul Huber, president of Norfolk Newspapers, died after a protracted period of ill health. Although Huber focused almost exclusively on financial matters, the *Pilot*'s editor and publisher had long enjoyed an effective working relationship. Huber had ranked Jaffé among the nation's most talented editorialists and as a result had compensated him at a rate that exceeded the salaries received by editors of the state's other principal papers, the *Richmond News Leader,* the *Richmond Times-Dispatch,* and the *Norfolk*

14. *London Independent,* 2 February 1991; Mason, interview by author, 18 September 1995; Jack Schaefer, *Shane* (Boston: Houghton Mifflin, 1949); *London Independent,* 2 February 1991; Schaefer, "A Brief Schaefer Bibliography," in *Shane: The Critical Edition,* n.p.

15. Dill, interview by author, 20 November 1992; Alonzo Dill to Lenoir Chambers, 7 April 1950, Chambers Papers; Mason, interview by author, 18 September 1995; Alonzo Dill, *Governor Tyron and His Palace* (Chapel Hill: University of North Carolina Press, 1955).

Ledger-Dispatch. Indeed, Huber knew of no other newspaper of comparable size that paid its editor so much.[16]

Both professionally and through his behind-the-scenes advocacy as a powerful leader of Norfolk's business community, Huber had backed Jaffé time and again, perhaps most notably in the bitter fight to secure the black beach. When Jaffé, in another matter close to his heart, had struggled to rally support for the construction of the Norfolk Museum of Arts and Sciences in the midst of the Great Depression and in the face of heated opposition (including that of the city council), Huber had again stood behind him. Huber had in late 1943, at his editor's urging, engineered Norfolk Newspapers' contribution of the largest single private-source sum received by the museum to that point in time.[17]

Jaffé may have aspired to succeed Huber as publisher. If he did, the board likely evaluated his candidacy seriously. He had a head for business. He had long followed Norfolk Newspapers' fiscal condition closely and had steeped himself in general economics through thorough reading of the *Wall Street Journal* and financial magazines. He had earned Slover's respect and confidence. He also held enough stock in the corporation to be considered a viable contender. But Slover instead nominated Henry Lewis, Huber's close associate whom he had tapped as his heir, and the matter was settled.[18]

Once again in the market for a senior associate editor, Jaffé learned through Virginius Dabney of the availability of Dabney's former subordinate, William Shands Meacham. Jaffé had had an acquaintance with Meacham, a native of nearby Petersburg, Virginia, for over twenty years, thought highly of his work, and believed he would make a compatible colleague. Meacham held strong journalistic credentials. He had begun his career in the mid-twenties at the *Ledger-Dispatch,* he later stated, "as a cub reporter (but one bold enough to hand in editorials which strangely enough were printed)." Between 1926 and 1936 he had served as the editor of the *Danville Register.* His work there had so impressed Jaffé that he had sent

16. *Pilot,* 26 September 1946; Paul Huber to Louis Jaffé, 6 January 1940, Jaffé Papers; Robert Mason, letter to author, 18 July 2000.

17. Louis Jaffé to Paul Huber, 1 January 1944, Jaffé Papers; *Pilot,* 26 September 1946, 1 August 1938; Wertenbaker, *Norfolk: Historic Southern Port,* 378–80.

18. Mason, interview by author, 18 September 1995; Chambers, Shank, and Sugg, *Salt Water & Printer's Ink,* 380.

Meacham an adulatory letter without knowing his identity. "Who are you and where do you come from?" Jaffé had written. He went on to express his gratitude to Meacham "for swinging the *Danville Register* smack into the liberal ranks, possessed of a progressive sophisticated viewpoint and a wallop." Meacham would later confide to Alice Jaffé that during his years in Danville he had modeled his editorial page on the *Pilot*'s.[19]

Throughout Meacham's tenure in the little cotton manufacturing and tobacco town, Jaffé had known that the young editor would encounter pressures from his paper's owners and advertisers to alter his liberal stances, a situation from which Jaffé had been comparatively insulated by Starke and Slover. He had mentored Meacham, lent him support, and gently urged him to continue his advocacy. When in 1930 labor militancy spread north from textile towns like Gastonia, Elizabethton, and Marion to the Riverside and Dan River Cotton Mills in Danville, Jaffé had known that Meacham would find himself on the front lines. The *Pilot*'s editor had affirmed his sympathy for labor but expressed his awareness of the limits to what Meacham could accomplish. "Nobody will expect the impossible of you," Jaffé had written. "All of us are far braver denouncing the grosseries of Fascist Italy than in denouncing the obscenities in our own backyards."[20]

Dabney, too, had appreciated Meacham's "graceful and practiced editorial style" and had brought him to Richmond, where he served as the *Times-Dispatch*'s associate editor between 1936 and 1942. Meacham also had long been interested in prison administration, and in 1942 Governor Colgate Darden had appointed him the first chairman of the Virginia Parole Board. When Darden's successor, William Munford Tuck, did not renew the appointment, the journalist-turned-penologist sought to return to his for-

19. Virginius Dabney to Louis Jaffé, 5 May 1948, Jaffé Papers; William S. Meacham to Lenoir Chambers, 4 October 1944, Chambers Papers; *Who's Who in the South and Southwest, 1950*, s.v. "William Shands Meacham"; Louis Jaffé to William Shands Meacham, 10 May 1927, Jaffé Papers; William Shands Meacham to Alice Jaffé, 13 June 1964, Louis Jaffé Jr.

20. Duane McCracken, *Strike Injunctions in the New South* (Chapel Hill: University of North Carolina Press, 1931), 114–26; Nancy J. Martin-Perdue and Charles L. Perdue Jr., eds., *Talk About Trouble: A New Deal Portrait of Virginians in the Great Depression* (Chapel Hill: University of North Carolina Press, 1996), 288–90; Heinemann, *Depression and New Deal*, 6–7; Louis Jaffé to William Meacham, 1 October 1930, Jaffé Papers.

mer profession in 1947. (Meacham later alleged that he had lost his job when he angered the new governor by refusing to release one of his constituents from prison. If the incident occurred, Tuck, whose memory for names was legendary in Virginia politics, certainly would never have forgotten such an offense.)[21]

Unknown to Jaffé, Meacham may have embellished his résumé somewhat. Although he claimed to have attended a branch of the College of William and Mary for three years, the registrar's department there could locate no record of his attendance. And despite his allusion to having taught at New York University, officials at that institution discovered no trace of his ever having served as full- or part-time faculty there.[22]

Despite Meacham's apparent suitability for the vacant position at the *Virginian-Pilot*, at close range Jaffé quickly grew disenchanted with his new associate. Meacham was prideful and easily angered over imaginary slights, and his methods of fact-finding and authoring editorials could not have differed more from Jaffé's. The new associate editor wrote facilely after only cursory research and quickly grew impatient if sources furnished more than superficial background on a subject. Probably only a few direct confrontations took place between Jaffé and Meacham, but their relationship was strained and at times unpleasant. Meacham foresaw that Jaffé's illness would soon force his retirement, and he deeply desired to replace him in the prestigious editorship of the *Virginian-Pilot*. This possibility must have troubled Jaffé, who knew that his liberal advocacy would be continued by Chambers and ardently wished for his former associate editor to succeed him.[23]

When in 1949 Alonzo Dill received an Ogden Reid Fellowship for

21. Dabney, *Across the Years,* 134; "Biographical Sketch of William S. Meacham," [1947?], Jaffé Papers; Robert Mason, interview by author, 5 December 1990; Leidholdt, *Standing Before the Shouting Mob*, 42–3; Mason, interview by author, 18 September 1995; Guy Friddell, *Opinions of an Old Contrarian* (Norfolk: Pilot Press, 1997), 126–7.

22. S. Garrison, interview by author, 27 September 1994; S. Aprill, interview by author, 24 September 1994.

23. Alice Jaffé to Louis Jaffé Jr., 1988, Louis Jaffé Jr.; Mason, interview by author, 5 December 1990; Leidholdt, *Standing Before the Shouting Mob*, 42–5; Alice Jaffé to Louis Jaffé Jr., 1988, Louis Jaffé Jr.; Harold Sugg, letter to author, 13 October 1990; William Meacham to Virginius Dabney, 30 April 1950, Dabney Papers.

a year's study abroad, Harold Sugg, the *Pilot*'s top political reporter, stood in for him. After graduating from Davidson College in the mid-thirties, Sugg had for a year edited the *Stanly News and Press* in Albemarle, a North Carolina textile town. Small-town journalism held little appeal for him, and he arrived at the *Pilot* in 1939. By 1946 he was covering city hall and the state legislative sessions. Like Dill, Sugg had earned a reputation throughout the paper for his writing ability. Sugg, too, considered himself fortunate to work closely with Jaffé. The new editorial writer admired particularly Jaffé's "brisk [and] informative" editorial conferences.[24]

Late in Jaffé's career, cracks began to emerge in Jim Crow's battlements, due in large part to the NAACP's legal activism and the decency and political courage of President Harry S. Truman. Scholars examining the southern intelligentsia during the postwar era have concluded that age figured prominently in their subjects' ability to adapt to changes in the South's racial landscape. Daniel Singal writes, "For those who came of age in the 1930s . . . it would be a relatively easy task; for others . . . just a few years older, it would take a long and hard struggle." Jaffé—then in his late fifties—might have been expected to adopt a more traditional attitude toward racial change, similar to that of Virginius Dabney. He did not.[25]

The Supreme Court's 1944 decision in *Smith v. Allwright,* which declared Texas's all-white primaries unconstitutional, amounted in Thurgood Marshall's view to the greatest victory of his career. Seeking to secure Fifteenth Amendment rights for blacks, the NAACP had for decades played a game of constitutional chess with crafty Lone Star authorities. Eyeing the state's hefty seven-figure black electorate, Marshall had remarked, "If we get a million Negroes voting in a bloc we are going to have some fun." Until *Smith,* the state's legislature had managed to stay one step ahead of the NAACP's legal staff through various chicaneries and deceits, ultimately repealing membership laws for political parties and devolving to them—as private voluntary organizations—the responsibility for conducting primary

24. Chambers, Shank, and Sugg, *Salt Water & Printer's Ink,* 374; *Who's Who in the South and Southwest, 1967–68,* s.v. "Harold Sugg"; Harold Sugg, letters to author, 2, 13 October 1990, 30 November 1990.

25. Daniel Joseph Singal, *The War Within: From Victorian to Modernist Thought in the South, 1919–1945* (Chapel Hill: University of North Carolina Press, 1982), 301.

elections. Texas's Democratic Party, which proscribed black participation, anointed the political leadership of the one-party state with near-total consistency. Thus, even though blacks possessed a legal right to vote in general elections, they remained for all intents and purposes disenfranchised. In a unanimous verdict in *Grovey v. Townsend* in 1935, the U.S. Supreme Court had upheld the constitutionality of the state's dubious primary elections. Nine years later, in *Smith,* the court in an eight-to-one decision reversed itself and ended Texas's lily-white primaries.[26]

No one savored the victory more than Walter White, who had seen Texas legislators such as Tom Connally and Martin Dies battle his initiatives throughout their careers. Nevertheless, the NAACP's leader must have pondered the irony that Justice Owen Roberts, who had authored the *Grovey* decision and served as the only holdout in *Smith,* had been nominated by Herbert Hoover only after his first choice, John J. Parker, had lost a narrow confirmation vote in the Senate due in large part to the onslaught that White had orchestrated.[27]

In 1935 Jaffé had underscored for his readers the unfairness of *Grovey,* and nine years later he relished the opportunity to take Roberts to task. Jaffé's attack on Texas's all-white primaries in the mid-thirties, while generally in accord with other southern liberal journalists' positions on suffrage restrictions, had predated by over five years the adoption of formal statements by the Commission on Interracial Cooperation and the Association of Southern Women for the Prevention of Lynching (ASWPL) opposing barriers to black voting. (Unlike its southern neighbors, Virginia had ended its all-white primaries in compliance with various court decisions in the late 1920s and early 1930s. The state continued to restrict black suffrage through literacy tests and the poll tax.)[28]

---

26. Williams, *Thurgood Marshall: American Revolutionary,* 109, 112.

27. Kermit L. Hall, ed., *The Oxford Companion to the Supreme Court of the United States* (New York: Oxford University Press, 1992), 737–8, 800–1; Key, *Southern Politics in State and Nation,* 621–4; Blaustein and Zangrando, *Civil Rights and African Americans,* 395–7; Sullivan, *Days of Hope,* 147–9; White, *Man Called White,* 105–10, 114.

28. Kneebone, *Southern Liberal Journalists,* 142; Hall, *Revolt Against Chivalry,* 225–6; Workers of the Writers' Program, *The Negro in Virginia,* 271–2; Key, *Southern Politics in State and Nation,* 564; Buni, *Negro in Virginia Politics,* 106; Tindall, *Emergence of the New South,* 558.

Justice Roberts, a native Pennsylvanian, had scolded his colleagues in a peevish dissent and argued that the era's greatest need was for "steadfastness of thought and purpose." The *Smith* decision, he grumbled, "tends to bring adjudications of [the] tribunal into the same class as a restricted railroad ticket, good for this day and train only." "Justice Roberts is mistaken . . . about the primacy of the era's need for steadfastness of thought and purpose," Jaffé wrote. "The far more important need in this or any other era is for basic justice. Judicial consistency ceases to be a jewel when it is invoked to perpetuate a denial of it. It was the opinion of the *Virginian-Pilot* that the 1935 decision denied it. We believe the present decision is sound." Liberal journalists such as Harry Ashmore joined the *Pilot* in supporting *Smith,* but southern senators opposed the decision to a man.[29]

The next year, New York passed an "anti-bias" law that created a State Commission Against Discrimination, the first such body in any state to act directly against racial and religious discrimination in private businesses and labor unions. The state assembly charged the commission with attempting to persuade offenders to end their discriminatory practices, but also invested it with quasi-judicial powers to issue cease-and-desist orders. The legislature empowered the commission to seek court action that would result in the fining and imprisonment of intractable lawbreakers. Supporters of the law believed it might help defuse the racial tensions that had triggered the many wartime riots, but Jaffé cautioned that he could "think of many sections in this country where an effort to give such a law sweeping and uncompromising enforcement" would also invite violence. He took a wait-and-see approach. "Something good may come of this law," he wrote. "If it does, it will come . . . as a by-product of its machinery of conciliation and persuasion sooner than from the invocation of its punitive disciplines. The wisdom and social insight of the law's administrators will have much to do with the law's ability to stand up against erosion. . . . New York has here become the testing ground for advanced experimental legislation in an extremely difficult and complex field."[30]

In 1946 Jaffé urged his readers to endorse a new advance in the

29. *Pilot,* 5 April 1944; Egerton, *Speak Now Against the Day,* 399; Ashmore, *Civil Rights and Wrongs,* 61.

30. *Pilot,* 12 March 1945.

civil-rights arena—nondiscriminatory seating on interstate transportation. In *Morgan v. Virginia* the Supreme Court, in a seven-to-one decision, struck down an Old Dominion statute mandating segregation on interstate carriers. Virginia's law owed at least part of its origin to the morning in 1899 when Governor James Hoge Tyler had awakened in an Atlanta-bound train and discovered with great consternation a "negro opposite him, above him, and in front of him." Three months later the General Assembly had acted to ensure that no Virginian would ever again suffer such mortification.[31]

Scornful of the state legislators' edict, Irene Morgan had in 1944 refused to move to the back of the Greyhound bus on her journey home to Baltimore from a trip she had taken to Gloucester County, Virginia. Local authorities had arrested her and fined her ten dollars in the red brick courthouse in tiny Saluda, near the mouth of the Rappahannock River. Spotswood "Spot" Robinson, the shrewd pipe-smoking Howard Law School professor, oversaw her failed appeal to Virginia's highest court and later assisted Thurgood Marshall and one of his revered mentors, William Hastie, in preparing the case the NAACP argued before the Supreme Court. With characteristic wit and his easy self-effacing manner, Marshall prevailed in his fourth appearance before the high court. The decision, which held that the Virginia law violated the Commerce Clause of the U.S. Constitution, amounted to a civil rights watershed; until the ruling, the justices had upheld the constitutionality of separate but equal accommodations.[32]

Although *Morgan* established an important and far-reaching precedent, it did not overstep Jaffé's gradualistic approach to civil rights, and he attempted to take the edge off the sharp criticism directed at the decision by hot-headed southerners. "The Supreme Court's decision both in its immediate and in its ultimate implications cuts into the segregation pattern that prevails in ten Southern States," he wrote, "but there is no reason for Southern over-excitement about it. The desegregation here ordered does not invade that hard-core of racial separatism, imbedded in Southern custom

31. Workers of the Writers' Program, *The Negro in Virginia*, 266.

32. Hall, *Oxford Companion to the Supreme Court*, 562–3; Williams, *Thurgood Marshall: American Revolutionary*, 145–6; *Pilot*, 5 June 1946; Jack Greenberg, *Crusaders in the Courts: How a Dedicated Band of Lawyers Fought for the Civil Rights Revolution* (New York: Basic Books, 1994), 109–10; Carl T. Rowan, *Dream Makers, Dream Breakers: The World of Justice Thurgood Marshall* (Boston: Little, Brown, 1993), 175.

and law, which southern majority opinion holds to be essential to the region's peace and which the majority opinion of the South will determinedly defend against dilution. The present decision invades a peripheral area of Southern segregation where a once rigid racial separatism has been undergoing gradual revision. Segregation of the races on the public carriers is beginning to generate tensions—some of them as serious as the tensions it was designed to avert." Jaffé believed the time was "ripe" to test whether an easing of Jim Crow laws would lead to improved race relations.[33]

In October 1947 a distinguished panel that included what the *Nation* termed a "Noah's Ark" of members—pairs of corporate heads, labor leaders, college presidents, Jews, Catholics, women, blacks, and southerners; University of North Carolina president Frank Porter Graham; and Methodist church leader and ASWPL principal Dorothy R. Tilly— issued a book-length report on civil rights entitled *To Secure These Rights*. President Truman had assembled the blue-ribbon advisory group after a Walter White–led delegation demanded federal action to end a spate of sadistic attacks on blacks. In1946 White had briefed Truman on the swelling number of hate groups circulating diatribes against blacks, Jews, Catholics, labor unions, and immigrants, as well as on the escalation of racial violence that year.[34]

In two incidents in Georgia and Louisiana, lynch mobs had taken the lives of five blacks—two of them war veterans—and a police chief in South Carolina had blinded a black ex-serviceman just back from duty in the South Pacific. In Columbia, Tennessee, five hundred National Guardsmen had mounted a military-style assault against a black neighborhood, Mink Slide. The NAACP's leader recalled that the grim-faced president had listened quietly to his presentation and then exclaimed, "My God! I had no idea it was as terrible as that! We've got to do something!" Bypassing powerful southern congressional leaders, Truman had created the panel with an executive order.[35]

---

33. *Pilot,* 5 June 1946.

34. Sosna, *In Search of the Silent South,* 150; Hall, *Revolt Against Chivalry,* 363.

35. White, *Man Called White,* 322–31; Wilkins, *Standing Fast,* 193; Blaustein and Zangrando, *Civil Rights and African Americans,* 372–9; Gail Williams O'Brien, *The Color of the Law: Race, Violence, and Justice in the Post–World War II South* (Chapel Hill: University of North Carolina Press, 1999), 7–55.

To Secure These Rights exceeded White's wildest expectations, and he called it "without doubt the most courageous and specific document of its kind in American history." His successor, former newspaperman Roy Wilkins, would recall in his memoirs that the NAACP used the report as a "blueprint [for its civil-rights activism] for the next two decades." Among its thirty-five unanimous recommendations, it included calls for ending "all discrimination and segregation . . . in . . . the armed forces," the "enactment by Congress of an antilynching act," "action by the states or Congress to end poll taxes," and—most controversially—the "elimination of segregation, based on race, color, creed, or national origin, from American life."[36]

Jaffé seemed to agonize over *To Secure These Rights*, which pushed him to examine in painful detail his own attitudes toward race relations. (The committee's deliberations had had precisely that effect on Frank Porter Graham.) Like many of his southern newspaper peers, Jaffé could have elected to ignore the recommendations or directed his readers' attention away from the panel's indictment of the South by resorting to an ad hominem attack on the North and its own racial problems. The report was bitter medicine, even for southerners who had devoted their lives to advancing human rights, but Jaffé swallowed it.[37]

He called *To Secure These Rights* a "document that belongs in the permanent collection of every thoughtful American" concerned about civil rights. "It is no easier to take exception to the manifesto's central thesis—that the privileges, sanctions, protections and opportunities of American citizenship should be extended to all members of the American family without prejudice or limitation on the ground of race, creed or color—," he wrote, "than it is to take exception to the essential professions of the Declaration of Independence, of the Bill of Rights and, indeed, of the religious doctrine which orders our paths to salvation."[38]

Jaffé did not attempt to justify his region's history of racism and racial violence, but he did "enter a kind of plea in extenuation." "Human

36. White, *Man Called White*, 333; Wilkins, *Standing Fast*, 200; President's Committee on Civil Rights, *To Secure These Rights: The Report of the President's Committee on Civil Rights* (New York: Simon and Schuster, 1947), 157, 160, 162, 166.

37. Ashby, *Frank Porter Graham*, 224–6; Sosna, *In Search of the Silent South*, 150–152.

38. *Pilot*, 31 October 1947.

beings and their social institutions," he contended, "always have been, still are, and are likely to remain imperfect; . . . men and women living in the contemporary social and economic frame are to a large extent prisoners of their blood and of their social past; and . . . though, considered in terms of pure democracy, our practices—especially in the South—fall far short of our copy-book and prayer-book professions, we have yet managed in the United States as fair and free a life for its people as exists anywhere on earth." He commended the authors of *To Secure These Rights* for acknowledging this.[39]

It would be unrealistic, he wrote, to believe that the federal government could by fiat eliminate all vestiges of racial suspicion, hatred, and unfairness. But, he declared, "many gross discriminations—civic, economic and political—that abridge the rights and liberties of our American minorities, especially our large Negro minority, need to be wiped out, should be wiped out by Federal legislation if relief is withheld by the States, and . . . this process of rectification has a long way to go before it can impinge on the raw inner-nerve of social separateness which will not bear touching save under the opiate of uncoerced approval voted by the peoples of the separate sovereign States." He finished by calling the report and its recommendations a "searching and useful contribution to our democratic therapy."[40]

Jaffé's strong editorial endorsement of the report's findings set him apart from nearly all of his peers in the southern press, even the region's most prominent liberal newspaper editors such as Hodding Carter, the Pulitzer Prize–winning editor of the *Greenville (Miss.) Delta Democrat-Times,* and future Pulitzer winners Dabney and McGill. Jaffé also came to the defense of Graham, whom many letter writers and southern newspapers excoriated for his membership on the panel. Jonathan Daniels perhaps came closest to joining Jaffé in sanctioning *To Secure These Rights.* Although Josephus Daniels blasted the committee's recommendations in one of his swan-song editorials (he died the following January), the younger Daniels soon came to support the report's findings and, like Jaffé, asserted that the federal government should ensure blacks' civil rights if southern states continued not to do so. By adopting positions that exceeded the tolerance of

39. Ibid.
40. Ibid.

most of their readers, Jaffé and Daniels opened themselves to charges of betraying their region. Their intellectual honesty and courage should not be underestimated.[41]

The NAACP's legal team continued to chip away at Jim Crow. In January 1948, in *Sipuel v. Board of Regents of the University of Oklahoma,* it scored another victory. Ada Lois Sipuel, the brainy and beautiful daughter of a minister, had been denied admission to Oklahoma's law school solely on the basis of her race. The university's president, George L. Cross, sympathetic to Sipuel's cause, had dictated for the NAACP's use a letter acknowledging that she would have been admitted had she been white; he had thus preempted state authorities from alleging that academic weaknesses, not race, accounted for her rejection. Cross recalled that when he arrived at the university in 1934 from the North, he had been informed that there was an "unwritten law that niggers can't be in Norman after sundown." Thurgood Marshall and his legal staff had found the "law" still on the books when they made their initial legal arguments in the university town. They could make no sleeping arrangements in Norman, nor could they find a restaurant that would serve them lunch. Marshall put Sipuel to work making sandwiches and secured accommodations in nearby Oklahoma City. Finding himself in a "dry" state, the NAACP advocate immediately laid in a prodigious stock of bootleg whiskey, which he used to entertain his staff and the deans of many of the nation's elite law schools, who delighted in the company of the charismatic raconteur and provided him with invaluable legal advice during late-night drinking/strategy sessions.[42]

The case followed a predictable pattern, with the NAACP encountering defeat in the state courts and prevailing in the U.S. Supreme Court on appeal. Only a few days after hearing arguments, the Court issued a terse decision, based entirely on *Gaines,* compelling Oklahoma to act without delay to furnish Sipuel with an education equal in quality to that provided

41. Egerton, *Speak Now Against the Day,* 470–1, 488; Ann Waldron, *Hodding Carter: The Reconstruction of a Racist* (Chapel Hill: Algonquin Books, 1993), 205–6; Barbara Barksdale Clowse, *Ralph McGill: A Biography* (Macon, Ga.: Mercer University Press, 1998), 138–9; Sloan and Anderson, *Pulitzer Prize Editorials,* 97–9, 105–7, 144–6; Eagles, *Jonathan Daniels and Race Relations,* 128–37.

42. Williams, *Thurgood Marshall: American Revolutionary,* 176–8; Rowan, *Dream Makers, Dream Breakers,* 145–9; Tushnet, *NAACP's Legal Strategy,* 120–1.

for white students. The verdict seemed to be a great victory for the NAACP until state authorities unexpectedly concocted a Potemkin "law school" in the capitol, where Sipuel would have attended classes as the only student. When Marshall eventually secured her admission to the University of Oklahoma's law school in 1949, white students welcomed her into the program warmly and assisted her with her studies.[43]

Jaffé apprised his readers that the *Sipuel* decision would force the integration of Virginia's graduate and professional programs and urged state lawmakers to engage in no subterfuge and carry out the Court's mandate without delay. He wrote that none of the southern states had "even in a nominal sense provided the equal facilities for graduate and professional education that the *Gaines* decision prescribed—perhaps because the Supreme Court was content to define the requirement of the Constitution on this point without setting a time within which to comply with it." The *Sipuel* verdict specified that states must redress inequities in graduate and professional education for blacks and whites immediately. "The dilemma posed by the Court's decision . . . is an all-Southern dilemma. The Virginia legislature which convenes today has the best of reasons for pondering the compulsions of the Supreme Court's new decision and for charting a State course that will at once comport with this decision and the best judgment of the people of Virginia."[44]

On February 2, 1948, President Truman, who had deliberated carefully over the contents of *To Secure These Rights,* delivered a State of the Union address. The heated criticism directed at the panel throughout the South had begun to cool; after all, the committee's membership had consisted of fifteen private citizens, not government officials. To his great credit, Truman, who undoubtedly had been taken aback at first by the boldness of the report, exhorted Congress to enact many of his panel's recommendations into legislation. Although Truman's speech and his nomination by the Democratic Party that summer at its steamy and raucous Philadelphia convention, where liberals emerged triumphant with a strong civil-rights plank, did not have as incendiary an effect on the South as Abraham Lincoln's elec-

43. Williams, *Thurgood Marshall: American Revolutionary,* 178–9.
44. *Pilot,* 14 January 1948.

tion to the presidency, it did trigger a revolt. Throughout the spring and summer, southern legislators—their sense of betrayal heightened by the fact that Truman came from a state that had added a star to the Confederate flag—competed in hurling vituperation at the president. Many of the region's delegates walked out of the Philadelphia convention in protest and headed straight to the all-white "Dixiecrat" convocation in Birmingham, where amidst rebel yells they dubbed South Carolina governor James Strom Thurmond the head of their new party.[45]

By this point, the animus between Truman and Virginia's powerful Senator Byrd, the undisputed leader of his state's political establishment, had grown palpable. Although he would not break with his party and openly endorse the Dixiecrats, Byrd, who had devolved into a dour and miserly reactionary, would maintain a "golden silence" regarding Truman's candidacy, thus conveying tacit dispensation for his many followers to vote for either Republican nominee Thomas Dewey or Thurmond.[46]

In this charged atmosphere, Congress considered a bill that would provide the states with $300 million of federal support per year for education. The government would distribute the moneys according to a formula that would provide the most revenue to the states with the poorest children. According to the measure's guidelines, Virginia, with its under-financed white schools and its unconscionably neglected black schools, would receive almost three times as much funding as Minnesota, which had nearly the same population. The bill would have a similarly salutary effect throughout the South, whose strapped schools stood in urgent need of assistance. Unthinkable as it seemed that any southern member of Congress would oppose the proposal, Byrd did just that. Asserting that the bill would increase the budget and that the federal government would at some future date use this support as leverage to force the integration of southern schools,

---

45. Egerton, *Speak Now Against the Day*, 416, 476–7, 495–501; Robert A. Garson, *The Democratic Party and the Politics of Sectionalism, 1941–1948* (Baton Rouge: Louisiana State University Press, 1974), 221–82; Blaustein and Zangrando, *Civil Rights and African Americans*, 380–4; Dewey W. Grantham, *The South in Modern America: A Region at Odds* (New York: HarperCollins, 1994), 199–201; Key, *Southern Politics in State and Nation*, 329–36.

46. Heinemann, *Harry Byrd of Virginia*, 262–3, 293–4.

Byrd joined Virginia's junior senator, garrulous Absalom Willis Robertson, and three other upper-house Dixie colleagues in casting ballots against the bill.[47]

Jaffé began his editorial response to his former ally's vote by stressing the importance of education to the stability of democratic institutions and his belief that the primary responsibility of a state lay in furnishing its children with adequate education. In the event that states or localities lacked the means to support their public schools, he asserted that the federal government should come to their aid. He then proceeded to dismantle Byrd's objections to the bill. "We do not share the fear that [the bill] is a diabolic Trojan Horse designed by Northern and Western conspirators to make a slick entry into the Southern States for the purpose of disrupting their established public school arrangements," he wrote. Regarding the senator's objection to the bill's expense, Jaffé pointed out that even if lawmakers had allocated $500 million, the figure would represent only 1 percent of the total federal budget. "That is not too large a proportion of the nation's revenue to apply to the rectification of education inequalities," he wrote. "The nation's most important resource is its children. . . . Educational facilities must be provided during a generation's school years. . . . Lost school cannot be recaptured."[48]

Byrd's Norfolk lieutenant, William "Billy" Prieur, a key cog in the senator's formidable machine, undoubtedly apprised him of the *Pilot*'s editorial, but history suggests that Jaffé's advocacy for education moved the senator not at all. A decade later, in a ploy devised by Byrd, Virginia would close many of its public schools in an attempt to subvert the Supreme Court's mandate in *Brown v. Board of Education*. Broadcast journalists Edward R. Murrow and Fred Friendly would devote one of their famous *See It Now* episodes to Norfolk's school closing and entitle it "The Lost Class of '59."[49]

---

47. Ibid., 279, 293; Grantham, *South in Modern America*, 205; *Pilot,* 7 April 1948; Heinemann, *Harry Byrd of Virginia,* 277–8.

48. *Pilot,* 7 April 1948.

49. Ibid.; Leidholdt, *Standing Before the Shouting Mob,* 61–2, 70, 83, 115; Forrest R. White, *Pride and Prejudice: School Desegregation and Urban Renewal in Norfolk, 1950–1959* (Westport, Conn.: Praeger, 1992), xxi; Edward R. Murrow and Fred W. Friendly, *The Lost Class of '59* (New York: CBS, 21 January 1959), videorecording; J. Fred MacDonald,

Despite Jaffé's support for *To Secure These Rights* and for many of Truman's civil-rights initiatives, he did not endorse the president's bid for re-election in November 1948. In Jaffé's view, Truman's "courage, sincerity, [and] unremitting industry" did not outweigh his weaknesses as a national leader and statesman. Nor had Dewey's campaign galvanized Jaffé's support, and he played "no intentional part in promoting the . . . Republican ticket." He did not, however, view the Dixiecrats ambivalently. He considered the movement at best "an ill-considered sortie up a magnolia-scented blind alley." At its worst he judged it a "device to give an aspect of nobility . . . to a knifing of Truman." He, like the rest of the nation's press, saw Dewey's election as a foregone conclusion. "The virtually unanimous finding of [the] most experienced takers of the public pulse" had divined a Dewey landslide, he wrote. Dewey's certain election did not distress Jaffé; he believed the New Yorker would function as a competent if somewhat unimaginative administrator.[50]

Jaffé surely was no less dumbfounded than his editorial peers and indeed the general public at the upshot of "Give 'em hell Harry's" 355-speech whistle-stop flaying of the "do-nothing 80th Congress." Only Alabama, Louisiana, Mississippi, and South Carolina had bolted the South's traditional Democratic solidarity. The overwhelming support of blacks also had figured prominently in Truman's victory. Roy Wilkins wrote, "The message was plain: white power in the South could be balanced with black power in the northern polls." Left with egg on his face like nearly every other editorialist in the country, Jaffé, speaking for the *Virginian-Pilot,* wrote that it was the "embarrassing task of this red-faced company to apply its logic to the explanation of President Truman's astounding victory, and its prescience to an estimate of what it portends." In Jaffé's opinion, Truman's "aroused fighting spirit . . . , tenacity . . . , high heart . . . , and fixity of purpose" accounted for his triumph.[51]

Senator Byrd, chagrined by the president's victory in the Old

---

Blacks and White TV: African Americans in Television Since 1948 (Chicago: Nelson-Hall, 1992), 100–2.

50. Egerton, *Speak Now Against the Day,* 491; *Pilot,* 19 October 1948, 1, 2 November 1948.

51. Garson, *Democratic Party and Sectionalism,* 310–4; Egerton, *Speak Now Against the Day,* 508–10; Wilkins, *Standing Fast,* 202; *Pilot,* 4 November 1948.

Dominion, continued to match his die-hard opposition to progressive federal initiatives such as the education-funding bill with his ruthless suppression of forward-thinking state resolutions. When in early 1950 Alexandria delegate Armistead L. Boothe, a World War II veteran and Rhodes scholar, proposed bills that would end state-enforced segregation on transportation in Virginia and create a much-needed state civil-rights commission, Byrd squelched them. At approximately this time, Byrd machine hard-liners also began to consider shutting down or privatizing schools and parks should their integration be mandated by the courts. "Nonsegregation would be most unwise and I will certainly oppose it every way I can," the senator wrote to a constituent.[52]

The demise of the Boothe bills, whose passage Jaffé had regarded as "highly desirable," did not surprise him. "The Virginia Democratic Organization makes haste slowly in the field of social-political reform," he observed drolly in late February 1950. "It allowed the Federal woman suffrage amendment to confer the voting right on Virginia women without ever troubling to arrange for approval of the Federal amendment by the Virginia General Assembly. It boarded the Federal social security train by a frantic special-session leap after all the other States had contracted for its services. It has only recently arrived at the point of not being frightened by the prospect of poll tax repeal."[53]

The manner in which the oldest legislative body in the Western Hemisphere had dispatched the bills, however, galled him. He described it as "slick, slippery and distasteful." The House Courts of Justice Committee had kept the measures from an Assembly vote and—contravening House rules—secreted the votes of the committee members from public record. "This is a committee procedure in high favor in Budapest on the Danube," Jaffé wrote. "It is entitled to nobody's respect when resorted to by Richmond on the James. By chance—certainly not by intent—the 'mercy killing' of the Boothe bills in the chamber of the House Courts of Justice Committee took place on the sixth day of Brotherhood Week and on the third day of

---

52. Wilkinson, *Harry Byrd and Virginia Politics*, 108; *Pilot*, 25 February 1950; Heinemann, *Harry Byrd of Virginia*, 318.

53. *Pilot*, 25 February 1950; Salmon and Campbell, *Hornbook of Virginia History*, 252.

Lent. The present and resurrectionary promises of these lay and religious observances invite us to believe—and we do so believe—that although the Boothe desegregation bill is dead as of 1950, it remains very much alive as of the years that lie ahead."[54]

Despite the pain Jaffé now endured on a daily basis and his reduced stamina and mobility, he retained his active intellect and penetrating curiosity. *Ledger-Dispatch* managing editor Charles F. Reilly Jr. later recalled that during this period, Jaffé continued his lifelong practice of asking tough questions and refusing to settle for easy answers. "That man Jaffé leaves me limp," one of Reilly's photographers complained. He explained that the editor had buttonholed him in the alley behind the newspaper building and asked so many questions he could not answer about his camera that the photojournalist had come to believe he knew nothing about his own craft.[55]

When the country's only remaining commissioned battleship, the USS *Missouri*—upon whose deck the Japanese had surrendered to the Allies in 1945—ran aground on a mud flat in Hampton Roads in January 1950 and to the Navy's humiliation could not be extricated for a fortnight, the national press descended on Norfolk. Reilly had served in the Coast Guard during the war; he had attended the Navy press conference on the mishap, boarded the vessel, and written a number of articles on the grounding. Consequently he felt that he knew more about the story than anyone else. Jaffé stopped him in a hallway and asked a battery of questions about the grounding—points that no journalist had yet investigated and that would prove to stump naval experts. Reilly immediately dispatched a reporter with a list of fifteen questions the press had not considered. "Have you been talking to Mr. Jaffé again?" she asked as she departed. (Jaffé later commended the reporter to Reilly and wrote her a note praising her work.)[56]

Reilly also recalled touring the aircraft carrier USS *Roosevelt* with the secretary of the Navy, military brass flanking the Joint Chiefs of Staff, and members of the press, including the *Pilot*'s editor. "The entire operation

54. *Pilot*, 25 February 1950.
55. Ibid., 13 March 1950.
56. Mason, *One of the Neighbors' Children*, 116–8; *Ledger*, 13 March 1950; Chambers, Shank, and Sugg, *Salt Water & Printer's Ink*, 373.

fascinated [Jaffé], and he was all over the ship firing questions with machine gun rapidity," Reilly recalled. He observed that only General Omar Bradley, who during World War II had commanded the largest number of combat troops ever to serve under a single American field commander, asked more questions than Jaffé. The editor asked to speak with a pilot about helicopters, and an aviator sat down with him for an hour. The roar of aircraft engines obscured their conversation from passersby, but as Reilly moved about on the flight deck, he could see the airman making hand gestures as he explained helicopter aeronautics to the newspaperman. The flight crews shut off the planes' engines just as the interview ended, and Reilly overheard the pilot apologize, "I am sorry I could not give you all the information you wanted, but I'll try to get the answers for you."[57]

On the morning of March 9, 1950, Louis Jaffé Jr., then aged three and a half, observed with surprise that his father had not dressed for work. Standing before his son, Jaffé, wearing pajamas and a bathrobe, calmly explained that he had to make a trip to the hospital. He seemed fine to young Louis, who "took him at his word" that he would shortly return. Physicians at Norfolk General Hospital examined Jaffé, almost certainly because of his heart disease, and admitted him for observation. The timing must have irked him, because he was in the midst of waging an editorial battle to abolish Virginia's poll tax. Throughout his newspaper career in Norfolk, he had fought for its repeal.[58]

The poll tax and a literacy test that rural officials twisted to disenfranchise blacks (many of these registrars would distribute to blacks blank pieces of paper and wait silently for them, unassisted by notes or prompting, to supply in the correct order information that state election procedures required) combined with apathy born of the Old Dominion's generally preordained election results and lifelong habits of not voting to make Virginia arguably the least democratic state in the nation. In 1931 the State Supreme Court of Appeals had declared illegal the "understanding" tests in which registrars asked blacks arcane civics questions that frequently neither these

57. *Ledger*, 13 March 1950.

58. Louis Jaffé Jr., interview by author, 1 November 1999; Chambers, Shank, and Sugg, *Salt Water & Printer's Ink*, 381–2; *Pilot*, 13 March 1950.

officials nor erudite Hampton Institute professors could answer, but only the NAACP's constant vigilance prevented authorities in Virginia's "black belt" counties from continuing to use the tests.[59]

By 1940, Virginia State College professor Luther Porter Jackson, founder and president of the Virginia State Voters League, had concluded that political apathy and the poll tax constituted the primary impediments to voting. In order to cast their ballots, Virginians had to pay an annual $1.50 suffrage tax. Should a prospective voter not have paid this fee in the preceding years, election laws levied a cumulative tax of up to $4.50. Voters had to remit their poll taxes half a year in advance of the general elections—about three months prior to the gubernatorial primaries—well before candidates announced and their campaigns aroused interest. Throughout Jaffé's editorial tenure, approximately 11.5 percent of potential voters in Virginia cast their ballots in the all-important Democratic primaries. (A Republican had last occupied the Governor's Mansion in the early 1870s.) Thus, 5 to 7 per cent of the adult population selected the state's political leader. In 1937 only 826 members of Norfolk's large black community paid the poll tax.[60]

In his exhaustive and witty 1949 treatise, Southern Politics in State and Nation, V. O. Key entitled a chapter "Virginia: A Political Museum Piece." "Of all the American states," Key wrote, "Virginia can lay claim to the most thorough control by an oligarchy." To a large extent, low voting numbers accounted for the Byrd machine's reign. Even in comparison with that of its southern neighbors, all of whom were characterized by tightly bridled electorates, voting turnout in the Old Dominion occupied the bottom position, far below the region's next worst.[61]

Although repeal sentiment had gathered steam with liberal journalists in the mid-1930s, Jaffé had urged poll-tax reform in the preceding decade, most notably in 1926, when newly inaugurated Governor Byrd commissioned a citizens' panel to recommend changes in Virginia gover-

59. Buni, Negro in Virginia Politics, 128–9; Low and Clift, Encyclopedia of Black America, 467; Key, Southern Politics in State and Nation, 580–1.

60. Buni, Negro in Virginia Politics, 124–33; Low and Clift, Encyclopedia of Black America, 467; Key, Southern Politics in State and Nation, 19–20, 580–1; Workers of the Writers' Program, Virginia: A Guide to the Old Dominion, 290; Dabney, Virginia: The New Dominion, 371–3; Workers of the Writers' Program, The Negro in Virginia, 271–2.

61. Key, Southern Politics in State and Nation, 19–20, 493, 564, 579–94.

nance. Jaffé's advocacy had borne no fruit, and he had then chided his peers in the press for not admitting that the South abridged blacks' Fourteenth and Fifteenth Amendment rights. Writing to fellow editor Walter S. Copeland in 1927, he had professed amazement that "Southern newspapers should so desperately pretend that their State election laws do not effectively defeat the intent of these amendments, when their party leaders make no bones about it and when they continue to oppose with all the power at their command any and all attempts to simplify the State election laws on the ground that to do so would be to undo the work that was done by the framers of the present constitutions when they contrived by ingenious provisions to exclude the Negro from the polls."[62]

During the 1930s, Jaffé had stirred up some outcry for the removal of voting barriers. In a 1936 editorial, "Virginia's Shackled Electorate," he had contrasted the state's lackluster voting turnouts with those of neighboring North Carolina, where twice as many citizens went to the polls. No doubt incurring Byrd's displeasure, he had pointed out that Virginia's constricted electorate made it particularly susceptible to "organization control." Early the following year, he had declared that the commonweath's poll tax was "not exceeded in severity in any other State." (In reality, Alabama and Georgia had enacted election laws that were in some ways even more restrictive.) Jaffé pointed out that although the state's legislators had concocted the tax at the turn of the century with the express purpose of eliminating black suffrage, the tax also played a prominent role in disenfranchising two-thirds of the state's whites in the depression years.[63]

When the co-owned *Ledger-Dispatch,* which supported the poll tax, asked the *Pilot* and other Old Dominion newspapers, "Are the States that have comparatively loose suffrage requirements as well governed as Virginia is?" Jaffé took editor Douglas Gordon to task. "Maybe yes," he wrote. "Maybe no. Perhaps just as well. But that is not the issue. The issue is one of democracy—not Democracy, politically organized and restricted.

62. *Pilot,* 14 September 1937, 20 October 1942; Heinemann, *Harry Byrd of Virginia,* 66–7; Kneebone, *Southern Liberal Journalists,* 141–3; Louis Jaffé to Walter Copeland, 28 November 1927, Jaffé Papers.

63. *Pilot,* 7 December 1936, 1 February 1937, 13 March 1950; Key, *Southern Politics in State and Nation,* 580; Virginius Dabney, "Civil Liberties in the South," *Virginia Quarterly Review* 16, no. 1 (winter 1940): 81–91; Tindall, *Emergence of the New South,* 640.

Italy may be as well-governed as Virginia. Some people think it is. But even if it were better governed than Virginia, we should still insist that it would be a negation of the democratic principle for Virginia to establish the Fascist electoral system and suppress the free play of public opinion."[64]

Poll tax opponents rejoiced when Virginia governor-elect James Hubert Price announced in January 1938 that he favored repeal of the levy. The unpretentious and popular former two-term Democratic lieutenant governor, who had alienated Byrd by embracing much-needed New Deal initiatives, flouted the senator's will further by not asking his blessing prior to declaring as a candidate. Sizing up Price as unbeatable, Byrd bestowed on him a reluctant and tepid endorsement. Price had staged a minor palace revolution, but machine insiders still controlled the General Assembly. A resolution introduced into the House of Delegates to abolish the poll tax died in the House Privileges and Elections Committee, and much of Price's legislative agenda met with a similar fate.[65]

The U.S. Congress stimulated electoral reform in the South by passing the Soldiers Vote Bill of 1942, which provided absentee ballots and invalidated poll taxes for servicemen and servicewomen in federal elections. Congress exerted even more pressure when it debated passage of the Geyer-Pepper bill, which advocated elimination of suffrage taxes for all voters in federal elections. The discriminatory electoral practices of southern states— Virginia's in particular—received prominent and embarrassing national attention. Despite his opposition to the poll tax, Dabney lobbied against the Geyer-Pepper bill, maintaining that it "would cause a frightful uproar in the South . . . and would contribute greatly to intersectional bitterness." He preferred that the region's states "resolve this knotty question for themselves."[66]

Jaffé did not bristle over the intrusion of the federal government into Dixie's affairs; instead he used the Soldiers Vote and Geyer-Pepper bills as leverage to goad the General Assembly to act. In late October 1942, he

64. *Pilot*, 12 September 1937.

65. Heinemann, *Harry Byrd of Virginia*, 187–92; Dabney, *Virginia: The New Dominion*, 506–9; Buni, *Negro in Virginia Politics*, 135–136.

66. Sullivan, *Days of Hope*, 114–20; Virginius Dabney, *Below the Potomac: A Book About the New South* (New York: D. Appleton-Century, 1942), 124; Kneebone, *Southern Liberal Journalists*, 142.

informed his readers that congressional legislation would "divide Virginia's electorate into two classes—a first class, its suffrage taxes paid, which could vote in all elections (local, State or Federal), and a second class, its poll taxes not paid, who could vote in Federal elections but not in local or State elections. This delectable prospect is near enough to realization to justify our State political leadership in giving it immediate attention," he wrote. "Silence on the poll tax issue will no longer serve. We urgently need a reordering of Virginia policy to fit changes that cannot be stayed." (Surprisingly, the Geyer-Pepper bill passed through the House with overwhelming support, but southern senators soon torpedoed it.)[67]

Jaffé again tackled the poll tax three days later. He argued that it violated the fundamental precepts of representative government and universal suffrage. Dismissing charges that many northern and midwestern congressional representatives supported abolition simply to curry favor with their black constituents, he wrote that the issue in fact centered on an "underlying and deeper controversy over the nature of the political state— whether the political state, in the fundamental American conception, belongs to the whole people without regard to religion, race, sex or wealth, or to a restricted group of the people who have contrived by one election barrier or another to constitute themselves a kind of governing caste."[68]

Today Jaffé's challenge appears unexceptional and unexceptionable; but from a contemporary standpoint and as the editor of a southern newspaper, he had staked out a controversial position. Other southern liberal journalists at this juncture—Dabney and Milton, for example—argued against the tax primarily on the grounds that its rescission would not threaten white political domination (in states such as Louisiana and North Carolina, annulment had not led to a conspicuous alteration in the racial balance of voters) and that it would serve to diminish the power of corrupt political machines that paid the taxes of their minions *en bloc*. (Interestingly, Dabney did not allude to the Byrd machine, which regularly had paid the poll taxes of many of its white constituents; instead he cited San Antonio's and Memphis's political machines, which respectively tapped Hispanic and black populations as wellsprings of their support.) Jaffé himself had

67. *Pilot*, 20 October 1942; Sullivan, *Days of Hope*, 118, 120.
68. *Pilot*, 23 October 1942.

previously maintained that poll tax reform or elimination would not lead to a fundamental change in the ratio of black to white voters, but by the early 1940s his editorials emphasized increasingly the unfair and anti-democratic nature of the tax.[69]

In this regard, Jaffé continued to serve, as he had throughout his career, as a trailblazer for many southern journalists. Time and time again he had placed himself in the forefront of the region's liberal press in attacking racial injustice and defending human rights. His sustained assaults on redbaiters, the Klan, religious fundamentalists seeking to proscribe the teaching of evolution, and fascism and Nazism predated those of other white Virginia journalists and nearly all other white southern newspapers. The same held true of his advocacy for state lynch laws, his subsequent support for federal antilynching legislation, and his early attacks on the poll tax.

Disseminated in many parts of the South via reprinting and imitated by a few disciples, Jaffé's editorials undoubtedly influenced readers outside the *Pilot*'s immediate sphere. Television in its infancy was ineffectual, particularly in the South, where it would remain so for many years; and radio news coverage—except for the reportage of Edward R. Murrow and a handful of other broadcast journalism pioneers—was transient and superficial. Newspapers and magazines comprised the dominant media by which the region's citizenry learned about itself and the world beyond the Magnolia Curtain.[70]

Some of Jaffé's most significant advocacy lay in the promulgation of his beliefs to his southern newspaper peers via newspaper exchange agreements. Although his editorials did not directly sway sizable numbers of editors to endorse his views immediately or without qualification, they broke the ice, set an agenda, and encouraged the interrogation of Jim Crow. Consequently they helped establish among his peers a climate for increasingly frank debate on the contravention of democracy and the Bill of Rights by southern mores and black laws.

69. Kneebone, *Southern Liberal Journalists,* 142–3; Virginius Dabney, *Below the Potomac,* 114–23; Key, *Southern Politics in State and Nation,* 594, 273, 63–75; *Pilot,* 14 September 1937.

70. MacDonald, *Blacks and White TV,* 73–4.

But without question, Jaffé's greatest attainment lay in his devotion to daily journalism and his steadfast commitment to Norfolk and the surrounding area. Almost lost today is an appreciation for the vital influence editorial pages exerted on readers during Jaffé's era, particularly in the South. Former *New York Times* national correspondent Dudley Clendinen, whose father edited a southern newspaper, recalled, "The mind of an editorial page editor could roam freely over terrain and through issues that were off-limits to reporters. The reputations of many Southern papers, in fact, were largely shaped by the individual prose, personality and point of view of their editorial page editors." For three decades, Jaffé took advantage of this prerogative to improve the lives of Norfolk's citizens and to ameliorate the community's injustices, particularly those suffered by the port city's large black population. "While the region tortured itself over the issue of race," Clendinen wrote, "the white newspaper editors of the South—the writing editors—had a role, a forum and an authority unequalled before or since. Those who had the courage and integrity to claim the moment, who saw right and spoke for it, were few in number, but they filled a tremendous void." Through his editorial and personal advocacy, informed by the anti-Semitism he had suffered, and magnified in its effectiveness by his partnership with P. B. Young—a relationship likely unique in the history of southern journalism—Jaffé championed racial understanding and served his community.[71]

In a rare divergence from daily journalism, in the mid-1940s Jaffé endorsed a statement in which the short-lived Committee of Editors and Writers from the South called for the elimination of voting barriers in the region. Assembled in Atlanta for a meeting chaired by Mark Ethridge, thirty-three editors, publishers, and academic and independent writers, including ten women and ten blacks, published a report entitled "Voting Restrictions in the Thirteen Southern States." In addition to Jaffé, over sixty people, including many of the region's best-known white moderates and liberals, such as Graham, Dabney, Lillian Smith, and Jonathan Daniels, signed the document. Prominent blacks signing the statement included P. B. Young and Charles

71. Dudley Clendinen, "In the South—When It Mattered to Be an Editor," *Media Studies Journal* 9, no. 1 (1995): 14–5.

Johnson. Many leading liberal white editors, however, including McGill, Carter, Graves, and Milton, abstained from endorsement.

In *Speak Now Against the Day,* the preeminent treatment of the South in the generation preceding the civil rights movement, John Egerton underscored the importance of the event. "There was significance in the fact that a nonpartisan assembly of articulate Southerners had recognized and publicly identified a principal cause of their region's chronic and crippling disadvantage in national life," he wrote. "In essence, this was their declaration: A handful of undemocratically chosen white men control the political machinery, the economic wealth, and the social structure of the South; all the others—the women, the blacks and other minorities, the white men with little or no money or property or education—are thereby deprived, in greater or lesser degree, of the constitutional right to take part in the democratic process."[72]

Until the day of his admission to Norfolk General Hospital on March 9, 1950, Jaffé had battled against the poll tax. His physicians ordered him to bed, but he did not comply and declined to relinquish the *Pilot*'s helm. Jaffé's work ethic alone did not account for his refusal to follow doctors' orders; throughout his career, he—like other journalists of his era, when six-day workweeks were routine—relished his time off. But that very evening, Byrd insiders in the General Assembly, engaging in their usual cozenage, were scheming to subvert the steadily strengthening sentiment in the state for the voting reform that Jaffé had championed.[73]

A resolution developed by a subcommittee of the House Committee on Privileges and Elections and passed by the House of Delegates called for an end to the suffrage tax but contained two poison pills for repeal supporters. One set the deadline for registration at February 1 for all elections during the year—nearly seven months prior to August primary elections and ten months before November general elections. The other required that registrants produce certificates documenting their completion of seven years of schooling or pass a literacy examination given under the direction of a local superintendent of schools. (In most areas, the Byrd machine's lieutenants—assembly-appointed circuit judges—indirectly selected the members of local

72. Egerton, *Speak Now Against the Day,* 259–61.
73. *Pilot,* 13 March 1950.

school boards to whom the superintendents reported.) The resolution contained a grandfather clause exempting registrants under the existing system—nearly all of whom were white—from the second requirement.[74]

The duplicity of the resolution galled Jaffé so much that he arose from his hospital bed to direct the *Pilot*'s campaign, collaborating with Meacham late into the evening to develop a lead piece to unmask the duplicity. "Poll Tax Repeal With a Couple of Atrocities" appeared early the following morning. It would be Jaffé's last editorial.

"The House Committee's plan would involve the public school system in the mumbo-jumbo of an impossible literacy test," he wrote. "Not one in 100 Negro citizens could produce a seventh-grade certificate. Not one in 50 white citizens could find the certificate if they ever had it. The poll tax repeal plan brought forth in the political agony of the House Committee on Privileges and Elections is a phony, and should be quickly voted down in the Senate."[75]

Norfolk's representatives attempted to amend the resolution, but Byrd insiders on the Senate Committee on Privileges and Elections, including the senator's son, Harry Flood Byrd Jr., took advantage of the assembly's rapidly approaching adjournment date to quash the discussion. Jaffé suffered a heart attack that day. It was his first, and both Chambers and Sugg believed that if he had obeyed his physician's instructions and remained in bed, he might have prevented or survived it. The repeal discussion expired in committee on March 11, and the next day, at the same hour the Speaker of the House declared the session over, Louis Jaffé's life ended.[76]

74. Wilkinson, *Harry Byrd and Virginia Politics*, 33; *Pilot*, 10 March 1950.

75. *Pilot*, 10 March 1950.

76. Ibid., 12 March 1950; Chambers, Shank, and Sugg, *Salt Water & Printer's Ink*, 381–2.

POSTSCRIPT: THE LEGACY OF LOUIS JAFFÉ

The day of Jaffé's funeral, Freddie Chinchilla, driving a Cadillac "as long as a Goss press," came to the newspaper building in search of someone to accompany him to the service. Future *Virginian-Pilot* editor Robert Mason accepted the invitation. Chinchilla's speakeasy across the street from the newspaper building had closed down or been closed down, and he had no commercial need to be seen paying his last respects to the leader of Norfolk's white journalistic fraternity, which had supplied him with many of his best and most appreciative customers. He came out of deference to Jaffé and in anticipation of what he hoped would be an exotic Jewish funeral. Mason recalled that Chinchilla departed from the service "shocked and disappointed" that an Episcopal minister, not a rabbi, had administered the last rites.[1]

In the heart of Norfolk's black district, the bells of many churches had tolled Jaffé's death. On the day of his funeral, many of the older merchants along Church Street closed their businesses in honor of "Mr. Jaffé." "To the minority group in particular, his name was known and revered throughout the length and breadth of this city and state," a *Journal and Guide* news report declared.[2]

Margaret and Christopher did not attend the funeral. Margaret's mental illness had become so debilitating that it had forced Christopher to commit her to the Seton Institute in Baltimore. She would remain institutionalized in various facilities for the rest of her life. Many years later Christopher's wife, Lorain, a trained psychologist, would reveal that Margaret's doctors had diagnosed her condition as schizophrenia. Christopher's wife would also disclose that during his attendance at Episcopal High School,

1. Mason, letter to author, 20 November 1992.
2. Suggs, *P. B. Young, Newspaperman*, 174; *Guide*, 14 March 1950.

Christopher had come to realize just how maladjusted his childhood had been. For the rest of his life he struggled with his conflicted feelings about his father. Without question his upbringing precipitated at least in part the addiction to alcohol and the extreme introversion he suffered. Later in life, he controlled his alcoholism and went on to have a successful career as a professor of sociology at a junior college.[3]

Across Virginia and throughout the South, editorialists paid homage to the *Pilot*'s deceased editor. Among Jaffé's peers, however, none had observed his human-rights advocacy more incisively than P. B. Young, Hamilton Owens, and Lenoir Chambers. Each of these newspapermen had appraised Jaffé's life's work from a different perspective. Young served as the leader of Norfolk's large black community and a racial spokesperson on a national level; Owens, despite his geographic detachment from the region, had acted as a catalyst for the southern journalistic renaissance and a touchstone for its key figures; Chambers, who had worked in day-to-day camaraderie with Jaffé for a decade and a half and down the hall from him for another six years, had known him intimately.[4]

In the *Norfolk Journal and Guide,* Young editorialized that "colored Americans particularly have ample cause to mourn Mr. Jaffé's passing." During Young's long career as the South's most prominent black editor, he had observed many Johnny-come-lately racial progressives, and he had watched many renowned figures in the region's white liberal press metamorphose into racial conservatives when they belatedly discovered that blacks intended to dismantle Jim Crow and fight to end their second-class citizenship. Jaffé, however, had "championed their cause at times when it was not the most popular thing to do," Young wrote. "Indeed, it is no exaggeration to say that Mr. Jaffé pioneered in blazing the trail of true liberalism [among] his newspaper contemporaries in the South and never once wavered in his stand."[5]

In Baltimore, where Jaffé had maintained his closest journalistic ties outside of Norfolk, the venerable *Sun* marked the passing of an old and

3. Dana Roeser to Alice Jaffé, 12 September 1974, Lorain C. Davis to Alice Jaffé, 23 September 1974, 16 October 1974, 8 December 1975, 10 May 1979, 12 February 1980, all Louis Jaffé Jr.

4. *Pilot,* 14 March 1950.

5. *Guide,* 14 March 1950.

cherished friend. "Observing the intellectual and social ferment which makes the South the most interesting section of the country today," Hamilton Owens wrote, "one finds it hard to realize that only a generation ago the best known leaders of that region were blustering apologists for every one of its shortcomings, including its ignorance and its poverty. . . . It is certain that among the first spokesmen for the more honest and more decent aspects of southern culture and for a more realistic appraisal of Southern needs was Louis I. Jaffé. . . . In this office, where Louis Jaffé had been known and admired for many years, the loss will be a real one. For us, he personified our best hope of what the South, with which we are so closely affiliated, might some day become."[6]

Although Chambers's editorial obituary chronicled Jaffé's advocacy, it also explored the character of the *Pilot*'s enigmatic editor. "He had fought his way up, against heavy handicaps, in the fine tradition of America when talent and determination unite to create opportunity," Chambers wrote. "He was only 62 when he died, the bodily machine broken but the spirit still flaming. . . . Somewhere in the shaping of this man—by inherent possession, by formal education, by rough experience, or by combinations not easily discernible—he absorbed the basic lessons of American life. He believed utterly in the stark necessity for freedom. He knew the inner meanings of the brotherhood of man. He took the old precepts of justice and democracy and a fair chance and applied them to the life about him. . . . His deep faith in the American dream and his brooding compassion for the men and women who were trying to make it come true were the very essence of his being. The causes for which he fought and the corruptions which he derided are all associated with this primary philosophy."[7]

Both Chambers and William Shands Meacham served as pallbearers at Jaffé's funeral. Looking at the two newspapermen standing alongside Jaffé's casket, Colonel Slover and publisher Henry Lewis knew that even in the midst of their grief they would soon have to appoint one of these two men to lead their flagship paper.[8]

Alice Jaffé met with Slover and lobbied hard for Chambers. She had

6. *Pilot,* 14 March 1950.
7. *Ledger,* 13 March 1950.
8. *Guide,* 14 March 1950.

both the motive and the means to take this action. As her husband's inner-most confidant, she knew that he had desired for Chambers to lead the *Pilot*. She ardently wished to see Jaffé's human-rights advocacy and support for cultural endeavors—causes with which she herself was deeply and per-sonally identified—continued. She also now controlled a sizable block of Norfolk Newspapers stock. Nearly four decades later she would confide to Louis Jaffé Jr. that his father had found Meacham a "disappointment." As she wrote, "Lenoir Chambers was of course the logical person" to serve as editor of the *Pilot*.[9]

Slover did in the end turn to Chambers. Chambers told Frank Por-ter Graham that he found it hard to move into his new office, for he could not help thinking of it as Jaffé's. He also confided to Owens how deeply he felt the loss of Jaffé. "I do not have to say to you how much I shall miss this man," he wrote. "We have faced together much of what life can bring. In the big issues, personal as well as public, he was a rock to lean on, and in all respects a delight."[10]

In May 1954 Chambers, nearing retirement age, stood at the *Pilot*'s helm when the Supreme Court issued its landmark desegregation decree in *Brown v. Board of Education*. The decision would serve as a litmus test for south-ern liberal newspaper editors. Hodding Carter said as much when he wrote that the *Brown* decision offered the South its greatest opportunity for lead-ership in this century. "But," Carter wrote, "most of the press, no less than most of the politicians, responded miserably." Alfred Hero surveyed fifty-three southern newspapers that summer; four accepted the decision, seven took no position but remarked on the trauma it would wreak in the South, and the remainder openly attacked it.[11]

When Henry Lewis died that October, Slover contemplated replac-ing him with John D. Wise. Such an appointment would have had deplor-

9. Alice Jaffé to Louis Jaffé Jr., 1988, Louis Jaffé Jr.; Robert Mason, letter to author, 2 November 1999.

10. Lenoir Chambers to Frank Porter Graham, 17 April 1950, Lenoir Chambers to Hamilton Owens, 18 May 1950, both in Chambers Papers.

11. Hodding Carter, *Their Words Were Bullets: The Southern Press in War, Recon-struction, and Peace* (Athens: University of Georgia Press, 1969), 64; Hero, *Southerner and World Affairs*, 395.

able consequences. As he had done in Richmond, the combative Wise would certainly have dictated an editorial policy that directly refuted the deeply held liberalism of Jaffé and Chambers. The courtly but uncompromising Chambers would have resigned, and many of the bright young men and women the *Pilot* had attracted as a result of its editors' reputations would no doubt have migrated gradually to other newspapers.[12]

Slover turned instead to his twenty-seven-year-old nephew, Frank Batten, who, despite an impressive education that included a degree from the Harvard Graduate School of Business Administration, had little newspaper experience. As in the case of Chambers, Slover made the correct decision. The young publisher and his senior editor would develop a warm and mutually respectful relationship and speak with the same voice. Over the next five years the *Pilot*—the state's only white newspaper and one of the few in the South to do so—urged compliance with *Brown*.[13]

In Richmond, James Jackson Kilpatrick, the brash young editor of the *News Leader,* displaying all of the restraint of an Edmund Ruffin, fomented defiance of the law and became the foremost propagandist of massive resistance. The scholarly Dabney, portraying himself as a moderate, inflamed passions by raising hot-button issues. In Norfolk, taking advantage of the long tradition of autonomy Norfolk Newspapers and its ancestors had granted their editors, Joseph Leslie of the *Ledger-Dispatch* backed his state's opposition to the new law of the land. In the fall of 1958, Governor J. Lindsay Almond shut down many of Norfolk's white schools rather than comply with a federal district court order mandating desegregation. Ten thousand of the city's schoolchildren found their schools closed.[14]

There was never a question about the editorial policy the *Virginian-Pilot* would chart in response to massive resistance. Chambers formulated his campaign almost precisely as Jaffé would have done. Motivated more by

12. Chambers, Shank, and Sugg, *Salt Water & Printer's Ink,* 380–1; Robert Mason, interviews by author, 5 December 1990, 17 April 1992; Robert Smith, interview by author, 2 October 1995; Luther Carter, interview by author, 10 October 1992.

13. Chambers, Shank, and Sugg, *Salt Water & Printer's Ink,* 380–1.

14. Leidholdt, *Standing Before the Shouting Mob,* 1–3, 5–6, 75; Dabney, "Virginia's Peaceable, Honorable Stand," 52, 55; Leidholdt, "Virginius Dabney and Lenoir Chambers," 57–60; Dabney, *Across the Years,* 234; Robert Mason, "V. Dabney: The Quintessential Virginian," *Virginia Quarterly Review* 55, no. 1 (winter 1979): 160–3.

noblesse oblige, in the best sense of those words, than by what he had termed his predecessor's "brooding compassion" for the common man, Chambers revisited the issue day after day for five years, informing and educating his readers, defusing the explosive situation, and excoriating irresponsible political leaders. No one at the *Pilot* wrote for ghosts, but Jaffé's legacy clearly was felt throughout the paper. "The *Virginian-Pilot* has a long record of trying to do what it could for justice and opportunity for Negroes," Chambers wrote. "My predecessor, Louis I. Jaffé, won a Pulitzer Prize . . . for editorial work directed for the control of lynching. . . . This is not a wildcat paper. It does not crusade. But it does try to appeal to reason and to encourage all educational processes that overcome prejudice in the end. It was doing so before May, 1954."[15]

The *Pilot*'s reporting staff took pride in Jaffé's Pulitzer and human-rights advocacy and in Chambers's stalwart and lonely editorial campaign. Former reporter Robert Smith recalled that as a result of the two editors' reputations, his peers believed that the newspaper could have a major impact on the South. Many believed that it could be a great paper, even surpassing the Washington and Atlanta presses. The *Pilot* covered the heady events surrounding massive resistance and Norfolk's school closing fairly, carefully refraining from sensationalism that would have inflamed tempers further.[16]

A less obvious but important part of Jaffé's legacy lay in the presence of Chambers on the scene, to take his long and courageous stand against the Byrd machine's defiance of the *Brown* mandate. Had not Jaffé brought Chambers to Virginia and his editorial post at the *Pilot,* a lesser successor might have joined the rest of the state's white press and the white public in their nearly unanimous opposition to the Court decision. Without Chambers's relentless and reasoned intercession, the denouement of massive resistance in Tidewater Virginia would not have taken place so peaceably.

Beyond a doubt, Frank Batten, who as an awestruck copy boy had

15. Leidholdt, *Standing Before the Shouting Mob*, 1–123; "Biographical data," 1959, Chambers Papers.

16. Smith, interview by author, 17 April 1992; Mason, interview by author, 17 July 1990.

delivered newspapers to the formidable Jaffé, felt his influence. Batten successfully garnered the support of Norfolk's business community for reopening the schools and served as a member of a delegation of the state's most powerful business leaders who petitioned Almond to end his recalcitrance. With deep personal reservations, Batten eventually ordered Leslie to cease his support for massive resistance, thus ending Norfolk Newspapers' tradition of editorial autonomy. At Leslie's request the young publisher himself wrote the *Ledger*'s editorial that reversed the paper's policy. Downplaying his writing, Batten later called it the "worst editorial that has ever been in the paper."[17]

Norfolk's capitulation to the federal mandate in 1959 pulled the props from massive resistance in Virginia and set the stage for its downfall across the South. Political scientist Francis Wilhoit observed that the "collapse of massive resistance in Virginia in 1959 was a decisive event in the history of the South's counterrevolution. And it is well to recall that the admission of black pupils to enter white schools, though doubtless resented by a majority of whites, took place [in Virginia] without mob violence or abuse of black pupils."[18]

In 1960, when Chambers won the Pulitzer Prize for Distinguished Editorial Writing for his advocacy to reopen Norfolk's schools, Stringfellow Barr's thoughts turned to Jaffé. "I wish Jaffé could have been alive to see you win it," Barr wrote to Chambers. "But given the kind of guy Louis was, he probably does know."[19]

Alice Jaffé saw the prize-winning editorial campaign as a continuation of her husband's work. She wrote to Chambers, "I feel happy not only about the well-deserved honor, but because of the special series of editorials singled out, in which the subject of human and racial justice followed the precedent of Louis' earlier prize. This series did much to influence current thought and action also, as did his. Yours was one of the very few voices raised in public utterance for schools, for law, for moderation, for intelli-

17. Frank Batten, letter to author, 22 September 1995; Leidholdt, *Standing Before the Shouting Mob*, 111–2, 118–9; Batten, interview by author, 25 September 1990.

18. Frances M. Wilhoit, *The Politics of Massive Resistance* (New York: Braziller, 1973), 148–9.

19. Stringfellow Barr to Lenoir Chambers, 3 May 1960, Chambers Papers.

gence—the voice never wavered through dark days and (I'm sure) abuse, and the words were as measured and firm as the voice itself."[20]

Jaffé's influence also lived on through Alice. From the first she had shared his liberal leanings; without his guidance, however, she probably would not have entered so actively into advocacy for blacks. In 1945 Alice helped found the Women's Council for Interracial Cooperation in Norfolk and served as its president. Throughout her many years of leadership with that organization, she worked tirelessly to increase interracial understanding and to provide blacks with increased opportunities for political and civic participation. Just as Jaffé would have done, she lobbied forcefully for the reopening of the schools during massive resistance. Later she served on the faculty of Old Dominion University's art department. Through her financial sponsorship and volunteer efforts, she would play a prominent part in Norfolk's cultural and civic endeavors until her death in 1993.[21]

Many additional fruits of Jaffé's journalistic advocacy far outlived him. Recreational facilities—the establishment and operability of which he spearheaded—brightened countless hours for black residents of Norfolk long after his lifetime. Over the years, citizens of all races have enjoyed the riches of the former Norfolk Museum of Arts and Sciences (now the Chrysler Museum of Art), in whose founding and subsequent financing Jaffé played such an instrumental part. And one of the broadest facets of his legacy springs from his leadership role in the genesis of Norfolk's first black college, which empowered underprivileged youth, and consequently their descendants in ever-widening ripples, to function as more responsible citizens and enjoy an improved quality of life.

Two decades after Jaffé's death, Robert Mason raised his hand at the national meeting of the American Society of Newspaper Editors; and the keynote speaker, Roy Wilkins, the executive director of the NAACP and former editor of the *St. Paul Appeal,* the *Kansas City Call,* and the *Crisis,* called

20. Alice Jaffé to Lenoir Chambers, 4 May 1960, ibid.

21. *Pilot,* December 1993; "The First Fifteen Years" (n.d.), Women's Committee on Interracial Cooperation Collection; Alice Jaffé to Norfolk City Council, 18 June 1952, Women's Committee on Interracial Cooperation Collection; Leidholdt, *Standing Before the Shouting Mob,* 98, 127; Parramore, Stewart, and Bogger, *Norfolk: The First Four Centuries,* 352, 364.

on him. As a result of the death of Walter White, the assassinations of Martin Luther King and Malcolm X, and the appointment of Thurgood Marshall to the Supreme Court, Wilkins served as the nation's most influential and respected civil-rights spokesperson.[22]

As a *Virginian-Pilot* staff writer, city editor, and—upon Jaffé's nomination—Sunday editor, Mason had written editorials for Jaffé and had come to know and admire him. Impressed by Mason's knowledge of southern history and his racial advocacy (some of which he had conducted as a small-town journalist living in close quarters with the men and women he wrote about), Chambers and Batten had persuaded him to give up the editorship and part ownership of a small North Carolina daily and positioned him to succeed Chambers. Back with the *Pilot,* he served consecutively as an associate editor and managing editor before assuming the paper's leadership in 1962.[23]

Wilkins had criticized the white press for its tendency to cover racial stories superficially and with its least experienced staff. Mason stated his name and newspaper affiliation and asked the NAACP's leader about the evidence he had assembled to support his claim. Wilkins, who had devoted his career to a brave and uncompromising battle for racial justice, stood on firm ground and would not have hesitated to dress down publicly a white journalist representing a paper that had impeded racial progress in any way.[24]

For blacks fighting for civil rights, much water had passed under the bridge since Jaffé's death many years earlier, but Wilkins invoked his name immediately. He exonerated the *Pilot* from his reproach: "It certainly doesn't apply to the *Norfolk Virginian-Pilot,* because yours is one of the newspapers—from the very beginning, with Louis Jaffé, when things began to emerge as a big national question—that has had a policy of keeping men on the race story who understood and who became acquainted with all of

22. Wilkins, *Standing Fast,* 48–50, 56–7, 155; Roland E. Wolseley, *The Black Press, USA* (Ames: Iowa State University Press, 1971), 138; David Lewis and Judy Miao, "America's Greatest Negroes: A Survey," *Crisis,* January 1970, 17–21.

23. Biographical note, Mason Papers; Mason, *One of the Neighbors' Children,* 146–47; Leidholdt, *Standing Before the Shouting Mob,* 43.

24. Paul Fisher and Ralph Lowenstein, *Race and the News Media* (New York: Praeger, 1967), 63.

the factors and personalities in the community. But I am afraid it is true of a good many other publications." Mason recalled that after the meeting he spent half an hour with Wilkins, reflecting on Jaffé's racial advocacy and influence.[25]

Jaffé's devotion to daily journalism had decreed that his fame would fade much more quickly than that of his book-author peers, whose writings scholars of southern history would one day mine, but Wilkins had not forgotten. His recollection and acknowledgment twenty years later comprised a simple but eloquent tribute from one old newspaperman and soldier in the battle for human rights to another.

25. *Proceedings of the American Society of Newspaper Editors*, 1969, Jaffé Papers; Mason, interview by author, 10 April 1989.

BIBLIOGRAPHY

PERSONAL COMMUNICATIONS

Abeles, Sally. Letters to author, 24 November 1992, 21 September 1995.

Agelastro, Peter. Interview by author, 11 July 1996.

Aprill, S. Interview by author, 24 September 1994.

Batten, Frank, Sr. Interview by author, 25 September 1990.

———. Letter to author, 22 September 1995.

Belkowitz, Shirley. Interview by author, 4 August 1997.

Burgess, Elisabeth. Interview by author, 25 September 1990.

———. Letter to author, 27 October 1992.

Carter, Luther. Interview by author, 10 October 1992.

Christein, Heidi. Letter to author, 14 April 1997.

Cohen, Sandor. Interview by author, 20 May 2000.

Cohen, Sharon. Interview by author, 19 May 1997.

Confidential interview in possession of author, 4 December 1985.

Confidential interview by author, 25 September 1996.

Daily, Daniel. Letter to author, 26 January 1996.

Dill, Alonzo. Interview by author, 20 November 1992.

Garrison, S. Interview by author, 27 September 1994.

Haspel, Michael. Letters to author, 26 March 1999, 7 April 1999.

Headspeth, Carol. Interview by author, 1 April 1996.

Higger, Daniel. Interview by author, 4 February 1998.

Jaffé, Louis I., Jr. Interview by author, 7 February 1996, 1 November 1999.

———. Letter to author, 7 June 2000.

Johnson, David J. Interview by author, 23 May 2000.

Lantor, Raynell. Interview by author, 8 July 1996.

Lazaron, Edna Sara. Interview by author, 19 August 1997.

Mason, Robert. Interviews by author, 10 April 1989, 17 July 1990, 5 December 1990, 18 September 1995.

———. Letters to author, 20 November 1992, 24 August 1995, 21 October 1995,

5 May 1996, 12 September 1996, 15 January 1998, 2 November 1999, 12 June 2000, 18 July 2000.

Phillips, Bud. Interview by author, 17 July 1995.

Porter, Celestyne. Interview by author, 18 May 1992.

Randle, Julia. Interview by author, 24 March 1998.

————. Letter to author, 27 March 1998.

Reeds, James A. Letters to author, 7 April 1999, 25 May 1999.

Rockaway, Robert. Letter to author, 8 April 1998.

Schindel, Martin. Letter to author, 26 March 1999.

Silverman, Alvin. Interview by author, 8 July 1996.

Stanton, Sheri. Letter to author, 23 October 1996.

Smith, Robert. Interview by author, 2 October 1995.

Stevens, Robert. Interview by author, 10 July 1996.

Sugg, Harold. Letters to author, 2, 12, 13 October 1990, 30 November 1990.

Tindal, Lina. Letter to author, 10 April 1996.

PERSONAL PAPERS AND MANUSCRIPT COLLECTIONS

Anderson, Sherwood. Papers. Department of Special Collections, Newberry Library, Chicago.

Bad Axe Colony Records. American Jewish Historical Society, Waltham, Mass.

Byrd, Harry F., Sr. Papers. Letters Received and Sent, Governor's Office, Executive Department, Archives, Library of Virginia, Richmond.

Chambers, Lenoir. Papers (#3827). Southern Historical Collection, Wilson Library, University of North Carolina at Chapel Hill.

Dabney, Virginius. Papers (#7690). Special Collections Department, University of Virginia Library, Charlottesville.

Ethridge, Mark F. Papers (#3842). Southern Historical Collection, Wilson Library, University of North Carolina at Chapel Hill.

Few, William, P. Papers. Duke University Archives, Durham, N.C.

Jaffé, Louis I. Personal Papers. Louis I. Jaffé, Jr.

Jaffé, Louis I. Papers (#9924). Special Collections Department, University of Virginia Library, Charlottesville.

Lankes, Julius Bartlett. Correspondence and papers regarding Julius J. Lankes (#10164). Special Collections Department, University of Virginia Library, Charlottesville. (Permission to quote provided by the children of J. J. Lankes.)

Mason, Robert. Papers (#4494). Southern Historical Collection, Wilson Library, University of North Carolina at Chapel Hill.

Murrow, Edward R., and Fred W. Friendly. *The Lost Class of '59*. New York: CBS, 21 January 1959. Videorecording.

NAACP Papers. Microfilm. Frederick, Md.: University Publications of America.

Perrow, Eber C. "Trinity College (N.C.) and Academic Freedom: A Report on the Meeting of the Board of Trustees, on December 1, 1903." Manuscript, 1958. Duke University Archives, Durham, N.C.

Powell, John. Papers (#7284). Manuscripts Division, Special Collections Department, University of Virginia Library.

Roy, Robert. "Reminiscences of Trinity." Durham: Duke University Archives, January 1939.

Shank, Joseph, comp. *Raw Materials on the History of Norfolk-Portsmouth Newspapers*. Norfolk: Norfolk Public Library, Sargeant Memorial Room, n.d.

Stebbins, Charles. Statement, March 1982. South Boston (Va.) Public Library.

Taylor, Welford Dunaway, and Richard Waller. *J. J. Lankes (1884–1960): Woodcuts of Rural America*. Richmond, Va.: University of Richmond Marsh Art Gallery and the Virginia Museum of Fine Arts, 1994.

Tuck, William, M. Papers. Earl Gregg Swem Library, College of William and Mary.

Wannamaker, William H. Papers. Duke University Archives, Durham, N.C.

Women's Committee on Interracial Cooperation. Collection. Archives, Norfolk State University, Norfolk, Va.

BOOKS

Aiken, Newton. *Newton Aiken Autobiography*. Baltimore: Baltimore Sun Library, 1979.

Alpher, Joseph, ed. *Encyclopedia of Jewish History: Events and Eras of the Jewish People*. New York: Facts on File Publications, 1986.

Anderson, Jean Bradley. *Durham County: A History of Durham County, North Carolina*. Durham: Duke University Press, 1990.

Anderson, James D. *The Education of Blacks in the South, 1860–1935*. Chapel Hill: University of North Carolina Press, 1988.

Anderson, Sherwood. *The Buck Fever Papers*. Ed. Welford Dunaway Taylor. Charlottesville: University Press of Virginia, 1971.

———. *Perhaps Women*. New York: Horace Liveright, 1931.

———. *The Sherwood Anderson Diaries, 1936–1941*. Ed. Hilbert H. Campbell. Athens: University of Georgia Press, 1987.

Angoff, Charles. *H. L. Mencken: A Portrait from Memory*. New York: Thomas Yoseloff, 1956.

Aptheker, Herbert, ed. *A Documentary History of the Negro People in the United States: From the NAACP to the New Deal*. New York: Citadel Press, 1973.

———, ed. *A Documentary History of the Negro People in the United States: From the New Deal to the End of World War II*. New York: Citadel Press, 1974.

Aronson, I. Michael. *Troubled Waters: The Origins of the 1881 Anti-Jewish Pogroms in Russia*. Pittsburgh: University of Pittsburgh Press, 1990.

Ashby, Warren. *Frank Porter Graham: A Southern Liberal*. Winston-Salem: John F. Blair, 1980.

Ashmore, Harry S. *Civil Rights and Wrongs: A Memoir of Race and Politics, 1944– 1994*. New York: Pantheon Books, 1994.

Baker, Richard Terrill. *A History of the Graduate School of Journalism, Columbia University*. New York: Columbia University Press, 1954.

Barbour, W. B. "Halifacts." Danville, Va.: J. T. Townes, 1941.

Beider, Alexander. *A Dictionary of Jewish Surnames from the Russian Empire*. Teaneck, N.J.: Avotaynu, 1993.

Bennett, David H. *The Party of Fear: The American Far Right from Nativism to the Militia Movement*. New York: Vintage Books, 1995.

Berman, Myron. *Richmond's Jewry, 1769–1976: Shabbat in Shockoe*. Charlottesville: University Press of Virginia, 1979.

Blaustein, Albert P., and Robert L. Zangrando, eds. *Civil Rights and African Americans: A Documentary History*. Evanston, Ill.: Northwestern University Press, 1991.

Blee, Kathleen M. *Women of the Klan: Racism and Gender in the 1920s*. Berkeley: University of California Press, 1991.

Bode, Carl. *Mencken*. Carbondale: Southern Illinois University Press, 1969.

Bowie, Walter Russell. *Learning to Live*. Nashville: Abingdon Press, 1969.

Boyd, William Kenneth. *The Story of Durham: City of the New South*. Durham: Duke University Press, 1927.

Brinkley, Alan. *Voices of Protest: Huey Long, Father Coughlin, and the Great Depression*. New York: Vintage Books, 1983.

Brooks, Lyman Beecher. *Upward: A History of Norfolk State University*. Washington, D.C.: Howard University Press, 1983.

Brundage, W. Fitzhugh. *Lynching in the New South: Georgia and Virginia, 1880– 1930*. Urbana: University of Illinois Press, 1993.

Bruns, Roger A. *Preacher: Billy Sunday and Big-Time Evangelism*. New York: W. W. Norton, 1992.

Buni, Andrew. *The Negro in Virginia Politics, 1902–1965*. Charlottesville: University Press of Virginia, 1967.

Caperton, Helena Lefroy, ed. *Social Record of Virginia*. Richmond: Garret & Massie, 1937.

Cappon, Lester J. *Virginia Newspapers, 1821–1935: A Bibliography with Historical Introduction and Notes*. New York: D. Appleton-Century, 1936.

Carrington, Wirt Johnson. *A History of Halifax County, Virginia*. Richmond: Appeals Press, 1924.

Carter, Hodding. *Their Words Were Bullets: The Southern Press in War, Reconstruction, and Peace*. Athens: University of Georgia Press, 1969.

Cash, W. J. *The Mind of the South*. New York: Vintage Books, 1991.

Chadbourn, James Harmon. *Lynching and the Law*. Chapel Hill: University of North Carolina Press, 1931.

Chalmers, David M. *Hooded Americanism: The First Century of the Ku Klux Klan, 1865–1965*. Garden City, N.Y.: Doubleday, 1965.

Chambers, Lenoir, Joseph E. Shank, and Harold Sugg. *Salt Water & Printer's Ink: Norfolk and Its Newspapers, 1865–1965*. Chapel Hill: University of North Carolina Press, 1967.

Clayton, Bruce. *W. J. Cash, A Life*. Baton Rouge: Louisiana State University Press, 1991.

Clowse, Barbara Barksdale. *Ralph McGill: A Biography*. Macon, Ga.: Mercer University Press, 1998.

Coleman, Kenneth, and Charles Stephen Gurr, eds. *Dictionary of Georgia Biography*. Vol. 1. Athens: University of Georgia Press, 1983.

Commission on Interracial Cooperation. *The Mob Still Rides: A Review of the Lynching Record, 1931–1935*. Atlanta: Commission on Interracial Cooperation, 1936.

Commission on the Study of Lynching. *Lynchings and What They Mean: General Findings of the Southern Commission on the Study of Lynching*. Atlanta: Commission on Interracial Cooperation, 1931.

Congregation Beth Ahabah Yearbooks, 1915–1917. Richmond, Va.

Cooke, Alistair. *Six Men*. New York: Alfred A. Knopf, 1977.

Cooke, James J. *The U.S. Air Service in the Great War, 1917–1919*. Westport, Conn.: Praeger, 1996.

Couch, W. T., ed. *Culture in the South*. Chapel Hill: University of North Carolina Press, 1934.

Cowan, Paul, and Rachel Cowan. *Mixed Blessings: Marriage Between Jews and Christians*. New York: Doubleday, 1987.

Dabney, Virginius. *Across the Years: Memories of a Virginian.* Garden City, N.Y.: Doubleday, 1978.

―――. *Below the Potomac: A Book About the New South.* New York: D. Appleton-Century, 1942.

―――. *Dry Messiah: The Life of Bishop James Cannon, Jr.* New York: Alfred A. Knopf, 1949.

―――. *Liberalism in the South.* Chapel Hill: University of North Carolina Press, 1932.

―――. *Richmond: The Story of a City.* Garden City, N.Y.: Doubleday, 1976.

―――. *Virginia: The New Dominion.* Charlottesville: University Press of Virginia, 1971.

Daniels, Josephus. *Editor in Politics.* Chapel Hill: University of North Carolina Press, 1941.

Davidson, Gabriel. *Our Jewish Farmers and the Story of the Jewish Agricultural Society.* New York: L. B. Fischer, 1943.

Davis, Kenneth S. *FDR: The New Deal Years, 1933–1937.* New York: Random House, 1986.

de Camp, L. Sprague. *The Great Monkey Trial.* New York: Doubleday, 1968.

Dill, Alonzo T. *Governor Tyron and His Palace.* Chapel Hill: University of North Carolina Press, 1955.

Dinnerstein, Leonard. *The Leo Frank Case.* Athens: University of Georgia Press, 1987.

―――. *Uneasy at Home: Antisemitism and the American Jewish Experience.* New York: Columbia University Press, 1987.

Dollard, John. *Caste and Class in a Southern Town.* Madison: University of Wisconsin Press, 1988.

Dorsey, George A. *Why We Behave Like Human Beings.* New York: Harper & Brothers, 1925.

Downs, Robert B. *Books That Changed the South.* Chapel Hill: University of North Carolina Press, 1977.

Downs, Robert B., and Jane B. Downs. *Journalists of the United States: Biographical Sketches of Print and Broadcast News Shapers from the Late 17th Century to the Present.* Jefferson, N.C.: McFarland, 1991.

Dreher, Carl. *Sarnoff: An American Success.* New York: Quadrangle/New York Times Book Company, 1977.

Dunford, Earle. *Richmond Times-Dispatch: The Story of a Newspaper.* Richmond: Cadmus, 1995.

Durden, Robert F. *The Launching of Duke University, 1924–1949.* Durham: Duke University Press, 1993.

Dykeman, Wilma, and James Stokely. *Seeds of Southern Change: The Life of Will Alexander*. Chicago: University of Chicago Press, 1962.

Eagles, Charles W. *Jonathan Daniels and Race Relations: The Evolution of a Southern Liberal*. Knoxville: University of Tennessee Press, 1982.

Edmunds, Pocahontas Wight. *Virginians Out Front*. Richmond: Whittet & Shepperson, 1972.

Egerton, John. *Speak Now Against the Day: The Generation Before the Civil Rights Movement in the South*. New York: Alfred A. Knopf, 1994.

Eichholz, Alice. *Ancestry's Redbook: American State, County & Town Sources*. Salt Lake City: Ancestry, 1992.

Emery, Michael, Edwin Emery, and Nancy Roberts. *The Press in America: An Interpretive History of the Mass Media*. 8th ed. Boston: Allyn & Bacon, 2000.

Encyclopaedia Judaica. Jerusalem: Keter, 1972.

Evans, Eli N. *The Lonely Days Were Sundays: Reflections of a Jewish Southerner*. Jackson: University Press of Mississippi, 1993.

———. *The Provincials: A Personal History of Jews in the South*. New York: Atheneum, 1974.

Fallows, James. *Breaking the News: How the Media Undermine American Democracy*. New York: Pantheon, 1996.

Fielding, Mantle. *Mantle Fielding's Dictionary of American Painters, Sculptors & Engravers*. Poughkeepsie, N.Y.: Apollo, 1986.

Fischer, Roger A. *Them Damned Pictures: Explorations in American Political Cartoon Art*. North Haven, Conn: Archon, 1996.

Fisher, Charles. *The Columnists*. New York: Howell, Soskin, 1944.

Fisher, Paul, and Ralph Lowenstein. *Race and the News Media*. New York: Praeger, 1967.

Fiss, Owen M. *The Irony of Free Speech*. Cambridge, Mass.: Harvard University Press, 1996.

Foner, Eric, and John A. Garraty, eds. *The Reader's Companion to American History*. Boston: Houghton Mifflin, 1991.

Fredman, J. George, and Louis A. Falk. *Jews in American Wars*. New York: Jewish War Veterans of the U.S., 1942.

Freidel, Frank. *F.D.R. and the South*. Baton Rouge: Louisiana State University Press, 1965.

Friddell, Guy. *Opinions of an Old Contrarian*. Norfolk: Pilot Press, 1997.

Friddell, Guy. *What Is It About Virginia?* Richmond: Dietz Press, 1966.

Fried, Lewis. *Makers of the City*. Amherst: University of Massachusetts Press, 1990.

Friendly, Fred W. *Minnesota Rag: The Dramatic Story of the Landmark Supreme*

Court Case That Gave Meaning to Freedom of the Press. New York: Random House, 1981.

Gall, Alice Crew. *In Peace and War: A Story of Human Service.* New York: Thomas Y. Crowell, 1942.

Gallo, Max. *The Night of the Long Knives.* Trans. Lily Emmet. New York: Harper & Row, 1972.

Garson, Robert A. *The Democratic Party and the Politics of Sectionalism, 1941–1948.* Baton Rouge: Louisiana State University Press, 1974.

Gatewood, Willard B., Jr. *Preachers, Pedagogues & Politicians.* Chapel Hill: University of North Carolina Press, 1966.

General Convention of the Protestant Episcopal Church, Constitution and Canons for the Government of the Protestant Episcopal Church in the United States of America. New York: General Convention of the Protestant Episcopal Church, 1919.

Goings, Kenneth. *"The NAACP Comes of Age": The Defeat of Judge John J. Parker.* Bloomington: Indiana University Press, 1990.

Golden, Harry. *Jewish Roots in the Carolinas: A Pattern of American Philo-Semitism.* Greensboro, N.C.: Deal Print, 1955.

Goodman, James E. *Stories of Scottsboro.* New York: Vintage, 1995.

Gould, Lewis L. *The Presidency of Theodore Roosevelt.* Lawrence: University Press of Kansas, 1991.

Graham, Frank. *Al Smith: American.* New York: G. P. Putnam's Sons, 1945.

Graham, Katharine. *Personal History.* New York: Vintage, 1998.

Gramm, Hans. *The Oberlaender Trust, 1931–1953.* Philadelphia: Carl Schurz Memorial Foundation, 1956.

Grant, Madison. *The Passing of the Great Race.* New York: Charles Scribner's Sons, 1916.

Grantham, Dewey W. *The South in Modern America: A Region at Odds.* New York: Harper Collins, 1994.

Grebstein, Sheldon Norman, ed. *Monkey Trial: The State of Tennessee vs. John Thomas Scopes.* Boston: Houghton Mifflin, 1960.

Green, Elna C. *Southern Strategies: Southern Women and the Woman Suffrage Question.* Chapel Hill: University of North Carolina Press, 1997.

Greenbaum, Masha. *The Jews of Lithuania: A History of a Remarkable Community, 1316–1945.* Jerusalem: Gefen, 1995.

Greenberg, Jack. *Crusaders in the Courts: How a Dedicated Band of Lawyers Fought for the Civil Rights Revolution.* New York: Basic Books, 1994.

Hagood, Johnson. *The Services of Supply: A Memoir of the Great War.* New York: Houghton Mifflin, 1927.

Hairston, L. Beatrice W. *A Brief History of Danville, Virginia, 1728–1954*. Richmond: Dietz Press, 1955.

Hall, Jacquelyn Dowd. *Revolt Against Chivalry: Jessie Daniel Ames and the Women's Campaign Against Lynching*. New York: Columbia University Press, 1993.

Hall, Jacquelyn Dowd, James Leloudis, Robert Korstad, Mary Murphy, Lu Ann Jones, and Christopher B. Daly. *Like A Family: The Making of a Southern Cotton Mill World*. New York: W. W. Norton, 1987.

Hall, Kermit L., ed. *The Oxford Companion to the Supreme Court of the United States*. New York: Oxford University Press, 1992.

Hand-Book of Durham, North Carolina: A Brief and Accurate Description of a Prosperous and Growing Southern Manufacturing Town. Durham: The Educator Company, 1895.

Hareven, Tamara K. *Eleanor Roosevelt: An American Conscience*. Chicago: Quadrangle, 1968.

Heinemann, Ronald L. *Depression and New Deal in Virginia: The Enduring Dominion*. Charlottesville: University Press of Virginia, 1983.

———. *Harry Byrd of Virginia*. Charlottesville: University Press of Virginia, 1996.

Held, Joseph, ed. *The Columbia History of Eastern Europe in the Twentieth Century*. New York: Columbia University Press, 1992.

Hero, Alfred O., Jr. *The Southerner and World Affairs*. Baton Rouge: Louisiana State University Press, 1965.

Herscher, Uri D. *Jewish Agricultural Utopias in America, 1880–1910*. Detroit: Wayne State University Press, 1981.

Hobson, Fred C. *Tell About the South: The Southern Rage to Explain*. Baton Rouge: Louisiana State University Press, 1983.

———. *Mencken: A Life*. Baltimore: Johns Hopkins University Press, 1994.

———. *Serpent in Eden: H. L. Mencken and the South*. Chapel Hill: University of North Carolina Press, 1974.

Hohenberg, John. *The Pulitzer Prize Story: News Stories, Editorials, Cartoons, and Pictures from the Pulitzer Prize Collection at Columbia University*. New York: Columbia University Press, 1959.

Hollis, Daniel Webster, III. *An Alabama Newspaper Tradition: Grover C. Hall and the Hall Family*. Tuscaloosa: University of Alabama Press, 1983.

Holloway, Betsy. *Unfinished Heaven: Durham, North Carolina: A Story of Two Schools*. Orlando: Persimmon Press, 1994.

Jacobs, Louis. *What Does Judaism Say About . . . ?* Jersualem: Keter, 1973.

Jackson, Kenneth T. *The Ku Klux Klan in the City, 1915–1930*. Chicago: Ivan R. Dee, 1992.

Jane's Fighting Ships of World War II. Avenel, N.J.: Crescent Books, 1995.

Jarman, T. L. *The Rise and Fall of Nazi Germany.* New York: New York University Press, 1956.

Jeansonne, Glen. *Gerald L. K. Smith: Minister of Hate.* New Haven: Yale University Press, 1988.

Johnson, Gerald W. *The Lines are Drawn: American Life Since the First World War as Reflected in the Pulitzer Prize Cartoons.* Philadelphia: J. B. Lippincott, 1958.

———. *South-Watching: Selected Essays by Gerald W. Johnson.* Ed. Fred Hobson. Chapel Hill: University of North Carolina Press, 1983.

Johnson, Gerald W., Frank R. Kent, H. L. Mencken, and Hamilton Owens. *The Sunpapers of Baltimore, 1837–1937.* New York: Alfred A. Knopf, 1937.

Johnson, Paul. *A History of the American People.* New York: Harper Collins, 1998.

Johnson, Walter C., and Arthur T. Robb. *The South and Its Newspapers, 1903–1953: The Story of the Southern Newspaper Publishers Association and Its Part in the South's Economic Rebirth.* Chattanooga: Southern Newspaper Publishers Association, 1954.

Keegan, John. *The First World War.* New York: Alfred A. Knopf, 1999.

Kegley, Mary B. *Wythe County, Virginia: A Bicentennial History.* Marceline, Mo.: Walsworth, 1989.

Kennedy, Ludovic. *The Airman and the Carpenter: The Lindbergh Kidnapping and the Framing of Richard Hauptmann.* New York: Viking Penguin, 1985.

Key, V. O., Jr. *Southern Politics in State and Nation.* Knoxville: University of Tennessee Press, 1984.

Killebrew, J. B., and Herbert Myrick. *Tobacco Leaf: Its Culture and Cure, Marketing and Manufacture: A Practical Handbook on the Most Approved Methods in Growing, Harvesting, Curing, Packing and Selling Tobacco, Also of Tobacco Manufacture.* New York: Orange Judd, 1897.

King, Florence. *Southern Ladies and Gentlemen.* New York: St. Martin's Press, 1975.

Kneebone, John T. *Southern Liberal Journalists and the Issue of Race, 1920–1944.* Chapel Hill: University of North Carolina Press, 1985.

Köhler, Wolfgang. *Gestalt Psychology.* New York: Horace Liveright, 1929.

Konvitz, Milton R., ed. *Judaism and Human Rights.* New York: W. W. Norton, 1972.

Kostyu, Joel A., and Frank A. Kostyu. *Durham: A Pictorial History.* Norfolk, Va.: Donning, 1978.

Krueger, Thomas A. *And Promises to Keep: The Southern Conference for Human Welfare, 1938–1948.* Nashville: Vanderbilt University Press, 1967.

Kurth, Peter. *American Cassandra: The Life of Dorothy Thompson*. Boston: Little, Brown, 1990.

Lankes, J. J. *Woodcut Manual*. New York: Crown, 1932.

Lefler, Hugh Talmage, and Albert Ray Newsome. *North Carolina: The History of a Southern State*. Chapel Hill: University of North Carolina Press, 1954.

Leidholdt, Alexander S. *Standing Before the Shouting Mob: Lenoir Chambers and Virginia's Massive Resistance to Public-School Integration*. Tuscaloosa: University of Alabama Press, 1997.

Levine, Bruce, et al. *Who Built America? Working People & The Nation's Economy, Politics, Culture & Society*. Vol. 2. New York: Pantheon, 1992.

Levinger, Lee J. *A History of the Jews in the United States*. Cincinnati: Department of Synagogue and School Extension of the Union of American Hebrew Congregations, 1930.

Levy, Leonard W., ed. *The World's Most Famous Court Trial: State of Tennessee v. John Thomas Scopes*. New York: Da Capo Press, 1971.

Lewis, Earl. *In Their Own Interests: Race, Class, and Power in Twentieth-Century Norfolk, Virginia*. Berkeley: University of California Press, 1991.

Lipstadt, Deborah E. *Beyond Belief: The American Press and the Coming of the Holocaust, 1933–1945*. New York: The Free Press, 1986.

Looking Back: Wise County in the Early Years. Wise, Va.: Lonesome Pine Office on Youth, 1992.

Loveland, Anne C. *Lillian Smith: A Southerner Confronting the South*. Baton Rouge: Louisiana State University Press, 1986.

Low, W. Augustus, and Virgil A. Clift, eds. *Encyclopedia of Black America*. New York: Da Capo Press, 1984.

MacDonald, J. Fred. *Blacks and White TV: African Americans in Television Since 1948*. 2d ed. Chicago: Nelson-Hall, 1992.

MacLean, Nancy. *Behind the Mask of Chivalry: The Making of the Second Ku Klux Klan*. New York: Oxford University Press, 1994.

Manchester, William. *Disturber of the Peace: The Life of H. L. Mencken*. New York: Harper & Brothers, 1951.

———. *The Glory and the Dream: A Narrative History of America, 1932–1972*. Vol. 1. Boston: Little, Brown, 1974.

Marshall, S. L. A. *World War I*. Boston: Houghton Mifflin, 1992.

Martin-Perdue, Nancy J., and Charles L. Perdue, Jr., eds. *Talk About Trouble: A New Deal Portrait of Virginians in the Great Depression*. Chapel Hill: University of North Carolina Press, 1996.

Mason, Robert. *One of the Neighbors' Children*. Chapel Hill: Algonquin Books, 1987.

Mayer, Egon. *Love & Tradition: Marriage Between Jews and Christians.* New York: Plenum Press, 1985.

McChesney, Robert W. *Corporate Media and the Threat to Democracy.* New York: Seven Stories Press, 1997.

McCracken, Duane. *Strike Injunctions in the New South.* Chapel Hill: University of North Carolina Press, 1931.

McGovern, James R. *Anatomy of a Lynching: The Killing of Claude Neal.* Baton Rouge: Louisiana State University Press, 1982.

McLoughlin, William G., Jr. *Billy Sunday Was His Real Name.* Chicago: University of Chicago Press, 1955.

McMillen, Neil, ed. *Remaking Dixie: The Impact of World War II on the American South.* Jackson: University Press of Mississippi, 1997.

McNeil, Genna Rae. *Groundwork: Charles Hamilton Houston and the Struggle for Civil Rights.* Philadelphia: University of Pennsylvania Press, 1983.

Mencken, H. L. *The Diary of H. L. Mencken.* Ed. Charles A. Fecher. New York: Vintage, 1991.

———. *A Mencken Chrestomathy.* New York: Vintage, 1982.

———. *Thirty-Five Years of Newspaper Work.* Ed. Fred Hobson, Vincent Fitzpatrick, and Bradford Jacobs. Baltimore: Johns Hopkins University Press, 1994.

Meredith, Henry Clarkson. *A History of the Norfolk German Club, 1868–1960.* Richmond, Va.: Whitlet & Shepperson, 1961.

Miller, Francis Pickens. *Man from the Valley.* Chapel Hill: University of North Carolina Press, 1971.

Mims, Edwin. *The Advancing South: Stories of Progress and Reaction.* Garden City, N.Y.: Doubleday, Page, 1926.

Minow, Newton N., and Craig L. Lamay. *Abandoned in the Wasteland: Children, Television, and the First Amendment.* New York: Hill and Wang, 1995.

Modlin, Charles E., ed. *Sherwood Anderson's Love Letters to Eleanor Copenhaver Anderson.* Athens: University of Georgia Press, 1989.

Morrison, Joseph L. *W. J. Cash: Southern Prophet.* New York: Alfred A. Knopf, 1967.

Morton, Richard L. *History of Virginia.* Vol. 2. Chicago: American Historical Society, 1924.

Moton, Robert Russa. *Finding a Way Out: An Autobiography.* College Park, Md.: McGrath, 1969.

Mott, Frank Luther. *American Journalism: A History, 1690–1960.* New York: Macmillan, 1962.

Myrdal, Gunnar. *An American Dilemma: The Negro Problem and Modern Democracy.* Vol. 2. New Brunswick, N.J.: Transaction, 1996.

O'Brien, Gail Williams. *The Color of the Law: Race, Violence, and Justice in the Post-World War II South*. Chapel Hill: University of North Carolina Press, 1999.

O'Brien, Michael. *Rethinking the South: Essays in Intellectual History*. Athens: University of Georgia Press, 1993.

Odum, Howard W. *Race and Rumors of Race: Challenge to American Crisis*. Chapel Hill: University of North Carolina Press, 1943.

———. *Southern Regions of the United States*. Chapel Hill: University of North Carolina Press, 1936.

Parramore, Thomas C., Peter C. Stewart, and Tommy L. Bogger. *Norfolk: The First Four Centuries*. Charlottesville: University Press of Virginia, 1994.

Pember, Don R. *Mass Media Law*. Boston: McGraw-Hill, 1998.

Perkins, George, Barbara Perkins, and Phillip Leininger, eds. *Benét's Reader's Encyclopedia of American Literature*. New York: Harper Collins, 1991.

Petsonk, Judy, and Jim Remsen. *The Inter-Marriage Handbook: A Guide for Jews & Christians*. New York: William Morrow, 1988.

Phagan, Mary. *The Murder of Little Mary Phagan*. Far Hills, N.J.: New Horizon Press, 1987.

Phillips, Cabell, ed. *Dateline: Washington, The Story of National Affairs Journalism in the Life and Times of the National Press Club*. Garden City, N.Y.: Doubleday, 1949.

Pollard, Edward Alfred. *The Virginia Tourist*. Philadelphia: J. B. Lippincott, 1870.

Porter, Earl W. *Trinity and Duke, 1892–1924: Foundations of Duke University*. Durham: Duke University Press, 1964.

Powell, William S. *North Carolina Through Four Centuries*. Chapel Hill: University of North Carolina Press, 1989.

Press, Charles. *The Political Cartoon*. Rutherford, N.J.: Farleigh Dickinson University Press, 1981.

Pride, Armistead S., and Clint C. Wilson II. *A History of the Black Press*. Washington, D.C.: Howard University Press, 1997.

Pringle, Henry F. *Alfred E. Smith: A Critical Study*. New York: Macy-Masius, 1927.

Putnam, Carleton. *Race and Reason: A Yankee View*. Washington, D.C.: Public Affairs Press, 1961.

Reed, John Shelton, and Dale Volberg Reed. *1001 Things Everyone Should Know About the South*. New York: Doubleday, 1996.

Reniers, Perceval. *The Springs of Virginia; Life, Love and Death at the Waters*. Chapel Hill: University Press of North Carolina, 1941.

Riley, Sam G. *Biographical Dictionary of American Newspaper Columnists*. Westport, Conn.: Greenwood, 1995.

Ripley, William. *The Races of Europe: A Sociological Study.* New York: D. Appleton, 1910.

Rockaway, Robert. *The Jews of Detroit: From the Beginning, 1762–1914.* Detroit: Wayne State University Press, 1986.

Roller, David C., and Robert W. Twyman, eds. *Encyclopedia of Southern History.* Baton Rouge: Louisiana State University Press, 1979.

Rouse, Parke. *We Happy Wasps: Virginia in the Days of Jim Crow and Harry Byrd.* Richmond, Va.: Dietz Press, 1996.

Rowan, Carl T. *Dream Makers, Dream Breakers: The World of Justice Thurgood Marshall.* Boston: Little, Brown, 1993.

Rubin, Louis D., Jr. Introduction to *I'll Take my Stand: The South and the Agrarian Tradition,* by Twelve Southerners. Baton Rouge: Louisiana State University Press, 1977.

———. *Virginia: A History.* New York: W. W. Norton, 1984.

Salmaggi, Cesare, and Alfredo Pallavisini, comps. *2194 Days of War.* New York: Windward, 1977.

Salmon, Emily J., and Edward D. C. Campbell, Jr., eds. *The Hornbook of Virginia History: A Ready-Reference Guide to the Old Dominion's People, Places, and Past.* Richmond: The Library of Virginia, 1994.

Salmond, John A. *Gastonia 1929: The Story of the Loray Mill Strike.* Chapel Hill: University of North Carolina Press, 1995.

Schaefer, Jack. *Shane.* Boston: Houghton Mifflin, 1949.

———. *Shane: The Critical Edition.* Ed. James C. Work. Lincoln: University of Nebraska Press, 1984.

Schevill, James Erwin. *Sherwood Anderson: His Life and Work.* Denver: University of Denver Press, 1951.

Schlegel, Marvin W. *Conscripted City: Norfolk in World War II.* Norfolk, Va.: Norfolk War History Commission, 1951.

Schoenburg, Nancy, and Stuart Schoenburg. *Lithuanian Jewish Communities.* New York: Garland, 1991.

Schweitzer, Albert. *On the Edge of the Primeval Forest.* New York: Macmillan, 1931.

Seabury, David. *Unmasking Our Minds.* New York: Boni and Liveright, 1924.

Shapiro, Herbert. *White Violence and Black Response: From Reconstruction to Montgomery.* Amherst: University of Massachusetts Press, 1988.

Shirer, William L. *Berlin Diary: The Journal of a Foreign Correspondent, 1934–1941.* New York: Alfred A. Knopf, 1941.

———. *The Nightmare Years, 1930–1940.* Vol. 2, *20th Century Journey: A Memoir of a Life and the Times.* Boston: Little, Brown, 1984.

———. *The Rise and Fall of the Third Reich: A History of Nazi Germany.* New York: Simon and Schuster, 1960.

Singal, Daniel Joseph. *The War Within: From Victorian to Modernist Thought in the South, 1919–1945.* Chapel Hill: University of North Carolina Press, 1982.

Sloan, Wm. David, and Laird B. Anderson, comps. *Pulitzer Prize Editorials: America's Best Editorial Writing, 1917–1993.* 2d ed. Ames: Iowa State University Press, 1994.

Sloan, Wm. David, and James D. Startt, eds. *The Media in America.* Northport, Ala.: Vision Press, 1996.

Smith, Alfred E. *Up to Now: An Autobiography.* New York: Viking, 1929.

Smith, Howard K. *Last Train from Berlin.* New York: Alfred A. Knopf, 1942.

Smith, Lillian. *How Am I to Be Heard? Letters of Lillian Smith.* Ed. Margaret Rose Gladney. Chapel Hill: University of North Carolina Press, 1993.

Smith, Rixey, and Norman Beasley. *Carter Glass: A Biography.* New York: Da Capo Press, 1972.

Snider, William D. *Light on the Hill: A History of the University of North Carolina at Chapel Hill.* Chapel Hill: University of North Carolina Press, 1992.

Sosna, Morton. *In Search of the Silent South: Southern Liberals and the Race Issue.* New York: Columbia University Press, 1977.

Southern Regional Council. *Race in the News: Usage in Southern Newspapers.* Atlanta: Southern Regional Council, n.d.

Spielvogel, Jackson J. *Hitler and Nazi Germany: A History.* Englewood Cliffs, N.J.: Prentice Hall, 1988.

Stopes, Marie Carmichael. *Married Love: A New Contribution to the Solution of Sex Difficulties.* New York: Eugenics, 1931.

Struggles in War and Peace, 1939–1966. Vol. 5, *The History of the Times.* London: Time Books, 1984.

Sturgill, Roy L. *Crimes, Criminals and Characters of the Cumberlands and Southwest Virginia.* Bristol, Va.: Quality Printers, 1970.

———. *Nostalgic Narratives and Historical Events of Southwest Virginia,* Bristol, Va.: R. L. Sturgill, 1991.

Suggs, Henry Lewis. *The Black Press in the South, 1865–1979.* Westport, Conn.: Greenwood, 1983.

———. *P. B. Young, Newspaperman: Race, Politics, and Journalism in the New South, 1910–1962.* Charlottesville: University Press of Virginia, 1988.

Sullivan, Patricia. *Days of Hope: Race and Democracy in the New Deal Era.* Chapel Hill: University of North Carolina Press, 1996.

Sunstein, Cass R. *Democracy and the Problem of Free Speech.* New York: Free Press, 1995.

Tate, Leland B., comp. *The Virginia Guide: A Manual of Information About Virginia.* Lebanon, Va.: Leland B. Tate, 1929.

Taylor, Welford Dunaway. *Robert Frost and J. J. Lankes: Riders on Pegasus.* Hanover, N.H.: Dartmouth College Library, 1996.

———. *Sherwood Anderson.* New York: Frederick Ungar, 1977.

Thomas, Emory M. *Robert E. Lee: A Biography.* New York: W. W. Norton, 1995.

Thompson, Dorothy. *I Saw Hitler!* New York: Farrar & Rinehart, 1932.

Tindall, George B. *The Emergence of the New South, 1913–1945.* Vol. 10, *A History of the South,* ed. Wendell Holmes Stephenson and E. Merton Coulter. Baton Rouge: Louisiana State University Press, 1967.

Tolnay, Stewart E., and E. M. Beck. *A Festival of Violence: An Analysis of Southern Lynchings, 1882–1930.* Urbana: University of Illinois Press, 1995.

Townsend, Kim. *Sherwood Anderson.* Boston: Houghton Mifflin, 1987.

Tushnet, Mark V. *The NAACP's Legal Strategy against Segregated Education, 1925–1950.* Chapel Hill: University of North Carolina Press, 1987.

van de Velde, Theodoor H. *Ideal Marriage: Its Physiology and Technique.* London: William Heinemann, 1930.

Wagman, Robert J. *The First Amendment Book.* New York: Pharos, 1991.

Waldron, Ann. *Hodding Carter: The Reconstruction of a Racist.* Chapel Hill: Algonquin Books, 1993.

Warren, Donald. *Radio Priest: Charles Coughlin, the Father of Hate Radio.* New York: The Free Press, 1996.

Watson, Elmo Scott. *A History of Newspaper Syndicates in the United States, 1865–1935.* Chicago: n.p., 1936.

Wertenbaker, Thomas J. *Norfolk: Historic Southern Port.* Ed. Marvin W. Schlegel. 2 ed. Durham: Duke University Press, 1962.

Western Union Traveler's Cable Code, Revised Edition. N.p., n.d.

Wheeler, Marjorie Spruill. *New Women of the New South: The Leaders in the Woman Suffrage Movement in the Southern States.* New York: Oxford University Press, 1993.

White, Forrest R. *Pride and Prejudice: School Desegregation and Urban Renewal in Norfolk, 1950–1959.* Westport, Conn.: Praeger, 1992.

White, Ray Lewis, ed. *Sherwood Anderson's Memoirs: A Critical Edition.* Chapel Hill: University of North Carolina Press, 1969.

———, ed. *Sherwood Anderson's Secret Love Letters.* Baton Rouge: Louisiana State University Press, 1991.

White, Walter. *A Man Called White: The Autobiography of Walter White.* New York: Viking, 1948.

————. *Rope and Faggot: A Biography of Judge Lynch.* New York: Alfred A. Knopf, 1929.

Wilhoit, Francis M. *The Politics of Massive Resistance.* New York: George Braziller, 1973.

Wilkins, Roy. *Standing Fast: The Autobiography of Roy Wilkins.* New York: Da Capo Press, 1994.

Wilkinson, J. Harvie, III. *Harry Byrd and the Changing Face of Virginia Politics, 1945–1966.* Charlottesville: University Press of Virginia, 1968.

Williams, Blanche Colton, ed. *O. Henry Memorial Award Prize Stories of 1927.* Garden City, N.Y.: Doubleday, Doran, 1928.

Williams, Harold A. *The Baltimore Sun, 1937–1987.* Baltimore: Johns Hopkins University Press, 1987.

Williams, Juan. *Eyes on the Prize: America's Civil Rights Years, 1954–1965.* New York: Viking, 1987.

————. *Thurgood Marshall: American Revolutionary.* New York: Times Books, 1998.

Williamson, William B. *A Handbook for Episcopalians.* New York: Morehouse-Barlow, 1961.

Wilson, Charles Reagan, and William Ferris, eds. *Encyclopedia of Southern Culture.* New York: Anchor, 1991.

Winfield, Betty Houchin. *FDR and the News Media.* Urbana: University of Illinois Press, 1990.

Wolseley, Roland E. *The Black Press, USA.* Ames: Iowa State University Press, 1971.

Woodward, C. Vann. *Tom Watson: Agrarian Rebel.* New York: Macmillan, 1938.

Workers of the Writers' Program of the Work Projects Administration in the State of Virginia, comps. *The Negro in Virginia.* Winston-Salem, N.C.: John F. Blair, 1994.

————, comps. *Virginia: A Guide to the Old Dominion.* Richmond: Virginia State Library and Archives, 1992.

Wright, George C. *Racial Violence in Kentucky, 1865–1940: Lynchings, Mob Rule, and "Legal Lynchings."* Baton Rouge: Louisiana State University Press, 1990.

Wyatt-Brown, Bertram. *Honor and Violence in the Old South.* New York: Oxford University Press, 1986.

————. Introduction to *Mind of the South,* by W. J. Cash. New York: Vintage, 1991.

Yarsinke, Amy Waters. *Norfolk's Church Street: Between Memory and Reality.* Charleston, S.C.: Arcadia, 1999.

Zangrando, Robert L. *The NAACP Crusade Against Lynching, 1909–1950.* Philadelphia: Temple University Press, 1980.

Zigrosser, Carl. *The Artist in America: Twenty-Four Close-Ups of Contemporary Printmakers.* New York: Alfred A. Knopf, 1942.

THESIS

Gruber, Robin. "From Pine Street to Watts Street: An Oral History of the Jews of Durham, North Carolina." Honors thesis, Duke University, 1986.

ARTICLES

Aiken, Newton. "Romances of American Journalism." *Editor and Publisher,* 3 March 1928, 10.

Anderson, Sherwood. "J. J. Lankes and His Woodcuts." *Virginia Quarterly Review* 7, no. 1 (1931): 18–26.

Bassett, John Spencer. "Stirring Up the Fires of Racial Antipathy." *South Atlantic Quarterly* 2, no. 4 (1903): 297–305.

Beers, Paul G. "The Lynching of Raymond Bird." N.p., n.d.

Bernstein, David, and Adele Bernstein. "Slow Revolution in Richmond, Va.: A New Pattern in the Making." In *Jews in the South,* ed. Leonard Dinnerstein and Mary Dale Palsson. Baton Rouge: Louisiana State University Press, 1973.

"Black Justice." *Nation,* 1 May 1935, 497.

Bonner, Marion. "Behind the Southern Textile Strikes." *Nation,* 2 October 1929, 351–2.

Bradsher, A. B. "The Manufacture of Tobacco in North Carolina." *Trinity College Historical Papers* 6 (1906): 12–21.

Brundage, W. Fitzhugh. "'To Howl Loudly': John Mitchell, Jr., and His Campaign against Lynching in Virginia." *Canadian Review of American Studies* 22, no. 3 (winter 1991): 325–42.

Clark, Thomas D. "The Post-Civil War Economy in the South." *American Jewish Historical Quarterly* 55, no. 4 (1966): 424–33.

Clendinen, Dudley. "In the South—When It Mattered to Be an Editor." *Media Studies Journal* 9, no. 1 (1995): 11–22.

Dabney, Virginius. "Civil Liberties in the South." *Virginia Quarterly Review* 16, no. 1 (winter 1940): 81–91.

———. "Dixie Rejects Lynching." *Nation,* 27 November 1937, 579–80.

————. "Nearer and Nearer the Precipice." *Atlantic Monthly,* January 1943, 94–100.

————. "Reflections." *Virginia Magazine of History and Biography* 93, no. 3 (1985): 279–90.

————. "Virginia." *American Mercury* 9, no. 35 (1926): 349–56.

————. "Virginia's Peaceable, Honorable Stand." *Life,* 22 September 1958, 54–6.

Davidson, Gabriel. "The Palestine Colony in Michigan: An Adventure in Colonization." *Publications of the American Jewish Historical Society,* no. 29 (1925): 61–74.

Davis, Margaret. "A Hut with Wattles Made." *Catholic World* (February 1943), 581–8.

"Deaths." *Duke Alumni Register,* April 1950, 103–4.

Dill, Alonzo. "A Glimpse of Parnassus: Travels of Louis I. Jaffé." N.p, n.d.

Dinnerstein, Leonard. "Atlanta in the Progressive Era: A Dreyfus Affair in Georgia." In *Jews in the South,* ed. Leonard Dinnerstein and Mary Dale Palsson. Baton Rouge: Louisiana State University Press, 1973.

————. "A Neglected Aspect of Southern Jewish History." *American Jewish Historical Quarterly* 61, no. 1 (1971): 52–68.

"Duke University Is Host to the State Press Association." *Duke University Alumni Register,* January 1933, 22.

"Editorial Paragraphs." *Nation,* 4 January 1922, 3.

"Editorial Paragraphs." *Nation,* 1 May 1935, 494.

"Editorials." *Crisis,* May 1937, 145.

Epstein, Joseph. "Mencken on Trial." *Commentary* 89 (April 1990): 31–9.

Evans, Eli N. "Southern-Jewish History: Alive and Unfolding." In *"Turn to the South,"* ed. Nathan M. Kaganoff and Melvin I. Urofsky. Charlottesville: University Press of Virginia, 1979, 158–67.

Ewing, Everett. "Romances of American Journalism." *Editor & Publisher,* 1 June 1929, 14.

"The Federal Anti-Lynching Bill." *Outlook,* 11 January 1922, 46–8.

Friedenwald, Herbert. "Agricultural Activities of Jews in America." *American Jewish Yearbook* 14 (1912): 92–3.

"Glad Rags." *The Astonisher: A Magazine of Facts and Near-Facts about South Boston and Halifax,* March 1926, 16–7.

Greenstein, Lillian R. "The Peddlers of Bay City." *Michigan Jewish History* 25, no. 1–2 (1985): 10–7.

Gurock, Jeffrey S. "Jacob A. Riis: Christian Friend or Missionary Foe? Two Jewish Views." *American Jewish History* 71, no. 1 (1981): 29–47.

Higham, John. "Social Discrimination Against Jews in America, 1830–1930." *Publications of the American Jewish Historical Society* 47, no. 1 (1957): 1–33.

Hunt, James L. "Law and Society in a New South Community: Durham County, North Carolina, 1898–1899." *North Carolina Historical Review* 68, no. 4 (1991): 427–60.

Jaffé, Louis I. "The Democracy and Al Smith." *Virginia Quarterly Review* 3, no. 3 (July 1927): 321–41.

———. "Duke University's Bid for Greatness." *McNaught's Monthly,* February 1926, 43–6.

———. "First Impressions of Germany." *Trinity Archive* 23 (December 1909): 137–46.

———. "A Glimpse of Holland." *Trinity Archive* 23 (October 1909): 14–20.

———. "Serbia and Its Jews." *American Israelite* 65 (1919): 1.

———. "To Europe on a Cattle Steamer." *Trinity Archive* 22 (February 1909): 161–75.

———. "Two Trinity Men in England." *Trinity Archive* 22 (May/June 1909): 313–36.

Jaffé, Margaret Davis. "Kitchen Etchings." *Catholic World,* June 1933, 291–7.

———. "Shut In." *Catholic World,* October 1926, 75–87.

Kilgo, John Carlisle. "An Inquiry Regarding Lynching." *South Atlantic Quarterly* 1, no. 1 (1902): 4–13.

Lankes, J. J. "Afternoon and Evening." *American Mercury* 11, no. 82 (October, 1930): 238–43.

Lavender, Abraham D. "Jewish Values in the Southern Milieu." In *"Turn to the South,"* ed. Nathan M. Kaganoff and Melvin I. Urofsky. Charlottesville: University Press of Virginia, 1979, 124–34.

Leidholdt, Alex. "Virginius Dabney and Lenoir Chambers: Two Southern Liberal Newspaper Editors Face Virginia's Massive Resistance to Public School Integration." *American Journalism* 15, no. 6 (1998): 35–68.

Lewis, David, and Judy Miao. "America's Greatest Negroes: A Survey." *Crisis,* January 1970, 17–21.

Lewis, Nell Battle. "Anarchy vs. Communism in Gastonia." *Nation,* 25 September 1929, 321–2.

Liebman, Charles S. "Orthodoxy in American Jewish Life." *American Jewish Yearbook* 66 (1965): 21–98.

Lisby, Gregory C. "Julian Harris and the *Columbus Enquirer-Sun*: The Consequences of Winning the Pulitzer Prize." *Journalism Monographs,* no. 105 (April 1988): 1–30.

Londow, E. Jacob. "Some College Questions." *Trinity Archive* 24 (February 1911): 175.

Lore, Ludwig. "Nazi Politics in America." *Nation,* 29 November 1933, 615–7.

"Louis I. Jaffé Gets Pulitzer Award for Best Editorial." *Duke University Alumni Register,* June 1929, 200–1.

"Louis Isaac Jaffé, '11, Honored." *Trinity Alumni Register,* January 1920, 295–6.

Mason, Robert. "Seeking to Undo Jim Crow." *Virginia Quarterly Review* 68, no. 2 (spring 1992): 385–6.

———. "V. Dabney: The Quintessential Virginian." *Virginia Quarterly Review* 55, no. 1 (winter 1979): 160–3.

Mencken, H. L. "The Library." *American Mercury* 8, no. 32 (1926): 506.

———. "The Library." *American Mercury* 30, no. 120 (1933): 506–10.

Miller, Kathleen Atkinson. "The Ladies and the Lynchers: A Look at the Association of Southern Women for the Prevention of Lynching." *Southern Studies* 2, nos. 2–4 (1991): 261–80.

Pekor, Charles, Jr. "An Adventure in Georgia." *American Mercury* 8, no. 32 (August 1926): 408–13.

Pleasants, Milton R. "How Trinity Students Help Themselves." *Trinity Archive* 27, no. 3 (December 1913): 108–11.

Price, George M. "The Russian Jews in America." *Publications of the American Jewish Historical Society* 48, no. 1 (September 1958): 28–62.

"Public Enemy Number One!" *Crisis,* March 1935, 22–3.

Rabinowitz, Howard N. "Nativism, Bigotry, and Anti-Semitism in the South." *American Jewish History* 77, no. 3 (March 1988): 437–51.

Rable, George C. "The South and the Politics of Antilynching Legislation, 1920–1940." *Journal of Southern History* 51, no. 2 (1985): 201–20.

"Reticence, Timidity Hamper Press Jaffé Tells Virginia Editors." *Editor & Publisher,* 27 July 1929, 20.

Rockaway, Robert. "Antisemitism in an American City: Detroit, 1850–1914." *American Jewish Historical Quarterly* 64, no. 1 (1974): 42–54.

Rogoff, Leonard. "Jewish Proletarians in the New South: The Durham Cigarette Rollers." *American Jewish History* 82, no. 1–4 (1994): 141–57.

Rudin, A. James. "Bad Axe, Michigan: An Experiment in Jewish Agricultural Settlement." *Michigan History* 56, no. 2 (1972): 119–30.

Sherman, Richard B. "'The Last Stand': The Fight for Racial Integrity in Virginia in the 1920s." *Journal of Southern History* 54, no. 1 (February 1988): 69–92.

———. "'The Teachings at Hampton Institute': Social Equality, Racial Integrity, and the Virginia Public Assemblage Act of 1926." *Virginia Magazine of History and Biography* 95, no. 3 (July 1987): 275–300.

Sledd, Andrew. "The Negro: Another View." *Atlantic Monthly* (July 1902), 65–73.

"Chamberlin and Martha Washington Hotel Advertisement." *Southern Progress: A Magazine of Opportunity and Patriotism.* July 1935, 8.

Stern, Malcolm M. "The Role of the Rabbi in the South." In *"Turn to the South,"* ed. Nathan M. Kaganoff and Melvin I. Urofsky. Charlottesville: University Press of Virginia, 1979, 21–32.

Stolberg, Benjamin. "Madness in Marion." *Nation,* 23 October 1929, 462–4.

"Topics in Brief." *Literary Digest,* 19 July 1924, 17.

"Topics in Brief." *Literary Digest,* 16 August 1924, 15.

Villard, Oswald Garrison. "The Nazi Child-Mind." *Nation,* 29 November 1933, 614–5.

"Virginians Speak on Jim Crow." *Crisis,* February 1944, 46–8.

"Virginia's Anti-Lynching Law." *Literary Digest,* 10 March 1928, 14.

White, Walter. "The Costigan-Wagner Bill." *Crisis,* January 1935, 10.

———. "Decline of Southern Liberals." *Negro Digest,* January 1943, 43–6.

Whitfield, Stephen J. "Jews and Other Southerners: Counterpoint and Paradox." In *"Turn to the South,"* ed. Nathan M. Kaganoff and Melvin I. Urofsky. Charlottesville: University Press of Virginia, 1979, 76–104.

PUBLIC DOCUMENTS AND PUBLICATIONS

Acts and Joint Resolutions of the General Assembly of the State of Virginia. Richmond: Division of Purchase and Printing, 1924, 534–5.

Acts and Joint Resolutions of the General Assembly of the State of Virginia. Richmond: Division of Purchase and Printing, 1926, 945–6.

Acts and Joint Resolutions of the General Assembly of the State of Virginia. Richmond: Division of Purchase and Printing, 1928, 715–6.

Air House: A History. Washington, D.C.: Center for Air Force History, 1994.

American National Red Cross Annual Report, 1918. Washington, D.C.: American National Red Cross, 1918.

American National Red Cross Annual Report, 1919. Washington, D.C.: American National Red Cross, 1919.

Camp Bullis: Admirably Suited to all Purposes of Military Training: A History of the Leon Springs Military Reservation, 1890–1990. Fort Sam Houston, Tex., 1990.

Circuit Court of Wythe County (Va.). Summons. 31 August 1926.

Circuit Court of Wythe County (Va.). Summons. 15 September 1926.

Circuit Court of Wythe County (Va.). Summons. 17 September 1926.

Darden, Colgate. "Message of Colgate Darden, Jr., Governor of Virginia, to the General Assembly of Virginia." Richmond, 12 January 1944.

Hussey, Ann Krueger, et al. *A Heritage of Service: Seventy-Five Years of Military Aviation at Kelly Air Force Base, 1916–1991*. Kelly Air Force Base, Tex.: Office of History, 1991.

Jaffé, Louis I. World War I draft registration (filed 5 June 1917). First Lee Ward, Richmond, Va.

Jaffe, Philip. Declaration of intention #41 (filed 8 March 1917). U.S. District Court, Western District of Virginia.

———. Naturalization petitions recommended to be continued (28 February 1928). U.S. District Court, Western District of Virginia.

———. Petition for naturalization #101 (admitted 5 March 1928). U.S. District Court, Western District of Virginia.

Lobb, Michael. *A Brief History of Early Kelly Field, 1916–1918*. Ed. Ann Krueger Hussey, Robert S. Browning III, and Thomas M. O'Donoghue. Kelly Air Force Base, Tex.: Office of History, 1988.

Maurer, Maurer, ed. *The Final Report and a Tactical History*. Vol. 1, *The U.S. Air Service in World War I*. Maxwell Air Force Base, Ala.: Albert F. Simpson Historical Research Center, 1978.

President's Committee on Civil Rights. *To Secure These Rights: The Report of the President's Committee on Civil Rights*. New York: Simon and Schuster, 1947.

Senate Subcommittee of the Committee on the Judiciary. *Punishment for the Crime of Lynching: Hearings on S. 24*, 74th Cong., 1st sess., 14 February 1935.

U.S. Bureau of the Census. 1900 census entry for Philip Jaffe's household. Durham Township, Durham County, N.C.

———. 1910 census entry for Philip Jaffe's household. South Boston, Halifax County, Va.

———. 1920 census entry for Phillip [sic] Jaffe's household. South Boston, Halifax County, Va.

NEWSPAPERS

Asheville (N.C.) Citizen, 1929.

Atlanta Journal, 1915.

Bad Axe (Mich.) Democrat, 1891.

Baltimore Afro-American, 1927.

Baltimore Evening Sun, 1929.

Baltimore Sun, 1926.

Bluefield (W. Va.) Daily Telegraph, 1920.

Bristol (Va.) Herald Courier, 1926, 1927.

Bristol (Va.) News Bulletin, 1926.

Chapel Hill (N.C.) Weekly, 1933.

Charlottesville (Va.) Progress, 1929.

Columbus (Ga.) Enquirer-Sun, 1929.

Danville (Va.) Register, 1928, 1933, 1935.

Duke Chronicle, 1926, 1933, 1937.

Durham (N.C.) Sun, 1911.

Durham (N.C.) High School Messenger, 1907.

Durham (N.C.) Morning Herald, 1933.

Elizabeth City (N.C.) Independent, 1929.

Frankfurter Allgemeine Zeitung, 1998.

Greensboro (N.C.) Daily News, 1929, 1930.

Halifax (Va.) Gazette, 1933.

London Independent, 1991.

London Times, 1991.

Louisville Courier-Journal, 1927.

Lynchburg (Va.) News, 1920.

Montgomery (Ala.) News Messenger, 1957.

New York Herald Tribune, 1942.

New York Times, 1927, 1933–35, 1981, 1991, 1994, 1995.

New York World, 1921, 1926.

Newport News (Va.) Daily Press, 1925, 1926.

Norfolk (Va.) Journal and Guide, 1923, 1926–28, 1931, 1935, 1939, 1940, 1950.

Norfolk (Va.) Ledger-Dispatch, 1929, 1944, 1950.

Norfolk (Va.) Virginian-Pilot, 1914, 1919, 1920–48, 1950, 1952, 1965, 1974, 1982, 1993.

Norton (Va.) Crawford's Weekly, 1927.

Petersburg (Va.) Progress-Index, 1933.

Philadelphia Tribune, 1930.

Raleigh (N.C.) News & Observer, 1903.

Richmond (Va.) News Leader, 1920, 1923, 1928, 1929.

Richmond (Va.) Planet, 1920, 1921, 1926, 1927.

Richmond (Va.) Times-Dispatch, 1913–15, 1917, 1918, 1920, 1923, 1927, 1928, 1934, 1937, 1939, 1943, 1958, 1959, 1963.

Roanoke (Va.) Times, 1926, 1933.

Smyth County (Va.) News, 1926.
Southwest Virginia Enterprise, 1926.
St. Louis Argus, n.d.
Stars and Stripes, 1919.
Trinity Chronicle, n.d., 1910, 1911.
Washington Post, 1983.
Whitesburg (Ky.) Mountain Eagle, 1927.

COMPUTER SOURCES

"Hallicrafters Skyrider Diversity" [cited 1 July 1999]. Available from http://ww1.photomicrographics.com/webpages2/pmi/dd1/default.htm

"Kovno" [cited 1 February 1997]. Available from http://www.jewishgen.org/shetlinks.kovno.html

"Sidwell Friends" [cited 1 July 1999]. Available from http://www.sidwell.edu/admissions/firstlook.html

"Titulus Fasciolae" [cited 3 October 1997]. Available from http://pub.xplore.it/nerone/nerone/ARCHIVIO/arch10.htm

Index